Vacation Guide & Atlas
Florida

Rand McNally & Company
Chicago • New York • San Francisco

ACKNOWLEDGMENTS

Photo Credits

Florida News Bureau, Department of Commerce, State of Florida, i, 2, 4, 5 (top and bottom), 6, 8, 9, 10, 11, 12, 17, 18, 21, 22, 24 (top and bottom), 25, 26, 29, 32, 35, 37, 38, 45 (top and bottom), 49, 53, 56, 65, 68, 69, 70, 72, 73, 74, 82, 83, 84, 85, 86, 90; Franke Keating, 13; Sylvia McNair, 14, 50; Florida's Silver Springs, 20; NASA, 28; Florida Citrus Commission, 40; Citrus Tower, Florida Towers Corporation, 41; Walt Disney Productions, 42; Cypress Gardens, 48; City News Bureau, St. Petersburg, 57; Ringling Museum, 59; Mario Pagliai, 62, 106; City of Miami Beach News Bureau, 77; Miami-Metro News Bureau, 80; Delta Air Lines, 98; Kentucky Tourist and Travel Division, 99.

Quoted Material

The following copyright holders have given permission for quotations from their works: Harper & Row, Publishers, Inc.—for the passage from *Florida— The Long Frontier* by Marjorie Stoneman Douglas, copyright 1947. Florida's Silver Springs—for the passage from *Eternal Spring* by Richard A. Martin, copyright 1966.

Copyright © 1984, 1981, 1979, 1977, 1975, 1973, 1972 by Rand McNally
(Formerly *Rand McNally Guide to Florida*)
All rights reserved
Library of Congress Catalog Card Number: 81-5118
Printed in the United States of America

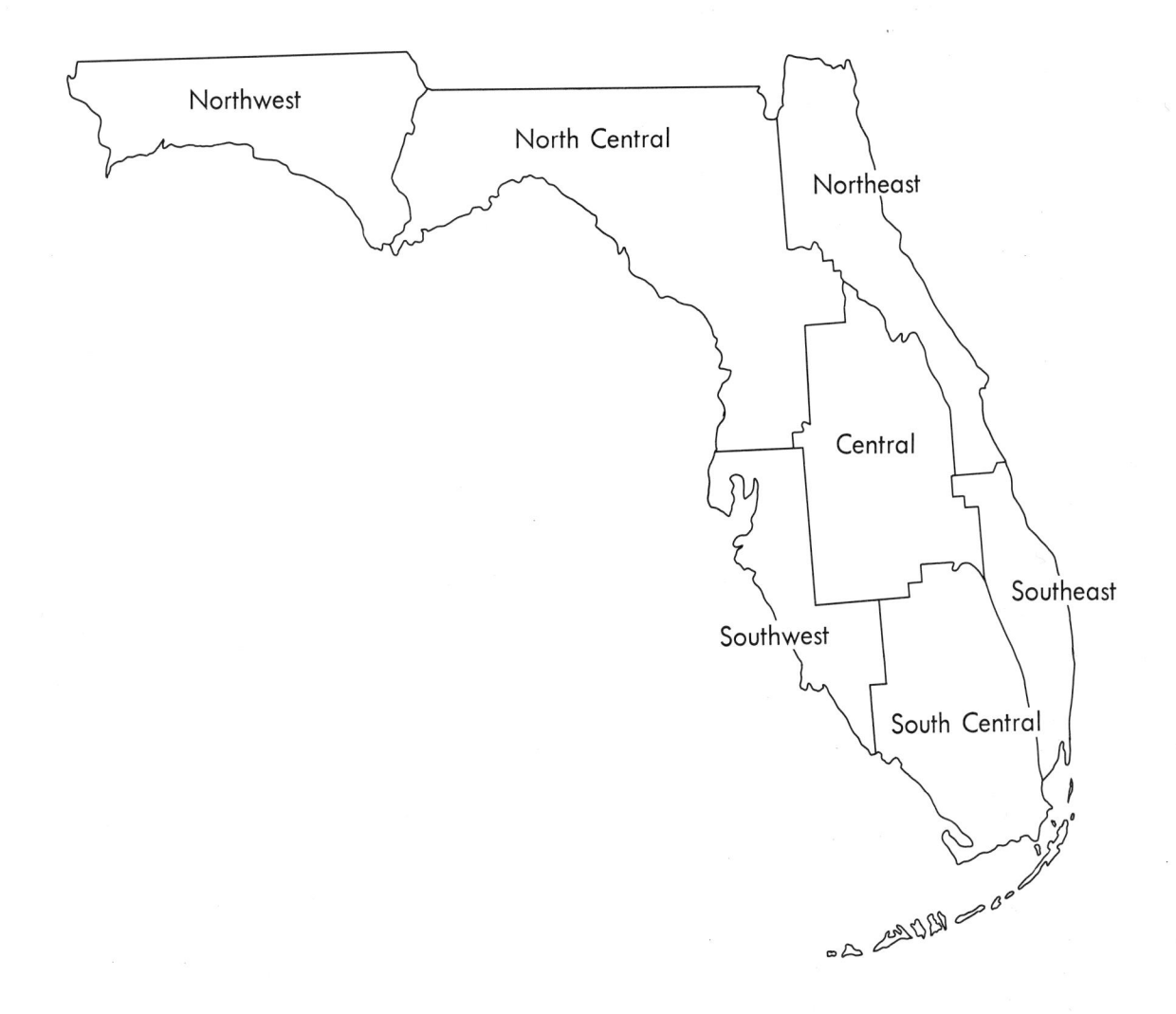

Map regions labeled: Northwest, North Central, Northeast, Central, Southwest, Southeast, South Central

CONTENTS

Introduction vi
Yesterday & Today 2
Northwest—The Panhandle 6
North Central—Woods & Rivers 14
Northeast—The Crown 26
Central—Lakes & Groves 38
Southwest—The Island Coast 50
South Central—Glades & Keys 62
Southeast—The Gold Coast 74
State Parks 86
On the Way 94
Island Hopping 101
Florida Facts & Features 107
Campgrounds 110
Accommodations & Restaurants 127
Index 150

MAPS & CHARTS

State Map iv
Mileage Chart v
Florida's Historic Highlights 1
Northwest Florida 11
Tallahassee 22
North Central Florida 23
Daytona Beach 30
Jacksonville 31
Northeast Florida 31
Walt Disney World—Orlando 43
Central Florida 46
Southwest Florida 55
Tampa—St. Petersburg 59
South Central Florida 67
Southeast Florida 78
Miami Metro Area 79
Routes to Florida 94–95
The West Indies 102
State Map—Campground Locations 114–115
Miami & Vicinity—Campground Locations 119

iii

FLORIDA

Population: 9,746,342
(1980 Census)
Area: 54,153 Sq. Miles
Capital: Tallahassee

Cities and Towns

- Alachua B-3
- Apalachicola H-3
- Apopka C-4
- Arcadia E-3
- Atlantic Beach B-4
- Auburndale E-4
- Avon Park E-4
- Bartow D-3
- Belle Glade F-5
- Blountstown H-3
- Boca Raton F-5
- Bonifay G-3
- Boynton Beach F-5
- Bradenton E-3
- Bristol H-3
- Bronson C-3
- Brooksville D-3
- Bunnell C-4
- Bushnell D-3
- Cantonment G-1
- Cape Canaveral D-5
- Cape Coral F-3
- Chattahoochee A-1, G-3
- Chipley G-3
- Clearwater D-3
- Clermont D-4
- Cocoa D-5
- Coral Gables G-5
- Crawfordville B-1
- Crescent City C-4
- Crestview G-2
- Cross City B-2
- Crystal River C-3
- Dade City D-3
- Dania F-5
- Daytona Beach C-4
- Deerfield Beach ... F-5
- De Funiak Sprs. ... G-2
- De Land C-4
- Delray Beach F-5
- Dunedin D-3
- E. Naples F-4
- Florida City G-5
- Ft. Lauderdale F-5
- Fort Meade E-3
- Ft. Myers F-3
- Ft. Ogden E-3
- Ft. Pierce E-5
- Ft. Walton Beach .. H-2
- Frostproof E-4
- Gainesville B-3
- Goulds G-5
- Green Cove Sprs. .. B-4
- Greenville A-2
- Haines City D-4
- Hallandale G-5
- Hialeah G-5
- High Springs B-3
- Holly Hill C-4
- Hollywood G-5
- Homestead G-5
- Inverness C-3
- Jacksonville B-4
- Jacksonville Beach B-4
- Jasper A-2
- Kenansville D-4
- Key West H-4
- Kissimmee D-4
- La Belle F-4
- Lake Butler B-3
- Lake City B-3
- Lakeland D-3
- Lake Placid E-4
- Lake Wales D-4
- Lake Worth F-5
- Lawtey B-3
- Leesburg C-3
- Live Oak B-2
- Macclenny B-3
- Madison A-2
- Marathon H-4
- Marianna G-3
- Mayo B-2
- Melbourne D-5
- Mexico Beach H-3
- Miami G-5
- Miami Beach G-5
- Miami Shores G-5
- Milton G-1
- Monticello A-2
- Moore Haven F-4
- Naples F-4
- New Port Richey ... D-3
- New Smyrna Beach .. C-5
- Ocala C-3
- Ochopee G-4
- Opa-Locka G-5
- Orange City C-4
- Orlando D-4
- Palatka B-4
- Palm Beach E-5
- Palmetto E-3
- Panama City H-3
- Pensacola H-1
- Perrine G-5
- Perry B-2
- Plant City D-3
- Pompano Beach F-5
- Punta Gorda F-3
- Quincy A-1
- Riviera Beach F-5
- St. Augustine B-4
- St. Cloud D-4
- St. Petersburg E-3
- Sanford D-4
- Sarasota E-3
- Sebring E-4
- Starke B-3
- Stuart E-5
- Tallahassee A-1
- Tampa D-3
- Tarpon Sprs. D-3
- Tavares C-4
- Titusville D-4
- Trenton B-3
- Venice E-3
- Vero Beach E-5
- Warrington H-1
- Watertown B-3
- Wauchula E-3
- W. Palm Beach F-5
- Pensacola H-1
- Wewahitchka H-3
- Winter Haven D-4
- Winter Park D-4

FLORIDA

Scale: 0 10 20 miles
One inch equals approximately 50.3 miles
© Rand McNally & Co. PRINTED IN U.S.A.

FLORIDA (WESTERN SECTION)

Scale: 0 5 10 20 30 miles
One inch equals approximately 57.8 miles
© Rand McNally & Co. PRINTED IN U.S.A.

84-1

HOW TO USE THIS GUIDE

In this book the state of Florida is divided into seven geographic sections. The maps on the Contents page and on the opening page of each sectional chapter indicate the boundaries of the sections, and each chapter lists the counties or portions of counties included. Cities and towns are listed alphabetically within the seven sectional chapters.

The Northwest section is the Panhandle, reaching to the Apalachicola River on the east. North Central Florida includes the "Big Bend" of the Gulf of Mexico, and extends to the Tampa—St. Petersburg metropolitan area. Northeast Florida is a strip of counties stretching from the Georgia border through the "Space Coast" area around Cape Canaveral. Central Florida covers the lush, verdant heart of the state. The Southwest and Southeast sections are the heavily populated strips along the two coasts, and South Central Florida is the large "wetland" of the Everglades and the Florida Keys.

Explanation of Symbols Used for Regional Maps

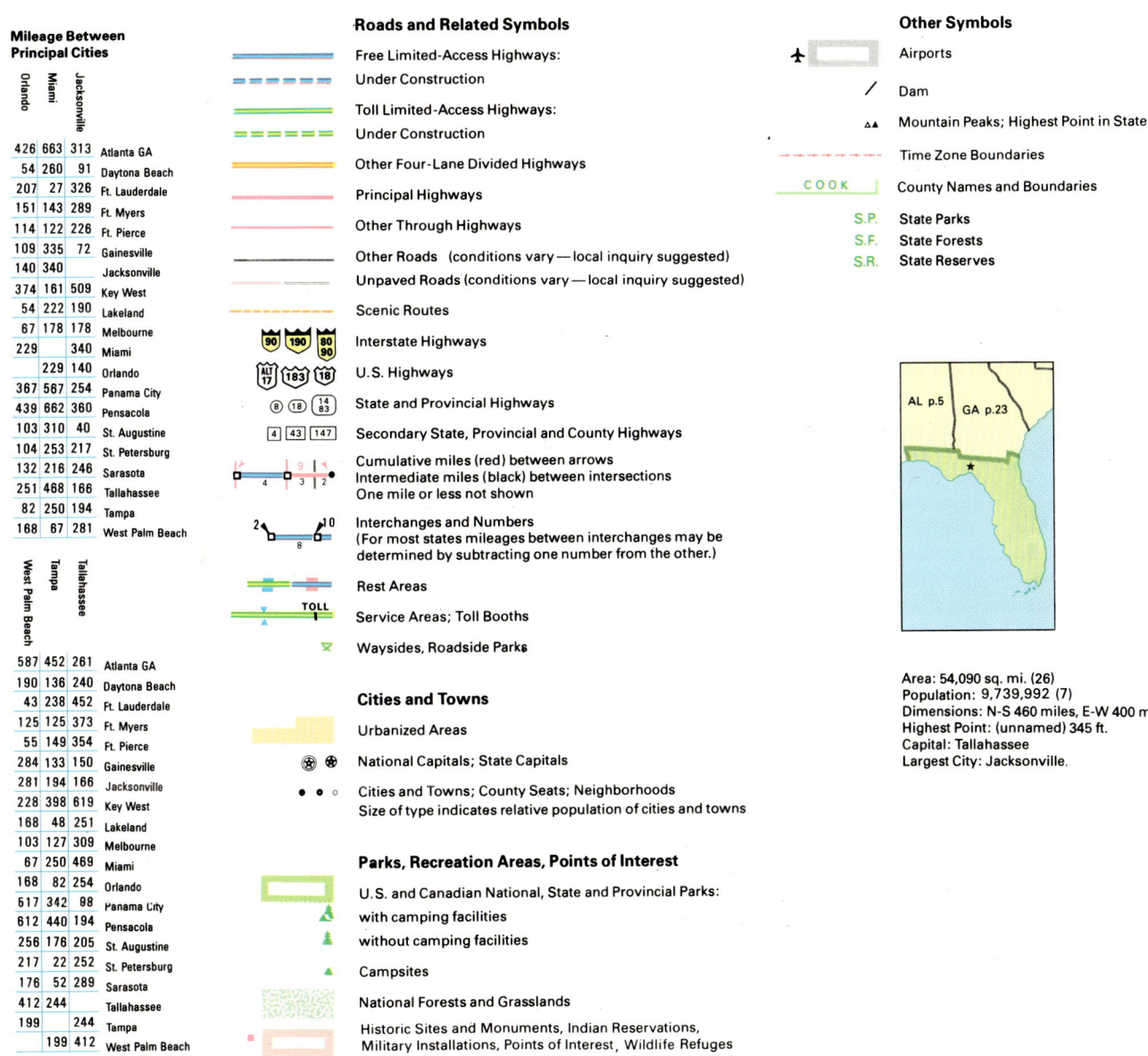

Mileage Between Principal Cities

Orlando	Miami	Jacksonville	
426	663	313	Atlanta GA
54	260	91	Daytona Beach
207	27	326	Ft. Lauderdale
151	143	289	Ft. Myers
114	122	226	Ft. Pierce
109	335	72	Gainesville
140	340		Jacksonville
374	161	509	Key West
54	222	190	Lakeland
67	178	178	Melbourne
229		340	Miami
	229	140	Orlando
367	567	254	Panama City
439	662	360	Pensacola
103	310	40	St. Augustine
104	253	217	St. Petersburg
132	216	246	Sarasota
251	468	166	Tallahassee
82	250	194	Tampa
168	67	281	West Palm Beach

West Palm Beach	Tampa	Tallahassee	
587	452	261	Atlanta GA
190	136	240	Daytona Beach
43	238	452	Ft. Lauderdale
125	125	373	Ft. Myers
55	149	354	Ft. Pierce
284	133	150	Gainesville
281	194	166	Jacksonville
228	398	619	Key West
168	48	251	Lakeland
103	127	309	Melbourne
67	250	469	Miami
168	82	254	Orlando
517	342	98	Panama City
612	440	194	Pensacola
256	176	205	St. Augustine
217	22	252	St. Petersburg
176	52	289	Sarasota
412	244		Tallahassee
199		244	Tampa
	199	412	West Palm Beach

Roads and Related Symbols

- Free Limited-Access Highways: Under Construction
- Toll Limited-Access Highways: Under Construction
- Other Four-Lane Divided Highways
- Principal Highways
- Other Through Highways
- Other Roads (conditions vary — local inquiry suggested)
- Unpaved Roads (conditions vary — local inquiry suggested)
- Scenic Routes
- Interstate Highways
- U.S. Highways
- State and Provincial Highways
- Secondary State, Provincial and County Highways
- Cumulative miles (red) between arrows
- Intermediate miles (black) between intersections
- One mile or less not shown
- Interchanges and Numbers (For most states mileages between interchanges may be determined by subtracting one number from the other.)
- Rest Areas
- Service Areas; Toll Booths
- Waysides, Roadside Parks

Cities and Towns

- Urbanized Areas
- National Capitals; State Capitals
- Cities and Towns; County Seats; Neighborhoods
- Size of type indicates relative population of cities and towns

Parks, Recreation Areas, Points of Interest

- U.S. and Canadian National, State and Provincial Parks:
- with camping facilities
- without camping facilities
- Campsites
- National Forests and Grasslands
- Historic Sites and Monuments, Indian Reservations, Military Installations, Points of Interest, Wildlife Refuges

Other Symbols

- Airports
- Dam
- Mountain Peaks; Highest Point in State
- Time Zone Boundaries
- COOK — County Names and Boundaries
- S.P. State Parks
- S.F. State Forests
- S.R. State Reserves

Area: 54,090 sq. mi. (26)
Population: 9,739,992 (7)
Dimensions: N-S 460 miles, E-W 400 miles
Highest Point: (unnamed) 345 ft.
Capital: Tallahassee
Largest City: Jacksonville

v

INTRODUCTION TO THE SEVENTH EDITION

Florida remains, in good times as well as bad, one of America's favorite playgrounds, and tourism there is alive and healthy. The many hues of license plates in parking lots are a slight hint of the diversity of the vacationers. And every quay will have boats from the Midwest as well as from the Atlantic coast and the Gulf of Mexico. In many new ways, and with the changing times, Flroida's preeminence in the world of travel is reaffirmed. This is still the place for all of North America to seek the sun.

And the rest of the world is coming, too, in larger numbers than ever before. South America is well represented; Spanish and Portuguese can be overheard every day at Walt Disney World, John F. Kennedy Space Center, and all the other popular spots; but so, too, are German, French, Japanese, and many other languages.

Some 274 Florida hostelries in 54 different cities now have bilingual or multilingual staff members. Orlando, Central Florida's bustling hub, claims a tourist information center that greets visitors in five foreign languages. Several attractions provide foreign-speaking guides or taped narrations in a variety of foreign tongues. Two Miami Beach banks have inaugurated free foreign currency exchange service for all area hotels, and Tampa's International Airport offers a currency exchange facility also.

Florida's primary appeal is her natural beauty, of course, but it also lies in the manner in which Floridians approach the welcoming of visitors. Some of the finest and best-managed tourist attractions in the world are here, along with outstanding hotels, restaurants, and entertainment. The State of Florida provides information and service invaluable to the traveler. And the information is truthful, even when it may be embarrassing. If accommodations are difficult to find in certain places or at certain seasons, the traveler will receive straight answers to questions from the personnel at the Department of Commerce's Division of Tourism at Tallahassee.

A vacation in Florida can be as luxurious or as simple as a person cares to make it. Yes, there are resorts expensive and lavish enough to attract the world's wealthiest travelers, but on the other hand there is no shortage of modestly priced motels, cabins, and campgrounds. In fact, by shopping around, families on a limited budget can find much finer accommodations for the price in this state than in most others.

This guide has been prepared with the traveling family in mind; we have tried to include all the points of interest that are attractive to people of all ages. Inevitably, errors do creep into guidebooks; many are simply the result of changes that occur after the book has gone to press. We will appreciate recieving letters from readers that inform us of any such changes, so that entries may be corrected in subsequent editions. Also, we will be grateful to have any inadvertent omissions or new points of interest brought to our attention.

To all of those who have helped in the gathering of information for this edition, a most sincere thank-you. Special acknowledgment is due to the following people: Joice Veselka, Gary Smith, Audrey Dunham, Debbie Geiger, Lilliam Morse, Rosetta Land, Dixie Davenport, and April Athey, all of whom work for the State of Florida in Tallahassee; Mary Mitchell, Pinellas Suncoast; Carol and Bob Binnie of Redington Shores; Jean Williams and Robert and Ellenor Strauhecker, Don CeSar Hotel, St. Petersburg Beach; Dick Dailey, St. Petersburg News Bureau; Leonard Brown and Michael Zmistowski, Greater Tampa Chamber of Commerce; Glenda Gilmore, Busch Gardens; Paul Lago, Trend Publications, Inc.; Bob Wannal, Orlando Area Chamber of Commerce; Stars Hall of Fame; Dick Weaver, Sea World; Tim Barber, Cocoa Beach Area Chamber of Commerce; G. J. Meguiar, TWA/NASA Tours, Kennedy Space Center; Howard Berger, Miami-Metro News Division; Ethel Blum, WKAT, Miami Beach; Herb Rau, *Miami News*; Barbara Booth, Third century U.S.A.; Larry Rogers, Key West Chamber of Commerce; and John McLeod, Amtrak. Special thanks as well to Sylvia McNair, who initiated work on this book, wrote the first edition in 1972, and has continued to give valuable assistance on this project to the Travel Guide Department staff.

The Editors
Travel Guides

FLORIDA'S HISTORIC HIGHLIGHTS

PRE-COLUMBIAN THROUGH THE CIVIL WAR

Before Columbus	Important Indian settlements showing highly developed culture existed in Florida since before the time of Christ. Sites of such settlements have been excavated in or near present-day towns of Crystal River, Fort Walton Beach, Marco, New Smyrna Beach, Safety Harbor, Tallahassee, and Terra Ceia.
1497–1512	Spaniards sighted Florida peninsula and began to put it on maps.
1513	Ponce de Leon landed near St. Augustine.
1516	Exploration of Florida by Spaniards began.
1528	Panfilo de Narvaez landed at Tampa Bay.
1539	Hernando de Soto explored Gulf Coast from Tampa to the north and west.
1559	First attempt at permanent colonization, by Tristan de Luna, near Pensacola. Colony was abandoned two years later.
1564	French built Fort Caroline on the St. Johns River.
1565	Spanish established a mission at St. Augustine, which has been settled continuously since then. They massacred the French forces at Fort Caroline.
1586	Sir Francis Drake, British seafarer, sacked and burned St. Augustine.
1660–1700	Spanish outposts (mostly mission towns) founded in northern Florida and along Gulf and Atlantic coasts; Fort San Marcos de Apalache (near present St. Marks) established about 1680, Pensacola in 1698.
1719	French captured Pensacola, later gave it back to Spanish and moved westward along the Gulf coast.
1740	British General Oglethorpe invaded Florida and besieged St. Augustine for 27 days.
1760–1830	Pirates made sporadic forages among Florida's bays and keys.
1763	Spanish traded Florida to British in exchange for Havana. Only settlements in the wilderness at that time were St. Augustine, Pensacola, and San Marcos de Apalache. British divided the land into East and West Florida.
1776–1778	Colonists from areas north of Florida who were loyal to the British fled from the Revolution and settled in Florida.
1781	Spaniards captured Pensacola from the British.
1783	Florida was returned to the Spanish by the British in exchange for the Bahamas. Florida's first newspaper, the *East Florida Gazette*, was published in St. Augustine.
1812	Spanish and Americans involved in border disputes. To strengthen American claims, a "republic" was proclaimed at Fernandina.
1813	Andrew Jackson captured Pensacola, then abandoned it.
1817	Gregor MacGregor, Scottish soldier of fortune, captured Fernandina. He withdrew, and leadership fell to Luis Aury, who declared Amelia Island to be annexed to Mexico. American forces drove him out and held the island until 1819.
1818	Andrew Jackson campaigned against Indians and runaway Negroes and accused the British of inciting them against the United States.
1821	Spain gave title to East and West Florida to the United States. Territorial government was established.
1824	First Territorial Legislature met in Tallahassee.
1835	Seminole War began with the Dade Massacre, lasted until 1842, with heavy costs and losses of life.
1836	First railroads in state began operation.
1838	Convention at St. Joseph drew up a state constitution.
1845	Florida joined Union as 27th state. David Yulee was the state's first U.S. representative, then elected senator, which office he held until Secession.
1851	Dr. John Gorrie of Apalachicola patented a process of making ice artificially. He is one of two Floridians whose statue is in the U.S. Capitol.
1860	First cross-state railroad was completed, between Fernandina and Cedar Key.
1861	Florida withdrew from the Union. Federal troops held Fort Taylor at Key West, Fort Jefferson in the Dry Tortugas, and Fort Pickens at Pensacola.
1861–1865	More than 16,000 Floridians served in the Civil War; losses by the spring of 1865 were more than 5,000. Few battles were fought on Florida soil, but damage to her economy was severe. Her property losses were estimated to be greater than those of any other state except Mississippi and South Carolina. Still, throughout the war Tallahassee was the only Confederate state capital east of the Mississippi to escape Federal occupation.

Castillo de San Marcos, more than 300 years old, stands guard over the old city of St. Augustine.

2 YESTERDAY & TODAY

YESTERDAY & TODAY

THE WAR BETWEEN THE STATES WAS AN IMPORTANT WATERSHED IN FLORIDA'S HISTORY. AT THE TIME OF SECESSION, HER STATEHOOD WAS ONLY 15 YEARS OLD, AND SHE WAS STILL PRIMARILY A PLANTATION STATE, CUT OFF BY GEOGRAPHY FROM THE MAINSTREAM OF THE YOUNG NATION SHE HAD JOINED. THERE WERE VAST MILES OF WILDERNESS, PUNCTUATED HERE AND THERE WITH A FEW SCATTERED FORTS LEFT OVER FROM THE HALF-HEARTED ATTEMPTS AT COLONIZATION BY THE SPANISH, FRENCH, AND BRITISH.

In 1880, after the Reconstruction years were over, the state's population was 269,493. It has been growing steadily ever since, doubling its numbers about every 20 years. Since World War II the increase has been even faster than that; by 1980 the population was more than five times that of 1940.

YESTERDAY

Almost immediately after the Civil War, tourism began to be important to Florida. Many new settlers discovered the advantages of Florida's climate and passed the word back home. Yankees, as well as Southerners, migrated here in great numbers. One of the state's first "press agents" was Mrs. Harriet Beecher Stowe, who came with her preacher husband to live in Mandarin, near the St. Johns River. She sent dispatches back to northern newspapers, some of which were later collected into two volumes, and her quaint, genteel Victorian language makes for fascinating reading today. She exorted her readers not to expect that everything about Florida would be perfect, yet gently suggested that this area would make an ideal winter home for those who could afford a second home. She described her activities as she sailed on the rivers, went picnicking, caught fish, and watched the seasons change. She waxed lyrical over the glories of orange trees:

> The orange-tree is, in our view, the best worthy to represent the tree of life of any that grows on our earth. It is the fairest, the noblest, the most generous, it is the most upspringing and abundant, of all trees which the Lord God caused to grow eastward in Eden.

Others, too, were discovering the lure of Florida. William Cullen Bryant visited Silver Springs and wrote of his delight in the experience. The poet Sidney Lanier prepared what may have been Florida's first guidebook, *Florida: Its Scenery, Climate, and History*, published in 1876. In 1884 Thomas Edison found the spot for his winter home in Fort Myers, and he soon persuaded Henry Ford and Harvey Firestone to join him there. A few of today's major tourist attractions were drawing visitors well before the end of the 19th century—Silver Springs, whose admirers spread its fame throughout the world; several spots in St. Augustine, including the St. Augustine Alligator Farm; Green Cove Springs; and others.

The Big Three business giants who did the most to develop settlement of Florida were Henry Plant on the West Coast, Henry Flagler on the East Coast, and Hamilton Disston, who purchased four million acres in the middle of the state. Disston did not live long enough to carry out all of his many plans for promoting central Florida, but he did contribute to later agricultural development of the state by financing studies on the scientific methods of growing rice, sugar cane, fruits, and vegetables, and breeding cattle.

Plant and Flagler developed their respective parts of the state by building railroads, establishing resort hotels, and promoting the sale of land. The first cross-state railroad was brought from Fernandina to the Cedar Keys in 1860. By 1884 there were 500 miles of railways in the state, and five times that much by 1891.

Henry Flagler's hotels marched down the East Coast—from St. Augustine to Palm Beach, finally to Miami. Meanwhile, Henry Plant built the ornate Tampa Bay Hotel (which today houses the University of Tampa) and invited notables from everywhere to attend its opening celebration—even his rival, Flagler. The story is told that upon receiving his invitation Henry Flagler wired Plant: "Where's Tampa?" Whereupon Plant replied: "Follow the crowd, Henry."

In the early part of the 1900s John Jacob Astor, William K. Vanderbilt, and other wealthy auto-racing enthusiasts found the packed sands of Daytona Beach to be ideal for indulging in their hobby. Soon John D. Rockefeller, Sr., chose Ormond Beach as the place where he was going to live to be 100 years old. (He missed it by a little over two years.) Florida was becoming more and more fashionable, and even the turmoil of World War I didn't lessen its popularity.

TODAY

The Gold Coast's boom period ended in the late twenties. Luckily tourism in Florida did not by any means lie down and die with the crash. The Depression years were hard, but people kept coming. And ever since World War II the economy of the state has steadily improved.

A characteristic of many of the popular Florida tourist attractions is that they have been—and a few still are—"mom-and-pop" businesses. Since the state is still relatively young, many of these original owners, or at least their sons and daughters, are still running things at the same old stand. This makes for a charming, personal, intimate relationship between the tourist and the Florida business community that has surely contributed to the state's drawing power. It is one of the factors that bring people back, year after year, to their own special, favorite vacation spot.

When the first resort hotels were opened, the owners supplied every sort of recreational facility that could be imagined, to make the guests feel pampered and appreciated. And through the years more and more facilities for entertainment and recreation have been added to the scene.

What can one do in Florida? Several hundred things could be listed. To start with, the water sportsmen can enjoy swimming, surfing, water skiing, canoeing, scuba diving, a dozen different methods of fishing, and at least as many ways of boating. On land there is tennis or polo or shuffleboard, golfing, biking, horseback riding, or hiking. Sorry—not much mountain climbing or (snow) skiing, though. For those who like their physical activity secondhand, there are big-league baseball, football, jai-alai, horse racing, dog racing, car racing, motorcycle racing, dune-buggy racing, and boat racing to watch. Or one can watch birds, photograph alligators, or collect shells; go to plays, concerts, art galleries, night clubs, circus performances, and visit museums covering every imaginable sort of collection; wander through some of the world's finest botanical and zoological parks; ride on dozens of amusement park rides; see legends and fairy tales brought to life through dioramas, wax museums, and reconstructed villages; visit forts and battlefields commemorating several wars; climb over ruins of pioneer plantations and mills; watch missile launches, porpoise shows, and performing birds. And wherever the visitor goes he or she can enjoy some of the finest food in the country.

There are probably more facilities per 100 square miles for having fun in this state than in any other place of similar size on earth—and more campgrounds, motels, hotels, restaurants, and shops to serve tourists as they seek that fun.

NATURE'S BOUNTY

But the phenomenal success that Florida has had for the past century in attracting tourists is basically rooted in the largess of nature in this subtropical corner of our nation. Market researchers tell us that most travelers come to Florida *primarily* to enjoy "the sun, sea, and sand." The first ambition of work-weary vacationers is to lie on the beach and relax. Once they have done that for a day or two, however, they find that there are many other ways to spend their time, and they begin to explore. That's when the discovery comes that almost everything one can do in Florida is dependent on, or made more enjoyable because of, the natural bounties on every hand. Nowhere do flowers, ornamental shrubs, and beautiful trees grow more profusely. No other state has so many deep, clear springs that feed sparkling rivers. No other state has so many acres of beaches—golden on the East Coast, sugar-fine and white on the beaches of the Panhandle, powdery and white on the Southwest Coast—or more beautiful waters bathing its shores. Nowhere are there so many miles of highways lined by groves of citrus trees. Nowhere else is there anything like the Everglades, with its complex community of plant and animal life, fresh and salt waters.

Tourism is without doubt the number one industry in the state: in 1982, for instance, the state had nearly 39.3 million visitors, and earned an income of $21.5 billion from tourism-related industries. Agriculture is nearly as important to the economy, bringing in nearly $4 billion annually in farm value of agricultural products, including the cattle and dairy industries, vegetable farming, forestry products, poultry and egg products, sugar cane, and tobacco. Horticulture is a large enterprise—Florida ranks first in the nation in production of foliage plants, and is second only to California in production of flowers. The state ranks second nationally in honey production.

Probably Florida's most valuable natural resource—more valuable than the orange and just about equal, perhaps, to the long hours of sunshine—is the fish. In 1981 Florida fishermen harvested over 214 million pounds of fish and shellfish. Marjory Stoneman Douglas, a newspaper woman who came to Florida in 1915 and became a staunch promoter of the area, described the importance of fishing this way:

> The single most important tourist attraction since the first tarpon was caught in the nineties with a light line and rod and reel is fishing. Like the large commercial fishing industry, it is carried on in every inlet and bay, river and lake in the state, and around all the coasts, especially on the west, from Tampa to Key West, headquarters of the great offshore shrimp-fishing fleet. With all the related industries of boats and boat yards, bait, tackle, marine supplies, to say nothing of taxidermists, sea-food restaurants, fish canning and fish export, the annual value of fish to Florida is almost impossible to estimate, except that it probably begins at a billion dollars. It is the reason why the great fish and shellfish breeding grounds of the lower coasts and the Everglades, in the face of speculative and industrial threat, must at all costs be preserved.

FUTURE THREATS

I don't believe that anyone who is sensitive to his surroundings can stay in Florida for more than a week without becoming aware of the environmental problems that must be solved if the state is to maintain the assets that draw people there. This is where great, glorious flocks of snowy egrets used to feed, before poachers killed them off for the feathers to adorn women's hats. Pink flamingos used to wander freely beside the highways; today they are rarely seen except in sedate groups within the landscaped grounds of the tourist attractions. Even the prolific alligator was seriously threat-

Florida's most important attractions: the sun, sea, and sand.

ened as a species until still state laws made it illegal to sell alligator products. And Florida's official marine mammal, the manatee, is severely threatened by increasing riverboat traffic in the state's rivers. A few nesting spots still remain for the American bald eagle—our national symbol—but our grandchildren may one day think the eagle is a mythical creature, something akin to the unicorn.

It may be, as the more optimistic segments of our population believe, that nature in general and the Everglades in particular are much tougher than some ardent environmentalists fear—and that man will not be able to damage the ecosystem of the Florida peninsula permanently no matter how foolishly he behaves. But even so, there really is no excuse for the kind of "brinksmanship" game that man so often tries to play with nature. If the breeding grounds for fish within the Everglades are destroyed, if the water supply is not managed with a great deal of prudence, if pollution problems are not taken seriously, then there is little doubt that the most endangered of all species in Florida may very well be man.

This state has always been all things to all people. To the fisherman, it is a bit of rock and sand surrounded by a sea of plenty. To the playboy, it's a resort where living is easy. To the sun worshiper, it's a guaranteed tan in mid-winter. To the retiree, it's a place where the climate is so mild and the pace so relaxed that the number of golden years may be doubled. To the golfer, it's a country club that is open 365 days a year.

And to the serious natural scientist, it has always been without peer as an outdoor laboratory. Beginning with John James Audubon they have come—the zoologists, botanists, and marine biologists; ornithologists, herpetologists, ichthyologists, horticulturists and agriculturists; the ecologists. They have studied nature, learned from it, worked with it, altered it. Stemming from these studies have come some of the state's most interesting places to visit—Marineland, the Seaquarium, Sunken Gardens, Caribbean Gardens, Orchid Jungle, Fairchild Gardens, Miami Serpentarium, The Dark Continent/Busch Gardens, Sarasota Jungle Gardens, the Marie Selby Botanical Gardens, Redland Fruit and Spice Park, the Thomas Edison gardens, Cypress Point Reptile Institute, Planet Ocean, Sea World of Florida, and many more.

More than a million and a half acres of Florida's land and water within the boundaries of Everglades National Park, the Gulf Islands National Seashore, Biscayne National Park, De Soto National Memorial, and Forts Castillo de San Marcos, Caroline, Jefferson, and Matanzas, belong by law to all the American people. But Floridians have always welcomed their countrymen to every inch of their homeland and have honored visitors and refugees from foreign shores as well. *Mi casa es su casa*: my house is your house. The hospitality here is limitless. Let us hope that all who came as guests are as gracious, and they they fully appreciate the treasure that is ours in both Florida's land and people.

Above: The osprey still have prime nesting areas in Florida's waterways.

Right: St. George Lighthouse, near Apalachicola.

Sailing is popular in the waters off Panama City.

6 NORTHWEST

NORTHWEST

THE PANHANDLE

FROM PENSACOLA—"WHERE FLORIDA BEGINS"—TO THE APALACHICOLA RIVER, NORTHWEST FLORIDA IS A JAUNTY THUMB STICKING OUT INTO ALABAMA. IT'S CALLED THE PANHANDLE OR THE MIRACLE STRIP. VISITORS FROM ALABAMA, GEORGIA, AND MISSISSIPPI CALL IT A SUMMER VACATIONLAND. MANY RETIRED SERVICEMEN ONCE CALLED IT THEIR TOUR OF DUTY AND NOW CALL IT HOME. IT'S THE SECTION OF FLORIDA THAT HAS THE LONGEST STRETCHES OF OPEN BEACH, PRESERVED IN ALL THEIR ORIGINAL, NATURAL BEAUTY.

Think of it—*100 miles* of snow-white, sugar-fine sand, stretching all the way from Pensacola Beach to Panama City and beyond, a great deal of it with not a building between the highway and the Gulf, just sand dunes topped with golden sea oats. Beyond the beach are incredible turquoise and azure and silver waters, a gentle surf rolling over a sandy bottom that slopes gently enough for a toddler to venture out—several hundred feet in many places.

And those waters cover some of the finest fishing grounds in the world. In summer dozens of fishing boat captains make a nice living squiring family groups around the Gulf and its bays and sounds; in the fall the serious fishermen come without their families and really get down to business.

Fishing is a continuous attraction on the Miracle Strip and tournaments are held the year around, with thousands of anglers competing for cash and trophies. The charter boats go out for sailfish and marlin; there is bottom fishing for snapper and grouper, or pier fishing, or freshwater fishing in the nearby lakes and streams.

Much of the land in the Panhandle is publicly owned. Eglin Air Force Base, 7 miles northeast of Fort Walton Beach, is the world's largest air force base in land area. There are 13 state parks in Northwest Florida, and a large portion of the beach area is owned or leased by the counties for public use. Recreational facilities include more than a dozen golf courses, two greyhound racetracks, and half a dozen amusement parks.

Pensacola, the Gateway City, has a heritage of recorded history that goes back more than four centuries—to August 14, 1559, when Don Tristan de Luna came ashore with 1,500 colonists from Spain. Since then the city has seen more than a dozen flag changes, back and forth among Spain, Great Britain, France, the United States, and the Confederacy. Its citizens are conscious of their rich heritage, and several annual events pay tribute to it. The most popular are the Fiesta of Five Flags, which begins in May, and the Seafood Festival in September. Pensacola is an aviation town too; the nearby Pensacola Naval Air Station is known as the birthplace of naval aviation.

In 1914 the infant Naval Air Station had 15 pilots, 12 mechanics, and 11 bi-wing seaplanes. Today the station employs several thousand military personnel and civilians. It is the home of the famed Blue Angels and the nation's only Naval Aviation Museum.

Traveling east from Pensacola along US 98, the Miracle Strip Parkway, the driver will cross long bridges known locally as the world's longest fishing piers, then continue along a narrow peninsula with the Intracoastal Waterway and Santa Rosa Island to the south. About 50 miles east of Pensacola is Fort Walton Beach, a city especially popular as a retirement center for service personnel. Right in the middle of town, at the side of the highway, is a prominent prehistoric Indian temple mound, proof that civilization existed in Northwest Florida thousands of years before any of the Five Flags were flown.

Across the mouth of Choctawhatchee Bay lies the beautiful little village of Destin. Some of its residents know very well the pleasures and delights of living here—their families have been in Destin for several generations. Some years ago this was a commerical fishing town; today there is one commercial fishing boat, and all it brings back is bait to sell to the hundreds of sports fishermen who embark from here. One of the most spectacular views in all of Florida can be seen only by going up in a plane over Destin. The East Pass Bridge, with Choctawhatchee Bay on the north and the Gulf of Mexico on the south, is an almost unbelievable sight from the air.

Another 50 miles or so east on US 98 will bring you to Panama City, the tourist capital and playground of Northwest Florida. More than eight thousand hotel and motel units are available in the immediate vicinity, and nightclubs, amusement parks, golf courses, and a large fleet of charter boats are available for a multifaceted vacation. The town's slogan is "Panama City is Florida's best-kept secret," but both the local boosters and the satisfied tourists who go home to sing its praises are making sure that the secret is not kept.

This area is especially popular with visitors from nearby southern states who come here for summer vacations. The "season" is from April 1 to Labor Day, and the motels are the fullest and the prices the highest during this period. But there are many hardy and canny Northerners who think that the Miracle Strip's "fireplace weather" during winter months is still a welcome change from blizzards and ice. These people have discovered the moderate prices, relaxed pace, and friendly welcome offered here during the off-season, and they enjoy a Florida vacation in the fall or even in the middle of the winter at bargain rates.

For even less money than the reasonably priced motel rooms, families can take advantage of several camping areas. One of the most popular is St. Andrews State Recreation Area, more than one thousand acres of sand dunes almost surrounded by water.

But Northwest Florida is much more than a strip of beautiful beach. Just a few miles north of the Miracle Strip Parkway are two principal routes: US 90 and I-10. If you leave either of these main routes, you can often travel for miles without seeing another person—through pine tree plantations, dairy farms, soybean fields, even wheat fields. There are little towns with sawmills and plywood factories. There are huge forest areas such as the Eglin Wildlife Management Area and the Blackwater State Forest. There are communities that look just as they did 25 years ago, with quiet main streets, small family-owned stores, and neat little churches—

towns whose economies depend on the agricultural trading area surrounding them.

The ten counties included in this section have over half a million people—nearly 7% of the state's total. The population is increasing here at a slower rate than in the rest of the state. About one-third of the total live in the Pensacola metropolitan area, one-third in other population centers, and one-third in rural areas. The population density here is only about half that for the state as a whole.

Four-laned US 90 follows roughly along an early trail that connected the Spanish mission settlements of the 1600s. Later on it was a stagecoach route. This section also had one of the earliest railroads in the state.

Part of this section of Florida is comparatively hilly; northwest of De Funiak Springs is the highest point in the state—345 feet above sea level. And to the east, along the Apalachicola River, are a few scenic bluffs.

For vacationing or for retirement, Northwest Florida has a flavor all its own. Its beaches are as wide and as white and its waters as clear and blue and fish-filled as any of those farther south, but the climate is a little more temperate, the pace a little less hectic, the atmosphere a little less "touristy" than in many other areas. Since most people come to Florida to enjoy sun and sea and sand, many of them have already discovered that this little corner has all of these things in abundance, plus a certain kind of natural, lighthearted, unspoiled charm that makes it unique.

CITIES & TOWNS
Map of this section on page 11.

CHIPLEY is the county seat and principal center of Washington, another rural county in the Panhandle. It is located on US 90 and Florida 77, about 50 miles north of Panama City. Three miles south of town off Florida 77, is **Falling Waters State Recreation Area.** A waterfall cascades into a 100 ft. sink, walls behind the fall are multihued. This was the site of the original—but unproductive—first attempt to find oil in Florida.

Chipley is watermelon country, and in late June the Panhandle Watermelon Festival is held in celebration of the crop.

CRESTVIEW is the county seat of Okaloosa County. It is located on US 90 and Florida 85, just north of I-10, about 30 miles north of Fort Walton Beach. Crestview is the center of a farm area producing soybeans, corn, wheat, cattle, hogs, and timber.

Each April or May Crestview holds an **Old Spanish Trail Festival.** Residents wear Spanish costumes, and events include a Spanish dinner, grand ball, beauty contest, fishing and golf tournaments, carnival, street dance, and parade.

DE FUNIAK SPRINGS is the county seat and population center of Walton County. It is located on US 90 and Florida 83, halfway between Pensacola and Tallahassee, and about 25 miles inland from the Gulf beaches. This is a beautiful old Southern town, surrounding a clear, circular, spring-fed lake bordered by a scenic drive. Excellent boating and fishing. Worth seeing here are a late 19th-century Chautauqua assembly building and an imposing Confederate memorial.

Each autumn the town hosts the **Walton County Fair,** with an art show featured as well. The **Chautauqua Festival,** held in May, includes entertainment, art and crafts displays, and a parade.

Ponce De Leon Springs State Recreation Area is located about 10 miles east of the town, at the intersection of US 90 and Florida 181A.

DESTIN is located in Okaloosa County, on a point of land between the Gulf of Mexico and Choctawhatchee Bay, on US 98, just east of Fort Walton Beach. A beach resort boasting some of the clearest blue water and whitest sand anywhere in the world, this is an old and famous center for serious sport fishermen, with several annual tournaments.

The month-long **Marlborough Cobia Tournament** begins in late March, or when the first cobia is caught.

On Ascension Day, May 12, is the colorful **Blessing of the Fleet,** in which local bishops bless the fishing boats. There are grand prizes and a number of special children's trophies. The **Marlborough Billfishing Tournament** in September and the **Deep Sea Fishing Rodeo** in October both offer prizes of several thousand dollars.

In 1971 the first steps were taken by the federal government to create the **Gulf Islands National Seashore.** The seashore encompasses a 150-mile stretch of offshore islands and keys between Destin and Gulfport, Mississippi, that has been set aside for recreational and conservation purposes under the direction of the National Park Service. The Florida section

Eden, a mansion near Grayton Beach.

of this new park consists of Johnson Beach on Perdido Key, a group of fort ruins and Naval Live Oaks reservation, on the mainland, beaches, and parts of Santa Rosa Island. All areas are accessible by car.

Nine miles east of town, on US 98, is the **Museum of the Sea and the Indian.** It offers exhibits of sponge diving and displays of Indian artifacts, as well as ponds filled with water flowers, birds, alligators, and fish. Cassette tours. Open daily; June through August, 8–6; September through May, 9–4. Admission $2.75, children 5–16 $1.50, under 5 free.

For an unforgettable view of the area, inquire at the airport about sightseeing rides.

FORT WALTON BEACH is the major center in Okaloosa County and is located on US 98 at the west end of lovely Choctawhatchee Bay. It shares honors with Pensacola, Destin, and Panama City for the excellent fishing waters off the famed and beautiful Miracle Strip. This stretch of incredibly white sand beaches along the Gulf is a moderately priced summer resort area especially popular with people from other parts of the South.

As you look about this attractive small city it is hard to believe that as late as 1940 Fort Walton Beach had a population of only 90!

Early each June Fort Walton Beach holds a fun-filled celebration called the **Billy Bowlegs Festival,** which includes the landing of a pirate captain and his crew, boat parade, treasure hunt, pirate balls, tournaments, parades, antique show, art show, and a Pirate Market. In February a **Beaux Arts Exhibit** features paintings and crafts.

Eglin Field is the largest (in area) air force base in the world. The main entrance to the base is 7 miles to the northeast of Fort Walton Beach. Tickets for tours of the base may be obtained from the Chamber of Commerce office in town. June through August tours are given on Wednesdays from 10–noon. Hunting is permitted on the Eglin Air Force Reservation to those with both an appropriate state or county license, which may be purchased at Fort Walton Beach courthouse or at various local department stores, and a current Eglin AFB permit, issued at Jackson Guard Station.

Nearby on Okaloosa Island is the **Gulfarium,** with its Living Sea, featuring exhibits of marine life in huge tanks and trained porpoise and sea lion shows. Snack bar and gift shop. Open winter, 9–4; summer, 9–6. Closed Thanksgiving and Christmas. Admission $6, children 4–11 $3, under 4 free.

Close to the center of the city, on US 98, near its intersection with Florida 85, is a recently excavated Indian mound and a museum operated by the city. **Temple Mound** has been designated a national historic landmark. **Indian Temple Mound Museum** has many displays covering 10,000 years of Indian life on the Gulf coast. Weeden Island ceramic artifacts and Fort Walton pottery are exhibited. Mound open daily, daylight hours. Free. Museum open Tuesday–Saturday, 11–4; Sunday, 1–4. Closed New Year's Day, Thanksgiving Day, and Christmas. Admission 50¢, children under 10 free. Indian crafts for sale.

Pirates Island has major rides, kiddie rides, restaurant, water flume, go-carts and bumper boats. Free gate and parking.

The bumper boat ride at Panama City Beach's Miracle Strip Amusement Park.

GRAYTON BEACH in Walton County, about 25 miles east of Fort Walton Beach by way of US 98 and Florida 30A, is the site of beautiful **Grayton Beach State Recreation Area,** a 356-acre park encompassing lakes and piney woods as well as the Gulf beach area.

On Choctawhatchee Bay at Point Washington, 5 miles from Grayton Beach, off US 98, is **Eden State Ornamental Garden,** a restored mansion on 11.6 acres of landscaped grounds.

MARIANNA is the county seat and principal city in Jackson County and is located on US 90 and Florida 71, just north of the now complete I-10. It is in the major peanut-producing region of the state. The town has several fine old Southern Colonial homes, and the surrounding countryside abounds with lovely lakes, fine forests, beautiful blue springs, and majestic rivers.

Near Marianna, **Three Rivers State Recreation Area** offers camping, fishing, and water sports.

Three miles north of town, on Florida 167, is **Florida Caverns State Park.** In addition to the caves, through which tours are conducted approximately every hour, the park offers picnicking, boating (ramp), swimming, fishing, nature trails, camping, a museum and a visitor center. Guide service through caverns $1.50, children 6–12 75¢.

NORTHWEST 9

Dozens of fishermen enjoy fishing off the 450-foot jetty at St. Andrews State Recreation Area.

MILTON is the county seat and major center of Santa Rosa County. It is on US 90 and Florida 87, about 20 miles northeast of Pensacola.

To the northeast lie **Blackwater River State Forest** and **State Game Management Area.** Recently developed is the 360-acre **Blackwater River State Park,** in the southern portion of the forest. In addition to Blackwater River, three other sandy-bottomed streams flow through the park. An old Indian trail, once used for Spanish-Indian trade, has been developed as a nature trail.

NICEVILLE is located on Florida 20 and 285, just north of Choctawhatchee Bay. East of town, on Florida 20, are **Fred Gannon Rocky Bayou State Recreation Area,** developed out of a former military park within Eglin Air Force Base, and **Basin Bayou State Recreation Area,** a park on Choctawhatchee Bay.

PANAMA CITY is the county seat and principal city of Bay County. It is located on US 98 and the Gulf's St. Andrews Bay and is the largest city between Pensacola and Tallahassee. An important commerical port (Port Panama City is a Foreign Trade Zone), industrial center, and resort city, it also boasts little theater groups and **Gulf Coast Junior College.**

Panama City is the amusement center of Northwest Florida, with superb fishing, water sports, amusement parks, golf courses, fine accommodations, and restaurants.

Points of interest for the visitor include use of the public boat ramp and fishing in the 5,000-acre lake impounded by **Deer Point Dam;** trips to nearby **Shell Island** (boats leave from Anderson's Pier at 9 am and 1 pm, mid-May to mid-September: adults $3.50, children $1.75); **Tyndall Air Force Base** (tours offered Monday through Friday excluding holidays; call for appointment); and the **U.S. Naval Ship Research and Development Laboratory.**

Gulf World, with a marine show and tropical gardens, is 8 miles west on US 98. It is open daily, Memorial Day through Labor Day from 9–9; April through late May 9–4:30.

The **Junior Museum of Bay County,** 1731 Jinks Avenue, has period furnishings in a reconstructed log cabin. Open Tuesday through Saturday, 9–4; closed holidays. Free.

The **Snake-A-Torium,** on US 98 in Panama City Beach, has guided tours and exhibitions of venom extraction. Open daily, 9 am–dusk. Admission $3.20, children 6–11 $2.15.

Across the bay, 3 miles east of Panama City Beach, on Florida 392, is **St. Andrews State Recreation Area,** with more than a thousand acres of beautiful pure white sand, as well as a 450-ft. pier.

There are several major family-oriented amusement parks in the vicinity. **Miracle Strip Amusement Park,** 12001 West US 98, has major rides, kiddie rides, a flume ride, 2 fun houses, refreshment stands, snack bar, arcade, shooting gallery, miniature golf, gift shops, and an observation tower. March–May and early September, open weekends;

June–August, open daily. Monday–Friday, 3–11; Saturday–Sunday, 1–11; admission, $8.95; under 11, $7.50. **Shipwreck Island,** a themed water park, is located across the street. Open 10–7:30; summer open daily, spring and fall open on weekends. Admission $8.50; 5–10, $5.50; under 5 free.

Petticoat Junction Amusement Park, at Long Beach Resort, has major rides, kiddie rides, refreshment stands, arcade, coal-burning steam engine ride; gun fights; and various attractions. Free parking. Admission for over 10, 50¢; all rides $6.50, under 3 free. Individual rides 60¢–$1.20. March–April, weekends only; May–Labor Day, daily. Phone 904/234-2808 for hours.

Also in the Panama City area is **Castle Dracula,** at 12390 West US 98, a wax museum of horror movie stars. Open March through September, 10–11. Admission $3, children 6–11 $1. The nearby **Wax and Historical Museum,** also known as International Archives, at 11073 West US 98, contains historical displays. Open daily, June through August, 9–11; March, April, May, and September, 9–5. Admission $3, children 6–11 $1.

From mid–May to mid–September the **Washington County Kennel Club** features greyhound racing nightly, except Sunday, at nearby Ebro Dog Track. Matinees every Monday and Saturday.

PENSACOLA is the major city in the Panhandle. Its metropolitan area has over one-third of all the residents of Northwest Florida—more than 200,000. County seat and principal center of Escambia County, the city is located on US 98 and

Seville Quarter, in the Pensacola Historical District

NORTHWEST 11

I-10, Pensacola Bay, and Santa Rosa Sound. At the western entrance to the Panhandle, it is the gateway to the 100 miles of beaches, islands, and peninsulas known as the Miracle Strip. The city has figured in much of the history of Florida, and it was settled briefly in 1559 by Spanish colonists before the establishment of the permanent colony at St. Augustine. In the four centuries that have passed it has lived under five flags and 17 changes of government. For information about **sightseeing tours** of the city, phone (904) 438-5078.

Since World War I, the Naval Air Station has been an important factor in Pensacola's economy, as has the city's harbor, the largest natural, landlocked deepwater harbor in Florida.

Much of the downtown area in the vicinity of Seville Square has been designated a national historic landmark—the **Pensacola Historical District.** Tours are available through restored old homes, antique shops, art galleries, museums, and archeological sites.

Plaza Ferdinand VII is the original central square of the old Spanish city. Nearby are the **Pensacola Historical Museum,** 405 South Adams Street, housed in old Christ Church—the oldest church building still standing in Florida, built in 1832—and the **Pensacola Museum of Art,** 407 South Jefferson Street, open Tuesday–Saturday, 10–5; closed holidays. Located in an old city jail. Entrance to both is free. Inquire about guided and self-guided tours at the historical museum, which is open Monday–Saturday, 9–4:30. Closed holidays. A free brochure, detailing a walking tour of the area, is available at the Tourist Information Office at 1401 E. Gregory Street.

On Zaragoza Street is the **West Florida Museum of History,** which includes a Hispanic Museum, a transportation building, and gulf coast history exhibits. Open Monday–Saturday, 10–4:30; closed Sundays, New Year's Day, Thanksgiving and Christmas.

North of the center of town, at 8382 Palafox Highway, is the **T. T. Wentworth Jr. Museum,** a private collection of thousands of items related to Florida history. Open only Saturday, Sunday, and holidays, 2–5. Free.

You can drive into the **U.S. Naval Air Station** and see strategic military points that have been defended at various times by Spanish, French, British, Confederate, and Union armed forces. The air station is known as the Cradle of Naval Aviation, because it was here that the first Navy flyers were trained for combat in World War I. Sites include the **Naval Aviation Museum** (open daily, 9–5; closed New Year's Day, Thanksgiving and Christmas); **Sherman Field** and the **Blue Angels;** the giant aircraft carrier **U.S.S. Lexington;** the 16th-century Spanish **Fort Barrancas,** now a part of Gulf Islands National Seashore; and the **Old Pensacola Lighthouse.**

Across Pensacola Bay lies **Santa Rosa Island.** At the western tip is **Fort Pickens,** 17 miles from Pensacola. This park, developed around the restored Fort Pickens, is a century-old scene of military activities and is today a focal point of interest of the history-rich **Gulf Islands National Seashore.** Campsites are located only a few yards from both the beach

Campers in St. Andrews State Recreation Area have all sorts of water sports just outside their tents.

Fort Pickens on Pensacola Bay has seen action in every major U.S. military conflict from the Civil War to World War II.

and the old fort itself. Tours of the fort and surrounding area are available.

About 10 miles southwest of the city is the **Big Lagoon State Recreation Area,** with opportunities for swimming, fishing, picnicking, boating, and nature study.

Bayview Park, on Bayou Texar, is a city-owned park with a playground, fishing pier, boat ramps, tennis courts, community centers, and picnic areas.

In addition to all its places of historic interest, Pensacola is worth visiting to see its docks and fishing fleets or to participate in its numerous sporting events. These include stock car, greyhound, and sailing races; shooting matches; golf and fishing tournaments. The main season for these events runs from April through November.

The city hosts quite a few annual festivals and events ranging from flower shows to stock car racing. In January it's the **Camellia Show;** in February **Mardi Gras;** in May the **American Amateur Golf Classic** and the **Fiesta of Five Flags;** in June the **Shark Rodeo;** in September the **Pensacola Seafood Festival;** in October the **Pensacola PGA Open;** in November the **Great Gulf Coast Arts Festival,** the **Blue Angels Air Show,** and the **Greek Festival Bazaar;** and in December the **Snowball Derby** (stock car racing).

If your special interest is hunting or fishing, you may wish to write for the "Authenic Map and Guide to Good Fishing and Hunting Around the City of Pensacola," from the Visitor Information Center, 1401 E. Gregory Street, Pensacola 32501.

PORT ST. JOE is the major population center of Gulf County, located on US 98 at St. Josephs Bay, near the southern tip of the Panhandle. Its major industries are fishing and the manufacturing of paper and paint.

South of town, about 1 mile, on US 98, is a state museum, **Constitution Convention,** marking the site where the first of Florida's five constitutions was written. Dioramas and exhibits of the convention and of the vanished city of St. Joseph are displayed. Open Monday–Saturday, 9–5. Closed Sunday, New Year's Day, Thanksgiving, and Christmas. Admission 25¢, children under 6 free.

To the southwest, **T. H. Stone Memorial St. Joseph Peninsula State Park** is bordered by the bay on one side and the Gulf on the other.

(Details on admission prices and hours have been included as a service to the reader and as a guide in planning activities. However, changes are inevitable in some cases, and the publisher cannot be responsible for any variations from the listed information.)

The mermaid is the symbol of Florida's Weeki Wachee, springs which are the setting for fabulous underwater shows.

NORTH CENTRAL

NORTH CENTRAL WOODS & RIVERS

TO DRIVE ACROSS NORTH CENTRAL FLORIDA IN EARLY SPRING IS TO INHALE THE SWEET FRAGRANCE OF NATURE UNSPOILED, TO LEARN AGAIN THAT THERE ARE ALTERNATIVES TO BUSTLING, BOOMING, BOISTEROUS CITY LIFE. IT IS GROVES OF BABY PINE TREES, PASTURES FULL OF CONTENTED COWS CARRYING WHITE BIRDS ON THEIR BACKS, ROADSIDE STANDS IN LITTLE VILLAGES OFFERING HOME-CANNED PRESERVES AND TUPELO HONEY AND PECANS. IT IS SWAMPS CHOKED WITH LILY PADS, THE WATER ECHOING WITH THE OCCASIONAL BARK OF AN ALLIGATOR OFF IN THE DISTANCE. CARPETS OF RED CLOVER. WILD IRIS.

The section designated here as North Central Florida is large in area, covering 24 counties. The northern sector is all woods and rivers; as you go farther south there are more lakes and the beginning of citrus groves. In recent years horse farms have added a new dimension to the economy and to the landscape. And everywhere there are the beautiful, bountiful springs of Florida—sources of fresh water, creating areas of incredible beauty.

LAND OF CONTRASTS

North Central Florida has contrasts—beautiful towns reminiscent of antebellum Dixie, such as Monticello and Tallahassee; sleepy, almost stagnant, backwater villages like Cross Creek (if you blink as you drive through you'll miss it, yet it provided inspiration for the highly successful books by Marjorie Kinnan Rawlings); the modern educational metropolis of Gainesville.

Approaching Monticello from either east or west, the tourist will notice beautifully trimmed ornamental plantings along the highway—many miles of them. The Mahan Nurseries, a large enterprise in the city, donated the shrubs and they are maintained by the State Highway Department. Masses of flowers are everywhere in the community, and it is not surprising to learn that there is an agricultural research center here. Even the high school complements the gracious old homes in the town; the building was designed in the architectural style of an antebellum mansion.

Then there is the Suwannee River with a photo-inviting vista around each curve. It rises in the Okefenokee Swamp in Georgia and flows 210 miles southwest into the Gulf of Mexico, fed by 55 known springs. Boat ramps are located about every 5 miles along the river, and there are numerous campgrounds, cottages, motels, and restaurants to serve those who wish to take advantage of the scenery.

"Big Bend" country curves from approximately Apalachicola to Homosassa. This is one area of shoreline that hasn't attracted land developers. Shallow, grass-choked bays, marshlands, and estuaries of numerous rivers and creeks are a barrier to change. It is still a better home for water birds, alligators, and oysters than for people. And the people who do make the little villages in the Big Bend their home know very well how lucky they are. They wouldn't trade their fishing and hunting wonderland for anyone's new suburban subdivision, with or without swimming pools.

You cannot be in North Central Florida long without being conscious of the importance of the timber industry. The highways are lined for hundreds of miles with tree farms, most identified by signs as being the property of a well-known paper or container manufacturer. Trucks pass by loaded with telephone-pole-sized logs. Exhibits explaining the story of forestry are displayed in Forest Capital State Museum, in Perry.

Tallahassee, Florida's Queen City, like a fine wine, ages well. She has most gracefully made the transition from the hoop-skirted Southern belle she was a few decades ago to the sophisticated modern woman she is today.

SILVER SPRINGS

One of the oldest, most beautiful, and most popular tourist attractions in the state is in North Central Florida—Silver Springs. During the tourist heydey of the 19th century, poets, authors, scientists, famous world travelers, and countless other visitors from all over the globe came to marvel at and enjoy the springs—and went away to sing their praises far and wide. Colorful steamboats brought them up the river from Palatka. Then, during the early part of the 20th century, when competition from railroads and automobiles had put the steamboats out of business, the popularity of the springs declined. Richard A. Martin, historian of Silver Springs, wrote this explanation:

> ... the promoters of the Hart Line steamboats had proved one thing—that people like their beauty spiced with excitement even in a natural attraction. Hart Line steamboats had provided the excitement. With their passing Silver Springs became, in the eyes of many tourists, no more than a picturesque pool tucked away in a remote Florida forest.

Florida is a state with some of the greatest natural beauty, as well as historic interest, anywhere in the world, and its residents and promoters have not hesitated to add the spice needed to attract visitors.

In North Central Florida more than half the people live in rural areas, about one-quarter in the metropolitan centers of Tallahassee and Gainesville, and the rest in other cities and towns of more than 2,500 people.

Like much of Florida, this section has many retired people. But they do not live in the glossy, highly advertised retirement havens like those of the southern part of the state. These are people of modest incomes, many of them rural or small-town folks, who have found that the climate here is beneficial, the living is easy, and the prices are comparatively moderate. The residents of this part of the state are, for the most part, happy that their dream spots have not yet been discovered by large numbers of people, and they can still hunt and fish, float down their rivers, and wander through their woods without running into traffic jams.

If you are driving to Florida, don't think of this section as something just to be rushed through on your way south; stop and enjoy it while you can. Twenty years from now it will be a different kind of place.

CITIES & TOWNS

Map of this section on page 23.

APALACHICOLA is the county seat and principal center of Franklin County. Located on US 98 and Apalachicola Bay of the Gulf of Mexico, at the southern tip of the Panhandle, it is almost entirely surrounded by water. The delightful meaning of the Indian name is "friendly people," and residents try to live up to the definition.

The principal product of this beautiful fishing village is seafood. A large portion of the state's shellfish is landed here, and Apalachicola's oyster harvest represents nearly 90% of Florida's total output. Each year on the first Saturday in November, a **Florida Seafood Festival** is held, with a parade of decorated boats, a seafood dinner, art and antique shows, visits to historic homes, tours of seafood factories, entertainment, a grand ball, and a fireworks display.

Beautiful bridges and causeways (toll $2) lead to St. George Island. Freshwater and saltwater fishing, swimming, and shell hunting are all excellent. **St. George Island State Park** has been developed on the eastern end that includes swimming, picnicking, and fishing facilities. The park also boasts miles of undeveloped beaches, dunes, and marshland.

In Apalachicola see **Trinity Church** and the **John Gorrie State Museum.** Trinity is one of the oldest churches in Florida and is known as the nation's first prefabricated church. Its sections and timbers were made in New York and shipped to Florida in the 1830s. **John Gorrie State Museum** displays scenes of local history and a replica of the first ice-making machine. Open daily 9–5. Admission 50¢, children under 6 free.

A few miles to the north, reached by way of US 98/319 east and Florida 65 north, is **Apalachicola National Forest,** covering more than half a million acres in Franklin, Liberty, Wakulla, and Leon counties. Oaks, pines, cedars, and cypress shade the many sparkling lakes and three large rivers in the forest. Fishing is good here for bass, bream, and perch. Boating, picnicking, and camping facilities are available, and there are several good swimming areas. Fees may be charged at recreation sites. Within the boundaries of the forest are **Silver Lake, Camel Lake,** and **Fort Gadsden State Historic Site,** a recreational park developed on the site of an abandoned fort once held by Indians and runaway slaves against American forces. For more information write Supervisor, 227 N. Brounough St., Tallahassee 32301, or phone (904) 681-7265.

BRISTOL is the county seat and principal village of Liberty County. This county is largely covered by Apalachicola National Forest and contains only a few small villages and less than 3,500 residents. Bristol is on Florida 20 across the Apalachicola River from Blountstown.

North of town (take Florida 12 northeast for about 3 miles, then turn north on secondary roads) is **Torreya State Park.** The park is set on rugged and picturesque bluffs overlooking the river. Special features include the rare Torreya evergreen trees, said to be the same wood as that used in the construction of Noah's ark; a fine antebellum mansion, **Gregory House;** and sites of Civil War gun pits. Open daily, 8–sunset. Admission 50¢.

BROOKSVILLE, county seat and principal population center of Hernando County, is at the junction of US 98 and US 41. Nearby is the **Chassahowitzka National Wildlife Refuge. Florida's Weeki Wachee** is 13 miles west of Brooksville on FL 50 at jct. US 19.

Rogers' Christmas House and Village, at 103 Saxon Avenue, includes five houses in a garden setting. The main house is filled with Christmas trees decorated with unique ornaments. Open Monday–Saturday, 9:30–5; Sunday, 10–5. Free.

Each spring the **Hernando County Fair** is presented at the county fairgrounds.

A 20-mile loop, beginning in Brooksville and proceeding north on US 41, around Chinsegut Hill, to Withlacoochee State Forest headquarters back to Brooksville, is called the **Dogwood Trail.** It is excellent for auto tours.

CEDAR KEY is on the Gulf of Mexico, 33 miles southwest of Bronson on Florida 24. The village, most populated settlement in Levy County, is on the largest of a group of about one hundred islands known as the Cedar Keys. Four of the islands have been established as **Cedar Keys National Wildlife Refuge.**

Cedar Key is a quaint fishing village and artists' colony, the most interesting stop in the north Gulf coast area. Thousands attend the **Art Festival** held here each April, and the **Seafood Festival** in October.

Settlement of the area goes back many centuries. Large Indian burial mounds have been found on nearby islands, and it also attracted the Spaniards, who built fortifications here. In the latter part of the 19th century Cedar Key was one of the largest cities in the state, a bustling port and summer resort. It was noted for its fine harbor and had a thriving industry in the manufacture of pencils from the cedar trees that gave the town its name. Then, in 1896, a hurricane devastated the port, and the town never quite recovered.

The interesting history of the area is preserved in **Cedar Key State Museum.** Open daily, 9–5. Admission 25¢, children under 6 free.

Storms and shifting currents have gradually shrunk the land area of Cedar Key over the years, and its residents are fiercely protective of what is left. The casual observer may not recognize its special appeal, but those who have become hooked on the town have no desire to be cured of their addiction.

Seafood meals in local restaurants are unsurpassed, featuring deviled crab, turtle steaks, scallops, swamp cabbage salad, and broiled pompano. Smoked mullet is a popular local specialty. Long-time residents will tell you that Cedar Key established its reputation for fine food and drink back when Gainesville was dry and Cedar Key was the nearest place to get a drink.

CHATTAHOOCHEE, in Gadsden County, is located on US 90 and the Georgia border, where the Apalachicola River meets Lake Seminole. The town sits on a high, rolling, wooded river bluff.

CHIEFLAND, the principal village in Levy County, is located on US 19/98 and US 27A, near the Suwannee River. In Ter-

Apalachicola, an important commercial fishing port, has a most picturesque waterfront.

ritorial days Indians and white settlers lived and farmed here harmoniously, side by side, and the town was named in honor of the tribal chief. It is now the center of an agricultural area producing peanuts, watermelons, tobacco, and corn, and claims the title of Watermelon Capital of the World. To celebrate this distinction there is an annual **Watermelon Festival** in June.

About 6 miles west of Chiefland is **Manatee Springs State Park,** a large park named for the strange, bulky aquatic mammals (the manatee is also known as the sea cow) once common to the area. It is a fully developed park, with a combination boardwalk and boat dock leading to the Suwanee River.

CRAWFORDVILLE, county seat of Wakulla County, is located on US 319 and Florida 365 at the eastern edge of **Apalachicola National Forest.**

Six miles northeast of town are **Wakulla Springs,** the state's deepest, producing millions of gallons of water daily. Glass-bottomed boats take visitors gliding over limestone formations and petrified bones of prehistoric animals. Hotel and restaurant facilities available. Swimming area (fee) jungle cruise, Floating Theater ($1; children 75¢), wildlife refuge. Open daily, 9:30–5:30. Admission to grounds free. Boat cruise $3.75, children $2.25; jungle cruise and boat tour $6, children $3.75.

CRYSTAL RIVER, in Citrus County, is located on US 19/98 and Florida 44, near the Gulf of Mexico and Homosassa Springs.

Fishing—both freshwater and saltwater—and hunting, are excellent.

The **Crystal River State Archaeological Site** marks one of the most important prehistoric Indian dwelling places in the state. This riverbank area was a ceremonial center for about 1,600 years. More than 450 burials have been found here since 1903. Some of the items found in the graves indicate that there was once trade and exchange of ideas and artifacts between these Indians and residents of areas as far away as Ohio and Mexico. The Visitor Center in the park permits visitors to view three different types of mounds through windows: temple, burial, and refuse mounds. Trails lead through the complex. Open daily, 9–5; grounds 8–sundown. Visitor Center, 50¢; under 6 free.

About seven springs of "Kings Bay" feed the Crystal River. Banana Island Spring, on the south side of Banana Island, is one of the finest freshwater dives in the state because of its size, visibility, ease of access, and potential for underwater photography. Manatees, a protected species of marine mammal native to Florida, frequent the spring.

DADE CITY, county seat of Pasco County, is on US 301, about 40 miles northeast of Tampa. Moss-hung oak trees, camphor trees, and lovely azalea bushes grace this pleasant community; extensive farmland, citrus groves, and cattle ranches surround it.

Each year in February this village is the setting for the **Pasco County Fair** and the **"Heart of Florida" Fair.**

At various times throughout the year exciting auto races

Mealtime for alligators at Homosassa Springs.

are held at the **Pasco County Fair Raceway.**

The town of San Antonio, 5 miles southwest, holds an unusual and interesting **Rattlesnake Festival and International Championship Gopher Race** on the third Saturday in October. This culminates a month-long snake-hunting contest, and prizes are awarded for the longest catch, the greatest number caught, etc. Gopher races, venom-milking contests, and other festivities are also featured. Indians from the area bring handicraft items for sale, and the merchants in Dade City have a special sidewalk sale during the Roundup Festival. Admission is charged.

Saint Leo Abbey, with **St. Leo College** on the grounds, is 5 miles southwest of Dade City on Florida 52. The Benedictine abbey has a Pilgrim Center designed as a replica of the Lourdes Grotto.

On US 301, 1 miles north of town, the **Pioneer Florida Museum** displays a schoolroom with furnishings and tools used by early settlers of the state. Open Tuesday–Sunday, 1–5. Donation $1.25.

GAINESVILLE, county seat and principal city of Alachua County, is located on US 441, just east of I-75, in the center of northern Florida. It is most famous as the home of the 34,500 student **University of Florida,** one of the largest universities in the Southeast.

Gainesville is in the heart of the pleasant rolling highlands of north Florida. The favorable climate and rich soil of the area make for a diversified agricultural industry, and the numerous freshwater lakes attract sport fishermen.

Spectator sports include drag racing at the **Gainesville Dragway** and intercollegiate sports at the university.

The university has several buildings on campus open to the public without charge. The **University Art Gallery** offers alternating public exhibits, open January–mid-December; Monday–Friday, 9–5; Sunday, 1–5; closed holidays and between exhibits. The Department of Music and the Florida Players provide a full schedule of musical and theatrical productions. The Dance Troupe also performs. Also on the grounds are the **Lake Alice Wildlife Preserve,** and **Century Tower,** which has one of Florida's only two carillons.

The **Florida State Museum** has a fine collection of fossils, Indian artifacts, dioramas of Florida history, a walk-through limestone cave, and a browsing library. Open Monday–Saturday, 9–5; Sunday, 1–5; Tuesday night until 9. Free.

Displays of Latin American art and artifacts are displayed at **Grinter Gallery,** open Monday–Friday, 9–3; free.

Near Gainesville, on US 301, is Cross Creek, a village made famous in the books of Marjorie Kinnan Rawlings (*The Yearling, Cross Creek*). Her cracker-style farmhouse, now the **Marjorie K. Rawlings State Historic Site,** has been named a national historic landmark. A small park nearby has facilities for picnicking and boating.

HOMOSASSA and HOMOSASSA SPRINGS are about 2 miles apart, located in Citrus County, on the Gulf of Mexico, at the junction of US 19 and Florida 490.

Homosassa Springs, the source of the Homosassa River, is a major tourist attraction. The park offers scenic boat trips, an underwater observatory, a botanical garden, alligators, waterfowl, and a new manatee rehabilitation exhibit. The Springs are open daily, 9:30–5:30; last boat to Nature Park leaves at 4. Admission $5, children 3–11 $2.75, under 3 free. Member Florida Attractions Association.

In Micanopy, 8 miles south of Gainesville on US 441, is **Payne's Prairie State Preserve,** a region of historical and natural importance. Indian artifacts found in the area have been dated to at least 7,000 B.C. Facilities in the preserve include swimming, picnicking, fishing, and boating. Scenic access is provided on the south rim.

West of the springs, on Florida 490, is the **Yulee Sugar Mill Ruins State Historic Site.** This 3,000-acre sugar plantation belonged to Florida's first U.S. Senator, David Levy Yulee, a man very active in many phases of the expansion of the new State of Florida. Picnic area.

LAKE BUTLER, county seat and principal center of Union County, is located at the intersection of Florida 100 and Florida 121, southeast of Lake City.

About 20 miles southwest is **O'Leno State Park,** a well-equipped recreational park on the Santa Fe River. The park is open daily, 8 am–sunset.

LAKE CITY, county seat and principal city of Columbia County, is located 5 miles southeast of the junction of I-75 and I-10. Tobacco auctions are held here in late July or August. The crops are harvested on nearby plantations that still retain a flavor of the Old South.

Lake City is on the edge of **Osceola National Forest,** an area of more than 157,000 acres. Ocean Pond is a major recreation area within the forest. There are camping, picnicking, and boating facilities here, as well as fine hiking, swimming, and fishing areas. Ponds and cypress swamps dot the forest. For more detailed information and a map of the area write Supervisor, 227 N. Bronough St., Tallahassee

18 NORTH CENTRAL

32301 or District Ranger's Office, U.S.D.A., Route 7, Box 95, Lake City 32055. Fees are charged at campgrounds and may be charged at other recreation sites.

About 20 miles southwest of Lake City, off Florida 137 between Branford and Fort White, is **Ichetucknee Springs State Park.**

LIVE OAK, county seat and principal city of Suwannee County, is located two miles south of I-10, at the junction of US 90 and US 129, about halfway between Tallahassee and Jacksonville.

In October Live Oak hosts the **Suwannee County Fair and Livestock Show.**

Fourteen miles west, on US 90 is **Suwannee River State Park.** Here the lovely Withlacoochee River flows down from Georgia into the Suwannee, merging with it in a beautiful Y-shaped fork. There are nature trails, Confederate earthworks, and an overlook along the Suwannee to accommodate camera bugs.

MONTICELLO is the county seat and principal center of Jefferson County. It is located at the junction of US 19 and US 90, about 25 miles east of Tallahassee. This area is rich in the production of watermelons, pecans, and Satsuma oranges.

Monticello is another town that pays tribute to the watermelon in June of each year with the **Jefferson County Watermelon Festival.** Along with a queen contest and parade are featured a watermelon-eating contest, horse show, dance, golf tournament, barbecue, and fireworks.

Many antebellum homes and beautiful gardens may be seen in Monticello, especially along Washington and Jefferson streets. A frame Greek revival structure, the **Wirick-Simmons House,** at Jefferson and Pearl Streets, is open to the public by appointment. Also see the Asa-May House on US 19 South. In late March the Jefferson County Historical Association sponsors a **Tour of Homes.**

The town's courthouse was modeled on Thomas Jefferson's Monticello, and the whole community has a gracious and cared-for appearance.

From May–October there is greyhound racing at the **Jefferson County Kennel Club.**

NEW PORT RICHEY, principal center of Pasco County, is just off US 19, about 6 miles north of Tarpon Springs.

Sports fishermen can follow the beautiful meandering Pithlachascotee River from the center of the town into the open waters of the Gulf for deep-sea fishing.

In late March the town holds a **Chasco Fiesta,** which honors the Calusa Indians who once inhabited this part of Florida. A **Merchant's Home Show** is held here in November.

OCALA, county seat of Marion County, is on US 27, 441, and 301, near I-75, at the western edge of **Ocala National Forest.** It is a pleasant, thriving city, set in an area of forests, lakes, and rolling hills. It is probably best known to millions of tourists because of its proximity to **Silver Springs.**

A tourist center for this part of the state, the city contains more than 100 motels, plus convention facilities, many fine restaurants, and a unique shopping center called Cascades. There are sparkling lakes and streams for fishing and water sports, camping facilities in Ocala National Forest, and fine golf courses. Nearby, at the **Ocala Fronton** in Orange Lake, jai-alai is played from January–March and mid-June–October.

If some of the towns in central Florida might remind the visitor of Kansas or Texas cow towns, surely Ocala today will make you think you are near Lexington, Kentucky. Hundreds of horse farms are located in Marion County, where some of the most famous thoroughbreds in racing are bred. Their lush pastureland occupies thousands of scenic acres, and many of the farms welcome visitors to tour the premises. For a tour map of farms and other area information, write to the Ocala-Marion County Chamber of Commerce, Box 1210, Ocala 32670, or phone (904) 629-8051.

OLUSTEE is located in Baker County, on US 90, between Lake City and Jacksonville, in the southeastern section of **Osceola National Forest.** Two miles east is **Olustee Battlefield State Historic Site,** where a monument marks the site of one of the most important Civil War battles fought in Florida. A museum on the grounds is open daily.

PERRY is the county seat and principal city of Taylor County. It is located at the junction of US 27 and US 221, about 50 miles southeast of Tallahassee. South of town is **Forest Capital Center,** a recreational and educational park covering six acres. **Forest Capital State Museum** is on the grounds; open daily, 9–5; 25¢.

In late September–early October Florida's billion-dollar forestry industry is honored in Perry at the **Florida Forest Festival,** an annual event which usually attracts some 50,000 visitors. The "world's largest free fish fry" is held at Forest Capital Park; the King Tree Parade consists of more than 250 units; a Forest Queen reigns over all; and educational displays are on view at the park. Other activities during the festival include the heavy equipment show, an art show, Gaslight Parade, and fireworks display.

ST. MARKS is located in Wakulla County at the end of Florida 363, off US 98, about 20 miles south of Tallahassee and north of Apalache Bay. There is a legend that Spanish explorers settled here as early as 1521, but no trace of the settlement remains.

To the west of St. Marks, on Florida 363, is the **San Marcos de Apalache State Historic Site,** memorializing a Spanish fort built more than three hundred years ago. Open daily, 9–5. Admission 50¢; under 6 free.

Just north and east of St. Marks, on US 98 east of Newport is **Newport Recreation Area.** There are well-developed campsites and a picnic area surrounded by moss-hung trees. Administered by the Florida Division of Forestry. South, off US 98, is a scenic drive to a lighthouse in the **St. Marks National Wildlife Refuge**—a bird-watcher's paradise. Open mid-March–mid-October, Sunday–Friday, daylight hours, free.

Southwest of St. Marks, off Florida 365 at the fishing community of Spring Creek is **Spring Creek Spring.**

SILVER SPRINGS in Marion County, is 6 miles east of Ocala, on Florida 40. The name applies to both the tourist attraction that has been drawing visitors for hundreds of years and to the little village, made up mostly of motels, which provide services for these visitors.

NORTH CENTRAL 19

The springs are surrounded by about 100 acres of landscaped grounds that border a section of Silver River and the deep blue pools fed by the underground waters. Every day 640 million gallons of crystal-clear water gush into the basin of the main spring. This major spring, plus about 15 lesser ones, feed the river. A tropical wilderness lies on either side of the river, complete with monkeys, birds, and jungle vegetation. A fleet of glass-bottomed boats makes regular cruises over the spring basin and down the river.

Long before white men were exploring North Central Florida, the Indian natives regarded the springs as sacred and maintained them as a shrine to their water gods. Ceremonies and festivities staged in the sacred groves attracted Indians from near and far. A number of white settlers "discovered" the area in the 1800's, and its fame gradually grew during the half-century following 1826, when a company of U.S. troops were stationed there.

In 1873, Harriet Beecher Stowe described her visit to Silver Springs in these words:

> There is nothing on earth comparable to it. We seemed floating through an immense cathedral where white marble columns meet in vast arches overhead and are reflected in the grassy depths below. The dusky plumes of the palmetto waving above, lit by torchlight, looked like fine tracery of a wondrous sculptured roof . . . Clouds of fragrance were wafted to us from orange groves along the shore; and the transparent depth of the water gave the impression that our boat was moving through the air. Every pebble and aquatic plant we glided over, seemed, in the torchlight, invested with prismatic brightness. What a sight was that!

Because of its "exceptional value in illustrating the natural history of the United States," Silver Springs has been designated a registered National Natural Landmark by the U.S. Department of Interior.

The history of Silver Springs and its development as a tourist attraction is fascinatingly told in a book entitled **Eternal Spring,** by Richard A. Martin, which is available at the gift stands.

The book also has an extensive listing of the plant life, fish, and animals of the area.

A word of advice: save plenty of time to enjoy Silver Springs fully. There is much there to see and do, and the grounds are a beautiful, peaceful place for relaxing and picnicking. More than a million and a half visitors a year come here, but the spacious grounds can accommodate them all.

Within the landscaped park is the **Senator Everett McKinley Dirksen** flower bed, which is beautiful in all seasons. Senator Dirksen advocated having the marigold as the national flower, and in his memory marigolds, which bloom

Glass-bottomed boats show the delights of the underwater world to millions of visitors to Florida's Silver Springs.

from late spring throughout the summer, flourish in the garden. During the rest of the year, pansies grow in bright patterns.

Admission to the park and all attractions $8.95, children 3–11 $6.75, under 3 free with adult. Open daily, 9–dusk. **Florida's Silver Springs** is a member of the Florida Attractions Association.

At Silver Springs there are five main areas. Take a 30 minute **Glass-Bottomed Boat Ride** or take the **Jungle Cruise** down the river.

The Jungle Cruise covers five miles, and, within this distance, the vegetation varies from the carefully tended and landscaped grounds surrounding the springs to wild and fearsome jungle. Visitors will see wild monkeys and alligators as well as myriad exotic animals, such as rhinos, zebras, and giraffes. The cruise takes about 40 minutes.

The third area on the grounds is **Cypress Point Reptile Institute,** which has a large collection of live reptiles and a venom laboratory that processes snake venom for many scientific and educational institutions. Also on the grounds is **Deer Park,** where various baby animals also make their residence. **The Antique Car Collection** boasts an abundance of classic and antique vehicles.

Wild Waters is a water theme park adjacent to the springs. Included here are picnicking facilities, flumes, a miniature-golf course, and wading and kiddie pools. Admission $6.50, children 3–11 $5.50, under 3 free. Open daily; late March–mid-September, 10–5; summer, 10–9.

On Florida 40 between Ocala and Silver Springs is **Six-Gun Territory,** a re-creation of a western frontier town with major rides, kiddie rides, gun fights, an amusement area, Indian dance performances, and various shows. Open daily, 9:30–5:30; ticket office closes at 3:45. Admission $6.95; children 4–12, $5.50; under 4 free. Fee includes shows and entertainment. All-day ticket for rides $3. Member Florida Attractions Association.

SOPCHOPPY is the largest village in Wakulla, a county devoid of populous centers. Almost all of the county lies within the borders of **Apalachicola National Forest.** Sopchoppy is on US 319, at the southern edge of the forest. Three miles south is **Ochlockonee River State Park,** a swimming, fishing, camping and picnicking area bounded by two rivers.

SUMATRA is located in Liberty County on Florida 65, at the southwestern edge of **Apalachicola National Forest.** Six miles southwest of town is **Fort Gadsden State Historic Site,** where an abandoned British fort was replaced under the direction of Andrew Jackson.

TALLAHASSEE is the capital of Florida, the county seat of Leon County, and the largest city in North Central Florida. It is located at the intersection of US 90 and US 27, at the eastern end of the Florida Panhandle.

The earliest known settlers of this wooded highland were an Indian tribe, now extinct, known as the Apalachee. Spaniards, Creek Indians, English, and Americans followed. In 1824 the site of the city was proclaimed as the governmental seat for the new Territory of Florida, and the legislative Council met there in November of that year, in a log house in the vicinity of the present-day Capitol.

Tallahassee has changed much since the WPA guide, **Flor-**

International Deer Ranch, Silver Springs.

ida, a Guide to the Southernmost State, was published in 1939. The population then was 10,700, and here is how the city was described:

> The business district, confined to two wide streets, followed a ridge northward from Capitol Square, and cross streets, shaded by oaks and magnolias, drop off precipitously into residential districts. Within and surrounding the area are old homes with spacious lawns that date back to Territorial days, some of them converted into business property, and tall-steepled brick and stucco churches that once sheltered citizens during Indian raids. Out the natural forest growth rise various State Government buildings of gray sandstone and yellow brick.
>
> Red clay streets intersect many paved thoroughfares, and horse- and mule-drawn vehicles are not uncommon sights. For two blocks, almost in the shadow of the Capitol dome, Adams Street is a noisy, crowded trading center on Saturdays when rural families attend to their weekly shopping. Store windows are plastered with signs, banners advertise bargain sales, and radios blare. Lunch counters and soft-drink stands do a brisk business. Parked along the high curbs are shining motors with liveried chauffeurs and rickety farm wagons acting as carry-alls for produce, groceries, and brown-faced children. Hitching posts and watering troughs still survive, and oats and baled hay are in demand along with gasoline.

Today Tallahassee possesses a quiet Southern dignity that somehow manages to superimpose a modern and sophisticated air upon its traditional setting; at azalea time (late March) Tallahassee's beauty becomes dramatic and spectacular. An annual festival, **Springtime Tallahassee,** is held to celebrate this blossoming and the city's founding. Special events held just before, during, and after the festival include art, music, and flower shows, lectures, dramas, variety shows, a P.G.A. invitational golf tournament, a horse show, a tour of old homes, etc., with a grand finale of entertainment and displays of arts and crafts in the parks.

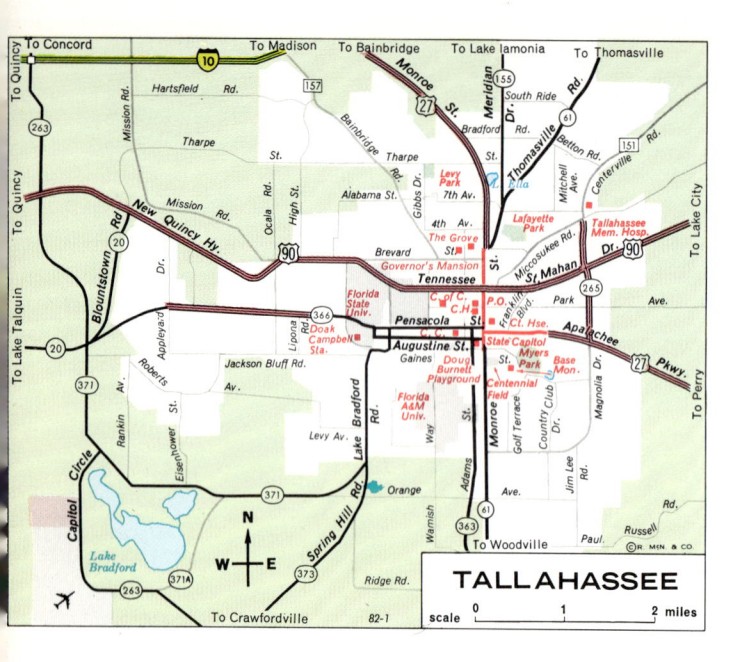

Other annual events include the **North Florida Fair** in the fall; and **Junior Museum Market Day** in November.

A young couple participating in "Springtime Tallahassee."

Anyone visiting the southeastern United States at any time between December and April should try to see the **Alfred B. Maclay State Ornamental Gardens** north of Tallahassee. Here is displayed a collection of camellias, rhododendron, and azaleas that is almost beyond belief. Admission ($1.50, children 75¢) is charged during the blooming season. The park is open all year.

Another small (11½ acres) state park, on the shore of Lake Jackson, northwest of Tallahassee, is the **Lake Jackson Mounds State Archaeological Site.** The area is historically interesting because it is the setting where the first Christmas Mass was celebrated in the New World (in 1539), and also because some important Indian temple mounds have been discovered here.

About 20 miles west of Tallahassee, off Florida 20, is **Lake Talquin State Recreation Area.** Recreational possibilities include fishing, boating, and picnicking at River Bluff Point.

Two universities, **Florida State** and **Florida A & M,** contribute much to the enrichment of cultural life in Tallahassee, particularly in the fields of art, music, and drama. But they contribute to the fun as well. Each year, during two weekends in April, eighty Florida State students perform in the three-ring **Flying High Circus.** Performances on Friday at 8 and on Saturday at 2 and 8; admission $4.50, under 12, $1.50.

A number of fine old homes and public buildings will interest architecture buffs, including the **Historic Old Capitol,** which stands on the second highest of the seven hills in the city and has been restored to its 1902 form. The Old Capitol, Florida's new 22-story capitol is an impressive modernistic structure immediately behind the historic capitol. Fountains, bench areas, and manicured gardens surround this Capitol Complex.

A part of traditional Tallahassee is the state-owned **Brokaw-McDougall House,** a handsome antebellum building with formal gardens, which now serves the state as a conference site. Visitors are welcome to view any of the rooms not in use.

You may also visit the **First Presbyterian Church,** at Adams Street and Park Avenue, the first church, as well as the first non-governmental building, built in Tallahassee. In the church are galleries where slaves worshipped. Open Monday through Friday, 8:30–4:30, Saturday to noon, Sunday to 1. Closed holidays.

The new **R. A. Grey Archives, Library, and Museum Building** is located in downtown Tallahassee just west of the Florida Supreme Court Building. It houses such treasures as Spanish gold, skeletons of giant mastedons, and many other pieces of Florida history. Open Monday–Friday, 9–4:30; Saturday, 10–4:30; Sunday and holidays, noon–4:30; free.

The **Little Gallery** at the Lewis State Bank has an outstanding program of exhibits, as does the **LeMoyne Art Foundation,** housed in a charming 1852 building at 125 North Gadsden Street. The latter is open Tuesday–Saturday, 10–5; Sunday, 2–5. Closed January 1, July 4, and Christmas. Free. Other cultural attractions include little theater groups that are active in the city.

The **Tallahassee Junior Museum,** at 3945 Museum Drive, on Lake Bradford, about 6 miles southwest of town, features nature trails and habitats, exhibit buildings, and an 1880 Pioneer Farm. Open Tuesday–Saturday, 9–5; Sunday, 2–5;

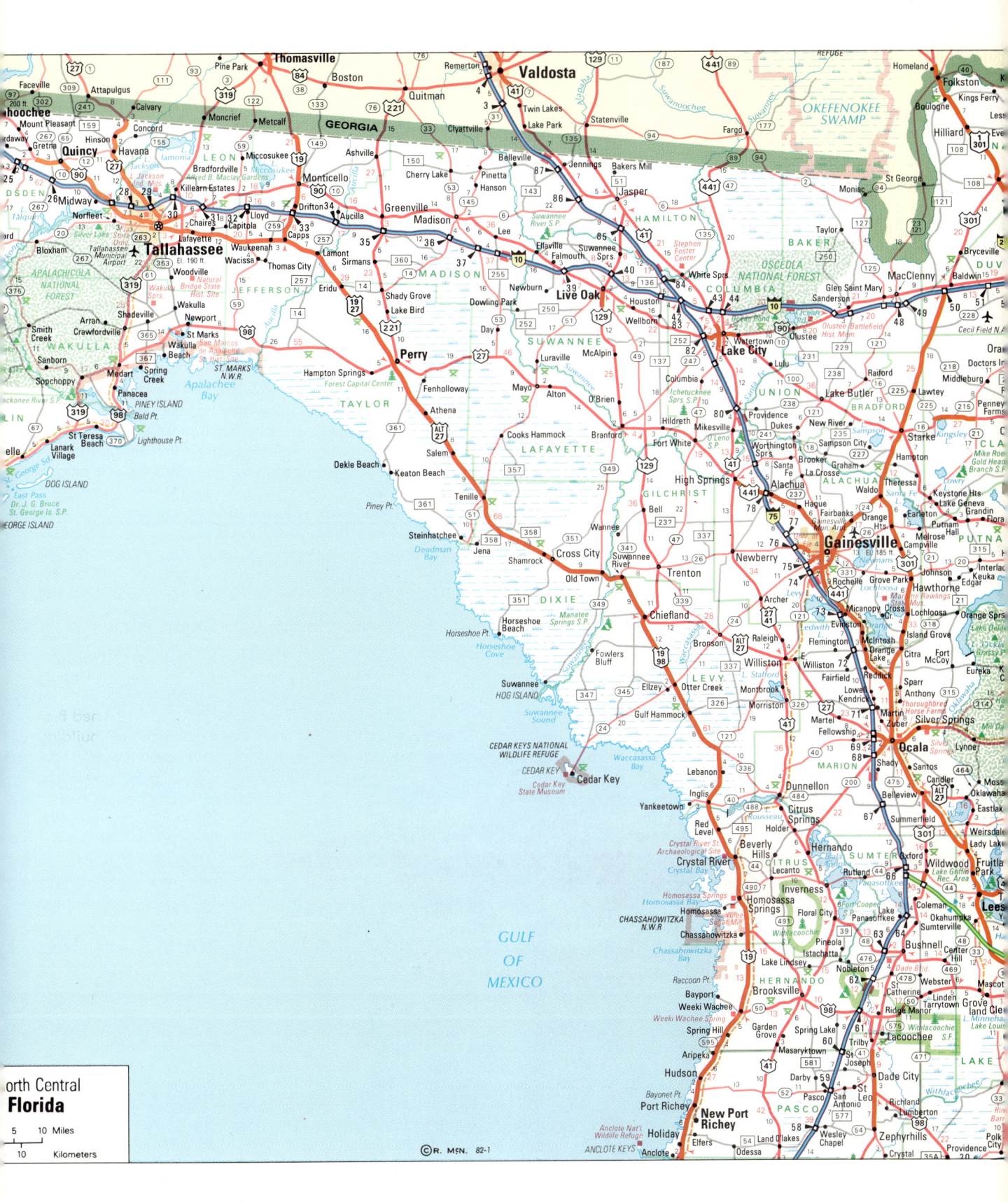

closed holidays. Admission $2; students and senior citizens, $1; under 4 free.

Ten miles southeast of Tallahassee, on US 319, is **Natural Bridge Battlefield State Historic Site.** During in the Civil War, boys from the West Florida Seminary joined Confederate troops in a battle here that saved Tallahassee from capture by Union troops. Each year near the March 7, 1865 anniversary of the skirmish, the Battle of Natural Bridge is reenacted by a group of volunteers.

About 15 miles southeast of Tallahassee, near the town

NORTH CENTRAL 23

of Wacissa off Florida 59, is the **Wacissa Springs Group.** The springs are scattered along the Wacissa River, in the Aucilla Game Management Area. In the group, Big Spring is popular with scuba divers. Also along the river is the 15-mile **Wacissa River Canoe Trail.**

WEEKI WACHEE in Hernando County, is on US 19 and Florida 50, 13 miles west of Brooksville.

A major tourist attraction known as **Florida's Weeki Wachee** has been developed around a crystal-clear natural spring, which is more than 130 feet deep and has a constant temperature of 72.2° F. The spring is used as a stage for spectacular water shows. Spectators sit in an auditorium built 16 feet below the surface and watch, through 2.-inch-thick plate glass windows, the Weeki Wachee "mermaids" perform in ballets, comedies, and skits. Each year a major new show is developed. Open daily, 9–6.

A Wilderness River Cruise may be taken down the Weeki Wachee River. Other popular attractions here are the Birds of Prey Show, a Tropical Rain Forest, the Pelican Orphanage, and the Exotic Wild Bird Show, featuring trained macaws and cockatoos.

A combination ticket covers general admission, all shows, and the river cruise: $6.95, children 3–11 $4.75, under 3 free. For special outings and group tour, write to the Tour

Left: Carillon Tower, Stephen Foster Center, White Springs.

Below: Six-Gun Territory, between Silver Springs and Ocala.

24 NORTH CENTRAL

The Pioneer farm at the Tallahassee Junior Museum depicts Florida farm life in the 1880s.

Development Department. Weeki Wachee is a member of the Florida Attractions Association.

Buccaneer Bay, a water park adjacent to Weeki Wachee, is open from mid-March through mid-September.

On US 19, 3 miles south of Weeki Wachee, is the **Foxbower Wildlife Exhibit,** with some eight hundred mounted species. Open daily, 9–5. Admission $2, children 6–14 $1, under 6 free.

WHITE SPRINGS is located in Hamilton County, on US 41 and the Suwannee River, just east of I-75. The mineral springs, which gave the town its name, first attracted visitors here some 150 years ago. Even before that the Indians were familiar with the medicinal power of the springs; the waters were considered so strong braves were forbidden to drink there.

On the edge of the Suwannee River is the **Stephen Foster State Folk Culture Center,** owned and operated by the State of Florida. A beautifully landscaped park contains a Carillon Tower, the Foster Museum, a permanent amphitheater, and an antique shop. Train and riverboat rides. Grounds open daily, 8–sunset; visitor center and tower, 9–5. Admission 50¢, under 6 free. Member Florida Attractions Association.

The Center is a setting for many events throughout the year, including an annual **Florida Folk Festival** on Memorial Day weekend, the **Jeannie with the Light Brown Hair** auditions in October, and **Christmas Concerts.** A complete schedule of events may be obtained by writing to the Stephen Foster Memorial Commission in White Springs.

ZEPHYRHILLS, in Pasco County, is located on US 301, about 20 miles northeast of Tampa.

Six miles southwest of town, on US 301, is **Hillsborough River State Park,** a facility with thick forests and many birds, nature trails, and a "swinging bridge" across the river. Recreational facilities, campsites, a public pond in which to swim, and a reconstructed fort across the highway. Inside the park is **Fort Foster,** a reproduction of a fort in operation during the Second Seminole War. Costumed park rangers present a living history program. Fee.

(Details on admission prices and hours have been included as a service to the reader and as a guide in planning activities. However, changes are inevitable in some cases, and the publisher cannot be responsible for any variations from the listed information.)

NORTH CENTRAL

Horse-drawn carriage pauses to give tourists a chance to visit the Oldest House in St. Augustine.

NORTHEAST

THE CROWN

FROM AMELIA ISLAND TO MELBOURNE, THE TRIP IS MORE THAN FOUR HUNDRED YEARS LONG. IT TAKES YOU FROM SPANISH SCHOONER TO SPACE SHIP, FROM PRIMEVAL WILDLIFE SANCTUARIES AND INDIAN MOUNDS TO ONE OF THE WORLD'S LARGEST BUILDINGS. NORTHEAST FLORIDA IS FAMOUS FOR ITS OLD FORTS AND PLANTATION RUINS—AND FOR AUTO RACING AND MISSILE TAKE-OFFS. IT HAS CHANGED ITS APPEARANCE DRASTICALLY SINCE THE SPACE AGE WAS LAUNCHED, BUT THEN IT IS USED TO CHANGE. EIGHT FLAGS HAVE FLOWN HERE DURING THE PAST FOUR CENTURIES.

Northeast Florida consists of eight counties; all but two (Clay and Putnam) are on the Atlantic coast, bordered by golden sand beaches and steel-blue surf. The mighty St. Johns River bisects most of the section. In 18 state parks some 10,000 acres have been set aside for public enjoyment. Some of these parks have historic interest—preserving old mills, plantations, forts, Indian mounds, some are wildlife preserves, havens of nature and outdoor natural history laboratories; some are simply beautiful spots for camping and recreation.

Coming in from the north, by boat or by car, the first important town is Fernandina Beach, on Amelia Island. Here you will hear the story of the eight flags: French, Spanish, English, Republic of Florida, Confederacy, the United States. The first six are easy to name, but what were the others? One was Mexico! And the eighth was a private little banner with a green cross on a white field run up by a Scotsman, General Sir Gregor MacGregor, who ruled the area for a few months in 1817.

From Fernandina Beach to Daytona Beach, Florida A1A is called the Buccaneer Trail. Along these magnificent waters, now prized for sport fishing and pleasure yachting, the major activities in earlier days were piracy, slave-trading, hijacking, smuggling, and wrecking.

Jacksonville, largest city in Florida in both area and population, is also the leading financial, industrial, transportation, and commercial city in the state. Its waterfront is 8 miles long, and there are more than 70 piers. It was known by the unromantic name of Cowford until after the United States purchased Florida, when it was renamed for Andrew Jackson.

MISSIONS TO MISSILES

St. Augustine has been a popular tourist spot and destination for school field trips for many years. It began early to capitalize on its claim as the oldest permanent settlement in the United States. Henry Flagler, the man who did so much to popularize Florida as a resort area a century ago, built two large hotels and established the headquarters of his Florida East Coast Railroad here.

As you wander slowly and quietly about the ruins of Castillo de San Marcos National Monument, a fort built about three hundred years ago, or visit the site of the first permanent Christian mission—established more than four hundred years ago—you will feel very far away indeed from the "Space Coast" to the south.

But it is there—the Kennedy Space Center with its giant Vehicle Assembly Building and the launching pads—barely two hours' drive from the Oldest House and the Oldest Store and the Oldest School.

On the western shore of the St. Johns River is Palatka, once a popular resort town for northerners who would take a train to Jacksonville and then made the 50-mile riverboat trip south. Today Palatka is an agricultural center, but the river is still both scenic and an important waterway for barges. The Ravine State Ornamental Garden is the setting for what must be the most spectacular show of azaleas in the world— 50 varieties of them, and more than 100,000 plants. A festival is held early each March when these blossoms put on their finest raiment.

Here, as in all parts of the state, fishing is superb, both in the St. Johns River and in lakes to the south.

Ormond Beach and Daytona Beach, cities of speed, where early auto racing records were set, are favorite resort spots for many northerners. Daytona has three beach fronts—one on the Atlantic and the others on each side of the Halifax River.

South of Daytona you reach the Space Coast. Two decades ago the little villages of Titusville, Cocoa, and Melbourne were shipping centers for citrus fruit, unknown to most travelers, who didn't see anything of importance on the map between Daytona Beach and Palm Beach. Motel rooms were reasonably priced and not very plentiful. But with the astronaut invasion came instant growth. Overnight, motels and service businesses sprang up all along the highway; new residents poured in; the area leapt into the 20th century. However, there are still two huge saltwater lagoons in Brevard County, with grassy flats, oyster bars, plentiful pompano and snapper, and speckled trout so large they are known as "gator" trout. Side by side with the huge missiles and rocket launching pads is the Merritt Island National Wildlife Refuge in which the Audubon Society holds an annual bird count—and has registered one of the highest counts in the United States.

Families still grow Indian River oranges and grapefruit in their backyards and fish for their supper from the ubiquitous bridges and catwalks. There are still long stretches of beaches unobstructed by buildings.

But these rural portions of Northeast Florida are fast disappearing. The eight counties have a total population of over one million, and only a small fraction of these people live in the outlying sections. Over one half million live in the metropolitan areas of Jacksonville and Daytona Beach, and a third of a million in other population centers of more than 2,500 people.

You'll find plenty of variety in Northeast Florida. Climb the walls of a fort in St. Augustine. Search with binoculars for a roseate spoonbill on Merritt Island. Go surfing at Daytona, or Sebastian Inlet. Search for buried treasure where the pirates once walked, or dive for sunken mementos of the Spanish ships. Watch a porpoise show. Take a houseboat down the Intracoastal Waterway. Go to the auto races. Pitch a tent beside the ocean. Or go fishing.

The Space Shuttle, Kennedy Space Center.

CITIES & TOWNS
Map of this section on page 31.

CAPE CANAVERAL is located in Brevard County, on Florida A1A, 6 miles north of Cocoa Beach and just south of the Cape Canaveral Air Force Station.

Port Canaveral, although not governed by the city, borders its north boundary. This is one of Florida's largest deep-water port by tonnage and is used to berth Polaris and Poseidon submarines while they are being armed. Trident submarines, the new billion-dollar marvels, occupy their own private harbor in the port. The dredging of this huge harbor gave Jetty Park the widest beach on the Atlantic Coast.

COCOA, in Brevard County, is on US 1, 4 miles east of I-95 and just southwest of Kennedy Space Center. Cocoa is a prominent shipping center for citrus products, and lovely orange groves line its major roads. Its population has more than tripled since 1950, when the first missile launching from Cape Canaveral took place.

The Houston Astros' spring training camp is at Cocoa, and the **Florida Grapefruit League** plays exhibition games here in March and April.

COCOA BEACH, Brevard County, is across the Indian and Banana rivers from Cocoa. Thousands of people come to Cocoa Beach each month to watch missiles being launched from Cape Canaveral.

South of Cocoa Beach, on Florida A1A, is **Patrick Air Force Base.** An interesting attraction on the base is the display of missiles tested at Cape Canaveral; the exhibit is located in front of the Air Force Technical Application Center.

At Canaveral Pier **surfing tournaments** are held during Easter and Labor Day weekends.

In November the entire downtown area of the city is taken over for the **Space Coast Art Festival.**

DAYTONA BEACH, largest city of Volusia County, is located on US 1, near the junction of I-95 and I-4.

For many years Daytona Beach has been a favorite resort area for visitors from all over the continent, especially from northeastern United States and Canada. The wide, flat, well-packed, white sand beaches form a natural speedway that has attracted motorists since the earliest days of the automobile, but areas and speeds for beach driving are now strictly regulated.

At the **Daytona International Speedway,** 3 miles west of the city on US 92, many different classes of autos are entered in nearly a dozen major annual racing events, mostly in January, February, and July. Highlights of the season are the **Daytona 500** in February, the **Daytona 200 Motorcycle Classic AMA Camel Pro Race** in March, the **Firecracker 400** on the Fourth of July, and the **IMSA National Championship** in November. Write to Drawer S, Daytona Beach 32015, for information.

Each January the little community of Daytona Beach Shores, south of Daytona Beach, hosts a **Canadian Festival,** when a planeload of VIPs are flown in from Toronto and entertained royally.

From February through July, jai-alai matches, with pari-mutuel betting, are held at the **Jai-Alai Fronton** nightly except Sunday. On Tuesday, Thursday, and Saturday matches are also held at noon. Greyhound races are held nightly except Sunday from early May through mid-September, also 1:30 on Monday, Wednesday, and Saturday, at the **Daytona Beach Kennel Club.**

Concerts, events, and shows are presented at the **Peabody Auditorium.** The **Daytona Playhouse** offers dramas, comedies, and musicals from September through early June; children's theater productions are also held during the season. Phone (904) 255-2431 for more information.

Bethune-Cookman College, founded in 1923, is a liberal arts institution currently enrolling about 1,700 students. Embry-Riddle Aeronautical University, Florida Technological University, and Daytona Beach Community College are also located here.

The **Museum of Arts and Sciences,** 1040 Museum Boulevard, has history and natural history displays, exhibits depicting Cuban life, and a planetarium (shows Saturday at 2:30 and Wednesday at 7:30, $2, under 12, 50¢; families, $4.50). Open Tuesday–Friday, 9–4; Saturday, noon–5. Closed New Year's Day, Easter, Thanksgiving, and Christmas. Admission $2, families $4.50, children under 12 50¢.

Five miles south and west of Daytona Beach, at Port Orange, are the **Sugar Mill Gardens,** ruins of an old English sugar mill built in 1763. The ruins include kettles and machinery and are now surrounded by beautiful, landscaped gardens. The mill was originally a Spanish mission, founded in 1602. Operated by Volusia County. Open daily, 9–5. Closed New Year's Day, Christmas. Free.

There are several amusement areas on the Boardwalk in Daytona Beach, all with free gate and parking. **Forest Amusement Park** has rides, a restaurant, gift shop, and beach. **Mardi Gras Fun Center** is a restaurant and arcade, with miniature golf. The **Midway Fun Fair** has a bathing beach, refreshment stand, penny arcade, and miniature golf. **Ocean Front Amusements** has rides, and a bathing beach.

Daytona Beach offers many facilities for such year-round pleasures as golf, yachting, sightseeing cruises, charter boats for deep-sea fishing, fishing from piers and bridges, and the three long, unexcelled beaches, one on the Atlantic Ocean and one on each side of the Halifax River.

DE BARY, in Volusia County, is just off I-4, about 30 miles southwest of Daytona Beach.

De Bary Hall, a showplace mansion built by German-born Baron Frederick De Bary in 1871 on the shores of Lake Monroe, was given to the state in 1967 by the Florida Federation of Art.

DE LAND, county seat of Volusia County, is located just south of the junction of US 92 and US 17, about 20 miles southwest of Daytona Beach.

It is the home of **Stetson University** (named for the Stetson hat tycoon), enrolling two thousand students, which annually cohosts in late February or early March, with the De Land Area Chamber of Commerce, the **Florida Community College Activities State Basketball Tournament.**

De Land is a beautiful, quiet, and culture-rich college town, with oak-lined residential streets and a surrounding countryside graced with citrus groves, lakes, and rolling hills.

Surfer enjoying the Atlantic waters near Cocoa Beach.

De Land Museum. has collections of shells, dolls, Indian artifacts, and changing exhibits. Open Tuesday–Saturday, 10–4; Sunday 2–4. Closed major holidays. Donations.

Nearby, on the St. Johns River, is the 1,649-acre **Hontoon Island,** near **Blue Spring State Park.** The island, developed for the boating public, has campsites and picnic areas. It is noted for its wildlife. Six miles south of De Land on US 17/92 is another portion of Blue Spring State Park; it contains the famous wintering spring for the endangered manatee. This part of the park offers swimming, food, picnicking, and nature walks.

DE LEON SPRINGS, in Volusia County, is 6 miles north of De Land on US 17.

The beautiful 50-acre **De Leon Springs State Recreation Area** features the spring said to be the **Great Healing Spring** discovered by Ponce de Leon in 1513. There are peacocks and many other species of birds, one of the oldest sugar mills in the New World, and semitropical trees and flowers. There are facilities for swimming, fishing, boating, and camping. Open daily, year-round, 8 am–sundown. Admission 50¢, under 6 free.

FERNANDINA BEACH, county seat and principal city of Nassau County, is in the northeastern corner of the state, on Amelia Island in the Atlantic Ocean, reached by Florida A1A.

It is one of the oldest communities in the state and in past centuries has been the home of pirates, slave traders, and smugglers. It counts eight flags in its history—those of France, Spain, Great Britain, and Mexico; a Patriot's Flag of the Republic of Florida (1812), the Green Cross of Florida (1817), the Confederacy, and the flag of the United States. The **Ame-**

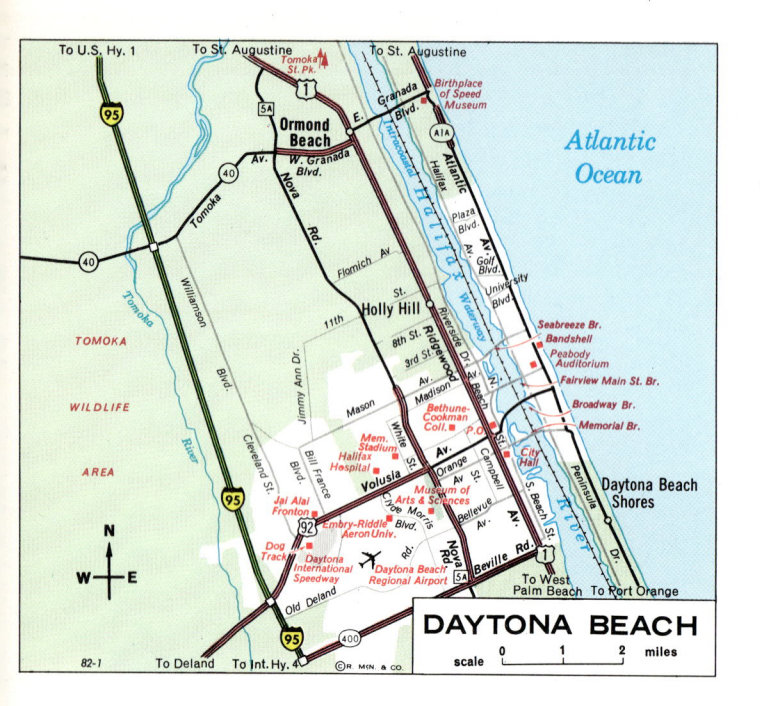

lia Island Lighthouse has been guiding mariners along Florida's coast since 1839.

The **Florida Marine Welcome Station,** on Atlantic Avenue at the Amelia River, is the Florida entrance to the Intracoastal Waterway. It is open Tuesday through Sunday from 8 am–noon, and 1–5. Closed holidays except July 4.

At **Fort Clinch State Park** an impressive museum (renovated in 1981) at the fort introduces the visitor to the military history of Fort Clinch, 50¢. For recreational pleasure there are more than a thousand acres of land, accented by magnificent beaches. A booklet is available that enables the visitor to take a self-guided tour through the fort, one of the nation's best-preserved relics of the Civil War. Swimming, boating, fishing, picnicking, camping.

Early in May the Fernandina Beach Chamber of Commerce holds the annual **Isle of Eight Flags Shrimp Festival,** with shrimp boat races, skydiving, an art show, a folk festival, mock pirate raids, a parade, and the blessing of the city's shrimp fleet.

The city has 14 miles of Atlantic coast sand beaches that are excellent for swimming, picnicking, and surf casting. At low tide, visitors can drive along the lovely beach. There is also a water slide and miniature golf course located here.

GREEN COVE SPRINGS, county seat of Clay County, is located at the junction of US 17 and Florida 16, on the west bank of the St. Johns River.

This town was one of the earliest health resorts in the state, and visitors to the spa used to come in by river steamer from Jacksonville. Among its frequenters were President Grover Cleveland and J.C. Penney.

Today the **Mineral Springs** are now the source of water for a large public swimming pool. Located in the city park, at Magnolia and Walnut streets, the spring produces about 3,000 gallons of mineralized water each minute. Open from June through September; daily noon–6. Admission 75¢, students 50¢, children under 6, 25¢. The city park is open all year. Free.

JACKSONVILLE. In 1968 the governments of Jacksonville and Duval County were merged, making the city of Jacksonville the largest in population in the state and the largest city in land area in the "lower 48" states. However, the Florida Supreme Court has since determined that the cities of Atlantic Beach, Neptune Beach, and Jacksonville Beach are still separate municipalities. Jacksonville is located at the mouth of the St. Johns River and the Atlantic Ocean, in northeastern Florida. Highways leading into Jacksonville are I-10, I-95, US 1, US 17, and US 90.

The little fishing village of **Mayport** lies directly at the mouth of the St. Johns River, and from here charter vessels and party boats leave daily for some of the finest fishing grounds on the eastern seaboard. A picturesque shrimp fleet makes its home here.

Jacksonville's presence of 16 insurance company headquarters has given it the nickname Hartford of the South. It is also a thriving seaport and bustles with factories, shipyards, and a naval air station. At one point in its history it boasted a moviemaking industry.

Almost every month of the year is marked by special annual sports or cultural events in Jacksonville. The Christmas-New Year season is ushered in by the **Gator Bowl Festival** and the **Gator Bowl Football Game** both held between Christmas and New Year's Day. For ticket information, write to Gator Bowl, Room 803, 11 East Forsyth Street, Jacksonville 32202.

In March is the annual **Delius Festival,** when the city's musical and civic groups honor Frederick Delius, English composer who once lived near Jacksonville.

Greyhound racing is held nightly except Sundays and Saturdays at the Jacksonville Greyhound Track, Orange Park or at Bayard. Pari-mutuel betting, no minors allowed. Phone 904/384-5439.

The beach at Little Talbot Island State Park

A major event in March, the **Tournament Players Championship,** is played at Sawgrass Country Club in nearby Ponte Vedra Beach. Also in March is the annual **River Run.**

An annual **Beach Festival** is held at Jacksonville Beach during the week after Easter. An annual 5-mile **Beach Marathon** takes place in August.

The Fourth of July is celebrated in Jacksonville with a night fireworks display over the St. Johns River and at Jacksonville Beach with a fireworks display over the ocean.

In July the **Jacksonville Kingfish Tournament** is held. From April through mid-September, 22 species of fish are eligible for entry in the **Annual Fishing Tournament,** sponsored by the Jacksonville Beaches Area Chamber of Commerce. Prizes go as high as $5,000.

Jacksonville's annual **Arts Festival** in April is one of the outstanding cultural events in the Southeast, with concerts, competitions in art and poetry, dance programs, and theater.

Jacksonville and All That Jazz one of the top jazz festivals with major performers, is held in October.

A **Bicentennial Flag Pavilion** at Jacksonville Beach displays the flags of all 50 states on an outdoor mall. Inside the pavilion are displays of all state seals.

Although Jacksonville was first platted in 1822 and developed as a major winter resort during Reconstruction days, a disastrous fire in 1901 almost obliterated the city and eliminated practically all of the early structures. Some outstanding postfire buildings are of interest, however, such as the Cohen Brothers Store, Klutho Apartments, Morocco Temple, and Riverside Baptist Church.

Two state parks open to the public are located in Jacksonville: **Kingsley Plantation State Historic Site** on Fort George Island, believed to be the oldest plantation house in Florida,

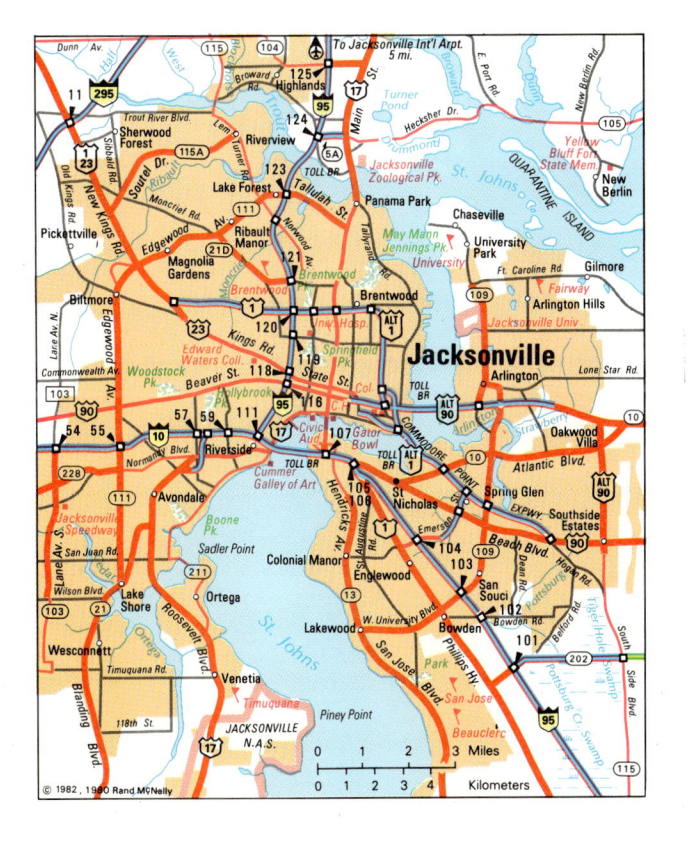

NORTHEAST 31

Sea oats on a beach near St. Augustine.

where slaves were trained for resale; and **Little Talbot Island State Park,** a lovely 2,500-acre island recreation area.

Kingsley Plantation is on Fort George Island, reached by Florida A1A; Little Talbot Island, just north of Fort George Island, is also on Florida A1A.

Kathryn Abbey Hanna Park, on the ocean and off Florida A1A, offers 450 acres of primitive woods, ½ mile of sandy beach, nature trails, freshwater lakes for fishing, and a shady 300-site campground. Fee.

Fort Caroline National Memorial is reached by taking Florida 10, 10 miles east from Jacksonville or 4 miles west from Florida A1A, then north on St. Johns Bluff Road and east on Fort Caroline Road. This is a 119-acre park along the St. Johns River, established in 1953 to commemorate an attempt by the French to settle in Florida. The fort was held successively by the French, Spanish, and English. The original site of the fort was washed away when the river channel was deepened in the late 19th century. The story of the area is shown in exhibits at a visitors' center. There is a replica of the original fort. Open daily, 9–5, free. Closed Christmas and New Year's Day.

The **Jacksonville Art Museum,** at 4160 Boulevard Center Drive, exhibits Oriental porcelains, pre-Columbian artifacts, and contemporary works. Open Tuesday, Wednesday, and Friday, 10–4; Thursday, 10–10; Saturday and Sunday, 1–5. Closed August and holidays. Free.

The **Jacksonville Museum of Arts and Sciences,** at 1025 Gulf Life Drive, has varied exhibits, including displays on Egypt, health, natural and physical sciences, as well as Science Theater, Children's Museum, and Planetarium shows. Open October through August, Tuesday–Friday 9–5, Saturday 11–5, Sunday 1–5. Closed major holidays. Admission, including Science Theater and matinee Planetarium shows, $2, youth 4–18 $1.

On the site of the former Cummer Mansion, the **Cummer Gallery of Art** includes a room transplanted intact from the original house, a collection ranging from ancient Greece to the 20th century, and 700 pieces of Meissen porcelain. Open Tuesday–Friday, 10–4, Saturday noon–5, Sunday 2–5. Closed major holidays. Donation.

More than 700 mammals, birds, and reptiles reside in natural habitats flanking the Trout River at the **Jacksonville Zoological Park,** at 8605 Zoo Road. Also available are a safari train, elephant rides, and picnic areas, and several amusement rides are on the grounds. Open daily, Memorial Day–Labor Day, 10–5:45; rest of year, 9–4:45. Closed New Year's Day, Thanksgiving, and Christmas. Admission $2.50, 4–12, $1, under 4 free.

Other points of interest in Jacksonville are **Jacksonville University,** with an enrollment of 2,600 students, and the **University of North Florida,** with 3,000 students.

KENNEDY SPACE CENTER was created when the federal government purchased more than 88,000 acres of land and water in the vicinity of Merritt Island on which to locate the John F. Kennedy Space Center, operated by NASA, plus the Cape Canaveral Air Force Station. All but one launch of Apollo, along with skylab, Apollo-Soynz and the space shuttle missions, were launched from the Kennedy Space Center. The incredible Space Shuttle is a spaceship that is launched like a rocket and landed like aircraft.

Two-hour "red" guided bus tours of the **Spaceport** depart regularly throughout the day from the Visitors Information Center, located 6 miles east of US 1, south of Titusville. Tours begin at 9:15 and the last tour departs 2 hours before dusk. This is one of Florida's most popular tourist attractions.

For charter tours and information, write Kennedy Space Center Tours, TWA Services, Inc., Visitors Center, TWA 810, NASA Tours Division, Kennedy Space Center, Florida 32899. Bus tours $4; 3–18, $2.25, under 3 free. Member Florida Attractions Association.

On Sundays, between 9 am and 3 pm, visitors may take the "blue" bus tour of **Cape Canaveral Air Force Station** and visit the **Air Force Space Museum,** where the world's largest collection of missiles and rockets is on display. Free.

Typical of Florida's historic contrasts, many Indian burial mounds have been found in the vicinity of the Space Center, and some of the artifacts uncovered indicate habitation of the region as long ago as the time of Christ.

Also, in ecological irony, many species of wildlife live and thrive in the 140,000-acre **Merritt Island National Wildlife Refuge,** existing side by side with the Space Age activities. Alligators, bobcats, raccoons, and more than two hundred species of birds fill the refuge. The local Audubon Society has registered one of the highest counts of bird species in the United States here; even American bald eagles have been sighted. The society sponsors bird-watching tours and an annual Christmas bird count for which Cocoa is the starting point. Citrus groves also flourish here.

Just north of the Space Center, including a portion of the Merrit Island Refuge, is **Canaveral National Seashore.** The seashore covers 67,500 acres, including 25 miles of beachfront. **Playalinda Beach,** at the south end, is most popular with swimmers, surfers, and beachwalkers. Parking is limited and on summer weekends the beach is apt to be crowded. The central portion of the seashore, about 14 miles, is undeveloped and roadless. Most of the land is marsh, or covered with scrub vegetation. Wildlife in the area includes loggerhead and green turtles, and many species of birds.

KEYSTONE HEIGHTS is in Clay County, at the junction of Florida 100 and Florida 21, about 25 miles northwest of Palatka. It is a pleasant little village, located on the edge of Lake Geneva.

Mike Roess Gold Head Branch State Park is 6 miles northeast of town, on Florida 21. It was one of the state's first parks, and its 1,481 acres offer nearly every sort of facility, including very comfortable housekeeping cabins.

MARINELAND, with a population of only 13 people, is nevertheless an incorporated village. It is in both Flagler and St. Johns counties, on Florida A1A, south of St. Augustine, and it consists entirely of various facilities and accommodations for visitors.

The performing porpoises, dolphins, and whales of **Marineland of Florida** have been delighting visitors since 1938, but Marineland has been a center for the scientific study of marine biology as well as an entertainment spot.

Huge tanks, called oceanariums, have been built on the shore of the ocean, open to the sun, where a constant supply of salt water simulates the conditions of the ocean floor. The natural illumination makes for the best possible observation and photography of the marine specimens. A circular oceanarium houses a permanent colony of porpoises, along with spotted groupers and smaller fish. A rectangular oceanarium is kept at a minimum temperature of 67 degrees, and holds tropical specimens from the Bahamas and the Keys. Approximately 3,000 specimens of nearly 150 species live in the two oceanariums.

Small showcase aquariums display beautiful and interesting, as well as dangerous and ugly, marine specimens in an exhibit called Wonders of the Sea. Marineland also includes Aquarius Theatre, electric eel shows, a shark exhibit, and the Margaret Herrick Shell Collection.

Six times each day (9:30, 11, 12:30, 2, 3:30, and 5) trained porpoises perform for visitors in the Porpoise Stadium, demonstrating their good memory, recognition of signals, and cleverness in performing stunts.

A single admission to the park is charged, covering performances and exhibits. Adults $6, children 3–11 $3.50, under 3 free. Member Florida Attractions Association.

The community of Marineland includes landscaped Whitney Park, a seaside motor inn, restaurant, snack bar, cocktail lounge, gift shop, film shop, a new oceanfront motor inn, and a new marina for visitors who arrive by way of the Intracoastal Waterway.

Three miles south of Marineland is **Washington Oaks State Ornamental Garden,** an oceanfront recreational area developed on a former estate. There are nature trails and a nature museum on the grounds.

MELBOURNE, in Brevard County, is on US 192, between I-95 and US 1, about 25 miles south of Cape Canaveral. In 1969 Melbourne consolidated with Eau Gallie. A causeway and bridge connect the city with Atlantic beaches and the Cape Canaveral area.

A fairly new (established in 1958) college, **Florida Insti-**

tute of Technology, now enrolls 7,500 students. Worth seeing on campus is the Dent Smith Trail, a botanical palm garden.

Fishing at ocean beaches and from causeways across Indian River is excellent, and the famous Indian River citrus crop is shipped to many northern markets.

In Indiatlantic, across the Indian River, the annual **Indiatlantic Art Show** is held in April. Each February the **Grant Seafood Festival** attracts more than 10,000 seafood lovers to the Melbourne area.

NEW SMYRNA BEACH is in Volusia County, on US 1 and the Indian River, about 10 miles south of Daytona Beach.

In the 18th century some 1,500 emigrants from Greece, Turkey, and the Island of Minorca settled here and planted an indigo crop. The majority of them eventually moved on to St. Augustine, but wild indigo still grows here.

At the junction of US 1 with Florida 44 is **New Smyrna Sugar Mill Ruins State Historic Site,** where a sugar mill was in operation until its destruction during the Seminole Indian hostilities in 1835. Free.

Also in town, on Riverside Drive north of Canal Street, are the coquina ruins of an **Old Fort** built by the Spanish.

Canaveral National Seashore is south of town.

Yaupon plants—of the holly family—grow on Turtle Mound. From this plant, Indians used to brew a potent concoction called the Black Drink, which was served in conch shell cups and used before certain ceremonies.

ORMOND BEACH, in Volusia County, is 6 miles north of Daytona Beach on Florida A1A.

This resort area, for many years the winter home of John D. Rockefeller, was important in the early days of auto racing. To commemorate the beginnings of auto racing (in 1902), the Birthplace of Speed Association and the Ormond Beach Chamber of Commerce annually sponsor an **Antique Car Meet** on Thanksgiving weekend. The city's Gasoline Alley Garage and Country Club is the center of activities, which include a Gaslight Parade, with horseless carriages driven by people in old-fashioned clothing; beach sprints; banquet; and contests.

Ormond Beach also hosts the **Women's South Atlantic Open** golf tournament in January. An important event here each November is the **Halifax Area Art Festival.**

Two miles north of Ormond Beach is **Tomoka State Park,** on the site of an early Indian village. It is surmised that the first Christian marriage in what is now the United States took place here, in 1567. The Marsh Museum houses artifacts, historic exhibits, and sculpture. The park has more than 900 acres of recreational area at the fork of the Halifax and Tomoka rivers.

PALATKA, county seat and largest city in Putnam County, is on the west bank of the St. Johns River on US 17 and Florida 100.

Legend has it that when white men first came to Florida, the alligators were so plentiful in this vicinity that a person could walk across the St. Johns River on their backs. Now the river is filled with bass.

The principal physical attraction of the city is **Ravine State Ornamental Garden,** 182 landscaped acres of trees, tropical and subtropical plants, ravines, streams, and lovely lakes.

The landscaping was performed during the 1930s, and the entire stock of the Winter Garden Ornamental Nursery—more than 40,000 azaleas and numerous other subtropical flowers—was purchased for the gardens. Records show that a grand total of more than 325,000 plants, trees, and shrubs were planted. Ravine Gardens is now a state park, with picnic grounds and nature trails. Open daily, 8–sundown; at 4 P.M. the park is closed to motorized vehicles. The first weekend in March the city holds an **Azalea Festival,** sponsored by the Palatka Jaycees, with a parade, powerboat races, golf tournament, skeet shoot, talent show, art show, and beauty pageant.

Other annual sports events include the **Palatka Horseman's Rodeo** in April and a **Mug Race** (sailboats) from Palatka to Jacksonville in May.

Fishing is exceptionally good in Crescent Lake and the St. Johns River, and this part of the county is known as the Bass Capital of the World. Camping, fishing, boating, and picnicking facilities are available at **Rodman Dam and Reservoir,** 17 miles south of Palatka, off US 19. For a full list of more than 45 fishing camps and resorts, write the Putnam County Chamber of Commerce, Box 550MG, Palatka.

ST. AUGUSTINE, county seat and largest city of St. Johns County, is on US 1 and the Atlantic Ocean in northeastern Florida, between Jacksonville and Daytona Beach.

This part of Florida was discovered by Ponce de Leon in 1513, and a permanent colony was founded by Pedro Menendez de Aviles in 1565. While the city's claim to the title of Oldest City can be justly disputed by some of the Indian pueblos in the Southwest, St. Augustine has long been called the nation's oldest permanent city.

A wide variety of events and attractions are to be found here, luring tourists of all ages and tastes. It attracts the history buff and curiosity seeker more than the sportsman, but the Chamber of Commerce does sponsor a summer-long **Fishing Tournament,** with prizes awarded in 17 categories of saltwater fish.

The Easter season is ushered in by an annual **Arts and Crafts Festival,** which is also held on Thanksgiving weekend, sponsored by the St. Augustine Arts and Crafts Council, and on Palm Sunday more than 250 shrimp boats and powerboats pass in review at Yacht Pier for the traditional **Blessing of the Fleet.** An **Easter Sunrise Service** is held atop the Castillo de San Marcos, and the entire week following Easter is a festival, with celebrations of religious and historic events. The festival week ends with an **Easter Parade.**

And every August a three-day **Days in Spain Festival** involves the whole city in a celebration of its founding. Fireworks displays, parades, and nightly entertainment are included in the festivities.

"Cross and Sword," Florida's official state play, a musical drama depicting the founding of St. Augustine, is presented nightly except Sunday from mid-June–late August at 8:30 in the St. Augustine Amphitheatre on Anastasia Island. Admission $5, under 12 $3, infants free.

Two national monuments are located here—**Castillo de San Marcos** in the city itself and **Fort Matanzas,** on Rattlesnake Island, 14 miles south of the city.

Construction of Castillo de San Marcos, the present stone fort, was begun in 1672 to replace the last of nine successive wooden forts which had existed here since 1565. It was built by the Spanish to protect their interests against the threat posed by the establishment of English colonies in the Carolinas and Georgia, only 200 miles away. The massive old walls are a vantage point from which the visitor can view the old City Gate and narrow streets of the quaint town. Open daily, last Sunday in October–last Saturday in April, 8:30–5:15; rest of year, 9–5:45. Closed Christmas. Admission 50¢, children 15 and under free with adults.

Fort Matanzas dates from 1742, but the area was the scene of a struggle between French and Spanish colonists in 1565, which ended in the slaughter of some three hundred Huguenots. ("Matanzas" is the Spanish word for "slaughter.") The fort, built of coquina blocks cemented together with oyster lime, was held by the Spanish, the English, then the Spanish again. By the time Florida was ceded to the United States by the Spanish in 1821, the interior of the fort was already in ruins. Open daily, last Sunday in October–last Saturday in April, 8:30–5:30; rest of the year, 9–6. Closed Christmas. Free.

St. Augustine will appeal especially to the avid sightseer, but there are so many facilities for leisurely family vacationing in the vicinity that the sightseeing can be done in a most relaxed fashion. Numerous excellent motels and hotels dot the area, and two state parks lie to the south of St. Augustine. **Anastasia** is a 1,035-acre park for campers on the Atlantic Ocean; and **Faver-Dykes,** also a camping area, is a 752-acre riverfront park on the site of an old Spanish plantation. A number of exceptionally attractive private camping resorts can also be found along Florida A1A south of St. Augustine, where the ocean surf lulls the campers to sleep.

There are several ways to acquaint yourself with the varied points of interest in St. Augustine.

Tours are available by sightseeing trains at 3 Cordova Street, daily, 8:30–6, closed Christmas. Horse-drawn carriage tours start at Bay Street near the entrance to Castillo de San Marcos Monument, every day, between 8:30 and 5; closed Christmas. Cruise boats leave from the Municipal Yacht Pier. Phone (904) 824-1806 for information.

You can also pick up literature at the **Visitors' Information Center** at 10 Castillo Drive, open daily, 8:30–5:30, near the City Gate, and follow the Visitors Guide for a self-guided walking tour. This guide lists nearly one hundred points of interest.

The old City Gate at St. Augustine marks the northern entry to America's oldest city.

The major area of historic interest in the city is known as The Restored Village, or as the **Museum San Agustin Antiguo.** In 1959 the State of Florida embarked on a program of restoration and reconstruction of a major part of the city to its appearance in the mid-18th century. The objective was "to obtain . . . as nearly accurate as possible a restoration of the ancient walled city St. Augustine." The Historic St. Augustine Preservation Board, at the corner of Cathedral Place and St. George Street, is in charge of the project. Many buildings are open to the public as museums or craft shops (where the old crafts are demonstrated and products are offered for sale); private citizens and organizations are encouraged to make use of other buildings as residences or business establishments that are compatible with the historic aspects of the area.

St. Augustine was, from the beginning, a charming, well-planned city, with gracious Spanish homes and picturesque walled patios and gardens. The original City Gate remains, and Castillo de San Marcos still stands at its side, symbolic guardian of the city, now carefully preserved by the National Park Service. And year by year the area between the Gate and the Plaza de la Constitucion—particularly along St. George and Cuna streets—is regaining its 18th-century appearance. Most of the buildings are open daily except Christmas, 9–5.

Nearby San Agustin Antiguo is **Casa del Hidalgo,** also known as the **Spanish National Tourist Office,** open Monday–Friday, 9–5; closed holidays, constructed by the government of Spain as an educational, cultural, and information center. It was built and furnished, at a cost of $300,000, to appear as a Spanish nobleman's home from the early 1600s. The building contains an exhibit of Spanish handcrafts. Open Tuesday–Saturday, 10–4:30. Closed holidays. Free.

More than 30 buildings have been restored or recreated during the first decade of the long-range project, which is planned to continue for many years to come. Professional art historians make expeditions to Spain and Mexico to collect authentic period furnishings and art objects for the interior decoration of the buildings.

A small admission charge is made at a few of the buildings, such as the **Oldest Wooden Schoolhouse,** the **Arrivas House,** and the **Rodriguez-Avero-Sanchez House,** now housing the Museum of Yesterday's Toys, both on St. George Street.

A block ticket may be purchased for the walking tour of the **Ribera House** (tickets may be obtained here); **Peso de Burgo-Pellicer Houses; de Mesa-Sanchez House; Gonzales–de Hita Houses; Gallegos House; Blacksmith Shop;** and **Gomez House.** Tickets $2.50, students over 18 with I.D. $1.25, 6–18 $1.25 or free with parent. Open daily, 9–5; closed Christmas.

Various aspects of early life in St. Augustine are depicted at the **Oldest House,** and **Tovar House,** operated by the St. Augustine Historical Society, the **Old Spanish Treasury,** and the **Old Sugar Mill.** Each of these has special exhibits, and admission is charged at all of them. These are not located in the Museum Village area.

The town is built around the **Plaza de la Constitucion,** which was established in 1598 and is thus the oldest public square in the United States. Near the Plaza are some fine examples of late 19th-century Spanish Renaissance architecture, from the period when St. Augustine was the resort playground for the wealthy. **Zorayda Castle,** built in 1883, was a copy of Spain's famous Alhambra. Today it houses a fantastic art collection. Open daily; June–late August, 9–9; rest of year, 9–5:30. Closed Christmas. Admission $2, children 6–12 $1, under 6 free. **Flagler College,** a liberal arts college for women, is in the 1888 building which was the elegant Hotel Ponce de Leon.

The **Lightner Museum,** an outstanding city-owned collection of antiques and hobbies, has been reopened in its customary home, the former Alcazar Hotel, which has been renovated. Both the Ponce de Leon and the Alcazar were built by Henry Flagler. The 300-room museum, at Cordova and King streets, contains natural science exhibits as well as a Victorian village. Exhibits include collections of artwork, porcelain, 19th century musical instruments, and Tiffany glass. The museum's grounds have lovely fountains and gardens. Open daily, 9–5. Closed Christmas. Admission $2, students 12–18 75¢, children under 12 free with adult.

Ripley's Believe It Or Not Museum, at 19 San Marco Avenue, is in the old Castle Warden. There are a full three floors of Ripley oddities here for visitors to view. Open daily, summer, 9–9; winter, 9–7. Admission $3.95, students 5–12 $2.25, senior citizens $2.75, under 5 free.

Potter's Wax Museum, 1 King Street, has more than 240 life-size figures of famous personalities. Open daily, June through August, 9–9; September through May, 9–5. Admission $3.75, children 6–12 $2, 5 and under free. Senior citizen rates available. Closed Christmas. Member Florida Attractions Association.

The **Oldest Store Museum,** 4 Artillery Lane, is a replica of a general store at the turn of the century. More than 100,000 unusual antique items of merchandise are displayed. Open Monday through Saturday, 9–5, Sunday, noon–5. Closed Christmas. Admission $2, children 6–12 $1. Member Florida Attractions Association.

St. Augustine Alligator Farm, on Anastasia Island, has been in operation since 1893. There is a zoo of Florida wildlife, especially alligators and crocodiles. Demonstrations of alligators wrestling. Open daily, 9–6. Admission $4.25, children 6–12 $2.25, under 6 free. Member Florida Attractions Association.

Six blocks north of the City Gate is **Fountain of Youth** where Ponce de Leon first landed. Indian burial grounds in the park are evidence of the culture that flourished here before the Spaniards came. Also here are a planetarium and a discovery globe, both offering shows throughout the day. Park open daily, 9–4:30. Closed Christmas. Admission $3, children 6–12 $1.50, senior citizens $2.50, under 6 free.

The rich, varied religious heritage of St. Augustine is visible everywhere. A beautiful, simple, illuminated, 200-foot stainless steel cross has been erected on a point of land at **Mission of Nombre de Dios,** where Father Lopez de Mendoza Grajales is believed to have planted a cross when the Spaniards first landed in Florida. The mission is regarded as the birthplace of Christianity in the United States. Also on the mission grounds are the Prince of Peace church, a statue of Father Lopez, a rustic altar, a diorama of the founding of St. Augustine, a mission chapel, Shrine of Our Lady of La Leche, and a shrine shop. Open daily, summer 8–8, winter 8–6. Closed Christmas. Donation.

Other religious landmarks include the **Old Protestant Cemetery,** opened during the yellow fever epidemic of 1821; the **Old Spanish Cemetery,** dating back to the late 1700s;

St. George Street is the heart of the charming restoration area known as San Agustin Antiguo.

the **St. Augustine National Cemetery,** established in the 1830s, thus the oldest documented National Cemetery in the country; **Flagler Memorial Presbyterian Church,** a beautiful example of Venetian Renaissance architecture; **Trinity Episcopal Church,** begun in 1825; and the **Cathedral of St. Augustine,** built by the Spanish in the 1790s, gutted by fire and remodeled in the 1880s, and completely refurbished for the quadricentennial in 1965.

St. Augustine has been an exciting place to visit for at least the past one hundred years—perhaps for the past four hundred. Its interest for the visitor is bound to increase even more in coming years as the cooperative planning and efforts of the Preservation Board, the city, the Historical Society, and the many private businesses, organizations, and individuals bring more and more of its vivid past into the living present.

TITUSVILLE is the county seat of Brevard County, located on US 1 at the entrance to the **Kennedy Space Center.** It is the service and shopping center for the aerospace complex and an important agricultural center for citrus fruits and commercial flowers.

Seven miles east of Titusville, via Florida 402, is **Canaveral National Seashore.** For further information write Supervisor, P.O. Box 2583, Titusville, Florida 32780.

(Details on admission prices and hours have been included as a service to the reader and as a guide in planning activities. However, changes are inevitable in some cases, and the publisher cannot be responsible for any variations from the listed information.)

NORTHEAST 37

Quiet lagoons and arched footbridges mark the pathways through the lovely and popular Cypress Gardens.

CENTRAL LAKES & GROVES

A DRIVE THROUGH THE HEARTLAND OF CENTRAL FLORIDA LEADS FROM THE TEMPERATE ZONE INTO THE SUBTROPICS, PAST DOZENS OF MAJOR TOURIST SPOTS, WITHIN A STONE'S THROW OF 20,000 LAKES AND AN ARM'S REACH OF MORE THAN 17,000,000 CITRUS TREES. HERE ARE THE LAKES AND HIGHLANDS OF FLORIDA, WHERE YOU ARE STILL NEVER MORE THAN 70 MILES AWAY FROM A SEASHORE. CENTRAL FLORIDA'S COLORS ARE THE GREEN AND GOLD OF AN ORANGE TREE. ITS SOUNDS ARE THE CARILLON OF THE SINGING TOWER AND THE MARCHING BANDS AT WALT DISNEY WORLD.

The population of the nine counties that make up Central Florida includes over one million people distributed almost equally among rural, urban, and metropolitan areas. Today, because of increasing industrial and recreational development, the area in and around Orlando-Winter Park is increasing its population much more rapidly than the surrounding areas.

There are several state parks in this section—Dade Battlefield, Highlands Hammock, Lake Griffin, Lake Louisa, Lake Kissimmee, Fort Cooper, and Wekiwa Springs, and the area does not lack for other attractions, many of them world-famous. It has no ocean beach, but the numbers of miles of lakeshore are virtually incalculable, and individual cities can boast of the numbers of lakes within their boundaries. (Winter Haven is the "city of 100 lakes"!)

THE 100-MILE MIDWAY

For years US 27 has led through such a rich area of recreational opportunities that its stretch from Leesburg to Sebring is a 100-mile midway. There are Lakes Harris and Apopka; the Citrus Tower, Cypress Gardens, Slocum Gardens, and the Florida Citrus Showcase; the Singing Tower and Chalet Suzanne; Highlands Hammock Park and Sebring auto races.

And now I-4 from Orlando to Tampa has developed into a second such midway, with Gatorland, Walt Disney World, EPCOT Center, Sea World of Florida, Circus World, Wet 'n Wild, and Stars Hall of Fame all close to the highway leading to The Dark Continent/Busch Gardens and the Tampa-St. Pete metropolis.

Citrus groves have been the mainstay of the economy here for years. The only way to really appreciate the extent of their importance—and their acreage—is to take the elevator to the top of the Citrus Tower in Clermont. The view is breathtaking—mile upon mile of trees in straight rows broken only by lakes—many, many lakes. Take a little time to learn about this great industry. Visit the Florida Citrus Showcase in Winter Haven or Donald Duck Citrus World at Lake Wales, where movies show the various steps in the production and distribution of citrus products. Take home candy and jellies for your friends. Stop at a roadside stand to buy fruit to eat on the spot. Many of them operate on the honor system, even leaving out a knife and napkins so that you can eat and run (but *do* leave payment in the box; let's keep this delightful practice alive).

Want to see a bit of the Old West right here in the Deep South? Come to see the Silver Spurs Rodeo in Kissimmee in July. This town is really a cow town, believe it or not. Cattle production ranks right up there with citrus production in economic importance to this part of the state.

Many of Central Florida's attractions were conceived, nourished, and groomed by a number of imaginative and devoted individuals and families. Dick and Julia Pope at Cypress Gardens and the late Bertha Hinshaw, who established Chalet Suzanne, are a few examples, as was the great Edward Bok, who presented the magnificent Singing Tower and Bok Tower Gardens to the people of his adopted land in fulfillment of his lifelong ambition to leave the world "a bit more beautiful." Standing on the highest spot in Central Florida, the tower is an exclamation point emphasizing the area's serene natural beauty.

Now the large, corporate investors have come—to develop huge new entertainment centers, national chain motels, franchised fast-food outlets, and city-size shopping centers. They have provided many new jobs and have given new impetus to tourism in Florida, but they unquestionably are changing the character of the area. It will be interesting to watch and see what effect all this will have on the Central Florida of the future.

A FUTURE THREAT

Much in the minds of Floridians is the general lowering of the central water table level in the state—due partly to a somewhat lessened rainfall, but more to the development of housing complexes and businesses. Finding an intelligent solution to this difficult problem will not be easy, and will require the active cooperation and participation of all concerned, including conservation groups, business developers, and government agencies, as well as of the long-time private residents.

Of course, the citrus growers need water for irrigation, and surely new housing, for residents and the growing number of people coming to Florida, is important. So, too, are the needs of the natural denizens—the alligators and birds must have a proper environment for survival. Whose need is greatest? It is a question that means across-the-board solutions, and involves the whole state of Florida, perhaps the nation. For, the whole nation drinks Florida orange juice, and a large number of citizens enjoy Florida as a vacationland. Think about it a little as you pass this way.

And to truly appreciate what Central Florida is and can be, stop at the Bok Tower Gardens for a half-day, an hour, or even a few minutes.

> Here all people are welcomed. All living things are respected. Here in quiet awe, the day is measured by the light of early morning, noon and sunset. The hours are marked by music from the bells. Not only do the birds sing, but the fish in the moat and the dashing squirrels give a greeting. There is majesty alike in the clouds in the sky and the lilies by the path. Both the Tower and a spider's web are masterful designs. This Sanctuary is a place. It may also be an experience to be cherished and long remembered.

CITIES & TOWNS
Map on this section on page 46.

APOPKA is located in Orange County, on US 441, about 15 miles northwest of Orlando.

One of the oldest towns in the state, it was settled in 1856 and originally named The Lodge, for its Masonic meeting place, built by slaves in 1859 and still used. Later it took its present Indian name, meaning "potato-eating place."

Apopka is known as the Indoor Foliage Capital of the World, or Fern City, because it produces 75% of all the foliage sold in Florida, and Florida leads all states in this industry. In early spring an annual **Art Show and Foliage Festival** is held.

Miss Apopka beauty pageant is held here in March.

Northwest of Apopka, in the village of Zellwood, a very popular **Sweet Corn Festival** is held each spring.

Apopka is surrounded by springs. Three miles east of town, off Florida 436 or I-4, is **Wekiwa Springs State Park.** Swimming, picnicking, fishing, boating, nature trails.

Six miles north of town, off Florida 435, is 200-acre **Kelly Park,** with camping and picnicking facilities and a swimming pool fed by Rock Springs. Open daily, 7 am–sunset.

Southwest of town is **Lake Apopka,** one of the largest in Florida and also regarded as one of the best bass-fishing lakes anywhere. Channels lead from it to form a waterway connecting it with other lakes and the St. Johns River.

ARCADIA, county seat and largest city of De Soto County, is located on US 17 and Florida 70, about 45 miles east of Sarasota. This area has good-sized cattle ranches, lush citrus groves, and phosphate strip mines. Weekly cattle auctions, on Wednesdays, feature chanting auctioneers. The All-Florida Championship Rodeo is held in March and on July 4.

AVON PARK, in Highlands County, is located on US 27 and Florida 64, about 25 miles south of Lake Wales. It lies almost in the geographical center of the state.

Avon Park was one of the early land developments in Florida. In the 1880s O.M. Crosby, of Danbury, Connecticut, selected this area for settlement. He went to England to recruit buyers and came back with a group of settlers who named the town for Stratford-on-Avon. Crosby established a newspaper, the *Florida Home Seeker,* which was widely distributed and in which he offered land for $25 an acre. Later he established a stage line to provide free transportation for prospective lot buyers—an early version of a practice which is still used to help lure new residents to the state! (One writer has wickedly suggested that this may have been the origin of the phrase "to take someone for a ride"!)

The area is as attractive today as it was a century ago, with 28 lakes within 3 miles of the town. Major products are citrus fruits, cattle, and commercial flowers.

Main Street of Avon Park is a mile-long mall planted with hundreds of tropical shrubs and plants. The city is the home of **South Florida Junior College.**

At **Lake Verona,** on east Main Street, are a sandy beach, playground, tennis courts, boating facilities, and picnic area. Free.

BARTOW, county seat of Polk County, is located on US 17 and Florida 60, about 15 miles south of Lakeland. There are several huge phosphate mines in the area, and the citrus and cattle industries are also important to the area.

In Bartow, at 495 N. Hendry Avenue, is the **Polk County Historical and Genealogical Library,** with one of the most extensive collections of material in the country for genealogical research. Open Monday through Friday, 8:30–5. Free. Closed holidays.

City recreational facilities include an Olympic-size pool and tennis, handball, and shuffleboard courts.

BUSHNELL, county seat of Sumter County, is located on US 301 and Florida 48, east of I-75, about 40 miles south of Ocala.

Southwest of town, on US 301, is **Dade Battlefield State Historic Site,** where an Indian ambush on December 28, 1835, touched off the Second Seminole War. The seven-year war, fiercest and costliest of all Indian wars waged by the United States, was caused by the unwillingness of the Seminoles to be driven from their lands to reservations in the West. More than a hundred soldiers were killed during this particular battle—only one survived to tell the story. Today a quiet picnic ground and museum mark the spot.

CLERMONT, in Lake County, is just off US 27 at Florida 50, about 20 miles west of Orlando.

Florida's gold—her citrus products.

40 CENTRAL

Clermont, with an altitude of 220 feet, claims to be the highest town in the Highlands of Central Florida. The town has 17 lakes within its city limits, and 100 or so in the immediate vicinity. **Lake Louisa State Park,** 7 miles southwest of Clermont, is a great fishing point.

One mile north of Florida 50, on US 27, is the 200-foot high **Florida Citrus Tower,** with observation decks from which to view the beauty of the 2,000 square miles of the surrounding countryside, its lakes and citrus groves. Within the Citrus Tower complex are a restaurant and service bar; a gift shop; a glass-blowing studio, where demonstrations are presented and objects offered for sale; a citrus processing exhibit and packing house; candy kitchen; and a citrus arcade. Carillon bells ring at regular intervals. Open daily, 8 am–6 pm. Admission $1.75, students 10–15 $1, under 10 free. Member Florida Attractions Association.

Adjacent to the tower is the **House of Presidents,** where wax figures of all the U.S. presidents are on display, in period settings. Open daily, except for the months of May and September, 9–5. Admission $2, children 8–15 $1, under 8 free with paying guest.

CYPRESS GARDENS—see **WINTER HAVEN**

DISNEY WORLD—see **LAKE BUENA VISTA**

EUSTIS, in Lake County, is just south of Ocala National Forest, on Florida 44, 30 miles from Orlando. It is set on the east shore of Lake Eustis. With 1,400 lakes within its boundaries, Lake County is aptly named.

In a state where festivals seem to be going on somewhere all the time, Eustis claims to have one of the oldest—an annual **Washington's Birthday Celebration,** held on the Saturday nearest to February 22, with a parade, fireworks, carnival, and other special events.

KISSIMMEE, county seat and largest city of Osceola County, is located on Tohopekaliga Lake, 10 miles east of Disney World, on US 192, east of I-4.

Kissimmee is in the heart of the Brahma cattle ranching area, and the Florida Cattlemen's Association has its headquarters here. Cattle were first introduced to this part of Florida in the 1820's, but they were tiny, scrubby things, described as being not much bigger than a donkey. Some Western movies might have just as appropriately been set in the Kissimmee of one hundred years ago as in Dodge City or Abilene.

A number of annual events bring visitors to town during all seasons. Perhaps the most well known is the performance of the **Silver Spurs Rodeo,** held in July and February. Professional cowboys and riders from throughout the country come to compete. The mid-winter rodeo is held in conjunction with the **Kissimmee Valley Livestock Show;** a parade is held one day in Kissimmee and the next day in St. Cloud, 10 miles east.

Early summer Kissimmee hosts an annual **Boat-a-Cade,** a trip down the Kissimmee River to the southern shore of Lake Okeechobee and over to the Atlantic; the **Official Florida State Air Show** is held in the fall; and the **Osceola Art Festival** is held in late September. St. Cloud also has an annual **Sidewalk Art Festival** held in late September.

The Florida Citrus Tower, Clermont.

Tupperware is a familiar name to almost every housewife. Kissimmee is the home of the famous plastics company that has made its fortune through merchandising parties in homes rather than from sales in stores. Worth seeing is their **Museum of Food Containers,** open to the public.

Indian and Florida relics, as well as relics of the Spanish-American war, may be seen at the **Indian World Museum.** The museum is open daily from 9–6. Admission $2.50; 13–16, $1.25; 5–12, 50¢; under 5 free.

Between Kissimmee and Orlando, on US 17/19, is Owen Godwin's **Gatorland Zoo,** boasting a daily feeding show. Thousands of alligators and crocodiles live in a natural habitat, along with other rare animals and birds. Miniature train rides. Open daily; in summer, 8–7; rest of year, 8–6. Admission $4, children 3–11 $3, under 3 free. Member Florida Attractions Association.

Alligatorland Safari is a jungle zoo located 9 miles south of Kissimmee on US 17/92. A 1,000-foot boardwalk leads through a swamp where monkeys swing through trees and beg for food. Gift shop. Open daily, 9–6. Admission $3; 3–11, $2; under 3 free.

In nearby St. Cloud is the **Reptile World Serpentarium,** with over 1500 specimens. Open Tuesday–Sunday, 9–5:30. Closed September, Thanksgiving and Christmas. Adults $3, 6–17 $2, 3–5 $1.

LAKE BUENA VISTA is the resort community growing at the doorstep of Walt Disney World, west of I-4, about 15 miles southwest of Orlando. Florida 535 leads to the city of Lake Buena Vista, US 192 to the entrance to Walt Disney World. (Both highways can be reached via well-marked exits on I-4.) **Lake Buena Vista Resort Community** is a uniquely planned

CENTRAL 41

vacation community, with resort villas, townhouses and treehouses, as well as a golf course and tennis courts. Also within this area is the **Walt Disney World Village**—an outstanding dining, entertainment and shopping area including the Empress Lilly Riverboat. The luxury hotels in this area are called the "Hotel Plaza" accommodations.

Walt Disney World is the largest and most elaborate tourist attraction ever conceived—in fact, it is such an expansive and imaginative a concept that it is hard to understand until you have seen it. The theme park, or **Magic Kingdom,** bears much similarity to Disneyland in California, but that is only a small part of the total Vacation Kingdom that is Walt Disney World.

The **Vacation Kingdom,** a resort and entertainment complex, covers 2,500 acres and includes Magic Kingdom, three hotels—Contemporary Resort, Polynesian Village, and Golf Resort, Fort Wilderness Campground, Discovery Island and River Country. Fine restaurants and supper clubs in the hotels book big-name entertainment. Complete convention and meeting facilities, along with banquet rooms, constantly attract bookings for several years in advance. The slogan is "Family conventioneering," and all sorts of master plans can be worked out to provide entertainment, recreation, accommodations, dining, and transportation.

Families who wish to camp can stay at the **Fort Wilderness Campground** on the shore of Bay Lake, a self-contained campground with its own utilities, shopping, restaurants, and recreation facilities. The cruises to **Discovery Island** are especially pleasant. The tropical island is an exquisite, quiet, cool, almost natural wilderness area abounding in colorful flowers and birds. Accessible by boat, bus, or car is **River Country,** an exciting recreation area with giant water flumes, tubing rapids, and cascading waterfalls. There are water slides suited to younger swimmers, as well as broad sandy beaches, nature trails, and shady picnic areas. All sorts of watercraft can be rented to travel about the lake: sailboats, motorboats, water speedboats, canoes, etc. There are miles of beaches, horseback riding trails, tennis courts, and many organized recreational activities. Two championship 18-hole golf courses are located at the Walt Disney World Golf Resort, which hosts several championship golf matches annually.

More than 7,500 acres of the 28,000-acre complex have been set aside for permanent protection as a conservation sanctuary, designed to protect the natural beauty of the area and its wildlife and, in addition, to inform the public on intelligent use of natural resources. In conjunction with this, the master plan of conservation calls for the use of most advanced methods of water and air pollution controls and of trash and sewage disposal.

The world famous **Magic Kingdom** is, of course, a Disney Masterpiece. The theme park is divided into six areas (or lands): **Main Street, U.S.A.; Adventureland; Frontierland; Liberty Square; Fantasyland;** and **Tomorrowland.** There are attractions, refreshment stands and restaurants, gift shops, and outdoor entertainment throughout the theme park.

Special entertainment events, such as firework displays, parades, shows featuring bands, singing groups and Disney characters, and the famous **Main Street Electrical Parade,** bring much variety to a stay in the Magic Kingdom. Meeting Mickey Mouse, Goofy, Pluto, as well as most other Disney characters, is also a thrill for children and adults.

EPCOT Center—Experimental Prototype Community of Tomorrow, which opened on October 1, 1982, is a permanent showplace for the technologies of tomorrow as well as for the nations of today. There are two major theme areas. **Future World** includes Spaceship Earth (Bell System); Universe of Energy (Exxon); World of Motion (General Motors); Journey Into Imagination (Kodak); The Land (Kraft); Horizons (General Electric); Communicore East and West, including Computer Central (Sperry); Energy Exchange (Exxon); FutureCom (Bell System); Travel Port (American Express); Electronic Forum; and Epcot Outreach. **World Showcase,** surrounding the World Showcase Lagoon, presently features pavilions from nine nations; Canada, the United Kingdom, France, Japan, American Adventure, Italy, Germany, China, and Mexico. Morocco and Scandinavia are scheduled to open within the next few years. These pavilions have spectacular restaurants (it is best to make advance reservations), entertainment, films, and shops.

A few words of advice on how best to enjoy your visit to the Magic Kingdom. First, if at all possible, plan to come at some time other than school vacation periods. If these most popular seasons are the only time you can come, and if you are staying outside of Walt Disney World, allow yourself plenty of extra time in the morning—get there early, if you can. Besides giving yourself a chance to beat the crowds, you are apt to enjoy cooler and pleasanter weather during the morning hours. Transportation within Disney World is easy. You may drive, or take a bus to the **Transportation Center** and board the monorail or the ferry boat to the Magic Kingdom. If you're EPCOT bound, either a bus or the separate monorail from the Transportation Center is available. The entire area is joined by an efficient network of monorail, boat, and bus systems.

Second, unless you will be satisfied with a very quick once-over, you will find that there is too much to cover in one day. You will enjoy your visit much more if you plan in advance to come for at least three days so that you won't feel the need to rush all day.

Third, if you are coming during peak seasons (Christmas or Easter, especially), you had better have advance reservations wherever you plan to stay—even at a campground. Although there are many new motels in Central Florida, it is very difficult to keep up with the increase in tourist travel. New attractions are constantly enticing more visitors, and consequently rooms are filled to capacity during the heavy seasons.

Once you arrive at Walt Disney World you will find excellent handicapped facilities, stroller rentals, baby care facilities (including rocking chairs for nursing mothers), some banking facilities, as well as many conveniences and services. The Magic Kingdom and EPCOT Center are open 365 days a year. The hours of operation depend on the season, allowing for extended hours during summer and holiday seasons.

There are special package rates depending on your needs. A 1-day passport costs $17, junior 12–17 $16, 3–11 $14; a 3-day passport costs $40, junior 12–17 $38, 3–11 $32; a 4-day passport costs $50, junior 12–17 $47, 3–11 $40; children under 3 are free. The three and four-day passports allow you to enter both the Magic Kingdom and EPCOT Center on the same day. There are also other package plans available.

For your convenience there is a Walt Disney World Central Reservations Office, Box 78, Lake Buena Vista, Florida 32830. Telephone (305) 824-8000. For general information write the Guest Letters Department, Walt Disney World, P.O. Box 40, Lake Buena Vista, Florida 32830. Telephone (305) 824-4500. Walt Disney World is a member of the Florida Attractions Association.

LAKELAND, largest city in Polk County, is located at the junction of US 98 and US 92, about 35 miles east of Tampa. There are 13 lakes within the city limits.

Lakeland is the major city of the Florida Highlands area, and the second largest in Central Florida. It is a thriving city, prospering from the citrus industry, phosphate mining, manufacturing, and tourism. The county produces one-fourth of the nation's citrus crop and three-fourths of its phosphate. For many years it has been a popular winter resort and retirement town, and many activities are planned for the entertainment of visitors. Its location makes it a good headquarters for the tourist who wishes to see a number of the major Florida attractions. Within an hour, you can drive to the Tampa-St. Pete area, Disney World and Orlando, or Lake Wales and Winter Haven.

Lakeland is the home of the Detroit Tigers spring training camp, and **Florida Grapefruit League** exhibition games are played here in March and April.

The special events calendar for Lakeland begins with the **Orange Cup Regatta,** outboard hydroplane races held annually on Lake Hollingsworth, in late February or early March.

There are two colleges in Lakeland: **South Eastern Bible College,** with 1,000 students; and **Florida Southern College,** that enrolls 1,900 students.

The campus of Florida Southern College boasts one of the largest collections of Frank Lloyd Wright buildings in the world.

A $13 million **Civic Center** was opened 1974, with excellent facilities for entertainment and conventions. Celebrity performances, rodeos, circuses, horse shows, ice hockey, and basketball games are held here, as well as trade shows.

LAKE PLACID is in Highlands County, on US 27, about midway between Sarasota on the Gulf coast and Fort Pierce on the Atlantic.

Lake Placid Day is held each Fourth of July, featuring a barbecue, games, children's beauty contest, and races.

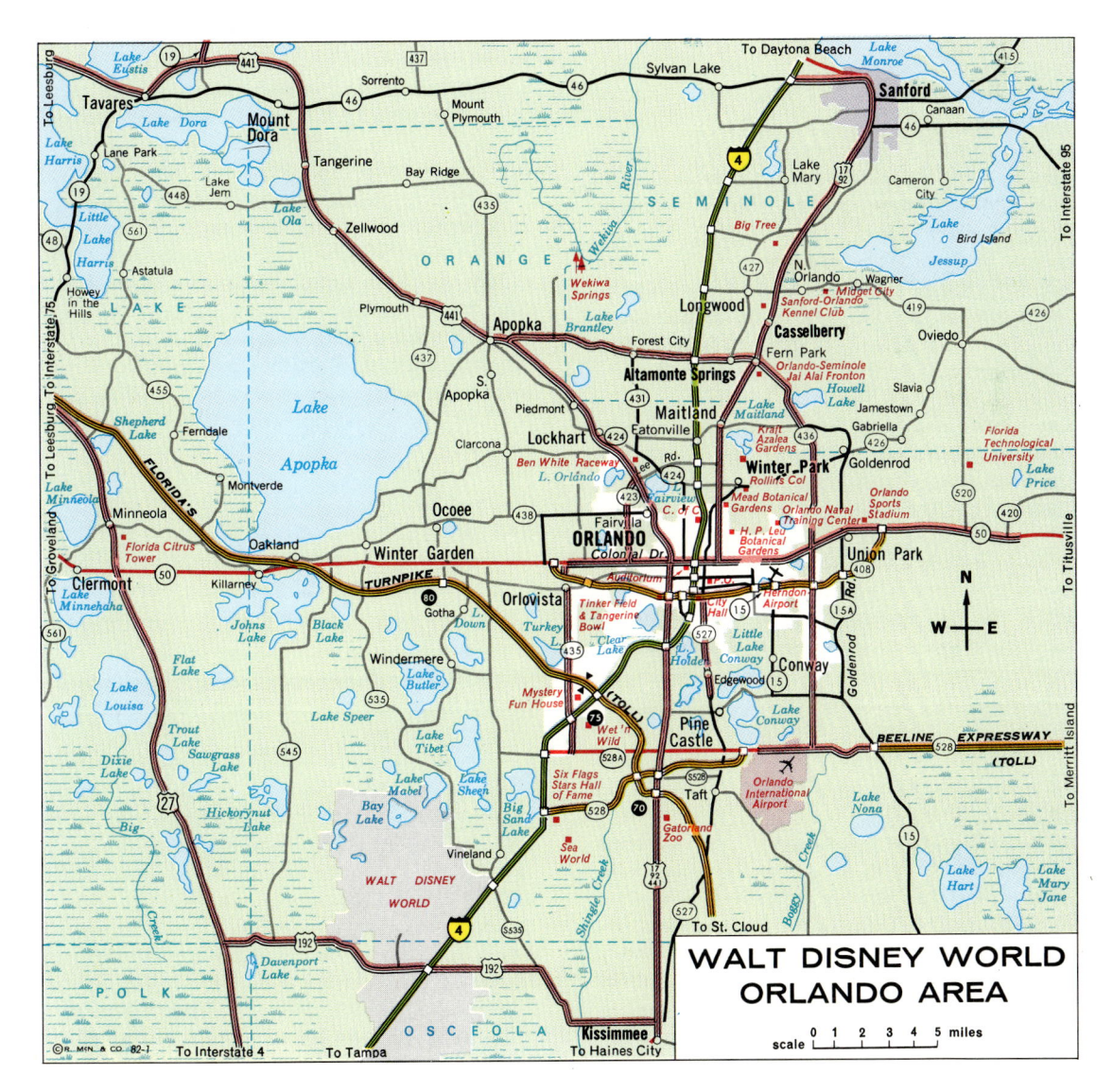

WALT DISNEY WORLD ORLANDO AREA

CENTRAL 43

South of town, on US 27, is **Plantation Paradise,** tropical gardens that specialize in the growing of pineapples. Open daily, 8–6. Closed Christmas. Free.

LAKE WALES is about 50 miles east of Tampa, on US 27 and Florida 60. It is one of the higher settlements in the state, with an elevation of 250 feet, and is surrounded by hilly countryside with 30 lakes and about 30,000 acres of citrus groves.

Lake Wales has been made known throughout the world by the philanthropy of Edward W. Bok, who created the **Bok Tower Gardens** and **Singing Tower.** This is a spot unlike any other. Pictures of it have surely been seen by everyone who has ever opened a book about Florida. A 205-foot tower built of Georgia marble and Florida coquina stone is set on the top of 290-foot Iron Mountain. Each afternoon at 3 o'clock the whole tower seems to burst into music as a 45-minute concert is played on the 53-bell carillon. Special recitals are performed at various times during the year, and Easter Sunrise Services are held here.

Around the tower is the 128-acre **Bok Tower Gardens,** a retreat from the noise and hurry of everyday life. About half the acreage is landscaped. There are no amusements or concessions; pets are not permitted; the entire purpose of the sanctuary is just what its name implies—a place for people to go to enjoy peace, rest, and beauty. Open daily, 8–5:30. Free; parking $2.50

Citrus World, on US 27, is the home of Donald Duck brand citrus products. Here visitors are welcome to stop for a cup of orange juice and take a movie "tour" through a citrus plant.

The **Black Hills Passion Play** is presented during the Lenten season each year from mid-February to mid-April on Tuesday, Thursday, Saturday at 7:30, Sunday at 6, some Wednesdays at 3, and also on Good Friday, in an amphitheater located 2 miles south of town. Admission $5–$8, under 12, $2.50–$4. It also has helped to make Lake Wales a major tourist center.

The history of this theater company is interesting. Josef Meier, the German-born actor who plays the Christ, is a seventh-generation Passion Play actor. The group came to the United States in 1932, and traveled from city to city in an effort to make a living. As America came out of the Depression, the Passion Play prospered, and in 1939 a permanent home was established in Spearfish, South Dakota. Each year since 1951 a winter season has been played in Lake Wales. The amphitheater is open for inspection year-round.

A phenomenon called **Spook Hill,** for which no explanation is offered, also exists in Lake Wales. At the bottom of the steep hill on Fifth Avenue one can turn off his motor and seemingly be propelled backwards in his car for as much as one hundred feet up the hill!

South of Lake Wales, near Babson Park, is an **Audubon Center,** with a nature trail and exhibit room. Open daily, November–April, 9–5; May–October, phone for hours, 813/638-1355. Closed New Year's Day and Christmas. Free.

One of the state's most renowned resorts is 4 miles north of Lake Wales, just off US 27A. **Chalet Suzanne** is outstanding because of its whimsical fairy-tale appearance, its collection of antiques and art objects from all over the world, and its superior cuisine. Especially well known are the soups, which are canned on the premises and sold in gourmet shops all over the country.

Lake Kissimmee State Park is 15 miles east of Lake Wales on Camp Mack Road. A living history interpretation of an authentic 1870s frontier cow camp is presented here each Saturday and Sunday afternoon. Also on the 5,030-acre site are sandhill cranes, an observation tower, fishing, and a boat ramp.

LEESBURG is the largest city in Lake County. It is located in the geographic center of the state, between two large lakes—Griffin and Harris—at the junction of US 27 and US 441.

The economy of the area is based on light industry and the processing of locally grown foods. Minute Maid frozen orange juice is processed here, and berries, grapes, and watermelons are other important crops in the vicinity.

Three miles north of town is **Lake Griffin State Recreation Area,** 423 acres developed for camping, boating, and recreation.

MOUNT DORA is in Lake County, on US 441, on Lake Dora across from Tavares and about 15 miles south of Leesburg.

Annual events include a **Sailboat Regatta** and **Antique Auto Show** in April, and in February an **Art Show.**

Mount Dora has an active art and writers' league, a good small library, and a fine Little Theater Group. However, fishing and boating are the main activities in this area of the state, where lakes are everywhere. There are two recreation areas nearby—**Gilbert Park,** on Lake Dora, and **Trimble Park,** between Lakes Carlton and Beauclair. Gilbert is a recreation park only, with boating and picnic areas. Free. Trimble is a county park with camping facilities. There is a charge for camping; obtain permit from the caretaker.

Shuffleboard, croquet, lawn bowling, and tennis are all popular pastimes in Mount Dora. Each October an **amateur invitational golf tournament** is held.

The Mount Dora Chamber of Commerce is now located in the historic old Seaboard Coast Line Railroad Station, which has been completely renovated for their use as an office, community meeting room, and service center for members and visitors. "The Depot" is at the foot of Alexander Street at Third Avenue, and visitors are always welcome.

An interesting building in town is the Donnelly Mansion, a good example of Victorian Steamboat Gothic architecture.

OKEECHOBEE, county seat and largest city of Okeechobee County, is located on US 441 and 98, at the northern end of Lake Okeechobee.

Okeechobee is the trading center for an area specializing in the growing of citrus fruits and winter vegetables, cattle raising, and the commerical breeding and gathering of frogs for frogs' legs. It is also the service center for fishing trips on Lake Okeechobee, second largest freshwater lake completely within the United States.

The town sponsors a fishing contest during the first three weeks in March. It comes to a close with the **Speckled Perch Festival,** held on the third weekend in March.

The Cattleman's Rodeo is held over Labor Day weekend.

One of the fiercest battles of the Seminole War was fought near here, on Christmas Day, 1837.

About 25 miles southwest of the city, via US 441 and Florida 78, the highway goes through the **Seminole Indian Reservation.**

ORLANDO, county seat and largest city in Orange County, located on I-4, US 17, US 441, the Florida Turnpike, and Florida 50, is the major city in Central Florida. During the past five years this has been one of the fastest growing metropolitan areas in the nation.

In a county with a thousand lakes, Orlando is often described as having the appearance of one big park—it has 54 lakes and 47 city parks within its limits!

The city was settled by army volunteers who stayed in the area after the Second Seminole War was ended. It began as a trading post in cattle country. Today it has a strong and balanced economy. It is a shipping center for citrus and vegetable crops; it is a major transportation center for mid-Florida; it is an important service center for the Kennedy Space Center and Cape Canaveral, with a number of missile-oriented industries; it is the location of Orlando Naval Training Center and Naval Training Device Center; and it is still a favorite winter colony for many northerners.

Orlando has called itself the City Beautiful. It is now adding new slogans—the Hub of the State, the Action Center of Florida. "The nice thing about Orlando is that it's completely surrounded by Florida," says the Chamber of Commerce. More and more, Orlando is becoming surrounded by tourist attractions that make this city an increasingly popular vacation headquarters and entertainment center.

Orlando celebrated its 100th birthday in 1975. Its slogan the City Beautiful was chosen in 1908, and its citizens have always been concerned with and proud of its beauty.

The opening of Walt Disney World, 15 miles to the southwest, gave the economy of this metropolitan area a huge boost, what with new construction, new permanent jobs created at Disney World itself, new motels and restaurants, built to accommodate the influx of tourists. Disney World, which almost immediately became the most popular tourist attraction in the world, has been joined by Sea World, Circus World, Stars Hall of Fame, and others, giving the thousands of visitors to the area even more reason to stay a few extra days and enjoy the hospitality of the Orlando area's 37,000-plus hotel/motel rooms, more than 1,000 eating establishments, and modern shopping facilities. Orlando encourages the visiting family to make the city its vacation base of operations from which to visit many other tourist attractions within a 100-mile radius.

Make your reservations before you head for Orlando— especially over major holidays. If you need special information or assistance, write to the Orlando Area Chamber of Commerce, P. O. Box 1234, Orlando 32802, or telephone (305) 425-1234.

Gray Line of Orlando operates **guided bus tours** to view the scenic areas of Orlando and Winter Park, as well as longer trips to St. Augustine, Kennedy Space Center, Walt Disney World, Cypress Gardens, and other popular spots. For information, phone (305) 422-0744.

Major city parks and recreation areas include **Eola,** on Central Boulevard, downtown; **Loch Haven,** Princeton Boulevard and Mills Avenue; **Wadeview,** at Osceola Avenue and Harding Street. In addition, there are five Orange County

The Singing Tower, Bok Tower Gardens, Lake Wales.

parks and recreation areas nearby.

In **Loch Haven Park** there are two museums. **John Young Science Center and Planetarium** is at 810 East Rollins Street. It is open Monday–Thursday, 9–5; Friday, 9–9; Saturday, noon–9; Sunday, noon–5. There are planetarium shows daily, Monday–Thursday at 2:30 and Friday at 2:30 and 8:30. Closed Christmas. Admission $2, children 4–18 and senior citizens $1.50. **Loch Haven Art Center,** 2416 North Mills Avenue, is open Tuesday–Friday, 10–5; Saturday, noon–5; Sunday, 2–5. Closed holidays. Free.

The **Orange County Historical Museum,** 812 East Rollins Street, has displays of tools, furniture, and other items of local history. Open Tuesday–Friday, 10–4; Saturday, Sunday, 2–5. Free.

A unique collection is exhibited at the **Cartoon Museum** at 4300 S. Semoran (Rte. 436), which has a permanent collection of cartoon art as well as occasional guest appearances and one-artist shows by well-known cartoonists.

At **Mystery Fun House,** located at 5767 Major Boulevard, you can participate in walk-through exhibits in 15 rooms. Open daily, 10–10. Admission $4.50, 4–12 $3.50.

The **Leu Gardens,** a 50-acre park now owned by the city, are located on Lake Rowena in the middle of the city. There are huge live oaks, tropical trees, azaleas, camellias, blooming shrubs, an orchid house, and a stream. Open daily, 9–5, closed Christmas. Admission $2, 5–12 50¢, under 5 free.

Just south of Orlando on US 17/19 is Owen Godwin's **Gatorland Zoo.**

The **Central Florida Civic Theatre** presents plays year-round. For the schedule or to make reservations, write 1010 East Princeton Avenue, Orlando 32803, or phone (305) 896-7365.

The **Florida Symphony Orchestra** plays from October through May. For information phone (305) 896-0331.

East of town on Florida 50 is **University of Central Florida,** on a 1,200-acre campus.

veloped by Six Flags, Inc., one of the nation's leading theme park operators. A multimedia presentation, restaurants, gift shop, and games area are part of the complex. Open daily, winter 10–10, summer 9–10. Admission $7.30, children 4–11 $5.20, under 4 free. Member Florida Attractions Association.

Circus World, at the intersection of I-4 and US 27, is a circus theme park. Daily circus performances, trapeze and tightrope shows, side shows, a menagerie, and magicians create the nostalgic atmosphere of the Big Top. A giant roller coaster, historic train cars, and circus museum displays are also here. Open daily, 9–6. Admission $11.50, children 3–11 $10.50, under 3 free.

A new addition to the rich collection of Orlando area attractions is **Wet 'n Wild,** a water-theme park located about 3 miles from Sea World. Features in the 12-acre park include a Surf Lagoon, White Water Slideways, a Jumper Pool, a Kamakaze Chute, and a large sand beach. Open daily; summer 9–9; rest of year, 10–5. Admission $8.50, children 3–12 $6.50, under 3 free; after 3 PM admission ½ price. Member Florida Attractions Association.

Orlando has many spectator sports events. The Minnesota Twins hold spring training here, and the **Florida Grapefruit League** plays exhibition games in March and April. In early March the Florida Citrus Commission sponsors the **Florida Citrus Open Invitational Golf Tournament.** Another popular golf tourney is the **Bayhill Classic** also in March. In October the **Walt Disney World National Team Championship Pro-Am Golf Tournament** takes place. Many other events are held year-round at the **Orlando Sports Stadium.**

Auto racing events take place at the **Central Florida Dragway** in Bithlo, about 20 miles east of Orlando on Florida 50, and off-road racing at the **Eastern Dunebuggy Association's course** on Florida 15A, east of the city. Jai-alai and dog racing in season add to the nighttime excitement.

In December the major sports events are the **Citrus Invitational Basketball Tournament,** in Rollins College Field House (for information write PO Box 5645, Orlando 32805) and the **Citrus Bowl Football Classic** (for tickets or other information write to **Citrus Bowl** (formerly Tangerine Bowl), Orlando P.O. Box 749 32802).

Festivals and expositions punctuate the year here, as they do in most Florida cities. The **Central Florida Fair,** held in late February and early March, is the state's second largest fair and has been held each year since 1912. In November there is a **Fiesta in the Park** at Eola Park.

SANFORD, county seat and largest city in Seminole County, is located northeast of Orlando on US 17/92 and I-4, on the St. Johns River at Lake Monroe.

Sanford is in a pleasant agricultural area of hills, lakes, rivers, and thick woods. It is a relaxed little city, convenient to Daytona Beach, Orlando, and Cape Kennedy. The citrus industry flourished here early, and many experiments in citrus culture were made. The industry was greatly hurt by killing frosts in 1894–95, and truck gardens replaced some of the groves. Today a diversified group of some 100 industries provide a good economic base.

The famous Sanford Zoo has been replaced by the new **Central Florida Zoological Park,** located on Lake Monroe 1 mile east of the US 17/92 interchange of I-4. More than 100

There are hundred of miles of fairways on an abundance of golf courses in the vicinity and, of course, unlimited opportunities for water sports on the more than 2,000 lakes.

Sea World of Florida is a beautifully landscaped park on a 135-acre site located near the intersection of I-4 and the Beeline Expressway. Developed by the creators of Sea World of San Diego, California, and Cleveland, Ohio, this is the largest marine park in the world, featuring major stadiums for whale, dolphin, seal, and penguin shows; an Undersea Fantasy show; a 660,000-gallon shark aquarium with a 135-foot tunnel; dolphin and seal feeding pools; and a 400-foot sky tower seating 60 people. The **Florida Festival** exhibit includes 40 booths, and features arts, crafts, live entertainment, and natural and manufactured Florida products. Sea World is open daily, 9 am–7 pm, with extended hours during peak season. All-inclusive admission $11.95, children 3–11, $10.95; under 3 free. Member Florida Attractions Association.

Six Flags' Stars Hall of Fame, next door to Sea World, is the world's largest wax museum devoted entirely to popular personalities and realistic sets from the entertainment world. Guests may actually take a screen test! The project was de-

46   CENTRAL

acres are developed as a zoological and botanical garden. On the grounds are nature trails and a picnic area.

Fort Mellon Park, on Lake Monroe, has a picnic area, playground, and tennis and shuffleboard courts. Open daily, 7 am–sunset. Free.

Eight miles southwest of town, in Longwood, is **Big Tree Park,** in which stands a giant cypress tree named **The Senator.** It is 125 feet tall and 47 feet around at the base, and is estimated to be about 3,500 years old. Open daily, daylight hours.

SEBRING, county seat and largest city of Highlands County, is located on Florida 17, just north of its junction with US 27.

This is a beautiful, planned city, with streets radiating from a central park known as The Circle. Three blocks from here is the county courthouse, a stately building situated in the center of a beautifully landscaped square. A tremendous banyan (Cuban mountain laurel) tree covers a large area on one side of the building. This tree was only 7 feet tall and 1 inches in diameter when it was planted here in 1928.

Sebring is surrounded by gently rolling hills covered with citrus groves.

Highlands Hammock State Park is 6 miles west of town, off US 27. This is a fantastic jungle area—3,800 acres of tropical wilderness, featuring rare orchids and other exotic plants; huge trees several centuries old; more than 11 miles of trails and catwalks through a cypress swamp; alligators, deer, and pond birds. Jeep-drawn trailers take spectators through the grounds, and guides explain the sights.

A camping area is available, as well as picnic facilities, a playground, and refreshment building. This is certainly one of the most interesting of Florida's fine state parks.

Every March Sebring hosts tens of thousands of auto racing buffs at the famous 12-hour endurance race of GT cars from all over the world.

TAVARES, county seat of Lake County, is located on US 441, between Lake Harris, Lake Dora, and Lake Eustis.

Tavares, Eustis, and Mount Dora make up the so-called Golden Triangle, a productive citrus-growing region, and Tavares has one of the largest fresh-fruit packing plants in the state. This is a popular retirement spot for trailer owners and apartment renters.

Cruise boats are available to take visitors among the waterways of the area.

The **Lake County Historical Society** has a collection of historical exhibits. Open Wednesday and Sunday, 1–4. Donation.

UMATILLA, in Lake County, is on Florida 19, known as the Backwoods Trail, a scenic auto route through the state, between Eustis and the Ocala National Forest.

Umatilla is the home of the famed Harry Anna Crippled Children's Hospital, sponsored by the Florida Elks Association. It is in the midst of a vast citrus growing area and has the second largest citrus processing plant in the state.

Umatilla is one of the entrance cities to **Ocala National Forest.** This forest, with more than 350,000 acres, is the only national forest with subtropical vegetation. Timber cutting is carried on in the thick pine woods. Many species of wildlife abound, and deer hunting is permitted in season. (State hunting license and Florida Public Hunt Area Permit are required.) There are more than 30 camping areas. One of them, on Florida 40, is **Juniper Springs** recreational area, where the springs form a scenic swimming pool and canoe stream. The Florida Hiking Trail passes through the national forest. For complete information, write to Ocala National Forest, PO Box 1050, Tallahassee 32302.

WAUCHULA, county seat and largest center in Hardee County, is located on US 17 and Florida 64A, 20 miles west of Avon Park.

The town calls itself the Cucumber Capital of the World. Each November the **Hardee County Fair,** naming a county queen and a "junior" pickle king and queen, is held. Cattle raising and citrus growing are also important in the area.

WINTER HAVEN is in Polk County, just off US 92, between Lakeland and Haines City. For many years it has been a popular tourist destination.

This is a progressive community, with a large community college and a fine hospital. Called the City of 100 Lakes, it actually does have nearly that many within the city limits, and 18 of them are joined by navigable canals. It is one of the major tourist cities of the state, claiming, with good reason, that it is "closer to everywhere." Besides tourism, the economy is based on citrus packing, canning, and shipping. There are five major citrus canneries and processing plants here; employing many people from the vicinity of Winter Haven. More than 17 million citrus trees, bearing one-fourth of Florida's total citrus crop, are grown in a 2,000-square-mile area of Central Florida.

The **Florida Citrus Showcase,** an interesting building with an orange geodesic dome, is an exposition hall for conventions and special events.

Each February Winter Haven hosts the **Florida Citrus Festival and Polk County Fair,** with many special events, including the **Florida Citrus Showcase Invitational** golf tournament.

The Boston Red Sox team has its spring training camp here, and the **Florida Grapefruit League** plays exhibition games in March and April.

On US 17, at 1530 6th Street N.W., is the **Museum of Old Dolls and Toys.** There are displays of dolls spanning three centuries, doll houses, miniature furniture, antique toys, and a miniature toy circus. Open Monday–Saturday, 10–5; Sunday and holidays, noon–5. Admission $2, children 8–15 $1, under 8 free.

Winter Haven has been a destination for millions of tourists over the past 30-odd years because of the drawing power and enduring popularity of **Cypress Gardens.** Mr. and Mrs. Dick Pope, Sr., developed this tropical wonderland of venerable, moss-draped cypress giants; rare and exotic plantings arranged amid grottoes, pools, and arched footbridges; and colorful and exciting water-ski shows. The gardens were started in the 1930s, and the smooth, quiet electric boats began gliding about the lagoons in 1933. Mrs. Pope started the water-ski shows in 1942, with her son and daughter and their teen-aged friends as performers, and soldiers from a nearby camp as spectators. There were six servicemen there for the first show—eight hundred for the second! Four regular performances have been given daily since 1946—a world record for any show. Spectators watch the skiers and stunt performers from the comfort of a 2,300-seat, all-weather stadium.

During **Cypress Gardens Festival Month** (June through July 4) activities include different waterskiing championships, the **Classic Car Meet,** and the **Miss Cheerleader USA** contest.

Also in Cypress Gardens is a 14-acre attractions area featuring new rides, shops, shows, and restaurants. In the "antebellum town", Southern Crossroads, is a cinema, a multimedia presentation, a children's funland, a dining area, and novelty shops. The Living Forest features a boardwalk through six acres of forest with an animal petting area, a baby animal nursery, a 'gator alley, an Exotic Bird Revue, ecology exhibits, live shows, and the aviary. The Gardens of the World botanical area boasts thirteen separate theme areas including the All-American Rose Garden.

A motel is adjacent to Cypress Gardens. Boat rides give excellent views of the Japanese Garden, Cactus Garden, and South Sea Island waterfalls. Gardens are open daily, 8 am–dusk. Four half-hour ski shows daily, at 10 am, noon, 2 pm, and 4 pm. Exciting shows are also presented throughout the four themed areas. Free wheelchairs and strollers and free parking. Admission $9.75, 6–11 $6.25, under 6 free. Member Florida Attractions Association.

WINTER PARK, in Orange County, is just off I-4 and US 17/92, 4 miles north of Orlando.

This is a lush suburb, settled by New Englanders in the 1800s and still preserving its original charm and beauty. It has long been a favorite retirement town for writers, artists, educators, and professional people.

At the southern edge of town is a 55-acre showplace of gardens and greenhouses, along trails through a chain of lakes and canals—**Mead Botanical Gardens.** Open daily, daylight hours. Closed Christmas. Free.

The world's slowest ride at Cypress Gardens.

The annual Sidewalk Art Festival in Winter Park.

Park Avenue, the shopping area of Winter Park, features over 120 shops and galleries nestled along gardens andbrick walkways. Known as little Europe, this section of Winter Park has attracted shoppers from all over the world.

The city has developed around **Rollins College,** and derives much of its character from the college atmosphere. The beautiful campus, featuring Spanish-Mediterranean architecture, houses the state's oldest institution of higher education. There is an interesting **Walk of Fame,** built of stones brought from the homes and birthplaces of famous people. The **Morse Gallery of Art** contains an outstanding exhibit of Tiffany paintings, stemware, jewelry, and windows. The **Beal Maltbie Shell Museum** includes shells of almost every known type. Dramatic productions are given throughout the school year in the **Annie Russell Theatre.** Other events include a **Bach Festival** in February.

An event that has steadily grown in fame and popularity is the annual **Sidewalk Arts Festival** in March. More than 300,000 visitors come to view the work of more than 450 artists and craftsmen representing all types of media.

A not-to-be-missed treat in Winter Park is to take a **Scenic Boat Tour,** Sundays 10 to 4, through 12 to 15 miles of waterways, past the Isle of Sicily, the Kraft Azalea Gardens, Rollins College, and beautiful estates.

In the area of sports, Rollins hosts a **Baseball Week Tournament** in the spring. In May the **Florida High School Championship Track Meet** is held at Showalter Field.

Horse racing, greyhound racing, and jai-alai are offered in nearby towns. In Casselberry, the **Seminole Raceway,** holds greyhound racing. The **Florida Jai-Alai Fronton,** in Fern Park, is the setting for this sport from mid-August through December. In Longwood, the **Sanford-Orlando Kennel Club** stages greyhound racing from late December through April.

(Details on admission prices and hours have been included as a service to the reader and as a guide in planning activities. However, changes are inevitable in some cases, and the publisher cannot be responsible for any variations from the listed information.)

The animals at The Dark Continent/Busch Gardens can be viewed from the monorail.

SOUTHWEST

THE ISLAND COAST

IT'S A STRIP OF CITIES AND TOWNS ALONG 180 MILES OF BAYS, HARBORS, SOUNDS, AND INLETS WITH BREEZE-BRUSHED ISLANDS, WHERE EXOTIC SEASHELLS ARE HARVESTED BY THE BUCKETFUL. FOOTPRINTS IN THE SAND HAVE BEEN LEFT BY PREHISTORIC INDIAN MOUND BUILDERS, 17TH-CENTURY SPANISH CONQUISTADORES, 18TH-CENTURY PIRATES, 19TH-CENTURY TYCOONS AND UTOPIANS, 20TH-CENTURY SUN WORSHIPPERS. HERE SHUFFLEBOARD IS A MAJOR SPORT AND PUBLIC BEACHES ARE MEASURED IN MILES, NOT FEET. HERE A BRIDGE IS A SIGHTSEEING POINT OF INTEREST AND A FISHING PIER IS A HISTORIC LANDMARK.

Suddenly we have left behind the groves and farms and ranches. There's Tampa—a major industrial metropolis, southern in climate, a trifle Cuban in appearance, but as busy and energetic as any northern center of commerce. St. Petersburg, the "Sunshine City," long famous as a retirement community—but with a lot of living going on. Sarasota, sophisticated, cultural, fashionable, and spotless. There are venerable and grand resorts such as the Belleview Biltmore in Clearwater and the Don CeSar in St. Petersburg. Fort Myers, "City of Palms," chosen retreat for industrial geniuses Thomas Edison, Henry Ford, and Harvey Firestone. Sanibel Island, where beachcombing is looked upon as the highest and noblest pursuit of man. Venice, originally planned as a retirement town for railroad workers, today winter home of clowns, aerialists, bareback riders, animal trainers, and all the other specialists of the circus world. Naples, wealthiest town on the west coast.

Southwest Florida is made up of six counties, plus about one-eight of the area of Collier County. It begins just above Tarpon Springs, at the northern boundaries of Pinellas and Hillsborough counties, and takes in a strip one county wide, south through Lee County, then the populated strip along western edge of Collier that lies between the Gulf and the Big Cypress Swamp, ending with Marco Island. About 20% of the state's residents live along this strip. Most of the population is concentrated in the metropolitan areas of Tampa, St. Petersburg, and Clearwater—and the number of people moving into the area is growing every day.

EARLY DEVELOPERS

Ponce de Leon sailed into Charlotte Harbor in 1513, the first of a long line of explorers and settlers who have sensed something magical about the climate, the waters, the flora, and the fauna of Florida. Not very much happened in Southwest Florida, however, until the latter part of the 19th century, when Henry B. Plant brought a railroad across to Tampa. Thomas Edison began to make his winter home in Fort Myers in 1887. St. Petersburg was founded by a Detroiter in 1875, and the first railroad came to that city in 1884. Naples, also, was "discovered" and platted in the 1880s, but it did not gain much attention or many residents until the Tamiami Trail was opened in 1928, making it accessible from Miami and Tampa. Mr. and Mrs. John Ringling built their fabulous Art Museum and Ca'd'Zan in the 1920s, in Sarasota. In 1924, Venice was founded by the members of a railroad labor union as a retirement community, but Florida's economic collapse destroyed that plan.

All of these most desirable places to live follow one another in a narrow line down the Gulf coast, bounded on the west by powder-fine, white beaches, gently sloping coastlines, islands basking in the sun, and waters which at times seem almost overflowing with mackerel, tarpon, redfish, trout, snook, and pompano. On the east the communities are rimmed by virgin cypress swamps, hammocks, sloughs, and strands—home of panthers, black bears, coons, otters, reptiles, and birds.

GROWTH VS. CONSERVATION

Nowhere in Florida has the struggle to achieve a balance between growth and conservation been more pronounced than in Southwest Florida. Nature's resources are so enticing and so bountiful that the constant pressure to make room for more and more people is almost inevitable. On the other hand, many of the people who have chosen this area for a home are aware that the natural environment can be easily damaged to the point of no return—that the bald eagles may stop nesting on Marco Island, that the wood storks might not return to Corkscrew Swamp Sanctuary, and that even the shells could disappear from Sanibel if greedy collectors insist on destroying living shellfish in order to clean out a beautiful specimen.

One conservation group dedicated to preventing irreversible pollution of the coastal bodies of water has proudly named itself the SOBs—for Save Our Bays. And some land promoters have found them to be formidable opposition. Such promoters simply refuse to believe that any lasting harm can be done by dredging and filling in order to change the shape of shorelines and create hundreds of additional waterfront lots. They look on the swamps and glades as unused expanses of land that ought to be made habitable for human beings.

It's a problem without easy solutions—because to see Southwest Florida is to love it, and there is no way to prevent increasing numbers of people from wanting to live here. But if the birds and animals and alligators have to move out to make room for people, if the beaches lose their shells and are filled end to end with littering picnickers, if the cypresses give way to manicured lawns and the wild orchids to formal hedges, then what will Florida have to offer that can't be found in a climate-controlled hotel in the midst of a northern city?

The resorts of Naples and Marco are irresistible partly because of the proximity of the wild, uncharted Ten Thousand Islands and the almost impenetrable Fakahatchee Strand, not in spite of it. Naples would not be Naples if it were no longer a gateway to the Everglades.

Perhaps the best way to introduce yourself to this region is to start with some of the spectacular zoological and botanical parks, such as The Dark Continent/Busch Gardens, Sunken Gardens, or Jungle Gardens. Here guides, signs, brochures, and tape recordings will awaken your interest, and before you know it you will be exploring on your own.

Much of the beauty of this area is grand and overwhelming—flaming sunsets, long stretches of beach, towering trees. But much more of it is subtle, minute, camouflaged. Tiny blossoms hiding behind huge leaves, timid baby birds, rare shells buried in the sand. Once you begin to discover these things, you'll be hooked. You'll tread more lightly, listen more carefully, look more sharply—and you will have discovered the magic that lured old Ponce de Leon.

CITIES & TOWNS
Map of this section on page 55.

BOCA GRANDE, in Lee County, is south of Venice on Gasparilla Island in the Gulf of Mexico, connected to the mainland by Florida 775 (toll bridge).

The island was for many decades a remote resort for the very wealthy, and it still has a number of millionaires' estates. The surrounding waters are excellent for tarpon fishing. The **Island Bay National Wildlife Refuge** is here.

BONITA SPRINGS, in Lee County, is located just off US 41, about 22 miles south of Fort Myers. This village has a beautiful location inland from the Gulf of Mexico, at the edge of Big Cypress Swamp, halfway between Fort Myers and Naples.

The **Naples-Ft. Myers Kennel Club** presents greyhound races nightly except Sunday from mid-December through mid-April, just south of town on Old US 41.

An outstanding tourist attraction is here—the **Everglades Wonder Gardens,** a large collection of native wildlife in a natural tropical setting. Guided tours. Open daily, 9–5. Admission $4, children 7–15 $1.75, senior citizen discount, under 7 free. Member Florida Attractions Association.

About 15 miles east of town on Florida 846 is the **Corkscrew Swamp Sanctuary.**

Delnor-Wiggins Pass State Recreation Area, 6 miles south, on the Gulf Coast, has boat ramps, fishing, and beaches.

BRADENTON, county seat and major city of Manatee County, is located on US 41 between Tampa and Sarasota, at the mouth of the mile-wide Manatee River. Many miles of waterways—both freshwater and saltwater—make this a fishing paradise.

Spanish explorer Hernando de Soto first set foot in the New World at Shaw's Point, just west of Bradenton, on May 30, 1539. The **De Soto National Memorial** Visitor Center, near the site of the landing, presents a movie about the De Soto expedition, and there are exhibits of Spanish weaponry. Self-guided nature walks along the beach. Open daily, 8–5. Free. Closed Christmas.

The **South Florida Museum and Bishop Planetarium** is located at 201 Tenth Street West, on the shore of the Manatee River at the south end of the Business Route 41 bridge. Dioramas tell the story of Florida from the Stone Age to the Space Age. There are good collections of Indian relics, prehistoric as well as more recent, and information about the different types of mounds built in Florida by the Indians before the arrival of the Europeans. There are also Civil War rooms and a health museum. Open Tuesday through Friday, 10–5; Saturday and Sunday, 1–5. Closed New Year's Day, Christmas and Thanksgiving. Planetarium shows daily except Monday at 3 pm, Friday and Saturday also at 7:30 pm. Combination admission $3, 6–18 $2, under 6 free. Admission to museum or planetarium $2, 6–18 $1.25, under 6 free. Under 6 not allowed in planetarium.

Nearby is **Lake Manatee State Recreation Area,** a 556-acre lakeside park with nature trails, picnicking, swimming, fishing, and a boat ramp.

Each spring the landing of De Soto is reenacted at Bradenton during a week-long **De Soto Celebration.**

The Pittsburgh Pirates' spring training camp is here, and the **Florida Grapefruit League** plays exhibition games here in March and April.

CAPE CORAL, in Lee County, is a fairly new, carefully planned, and rapidly growing community located at the mouth of the Caloosahatchee River. It is Florida's second largest city in area.

The community hosts an annual **Oktoberfest.**

The Cape Coral Golf and Country Club hosts intercollegiate tennis and golf tournaments, and the Yacht and Racquet Club has a fishing pier and plentiful boat dockage.

CLEARWATER, county seat of Pinellas County, occupies the central part of the peninsula lying between Tampa Bay and the Gulf of Mexico.

The area was originally named Clear Water by the Indians, for the sparkling waters fed by active springs. It is today a clean, bright, flourishing tourist city, with many renowned restaurants, three miles of powdery white sand beach, a number of fashionable shops, all sorts of water sports, and a generally relaxed atmosphere. The tourist accommodations run the gamut from modest motel apartments with kitchenettes, catering to families, to the classic and famous old resort, the **Belleview Biltmore,** a huge wooden structure established in 1897.

The Philadelphia Phillies hold spring training here and play in **Florida Grapefruit League** exhibition games in March and April.

For ten days in mid-March the town jumps with its annual **Fun 'n Sun Festival.**

For two weeks in late September the city celebrates a **Jazz Holiday,** with Big Bands, jazz dancing, and yacht and bicycle races.

Deep-sea fishing, boating, and golfing are among the activities popular with visitors to Clearwater. Many of the state's outstanding tourist attractions are only a short distance away. The city's cultural life is enriched by the Florida Gulf Coast Art Center, the Showboat Dinner Theatre, the Royalty Theatre, and concerts by the Clearwater Symphony Orchestra. The **Performing Art Center and Theatre** is scheduled to open January, 1984.

In the adjoining village of Indian Rocks Beach, on Florida 699, is an intriguing and unusual tourist attraction called **Tiki Gardens.** Here "Trader Frank" Byars and his wife Jo, have created a Polynesian-style village out of a Florida mangrove jungle. A boardwalk leads through the tropical tangle, and at various spots along the way the stroller is surprised by a

Sea, sand, and beach activities draw thousands of visitors each year to Clearwater Beach.

towering "tiki" (Polynesian idol), a charming South Seas palm-thatched "chapel," a languid lagoon, or a preening peacock. A flock of nearly 50 of these exotic birds roams the grounds, happily nibbling on whatever beautiful and rare flowers they can find. Ten shops on the grounds give the tourist the opportunity to buy souvenirs imported from all over the world. Especially attractive and reasonable is the collection of Hawaiian-made clothing—lovely long cotton gowns and brightly flowered men's jackets. Tiki Gardens is the Hong Kong of Florida. Excellent Oriental and Polynesian dishes are served at Trader Frank's Restaurant. Gardens open daily, 9:30 am–10 pm. Admission $2, children 3–11 $1, under 3 free. Member Florida Attractions Association.

Near Clearwater, in Belleair, is the **Florida Gulf Coast Art Center,** at 222 Ponce de Leon Boulevard. The center exhibits regional and national artwork. Open September to June, Tuesday through Saturday 10–4; Sunday 2–5.

Another local highlight worth seeing is the **Kapok Tree Inn,** on Florida 593, one mile north of Florida 60. Here a gigantic Kapok tree, planted in 1888, serves as the nucleus of an elaborate network of gardens and glass-enclosed dining rooms where thousands of visitors daily come to stroll, browse in the shops, and eat the delicious and reasonably priced meals.

DUNEDIN, in Pinellas County, is a suburb just north of Clearwater. Its early settlers were Scottish, and the community has maintained this heritage. Each spring the city hosts a **Highland Games & Festival,** featuring a kilted bagpipe-playing Highlander Band; dances; and sporting events. The Toronto Blue Jays hold spring training here and play **Florida Grapefruit League** exhibition games in March and April.

Two miles offshore (but within Dunedin's city limits) lies 1,700-acre **Caladesi Island State Park.** It is a barrier island in the Gulf of Mexico, accessible only by boat. All activities are water oriented, and camping is prohibited at present. A ferry operates daily on the hour to the island; last on-the-half-hour return trip is at 4:30 pm. No vehicles are allowed on the island.

ELLENTON in Manatee County, is just north and east of Bradenton.

On US 301 is the **Gamble Plantation State Historic Site,** the oldest building on Florida's west coast, restored and furnished in the period when the estate was a huge sugar plantation. The house served as a hideout for Judah P. Benjamin, Secretary of State for the Confederacy, toward the close of the Civil War. War relics are on display. Open for tours daily, 9–5. Admission 50¢. Children under 6 free.

FORT MYERS, City of Palms, county seat and largest city in Lee County, is on US 41 and the Caloosahatchee River, in southwestern Florida, just north of the Everglades.

"There is just one Fort Myers, and 90 million people are going to find it out." This was Thomas Edison's opinion of the town he adopted as his winter home. Palm-lined boulevards, miles of white bathing beaches with gentle slopes, and refreshing surf with no undertow, complemented by a network of exotic offshore islands—Sanibel, Captiva, Estero, Pine, Gasparilla, and others—freshwater fishing in three rivers.

SOUTHWEST 53

Fort Myers does indeed have a lot going for it.

The number one tourist attraction is **Thomas A. Edison's Winter Home.** The house, his laboratory, gardens, and a museum, are open to the public, preserved as they were during the half-century when Edison lived and worked there. The power of Thomas Edison's personality and intellect is evident everywhere—in the exhibits of his hundreds of patented inventions; in the 14 acres of botanical gardens filled with exotic species from all over the world; in the swimming pool, built of concrete reinforced with bamboo rather than steel; in the house built without a kitchen because Mr. Edison didn't like to smell cooking odors; in his magnificent banyan tree, the largest tree in Florida. The casual remarks of a number of the employees of the attraction who knew Mr. Edison personally and somehow seem to feel that they are still working for him make a visit here an intimate experience. Guided tours are conducted every half-hour. Open daily, Monday–Saturday, 9–4; Sunday, 12:30–4. Closed Christmas. Admission $3, children 6–17 $1, under 6 free. Member Florida Attractions Association.

A unique gift shop on US 41 in North Fort Myers that attracts thousands of visitors is the **Shell Factory,** where innumerable souvenirs, many of them made of shells, as well as specimen shells and coral collected from everywhere, are displayed and sold. One Miami resident told me, "I always say I'll just look—I don't need any more shells; but I always find one I can't resist." Open daily, 9:30–6. Free.

At the City Yacht Basin there are complete docking facilities for 200 boats. Nearby at 2254 Edwards Drive, the **Tourist Center** of Fort Myers offers an attractive lounge and various facilities for recreation for tourists, winter residents, and new retirees.

A not-to-be-missed activity in Fort Myers is the **Everglades Jungle Cruise,** a three-hour trip up the Caloosahatchee and Orange rivers into a wilderness area where racoons, alligators, snakes, and turtles are seen regularly. Tours leave the City Yacht Basin daily, December through August, 10 am and 2 pm; October through November, 10 am only. No cruises on Christmas or in May or September. Adults $7, children $3. Refreshments aboard.

A longer jungle cruise can be taken from Orange River Dock, 7 miles east of town, aboard the riverboat the **Lazy Bones.** This is a five-day vacation, for adults (16 and over) only, operated from November through May. Includes home-cooked meals and swamp-buggy and air-boat rides. Fee is $350 per person. Write to Box 434 MG, Route 29, Fort Myers 33905, or telephone (813) 694-3401 for details or reservations for these and other trips.

Fort Myers has a full calendar of sporting events and special festivals to attract the visitor. Winter months are filled with golf, shuffleboard, and fishing tournaments. An annual **Southwest Florida Championship Rodeo** is held in January. In March and April the Kansas City Royals play **Florida Grapefruit League** exhibition games here.

Two festivals are held in February—the **Edison Pageant of Light,** with dances, flower shows, yacht regatta, and other events, and the **Shrimp Festival** at Fort Myers Beach, when beautifully decorated boats pass in review.

In Estero, fifteen miles south of Fort Myers, is the **Koreshan State Historic Site.** The park was given to the State of Florida by the last surviving member of the Koreshan Unity, a Utopian community established in 1894 by Dr. Cyrus R. Teed and 200 of his followers. The religious group established Pioneer University in the Florida wilderness, built homes, roads, trails, and footbridges, and transformed the pineland into a tropical paradise. Documents, art objects, and other relics are displayed in the Art Hall.

MARCO, Collier County, is reached by Florida 951 and 92 south of Naples. There are two bridges that lead to the island from the mainland.

This beautiful tropical island at the end of the populated strip on the southwestern coast of Florida is one of the newest areas of the state to be undergoing rapid growth. The only amazing thing about its present development and popularity is that it didn't happen long ago. Easily one of the most appealing places on the Gulf coast, with broad beaches, a climate beyond compare, soft breezes, abundant wildlife, magnificent seafood, and the lure of remoteness from noise, bustle, and pollution—it is just now being "discovered" and developed into a full-fledged resort city.

At the north end of the island is the little village of "Old" Marco; at the southeastern end is Goodland, another small settlement of modest cottages and trailer homes. Goodland has actually existed in its present location only since 1949, when the entire village was moved, house by house, from the area then called Caxambas, where the Marco Beach Hotel now stands. Even Marco Lodge, the home of a justly famous restaurant, was moved to its present spot in Goodland from the north end of the island.

The two little villages retain their charm, with friendly, family-owned businesses. In between them are the new streets, boat slips, and modern homes, with the luxurious resort, **Marriott's Marco Beach Hotel and Villas,** dominating the skyline to the southwest. A public beach leads from the hotel to a cluster of high-rise condominium apartments, and an airport services local shuttle planes to Tampa and Miami.

This is a waterland playground, and the major leisure-time activities are boating, fishing, swimming, sunbathing, and beachcombing. The Ten Thousand Islands begin here and lie along the rest of the coast to the southern tip of the state. (Incidentally, if you are staying at the hotel you will find plastic bags in your closet. They're not really meant for your wet bathing suit, although you're welcome to use them for that—they're for collecting shells!)

Marco Island was the home of Calusa Indians during the period from perhaps 500 B.C. to A.D. 1700, and a number of very important archeological finds have been made here, including pieces of ceremonial face masks, carved animals, tools, children's toys, and weapons.

The present developers and residents of Marco Island are attempting to strike a balance between economic and population growth on the one hand and environmental protection on the other. If they are successful, some valuable lessons may be learned here. An experiment is being carried out with artificial bald eagles' nests, in the hope that more of the great birds can be persuaded to make their homes here. A booklet published by the Rotary Club of Marco Island boasts: "This is going to be a community where man will live with and enjoy all the greatness of his natural surroundings without destroying it instead."

Near Marco, on the mainland, is **Collier-Seminole State**

Park and a few miles further on is Everglades City, the western gateway to **Everglades National Park**.

NAPLES, county seat and principal city of Collier County, is on US 41 and Alligator Alley (Florida 84), at the edge of the Big Cypress Swamp. It is one of the wealthiest and most attractive cities on the west coast, and its history as a resort area dates back to 1887, when the Naples Town Improvement Company was founded and the first lots were sold. An early brochure described the community as one "where roses bloom in December, where sickness is the exception and health the rule and where surf bathing is enjoyed in January."

The only approach to the isolated village was by boat until a rough road was built to Fort Myers. Finally, in 1928, the Tamiami Trail connected Naples to other communities.

Most of Naples is quite new—only 10 to 20 years old, in fact. The town had only about 1,500 residents in 1950, and in 1960 Hurricane Donna swept away quite a bit of what was already there. Today there are many high-rise condominiums and residential clubs at the north end of town and new homes to be seen in all directions.

The most distinguishing feature of this lovely city is the palm-shaded public beach that stretches for seven miles along the west side of town. Nearly 30 avenues lead from First Street to the beach, and anyone can drive his car up, park it at the side of the street, and stroll along the beach to his heart's content. At the end of 12th Avenue South is the **Naples Pier**, a 1,000-foot fishing pier that has been a favorite landmark since 1887 (through the present structure was built after Hurricane Donna). Open daily, free.

Third Street is a most distinguished shopping area, lined with glamorous shops of all sorts. It is in the Olde Naples area, a showcase of historic homes. The most luxurious residential area is at the south end of town at Port Royal.

The **City Recreation Center** in downtown Cambier Park has facilities for tennis, shuffleboard, basketball, softball, and indoor activities.

Jungle Larry's African Safari and Caribbean Gardens is a 200-acre botanical-zoological park located at Fleischmann Boulevard and Goodlette Road. The gardens were started in 1917 by Dr. Henry Nehrling, a German horticulturist. Between 1929 and 1951 they were left unattended, then were purchased and improved by Julius Fleishmann, who added orchids, rare flowering trees, and colorful water birds. The zoological collection was added by Larry Tetzlaff during the past few years, and which includes rare specimens of tiglons (half-tiger, half-lion), and lepjags (half-leopard, half-jaguar). Circus Africa shows at 11:30, 2 and 4. Open daily, 9:30–4:30, park closes at 5:30. Admission varies. Member Florida Attractions Association.

Annual events in Naples include golf tournaments, as well as **Swamp Buggy Races** in February and October.

PUNTA GORDA, county seat of Charlotte County, is on US 41 and 17 at the mouth of the Peace River. North across a mile-long bridge is its sister city, **PORT CHARLOTTE,** largest community in the county.

This has been a popular resort area for many years. At one time vacationers came from New York City by railroad to enjoy the fine fishing on the Peace River and in Charlotte Harbor. Early settlers got their mail and supplies by boat from the Cedar Keys, and shipped out oranges, furs, and alligator hides in return.

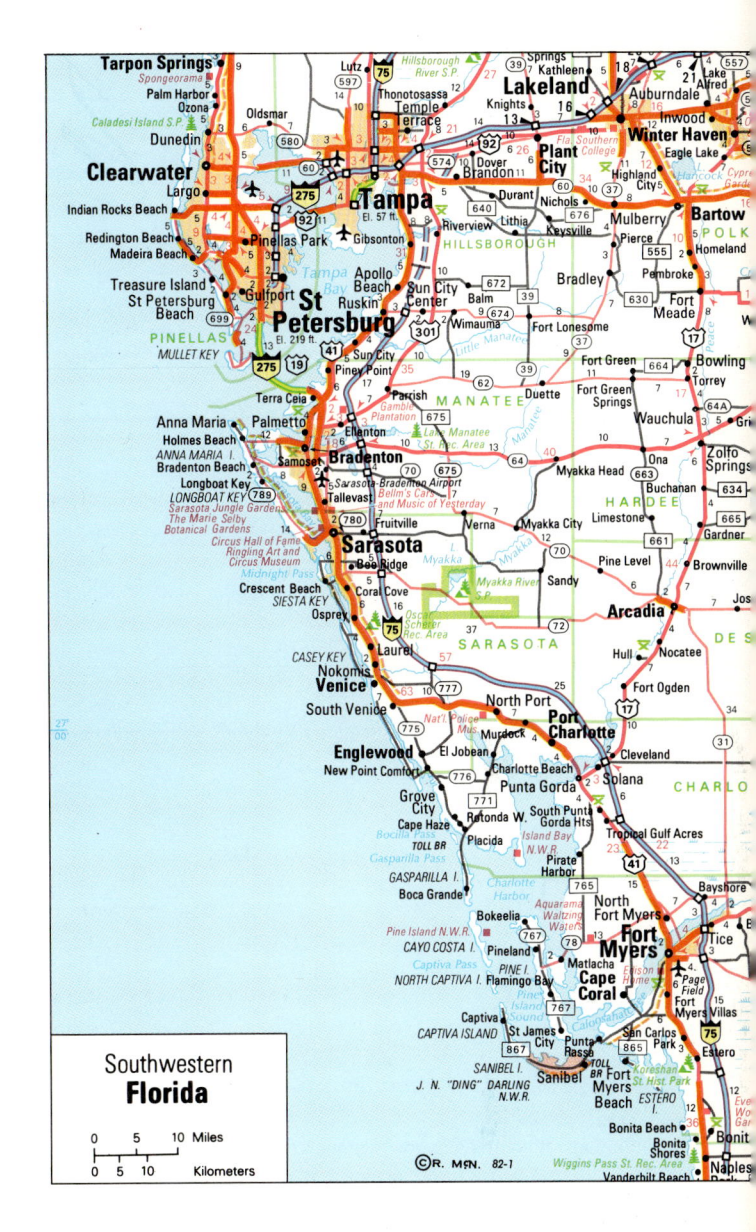

Today it is still an ideal location for the sportsman interested in hunting, fishing, shelling, boating, or any other water-related activities.

Eight miles southeast of town is the 65,300-acre **Cecil M. Webb Wildlife Management Area,** where fishing and frogging are carried on all year. For information about hunting seasons and regulations, write Florida Game and Fresh Water Fish Commission, South Florida Region, 2202 Lakeland Hills Boulevard, Lakeland 33801.

Ponce de Leon discovered Charlotte Harbor in 1513. In 1521 de Leon returned with two shiploads of colonists. The colony lasted five months. Its ill-fated history is memorialized at the **Ponce de Leon Park** at 1625 West Marion Avenue. Open daily until sundown. Free.

For further information about the area, write to the Charlotte County Chamber of Commerce, 2702 Tamiami Trail, Punta Gorda, or phone (813) 627-2222.

The **American Police Hall of Fame and Museum** is at 14600

SOUTHWEST 55

Coming in by boat for a picnic on Marco Island.

South Tamiami Trail, in North Port, 11 miles northwest of Port Charlotte on US 41. Open daily, 9:30–4:30. Admission $1.50, children 3–16 50¢, under 3 free. Police officers and family free.

SAFETY HARBOR is in northeastern Pinellas County, just north of Clearwater.

Though Pinellas County claims to be the fastest-growing county in the state, and most of it is completely built up, Safety Harbor is still a small, sleepy, rural town, with a quiet main street, frame houses, and shaded yards. The area and the group of mineral springs around which the town has grown up were well known to the Indians, the early Spanish explorers, and to pirates. It was settled by Dr. Odet Philippe, a surgeon in Napoleon's navy, in 1823.

He was buried in **Philippe Park,** one mile north of the village center, near a large temple mound built in prehistorical times by Timucua Indians.

The **Safety Harbor Spa** has been built over the Espiritu Sanctu Springs. This is a health spa patterned after the type of health resort popular for many generations in Europe, with mineral baths and mineral waters to drink. Each guest has a physical examination and a special diet and health regimen are prescribed for his or her needs.

ST. PETERSBURG, largest city in Pinellas County, is on US 19 at the southern end of the peninsula between Tampa Bay and the Gulf of Mexico. The St. Petersburg Beach area, a burgeoning residential and motel community across Boca Ciega Bay, is connected to the mainland by bridges and causeways.

Surrounded by sparkling water, St. Petersburg, fourth largest city in the state, has for many years been one of the most popular retirement and resort cities in the nation.

There are hundreds of outstanding accommodations for the tourist or winter resident, fine restaurants, all kinds of vacation activities, and many fine tourist attractions. In addition to what is available within St. Petersburg, all of the facilities of central and southwestern Florida are within a few hours' drive. It is easy to see why this part of the state has enjoyed such popularity as a vacation headquarters.

At the waterfront a spectacular modern building in the shape of an inverted pyramid dominates the skyline and provides a center for entertainment and sightseeing both on water and on land. **Pier Place** has shops, several restaurants, nightly dancing, and an observation tower, and is within walking distance of **Bayfront Center** and many of the most popular attractions in St. Petersburg. **The Pier,** at 800 Second Avenue N.E., also boasts entertainment, restaurants, boutiques, an observation deck and a community center.

Gray Line offers elegant sightseeing cruises in the area. Choose either luncheon, dinner, or dancing. Call (813) 866-3002 for information and reservations.

For sheer beauty, **Florida's Sunken Gardens,** at 1825 Fourth Street North, are unsurpassed. The gardens were started about 70 years ago, when George Turner purchased property for a new home that included a huge sink hole with a shallow lake at its bottom. He proceeded to drain the lake and use the rich mucky bottomland for gardening. Local residents made the area such a popular spot for strolling that Mr. Turner added exotic plants, fenced in the gardens, and initiated a 15¢ admission charge. This is how one of Florida's oldest attractions was established.

The lover of birds and flowers can happily spend many hours wandering through the gardens. There are two walk-through aviaries filled with spectacular birds. Take plenty of color film if you are a photographer, but if you're content with professional pictures you can buy a beautiful full-color pictorial guide in the gift shop.

Plantings are changed and renewed all year, so that the gardens are always in full dress—some 50,000 annuals are planted each year. But an especially memorable time to visit is in early spring, when camellias, gardenias, azaleas, and rhododendrons are all bursting with color. An additional feature at the Sunken Gardens is the "King of Kings"—a collection of wax sculptures telling the story of Christ. Open daily, 9 am–5:30. Admission $4.50, children 6–12 $2.50, under 6 free. Member Florida Attractions Association.

Moored at 345 Second Avenue N.E., in Vinoy Basin adjacent to Municipal Pier, is **MGM's** *Bounty,* the wooden ship built for the movie "Mutiny on the Bounty." Fully and authentically outfitted, it is a fascinating marine museum. As wooden ships are becoming more and more scarce, this is a rare opportunity to see at first hand what life was really like aboard these romantic vessels. The gift shop on shore features rare, original wood carvings created by residents of Pitcairn Island, descendants of the mutineers, and samples of the fast-disappearing art of scrimshaw. Also on shore is a replica of the long boat in which Captain Bligh made the incredible 3,600-mile journey after the mutiny. Open daily, 9 am–10 pm. Admission $4, children 4–12 $2.25, under 4 free. Member Florida Attractions Association.

Next door, at 335 Second Avenue N.E., is the **St. Petersburg Historical Museum,** with a large collection of early St. Petersburg documents and articles, Indian artifacts, and Civil War items. Most of the Indian materials are from the early 1500s, reflecting the important Weeden Island and Safety Harbor cultures. Open Monday–Saturday, 11–5; Sunday, 1–5. Closed January 1, Thanksgiving, Christmas Eve and Christmas. Admission 75¢, children 6–15 25¢, under 6 free.

Three other houses with interesting collections and furnishings are administered by the St. Petersburg Historical Society: **Grace S. Turner House** at 3501 Second Avenue South, **Haas Museum** at 3511 Second Avenue South, and **Lowe House,** 3527 Second Avenue South. All three are open Tuesday–Sunday 1–5. Closed the month of September and major holidays. Combination ticket $1, 12 and under 25¢.

The **London Wax Museum,** at 5505 Gulf Boulevard in St. Petersburg Beach, is a collection of wax sculptures of persons important in American history. Open Monday–Saturday, 9–9; Sunday, noon–9. Admission $3, children under 13 $1.50, 4 and under free.

An interesting area on five islands, reached by Pinellas Bayway (toll 65¢), is **Fort De Soto Park.** Camping, picnicking, and recreational facilities are on the grounds of a historic fort. Residents will tell you (unless they want to keep the secret) that this is one of the most beautiful and best maintained public parks to be found anywhere.

In St. Petersburg Beach, at the end of the Bayway (54th Avenue South) stands an elegant and striking *"pink palace,"* the Don CeSar Hotel. Restored as a resort, this fine old building has been placed on the National Register of Historic Landmarks.

The **Museum of Fine Arts,** 225 Beach Drive North, is open Tuesday–Saturday, 10–5; third Thursday of each month, 10–9; Sunday, 1–5. Closed Christmas and New Year's Day.

MGM's Bounty, anchored at St. Petersburg.

Donation. Free guided tours, daily except Monday at 2.

At St. Petersburg Junior College, 6605 Fifth Avenue North, **Planetarium** programs are presented on Friday evenings during September–April; free. Also ranking as a sightseeing attraction is the **Sunshine Skyway Bridge** at the end of 34th Street South. Toll $1 per car. Fifteen miles of bridges and causeways connect St. Petersburg with the Bradenton-Palmetto area.

An unusual facility in St. Petersburg is the **Science Center of Pinellas County, Inc.,** at 7701 Twenty-Second Avenue North. The center provides scientific training to students from kindergarten age through adults, in working laboratories. Visitors are welcome to visit year-round from 9–4, Monday through Friday. Closed holidays. Free.

Bayfront Center, at 400 First Street South, is one of the finest entertainment complexes in the nation, with its five-million-dollar auditorium and arena. Many exciting performances—Broadway plays, musicals, ice shows, circuses, and concerts—are offered here.

Other municipal facilities include the expanded 700-acre **Lake Maggiore Park,** at 1101 Country Club Way South; **Municipal Marina** at 300 Second Avenue S.E. for day and night fishing; **Boyd Hill Nature Trail,** 1101 Country Club Way South (admission 75¢, under 18 35¢); and the spectacular **North Shore Olympic Pool** at 901 North Shore Drive N.E.

St. Pete's location makes it a natural spot for the water sports enthusiast, and as an added incentive for fishermen the **Suncoast Tarpon Roundup** awards an impressive gift to the fisherman landing the largest tarpon during the May–August season. There are 19 courses in Pinellas county for golfers to enjoy.

Almost every type of spectator sport is available in St. Petersburg: The New York Mets and the St. Louis Cardinals have spring training here and play **Florida Grapefruit League** exhibition games in March and April. Stock car racing is held on Saturday nights, March–November, at the **Sunshine Speedway.** Greyhound races take place Monday, Wednesday and Saturday afternoons; and nightly except Sunday and Good Friday, January through early May, at **Derby Lane.** There are numerous sailboat and outboard races during January, February, March, April, and May, and an annual **Southland Sweepstakes Regatta** in February.

A huge festival, billed as "the South's largest," takes place each spring during the last week in March and the first week in April. There are literally hundreds of sporting, social, musical, and special events. This **Festival of States** is climaxed by the Parade of States, with bands from all over the country competing for the Florida Governor's Cup.

SANIBEL, in Lee County, is an island in the Gulf of Mexico, west of Fort Myers, accessible from the mainland by County Route 867 (round trip toll $3) and connected by bridge to its small sister island, Captiva.

As you drive off the causeway onto Sanibel a charming building housing the Sanibel-Captiva Islands Chamber of Commerce catches your eye. If you go inside you will find seven huge wall panels on which all the motels on the islands list their vacancies. But you will be well advised to make reservations far in advance if you want to stay on the islands. This is a most popular vacation area, and it's easy to see why.

SOUTHWEST 57

The conservation-minded residents of this unique two-island community have been unusually foresighted, or lucky, or both. They recognized early that in order to preserve the distinctive natural qualities of these islands, stringent restrictions must be placed on land development. An active, hardworking group called the Sanibel-Captiva Conservation Foundation is "dedicated to the belief that people, if they have the will to preserve it, can enjoy rather than destroy the world around them." It operates a **Conservation Center** on a 207-acre tract, with nature trails around the Sanibel River, naturalist's presentations, tours, and a gift shop. The center, open daily except Sunday and holidays, 9–5, $1, under 12, 50¢; is at 3333 Sanibel-Captiva Road.

About half of the 15,000 acres on the island are now publicly owned by the federal government, the State of Florida, and Lee County; and the Conservation Foundation is working to add more land to these holdings. Sanibel has been declared "scenic and unique" by the State, and very strict regulations have been enacted to protect its beauty.

What is it that makes Sanibel unique? First of all, its particular location, together with the direction of the winds and the tides, have made it the best area for shell collecting in the Western Hemisphere. According to the shelling experts, only Japan, Australia, and the Philippines have beaches that can compare with these. Secondly, more than two hundred different species of birds have been identified here, as well as alligators, many varieties of both freshwater and saltwater fish, and other types of wildlife. The entire island plus much of the surrounding area has been closed to hunting since 1949. Thirdly, the restraint of the residents has kept the buildings from encroaching upon the secluded beaches.

Much of the western side of the island is set aside as the **J. N. "Ding" Darling National Wildlife Refuge,** where a one-way road leads through the bayous, separating the fresh water from the salt. Signs advise the traveler that a Florida fishing license is required for fishing on the left (freshwater) side of the road. Much of the interior of the island is mangrove wetland, dotted by tropical hammocks. Marked canoe trails lead through the swamp.

Most of the motels on Sanibel and Captiva are small and not part of chains; many of the units have kitchenettes. The pace here is relaxed, the atmosphere is intimate, the lifestyle consists of enjoying the environment deeply and fully. Nowhere in the state are people more interested in preserving their natural heritage.

For about 40 years the first weekend in March has been set aside for the **Sanibel Shell Fair,** an event that now attracts more than 11,000 visitors, including most of the serious conchologists in the eastern United States. Free. The **Fall Festival of the Islands** held in October features a fish rodeo, sailing regatta, and other events.

SARASOTA, county seat and largest city in Sarasota County, is on US 41 and the Gulf of Mexico about 30 miles south of St. Petersburg and Tampa.

The first impression one has of Sarasota is of bright white buildings, brilliantly colored foliage, sparkling water, clean streets. The whole city gleams. The second impression is one of sophistication and a great deal of cultural emphasis—art, theater, music. More than a dozen recognized art schools give instructions in all media here, and many galleries offer art objects for sale in all price ranges. The Sarasota Art Association is one of the oldest and largest such groups in the state. **The Players,** Sarasota's Community Theater, at the Civic Theater on Ninth Street, has been performing dramas, comedies, and musicals each year for almost 50 years; and the repertory company of the Asolo Theater has a season that runs from mid-December–mid-July (7–9 plays). The **Sarasota Opera Company** performs from mid-January to mid-February at the Sarasota Theatre of the Arts at 61 N. Pineapple Avenue. Concerts are given regularly by the **Community Concert Association,** the **Florida West Coast Symphony,** a concert band, and other groups. The **Golden Apple Dinner Theatre** presents Broadway entertainment and Saturday matinees for children.

A startling ultramodern building on the bayfront at 777 N. Tamiami Trail, is the **Van Wezel Performing Arts Hall,** designed by architects associated with the Frank Lloyd Wright Foundation. It is shaped like a gigantic seashell, colored purple on the outside and lavender on the inside, seats as many as 1,800 people, and is said to be almost perfect acoustically.

The first citizen of Sarasota in past years was circus king John Ringling, who built a great Venetian-style mansion on the bay and named it **Ca'd'Zan** ("house of John" in Venetian dialect). The **Residence** was willed to the State of Florida and is now open to the public as a part of the complex on Mr. Ringling's estate known as the **Ringling Museums.** The other components are the **John and Mable Ringling Museum of Art,** the **Museum of the Circus,** and the **Asolo Theater.**

Ca'd'Zan is a treasure house of marble floors, custom-built furniture, rare windows and chandeliers, gold and silver fittings. The Museum of Art, Florida's official art museum, is an Italian Renaissance building surrounding a sculpture-dotted garden courtyard, and it contains a large and important collection of baroque art, paintings by Rubens, and paintings and drawings by other great masters. The Museum of the Circus is an imposing exhibit of wild animal wagons, bandwagons, circus posters and handbills, and historic objects that tell the story of the circus from ancient Rome to the Greatest Show on Earth. The Asolo Theater was an 18th-century theater built near Venice, the home stage of Eleanor Duse. It was purchased and moved here in 1950 to an air conditioned building, and it is now used by the State Theatre of Florida.

Plan to spend most of the day touring the Ringling Museums and enjoying the extensive, landscaped grounds. Don't miss the "Dwarf Garden" of small-scale sculpture between the museum and the theater, Mrs. Ringling's rose garden, and the spectacular banyan trees. Open Monday–Friday, 9 am–7 pm; Saturday, 9–5; Sunday, 11–6. Combination ticket $4.50; 6–12, $1.75; children under 6 free.

Both north and south of the Ringling Museums is the University of South Florida Sarasota Campus, with **New College,** its undergraduate liberal arts division, established north of the estate of John Ringling's brother Charles. Outstanding artists are invited here for a summer music festival.

Opposite the Ringling Museums, at 5500 North Tamiami Trail, is **Bellm's Cars and Music of Yesterday.** As the name implies, the collection consists of autos, cycles, race cars, band and dance organs, nickelodeons, hurdy gurdies, calliopes, and phonographs. Open Monday–Saturday, 8:30–6; Sunday, 9:30–6. Admission $4.50, children 6–16 $2, under 6 free. Member Florida Attractions Association.

The **Sarasota Jungle Gardens,** at 3701 Bayshore Road, off Myrtle Street, is a 15-acre park filled with more than five thousand varieties of rare tropical plantings from all over the world—tall palms, delicate orchids, flame vines, birds of paradise. Alligators, macaws, myna birds, and a huge flock of hot pink flamingos roam the formal gardens and jungle paths. Open daily, 9–5. Admission $4.50, children 6–16 $2.50, under 6 free. Member Florida Attractions Association.

The **Marie Selby Botanical Gardens** are located at the intersection of South Palm Avenue and US 41. Open daily, 10–5. Closed Christmas. Admission $3.50, children under 16 free with adult.

About 14 miles east of Sarasota, on Florida 72, is a 28,875-acre wildlife refuge called **Myakka River State Park.** Much of the area was donated to the State of Florida by Chicago socialite Mrs. Potter Palmer. There are various ways to tour the park—a scenic 7-mile paved drive through the forests and marshlands can be traversed by car or bicycle; a 1-hour sundown train ride takes visitors to a bird observation tower; guided boat tours are made daily at 1 and 4 pm. Tram and boat tours, $5; under 12, $2. This is a truly natural refuge; very little has been altered or added.

About 10 miles south of Sarasota, neary Osprey, is the **Oscar Scherer State Recreation Area,** on US 41. The park was built and is operated by a concessionaire, Restaurant Associates Industry. Great care was taken to conserve the natural environment of the park.

St. Armands Key, a nearly round island between Sarasota and Lido Beach, is a striking shopping and dining area, with more than a hundred fine shops and boutiques arranged around a small circular park.

Sarasota has many facilities for golf, tennis, and water sports, and a number of tournaments are held here in these sports. The Chicago White Sox do their spring training and play in **Florida Grapefruit League** exhibition games here.

Greyhound races are run nightly except Sunday from May to Labor Day at the **Sarasota Kennel Club.**

An annual event peculiar to Sarasota is the **Sailor Circus** in April, when more than two hundred Sarasota school children participate in a regular circus of aerial acrobatics—skills learned as a part of the public school physical education program. The **Medieval Fair** is also held in mid-March at the Ringling Museums.

The **King Neptune Frolics** is a festival that has been celebrated each spring in Sarasota for more than 50 years. It consists of water sports, sailing shows, boat parades, a fish fry, fireworks display, and a Grand Night Parade.

TAMPA, county seat and principal city in Hillsborough County, third largest city in the state, is located on I-75, I-4, and US

Ca'd'Zan, the Ringling residence, from Sarasota Bay.

SOUTHWEST 59

41, on the east shore of Tampa Bay.

More than any of the other major cities in Florida, Tampa retains the Latin color and flavor that attest to its Spanish origin. Its earliest explorers were Panfilo de Narvaez in 1528 and Hernando de Soto in 1539. Other Spaniards ventured in from time to time, but they were wiped out by the Indian natives who had no interest in being conquered or converted.

The settlement of the Tampa area by Americans began with the establishment of Fort Brooke in 1824. The first railroad and the first bank came to the city in 1882–83, and industry began to flourish. Tampa is today the leading industrial city in the state. Phosphate mining, commerical fishing, tourism, and cigar-making have all contributed to its growth.

The year 1886 saw the beginning of cigar-making in Tampa, when Vincente Martinez Ybor moved his factory here from Key West. Along with the cigar industry grew the settlement of **Ybor City** (now within the city limits of Tampa), a "little Havana" where Cuban immigrants established homes and businesses. Here, in 1898, Cuban freedom fighters and Teddy Roosevelt's Rough Riders made plans and sought support for the struggle for Cuban independence.

Today Ybor City is a Cuban, Spanish, and Italian enclave—with wrought-iron balconies, multicolumned buildings, plazas, arcades, and sidewalk coffee shops. Small cigar factories, where skilled craftsmen still make cigars by hand, line Seventh Avenue. A world-famous establishment, **The Columbia,** under the same management for more than 70 years and one of the largest restaurants in the country, has been attracting gourmets to Ybor City for many years.

The old V. M. Ybor Cigar Factory, once the world's largest, has been transformed into a major new tourist attraction called **Ybor Square.** Shops, a Nostalgia Market, ice cream parlor, Garden Patio, a restaurant, and a theater have been created in an architecturally fascinating building that is steeped in the Latin ethnic history of the neighborhood. Open Monday–Saturday 10–9, Sunday noon–6. Free.

Ybor City State Museum, 1818 9th Avenue, located in a former bakery, tells the story of the cigar. There are rotating exhibits in the visitors center; open daily 9–noon and 1–5; 25¢, under 6 free.

In 1891 railroad tycoon Henry B. Plant opened an elaborate, palatial, Moorish-style resort hotel, patterned after Spain's Alhambra. Today the former Tampa Bay Hotel houses the **University of Tampa.**

Transportation has played an important part in Tampa's development. Shortly after the railroad line reached the city a deep channel was cut in the Tampa Bay harbor, and in 1914 the first commercial airline was established here, scheduling a 23-minute flight between St. Petersburg and Tampa. Thus it is perhaps fitting that a new, ultramodern **Tampa International Airport** should set an example for others. Here the time spent getting from car to plane is cut to a minimum by careful traffic engineering that directs the driver to a parking area close to an elevator, which whisks him directly to the ticket counter of his chosen airline. Then, only a few steps away, a "horizontal elevator" shuttles him off to a planeside waiting room. The latest word in convenience, plus the creative merging of engineering, architectural, and decorating talent, make the airport a tourist attraction as well as an efficient terminal.

The largest and best-known attraction in Tampa is **The Dark Continent/Busch Gardens,** on Busch Boulevard between 30th and 40th streets, where Anheuser-Busch, Inc., has created a 300-acre wild animal kingdom, a transplanted African veldt. There are three ways to view the veldt: by monorail, steam train, or sky ride. Animals include lions, gazelles, antelopes, wildebeests, hartebeests, waterbucks, giraffes, zebras, elephants, and dozens of other African species. Other features include an orangutan show, thrill rides, boat rides, and Claw Island—home of Busch's Bengal tiger family. The Moroccan Village features shops for every taste and purse.

On the grounds of the Anheuser-Busch brewery is a lavish 15-acre tropical garden in which there are more than 150,000 plants, trees, and shrubs. In the midst of the garden is a glass-enclosed, seven-sided Hospitality House, where complimentary beer is served—to adults only—and attendants do check carefully! Other points of interest include a tour of the plant, a trained bird show, patio and gift shop, an exotic birdhouse topped by a geodesic dome, a storybook lane, a small animal zoo, lagoons and arbors, and the Old Swiss House restaurant and rathskeller.

Busch Gardens' recently opened Timbuktu is a 7-acre recreation of the African town that includes dolphin shows, thrill rides, and a restaurant. Timbuktu's architecture and its desertlike atmosphere reflect the town's appearance during the 16th century. The newest addition, located near Busch Gardens, is a 13-acre **Adventure Island** "the ultimate in water parks." Palm trees, lush tropical lagoons, a 300-foot body flume, several smaller flumes, wave pools, swimming pools, and extensive picnic areas are all part of the attraction—open March through October; $8.25; children under 3 free; children 9 and under must have adult supervision. You will regret it if you try to "do" Busch Gardens in less than a day. Take your time and relax. It's well worth it. Open daily, 9:30–6; extended hours during summer and selected holiday seasons. Admission (includes shows, rides, attractions): $12.50, children under 3 free. Parking, $1. Member Florida Attractions Association.

There are a number of fine museums in Tampa. The **Henry B. Plant Museum,** in the main building of the University of Tampa, is open Tuesday–Saturday, 10–4. Closed holidays. The newest cultural center is the **Tampa Museum,** located on Hillsborough River behind the Curtis Hixon Convention Center, open Tuesday, Thursday and Friday 10–6; Wednesday 10–5; Saturday 9–5; Sunday 1–5; closed holidays; free. The recently-opened **Museum of Science and Industry,** at 4801 E. Fowler Avenue, features participatory exhibits themed around the sun, energy, and scientific and industrial subjects. Open daily 10–4:30; closed Thanksgiving, Christmas, and January 1. May be fee.

Art exhibits can be found at the **University of South Florida,** 4202 Fowler Avenue. Free planetarium shows are held at the university in the Physics building, but reservations must be made in advance.

The 1400-seat **Tampa Theatre,** on the National Register of Historic Places, is operated by the City of Tampa and has programs in the performing arts, live theater, and films.

Spectator sports here include baseball—the Cincinnati Reds play **Florida Grapefruit League** exhibition games in March and April; horse racing at the **Tampa Bay Downs** track, December through April; jai-alai at the **Tampa Fronton,** January through June; greyhound racing at the **Tampa Track,** September to early January; auto racing at the **East Bay Racetrack,** early March through late November; professional football in the summer and fall, and professional soccer March through August at the **Tampa Stadium.** There are golf tournaments, fishing tournaments, horse shows, and University of South Florida basketball games on campus.

Each February the city enjoys a gay and colorful 70-year-old tradition known as the **Gasparilla Pirate Invasion,** when a fully rigged pirate ship sails into the bay and "captures" the city. Also in February the **Florida State Fair** is held at the landscaped fairgrounds.

Climaxing a series of horse shows is the **American Invitational Horse Show** in March. The **Sarasota Jazz Festival** is held here in early May.

Equally interesting, and indigenous to Tampa are **Fiesta Day** in February and the **Latin American Fiesta** that has been held each March for almost a half-century.

The **Tampa Tarpoon Tournament** is held from June through September.

TARPON SPRINGS, in Pinellas County, is located on US 19 and the Gulf of Mexico, about 10 miles north of Clearwater.

This 100-year-old village is populated largely by people of Greek descent, and the economy is based on fishing, tourism, and light industry. Tarpon Springs is one of the world's largest sponge markets. The center of this industry had been in Key West until the early 1900s, when the Greek sponge fisherman discovered more favorable conditions here and migrated, along with some five hundred persons from Greece.

The **Spongeorama Exhibit Center** is at Sponge Docks. Here visitors can see a working sponge factory, a Display Museum, and specialty shops. Free admission to the complex; $1, 4–11 50¢, under 4 free for the 30 minute sponge diving trip at the Cinematic Theater. Open daily, 10–5:30, last show starts at 5.

All along the waterfront are sponge boats, decorated with Greek designs. The street is filled with curio shops and restaurants. Nearby is the **Sponge Exchange.**

St. Nicholas Greek Orthodox Cathedral, at 36 North Pinellas Avenue, is a beautiful example of neo-Byzantine architecture. The cathedral has icons, stained glass, and sculptured marble. Open daily, 9–5. Free.

In the **Universalist Church,** at Grand Boulevard and Read Street, are 11 paintings by George Inness, Jr., the celebrated American landscape painter. Guided tours are conducted every half-hour, October through May, Tuesday–Sunday, 2–5 P.M. Donations.

Two miles south of town on US 19A is **Noell's Ark Chimpanzee Farm.** Open daily, 10 am–dusk; $3, children, $2.

The **A. L. Anderson Park** on US 19 has a picnic area and playground.

Each January 6, which is **Epiphany,** or Greek Cross Day, the Greek community celebrates with an early service at St. Nicholas Greek Orthodox Cathedral, followed by a ceremony called Diving for the Cross. Following this a feast is held at Craig Park. Another important annual religious observance is **Greek Easter Week.**

In mid-April an **Arts and Crafts Show** is held and in mid-May a **Seafood Festival** is held at the Sponge Docks.

TERRA CEIA, in Manatee County, is on US 19, just south of the Sunshine Skyway Bridge and north of the intersection with US 41.

The **Madira Bickel Mount State Archeological Site** here is an important dig. Apparently Indians occupied the area from about A.D. 1 to 1600. Excavations have uncovered shell mounds, burial mounds, and temple mounds. Artifacts including pottery, shell beads, and shellcups have been found. Open daily, 8–sundown. Free.

VENICE, in Sarasota County, is on US 41, about 20 miles south of Sarasota.

Venice is an open, pleasant, gulfside community, known widely as the winter home of the Ringling Bros.-Barnum & Bailey Combined Shows, Inc. A **Clown College** offers a seven-week course.

Venice was one of Florida's earliest planned cities. The Seaboard Railroad completed its tracks into the little village in 1911, and the railroad men who came there were much impressed with the area. In the early twenties the Brotherhood of Railroad Engineers selected Venice as the site for a retirement haven for its members. The city was beautifully planned, with wide streets and numerous parks. The dream of the Brotherhood ended in bankruptcy, but the natural beauty and the wise early planning have resulted in a city that has continued to grow and attract both residents and tourists. There are many fine facilities for golf, tennis, shuffleboard, and all kinds of water sports.

Each October the whole community frolics at the **Venetian Sun Festival.**

Southeast of Venice on US 41 is **Warm Mineral Springs and Cyclorama,** a health spa with white sand beaches, bathhouse, picnic sites.

(Details on admission prices and hours have been included as a service to the reader and as a guide in planning activities. However, changes are inevitable in some cases, and the publisher cannot be responsible for any variations from the listed information.)

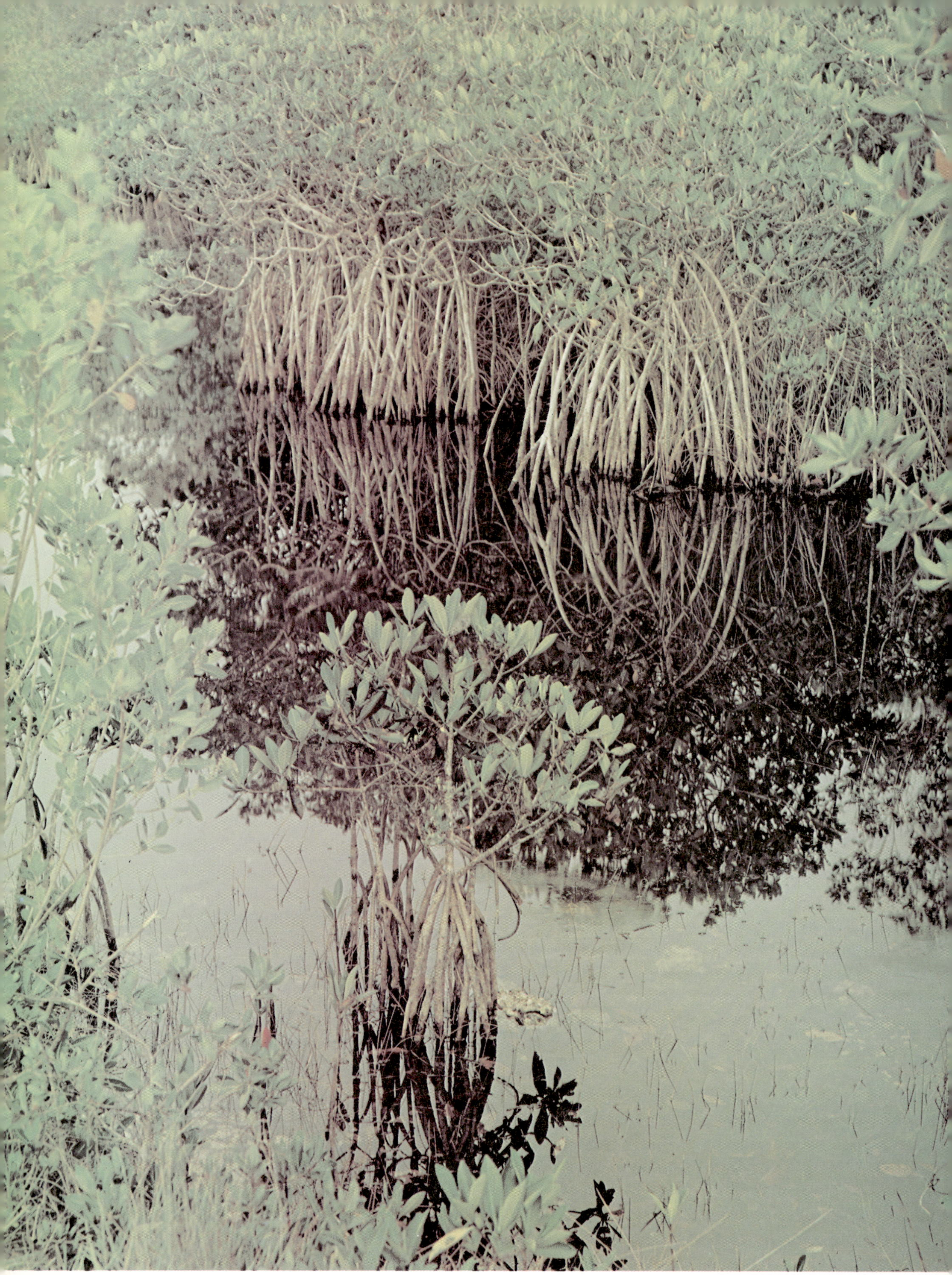

SOUTH CENTRAL — GLADES & KEYS

THE FLORIDA KEYS: PLAYGROUND FOR SPEAR FISHERMEN AND SCUBA DIVERS. THE EVERGLADES AND BIG CYPRESS SWAMP: VAST AND MYSTERIOUS PRESERVES WHERE PLANTS AND ANIMALS CONSPIRE TO KEEP HUMANS FROM TAKING OVER. THE RICH AGRICULTURAL MUCKLANDS LYING TO THE WEST AND SOUTH OF LAKE OKEECHOBEE: AMERICA'S WINTER VEGETABLE GARDEN. THESE THREE DISTINCT BUT CLOSELY RELATED TYPES OF LAND FORMS MAKE UP SOUTH CENTRAL FLORIDA.

Anyone who likes bright sunshine, gorgeous sparkling waters, and a carefree, casual atmosphere will immediately fall in love with the Keys. Anyone who eats vegetables will quickly recognize the obvious importance of the farmlands of South Central Florida to all of us. But the Everglades must be approached with patience and understanding to be appreciated. Many tourists, especially some who have seen and loved other national parks, are disappointed when they first visit this one, the third largest in the National Park System. Where are the sweeping vistas, the towering trees, the deep waters? Most of all, where are the tropical forests of ancient cypresses and regal palm trees? For some reason, it seems that the majority of people visiting the Everglades for the first time have a complete misconception about what they will see. The groves of large, lovely, moss-hung live oaks and cypresses and banyans grow in other parts of the South—not here.

Here the interest is in the tiny aspects of nature, not the grandiose. You must stand very still and wait, and look and listen sharply. Whoosh! You thought that was just a stick poking up out of the pond way over there, but it was a little heron, and he just swooped down on an unwary fish. What's that moving in the grass? A tiny alligator! Be careful—its mother is probably close by.

EVERGLADES

As you enter the park at its eastern edge and travel along the 38-mile road to Flamingo, you will at first be looking out across grassy meadows, broken now and then by little islands of hardwood trees—primarily mahogany. At several points along the highway and at Flamingo you can walk out on trails and boardwalks and be surrounded immediately by the world of the Everglades. The important rule is to set your pace to "slow." Take a walk along a boardwalk. See the lizards? That owl's nest up there? The huge ferns? The vines and mosses and air plants that all make their home in that tree? You will soon be recognizing new species, such as the strangler fig and the gumbo-limbo tree (that's the one they call the tourist tree, because it's always red and peeling!)

As the fresh water becomes brackish, then salt, everything gradually changes. No more saw grass. Mangrove trees replace the palms and mahoganies.

In Everglades National Park one can get almost an entire university education in natural history and ecology in a few weeks' time. But if your taste does not run to this sort of thing, and if you really prefer not studying on your vacation time, don't despair. There is plenty of excitement to be found in this unusual park, where even a quiet, peaceful ride over the waters will bring you within chatting distance of an alligator.

THE FARMLANDS

Homestead, the gateway city to both the Keys and the Everglades, is the leading agricultural center of South Florida. Its annual county fair and a rodeo are important social events. Vegetable and fruit stands are plentiful on all the roads leading into town, and even the principal tourist attractions are agricultural—the Fruit and Spice Park and the half-century-old Orchid Jungle.

Farther north, around Lake Okeechobee, are such towns as Clewiston, sugar cane center, and Belle Glade, where at least 30 different kinds of vegetables are grown and shipped. The Everglades Experiment Station here is constantly studying how to make the most productive use of this rich muckland.

On the western edge of the Big Cypress Swamp is Immokalee, which has the state's second largest Farmers' Market. It now holds second place in the state in the volume of vegetable crops produced for northern markets and is working hard to become Number One. There are 25 vegetable packing and processing plants in the town. The population almost doubles here during the fall and spring harvest season, when thousands of migrant workers are employed. Cattle ranching is also important, and there are at least 40 cattle ranches in the immediate vicinity. Oil wells nearby also contribute to the economy.

Sixteen miles west of this village is one of the most unusual spots in all of Florida, the Corkscrew Swamp Sanctuary. Here the National Audubon Society has acquired and is protecting the largest remaining stand of virgin bald cypress—the oldest trees in eastern North America. Big Cypress is also a national preserve, the only one in the Southeast.

The South Central section of the state is as large in acreage as some of the other sections, but has only a few hundred thousand total population. The populated villages are increasing in size, however, and the area has greatly increased its numbers in the past few decades. There are no large metropolitan centers in this section; most residents live in small towns or rural areas.

THE KEYS

In the Florida Keys the sweep of coral rock, the waters which sparkle in every shade of blue and blue-green, the spectacular high and long bridges linking the islands, the boats everywhere are guaranteed to impress the most jaded traveler. This land is truly made for pure enjoyment, for relaxation, for feasting the eyes. And for gastronomic feasting too, with supreme seafood and all sorts of tropical fruit delicacies on every hand.

The 106 miles from the mainland to Key West can be covered rather quickly, if all you want to do is get down to the tip. But you'll be tempted to stop at many points along the way. The Key Deer and Great White Heron national wildlife refuges are worth stopping for. John Pennekamp Coral Reef State Park offers experiences unlike those to be found in any other state parks, anywhere, and Bahia Honda State Recreation Area is one of the world's most beautiful waterfront camping areas.

If you are going to Key West, do be sure to save enough time to really see it. You'll be surprised at how much there is to do in this relatively small city. And even this remote but exciting city is not the last outpost of civilization in Florida, though it is the last one that can be reached by highway. Stretching nearly 70 miles farther to the west are many more little islands, first the Marquesas Keys, then the Dry Tortugas. Seaplanes and boats leave Key West regularly to take history buffs, bird watchers, marine scientists, photographers, and travelers who have already seen everyplace else, to visit Fort Jefferson National Monument. Are you a placedropper? If so, you'll really make an impression if you come back from your next vacation with slides of the Dry Tortugas.

CITIES & TOWNS
Map of this section on page 67.

BELLE GLADE is located on US 441 at the southeastern tip of Lake Okeechobee, in Palm Beach County. This is the trading center for a rich truck-farming area producing 32 varieties of vegetables for the residents of northern cities to enjoy throughout the winter. It claims the title of Winter Vegetable Capital of the World. Palm Beach County is the largest sugar-producing county in America. Beef cattle are also important to the economy of the area.

This agricultural land has been reclaimed by drainage from former swampland.

The Port of Belle Glade is on the **Lake Okeechobee Waterway,** a cross-state channel for cruisers, yachts, and barges navigating between the Atlantic Ocean and the Gulf of Mexico. A 40-acre island marina in the lake provides boat launching and storage facilities. Camping and picnic grounds, as well as an excellent municipal golf course and country club, are available for visitors. Bass fishing is excellent here.

Each year during April Belle Glade holds the **Black Gold Jubilee Celebration.** Activities include golf, fishing and tennis tournaments, a marathon, a parade, exhibits of arts and crafts, a puppet show, and a children's art show.

Belle Glade Marina is the setting for many popular water events during the year.

About 10 miles west of Belle Glade, near Lake Harbor, is the **Everglades Reclamation State Historic Site,** commemorating the first attempt to manage the Everglades for agriculture.

North of Belle Glade, in Pahokee, is the **Pahokee State Recreation Area,** which includes an enclosed harbor. The **Pahokee Observation Tower,** atop Hoover Dike, affords panoramic views of Lake Okeechobee and the surrounding agricultural area.

CLEWISTON, the largest community in Hendry County, is located on US 27 and the southwestern shore of Lake Okeechobee. Clewiston calls itself America's Sweetest Town. About 75,000 acres of sugarcane are harvested here annually and processed at the facilities of the U.S. Sugar Corporation, a mile south of US 27.

Access to Lake Okeechobee, with some of the finest bass fishing in the Southeast, is provided at Clewiston.

EVERGLADES CITY, in Collier County, is located 4 miles south of US 41 on Florida 29 and the Gulf of Mexico. This stretch of US 41 joining Miami and Tampa and crossing the state just north of Everglades National Park is known as the Tamiami Trail.

This is the Western Water Gateway city to **Everglades National Park,** a 2,100 mile subtropical wilderness, the largest in North America. The only access into the park from here is by water. This is a tranquil fishing and fishing resort town, only 85 miles from Miami but a million miles away from the rush and tension of city life.

Stop at the **Everglades Area Chamber of Commerce Welcome Station,** at the junction of US 41 and Florida 29. Here you can pick up literature that will introduce you to this fascinating and unique area.

Everglades City, "Florida's Last Frontier," is primarily a service center for visitors to the national park and for boaters exploring the rich fishing waters surrounding the Ten Thousand Islands, which lie offshore from here.

Mangrove trees have created these islands. The trees thrive in the brackish water, and the islands are built by bits of shell, driftwood, and seaweed trapped in the matted, sprawling roots. As the cylindrical tree seeds mature and fall into the water, they float upright until they meet resistance, then take root. Since new islands are continually being started this way, they are impossible to count and may actually number as many as 20,000.

Everglades National Park Boat Tours originate at the Gulf Coast Ranger Station in Everglades City. Small motorboats travel the waterways into the mangrove wilderness. The trips take about 1 hours; schedules vary at different seasons. Plan to make reservations during the winter months. Larger boats take 2½-hour voyages among the Ten Thousand islands. Adults $6, children 6–12 $3 for either tour.

Knowledgeable national park rangers point out the wildlife and plant life. Huge flocks of egrets, herons, anhingas, and cormorants live here, and sometimes passengers are fortunate enough to see the rarer roseate spoonbills and American bald eagles. A flock of birds taking flight in front of you as your boat rounds a bend is a breathtaking sight. Even if you never were a bird watcher before, you'll be one before you finish your ride. You, too, will begin to recognize the split-tailed Everglades kite, the osprey, the laughing gull with his black-tipped wings, the little blue heron with his dusky, unusual coloring.

All these tours are very popular. Make reservations in advance, if possible, by writing to Everglades National Park Boat Tours, Everglades City, Florida 33929, or by telephoning (813) 695-2591.

There are several motels in Everglades City, as well as camping facilities, boat rentals, and a small airstrip.

About 20 miles northwest of Everglades City, off US 41, is **Collier-Seminole State Park.** Covering nearly 6,500 acres, this park has some of the densest jungle in Florida and has

64 SOUTH CENTRAL

Mangrove trees have created the Ten Thousand Islands, which may in fact number many more than that.

been described as a miniature Everglades National Park. There is a 1,100-foot catwalk through the mangrove swamps, and a commemorative monument to the men who took part in the Seminole Wars. The park has facilities for camping, picnicking, fishing, and boating.

East of Collier-Seminole Park and on the other side of the Tamiami Trail is a registered natural landmark called **Big Cypress Bend,** 650 acres of virgin cypress swamp. This is a miniature version of the much larger Corkscrew Swamp Sanctuary, with a 2,000-foot boardwalk leading through the primeval wilderness to a tropical pond, Lake Surprise. There is a small admission charge.

North of the Tamiami Trail on Florida 29, 3 miles beyond the Collier County Welcome Station, a 13-mile loop called **Janes Scenic Drive** leads west from the village of Copeland. The road follows an old logging trail through a portion of the wild and bewitching **Fakahatchee Strand** and the **Big Cypress Swamp.** There are bald cypresses and a large stand of royal palm trees. Orchids, bromeliads, and other air plants grow in profusion within the swamp.

By act of Congress, in 1974, some 570,000 acres of land north of Everglades National Park were authorized to be the **Big Cypress National Preserve.** The purpose of this act was to assure a supply of fresh water to the Everglades and help protect the area's "natural and ecological integrity in perpetuity."

Four miles east of the Welcome Station is the village of **Ochopee,** a spot famous for having the nation's smallest post office—measuring 8 feet 4 inches by 7 feet 3 inches.

At various points along the Tamiami Trail are **Micco Sukee Indian villages** where handicrafts are sold, and arrangements can be made for taking **airboat rides** out into the wetlands. No airboat rides are permitted within the boundaries of Everglades National Park.

Thirty-two miles east of Ochopee, where the park boundaries nearly abut the Tamiami Trail, is the **Shark Valley Loop Road.** Here guided tram tours take visitors 7 miles into the park to a 25-foot-high observation tower. Usually a dozen or more alligators of all sizes are basking in the sun beneath the tower. Typical Everglades birds can be spotted. Tram rides, when water conditions permit, $3.85, children, $2; bikes may also be rented.

EVERGLADES NATIONAL PARK. See Everglades City, above, and Flamingo, below. These are the two settlements at either side of the park, and points of interest within the park are described under the two listings.

FLAMINGO, in Monroe County, is at the southern tip of the Florida mainland, about 50 miles southwest of Homestead, across Everglades National Park. Its only land access is by way of Florida 27, over a 38-mile road traversing the park from its entrance. Facilities include an excellent lodge and dining room, museum, large marina, boat tours, extensive campground and picnic area, gas station, and fishing boat rentals.

The **Visitor Center** at the east end of the park has interpretive displays, a book shop, and rest rooms. A short film introduces the visitor to the Everglades.

Two trails lead out from the **Royal Palm** area: the **Anhinga Trail** leads to a pond where alligators, birds, turtles, and other wildlife can be observed; the **Gumbo-Limbo Trail** leads

SOUTH CENTRAL

through a tropical hardwood hammock.

Other points to stop along the highway to Flamingo are **Long Pine Key,** where there are campgrounds and a picnic area; **Pineland Trail,** through the pinewoods; **Mahogany Hammock,** with an elevated boardwalk into a fascinating hardwood forest; **Paurotis Pond,** beside a stand of rare palms; **Nine Mile Pond** wildlife area; **West Lake Trail,** a boardwalk into the tropical mangrove swamp.

At Flamingo, rangers conduct nature walks along the shore, identifying plant and animal life. There are also a number of sightseeing boat trips. Prices, hours, and length of tours vary. For schedules and tickets, inquire at the Flamingo Visitors Center, or phone (305) 247-6211. For inn reservations phone (305) 253-2241. Talks, films, and slide shows are given nightly during the winter season by the Ranger Naturalist.

On a clear day the Florida Keys, 25 miles to the south, can be seen across the water from Flamingo.

FLORIDA KEYS. From Key Largo, where US 1 enters the Florida Keys, to Key West, the southernmost city in continental United States, the driver travels a 106-mile highway, crossing 42 bridges over the sea. Despite the relatively long distance, however, it is virtually impossible to think of the Keys as a group of separate and individual communities, so we shall treat them here as a single entity, listing points of interest in geographical order.

The highway follows the former roadbed of Henry Flagler's East Coast Railroad, which was completed in 1912, making Key West accessible by land for the first time. Much of the highway travels over bridges, causeways, and strips of land so narrow that one can feast one's eyes on a panorama of water on both sides of the highway—the Atlantic to the left as you go away from the mainland, and the Gulf on the right. Usually the ocean waters will range from cobalt to sapphire, while the Gulf is various shades of aquamarine. Patches of seaweed beneath the water create areas that are reddish in the sunlight. On a sunny day—and most of them are in the Keys—the incredible brilliance of these colors is so startling that your first view of one of these vistas will almost certainly take your breath away.

The islands closest to the mainland are known as the Upper Keys, and they include Key Largo, Plantation Key, Upper and Lower Matecumbe Keys, and Long Key. The population centers here are the unincorporated communities of Key Largo, Tavernier, and Islamorada.

From **KEY LARGO** charter boats take off for **John Pennekamp Coral Reef State Park** carrying skin and scuba divers, as well as sightseers who prefer to do their viewing from above the water in glass-bottomed boats.

This unique park covers more than 52,000 acres of underseas coral reef, where many colorful species of marine life swim among coral canyons and waving sea fans. Pennekamp was the first underseas park in the continental United States, but other states are now following Florida's example and establishing similar offshore parks.

An air-conditioned glass-bottomed boat, carries passengers over the reef to look at the living coral and other tropical marine life. The trips take approximately 2 hours, leaving at 9 am, noon, and 3 pm. Fare: adults $6.50, children 3–12 $3.50, under 3 free.

The authority of the state park system protects the fragile and incredibly beautiful seascape from treasure hunters and vandals, and the area offers every sort of water sport, including underwater photography. A land area on shore has marine facilities, concessions, and a fine campground.

Private entrepreneurs on the shore also provide camping, boating, diving, and food services.

At the south end of Key Largo is the community of **TAVERNIER.** From here boat trips into the Everglades are conducted by the National Audubon Society. A shaded picnic area and a beach are available in the **Harry Harris County Park** 2 miles north of the village. Free.

Farther along US 1 toward Key West is Windley Key. Here the **Theater of the Sea** features dolphin shows, bottomless boat rides, and aquaria. Open daily, 9:30–4. Admission $5.25, children 5–12 $3.25, under 5 free.

The unincorporated village of **ISLAMORADA** occupies Upper Matecumbe Key. **Wells Studio Gallery** has exhibits by local artists, including watercolors of the area (free admission). Giant turtles and conchs can be seen at the **Turtle Kraals** at Sid and Roxie's Cannery. Open daily, 8–5:30. Free. (*Kraal* is a South African word derived from the same root as "corral.") Offshore of both Upper and Lower Matecumbe Keys are colorful living coral reefs, the **Underwater Coral Gardens.** The gardens as well as the wreck of a Spanish ship, *Herrera,* may be reached by charter boat.

Major fishing tournaments with numerous prizes in a wide variety of categories are held in Islamorada during the year, including a **Bonefish Tournament** in September, a **Shark Tournament** and a **Sailfish Tournament** in December. The **Indian Key Festival** commemorates the Seminole attack of August 7, 1840, against the white settlers. The festival is in August, at **Indian Key State Historic Site.**

Beside the highway is **Hurricane Monument,** at Matecumbe Methodist Church, a memorial to the veterans of World War I and to Overseas Highway construction workers who were victims of the 1935 hurricane. Within the monument is a crypt containing the bodies of a few of the World War I veterans. Opposite this memorial, on the bay side, is the **Islamorada Public Beach.**

Lignumvitae Key State Botanical Site, accessible by boat only, is located in the Gulf opposite Islamorada. The grounds keeper runs tours of the area. In addition to the plant life on the site is the restored 19th-century Matheson Mansion.

Fifteen miles south of Islamorada is **Long Key State Recreation Area,** a convenient spot for camping while exploring the Keys. Fishing and boating are delightful in the area.

Crossing the bridge from Long Key to Conch Key, the tourist enters the Middle Keys. From here on, spearfishing is a major sport; it is not permitted in the Upper Key waters. The Middle Keys (Conch, Duck, Grassy, Crawl, Fat Deer, Vaca, Knight, Pigeon, Little Duck, Missouri, Ohio, Bahia Honda, and West Summerland Keys) include two communities— **MARATHON** and the new city of **KEY COLONY BEACH.** Both are on Vaca Key.

Developers have recently poured millions of dollars into the area, and the community now has a new terminal building at the airport, 18-hole golf course, night clubs, and a convention hall.

On Grassy Key, 6 miles north of Marathon, is **Flipper's Key West** (formerly Flipper's Sea School).

DE SOTO
Nocatee
Fort Ogden
CHARLOTTE
GLADES
Venus
BRIGHTON INDIAN RESERVATION
Lakeport
Palmdale
Cypress Knee Museum
LAKE OKEECHOBEE
14 ft. above sea level
MARTIN
Indiantown
St. Lucie Canal
Port Mayaca
Sand Cut
Canal Point
Pahokee
Pahokee Rec. Area
Bryant
Port Salerno
St. Lucie Inlet
Gomez
Hobe Sound
Jupiter Island
JUPITER ISLAND
Jonathan Dickinson S.P.
Jupiter Inlet Beach Colony
Tequesta
Jupiter
Juno Beach
Palm Beach Gards.
N.Palm Beach
Lake Park
Palm Beach Shores
Flagler Museum
Riviera Beach
West Palm Beach
Palm Beach
Citrus Center
Moore Haven
Hicpochee
Suwannee
Everglades Tropical Gards.
Clewiston
Harlem
Lake Harbor
South Bay
Belle Glade
West Palm Beach Canal
Lion Country Safari
Haverhill
Loxahatchee
Royal Palm Beach
Lake Worth
Greenacres City
Lantana
Hypoluxo
Boynton Beach
Golf
Ocean Ridge
Gulf Stream
Delray Beach
Highland Beach
Boca Raton
Bayshore
Alva
Denaud
La Belle
Goodno
Buckingham
Fort Myers
Tice
Lehigh Acres
Page Field
Fort Myers Villas
HENDRY
Felda
LEE
Okeelanta
PALM BEACH
LOXAHATCHEE N.W.R.
North New River Canal
Hillsboro Canal
Miami Canal
San Carlos Park
Estero
Koreshan St. Hist. Park
ESTERO I.
Corkscrew
Immokalee
L. Trafford
Everglades Wonder Gardens
Corkscrew Swamp Sanctuary
Bonita Springs
Bonita Shores Rec. Area
Naples Park
Golden Gate
COLLIER
Sunniland
BIG CYPRESS SEMINOLE INDIAN RESERVATION
Coral Springs
Margate
Deerfield Beach
Lighthouse Point
Pompano Beach
Tamarac
BROWARD
Oakland Park
Hugh Taylor Birch Rec. Area
Fort Lauderdale
ALLIGATOR ALLEY
TWO LANES (EVERGLADES PKWY.)
TOLL
Naples
East Naples
Naples Manor
Marco
Big Marco Pass
Caxambas Pass
Collier Seminole S.P.
Goodland
Gullivan Bay
Cape Romano
Jerome
Copeland
Ochopee
BIG CYPRESS NATIONAL PRESERVE
Ft. Lauderdale-Hollywood Int'l. Arpt.
South New River Canal
Davie
Miramar
John U. Lloyd Beach S.P.
Dania
Hollywood
Hallandale
Carol City
Ojus
North Miami Beach
Opa Locka
Surfside
Tamiami Canal
THE EVERGLADES
HOMESTEAD EXTENSION FLORIDA'S TPK.
Miami Sprs.
Hialeah
Miami Beach
Everglades City
Monroe
TEN THOUSAND ISLANDS
Chokoloskee
Chevalier Bay
Alligator Bay
Miami Int'l. Arpt.
Sweetwater
Miami
Seaquarium
Coral Gables
KEY BISCAYNE
Bill Baggs Cape Florida State Rec. Area
Key Biscayne
Parrot Jungle
Serpentarium
Kendall
South Miami
Chekika Rec. Area
Richmond Hts.
Perrine
Cutler Ridge
Monkey Jungle
Princeton
Goulds
Naranja
Orchid Jungle
Biscayne Bay
SANDS KEY
Big Lostmans Bay
DADE
Homestead
Coral Castle
Leisure City
Homestead A.F.B.
ELLIOTT KEY
Islandia
Biscayne Nat'l. Park
OLD RHODES KEY
INTRACOASTAL WATERWAY
Florida City
Highland Pt.
EVERGLADES NATIONAL PARK
Long Pine Key
Shark Pt.
Ponce de Leon Bay
MONROE
Whitewater Bay
North West Cape
TOLL BR.
Barnes Sound
KEY LARGO
Cape Sable
MANGROVE SWAMP
Flamingo
Middle Cape
John Pennekamp Coral Reef S.P.
East Cape
OYSTER KEYS
Key Largo
Florida Bay
Sunset Point
Tavernier
Plantation
UPPER MATECUMBE KEY
PLANTATION KEY
Islamorada
Theater of the Sea
Lignumvitae Key St. Botanical Site
LONG KEY
Layton
LOWER MATECUMBE KEY
FLORIDA KEYS
CONTENT KEYS
NAT'L. KEY DEER REFUGE
GREAT WHITE HERON N.W.R.
Flipper Sea School
Duck Key
Long Key Rec. Area
VACA KEY
Key Colony Beach
Marathon
GREAT WHITE HERON N.W.R.
JOHNSTON KEY
BIG TORCH KEY
BIG PINE KEY
NO NAME KEY
CUDJOE KEY
SUGARLOAF KEY
Summerland Key
MUD KEYS
SNIPE KEYS
Ramrod Key
Big Pine Key
Bahia Honda Rec. Area
KEY WEST N.W.R.
Stock Island
INTRACOASTAL WATERWAY
Key West
Key West Aquarium
Key West Int'l. Arpt.
Key West N.A.S.
828012-3
©R. McN. 82-1
South Central Florida
0 5 10 Miles
0 5 10 Kilometers

Visitors are taken on a guided tour. The walk is a relaxed, informal, and intimate experience. Participants are encouraged to stop, interrupt, and ask questions whenever they wish. There are three water shows (daily at 10, noon, and 2), and beautifully landscaped grounds with a tidal pool, waterfalls, and birds and animals. Phone for hours and fees, (305) 294-8827.

A facility has been established at Marathon Airport by the U.S. Custom Service. Its purpose is to clear persons through customs who put in here by boat from the West Indies and the Bahamas.

Several major fishing tournaments are held annually at Marathon and Key Colony Beach, including billfish, tarpon, bonefish, sailfish, and shark. Write to the chambers of commerce in the two communities for details.

From Marathon's airport, air taxi tours are available for a bird's eye view of the area. These give passengers magnificent opportunities for aerial photography of land, water, and underwater sights.

Directly beyond Marathon, connecting Pigeon and Bahia Honda Keys, is the famed and spectacular Seven-Mile Bridge. From here on the shape, geology, topography, and flora of the Keys differ considerably from those of the Keys already traversed. Nearly 80 acres of land are available for camping and picnicking in the beautiful, tropical **Bahia Honda State Recreation Area.** This is Florida's southernmost park, and it includes all recreational facilities in a lush tropical setting.

Beyond the West Summerland Keys begins the area of the Lower Keys. There are Big Pine, Torch, Ramrod, Summerland, Cudjoe, Sugarloaf, Saddlebunch, Shark, Big Coppitt, Rockland, Boca Chica, Stock, and Key West.

On Big Pine Key is the highest point in the Keys. Here pine trees are growing, an unusual sight in this area, since pines do not normally thrive in a saltwater environment, as well as similarly out-of-place cacti.

In the vicinity of Big Pine Key are the **Great White Heron National Wildlife Refuge** and the **Key Deer National Wildlife Refuge.** If you are patient, and lucky, you may spot some of the rare, tiny Key deer running wild. Your chances are fairly good of seeing a flight of lovely pink roseate spoonbills rising above green waters. Information is available at the Ranger Station, open Monday–Friday, 8–5. Free. Refuge areas are open daily, daylight hours.

About 20 miles of relatively undeveloped land lies between Summerland Key and Key West, the terminus of US 1 and the southernmost U.S. city outside the state of

This Spanish Colonial house in Key West was author Ernest Hemingway's home for 30 years.

Visitors aboard the Conch Tour Train as it travels along Roosevelt Boulevard, Key West.

Hawaii. The largest city in Monroe County, **KEY WEST** is one of a handful of cities throughout the world whose name immediately conjures up a distinctive vision, even to those who have never been there.

This picture is a kaleidoscope of many pieces—some quaint, picturesque, nostalgic; some exotic and exciting; some mysterious, filled with intrigue, even frightening. Key West's location—more than a hundred miles by land from the mainland of Florida, cut off from the rest of the state even further by the Everglades, much closer by air or water to Havana than to Miami, nearer to Yucatan than to New Orleans—may account for part of its mystery. Its history—shaped by Indians, Spanish conquistadores, pirates, Bahamians, Cubans, West Indians, New England seafarers and other Americans—partially explains its colorfulness. The harshness of the elements, which have dumped in its harbors and on its shores the litter of shipwrecks and hurricanes, undoubtedly helps to intensify an aura of danger hovering over the city.

Yet, when you get there its pastel, tropical, sleepy charm will make the tales of adventure, which begin with the first Spanish explorers and continue into present-day Cuban involvement, seem totally unreal.

But no matter how you care to explain its allure, alluring it is, a refuge for artists and writers, but also a major tourist city with an array of accommodations, food, recreation, shopping, historic landmarks, and wonders of nature to rival centers many times its size.

To see the whole city in comfort, get an overview of its history, and decide on which of its many faces you want to investigate further, begin your visit with a 1¾-hour, guided sightseeing tour on the **Conch Tour Train**. There are two depots, one at **Old Mallory Square**, 303 Front Street, and one on North Roosevelt Boulevard at the **Quality Inn**. The price of the tour is reasonable, the lecture is amusing and informative, and the tour will introduce you to dozens of points of interest in old and new Key West. The trains run daily, all year 9–4. Tickets $6, children 3–11 $3, under 3 free. Member Florida Attractions Association.

Also located at Mallory Square is the **Old Town Trolley,** streetcar sightseeing tours.

Both the Chamber of Commerce and the Conch Train depot are in Mallory Square, as are the **Municipal Aquarium** and the **Key West Hospitality House,** where all your questions about the city can be answered. The Aquarium houses octopus, sharks, and barracudas, along with smaller native tropical fish. Open daily, 9–5. Admission fee.

The **Waterfront Playhouse,** in Mallory Square, offers theatrical productions during a season that runs from November through April.

Across the street and down a few steps from Mallory Square is **Pirate's Alley,** a group of imaginative and sophisticated art galleries, craft shops, boutiques, and gift stores. (Would you believe that you can buy excellent examples of Eskimo soapstone carvings in *Key West,* of all places?) The shops are housed in a number of old Key West buildings that have been moved here from various parts of town and placed

SOUTH CENTRAL 69

informally around a courtyard. The area was developed by David Williams Wolkowsky, owner of the Pier House Motel and a third-generation Key Wester whose grandfather migrated here from Russia and, starting as a pushcart peddler, became a successful Key West merchant.

Among the most popular attractions for visitors in Key West are the **Ernest Hemingway House** and the **Audubon House,** where their respective famous residents did much of their work. Both houses are fine examples of Key West architecture; both have beautiful gardens. The Audubon House is more of a museum of Key West at the time of Audubon, while the Hemingway House is a preservation of the great writer's home. Both are furnished in period pieces and contain interesting memorabilia. Some of Audubon's original work is on display, and many of the plants collected and planted by Hemingway still thrive today. Audubon House, at Whitehead and Greene streets, is open daily, 9–noon and 1–5. Admission $2, children 6–12 75¢, under 6 free. Hemingway House is about seven blocks away, at 907 Whitehead Street. Open daily, 9–5. Admission $2, children $1.

At 221 Duval Street, **Artists Unlimited,** housed in a historic building constructed by ship's carpenters, displays choice art work and a tropical garden; and the **Key West Art Center,** at 301 Front Street, features paintings and ceramics by local artists.

At 529 Front Street visitors may watch the various steps taken in the manufacture of materials by **Key West Hand Print Fabrics.** Articles of clothing made from these fabrics are choice souvenirs to carry home from Key West. Open Monday–Friday, 9:30–5:30. Closed holidays. Free. Retail shop open Monday–Saturday, 9:30–5:30 and Sunday, 11–4.

At the **Key West Fragrance and Cosmetic Store,** 528 Front Street, you can buy aloe-based cosmetics. The factory is located on Green Street.

At the end of Margaret Street, at the docks, a picturesque fleet of shrimp boats tie up, and turtle kraals, or tanks, house the giant sea turtles that are awaiting processing into turtle steaks and turtle soup.

Duval Street has quite a number of venerable buildings that date back to the 1820s and 1830s. Over the years, many of them had been modified and allowed to deteriorate, but a recent restoration project has turned two blocks of the street into what the residents call the New Old Key West. The facelifting the houses were treated to recreates an authentic Bahamian motif, and the restored buildings, now housing imaginative shops and restaurants, give visitors the opportunity to experience the flavor of a tropical island of a century and a half ago.

The **Oldest House Museum,** built in 1829 on Duval Street, was the home of early wrecker and sea captain Francis B.

Sooty tern nesting on Bird Key, in the Dry Tortugas.

Watlington. It has antique furniture, old toys and dolls, the original outside kitchen, and a six-foot-long model schooner. Open daily except Wednesday, 10–4. Admission fee.

Key West Cemetery, with its monument to the victims of the torpedoing of the USS *Maine* (remember the *Maine*?) and **Bayview,** a park with a memorial to Jose Marti, hero of Cuba's fight for independence, are worth a visit.

The **Lighthouse Tower and Museum,** at 938 Whitehead Street, is open daily, 9:30–5. Closed Christmas. Admission $2, children 7–15 50¢, under 7 free.

The **East Martello Gallery and Museum,** on South Roosevelt Boulevard, is housed in a structure that is most unusual, but admirably suited for the collection it contains. The old fort was built by Union forces in control of the island during the War Between the States. This tower, East Martello, and its twin, West Martello (which houses the Monroe County Beach and Garden Center), were never completed because the design became obsolete with the adaptation of rifled cannon with exploding shells. The term *Martello Tower* designates masonry forts built chiefly on seacoasts, generally with thick walls and entrances high off the ground. An outer circular building with vaulted rooms surrounds a courtyard with a square tower in the center.

Today the museum is filled with a well-arranged collection of Key West historical items. The history of this intriguing city unfolds before you as you look over the cigar-making and sponge-diving tools; ties and rails from the Overseas Railway and photos of the celebration when the railway was completed in 1912; railings and beds from the old Civil War hospital; examples of many designs of the "gingerbread" spindles that adorn Key West verandas and balconies; Hemingway memorabilia. In addition to the historical exhibits are fine paintings, woodcuts, ceramics, and other locally fashioned products. Open daily, 9:30–5. Closed Christmas. Admission $2.50, children 7–15, 50¢, under 7 free.

Recreation in Key West is varied. Glass-bottomed boats take visitors on cruises over the living coral reef off Key West. Charter boats with guides may be engaged for deep-sea fishing. Local restaurants will prepare your catch for your gustatory pleasure, or you can barbecue it at any of the ubiquitous roadside picnic parks.

Fishing tournaments, powerboat races, and sailing regattas are regular events in Key West—for details write to the Chamber of Commerce. Some events include **Hemingway Days** in mid-July; **Raft Races** and **Fantasy Festival** both held in October; and the **International Powerboat Races** in November.

The coral reef of Key West is not exactly compatible with pleasant white sand beaches so there is no swimming at the city's edge, but swimming can be enjoyed at the following areas: **Smather's Beach,** on Roosevelt Boulevard; **Monroe County Beach**; **South Beach**; and the **City Swimming Area.** Swimming is free.

Everywhere in the Keys are thousands of varieties of shells, rocks, driftwood, and coral of interest to those addicted to beachcombing. Or you may buy your specimens from divers who clean and sell their wares at Southernmost Point. You may want to be a typical tourist and prove that you have made it to the very tip of continental United States by having your picture taken at the sign at the point.

By no means the least of Key West's attractions is its food. Seafood delicacies include conch chowder and conch salad, snapper casserole, Florida crawfish (said by native gourmets to surpass the flavor of Maine lobsters), green turtle soup and green turtle steak, shrimp broiled with wine and buttered bread crumbs, or your own catch-of-the-day spread with tartar sauce, wrapped in foil, and roasted over coals in an outdoor barbecue oven.

A dish apparently indigenous to the city is *bollos*—fried, puffy balls sold by the sackful at outdoor stands. A little like hush puppies, maybe, but fragrant and tasty with hints of onion and garlic. Eat them while they're still hot and crisp.

Avocados (for salad) and limes (for Key lime pie) are only two of the more than a dozen edible tropical fruits available here to eat "as is," made into desserts, or used as a base for various fruit juice mixtures. Indulge your curiosity; your taste buds will love it even if your waistline suffers.

A good time to visit Key West is during the month of February through most of March when the city celebrates **Old Island Days** with a number of unique events—such as a conch shell-blowing contest!

Sixty-eight miles west of Key West, in an isolated wilderness accessible only by boat or seaplane, and with no facilities for accommodating visitors, is **Fort Jefferson National Monument,** at Tortugas Harbor on Garden Key. Planes, which carry five passengers, may be chartered at Murray's Marina, Stock Island. The trip is $75 for adults, reduced price for children, with a two-passenger minimum per trip. Phone (305) 294-6978 to make arrangements.

Construction of the fort started in 1846 and went on for nearly 30 years, but, like the East and West Martello towers, was never completed. For about ten years (until 1874) it was used as a federal prison. In 1898 the U.S. Fleet was stationed in Tortugas Harbor, and the ill-fated battleship *Maine* sailed from there to Havana. The fort was again used briefly during World War I, but has stood abandoned since, a monument to the wasted money and lives sacrificed during the construction of this useless fortification.

Today, by contrast, the seven Dry Tortugas Islands which form the southernmost tip of the Florida Reef serve a valuable purpose as a refuge for terns, boobies, and frigate birds, and as a flyway for songbirds and others migrants. Brilliant tropical fish and crustaceans abound in the crystal-clear waters covering natural sea gardens surrounding the islands. Charter boats and seaplanes to explore the area are available from Key West.

HOMESTEAD, in Dade County, is 30 miles southwest of Miami, at the end of a line of suburbs. US 1 leads from Miami through Homestead and on to the Keys. Key Largo is 29 miles south. Florida 27, the only road through the Everglades, runs southwest from Homestead to Flamingo, 50 miles away at the tip of the mainland.

Perhaps eventually the metropolitan sprawl of Miami will engulf the village, but as yet it is a distinct community. Its character is agricultural, and the tourist who stops to look the little city over will probably be startled to find this typical "Small Town, USA" sitting amidst the urban/resort strip on the East Coast, the fishing/boating paradise of the Keys, and the tropical wilderness wildlife sanctuary of the Everglades—a stone's throw from each of them, but very different from them all.

The famous Seven-Mile Bridge is an important landmark along the 106-mile journey from Key Largo to Key West.

Ten miles east, on Biscayne Bay, is Homestead's **Bayfront Park,** several hundred acres of beach area with boat rentals, swimming, fishing, and picnicking. In the bay, accessible only by boat from Bayfront Park, is **Biscayne National Park,** a primitive tropical island area. No fresh water is available. For information write P.O. Box 1369, Homestead 33030; or phone (305) 247-7275.

Florida has been peopled with a good many extreme individualists over the years—those who have come here to "do their own thing." Many were eccentrics; some were geniuses; a few were both. **Coral Castle,** about 2 miles north of Homestead on US 1, was built by such an eccentric genius. A weirdly beautiful "coral museum" fairyland was created here by an unschooled recluse who was seeking escape and solace from the anguish of an unrequited love. Open daily, 9–5. Admission $4.50, children 6–14 $2.50, under 6 free.

Also north of town (follow the signs) is the exotic **Orchid Jungle.** Here four generations of Fennells have established and maintained this incredible orchid-growing business. Today more than a quarter of a million plants are growing, most of them in a natural state in the trees out of doors, requiring no care whatsoever. In addition to these, thousands of potted plants are raised for sale. The blooming season of different types of orchids varies throughout the year, so that there is always a magnificent display of flowers to be seen. Open daily, 8:30–5:30. Closed Thanksgiving and Christmas. Admission $3.50, 13–17 $2.80, 6–12 $1.25.

Chekika State Recreation Area is at S.W. 237th Street and Grossman Drive; camping, picnicking, swimming, fishing, and nature trails.

An entirely different type of park is about 5 miles north of Homestead on Florida 27 and 1 mile west, the **Preston B. Bird & Mary Heinlein Fruit and Spice Park.** It is a demonstration plot and information center for the cultivation of tropical fruits, spice trees and shrubs. Guided tours: November–May 1 on Wednesday, Friday and Saturday at 10:30, Sunday at 1 and 3:30; summer by appointment only. Park and store open daily, all year 9–5; closed New Year's Day, Thanksgiving and Christmas. Free.

Two miles south, in Florida City, is **Florida Pioneer Museum,** displaying antiques and Indian artifacts. Open daily, October through May, 9–5. Open Sunday only, June through October. Closed holidays. Admission $1.50, under 12 75¢.

In February of each year Homestead hosts **Rodeo and Frontier Days** at the Arena, with all of the popular riding events. For details write to the Homestead Chamber of Commerce. Other annual events are the **Wheelmen's Rendezvous** in the spring, five days of bicycle fun highlighting a 50-mile endurance race to Flamingo, and a big **Veterans Day Parade.**

IMMOKALEE is located in Collier County of Florida 29, about 20 miles north of Alligator Alley, Florida 84, the arrow-straight tollway traversing the Everglades from US 27 to the outskirts of Naples.

This agricultural community celebrates its vegetable crops with a **Harvest Festival** in March, featuring a parade and the selection of a queen.

Cattle ranches and oil wells lie to the north of Immokalee, and Big Cypress Seminole Indian Reservation lies to the east. Sometimes, when the village fills up with cattlemen, oilmen, and Indian farmers, the visitor may think he has been transplanted to a western town.

About 16 miles west of town, at the north end of Big Cypress Swamp, is a unique preserve maintained by the National Audubon Society—the **Corkscrew Swamp Sanctuary.** Here is the country's largest remaining stand of virgin bald cypress, trees which once thrived throughout southeastern United States. This stand includes trees believed to be at least seven hundred years old. From a raised boardwalk, visitors may enjoy the beauty of wild orchids, air plants, ferns, and mosses; beautiful subtropical birds, alligators, and other wildlife. Within the sanctuary is a favorite nesting place of the rare wood stork.

The Audubon Society rescued this irreplaceable natural treasure from the logging industry in 1954, but it faces an ongoing struggle to save the wilderness from destruction through loss of the life-giving waters of the swamp. Drainage for real estate developments, proposed new canals and jetports, forest fires—all threaten the sanctuary's existence.

The sanctuary is open daily, 9–5. Admission $4 (plus tax), students $2, children under 12 free. An illustrated booklet enables the visitor to take a self-guided tour, but rangers are usually around to answer questions. A picnic area is provided. Phone (813) 657-3771 for additional information.

ISLAMORADA, KEY COLONY BEACH, KEY LARGO, KEY WEST, MARATHON—see **FLORIDA KEYS**

MOORE HAVEN is the county seat and principal center in the very sparsely populated Glades County. It is located on US 27 just west of Lake Okeechobee.

From January to March of each year, bass anglers who fish in Lake Okeechobee and the waters that empty into it may take part in the **Chalo Nitka Fishing Contest.** Each March the week-long **Chalo Nitka Festival** is held. (*Chalo Nitka* means "big bass" is Seminole.)

Twelve miles north of Moore Haven, off Florida 78, is a **Brighton-Seminole Indian Reservation.**

PALMDALE is located on US 27, 18 miles northwest of Moore Haven. One mile south of town is **Cypress Knee Museum,** which calls itself a three-in-one attraction. There are the museum itself displaying hundreds of these curious knee formations (it is surprising to learn that they have been found in at least 22 states); a factory in which the knees are fashioned into decorative objects for sale; and a catwalk into the swamp. Tours daily, 8 am–sundown. Admission $1, under 12 and over 80 free.

TAVERNIER—see **FLORIDA KEYS**

(*Details on admission prices and hours have been included as a service to the reader and as a guide in planning activities. However, changes are inevitable in some cases, and the publisher cannot be responsible for any variations from the listed information.*)

Lighthouse at Fort Jefferson, Garden Key.

Bahia Honda State Park

The lighthouse at Cape Florida, Key Biscayne, is one of the oldest structures in southern Florida.

SOUTHEAST

THE GOLD COAST

A NARROW STRIP OF GOLDEN SAND BETWEEN THE STEELY SAPPHIRE SURF OF THE ATLANTIC AND THE LIGHT BROWNS AND RICH DARK GREENS OF THE EVERGLADES. THE MOST HIGHLY ADVERTISED AND BALLYHOOED PIECE OF REAL ESTATE EVER PROMOTED IN THE HISTORY OF MAN. AMERICA'S RIVIERA—ABOUT 2,000 SQUARE MILES OF RESORTS, YACHT BASINS, RACETRACKS, RESTAURANTS, MARINAS, GOLF COURSES, AND OTHER ASSORTED PLEASURE PALACES AND RELATED BUSINESS, ALL CREATED ON TOP OF LAND SCOOPED OUT OF THE BOTTOM OF THE BAYS, DUMPED INTO MANGROVE SWAMPS, AND DRAINED INTO COUNTLESS CANALS. THIS IS SOUTHEAST FLORIDA.

It includes St. Lucie and Martin counties, plus the oceanfront strip about 10 miles wide that contains most of the population of Palm Beach, Broward, and Dade counties. Today this strip is where more than one-third of all of Floridians live—and most of them within the metropolitan sprawl that begins north of Palm Beach and extends in an unbroken line of cities south to Goulds.

Southeast Florida had nothing going for it to start with except a frost-free climate, balmy breezes, and wide beaches. Otherwise the terrain was almost impenetrable, the mosquitoes and sand flies were voracious, and during part of the year the heat and humidity were overpowering.

THE PIONEERS

But a number of people saw its potential, and little by little, after the Civil War, settlers (mostly Yankees) came to the frontier coast south of Cape Canaveral to try to make their fortunes out of pineapple and coconut plantations. By 1881 boats were going back and forth regularly between Titusville and Lake Worth. The few, scattered pioneers visited each other by sailboat or by foot. Trade boats, which operated like peddlers' carts, brought general store supplies to the settlers; the captains were usually notary publics also, with the power to perform marriages when needed. Floating dental offices brought services periodically. Whatever the people needed came by boat—if at all—and this maritime traffic covered a vast range of activity. The story is told of one steamer on its regular run on the Indian River: the crew heard cries for help and, on shore, saw a man treed by a big, black bear. They quickly came to the rescue by shooting the bear!

In 1893 the Northeast Coast was being served by Henry Flagler's railroad. Indian River oranges were already an important crop, and were being shipped out by rail. From the Indian River ports, which included Sebastian, Fort Pierce, Jensen, and Stuart, two and a half million pounds of fish were being shipped annually to markets in the north.

The most glamorous and exclusive of all Florida resorts is conceded to be Palm Beach. It owes its name and a great deal of its beauty to a shipwreck that occurred off its shores during its earliest days of settlement. The boat was carrying a full load of coconuts, and the foresighted pioneers planted the cargo that washed ashore. The village got its own post office and was officially named Palm Beach in 1886.

In 1888 the first railroad came down to the Southeast—an 8-mile spur that reached to the north shore of Lake Worth. (This is the saltwater lake that separates Palm Beach from West Palm Beach.) There was no means of turning around, so trains headed down and rolled backward for the return trip. The line was known locally as the Celestial Railroad, because its four stops were Jupiter, Mars, Venus, and Juno. Transportation routes reached farther south in 1893, when a stage line, or "hack line," was established between the southern shore of Lake Worth and the northern end of Biscayne Bay.

HENRY FLAGLER

The development of the entire East Coast of Florida is generally credited to Henry Flagler and his hotels and railroads, but pioneers were settling and building up the region—and attracting tourists—before the railroad was built. Some of the early residents felt a certain degree of resentment over the credit given Flagler for "creating" the Gold Coast.

Another very important factor in opening up this part of the state was the creation of the Intracoastal Waterway. Dredging of the bays and channels along the mainland was begun in 1883. The waterway reached Palm Beach by 1898, and made it all the way down the coast by 1912. With the completion of this channel, small boats were able to make the entire trip from Fernandina to the Keys.

Although a great deal of valuable acreage was given to the canal company in return for its investment in digging the canal, most of the land was sold off before prices got high enough for the company to realize much profit.

In 1927 the Florida Inland Navigation District was created, to clean out and deepen the whole waterway. It is now unsurpassed as a luxury cruise route, and many millions of dollars have been invested in the marinas, yacht clubs, docks, wharves, waterfront shopping centers, cabanas, and dozens of other shore-front services for boaters.

The development of the Southeast Coast paralleled the building of hotels and the establishment of transportation routes. In 1894 the final segment of the railroad to Palm Beach was completed and the Royal Poinciana Hotel was opened. Every imaginable form of entertainment was provided for Palm Beach tourists—bathing, bicycling, riding, golfing, sailing; teas, dances, concerts, and fancy dinners; hunting trips and fishing expeditions. Across the island on the ocean shore, Mr. Flagler bought a hotel called the Palm Beach Inn. Less pretentious than the Royal Poinciana, it opened in 1896 and was enlarged and renovated over several years. The hotel was destroyed by fire in 1903, was rebuilt the same year and was renamed The Breakers. That structure, too, was destroyed by fire, in 1925, each time being rebuilt on a greater scale. Mr. Flagler began work on his own palatial Whitehall in 1900, and moved in 1902.

Meanwhile a woman named Julia D. Tuttle, who has earned a notable spot in history as the "Mother of Miami," bought a tract of land along the Miami River and started pestering Flagler to extend his developments to the area around Biscayne Bay. In return for his bringing in a railroad she promised to give him half her land. At first Flagler was not much interested, but the Big Freeze of 1894, which ruined citrus crops and other vegetation as far south as Palm Beach, made Miami look a lot more attractive for residential and agricultural development.

In 1895 the Flagler interests began to build the new Miami. Hundreds of workers were brought in, to live in crude shacks and tents hastily thrown together for them. In 1896 the railroad extended from Palm Beach to Miami and the first Miami newspaper, *The Metropolis,* was started. Seven years later a second paper, the *Evening Record,* forerunner of the *Miami Herald,* began publication. By the turn of the century Flagler had a railroad, a hotel, electric plants, waterworks, and land companies in Miami.

Soon a hotly debated political issue arose—whether or not Miami should be a "dry" town. Even Carrie Nation came to town to raid some of the joints in North Miami—and the drys were victorious for the time being.

During the Spanish-American War troops were encamped at Palm Beach and Miami. The war itself lasted only a few months, but there were heavy casualties in the Florida camps from malaria, yellow fever, and typhoid.

COLLINS AND MIAMI BEACH

Present-day Miami Beach was created by a horticulturist, John S. Collins, who came down from New Jersey to invest in avocado planting. He bought a great deal of the land on the island across the channel from Miami, but soon found that mangrove swamps were a very difficult kind of terrain in which to plant the trees. He then envisioned a different kind of future for his island, but realized that first of all it would have to be made accessible by bridge. He encountered difficulty in obtaining permission to build a bridge, since the boating interests opposed the plan, so he devised a scheme to demonstrate the necessity for a bridge. He brought an automobile to the edge of the bay and demanded that it be ferried across. Since ferryboats of the time were not built to carry such a heavy load, he was able to argue, successfully, that a bridge was essential in order to gain access to his property.

When Collins had almost exhausted his funds on the building of the bridge, he got additional financing from Carl Fisher of Indianapolis, the businessman who had helped to form the Prestolite Company of America. The bridge was finished in 1913; land was dredged up from the bottom of Biscayne Bay to fill in the mangrove swamp; and the land promotion of Miami Beach began.

After World War I, Florida tourism began to boom, as travelers from the north with money to spend piled into their roadsters and headed south on the Dixie Highway (another Fisher project). The big promotion and ballyhoo advertising for Miami Beach started in 1919. Meanwhile, other promoters were hawking their wares in Coral Gables, Boca Raton, Hollywood, and Fort Lauderdale. Between 1920 and 1925 the population of Florida's East Coast increased by more than 50%!

Along with all the legal entertainment offered the tourist, gamblers, bookies, and bootleggers were getting their piece of the action, too.

THE BUBBLE BURSTS

The collapse of the Florida land boom resulted from a series of disastrous events. First fire tragically destroyed both The Breakers and the Palm Beach Hotel. Not long after that a large ship sank in the Miami ship channel and blocked passage for some time for 70 boats stuck within the harbor and 60 more waiting outside to come in. Then the railroad line needed repairs, and passage by rail was greatly slowed down. In 1926 a crippling hurricane struck Miami; and a second one, just about as devastating, hit in 1928. All of these blows to the East Coast were quickly followed by the stock market crash in 1929—and the bubble had finally burst.

Although lean years followed the glorious twenties, the Gold Coast had been advertised so successfully and widely throughout the world that millions of people remembered its delights and hung onto their dreams about this beautiful tropical paradise.

One "industry" of the twenties survived the crash—rum-running from the Bahamas. All through the Prohibition years, liquor was being brought in by the boatload. The Bahamas government was not interested in doing anything to interfere with this profitable trade; their liquor tax income was soon more than a million dollars a year. Before long the local folklore about liquor smuggling began to match the wild tales of earlier years about piracy and wrecking along the coast. Miami and Palm Beach never stopped being wideopen towns for liquor. The Eighteenth Amendment, somehow, was not as effective as Carrie Nation had been.

WORLD WAR II AND AFTER

World War II saw the posting of thousands of servicemen and women in Florida; there were 34 Armed Services establishments between Fernandina and Key West. Tourist hotels were converted to barracks; golf courses and parks were used as parade grounds. Countless numbers of those who saw service here during the war years later returned to establish homes—some of them simply never left!

The postwar years have seen all of the Southeast Florida cities reach maturity. Miami is no longer just a tourist town—it is a vibrant, exciting, major city with a life of its own that is not dependent on visitors or winter residents to keep it alive. It is an international city, an important center for trade and transportation between this country and many others throughout the world.

Southeast Florida is a product of the 20th century. Without heavy machinery to shift about large quantities of rock and soil, without the generation of vast quantities of electrical energy, without modern fast transportation—most of all, perhaps, without air conditioning, man could not have made this territory conform to his standard of living.

But along with the tycoons and the promoters and the industrial giants, let us not forget the influence of some of the gentler souls. There was President B. F. Ashe, who brought the University of Miami through its lean times almost single-handedly. There were horticulturists David and Marian Bell Fairchild, ecologist John C. Gifford, landscape architect Ernest F. Coe, all of whom saw how man's efforts could cooperate with and enhance those of nature. There were newspaperman

John Pennekamp, for whom the nation's first underwater park was named, and his colleague Marjory Stoneman Douglas, one of Florida's most eloquent chroniclers and advocates. These people, too, helped to shape both the physical appearance and the personality of Southeast Florida. May their names be remembered as long as those of Henry Flagler and John S. Collins!

CITIES & TOWNS

Map of this section on page 78.

BOCA RATON, in Palm Beach County, is about 15 miles north of Fort Lauderdale. Since 1960 its population has increased nearly seven-fold, although it was first settled in the late 1800s, when mail between Miami and Palm Beach (66 miles) was delivered by the famous "barefoot mailmen." The luxurious Boca Raton Hotel and Club was built during the 1920s, and its developer had hoped to build a splendid dream city on several thousand acres of farmland. This plan was stopped by the 1926 real estate crash, and the village remained tiny and quiet for more than 30 years. The name comes from a Spanish phrase meaning "mouth of the sharp-pointed rocks."

Florida Atlantic University occupies a 1,200-acre campus at the western edge of town. It was established in 1964 and has a current enrollment of nearly 9,200 students.

CORAL GABLES, in Dade County, is a Miami suburb immediately south of the city, on US 1 and US 41. Its name comes from the coral rock which underlies the entire area, covered over by only a few inches of soil.

A visitor to the substantial, prosperous, manicured Coral Gables of today would not guess that it was conceived and born amid some of the most outrageous, flamboyant, hard-sell promotion ever seen—even in a state full of towns that came to life at the hands of similar razzle-dazzle midwifery.

Today's promoters use TV and sports personalities to help sell their developments; Coral Gables was pitched by such giants as orator William Jennings Bryan, opera singer Mary Garden, and orchestra leader Paul Whiteman.

To make the most of your visit to this beautiful town, stop at the Coral Gables Chamber of Commerce, 50 Aragon Avenue, or at the City Hall Information Desk, and pick up a Self-Guided Tour map. More than one hundred points of interest are covered on the tour.

Pelicans await the catch from a Miami Beach pier.

The **Venetian Municipal Pool,** 2701 DeSoto Boulevard, is surrounded by shaded porticos and loggias, palm trees, and Spanish-style stone and ironwork. It is open Saturday–Sunday all year, 10–4:45. On Monday–Friday the hours open are: June–August 11–7:45, September–October and April–May 11–5:45, November–March 10–4:45. Admission $2.50, children 2–12 $1; under 2 free. Closed Thanksgiving and Christmas. Swimming is also available at Matheson Hammock Beach and Park, 9610 Old Cutler Road. Open daily, 6–sunset, $1.

Fairchild Tropical Garden, 10901 Old Cutler Road, is probably Coral Gables best-known attraction. Tram tours through the 83-acre garden are conducted by knowledgeable guides. There are a Rare Plant House containing tender exotic plants, a museum displaying items made of palm products, and a bookshop featuring literature on tropical horticulture. Open daily, 9:30–4:30. Closed Christmas. Admission $3, children under 13 free with parent. Hourly tram tour $1, children under 13, 50¢.

The **University of Miami,** in Coral Gables, is the largest independent university in southeastern United States, with a current enrollment of over 18,000 students. The school was founded during Florida's boom years of the 1920s. It nearly went under during the Depression, but it has survived and grown to great prestige. Its modern campus is expanding rapidly. Worth visiting is its **Lowe Art Museum,** where there are fine collections of Oriental, American, European, and primitive art. Open Tuesday–Friday, noon–5; Saturday, 10–5; Sunday, 2–5. Closed Christmas and January 1. Fee. Also on the campus is **Gusman Concert Hall,** which hosts ensembles, recitals, concerts, lectures, and forums, as well as performances by distinguished alumni and guest artists.

Adjacent to the St. James Evangelical Lutheran Church, at 110 Phoenetia Avenue, is the **Garden of Our Lord,** where flowers, shrubs, and trees, native to the Holy Land and mentioned in the Bible, are grown.

Each January Coral Gables hosts a popular **Sidewalk Art Show.**

During the winter months Coral Gables hosts a number of golf, tennis, and bowling tournaments. In November and December the Junior Orange Bowl Festivities attract more than 4,000 young participants who take part in football, bowling, tennis, and golf tournaments. The festival is climaxed by a **Junior Orange Bowl Parade** and **Queen's Ball** in late December.

DANIA, in Broward County, is on US 1 just south of Fort Lauderdale. Its 2-mile-long public beach on the Atlantic Ocean is shaded with palm trees and complete with a pavilion, cabanas, a cafe, and a picnic area.

Calling itself the Antique Center of the South, Dania has more than 50 shops for antique-hunters.

Lloyd Beach State Recreation Area is a beautiful oceanfront park located north of Dania, off Florida A1A.

On Dania Beach Boulevard is the **Dania Jai-Alai Palace,** where games are played nightly except Sundays and Tuesdays from July through December, nightly except Sunday from January through mid–March, and nightly except Sundays and Wednesdays from mid–March-mid–April. Phone 305/927-2841 for matinee schedule.

DELRAY BEACH, in Palm Beach County, is on US 1 about 15 miles south of Palm Beach.

This beautiful town on the ocean has extensive facilities for swimming, boating, golf, tennis, picnicking, yachting, and both freshwater and deep-sea fishing. The Chamber of Commerce hosts an annual tennis tournament in June; and an annual festival in the spring, the **Delray Affair,** features displays of arts, crafts, flowers, and produce.

Morikami Park includes a one-half mile self-guided nature trail, picnic facilities, a Japanese Garden, and the **Museum of Japanese Culture,** which has permanent and changing exhibits including a tea ceremony room, and bonsai collection. Open Tuesday through Sunday, 10–5. Free.

The **Loxahatchee National Wildlife Refuge,** 13 miles northwest of the city, is a wetland area of nearly 150,000 acres where Everglade kites, cranes, herons, and alligators abound. There are two recreation areas, **Twenty-Mile Bend** (boat launch) at the north end and **Loxahatchee** at the south. Open daily, during daylight hours. Office open Monday–Friday, 8 am–4:30 pm. Closed holidays. Free.

Another recreation area, **Lake Ida County Park**, is at the northwest edge of town. Free.

West of Delray Beach a large area is devoted to flower farming. Acres of gladioli, chrysanthemums, and other varieties are grown commercially.

FORT LAUDERDALE is the county seat and largest city in Broward County. It is located on US 1 and the ocean, about 20 miles north of Miami.

For many years Fort Lauderdale has been a favorite spot for boaters. There are more than 160 miles of navigable waterways—rivers, inlets, canals—providing home port for more than 25,000 boats. Even if you don't own your own, you can charter one of almost any size by the hour, day, week, or season. Half a dozen harbors are available for visiting yachtsmen; probably the most famous is Bahia Mar, a large complex for entertainment which includes the largest marina in the state. **Hugh Taylor Birch State Recreation Area,** on the ocean at East Sunrise Boulevard and Florida A1A, is a beautiful 180-acre recreation area. A 3-mile train ride goes through the park.

Fort Lauderdale has an abundance of facilities for sightseeing—**Gray Line** offers bus tours, trains, boats. **The Voyager Sightseeing Train** makes four daily 1½ hour tours through the city, at 10, noon, 2, and 4. Fee $3.95, children 3–11 $1.75, under 3 free. Narrated Safari Tour Tuesday, Thursday, and Saturday, at noon. Phone (305) 467-3149 for schedules and fees.

The **Jungle Queen** takes passengers on three-hour sightseeing cruises into the Everglades. Daytime trips leave from Bahia Mar Yacht Basin at 10 and 2; $3.50, under 12 $1.75. Call (305) 462-5596 for reservations and ticket prices regarding the night cruises.

The **Paddlewheel Queen** takes passengers on a 2½-hour narrated cruise on the Intracoastal Waterway, leaving daily at 2 pm. Tickets $4.50, children 3–11 $3.50. There are also dinner-dancing cruises leaving nightly at 7:30. Tickets $20.50, children $17.50. Closed two weeks in September and Thanksgiving and Christmas.

Ocean World, a large complex at 1701 S.E. 17th Street Causeway, includes aquatic exhibits, marine shows, sky rides. Open daily, 10–6; ticket office open till 4:30 Admission $6.50, children 6–14 $3.50, under 6 free.

About 15 miles west of the city, via Florida 84 and 823, visitors are welcome at the **Flamingo Gardens.** A tram ride goes through a natural jungle hammock, and pink flamingos and East Indian peacocks wander freely about. Gift shop, petting zoo, and museums. Open daily, 9–5. Admission to gardens free; combination ticket for tram, petting zoo, and museums $3, 5–12 $1.50, under 5 free.

The **Gold Coast Railroad,** 3398 S.W. Ninth Avenue, takes passengers on a 5 mile 45-minute trip on a steam train. A museum car holds railroad mementos; also on the train is the private railroad car used by presidents Roosevelt, Truman, and Eisenhower. Open Sunday, 1–5. Closed most holidays. Admission $4, children 3–12 $2, under 3 free.

Fort Lauderdale is the home of the New York Yankees spring training camp, and **Florida Grapefruit League** games are played here in March and April. The **Fort Lauderdale Strikers** soccer team plays here from April through August.

There are many annual events; a partial list includes the **Las Olas Art Festival** in March, the **Hall of Fame International Diving Meet** in May, the **Miss Florida-USA Pageant** in August and the **New River Raft Race** in October. The **Annual Fort Lauderdale International Boat Show** and the **Broward County Fair** both take place in November. The **Winterfest** with a boat parade is held in December.

The Fort Lauderdale **Museum of the Arts** at 426 E. Las Olas Boulevard is open Tuesday–Friday, 10–4; Saturday, 10–4:30; Sunday, 12–5. Closed holidays. Admission $1, senior citizens 75¢, students with ID 50¢.

And to thousands of college students Fort Lauderdale is best known for the unofficial but nonetheless time-honored annual spring vacation invasion, when the beaches are carpeted end-to-end with sun-worshiping students seeking their first breath of fresh, warm air after a long, hard winter.

FORT PIERCE, county seat and population center in St. Lucie County, is located on US 1 and Florida 68, about 50 miles south of Melbourne, on the west side of the Indian River. It is a packing and shipping center for citrus and vegetables, and the shopping center for the growers and ranchers in the "backcountry" nearby. Across the river are public beaches.

All up and down the Indian River, a favorite pastime is

SOUTHEAST 79

fishing from the bridges, and cars crossing them have to thread their way carefully between lanes of men, women, and children dropping in their lines and flipping out the catch. The St. Lucie River provides freshwater fishing and many charter boats are available for deep-sea fishing.

Fort Pierce Inlet State Recreation Area, including Pepper Beach, is north of town on Florida A1A. There are 32 acres with a sand beach, picnic area, rest rooms, and a concession stand. Housed within the park, in a building on the ocean, is St. Lucie Visitor Center, where local history is illustrated in a 60-foot-long mural, and treasures taken from the sea are displayed. The center is open Wednesday–Sunday, 9–5. Admission 50¢, children under 12 free. Also part of the park is 958-acre Jack Island, located nearby off the east shore of the Indian River and reached only by a foot-bridge from a parking lot off Florida A1A. This park is a remarkable wildlife and plant sanctuary, made up of salt marsh, high marshlands, and small hammocks. Fishing around the island is excellent. More than a hundred varieties of birds have been spotted here.

St. Lucie County Historical Museum, at 414 Seaway Drive, has exhibits relating to local history.

Annual events in town include **"On the Green" Arts and Craft Show** in January, and the **St. Lucie County Fair,** in February.

Jai-alai games are performed from March through September at the **Fort Pierce Fronton.**

HALLANDALE, in Broward County, just off I-95, is a suburb north of Miami and south of Hollywood.

Horse races are held daily except Sunday in February, and April at **Gulfstream Park,** on US 1 and Hallandale Beach Boulevard. The Garden of Champions, where bronze plaques honor famous thoroughbreds, is a popular tourist attraction all year, daily 10–4.

The **Hollywood Greyhound Track** is also on US 1 in Hallandale. Dog races are held nightly except Sunday from December to April. Closed Christmas.

For three weeks in March, the Hallandale Chamber of Commerce sponsors the **Florida Derby Festival** leading up to the running of the Florida Derby at Gulfstream Park.

Bargain-hunters will enjoy **Discount Fashion Row,** a group of some 60 warehouse and "sample" ready-to-wear shops grouped along the railroad tracks at NE First and Second Avenues and Third Street.

HIALEAH, in Dade County, on US 27, is a suburb immediately northwest of Miami.

The **Hialeah Park** is world renowned. Thoroughbred horses race here in January, February, and the first week in March, daily except Sunday. On the final day of racing, which is in early March, the Flamingo Stakes adds $100,000 for the best three-year-old horses covering a distance of 1⅛ miles. This is considered the first stiff trial for Kentucky Derby contestants.

A tram tour shows visitors through the grounds. Besides the tracks, paddocks, and walking ring, there are exhibits of carriages and stagecoaches, a Shipwreck Aquarium, tropical gardens, and a flamingo colony. Park open daily, during racing season, 10:30–6; rest of year, 9:30–5. Tram runs in the summer ($2, under 12 $1). Closed one month preceding and following race meets. Every Saturday night throughout the year, late model stock cars race at the **Hialeah Speedway.**

HOLLYWOOD, in Broward County, is on US 1 and I-95, just south of Fort Lauderdale.

Golf and swimming facilities are outstanding in Hollywood, with 17 golf courses in the area and a 6-mile-long public beach with a 2-mile concrete "Broadwalk."

Each spring contenders for the Kentucky Derby compete at Hialeah Park.

The **Okalee Seminole Indian Village** is on US 441 in Hollywood. Here Indians in native dress make and sell dolls, baskets, beadwork, and clothing. Small zoo, alligator wrestling.

A **Seven Lively Arts Festival** is held in March. Art, music, drama, literature, photography, dance, and comedy are highlighted, each on a different night.

JUPITER, in Palm Beach County, is located on US 1 and Florida 706, about 15 miles north of Palm Beach.

Jupiter Lighthouse and Museum, built in 1860, is one of the oldest lighthouses on the Atlantic coast. Open Sundays, noon–2:30 pm. Closed Christmas and January 1. Free.

The historic museum **Dubois Home** is located on Jupiter Inlet across from the lighthouse. Open Sundays, 1–3:30 pm. Free guided tours.

On Jupiter Island, accessible only by boat, is the **Joseph Verner Reed Wilderness Sanctuary**, a 120-acre bird preserve maintained by the Audubon Society. There are several Indian shell mounds on the island. Open daily, free.

Five miles north of town is **Jonathan Dickinson State Park**, a very large park with complete facilities, including cabins, bike rentals, guided tours. A 1½-hour jungle boat cruise starts at 11 am and 1 pm every day except Monday and Tuesday. The cost of the tour is $6, children under 12, $3.

Also about five miles north of Jupiter, via US 1, is the **Hobe Sound National Wildlife Refuge.** The reguge has sea turtles nesting at the beach, nature trails, and a visitor center.

KEY BISCAYNE, in Dade County, is an island just southeast of Miami, connected to the mainland by the Rickenbacker Causeway (toll 25¢ round trip).

Crandon Park is a popular spot with Miami residents for ocean swimming. There is an extensive beach, along with bathhouse, cabanas, picnic grove, small amusement park, marina, golf, roller skating, and a miniature train ride.

Bill Baggs Cape Florida State Recreation Area is at the southern end of Key Biscayne, with facilities for picnicking, swimming, fishing, and an old lighthouse. Admission 25¢.

MIAMI is the county seat and principal city of Dade County. The Greater Miami Metropolitan Area is the most heavily populated part of the state.

Miami is located on the southeast coast of Florida, served by routes I-95, US 1, and Florida A1A from the north, US 41, the Tamiami Trail, from the west, and US 27 from the northwest and inland Florida. A good network of expressways takes the motorist through and around the city or quickly and conveniently into the downtown area.

To many northern visitors "Miami" means the glamour, fun, and sand of the Gold Coast, but the city of Miami has, in addition, a life of its own that pulses independently of the tourism which has helped it to grow to its present stature. It is an exciting, cosmopolitan, progressive, vigorous, and well-rounded major city. Its appearance is, for the most part, gleaming and modern, largely because it is a very young city. A number of its older residents still remember the tropical fishing village that Miami was well into the 1920s—a sleepy, muggy settlement of less than 30,000 inhabitants tucked between the Everglades and the ocean, with little to foretell its rapid transition into a cultural, industrial, and resort leader of the South.

Miami's residents work in every sort of occupation, and at the end of the day they're on vacation—back to the family swimming pool and/or pleasure boat, to golf courses that are open 365 days a year, to flower gardens that won't quit blooming. (While northerners are pampering little shoots in an effort to coax them to grow into respectably tall saplings, Miamians are digging out trees planted only a few years before whose spreading roots are threatening to crack the sidewalk or the bottom of the swimming pool.)

Miami is a major international city, outranked only by New York City as an entry and exit point for international travelers who come and go by air and sea. More than half a million foreign travelers come into Miami yearly. One-third of the area's residents are "Latinos," and Spanish is heard almost as frequently as English.

For the tourist, Miami has more attractions than almost any other city in the world. This fact, plus the miles of hotel accommodations in Miami and her sister city, Miami Beach, plus the unrivaled sea and sun and sand, make the Miami area the standard of resort luxury.

Besides the attractions listed below, all of those in the Southeast Florida section and the South Central Florida section are within easy driving distance from Miami. So if you're vacationing in or near Miami, don't neglect to consider driving south to the Everglades and Keys or north along the Atlantic coast.

The visitor has a wide range of choices of methods for getting acquainted with the area. The **Metro-Dade Department of Tourism**, at 234 W. Flagler Street, Phone (305) 579-4694, will furnish booklets and maps for guides on your own auto tour, or you may choose a **guided sightseeing tour** by American Sightseeing bus, phone (305) 871-2370 or by A-1 bus, phone (305) 573-0550; by cruise ship (Bayfront Park, Miamarina, phone 379-5119; or by helicopter (1050 MacArthur Causeway, phone 377-0934).

At the north end of the city is **Greynolds Park**, on West Dixie Highway north of N.E. 172nd Street and South of Miami Gardens Drive (two sections) at 17530 W. Dixie Highway. Facilities include barbecue grills, picnic tables, an observation tower, paddle boat rentals, and a golf course. Open daily, daylight hours.

Near Greynolds Park, at 16711 West Dixie Highway in North Miami Beach, is the **Cloisters of the Monastery of St. Bernard de Clairvaux,** a 12th-century structure with 6 acres of formal gardens, purchased by William Randolph Hearst in Segovia, Spain. It was disassembled, brought to Florida, and reassembled after Hearst's death. Open Monday–Saturday, 10–5; Sunday, noon–5. Closed New Year's Day, Easter and Christmas. Admission $3, senior citizens $2, children 6–12 75¢, under 6 free.

Bayfront Park is in downtown Miami, on Biscayne Boulevard, south of the MacArthur Causeway. Within the park are a library, a marina, auditorium, and the John F. Kennedy Memorial Torch of Friendship. The **Miamarina**, with its more than two hundred berths for pleasure craft, offers all sorts of dining and other facilities especially for the convenience of boaters. Park is open daily.

On Virginia Key, along Bear Cut and the Atlantic Ocean, on the north side of Rickenbacker Causeway, is **Virginia Beach Park.** Open daily, 6 am–sundown. Free.

SOUTHEAST

Coconut Grove Bayfront Park, on South Bayshore Drive, and adjacent **Dinner Key** recreation area also offer boating, picnicking, marina, and recreational facilities. Miami's city hall is also located here.

The Barnacle State Historic Site, in Coconut Grove, is situated in a 5-acre park on the bay. The home was that of pioneer settler Ralph Munroe, founder of Biscayne Bay Yacht Club and boat builder.

The **Japanese Garden,** on Watson Island on the MacArthur Causeway, was a gift donated to the city in 1961 by the late Tokyo industrialist Kiyoshi Ichimura. It includes a circular garden, a teahouse where visitors may take part in a traditional, leisurely Japanese tea ceremony, decorative bridges, an arbor, a lagoon, rock garden, pagoda, and Oriental statuary. Open daily, 9–6. Free.

A unique facility on Virginia Key is the **City of Miami Marine Stadium,** from which viewers may watch powerboat races and rowing and sailing regattas, The stadium seats also afford one a gorgeous view of sunsets over the skyline of Miami.

On the Miami side of the Rickenbacker Causeway is **Villa Vizcaya Museum and Gardens,** a Venetian-style palace built by International Harvester magnate James Deering to house priceless European and Oriental art treasures. It is now operated as a museum by the Dade County Park and Recreation Department. A 90-minute sound and light show has also been added, Saturday and Sunday at 8. Open daily, 9:30–5; ticket window open till 4:30. Closed Christmas. Admission $5, children 6–11 $3.50, under 6 free. Gardens only, $3.50. Member Florida Attractions Association.

The **Museum of Science and Space Transit Planetarium,** at 3280 South Miami Avenue, is a major museum, with coral reef exhibits, pre-Columbian art in the Plaza Maya gallery, beautifully mounted specimen fish, films, and space exhibits. A live "Animal Exploratorium" (Tuesday–Sunday, noon–4), and an observatory (Friday–Sunday) 7:30 pm–10 pm; Sunday also from 2–5) are also featured. Open Sunday–Thursday, 10–6; Friday and Saturday 10–10. $1.50, senior citizens and children under 12, $1. Closed Christmas. Admission charged ($3, senior citizens and under 12, $1.50) for planetarium shows; phone (305) 854-2222 for schedule.

In the same building is the **Historical Museum of Southern Florida,** featuring local historical exhibits on the early Indians, white settlers, archeological digs, the coming of the railroad, aviation, education, and ships and boats. An art deco theater is also featured. Open Monday–Saturday, 10–6; Sunday noon–6. Closed Christmas. $3; children, $2. Scheduled to move into the new Miami-Dade Cultural Center.

The new **Miami-Dade Cultural Center,** located on Flagler Street between 1st. and 2nd Avenues, phone (305) 372-7666

Vizcaya, an Italian-style mansion built by James Deering, is now the Dade County Art Museum.

has completed many of its offices. The Center is scheduled to house the Historical Museum of Southern Florida, the Miami-Dade Public Library System, and the Center for Fine Arts (scheduled to open January 1984).

The **Miami Wax Museum,** 13899 Biscayne Boulevard, displays dozens of life-size wax sculptures in more than 40 large dioramas illustrating events in history from the landing of Columbus to the first landing on the moon. Continuous self-guided recorded tours. Open Monday–Saturday, 9:30–9:30; Sunday, 10:30–9:30. Admission charged, phone (305) 945-3641 for rates. Member Florida Attractions Association.

Three major Miami attractions are the Miami Seaquarium, the Serpentarium, and the Parrot Jungle.

The **Seaquarium** is located on Virginia Key, just off the Rickenbacker Causeway. Under the Golden Aquadome—a Miami landmark whose design was created by the renowned and brilliant designer-engineer-ecology spokesman R. Buckminster Fuller—porpoises and sea lions perform for delighted audiences in expertly produced shows. Additional shows are presented daily at the movie set where the Flipper movies and TV series were filmed. The massive stadium surrounding a refrigerated pool houses performing killer whales. Shows are continuous, every ½ hour, from 10–4 every day. A monorail offers an aerial tour across and around the 50 acres of landscaped park grounds. Fish, turtles, and waterfowl can be seen on the grounds and in dozens of aquarium tanks. Sharks swim in the channels traversing the grounds. In addition to its value as a place of entertainment and education, the Seaquarium provides space and facilities for a great deal of serious marine research. Open daily, 9–6:30. Admission $8, children 6–12 $4, under 6 free. Member Florida Attractions Association.

The **Miami Serpentarium,** 12655 South Dixie Highway, is an outdoor laboratory of reptilian life. Tours are conducted throughout the day, through natural areas housing snakes, tortoises, lizards, and crocodiles. Lecturers explain the many uses of snake venom in scientific research, and demonstrations of "snake-milking," or venom extraction, are given during each tour. Open daily, 9–5. Admission $6, children 6–13 $2, under 6 free. Member Florida Attractions Association.

The **Parrot Jungle,** at 11000 S.W. 57th Avenue, features bird shows in a beautiful amphitheater; trained parrots and macaws ride bicycles, roller skate, work puzzles, and perform other amazing tricks. Dozens of varieties of colorful tropical birds fly free in a lush jungle setting. Open daily, 9:30–5. Phone (305) 666-7834 for rates. Member Florida Attractions Association.

Planet Ocean, at 3979 Rickenbacker Causeway, is just across the street from the Seaquarium. More than one hundred exhibits here tell the fascinating story of the ocean. Open daily, 10–6. Admission charged, phone (305) 361-5786 for rates.

Metrozoo, a cageless zoo south of the city, now covers about 200 acres of tropical gardens full of exotic animals. Monorail (fee), free flight aviary, restaurant and mini parks are also featured. Daily, 10–5:30, ticket office closes at 4. Admission $4.50; 2–12 $2, under 2 free.

South of Miami, 3 miles west of Goulds, is the **Monkey Jungle,** a rain forest where visitors watch the monkeys from inside "people cages." Also chimpanzee performance shows. Open daily, 9:30–5. Admission $5, senior citizens, $4, children 5–12 $2.50, under 5 free. Member Florida Attractions Association.

Miami Beach, the world's most luxurious resort strip.

Miami is unsurpassed in the number and variety of spectator sports events offered. The Baltimore Orioles have their spring training camp here, and **Florida Grapefruit League** exhibition games are played at the Miami Stadium, 2301 N.W. 10th Avenue. Greyhound races are held from late April through June and September and October at the **Flagler Dog Track.** There are also races at **Biscayne Dog Track** in Miami Shores. Jai-alai games from late December to mid-September nightly except Sunday at the **Miami Fronton,** N.W. 36th Street at 37th Avenue. Matinees Monday, Wednesday, and Saturday.

The Miami Dolphins and the University of Miami both play home football games in the Orange Bowl Stadium at 1400 N.W. Fourth Street, home of the annual **Orange Bowl Festival.** In addition to the New Year's Day championship football game, the four week festival includes the Orange Bowl Parade on New Year's Eve and the Junior Orange Bowl festivities in Coral Gables.

Other important powerboat and sailboat races, as well as fishing and golfing tournaments, are held in Miami throughout the year. Write to the Metro-Dade Department of Tourism, 234 W. Flagler Street, Miami 33130, for more information.

Symphony concerts are presented during most of the year by the Miami Beach Symphony. Opera, ballet, and theater performances are numerous, as are big-name shows in the various hotels, supper clubs, and auditoriums.

SOUTHEAST 83

MIAMI BEACH, in Dade County, on Florida A1A, is an island east of Miami and connected to it by several causeways.

"Sun and fun capital of the world," "convention capital of the world," "resort capital of the world,"—by any name, Miami Beach is synonymous with pleasure. The name immediately conjures up a vision of fashionable sportswear; glittering nightclubs; luxurious hotels on the beach, each with a stretch of white sand, plus outdoor and indoor swimming pools.

Aside from the fine hotels and superb convention facilities, most of the points of interest for the tourist are located in the surrounding towns and cities listed elsewhere in this section, but a few are close at hand. The **Bass Museum of Art,** 2100 Collins Avenue, has a fine collection of paintings. Open Tuesday–Saturday, 10–5; Sunday, 1–5. Closed major holidays. Phone (305) 673-7533 for rates. The **Miami Beach Garden and Conservatory,** 2000 Convention Center Drive, has special garden displays at Easter and Christmas, a conservatory, and a craft shop. Open daily, 10–3:30. Free. The **Lincoln Road Mall** is a landscaped shopping area.

Various boat cruises take visitors on sightseeing trips which include: **Haulover Dinner Cruise** 947-6105, **Nikko Gold Coast Cruises** 945-5461, and **Island Queen** 379-5119.

Symphony and popular music concerts, Broadway shows, and other events are held during most of the year at the **Miami Beach Theater of the Performing Arts.**

Part of the heritage of Miami Beach is the **Art Deco District,** a one-square-mile area now being restored, devoted to the resort architecture of the 1920s, 1930s and 1940s. Walking and group tours are available through the Miami Design Preservation League office at 1300 Ocean Drive.

Annual events in the city include the **Miami International Boat Show** and the **Miami Beach Festival of the Arts,** both held in February. Also the **Art Deco Weekend** is held in mid-January and the **South Florida Auto Show** takes place in November.

PALM BEACH is on a 14-mile-long island between Lake Worth and the Atlantic Ocean on Florida A1A about 70 miles north of Miami. It is the home of the wealthiest, most exclusive, and socially prominent people on Florida's Atlantic coast.

Whitehall, the **Henry Morrison Flagler Museum,** on Whitehall Way, off Coconut Row, is the former home of the man who founded Palm Beach. It was built in 1901, and Henry Flagler and his wife lived there until his death in 1913 and hers in 1917. For a time it was converted to a luxury resort hotel, and most of the art treasures were removed. Today many of them have been replaced. This home, which cost four million dollars to build and furnish, was one of the truly magnificent private residences of the world. Open Tuesday–Saturday, 10–5; Sunday, noon–5. Closed New Year's Day, Christmas. Admission $3, children 6–12 $1, under 6 free. On the grounds is Mr. Flagler's private railroad car, the **Rambler,** which is open free.

In Palm Beach are a number of formal gardens worth seeing. One of the country's great resorts, **The Breakers,** is on Florida A1A overlooking the ocean.

POMPANO BEACH, in Broward County, is on US 1 between Miami and Palm Beach. It is a tourist center with miles of motels.

It is also a major sports center, with the Texas Rangers holding spring training here. The **Pompano Park Harness**

Henry Flagler, principal developer of Florida's east coast, built this impressive home in Palm Beach.

Raceway is the number one harness track in Florida, with racing nightly except Sunday in winter and quarter horse racing in summer. The Chamber of Commerce sponsors year-round fishing tournaments. There are five golf courses in the area.

From November to May visitors may see the **Goodyear Blimp.** The blimp leaves from Pompano Air Park.

Each year on the Sunday before Christmas the Coast Guard Auxiliary and the Chamber of Commerce sponsor a **Christmas Boat Parade,** in mid-December, with more than a hundred beautifully decorated boats carrying carolers and other musicians along the Intracoastal Waterway. The Chamber also sponsors an outdoor art show in March, and a **Fishing Rodeo** in May.

SEBASTIAN, in Indian River County, is on US 1, 10 miles north of Vero Beach. Nearby is the **Pelican Island National Wildlife Refuge.** In February is the gourmet **Grant Seafood Festival.**

On Florida A1A, one mile below the Sebastian Inlet Bridge, is the **Sebastian Inlet State Recreation Area,** within which is **McLarty Museum.** The museum tells the interesting story of treasure diving, and the park is a fine recreational center.

STUART is the county seat and principal center of Martin County, on US 1 about 20 miles south of Fort Pierce. The numerous waterways in the area provide excellent fishing and boating.

There are two interesting museums on Hutchinson Island, across the St. Lucie and Indian rivers. The **House of Refuge** displays nautical artifacts, shipwreck relics, and live turtles. Open Tuesday–Sunday, 1–5. Closed Christmas. Admission 50¢, children 6–13 25¢, under 6 free. **Elliott Museum** has an art gallery, country store, gracious living wing. Open daily, 1–5. Admission $1, children 6–13 50¢, under 6 free.

VERO BEACH, county seat and principal center of Indian River County, is on US 1 about 15 miles north of Fort Pierce. it is an important center for shipping the famous Indian River citrus fruit. A landmark in town is the **Driftwood Inn.**

Recreation facilities are available at Pocahontas Park, at 14th Avenue and 21st Street.

Vero Beach is the winter home of the Los Angeles Dodgers and summer training camp for the NFL New Orleans Saints.

WEST PALM BEACH is the county seat and largest city in Palm Beach County. It is on I-95, about 70 miles north of Miami, due east of Lake Okeechobee. It is a major, bustling resort city, larger and less exclusive than its sister city, Palm Beach.

Seventeen miles west of the city on US 98 and US 44, or via exits 8 and 9 from the Florida Turnpike, is **Lion Country Safari,** a wildlife preserve where lions, zebras, antelopes, elephants, giraffes, ostriches, and other wildlife imported from Africa roam free as cars drive through. Open daily, 9:30–4:30. Admission includes rides and tours. Phone (305) 793-1084 for rates. Member Florida Attractions Association.

Norton Gallery and School of Art, 1451 South Olive Avenue, has exhibits of jade, oriental art, sculpture, and paintings. Open Tuesday–Saturday, 10–5; Sunday, 1–5. Closed major holidays. Donation.

The **Science Museum and Planetarium,** at 1141 West Lakewood Road, has land, sea, and space exhibits, plane-

The House of Refuge, in Stuart.

tarium shows. Open Tuesday–Saturday, 10–5; Sunday and Monday, 1–5; Friday evenings, 6:30–10:30. Closed holidays. Museum admission $2, senior citizens and children $1. Planetarium shows at 3, Friday at 7, $1.

There are many facilities for swimming golf, and boating in West Palm Beach. The Atlanta Braves and Montreal Expos do their spring training and play in **Florida Grapefruit League** games here. There is auto and stock car racing at the **Palm Beach Fairgrounds Speedway.** Greyhound races are held from November to April, at the **Palm Beach Kennel Club.** There are jai-alai games at the **West Palm Beach Fronton** from November to March, and polo games at **Gulfstream Polo Fields** from January to April. The **South Florida Fair and Exposition** is held at the fairgrounds each January.

(Details on admission prices and hours have been included as a service to the reader and as a guide in planning activities. However, changes are inevitable in some cases, and the publisher cannot be responsible for any variations from the listed information.)

Evening silhouettes accent the beauty and special quality of Florida's excellent state parks.

STATE PARKS

FLORIDA'S EXCELLENT SYSTEM OF STATE PARKS INCUDES HISTORICAL MEMORIALS TO SUCH DIVERSE EVENTS AS THE FIRST CONSTITUTIONAL CONVENTION AND THE INVENTION OF THE FIRST ICE-MAKING MACHINE; NATURE PRESERVES WITH OCEANFRONT CAMPING, TROPICAL HARDWOOD HAMMOCKS, OR DEEP, SPARKLING SPRINGS; GORGEOUS BOTANICAL DISPLAYS. BUT THEY ARE ALL PLACES OF BEAUTY DESIGNED FOR RECREATION.

A number, but not all, of the state parks charge a nominal admission fee. For $25, plus tax, you may purchase a Sunshine Ticket sticker, good for one calendar year, which will admit your car and all occupants to all state parks.

Overnight camping areas are provided at about half the parks. Tables and grills are provided, as well as rest rooms with hot and cold water, showers, toilets, lavatories, and sometimes laundry facilities. Camping fees vary from $6 to $8 per night depending on park location. An additional $2 per night is charged for electricity, if used. Campsites are available on a first-come, first-served basis, but 50 percent of the campsites in each park may be reserved in advance.

Stays are limited to two weeks. Checkout time is 2 pm. A person 18 years of age or older must be present in each group. Campsite reservations may be made by telephone year-round for any of 22 parks, and during summer months only at two other parks.

An annual family camping permit is available to Florida residents only, which can be obtained from the Florida Department of Natural Resources, Tallahassee, or at any state park with camping facilities, for $150 plus tax. An additional fee of $2 per night is required for the use of electricity.

There is no additional charge at any park for picnicking, except for after-hours use or for large outings. Swimming and fishing are free. A state fishing license is required for freshwater fishing in Florida.

No pets are permitted in the campgrounds or on the beaches; they may be taken into the picnic areas only if they are leashed and well behaved.

For further information about state parks, write to the Florida Department of Natural Resources, Division of Recreation and Parks, Bureau of Education and Information, Room 613, 3900 Commonwealth Blvd., Tallahassee 32303.

PARK	NEAREST CITY	SECTION
Anastasia	St. Augustine	Northeast
Bahia Honda	Marathon	South Central
The Barnacle	Coconut Grove	Southeast
Basin Bayou	Niceville	Northwest
Big Lagoon	Pensacola	Northwest
Bill Baggs Cape Florida	Key Biscayne	Southeast
Blackwater River	Milton	Northwest
Blue Spring-Hontoon Island	De Land	Northeast
Bulow Plantation	Bunnell	Northeast
Caladesi Island	Dunedin	Southwest
Cedar Key	Cedar Key	North Central
Chekika	Homestead	South Central
Collier-Seminole	Everglades City	South Central
Constitution Convention	Port St. Joe	Northwest
Crystal River	Crystal River	North Central
Dade Battlefield	Bushnell	Central
Dead Lakes	Wewahitchka	Northwest
Devil's Millhopper	Gainesville	North Central
Dr. Julian Bruce	Apalachicola	North Central
Eden State Garden	Grayton Beach	Northwest
Everglades Reclamation	Lake Harbor	South Central
Falling Waters	Chipley	Northwest
Faver-Dykes	St. Augustine	Northeast
Flagler Beach	Flagler Beach	Northeast
Florida Caverns	Marianna	Northwest
Forest Capital	Perry	North Central
Fort Clinch	Fernandina Beach	Northeast
Fort Cooper	Inverness	Central
Fort Gadsden	Apalachicola	North Central
Fort Pierce Inlet	Fort Pierce	Southeast
Fred Gannon	Niceville	Northwest
Gamble Plantation	Bradenton	Southwest
Grayton Beach	Grayton Beach	Northwest
Highlands Hammock	Sebring	Central
Hillsborough River	Zephyrhills	North Central
Hugh Taylor Birch	Fort Lauderdale	Southeast
Ichetucknee Springs	Lake City	North Central
John Gorrie	Apalachicola	North Central
John Pennekamp	Key Largo	South Central
Jonathan Dickinson	Jupiter	Southeast
Kingsley Plantation	Jacksonville	Northeast

PARK	NEAREST CITY	SECTION
Koreshan	Estero	Southwest
Lake Griffin	Leesburg	Central
Lake Jackson Mounds	Tallahassee	North Central
Lake Kissimmee	Lakes Wales	Central
Lake Louisa	Clermont	Central
Lake Manatee	Bradenton	Southwest
Lake Talquin	Tallahassee	North Central
Lignumvitae Key	Islamorada	South Central
Little Talbot Island	Jacksonville	Northeast
Lloyd Beach	Dania	Southeast
Long Key	Islamorada	South Central
Maclay State Garden	Tallahassee	North Central
Madira Bickel Mound	Terre Ceia	Southwest
Manatee Springs	Chiefland	North Central
Marjorie K. Rawlings	Cross Creek	North Central
Mike Roess Gold Head	Keystone Heights	Northeast
Myakka River	Sarasota	Southwest
Natural Bridge	Woodville	North Central
New Smyrna	New Smyrna Beach	Northeast
Ochlockonee River	Sopchoppy	North Central
O'Leno	Lake Butler	North Central
Olustee Battlefield	Olustee	North Central
Oscar Scherer	Osprey	Southwest
Pahokee	Pahokee	South Central
Payne's Prairie Preserve	Micanopy	North Central
Ponce de Leon	De Funiak Springs	Northwest
Ravine State Garden	Palatka	Northeast
St. Andrews	Panama City	Northwest
San Marcos de Apalache	St. Marks	North Central
Sebastian Inlet	Sebastian	Southeast
Stephen Foster	White Springs	North Central
Suwannee River	Live Oak	North Central
T. H. Stone Memorial	Port St. Joe	Northwest
Three Rivers	Sneads	Northwest
Tomoka	Ormond Beach	Northeast
Torreya	Bristol	North Central
Washington Oaks	Marineland	Northeast
Wekiwa Springs	Apopka	Central
Wiggins Pass	Bonita Springs	Southwest
Ybor City	Tampa	Southwest
Yulee Sugar Mill	Homosassa	North Central

STATE PARKS 87

NORTHWEST

BIG LAGOON State Recreation Area is on Florida 292, approximately 10 miles southwest of Pensacola. It consists of 698 acres bounded by Big Lagoon. Facilities: swimming, fishing, picnicking, boating, and nature study.

BASIN BAYOU State Recreation Area is on Florida 20, 18 miles east of Niceville. This is a 287-acre park fronting on Basin Bayou and the Choctawhatchee Bay. Facilities: camping, picnicking, swimming, fishing.

BLACKWATER RIVER State Park is on US 90, 15 miles northeast of Milton. It is a 360-acre recreational park on the Blackwater River, in Blackwater River State Forest. The terrain is hilly, and there are several sandy-bottomed streams. A nature trail follows the route used by General Andrew Jackson when he was on his way to occupy Pensacola. Facilities: camping, picnicking, swimming, fishing, nature trails.

CONSTITUTION CONVENTION State Museum is in a 13-acre park on US 98 in Port St. Joe. Dioramas and exhibits of Florida's first state constitution convention, as well as of the vanished city of St. Joseph, are featured. The first of Florida's five constitutions was written here in 1838–39. Facilities: museum, guided tours.

DEAD LAKES State Recreation Area, a 41-acre park, is on Florida 71 north of Wewahitchka. Named for countless dead cypress, oak, and pine trees once drowned by a natural overflow of the Chipola River, the Dead Lakes area is popular for catching bass, bream, and perch. Facilities: camping, picnicking, boating, fishing, nature trails.

EDEN STATE ORNAMENTAL GARDEN, 11.6 acres of landscaped grounds surrounding a restored mansion, is 1 mile off US 98 at Point Washington on Choctawhatchee Bay, 5 miles from Grayton Beach. Admission to house: adults 50¢, children under 6 free. Facilities: picnicking.

FALLING WATERS State Recreation Area is near Chipley, on Florida 77A. This 155-acre park is developed around a waterfall that surges over a multicolored rocky hill into a 100-foot sink. There are limestone caverns and caves. Facilities: camping, picnicking, swimming, nature trails.

FLORIDA CAVERNS State Park is in Marianna, on Florida 167. It is a park of 1,783 acres surrounding a limestone cavern with dramatic stalactites and stalagmites. There is a network of colorful limestone caves through which guided underground tours are conducted (adults $1.50, children 6–12 75¢). A beautiful white sandy beach encircles Blue Hole Springs, where swimmers enjoy 70-degree water. Facilities: camping, picnicking, swimming, fishing, boating, skin diving, scuba diving, nature trails, snacks, gift shop.

FRED GANNON ROCKY BAYOU State Recreation Area is 3 miles east of Niceville, on Florida 20. This 632-acre park is located within the Eglin Air Force Reservation. Facilities: camping, picnicking, swimming, fishing, boating, nature trails.

GRAYTON BEACH State Recreation Area, on Florida 30A at Grayton Beach, has 356 acres of pine woodlands, freshwater lakes, sand dunes, and a mile of white beach on the Gulf of Mexico. Facilities: camping, picnicking, swimming, fishing, boating, skin diving, scuba diving, snacks, gift shop.

PONCE DE LEON State Recreation Area is a 370-acre park located 10 miles east of De Funiak Springs at the intersection of US 90 and Florida 181A. Facilities: picnicking, swimming, fishing.

ST. ANDREWS State Recreation Area is 3 miles west of Panama City Beach, on Florida 392. On a 1,063 acre point of land between St. Andrews Bay and the Gulf of Mexico, the park has dunes and wide beaches. A restored "Cracker" turpentine still is on display. Facilities: camping, picnicking, swimming, boating, skin diving, scuba diving, boat rentals, bicycle rentals, nature trails, museum, snacks, gift shop.

T. H. STONE MEMORIAL—ST. JOSEPH PENINSULA State Park is on Florida 30E, near Port St. Joe. Within its 2,516 acres is a 20-mile beach on St. Josephs Peninsula, with the Gulf of Mexico on one side and St. Josephs Bay on the other. Facilities: camping, picnicking, swimming, fishing, boating, skin diving, scuba diving, nature trails, bicycle rentals, snacks, gift shop, family cottages

THREE RIVERS State Recreation Area is an 834-acre park on US 90, 1 mile north of Sneads, situated on a lake near a dam in an evergreen forest. Facilities: camping, picnicking, swimming, fishing, boating, nature trails, snacks.

NORTH CENTRAL

ALFRED B. MACLAY STATE ORNAMENTAL GARDEN is on US 319, 5 miles north of Tallahassee. A masterpiece of floral architecture, the estate covers 308 acres. The Lake Hall recreation area, a nature trail, and surrounding woodlands are open year-round. The gardens are open to the public only during the blooming season, January through April. Admission $1.50, students and children 75¢. Camellias, gardenias, and azaleas are the main flowers. Facilities: picnicking, swimming, fishing, boating, Maclay House museum, snacks.

CEDAR KEY State Museum is on Florida 24 at Cedar Key. The St. Clair Whitman Museum, on 109 acres, houses exhibits and dioramas of this once busy port city, as well as Mr. Whitman's large and interesting shell collection. Open daily, 9–noon and 1–5. Admission 50¢.

CRYSTAL RIVER State Archaeological Site is a 14-acre park northwest of Crystal River on US 19/98. It is one of the most important pre-Columbian sites in Florida. It was an Indian ceremonial center for almost 1,600 years. More than 450 burials have been found here since 1903. Some of the grave goods indicate this tribe traded with Indians who lived north of the Ohio River, hundreds of miles away.

The museum building permits visitors to view mounds through plate glass windows. Trails lead from the museum through the mound complex. Open daily, 9–5. Admission 50¢.

DEVIL'S MILLHOPPER State Geological Site is just north of Gainesville on State Road 232. The 118-foot-deep, 500-foot-wide cavity here is the largest naturally drained sinkhole in Florida. Exhibits in a museum explain the geological and natural history of the area; also living displays. Trails lead into the sinkhole from an observation boardwalk. Facilities: museum, nature trails.

DR. JULIAN BRUCE ST. GEORGE ISLAND State Park, east of Apalachicola near Eastpoint, is on 1,883 acres. The island was inhabited by man only in this century. It comprises miles of undeveloped beaches, dunes, forest, and marshland. Facilities: picnicking, swimming, fishing, hiking, backpacking, skin diving, scuba diving.

FOREST CAPITAL State Museum is on a 14-acre tract south of Perry on US 98/27A, part of the recreational and educational complex that makes up the Forest Capital Center. Facilities: picnicking.

FORT GADSDEN State Historic Site is on Florida 65, northeast of Apalachicola. The 78-acre park is on the site of a British fort that was occupied by Indians and runaway slaves and destroyed by American forces in 1816. Of the 300 men, women, and children in the fort at the time of attack, only about 30 survived. In 1818 Andrew Jackson directed Lt. James Gadsden of the Engineer Corps to rebuild a fort there as a provisions base. This garrison was maintained, despite Spanish protests, until Florida was ceded to the United States. A plaque commemorates an Indian maiden, Milly Francis. Facilities: picnicking, fishing, boating, nature trails.

HILLSBOROUGH RIVER State Park is 6 miles southwest of Zephyrhills on US 301. This is a large vacation park near the Tampa-St. Petersburg area—2,964 acres in an unusually beautiful forest. Nature trails are reached by a "swinging bridge" that spans the spring-fed river that flows through the park. Many varieties of bird and plant life. In the park is **FORT FOSTER** State Historic Site, a replica of the original fort, open on weekends and holidays for a living history presentation by park rangers costumed in authentic uniforms of soldiers stationed at the fort during the Second Seminole War. Facilities: camping, picnicking, swimming, fishing, boating, boat rentals, bicycle rentals, canoe rentals, miniature golf, nature trails, snacks, gift shop, family cottages.

ICHETUCKNEE SPRINGS State Park is a scenic woodland park of 2,241 acres along the Ichetucknee River, a 3-mile spring-fed run, located off Florida 137 west of Fort White and southwest of Lake City. Facilities: picnicking, swimming, tubing, skin diving, scuba diving.

JOHN GORRIE State Musuem is on a one-acre lot in Apalachicola, on US 319/98. It honors the inventor of the first ice-making machine, a replica of which is on display. Dr. Gorrie settled in Apalachicola in 1833. As he cared for patients suffering from malaria, he felt that if he could lower the room temperature he might control their fevers. He built a cold-air machine that was the forerunner of the compression refrigerator, and by 1844 mechanical refrigeration was cooling two rooms set aside in his home for hospital purposes. He found that the pipes of the machine were clogged with ice. By 1845, Dr. Gorrie was producing ice in blocks. He patented the machine in 1851 but could not raise any funds to produce it commercially and died in 1855 without achieving recognition for his efforts. Displays also depict scenes of local history. Open daily, 8–5. Admission.

LAKE JACKSON MOUNDS State Archaeological Site, a park of 11 acres on US 27, is 4 miles northwest of Tallahassee. Hernando de Soto and his men spent the winter of 1539–40 here, and probably held the first Christmas service in the United States. The site is also important archeologically, as excavations have uncovered a type of structure never before found in Florida. There are several temple mounds here that were once surrounded by the Indian village, and evidence that people inhabited the area as early as 1300 years before Christ. Facilities: picnicking, nature trails.

LAKE TALQUIN State Recreation Area is located 20 miles west of Tallahassee off Florida 20. Facilities: picnicking, fishing, boating.

MANATEE SPRINGS State Park is on Florida 320, 6 miles west of Chiefland. There are 2,074 acres surrounding one of the most beautiful springs in the country, which pours out 116 million gallons per day into the Suwannee River. Facilities: camping, picnicking, swimming, fishing, skin diving, scuba diving, boating, boat rentals, canoe rentals, bicycle rentals, nature trails, snacks.

MARJORIE K. RAWLINGS State Historic Site is on US 325 in Cross Creek. The home of the author of *Cross Creek* and *The Yearling* has been preserved as a museum, and there is a small park nearby. Open daily, 9–5. Admission 50¢. Facilities: picnicking, boating.

NATURAL BRIDGE BATTLEFIELD State Historic Site is on US 319, 6 miles east of Woodville. In 1865, the battle fought here saved Tallahassee from capture by Federal forces, making it the only Southern capital east of the Mississippi that did not fall into Union hands. Cadets from the West Florida Seminary (now Florida State University) were among those who fought, earning one of the three Confederate battle streamers awarded to schools during the war. Facilities: picnicking, fishing.

OCHLOCKONEE RIVER State Park is on US 319, 3 miles south of Sopchoppy. Its 392 acres are bounded by the Sopchoppy and Ochlockonee rivers. It is a heavily wooded area, honeycombed with small ponds. Facilities: camping, fishing, picnicking, swimming, boating, nature trails, snacks.

O'LENO State Park is a 5,898-acre recreational area on US 41, 20 miles southwest of Lake Butler. A graceful suspension bridge spans the beautiful Santa Fe River, which disappears underground in the park, then reappears several miles to the west. Facilities: camping, picnicking, swimming, fishing, boating, nature trails, group camping cabins and mess hall.

OLUSTEE BATTLEFIELD State Historic Site is a 270-acre park on US 90, 2 miles east of Olustee. The major engagement of

STATE PARKS 89

the Civil War in Florida was fought February 20, 1865, on the Battlefield of Olustee, between 5,000 Confederate soldiers and 5,500 Federals. Museum.

PAYNE'S PRAIRIE State Preserve is 8 miles south of Gainesville on US 441, in Micanopy. This 18,000-acre preserve has significant natural and historical value. An observation tower and a Visitor Center are on the site. Facilities: picnicking, fishing, swimming.

SAN MARCOS DE APALACHE State Historic Site is a 7-acre park in St. Marks, on Florida 363, where a Spanish fort was built more than three hundred years ago. It was held at various times by Spanish, English, United States, and Confederate forces. Andrew Jackson's capture of the fort, in 1818, was instrumental in the United States' acquisition of Florida the following year. Facilities: museum, nature trails.

STEPHEN FOSTER State Folk Culture Center, at White Springs, commemorates the composer and promotes Florida's folk culture through annual programs. There is a museum on the grounds, and Foster's songs are played at a carillon tower. Facilities: boat tours, picnicking.

SUWANNEE RIVER State Park is an 1,831-acre tract on US 90, 14 miles northwest of Live Oak. Towering moss-hung oaks and cypresses line the banks of the river that Stephen Foster made famous. An overlook gives a view of the confluence of the Withlacoochee with the Suwannee. Confederate earthworks can be seen in the park. Facilities: camping, picnicking, swimming, fishing, boating, nature trails, snacks.

TORREYA State Park is on Florida 12 between Bristol and Greensboro, a 1,063-acre recreational and botanical park overlooking the Apalachicola River. The park is named for a tree that grows only in a 20-mile radius of the park. An antebellum plantation mansion, Gregory House, is open daily, guided tours available. Park is open 8 am—sunset. Facilities: camping, picnicking, fishing, nature trails.

YULEE SUGAR MILL RUINS State Historic Site is a 6-acre park on Florida 480 in Homosassa. Standing on what once was part of a 5,100-acre plantation belonging to David Levy Yulee (1810–1886), Florida's first U.S. Senator, the ruins of the Yulee sugar mill, constructed in 1851, are all that remain of this early Florida promoter's enterprises in this part of the state. Facilities: picnicking.

NORTHEAST

ANASTASIA State Recreation Area covers 1,035 acres on Florida A1A, just across the Matanzas River from St. Augustine on Anastasia Island.

Within the park are the coquina veins from which the Spaniards quarried rock in the 17th century for the construction of Castillo de San Marcos. Facilities: camping, picnicking, swimming, fishing, boating, skin diving, scuba diving, nature trails, snacks, gift shop.

BLUE SPRING and **HONTOON ISLAND** State Parks are next to each other, and are administered as a unit. **Blue Spring** is

Alfred B. Maclay State Ornamental Gardens, Tallahassee.

a 945-acre area located off I-4 and US 17/92, about 6 miles south of De Land, and contains one of the largest springs in the state of Florida. A group of manatees migrate to Blue Spring each winter. Facilities: camping, picnicking, swimming, fishing, skin diving, scuba diving, boating, boat rentals, snacks, nature trails.

Hontoon Island is a 1,650-acre park located in the St. John's River, off Florida 44, 6 miles west of De Land. Accessible only by boat. There is an observation tower with a view of 20 miles in every direction. The island is a bald eagle sanctuary, and contains a cypress swamp, a large open savannah, and hammocks of pine, oak, and palm trees. An Indian ceremonial mound was probably built by the Timucua Indians, earliest known residents of the island. A totem pole found near the park is the only one yet discovered in the Southeast. No vehicles. Free ferry. Facilities: camping, picnicking, fishing, boating, boat rentals, bicycle rentals, family cottages, nature trails, snacks.

BULOW PLANTATION RUINS State Historic Site is a 109-acre memorial park on Florida S-5A, southeast of Bunnell. During the early 19th century, Bulow Plantation covered 6,000 acres. In December 1835, with the outbreak of the Seminole War, militia were quartered at the mansion, Bulow Ville. When the soldiers retreated to St. Augustine the Indians laid waste to the entire area, including the manor.

On the grounds are the ruins of a coquina sugar mill, several well-preserved wells, a unique springhouse, and the crumbling foundation of the mansion. Facilities: picnicking, fishing, museum, nature trails, snacks.

FAVER-DYKES State Park is east of US 1, 15 miles south of St. Augustine. There are 752 acres here of beautiful woodlands and marsh overlooking the Matanzas River and Pellicer Creek.

This area was at one time part of the vast Hernandez Spanish Land Grant holdings. Facilities: camping, picnicking, fishing, boating, nature trails.

FLAGLER BEACH State Recreation Area is a 145-acre park on Florida A1A at Flagler Beach. This is believed to be the area in which French Huguenot Jean Ribault landed his flagship in 1565. Facilities: camping, picnicking, swimming, fishing, skin diving, scuba diving, boating.

FORT CLINCH State Park is on Florida A1A at Fernandina Beach. Fort Clinch was one of a chain of masonry forts on the Atlantic coast. It was built by the United States on the northern tip of Amelia Island, overlooking the entrance to Cumberland Sound. Construction began in 1847, with its primary purpose being to guard passages through Cumberland Sound into the deepwater harbor of Fernandina.

Construction was incomplete when the Confederates seized it in 1861. It was evacuated in 1862 when a combined Federal naval and army attack threatened. Federal forces possessed Amelia Island during the remainder of the Civil War.

It was again strengthened and used during the Spanish-American War, and found limited use during World War II as a communications and security post. Fort Clinch was acquired by the state in 1936 for development as a state park. Museum closed for renovation. Facilities: camping, picnicking, swimming, fishing, boating, skin diving, scuba diving, guided tours, nature trails, snacks.

KINGSLEY PLANTATION State Historic Site, 14 acres on Fort George Island, Jacksonville, on Florida A1A, is believed to be the oldest plantation house in Florida. It has been restored as a house museum with exhibits and furnishings that illustrate the history of the area. The first plantation was established here in 1763, but the present structure was built in 1813 by Zephaniah Kingsley. Open daily, 9–11, 1–4. Admission 50¢, under 6 free with adult. Facilities: picnicking.

LITTLE TALBOT ISLAND State Park is a 2,500-acre recreational park on Florida A1A in Jacksonville. A wide, smooth beach borders the ocean side of the island, and high white sand dunes are a contrast to the thick forest in the northern section of the park. Facilities: camping, picnicking, swimming, fishing, boating, skin diving, scuba diving, snacks.

MIKE ROESS GOLD HEAD BRANCH State Park, on Florida 21, about 6 miles northeast of Keystone Heights, was one of the state's first parks, developed on 1,481 acres donated by the late Mike Roess. Featured are an old mill site, lovely lakes, and a dramatic ravine. Facilities: camping, picnicking, swimming, fishing, skin diving, scuba diving, boating, boat rentals, bicycle rentals, canoe rentals, nature trails, snacks, cottages.

NEW SMYRNA SUGAR MILL RUINS State Historic Site, 17 acres on US 1 and Florida 44 at New Smyrna Beach. Arched doors and window openings in thick coquina walls are all that remain of a sugar mill that represents the expansion of the plantation economy in Florida before the Seminole Wars. The plantations in the area of New Smyrna were destroyed in late 1835, or during January of 1836, in the Indian hostilities, and it is probable that the sugar mill suffered the same fate. The ruins and general layout are similar to those at the Bulow Plantation Ruins, and the mill is known to have been under construction at the time of a visit of John James Audubon in 1831. Facilities: nature trails.

RAVINE STATE ORNAMENTAL GARDEN, Twigg Street, Palatka. These grounds are alive with color at the time of the annual Azalea Festival in the spring, when 100,000 magnificent azaleas are in bloom. There are also more than 300,000 other ornamental plants. Near the entrance is the Court of States, with the Civic Center at one end and an obelisk at the other. A drive runs along three ravines, and there are more than 6 miles of trails. Facilities: picnicking, nature trails.

TOMOKA State Park consists of 915 acres on North Beach Street, Ormond Beach, an area at the confluence of the Halifax and Tomoka rivers where the Timucuan village of Nocoroco once stood. Later the area was part of a vast plantation owned in the late 1760s by Richard Oswald, a British subject who later met with Benjamin Franklin, John Jay, and John Adams to draft the treaty of peace which ended the Revolutionary War and granted the United States her independence. There is a statue of the legendary chief Tomokie drinking from a sacred cup—symbolizing the Indian belief that the surrounding waters possessed curative powers. Facilities: camping, picnicking, fishing, boating, canoe rentals, guided tours, museum, nature trails, snacks, gift shop.

WASHINGTON OAKS STATE ORNAMENTAL GARDEN, 341 acres, on Florida A1A, 3 miles south of Marineland. The plantation was named for a relative of the first president of the United States, who inherited it from General Hernandez, a hero of the Seminole War. In 1936 it was purchased by Owen D. Young, chairman of the board of General Electric Corporation and a member of President Hoover's cabinet, and Mrs. Young. A visitor's center contains historical exhibits, and there is a nature museum. Other facilities: fishing, picnicking, nature trails.

CENTRAL

DADE BATTLEFIELD State Historic Site consists of 80 acres on US 301, Bushnell. Here in 1835 Maj. Francis L. Dade and a company of more than one hundred men were ambushed by a band of Seminoles. Almost all were killed, and the battle touched off the fiercest and costliest Indian war ever waged by the United States—the Second Seminole War. Facilities: picnicking, museum, nature trails, tennis, playground.

FORT COOPER State Park is located in Inverness on Old Floral City Road. In the park is the site of 1836 Fort Cooper. Facilities: picnicking, swimming, fishing, nature trails, tours.

HIGHLANDS HAMMOCK State Park is a 3,800-acre preserve, 6 miles west of Sebring, off US 27. Convenient boardwalks through the hammock provide excellent observation points from which to watch the wildlife that abounds amid the tropical hardwood trees, shrubs, orchids, and air plants. Conducted wildlife tours are taken on a "trackless train." Facilities: camping, picnicking, fishing, bicycle rentals, museum, nature trails, snacks.

LAKE GRIFFIN State Recreation Area, 423 acres on US 27/441 3 miles north of Leesburg, includes one of the largest lakes in Central Florida. Facilities: camping, picnicking, fishing, boating, canoe rentals, nature trails.

LAKE KISSIMMEE State Park is 15 miles east of Lake Wales on Camp Mack Road. Living history interpretations of a 19th century cow camp are presented here on Saturday and Sunday. Facilities: camping, picnicking, fishing, boating, nature trails.

LAKE LOUISA State Park is 7 miles southwest of Clermont on Lake Nellie Road. Facilities: picnicking, swimming, fishing.

WEKIWA SPRINGS State Park is a large recreational park—6,396 acres—3 miles east of Apopka, off Florida 436 or I-4. This park is one of the most popular in the state, a large, unspoiled woodland area of open forest and jungles. Facilities: picnicking, swimming, fishing, boating, skin diving, scuba diving, nature trails.

SOUTHWEST

CALADESI ISLAND State Park is 2 miles offshore from Dunedin (but within the city limits). The 607-acre island is accessible only by boat. A ferry operates daily on the hour to the island; last on-the-half-hour return trip is at 4:30 pm. There is a fine view from a 60-foot observation tower. Facilities: picnicking, swimming, fishing, boating, skin diving, scuba diving, nature trails. No vehicles.

GAMBLE PLANTATION State Historic Site is on 5 acres in Ellenton, on US 301. The restored mansion, built between 1845 and 1850, was originally part of a sugar plantation. It is a two-story structure with walls nearly 2 feet thick. It is built of brick, "tabby" (oyster shell lime combined with sand), and lumber. Confederate Secretary of State Judah P. Benjamin delayed his capture by taking refuge here. Facilities: guided tours, picnicking.

KORESHAN State Historic Site is a beautiful park of 305 acres on the river and bay at Estero, on US 41. The tropical pineland was transformed and beautified by the members of Koreshan Unity, a Utopian group who came to this part of the state in 1893. Roads, trails, and footbridges lead through a forest of ornamental trees, shrubs, and plantings that teem with birds and other wildlife. There is an Art Hall where documents and relics relating to the Koreshan Unity are displayed. Facilities: camping, picnicking, boating, fishing, nature trails, guided tours, museum.

LAKE MANATEE State Recreation Area is 15 miles east of Bradenton on Florida 64. Facilities: picnicking, swimming, fishing, boating, nature trails.

MADIRA BICKEL MOUND State Archeological Site, on US 19, Terra Ceia, is a 10-acre area where Indians lived from about A.D. 1 to 1600. The mound itself is 100 by 170 feet at the base and 20 feet high. The low burial mound in the monument area was built during the Weeden Island period (A.D. 700–1400). The Safety Harbor period (A.D. 1400–1600) is the final period of occupancy of the site, when the Madira Bickel Mound was built. It is a mixture of shells, black dirt, animal bones, and pottery. It apparently was constructed as a foundation for a building, perhaps a chief's residence or a temple. Indians were living at this site when the Spaniards first arrived in Florida, in the early 1500s. Open daily, 8–sundown. Free. Facilities: nature trails.

MYAKKA RIVER State Park, a 28,875-acre preserve located on Florida 72, 17 miles east of Sarasota, is the natural home of large flocks of birds of all varieties, and of other wildlife. Large rookeries and a bird tower are on the grounds. An area of 7,500 acres has been set aside as a wilderness preserve, with all visitors required to register, pay an entrance fee, receive instructions, and check out when leaving. Only 20 persons are admitted on any one day. The park's northern entrance is open only on weekends.

Guided boat tours and train tours are offered daily. Facilities: camping, picnicking, fishing, boating, boat rentals, canoe rentals, bicycle rentals, museum, nature trails, snacks, family cottages.

OSCAR SHERER State Recreation Area covers 463 acres on US 41, 2 miles south of Osprey, where South Creek empties into Dryman Bay. Much of the land has been left in its natural state, and alligators, muskrats, raccoons, possums, gophers, and occasionally wild hogs and Florida panthers have been spotted. There are also many species of birds, including quails and bald eagles. Campsites have been left naturally screened for privacy. Facilities: camping, picnicking, fishing, swimming, boating, canoe rentals, bicycle rentals, nature trails, snacks, gift shop.

WIGGINS PASS State Recreation Area, 6 miles south of Bonita Springs, is reached via County Road 901, off US 41. Facilities: picnicking, swimming, fishing, boating.

YBOR CITY State Museum is housed in the Ferlita Bakery building at 1818 9th Avenue in the Ybor City section of Tampa. Exhibits tell the stories of the immigrants who came to Tampa to work in the cigar factories. A cigar maker demonstrates the art of rolling cigars.

SOUTH CENTRAL

BAHIA HONDA State Recreation Area is on Bahia Honda Key, south of Marathon and the Seven Mile Bridge, 276-acres on the ocean. This is Florida's southernmost park. Over 80 acres of land are set aside for camping, and picnicking. Facilities: camping, picnicking, swimming, fishing, skin diving, scuba diving, boating, boat rentals, snacks, gift shop.

CHEKIKA State Recreation Area is a 640-acre park on S.W. 237th Street and Grossman Drive, north of Homestead. Three million gallons of water flow daily from the area's artesian springs. Facilities: camping, picnicking, swimming, fishing, nature trails.

COLLIER-SEMINOLE State Park is a 6,423-acre preserve on US 41, 17 miles south of Naples, and 20 miles northeast of Everglades City. Big Cypress Swamp joins the Everglades here; the land ends and the world of water begins. It is historically significant as the last refuge of the Seminole, and some Indian villages are nearby. Facilities: camping, picnicking, fishing, boating, nature trails. A wilderness preserve of 4,760 acres has restricted use for canoeing, fishing, and primitive camping.

EVERGLADES RECLAMATION State Historic Site is located near Lake Harbor, approximately 10 miles west of Belle Glade on US 27, on the site of the Miami Lock and Keeper's House. It commemorates the first attempt to manage the everglades for agriculture.

JOHN PENNEKAMP CORAL REEF State Park is an area of about 55,000 acres, mostly under water, at Key Largo. This was the first underwater state park in the United States, featuring part of the only living coral reef formation in North America. A variety of water activities are available, and frequent boat trips link the land area to the reef. Glass-bottomed boats make two-hour trips over the coral reef, daily, weather permitting, at 9, noon, and 3. Tickets $5, children $3. Escorted scuba and snorkel tours are available. Brilliantly colored living coral and the wrecks of many ships can be seen. Facilities: camping, picnicking, swimming, skin diving, scuba diving, fishing, boating, boat rentals, canoe rentals, nature trails, snacks, gift shop.

LIGNUMVITAE KEY State Botanical Site, accessible by boat only, is located in the Gulf opposite Islamorada. A 19th-century restored mansion is on the grounds. Facilities: boating, skin and scuba diving, nature trails, guided tours.

LONG KEY State Recreation Area is on US 1, at Long Key, 15 miles south of Islamorada. Facilities: camping, picnicking, fishing, boating, swimming, skin diving, scuba diving, nature trails.

PAHOKEE State Recreation Area is a 30-acre camping park in the center of the town of Pahokee on the Hoover Dike on Lake Okeechobee, developed for the convenience, primarily, of boaters. Facilities: camping, picnicking, swimming, boating, fishing, snacks.

SOUTHEAST

THE BARNACLE State Historic Site is located in Coconut Grove, on Biscayne Bay, at 3485 Main Highway. The park contains the home of pioneer settler Ralph Munroe, boat builder and founder of Biscayne Bay Yacht Club. Facilities: nature trails.

BILL BAGGS CAPE FLORIDA State Recreation Area is on Key Biscayne, off US 1. The Historic Cape Florida Lighthouse, one of the oldest buildings in southern Florida, is situated in a 406-acre park with a dramatic beach setting. Tape recordings guide you through the grounds, lighthouse, and museum, telling the story of a dramatic burning of the lighthouse during the Seminole War—the lighthouse keeper lived to tell the tale. Guided tours available. Facilities: picnicking, swimming, fishing, boating, skin diving, scuba diving, nature trails, snacks.

FORT PIERCE INLET—ST. LUCIE MUSEUM State Recreation Area is a complex that includes Jack Island, St. Lucie State Museum, and Pepper Beach. The large museum is located on several hundred feet of ocean frontage, north of Fort Pierce on Florida A1A. It features exhibits of salvaged treasure and a 60-foot mural interpreting the history of the area. The park is a wildlife sanctuary. It can be reached only by footbridge from A1A, and only foot traffic is allowed. Huge flocks of birds abound—119 species have been identified. Facilities: picnicking, swimming, fishing, boating, skin diving, scuba diving, nature trails, guided tours, snacks, observation tower.

HUGH TAYLOR BIRCH State Recreation Area is a 180-acre park in Fort Lauderdale, on Florida A1A. Miles of glistening sand beach lie open to the Atlantic on the east, with quiet lagoons and inland waterways at the western approach. A 3-mile ride on a miniature train offers a close-up view of the many scenic attractions. Tickets $2, children $1.25. Facilities: picnicking, swimming, fishing, boating, skin diving, scuba diving, nature trails, snacks.

JONATHAN DICKINSON State Park is on US 1, 3 miles north of Jupiter. In 1696 a group of Quakers bound from Jamaica to Philadelphia were shipwrecked off Jupiter Island and captured by a fierce group of Indians. They eventually persuaded their captors to guide them northward, and reached St. Augustine, and from there they finally made it to Philadelphia. Leader of the 24 survivors was Jonathan Dickinson, who wrote of their adventures among the Indians. The site of their original landing is now marked by beautiful high white sand hills where all manner of wildlife can be seen. A cruise lasting nearly 2 hours is available Tuesday through Sunday, December through March. Tickets $6, children $3. Facilities: camping, picnicking, swimming, fishing, boating, boat rentals, canoe rentals, bicycle rentals, nature trails, guided horseback tours, snacks, gift shop, pony rides, family cottages.

LLOYD BEACH State Recreation Area is a 243-acre park located between Dania and Fort Lauderdale off Florida A1A. This is the territory once traveled by the almost legendary barefoot mailman. Facilities: picnicking, swimming, fishing, boating, skin diving, scuba diving.

SEBASTIAN INLET State Recreation Area is on Florida A1A, 1 mile below the Sebastian Inlet Bridge. **McLarty Museum** is built in the shape of a four-pointed star and is located at the site of salvage camps set up by the survivors of a Spanish treasure fleet that was downed in a hurricane in 1715. From this fleet has come one of the world's richest recoveries of treasure, much of it not brought up until the late 1950s. Replicas of gold, silver and Spanish artifacts are displayed. A diorama, slide show, and illustrations tell the story of the area's interesting history. Museum open Wednesday–Sunday, 8–5, admission 50¢. Facilities: camping, picnicking, swimming, fishing, boating, nature trails, guided tours, snacks.

CANADA
MEXICO
WASHINGTON
MONTANA
NORTH DAKOTA
IDAHO
OREGON
SOUTH DAKOTA
WYOMING
NEVADA
NEBRASKA
UTAH
COLORADO
KANSAS
CALIFORNIA
ARIZONA
NEW MEXICO
OKLAHOMA
TEXAS
Bellingham
SEATTLE
OLYMPIA
SPOKANE
Coeur d'Alene
Yakima
PASCO
PORTLAND
SALEM
Pendleton
Eugene
Grants Pass
Shelby
GREAT FALLS
Missoula
HELENA
BUTTE
BILLINGS
Miles City
BISMARCK
Jamestown
BOISE
Idaho Falls
Twin Falls
POCATELLO
Sheridan
Buffalo
RAPID CITY
CASPER
Redding
Winnemucca
Elko
Ogden
Rock Sprs
SALT LAKE CITY
Laramie
CHEYENNE
North Platte
Grand Island
Kearney
RENO
SACRAMENTO
OAKLAND
SAN FRANCISCO
Sterling
DENVER
Limon
Grand Jct
COLORADO SPRINGS
PUEBLO
Cedar City
LAS VEGAS
Trinidad
Barstow
Kingman
Flagstaff
Gallup
SANTA FE
SANTA MONICA
LOS ANGELES
San Bernardino
Tucumcari
AMARILLO
Clinton
ALBUQUERQUE
SAN DIEGO
PHOENIX
Yuma
Casa Grande
LUBBOCK
TUCSON
Lordsburg
Las Cruces
Nogales
EL PASO
Pecos
Abilene
Ft Stockton
SAN ANTONIO
Laredo
5
90
82
182
84
15
94
86
80
505
580
25
76
70
17
40
10
8
19
27
20
35
37
82-1

UNITED STATES INTERSTATE HIGHWAYS

- COMPLETE
- UNDER CONSTRUCTION
- PROPOSED
- 90 TOLL
- 90 FREE

© RAND MCNALLY & CO.

National System of Interstate and Defense Highways

Designed to accommodate the traffic needs of the future, the Interstate Highway System is the nation's key highway network. The system is now over 90 percent complete and will provide 42,500 miles of expressways throughout the United States, serving both civilian and defense requirements.

ON THE WAY

FAMILIES DRIVING TO FLORIDA FROM RELATIVELY LONG DISTANCES MAY FIND IT NECESSARY TO PLAN FOR SOME CHANGES OF PACE AND CHANCES TO RELAX ALONG THE WAY. CHILDREN CAN GO STIR-CRAZY WHEN CONFINED IN AN AUTOMOBILE ON A LONG TRIP, AND EVERYONE WILL ENJOY THE VACATION MORE IF THERE IS SOMETHING INTERESTING TO SEE AND DO EVERY DAY, ON THE WAY TO AND FROM FLORIDA, AS WELL AS WHILE YOU ARE THERE.

A good plan for traveling which covers the ground without wearing out all the passengers is to get an early start, whip off several hours of driving on the fast routes, then head for an interesting destination by early afternoon and relax for the rest of the day. Or, perhaps you would prefer to put in one solid day of driving (if your young ones will sit still for it) and relax most of the next day.

This section is a listing of major points of interest along the three Interstate routes that carry most of Florida's tourists into the state: I-95 from the Northeast, I-75 from the Midwest, and I-10 from the Southwest.

These suggestions are not meant to be a recommended itinerary; they are offered as a variety of types of attractions tht may tempt you to get off the expressways for a while and do something special.

FROM THE NORTHEAST

Interstate 95 begins on the Canadian border, near Houlton, Maine, and follows a route along the Atlantic Coast in Maine, goes through Boston south to New London, Connecticut, and then traces the coast again to New York City. Traveling from New York to the northern boundary of Florida, you could enjoy stops at any of these points.

The **Edison National Historic Site** is in West Orange, New Jersey, a few miles west of I-95, just off I-280 at Main Street and Lakeside Avenue. This will be of special interest if your trip in Florida will take you to the Edison Winter Home in Fort Myers. Guided tours are offered of both the Edison Laboratory and Glenmont, Edison's home from 1886 to 1931. Many of his inventions are on display, and the 23-room house is furnished as it was when he lived there. Edison Laboratory open daily; Glenmont open daily except Sunday. Both closed holidays.

The **Morristown National Historical Park,** Morristown, New Jersey, on US 202, is a 1,677-acre park at the site of George Washington's military headquarters during the Revolution. There is much to see here, starting with the Historical Museum in the heart of the town. Two elegant mansions can be toured—Ford Mansion, which was Washington's headquarters, and Wick House, with its 18th-century kitchen garden.

This is one of the most informtive and interesting of all Revolutionary War memorial areas. Beautiful plantings are picturesque in all seasons, and battlefields are nearby.

Princeton, New Jersey, is on US 206 a few miles east of the proposed route I-95. This is an old town, settled in 1685, which figured prominently in the Revolutionary War. There are guided tours through the campus of **Princeton University.** Also worth seeing are the **Princeton Battle Monument,** the **Princeton Cemetery,** and **Morven,** a mansion built in 1701 that is now the governor's residence.

Washington Crossing State Park is 8 miles northwest of Trenton on New Jersey 29 and the Delaware River. It is a good-sized recreational park which commemorates the famous crossing. There are a flag museum and a restored Colonial inn.

In **Trenton** one can obtain a brochure from the Chamber of Commerce, 88 East State Street, for a "Guide Yourself tour" of a number of places of importance in Revolutionary War history, including a Colonial Barracks, Trenton's oldest house, and the Trenton Battle Monument. The state buildings are also interesting.

In **Camden,** directly across the Deleware River from Philadelphia, visit **Walt Whitman's Home State Historic Site,** a house containing original furnishings and Whitman mementos.

If you do not have time to stop in **Philadelphia** for a day or more and really explore it, you will still enjoy a short walk in the vicinity of Independence Square, to see Independence Hall, where the Declaration of Independence was signed; Congress Hall, where the U.S. Congress met during the 1790s; and Old City Hall, home of the first U.S. Supreme Court.

Six miles northwest of Wilmington, Delaware, on Delaware 52, is the **Henry Francis du Pont Winterthur Museum,** the finest museum of its kind in the country. More than one hundred rooms are authentically and beautifully furnished with furniture and furnishings of the 1640–1840 period. Various portions are open for guided tours at different seasons of the year; prices and hours vary. Reservations are necessary for tours of the main museum, and children under 12 are not admitted on these particular tours. Write for reservations to Winterthur Museum, Winterthur 19735. Equally outstanding are the 60-acre Winterthur Gardens. The Garden Pavilion serves a cafeteria-style luncheon.

About 25 miles south of I-95 is the lovely Colonial town of **Annapolis,** Maryland. Walking tours are conducted by Historic Annapolis, Inc., 64 State Circle. Tours are at 10, 1:30, and 3, daily, during the summer; rest of the year, 10 and 1:30, Monday–Friday.

If you are going to spend only a limited time in **Washington, D. C.,** you will make the most of it by taking a Gray Line Tour, phone (202) DI 7-0600, the White House bus line tour, phone (202) 393-1616, or a tour in a Landmark Services' Tourmobile. The tourmobiles, conducted by a National Park Service concession, leave from the Washington Monument, daily in summer, 8–7; rest of year, 8–5.

In nearby Virginia, **Mount Vernon,** the beautiful plantation home of George Washington, is a short drive south of the Washington city limits along the Mount Vernon Memorial Highway, or it can be reached by a boat trip on the Potomac, leaving from Pier 4, Main Avenue and Sixth Street S.W. Phone (202) 554-8000. The lovely Georgian Colonial presidential home has been restored with great care and authen-

The Jekyll Island Hotel (Georgia) was formerly a clubhouse for the island's millionaire residents.

ticity, and appears much as it did when the first president died. Open daily, summer, 9–5; winter, 9–4.

Fredericksburg, Virginia, a fascinating pre-Revolutionary town, was George Washington's boyhood home. An important Civil War battle was fought in the area, also. Information about self-guided tours, combination admission tickets for admission to historic homes, and maps are available at the Fredericksburg Information Center, 706 Caroline Street.

Richmond, also, figured in both the Revolutionary and Civil wars. Many museums and carefully preserved buildings have collections important to the history of this capital city of the Confederacy. The Richmond Chamber of Commerce, 201 East Franklin Street, has maps and folders about points of interest within and around Richmond. Several fine old plantation houses are nearby.

Fifty miles southeast of Richmond, via US 60, is **Williamsburg,** the most outstanding center of Colonial restoration in the nation. For more than 30 years John D. Rockefeller, Jr., financed and devoted his efforts to the authentic re-creation of this early American town. Shops, gardens, public buildings, and homes are restored to their original 17th- and 18th-century appearance. Sightseeing information, guidebooks, free bus service, and a free film about the city are available at the Colonial Williamsburg Information Center, Colonial Parkway and Virginia 132. Combination tickets are avilable to exhibition buildings.

Six miles from Williamsburg is **Jamestown,** site of the first permanent English settlement in the New World. Jamestown Island is a national memorial, preserved and administered jointly by the National Park Service and the Association for the Preservation of Virginia Antiquities. Guide leaflets and information for a walking tour are available at the Visitor Center, where dioramas, models, and relics are on display.

About 25 miles southeast of Williamsburg, by way of I-64, is the huge marine and naval area known as the **Port of Hampton Roads,** consisting of the three cities of Newport News, Norfolk, and Portsmouth. These cities, along with Hampton, Chesapeake, and Virginia Beach, all cluster around the mouth of the James River. There is a huge shipbuilding industry, and a number of naval installations make the area a sailors' town. There are harbor cruises and several unusual museums.

In North Carolina, I-95 goes through **Rocky Mount,** one of the world's largest bright-leaf tobacco centers. Tobacco auctions are held in 16 different warehouses in the fall.

A 70-mile detour from I-95 by way of US 501, in South Carolina, will take you to **"The Grand Strand,"** a 50-mile drive through beach resorts along the Atlantic coast. **Myrtle**

Thoroughbreds on a Kentucky horse farm.

Beach State Park and **Huntington Beach State Park** provide a variety of recreational facilities. At the end of this strand is **Georgetown,** where the spectacular **Brookgreen Gardens** are worth visiting. Open daily, 9:30–4:45.

From **Charleston** (about 50 miles southeast of I-95 via I-26), at the Municipal Marina, 2¼-hour boat tours sail about the harbor with a stopover at **Fort Sumter National Monument.** This fort was the scene of the shooting which set off the Civil War. Open daily. Closed Christmas. Free.

Lovely old **Savannah,** Georgia, founded in 1733, was one of America's early planned cities. The route of I-95 will pass a few miles to the west. Well-marked walking and driving tours are outlined in leaflets that may be obtained at the Chamber of Commerce, 301 West Broad Street. Much is being done to restore the city's important landmarks and interesting buildings.

In Georgia I-95 hugs the seacoast. Off to the east are the famous **Sea Islands,** about a dozen islands with a romantic history. On Sea Island itself is the renowned resort, The Cloister, and on adjacent St. Simons Island is the beautiful old King and Prince Hotel. Both resorts have beach clubs, golf courses, and tennis courts.

The area is rich in folklore; the claim is made that "there are more than 20 known ghosts here." **Fort Frederica National Monument,** on St. Simons Island, is the site of the settlement founded by Gen. James Oglethorpe. His efforts here were aided by John and Charles Wesley, founders of the Methodist Church. The Battle of Bloody Marsh, fought nearby, was part of the struggle between the early English and Spanish settlers for control of the Georgia and northern Florida area.

Jekyll Island, just south of St. Simons, is a magnificent state park. The island was an exclusive resort inhabited by some of the nation's wealthiest families until the early 1940s. Then, during World War II, the threat of submarine warfare in the waters nearby caused the government to quietly suggest to these people that it would be a good idea not to have such a concentration of top business management vacationing in an area so exposed. The entire island was later sold to the state for a fraction of its value, and today it comprises one of the finest publicly owned vacation resorts to be found anywhere. There are many motels and restaurants as well as all sorts of recreational facilities and meeting and convention halls.

Southwest of Brunswick is the eerie, wild, and awe-inspring 60,000-acre **Okefenokee Swamp.** About 80 percent of the area has been set aside by the federal government as a National Wildlife Refuge. **Okefenokee Swamp Park,** 8 miles south of Waycross on US 1/23 and Georgia 177, is the north entrance of the swamp. Boat tours are available, for all day or for shorter trips. Boardwalks, 90-foot observation tower, museum, and picnic area are in the park, but there are no overnight accommodations. Open daily, spring and summer, 9–6:30; fall and winter, 9–5:30.

FROM THE MIDWEST

Interstate 75 begins at Sault Ste. Marie, in the Upper Peninsula of Michigan, and proceeds south through Detroit to Cincinnati. The route continues through Atlanta to Tampa, and, when it is completed, will extend all the way to Miami. Travelers from all over the Midwest can join this route at any convenient junction. Those coming from Chicago, for example, can take I-65 to Nashville, then head southeast on I-24 to pick up I-75 at Chattanooga.

The **Henry Ford Museum and Greenfield Village** is south of US 12 in Dearborn, Michigan, just west of I-75. This is an incomparable collection of restored houses and public buildings of the 17th, 18th, and 19th centuries, displaying many aspects of Americana, particularly early American crafts and businesses. Open all year. Separate admission prices for various attractions.

About 40 miles east of Toledo, Ohio, by way of Ohio 2 is Port Clinton, embarkation point for **Put-in-Bay,** on South Bass Island in Lake Erie. Both a ferry and the "world's shortest airline" take passengers across to the island. This is a relaxed, off-beat resort area, a popular yachting stop in summer and an ice-fishing headquarters in winter. A 352-foot tower, commanding a fine view of southern Ontario, Lake Erie, and northern Ohio, commemorates Commodore Perry's battle victory during the War of 1812 and the century and a half of peace since then between Great Britain and the United States.

About a hundred miles south of Toledo and 50 miles north of Dayton, just off I-75, is Wapakoneta, home town of Neil Armstrong, first man to step on the moon. Housed in an interesting, modern building is the **Neil Armstrong Air and Space Museum.** It offers a brief introduction to the fascinating world of space flight, which can be explored more thoroughly at the Kennedy Space Center in Florida.

Eleven miles east of I-75 at Dayton, at the Wright-Patterson Air Force Base in Fairborn, is the **Air Force Museum.** Here are gathered more than one hundred historic pieces of aircraft, dating from early Wright brothers models to Space Age missiles. Open daily, Monday–Friday, 9–5; Saturday and Sunday, 10–6. Closed Christmas. Free.

On I-71, at Kings Mills, 20 miles north of Cincinnati and 7 miles east of I-75, is a 1,600-acre recreation and entertainment complex called **Kings Island.** There are six theme areas: International Street, a shopper's mart; Oktoberfest, a German beer garden; a re-creation of an old amusement park; a Rivertown area; a 100-acre wildlife preserve, viewed from a monorail; and the Happy Kingdom of Hanna-Barbera, featuring such popular cartoon characters as Yogi Bear and the Flintstones. Other attractions include live entertainment, a 330-foot replica of the Eiffel Tower, more than 60 rides, the world's largest roller coaster, two golf courses, and a campground. Open daily from Memorial Day through Labor Day; weekends late April, May, September, early October. One-price admission for all attractions.

Cincinnati is one of the oldest settlements in the Midwest, dating back to 1788. Its strategic location on the Ohio River has given it importance throughout the history of the United States.

Among the many points of interest worth visiting are the **William Howard Taft National Historic Site,** 2038 Auburn Avenue, birthplace and boyhood home of our 27th president; the **Cincinnati Zoo** at 3400 Vine Street, with over 2,000 animals; and the **Contemporary Arts Center,** at 115 East Fifth Street, with changing exhibits.

Cincinnati is the home port of the charming riverboat the *Delta Queen,* and her new sister, the *Mississippi Queen.* These are the only overnight paddlewheelers still plying our country's inland waterways. Phone (513) 621-1445 for information about cruises.

Those traveling on I-65 will becoming through **Louisville,** Kentucky, where the stern-wheeler *Belle of Louisville* takes passengers on memorable river excursions, leaving from Riverfront Plaza, at the foot of Fourth Street. **Churchill Downs,** home of the Kentucky Derby, at 700 Central Avenue, is open to visitors except during races. Closed holidays. Free museum displaying track's history and photos of Derby winners.

Mammoth Cave National Park is in southwestern Kentucky, a few miles west of I-65. It is open all year, and is particularly interesting to visit during the winter, when it is much less crowded. The cave has a constant temperature (54 degrees) year-round. Tours of varying lengths are offered. This is an exceptionally pleasant place to make an overnight stop during a winter trip to Florida by car.

Interstate 65 continues into Tennessee and passes through Nashville. Twelve miles east of the city on US 70 is **The Hermitage,** home of Andrew Jackson, seventh president of the United States. This is the only presidential home completely furnished with original pieces.

Those traveling on I-75 will be passing **Lexington,** a beautiful Middle South city. Blue Grass Tours, Inc., 410 West Vine Street, take visitors on tours of historic points and Thoroughbred horse farms in the surrounding countryside. Trips last from 2½ to 3 hours and are conducted year-round. Phone (606) 252-5744.

At the point where Kentucky, Tennessee, and Virginia meet, a few miles east of I-75, is **Cumberland Gap National Historic Park.** This is both a dramatically beautiful and a historically significant pass in the Cumberland Mountains. Exhibits at the Visitor Center tell the story of the area.

Continuing on down through Tennessee, I-75 passes near a number of attractive points of interest: the planned residential city of **Norris,** built by the federal government in 1933; **Norris Dam,** the first dam built by the TVA; **Oak Ridge,** with its **American Museum of Science and Energy;** and **Great Smoky Mountains National Park.** The national park, at the top of the Appalachian Mountains, is beautiful in all seasons but especially breathtaking in the spring and fall.

From Nashville, those who have been traveling on I-65 should turn southeast on I-24 to meet I-75 in Chattanooga. Everyone in eastern U.S.A. must have seen the huge letters painted on barn roofs throughout the countryside proclaiming: "SEE ROCK CITY." Sometimes the signs locate **Rock City,** "atop Lookout Mountain, Chattanooga." Fairyland Caverns, Mother Goose Village, the swinging bridge, and the observation point from which seven states can be seen make Rock City well worth a stop. Open daily, 8:30 am–sundown. There are also many other points of interest in and around Chattanooga. For information stop at the Convention and Visitors Bureau, 1001 Market Street.

As you cross the state line into Georgia you may be thinking "we're almost there" (meaning Florida). But Georgia is a large state, and you have about 350 more miles to go before reaching the northern border of Florida. It is also a beautiful and historic state, and you should give yourself the pleasure of investigating some of its attractions.

Interstate 75 passes through one part of the **Chattahoochee National Forest,** a huge tract in two segments which covers most of northern Georgia. The forestland includes parts of the piedmont plateau, river valleys, and mountain slopes. For information on camping and other recreation write to the headquarters: 601 Broad Street Northeast, Gainesville, Georgia 30501.

On Georgia 225, just off I-75 near Calhoun, is **New Echota,** a restoration of the Last Eastern Cherokee Capital. It is from here that the Cherokees were forced to migrate to Oklahoma over the "Trail of Tears," a march that resulted in the death of one-third of the Indians en route. The buildings are furnished authentically. Open all year. Free.

For those interested in the story of prehistoric Indian mound dwellers, there are two extraordinarily fine archeological sites and museums along the I-75 route: **Etowah Mounds,** near Cartersville, and **Ocmulgee National Monument,** at the southern edge of Macon, Georgia. Both of these finds have been very important in the study of the early Indian cultures of this part of the country.

Atlanta is a city rich in history and in tourist appeal. Outstanding points of interest are **Underground Atlanta,** a restoration of the original city now beneath the level of modern streets; **Stone Mountain Park,** a memorial park featuring mountainside carvings of Jefferson Davis, Robert E. Lee, and Stonewall Jackson; **Six Flags Over Georgia,** an extensive entertainment complex, and Atlanta's **Cyclorama**—the world's largest painting, re-creating the Battle of Atlanta.

Various Gray Line tours cover these and other interesting places in Atlanta. Also, special group tours can be arranged to make a 150-mile round trip to the **Little White House** in Warm Springs, where Franklin D. Roosevelt went for relaxation and therapy; and to the remarkable **Calloway Gardens.** Both places can be reached by car, also, of course.

A scenic 75-mile loop off I-75 called the **Andersonville Trail** leads west from Perry to Marshallville, south through Montezuma and Americus, and east to rejoin I-75 at Cordele. En route are the **Camellia Gardens** at Marshallville, **Whitewater State Park, Andersonville National Historic Site,** antebellum homes in Montezuma and Americus, and **Georgia Veterans Memorial State Park.**

At Cordele you are only about two hours away from Florida.

FROM THE SOUTHWEST

Interstate 10, when completed, will traverse the country coast-to-coast from Los Angeles to Jacksonville. Listed here are a few of the major points of interest along this general route between San Antonio, Texas, and Pensacola.

In San Antonio the number one tourist attraction is, of course, **The Alamo.** The fascinating museum is open Monday–Saturday, 9–5:30; Sunday, 10–5:30. Closed Christmas Eve day and Christmas. Free. Starting from this point, a walking tour takes you past many historic buildings. San Antonio was founded in 1718, and the original Alamo was built then. Other restored structures date from about 1750. An auto tour along the well-marked **Mission Trail** leads to four early 18th-century Spanish missions. It is interesting to compare these historic spots with the places in Florida also settled by early Spanish explorers and missionaries.

Circus buffs (especially those who are planning to visit Sarasota) will be interested in visiting the **Hertzberg Circus Collection** at 210 West Market Street. Open Monday through Saturday, 9–5:30; Sunday, 1–5. Closed major holidays. Free.

Two hundred miles east of San Antonio is another Texas city with close ties to Florida— Houston, home of the **NASA Lyndon B. Johnson Space Center,** from which the space flights taking off from the Kennedy Space Center have been controlled. The center is actually about 26 miles southeast of the city, in Clear Lake. A Visitor Orientation Center has exhibits of space flight equipment and other displays related to such projects as Mercury, Gemini, and Apollo. Open daily, 9–4. Closed Christmas. Free.

Within the rapidly growing city of Houston, two favorite tourist spots are the **Astrodome,** a $31-million stadium of unique modern design, and **Astroworld, USA,** a 65-acre entertainment and recreation center. Hours vary with the seasons. One price combination ticket to Astroworld.

Baton Rouge, capital of Louisiana, is a seaport, industrial center, oil well center, and seat of the state government, the **State Capitol,** at North Third Street and Boyd Avenue, built during the administration of the controversial governor Huey P. Long, is a fabulous skyscraper unlike any other state capitol. The beautiful campus of **Louisiana State University** is also worth visiting.

From Baton Rouge I-10 will lead across the south shore of Lake Pontchartrain to **New Orleans,** a city which combines its quaint and charming heritage with modern sophistication in a way that is utterly captivating to most tourists. It is one of the few cities in the United States with a strong French heritage, which has been enriched with many other elements and cultures.

Space limitations make it impossible to do any more than skim the surface of the charm of New Orleans. If you have never been there, and if it is possible to work it into your itinerary while traveling to Florida, be sure to do so. Even if you can spare only half a day or an evening and overnight, careful planning can made your short stop most rewarding. New Orleans certainly ranks among America's most beguiling cities for the tourist, and a brief visit is certain to whet your appetite for a return trip.

The oldest part of the city, much of it settled in the 1700s, is the French Quarter, or *Vieux Carre* (literal translation is "old square"). This section is the heart and soul of New Orleans. The restoration and preservation of historic buildings here has been eminently successful. New structures have been combined with restorations in such a way as to preserve the original atmosphere. A good example is the award-winning Provincial Motel, at 1024 Chartres Street.

Within the Vieux Carre are the restaurants (e.g. Brennan's and Antoine's), the jazz museums, and jazz emporiums whose fame is world-wide. Here is the French Market, where all good lovers of N'Aw-le-uns night life end their evenings with doughnuts and coffee. Here streets are blocked off from auto traffic and set aside for strolling during evening hours.

The only way to really explore the French Quarter is on foot. You can pick up a map and brochure at the Tourist and Convention Commission, 334 Royal Street, and set out on your own.

But there is much more to New Orleans beyond the boundaries of Vieux Carre. **Gray Line** tours will introduce you to the rest of the city. Three-hour tours, beginning at 9 am and 1:30 pm, take passengers through the Vieux Carre, the garden district, the university section, and the lakefront area. For information and reservations, phone (504) 525-0138. Various harbor cruises have an overview of the city from a different vantage point. Longer cruises take passengers deep into the bayou country south of the city.

Campers will enjoy the beautiful **Fountainebleau State Park** covering over 2,700 acres on the northern shore of Lake Pontchartrain. The longest overwater highway in the world now traverses the lake, north and south, a 24-mile double causeway (toll).

The enticing beaches of Gulfport and D'Iberville, Mississippi, will tempt you to stop awhile for a picnic or a swim, and Mobile, Alabama, will be most difficult of all to pass by. **Bellingrath Gardens,** 20 miles south of the city, is especially worthwhile. This is an 800-acre estate with about 75 acres of landscape plantings. The gardens are open daily, 7 am–dusk.

The distance from New Orleans to Pensacola is slightly over 200 miles—but the drive along the Gulf shore is so beautiful your chauffeur may take quite a few hours to make the trip.

ISLAND HOPPING

ONLY MINUTES AWAY FROM FLORIDA BY AIR LIE THE SHIMMERING, SANDY, SUN-KISSED BAHAMAS, AND STRETCHING SOUTH AND EAST ARE THE WEST INDIES—THOSE THOUSANDS OF TROPICAL ISLANDS, KEYS, REEFS, AND ATOLLS THAT TOGETHER FORM A HUGE RIGHT-HANDED PARENTHESIS ENCLOSING THE CARIBBEAN SEA.

The Bahamas are comprised of some 700 islands and 2,000 keys and reefs, scattered along a route about 750 miles long. They are not Caribbean islands (they are located in the Atlantic Ocean, north of the Caribbean Sea), but they are, properly, part of the "West Indies." According to accepted historic theory it was on San Salvador in The Bahamas that Christopher Columbus first set foot in the New World, on October 12, 1492.

South of The Bahamas are the Greater Antilles, a group of islands consisting of the comparatively large land bodies of Cuba, Jamaica, Hispaniola (Haiti and Dominican Republic), and Puerto Rico. East and south of these curve the Lesser Antilles, which are divided into the Leeward and the Windward Islands. While the Virgin Islands, just east of Puerto Rico, belong geologically to the Greater Antilles, because of their small size they are grouped with the Lesser Antilles.

Many nations and political entities are represented in the West Indies. There are a number of independent republics, as well as self-governing protectorates of the United States and the British Commonwealth. Netherlands, France, and Venezuela hold islands that are not considered colonies, but overseas "departments" (states). Thus the tourist who books passage on one of the numerous cruise ships that sail out of Florida's harbors, or the visitor who plans an island-hopping expedition via the airways, can easily and comfortably make the Grand Tour of several nations within a rather short time span. Interesting combinations of cultures exist side by side: in the Spanish-speaking Commonwealth of Puerto Rico, whose natives enjoy dual citizenship in Puerto Rico and the United States; in exotic French-African Haiti; on the island of St. Martin-Sint Maarten, which is divided in ownership between France and Netherlands and where the two cultures exist in proximity and harmony with no border formalities. There are also islands that were once held by Denmark and Sweden. Curacao, one of the Netherlands Antilles, is an outstanding example of the West Indian melting pot—boasting of at least 40 different nationalities and races.

Most of the islands require no passport for U.S. and Canadian tourists; some require visas. All do want visitors to produce some proof of identity and, ordinarily, a return ticket.

Cuba is not covered in this chapter, as it is difficult for U.S. citizens to obtain permission to travel there. It *is* fairly easy for visitors from Canada, the United Kingdom, and many other countries to book trips there. Other Caribbean islands omitted from this section are the several offshore Venezuelan islands, which are generally approached by way of the mainland of South America.

Also not covered are the Mexican islands, such as Isla Mujeres, Cozumel, and Cancun, which can now be reached by direct flight from Miami.

THE BAHAMAS

Bahamians consider themselves to be separate and distinct from the rest of the West Indian islanders—largely because The Bahamas are actually in the Atlantic Ocean rather than in the Caribbean. But there is much similarity in culture, accent, music, and religion between these people and the residents of Jamaica and other islands. There is an "Englishness" that has pervaded through the years, has melted through so many diverse cultures, and has softened and civilized the manner—so that any traveler who blusters in will soon be gratefully responding to the innate courtesy of the islanders.

About 85% of the population is descended from Africans who came from the plantations of the South or who managed to escape from slave ships putting into harbor in the islands. Other early residents of The Bahamas were Loyalists, who came here from America during and after the Revolution.

The history of the islands is filled with tales of renegade sailors, smugglers, and pirates who hid out in the many hundreds of bays, inlets, and harbors and made the islands their headquarters. A permanent, well-ordered British colony was established in 1718. During the Civil War the Bahamians made a very good business out of running guns through Northern blockades to Southern ports. After the war ended the pace was slow in the islands for a number of decades, but the enactment of Prohibition in the United States was a spur to the economy of The Bahamas, where "rum-running" proved to be extremely profitable.

Today the economy is solidly based on tourism. With a climate that is nearly perfect all year-round; powdery white beaches lapped by warm, azure waters; abundant fishing; and many other natural blessings, the islands attract visitors during all seasons.

Resorts run the gamut from very luxurious to fairly modest cottages and guesthouses. Food is not cheap on the islands, as most of it is imported, but visiting families can cut their costs considerably by renting a cottage or apartment with kitchenette facilities. Best—and tastiest—buys in local restaurants include conch chowder, conch salad, and Bahamian grouper. If you will be staying in hotels, you may find that the most reasonable way to enjoy a holiday in The Bahamas is to book reservations on a package tour.

Golf, tennis, swimming, water skiing, snorkeling, surfing, and scuba diving are the favorite activities, and lessons are available for learning all of these skills. There are sailboats, schooners, motorboats, and yachts for rent or charter. Magnificent fishing, of course. Also for rent are cars, bikes, motor scooters, horses, and horse-drawn carriages. There are regular flights and boat rides between the islands.

Except for the Biminis, **Grand Bahama Island** is the nearest to the Florida mainland, and it is the most recently developed and modern resort area. **Lucaya** offers luxury hotels and motels, and 2 miles away is **Freeport,** famous for its gambling casinos and the fascinating array of shops in the **International Bazaar.** There are many fine hotels, restaurants, and night clubs featuring big-name acts.

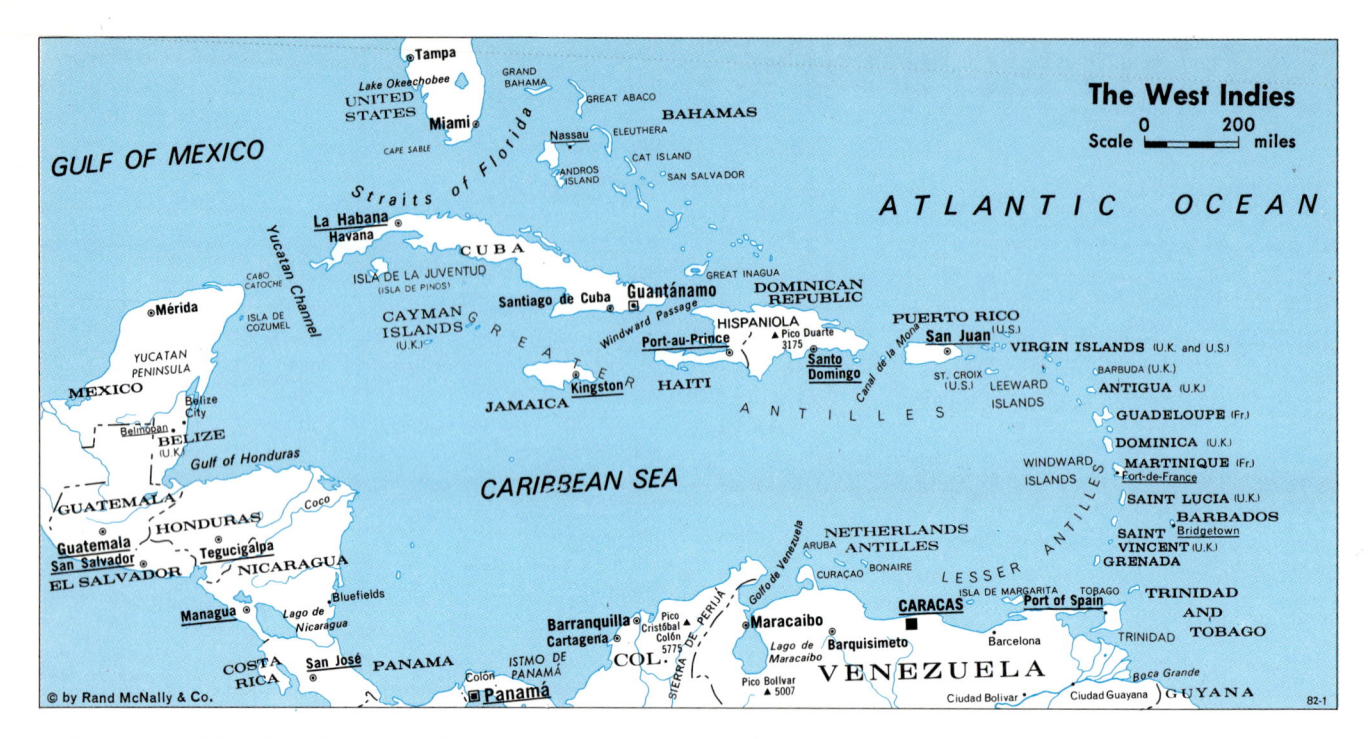

Nassau, on **New Providence Island,** is the capital and nerve center of the country. Several points of interest here should be on your list: **Bay Street,** with its fine shops featuring European goods at prices 20 to 45 percent lower than those in the States; **Woodes Rogers' Walk,** on the waterfront, where fresh fruits, vegetables, fish, and shells are sold; and **Prince George Wharf,** where the cruise ships dock. Leading tourist attractions are **Fort Charlotte,** the dolphin shows and marine exhibits at the **Seafloor Aquarium,** the Flamingo Parade at **Ardastra Gardens,** and a number of night clubs that feature native entertainment. Exceptionally good bargains in Nassau are the locally made straw goods and conch shell jewelry.

Across a toll bridge from Nassau is **Paradise Island,** a beautiful resort area with huge, luxurious hotels, a casino, bathing beach, and the renowned and unique **French Cloister and Versailles Gardens,** brought here by A & P heir Huntington Hartford. Boats take passengers across to the beach from Nassau, and the same boats make trips to the **Sea Gardens,** a beautiful reef of coral and sponges.

The rest of the Bahama islands are known collectively as The Family of Out Islands. Many of them are easily accessible by boat or Bahamasair. All of those listed here have facilities that make them popular vacation spots. There are **Abaco** and its cays, at one time a stronghold of pirates; **Andros,** where skindiving over the huge Barrier Reef is a not-to-be-forgotten experience; the very exclusive **Berry Islands;** the **Biminis,** claiming to have the finest fishing waters in the Western Hemisphere; hilly **Cat Island,** dotted with ruins of plantation mansions; long, skinny **Eleuthera,** 110 miles by 2 miles, settled more than three hundred years ago by the Eleutheran Adventurers, a brave group who fled from Bermuda in search of religious freedom (rent a houseboat there for a very different kind of holiday); **Harbour Island,** the oldest resort center in the Bahamas; the yachting center of **Spanish Wells;** the **Exuma Cays,** 100 miles of little islands with towering white limestone cliffs—where great resort hotels sit next to ancient, primitive villages; **Long Island,** dominated by two huge Moorish-style churches; and **San Salvador,** Columbus's landing place, which is marked by several monuments.

JAMAICA

South of the Bahamas and Cuba lies the lush emerald island of Jamaica, a land of towering blue mountains, fertile plantations, dense jungles, dark rain forests, white beaches, and sparkling rivers. Each visitor who sees it for the first time feels as though he is its original discoverer. It's a resort; it's an exotic foreign country; it's an adventure.

Columbus came here, to Discovery Bay, in 1494, and the Spanish who followed him wiped out the original inhabitants of the island—the Arawak Indians. Slaves from Africa were brought in, and the Spaniards half-heartedly farmed the land for more than a century. In 1655 the English attacked the island, and after a three-year struggle the Spanish left. Under English colonization, the great plantations flourished. The slaves were freed in Jamaica in 1833, and more than 80% of present-day Jamaicans are descended from these slaves. But the culture of the island is heavily British. In 1962 the island became an independent nation, a member of the British Commonwealth. Today, although poverty and underemployment are still prevalent, the country is as nearly self-sufficient as any in the Caribbean, with an economy based on agriculture, mining, and manufacturing, reinforced with a healthy tourist business. The modern waterfront is a good example of the new strength in the economy.

Superb fishing and all sorts of water sports make Jamaica a year-round playground. There are excellent golf courses spotted throughout the island, and numerous tennis courts.

Jamaican food is varied, excellent, and spicy. Try curried goat, codfish and ackee, boiled green bananas and mackeral. You'll be surprised—this is really gourmet fare! You can choose from a dozen or more tropical fruit drinks—with or without rum—for your afternoon cooling-off break.

Many visitors rent small cottages for their stay in Jamaica, and these often come complete with a daytime housekeeper. Most of these women are fine cooks who will prepare foods to your order, either Jamaican or American style. "Nanny" service is readily available for small children, at very reasonable rates. Arrangements for these services can be made before you leave home, either through your travel agent or the Jamaica Tourist Board.

Kingston, the capital, is a major city with a large, excellent, beautiful harbor. Fascinating glimpses of the island's romantic past can be seen at the **Institute of Jamaica,** the **Arawak Museum,** the **Folk Museum,** and various old mansions. **Port Royal,** across the harbor, opposite the city, has several interesting historic landmarks: **Fort Charles, St. Peter's Church,** and the **Giddy House.** Once the home of ruthless pirates, Port Royal was known as "the wickedest city in the world." Many devout natives are still convinced that it was divine retribution for the sins committed there that swept most of the city into the sea during an earthquake in 1692.

Perched on a mountainside above Kingston is the **Blue Mountain Inn,** an old plantation house whose furnishings, service, and food are among the most outstanding in the Western Hemisphere.

Spectator sports here include horse racing at **Caymanas Park** (all year) and cricket, rugger (rugby), and soccer. There are several movie theaters and night clubs. Also worth visiting are the **Victoria Crafts Market,** the **Royal Botanic Gardens and Zoo,** and the **University of the West Indies.**

The beaches on Jamaica's north shore are pure white powder, and there are hundreds of deep-blue coves and inlets, many of them fed by sparkling waterfalls that come tumbling over magnificently sculpted cliffs and rocks. **Montego Bay,** in the northwest corner of the island, is Jamaica's top resort center and second largest city. There are first-class hotels and resorts, with extensive facilities for sports and entertainment. On land near the city are several old "great houses" and the intriguing **Cockpit Country**—a largely unexplored area inhabited by descendants of runaway slaves.

Ocho Rios, 64 miles east of "Mobay," is a newer resort town, surrounded by many places of spectacular natural beauty. Farther to the east is picturesque **Port Antonio,** the oldest but quietest of Jamaica's north-shore resort centers. Some of the cruise ships dock here, but there are no international airport facilities. The fact that it is less crowded makes it the first choice of many Jamaica-lovers. The tropical vegetation in this area is rich and plentiful, and lofty mountains seem to lead straight down to the white beaches. **Rafting down the Rio Grande** is a glamorous and memorable way to spend an afternoon.

Other resort developments are rapidly gaining popularity in and around **Runaway Bay, Negril,** and **Paradise Park.** Negril, with its relaxed and casual ambience, has become the "in" spot for young people.

There are many conducted tours to all parts of Jamaica from the major resort centers, with visits to tropical plantations, caves and grottoes, country markets, or a rum distillery.

THE CAYMAN ISLANDS

These three small British islands northwest of Jamaica, with a total population of 14,000, are becoming an increasingly popular resort area. **Grand Cayman,** the largest, is about 22 miles long and 8 miles wide; **Little Cayman** and **Cayman Brac** are each 10 to 12 miles long. The atmosphere of the islands reflects the heritage left by the original Scottish settlers. **George Town** is the capital and largest center; it has only 2,000 people.

The islands have wide and secluded beaches, rich fishing waters, and beautiful coral reefs and marine gardens. There are more than a dozen good hotels and numerous guesthouses.

Visitors can avail themselves of duty-free shopping, and native-made goods include straw and sisal work and ornaments made of seashells and tortoise shells.

Sightseeing spots include the ruins of **Fort George,** the restoration of **Pedro's Castle, Kiemanus Museum,** and the Caribbean's only **Turtle Farm.** Shelling and beachcombing yield interesting finds. Sports popular with tourists here are swimming, skin diving, sailing and motor-boating, and truly outstanding fishing. There are three outdoor cinemas and a few night clubs.

HAITI

The independent republic of Haiti occupies the western third of Hispaniola, the large island east of Jamaica. The official language is French, but what is spoken is a sort of Creole patois. More than 90% of the population is black.

Haiti is the most mountainous country in the Caribbean, and there are a number of cool hill resorts in the countryside. Residents are becoming increasingly tourist-conscious; much English is spoken and the service is excellent. It is, nevertheless, an out-of-the-ordinary, exotic, very different kind of place that will not appeal to everyone but will delight the really adventuresome traveler.

The economy is based on coffee, bauxite, sugar, sisal production, tourism, and some manufacturing.

Port-au-Prince, with a population of more than half a million, is the capital and chief port. Several hotels are located in resort towns in the hills above the city.

The second city is **Cap Haitien,** 170 miles away. Here is the palace of **Sans Souci,** built by Henri Christophe, the former slave who became president of Haiti after the slave uprisings in the early 1800s, and then later declared himself king. A few miles out of town, in the mountains, is Christophe's fabulous fortress called **La Citadelle Laferrière.** The ruins of both of these structures can be explored.

The scenery of Haiti is spectacular, and the same water sports offered by other Caribbean Islands are available for tourists here.

DOMINICAN REPUBLIC

The Dominican Republic, which occupies the eastern two-thirds of the island of Hispaniola, became an independent republic in 1844. The official language here is Spanish, but many residents also speak English, French, or Portuguese.

This is an agricultural country, whose principal products are sugar, coffee, cocoa, and tobacco. Bauxite, also, is exported. Since the land offers much in natural beauty and there are some fine old homes to explore, representing excellent examples of Colonial architecture, the Dominican Republic is now attracting large numbers of tourists.

The capital and chief seaport is **Santo Domingo,** a city of more than 1,000,000 people. Worth seeing are the tomb of Columbus in the **Cathedral;** the **Alcazar de Colon,** which has been reconstructed and furnished with period furniture; the **National Pantheon,** a former Jesuit convent; and the **National Museum,** which has fine displays of pre-Columbian art. The oldest university in the Western Hemisphere is located here.

Visitors will also enjoy the beach areas and the casinos.

PUERTO RICO

The Commonwealth of Puerto Rico is a Spanish-speaking nation that has a special association with the United States; Puerto Ricans are citizens of their own country and also enjoy most of the rights and privileges of U.S. citizens. The island was discovered by Columbus in 1493 and colonized by Ponce de Leon. The Spanish held it until 1898, when they ceded it to the United States. It became independent in 1952.

Fourth-largest island in the Caribbean, it measures 100 miles long by about 35 miles wide. It had a plantation culture—sugar cane and coffee—until after World War II. Since then, an industrialization program has been changing its face.

The capital city, **San Juan,** with a half-million people, has some of the most interesting historic spots to be found in the islands. **Old San Juan,** a seven-block area once enclosed within the City Wall, was founded in 1521—making it the oldest city under the American flag. It has been declared an Ancient and Historic Zone. Flanked by two forts—**El Morro** (dating back to 1595) and **San Cristobal** (1766)—the area contains lovely restored old residences, a fascinating shopping area, good restaurants, many historic buildings, museums, plazas, parks, and a cathedral. The two forts and most of the City Wall are owned and administered by the National Park Service, which conducts guided tours several times a day.

Shopping is good in Puerto Rico, not only for imported duty-free goods, but for locally made handicrafts, art objects, fashions, rum, and cigars.

In the newer sections of San Juan see the **Capitol, Fort San Jeronimo** (which contains a military museum), the **Sea Aquarium, Ponce de Leon Museum,** and the **Monolero,** a 9-acre landscaped zoo. A two-hour guided boat trip cruises through the peaceful Torrecilla Lagoon; ferry cruises explore San Juan Bay; the **Bacardi Rum** plant welcomes visitors on guided tours. **The University of Puerto Rico** has fine modern architecture, a good museum, and botanical gardens. The annual **Casals Music Festival** is an important event.

Sports in Puerto Rico include swimming, boating, snorkeling, scuba diving, deep-sea fishing, surfing, tennis, and golf. Spectators can enjoy races and cockfighting.

There are many fine hotels, restaurants, and sightseeing points of interest scattered throughout San Juan—and "out on the island" as well. San Juan has luxurious supper clubs and gourmet restaurants that represent many countries and cultures—European, Asiatic, and Latin American. Many sightseeing tours are available. Other interesting towns are **Ponce, Mayaguez, Guanica, Isabela,** and **Dorado.**

There is airline service between Puerto Rico and the Virgin Islands.

VIRGIN ISLANDS

British Virgin Islands consist of 4 large and about 40 smaller islands; the United States administers 3 big ones and about 60 little ones. They are separated by less than a mile at one point—the British group is east of the American. British Virgin Islands were held briefly by the Spanish, then by the Dutch until 1666. They have been a British colony since then. The American islands have been held by England, Spain, Holland, France, a number of pirates, and Denmark. The United States bought them from Denmark in 1917.

These islands have an ideal climate. There is no real rainy season.

The economy of the islands is based on rum and tourism. There are many first-class and luxurious hotels and restaurants, free-port shopping, beautiful scenery, a full complement of recreational and sports facilities, and fine old colonial buildings to admire in **Christiansted** and **Frederiksted.**

The major British Virgin Islands are Tortola, Virgin Gorda, Anegada, and Beef Island; the American are St. Thomas, St. Croix, and St. John.

BRITISH LEEWARDS

The northern group of the Lesser Antilles is known as the Leeward Islands. The British Leewards are Antigua, St. Kitts, Nevis, Anguilla—all self-governing states—and the crown colony of Montserrat.

The climate of these islands is less humid than in most of the Greater Antilles. **Antigua,** a hilly island with splendid views of neighboring islands, has more than 350 beaches, backed by palm trees. Much of the soil is thin, sandy, and rocky, but part of the island also has lush sugar fields and tropical fruit orchards. The most famous tourist attraction on this island is **Nelson's Dockyard,** an 18th-century restoration, where *Son et Luniere* shows about Lord Nelson's adventures are shown. The island has about 25 resort hotels and a number of luxury restaurants and nightclubs. A colorful carnival held each August attracts visitors.

St. Kitts-Nevis-Anguilla is one unit politically. **St. Kitts** is a mountainous, fertile island, and the best way to explore it is on horseback. **Nevis,** a volcanic island which today is a quiet resort area, is interesting to U.S. citizens as the birthplace of Alexander Hamilton. Its many decaying old mansions suggest its grand past. **Anguilla** is a flat coral island. All three islands have good hotels and recreation facilities, but not much in the way of exciting entertainment.

Montserrat, which was settled by Irish people during the 17th century, calls itself the Emerald Isle of the West. It produces much more of its own food—including meat and poultry—than most of the Caribbean islands.

FRENCH LEEWARDS

Scattered among the British Leewards are the two islands—Grande-Terre and Basse-Terre—that make up **Guadeloupe;** St. Martin (which shares its island area with the Dutch Sint Maarten), and St. Barthelemy, plus a few tiny islets. St. Martin and St. Barthelemy are dependencies of Guadeloupe, which, in turn, is a department of France. Guadeloupe—

104 ISLAND HOPPING

once held briefly by Britain, then by Sweden—has been French since 1674.

Marvelous Creole and French cooking is featured at a number of fine restaurants in Guadeloupe. There are a dozen cinemas and many clubs with floor shows, good department stores carrying luxury imports from France, and the usual facilities for sports and recreation.

BRITISH WINDWARDS

Dominica, St. Lucia, St. Vincent, Grenada, and the Grenadines, curving south of the Leewards to within 100 miles of the South American coast, are self-governing members of the British Commonwealth. Dominica, St. Lucia, and Grenada are independent countries. There are first-class hotels and recreation facilities, but these islands are still largely unspoiled and unexploited.

Dominica has volcanic peaks, forests, lakes, waterfalls, and huge rocks; it is more a mountain resort and botanist's paradise that a beach resort. Here live the few last surviving descendants of the ancient Carib Indians. **St. Lucia** has more of the classic tropical island beauty. Its history is varied; its rule changed hands 14 times. **St. Vincent** is volcanic, mountainous, with lush groves and fields, and luxurious beaches as well. **Grenada** also has dazzling scenery and magnificent sand beaches. Known as the Isle of Spice, it produces large crops of cloves, mace, and nutmeg.

FRENCH WINDWARD

Martinique, the only French Windward island, lies between Dominica and St. Lucia. There is spectacular scenery in the northern sector—volcanic mountains, rain forests, and a lovely coastline with many bays and inlets. French, or rather a Creole patois, is spoken. An overseas department of France, Martinique has been in the hands of that country since 1816. Exports include bananas, sugar, rum, cocoa, and coffee.

There is a handful of first-class hotels and restaurants that are marked by old-world French charm, and the usual recreation facilities are available.

BARBADOS

Barbados, easternmost of the West Indian islands, was settled by the British in 1627, governed as a crown colony for more than three hundred years, and has been an independent member of the British Commonwealth since 1966. It is a very West Indian—and, at the same time, a very English—land, known throughout the Caribbean as Little England. Tourism is its major industry, and it is the home of many wealthy expatriates and film stars.

Over a quarter of a million people live here, a high proportion of them of British descent. It is a neat and flat island, not as flamboyant as Jamaica and Trinidad. Beautiful beaches ring the island; the interior has soft hills reminiscent of Scotland. This is an interesting and lovely foreign country to become acquainted with; it is also an idyllic resort. There are several dozen good hotels and guesthouses, good facilities for recreation and entertainment. There is excellent local cuisine available at numerous restaurants. Many hotels and restaurants specialize in American and European menus.

TRINIDAD AND TOBAGO

The traveler who gets to **Trinidad** has almost made it to South America; only 7 miles of water separates Venezuela from Trinidad's southwestern tip.

Columbus discovered this island in 1498 and claimed it for Spain, but it wasn't colonized until 1592. Spain badly mismanaged it because she regarded it merely as a jumping-off place for other, more important places in the Caribbean area. The British took it over in 1797.

Tobago, on the other hand, changed hands more times than any other West Indian island. At various times it was controlled by the British, Carib Indians, Dutch, Jamaican privateers, and French from Grenada. It has been British since 1814.

Slaves were treated somewhat less badly in Trinidad than in other Caribbean countries, and their emancipation came in 1834. Following this, several thousand Negroes emigrated to the island from the United States.

Since 1962 the two islands have been combined into one independent country, with a population of more than a million. It became a republic on August 1, 1976. Theirs is one of the most prosperous countries in the Caribbean and the second-largest oil-producer in the British Commonwealth.

These are lands of stunningly colorful and exotic flowers, scenery, and tropical birds. Almost as exotic are the music and dances for which Trinidad is famous—calypso (folk music), the steel bands, the limbo dancing.

In Trinidad **Port of Spain** is the main tourist spot and one of the best places to shop in the West Indies. The shops are mostly on Frederick Street; the **Central Market** has locally made crafts. Visit the **National Museum and Art Gallery,** home of a fine natural history museum; the **Queen's Park Savannah,** a 199-acre recreation area; the **Botanic Gardens;** the **National Museum and Art Gallery.** The **Holy Trinity Cathedral** dates from 1823 and the **Roman Catholic Cathedral** from 1832.

A unique phenomenon is **Pitch Lake,** at the village of La Brea—109 acres of natural asphalt. As you stand looking at it you will think you are in the hottest place on earth.

Tobago, a delightful tropical island northeast of Trinidad, has a population of more than 34,000. Climb the **Tobago Lighthouse** at **Fort King George,** in the capital city of Scarborough. There are great views in all directions.

Surrounding the island are coral reefs with abundant sponges and multicolored tropical fish.

There are fine hotels in Trinidad and Tobago, as well as restaurants, night clubs, facilities for water sports, golf, tennis, hunting, and spectator sports.

The biggest event of the year is the **Carnival,** held in Port of Spain, Trinidad, on the Monday and Tuesday before Ash Wednesday.

Another festival worth seeing is held on the seventh to the ninth days after the Moslem New Year (this falls during the spring months)—**Hosein.** It is marked by a parade with elegant floats and exciting drum music.

NETHERLANDS ANTILLES

Netherlands Antilles is not a colony, but part of the Kingdom of Netherlands. It consists of six small islands, located in two widely separated areas of the Caribbean Sea. Three of them—**Sint Eustatius, Sint Maarten,** and **Saba**—are tucked among the British and French Leeward Islands. The other three—**Aruba, Bonaire,** and **Curaçao**—lie far to the southwest of the Windward Islands, just off the coast of northwest Venezuela and only a few miles from Colombia.

These islands are somewhat more economical for a holiday than many of the better-known West Indian resorts. The three northern islands are friendly, relaxed, have a pleasant climate, and feature small, modest resorts. English is spoken more commonly than Dutch. Sint Maarten, the major resort destination and most sophisticated, is especially interesting because it shares the island with the French St. Martin.

Aruba has marvelous beaches and a coral reef, abandoned gold mines, casinos and nightclubs, and good shopping. The island is also the site of one of the world's major oil refineries.

Bonaire, known as the Flamingo Island, has one of the world's largest colonies of pink flamingos. It offers similar diversions to those on Aruba, plus extensive coral beds. Scuba diving is the major activity.

Curaçao is an important commercial and oil-refining center. More oil is transshipped from Curacao, Bonaire, and Aruba than from any other country. Curacao is also an outstanding resort island. The official language is Dutch, but there is also a native language called *Papiamento*. The capital, a picturesque city with 17th-century gabled Dutch houses, is **Willemstad.** Points of interest include the **Schooner Market,** where fruits and vegetables from South America are sold; the **Protestant Church,** dating from 1769; **Mikve Israel Synagogue,** built in 1732 and the oldest Jewish house of worship in the hemisphere; the **Curaçao Museum,** and several restored country houses.

There are a number of fine restaurants and hotels, nightclubs, and casinos.

For further information about visiting these islands, write to the offices listed below.

Antigua Department of Tourism and Trade, 610 Fifth Avenue, New York 10020

Aruba Tourist Bureau, 1270 Avenue of the Americas, New York 10020

Bahamas Tourist Office, 30 Rockefeller Plaza, New York 10020

Barbados Tourist Board, 800 Second Avenue, New York 10017

Bonaire Dutch Antilles Tourist Information Office, 685 Fifth Avenue, New York 10022

Caribbean Tourism Association, 20 E. 46th Street, New York 10017

Cayman Islands Department of Tourism, 420 Lexington Avenue, New York 10017

Curaçao Tourist Board, 685 Fifth Avenue, New York 10020

Dominican Tourist Information Center Inc., 485 Madison Avenue, New York 10022

Eastern Caribbean Tourist Association, 220 E. 42nd Street, New York 10017

French Travel Board, 610 Fifth Avenue, New York 10020

Grenada Tourist Information Office, 141 E. 44th Street, New York 10017

Haiti Government Tourist Bureau, 30 Rockefeller Plaza, New York 10020

Jamaica Tourist Board, 2 Dag Hammarskjold Plaza, New York 10017

Puerto Rico Tourism Company, 1290 Avenue of the Americas, New York 10019

St. Maartin Tourist Information Office, 455 Park Avenue #903, New York 10022

Trinidad & Tobago Tourist Board, 400 Madison Avenue, New York 10017

Virgin Islands (U.S.) Government Tourist Office, 10 Rockefeller Plaza, New York 10020

A visitor to St. Thomas, American Virgin Islands, can see the mountains of the British islands across Sapphire Bay.

FLORIDA FACTS & FEATURES

FLORIDA LAW AND YOU

RESIDENCE

If you wish to become a legal resident of Florida you must move to Florida and establish a domicile, or place of permanent abode. You are also urged to visit the county courthouse and obtain from the office of the circuit court an affidavit of intent to establish residency. You cannot be a voter in another state and claim your residence in Florida.

Requirements for legal residency in Florida vary according to the purpose for which residency is desired: for voting, for Old Age Assistance, for jury duty, for admission to a state mental hospital, for attending a state institution of higher learning without paying nonresident tuition fees, to obtain a divorce. Inquire at the local county or municipal courthouse for the details of the residency requirements.

BOAT REGISTRATION

Valid out-of-state registration of pleasure yachts and boats is accepted for a period of 90 days. If residency is established boats must be registered immediately with the tax collector at the local county courthouse. This registration must be renewed yearly.

FISHING REGULATIONS

Licenses are not necessary for sports fishing in salt waters. Minimum legal lengths are as follows: bluefish, 10 in.; flounder, 11 in.; mackerel, 12 in.; mullet, 11 in.; pompano, 9½ in.; trout, 12 in.; redfish, 12 in.; snook, 18 in.; crawfish, carapace measurement of more than 3 in. and tail measurement of 5½ inches; stone crab, 2¾-inch forearm; oyster, 3-inch long shell. Bag limits: sailfish, 2 per day; tarpon, 2 per day; snook, 2 per day, shad, 10 per day; striped bass, 6 per day. Closed seasons: crawfish, April 1–July 25; oysters, June 1 to September 1; stone crabs, May 15 to October 15.

For freshwater fishing, all Florida fishermen over the age of 15 and under 65 must obtain licenses: nonresident fee— 1-year, $10.50; 14-day, $7.50; 5-day, $5.50. The only legal methods of taking freshwater fish are by pole and line, rod and reel, bob, spinner, troll, or trotline with cut bait. The use of goldfish or carp and minnows of bass for bait is prohibited. The daily bag limit is 41 game fish per day, but not more than 10 bass, 15 pickerel, or 50 panfish. Check locally for the point at which fresh water begins.

MOTOR VEHICLE REGULATIONS

Speed limits are 55 miles per hour, or as posted. When you are traveling through Florida as a tourist you may use an out-of-state driver's license. However, as soon as you become a resident, accept employment, or place children in school you must immediately secure a Florida driver's license, and there is no grace period.

License plates for cars are issued during the month of birth of the car owner. Florida will honor license plates from other states until the expiration date or until you are either in business, employed, or have children in public school in Florida.

If you become a legal resident of Florida, you should secure a Florida Title Certificate for your car as well as license plates. It is recommended, but not required, that you carry liability insurance on your vehicle.

All mobile homes and travel trailers in rental parks must carry Florida license plates, except those owned by bona fide tourists who have current tags from their home state. Mobile homes located in subdivisions or on private lots owned by the mobile home owner may be taxed as real estate, and if the owner is otherwise eligible, he may claim homestead exemption.

FLORIDA ATTRACTIONS ASSOCIATION

Certain tourist attractions in this book have been listed as "Member Florida Attractions Association." As the tourist travels throughout the state, he will see this designation applied to 44 such entertainment areas and establishments.

The Florida Attractions Association was formed in 1949 by the proprietors of five of the leading attractions, to set up and observe a set of standards both for their own betterment and to protect the interests of Florida's millions of visitors. They recognized the need to formulate principles of ethical, wholesome, and reliable operation that would establish them as respectable in the minds of visitors who saw their membership designation.

Florida Attractions Association members are closely scrutinized prior to admission, and then are policed by the group to assure continued high quality of operation. Such factors as members' advertising, relations with the communities of which they are a part, and even their housekeeping, are matters of concern. Committees study and report on everything from mutual public relations opportunities to the conditions under which wildlife is kept and displayed.

Members are located in all parts of the state, and "their appeals range from the historic aspects of St. Augustine to the crystal-clear springs that are great natural attractions, from the appeal of wild animals and reptiles to the fascination and beauty of tropical gardens, water skiers, trained birds, and a wide array of other novel and unusual presentations."

Thus the traveler can be quite confident, as he travels about in Florida, that he will find family entertainment that offers good value for the price of admission at the places that are members of this association, as well as at the various attractions that are operated by the state and federal government, or individual cities and counties. Of course there are also many other privately operated attractions that are of high quality and fair price, but membership in the association is an indication that these attractions have been carefully screened and policed by their peers.

GOING BY TRAIN

Amtrak offers year-round train service to both the east and west coasts of Florida from New York and Chicago, as well as from points along the way. Within Florida, Amtrak services 22 cities. During the winter season various extras are added. Consult your travel agent for specific details.

There are package tours which include hotel rooms, guide and driver service, and admission to such tourist attractions as Cypress Gardens, Kennedy Space Center's TWA/NASA Tour, Sea World, and Walt Disney World. You can combine your train trip with a cruise—a Rail and Sail holiday.

The thoroughly modernized Silver Meteor is a premium train running between New York and Miami, and New York and St. Petersburg.

A Week of Wheels Plan includes discounts on car rental, with the amount of discount based on the number of persons in the party. Cars may be picked up at Orlando, Tampa, West Palm Beach, Fort Lauderdale, or Miami, and dropped off either at the same city or one of the others.

GOING BY PLANE

Hundreds of airports across the United States offer airline service to Florida, so if it's air travel you want, you won't have any trouble finding it. The most obvious advantage of going by plane is speed. It takes only four and a half hours to fly nonstop from Los Angeles to Miami, a little less than three hours from Chicago, and just two and a half hours from New York. The same trips by land would, of course, take days.

International airlines serving Florida include Air Canada; Air France; British Airways; and Trans World Airways. U.S. airlines servicing major cities in the state are Braniff; Continental; Delta; Eastern; National; Northwest Orient; Republic; and United. Other cities within Florida are served by Air Florida, PBA, and several other local airline companies. Flights can be arranged easily by calling either your local travel agent or the airline of your choice at your nearest airport.

Many of the airline companies offer package tours for your trip to Florida. These can consist of your airline ticket, airport/hotel transfers, accommodations, meals, a rental car, sightseeing tours, and discount coupons for attractions in the area of your destination. Golf holidays and tennis holidays are also available as special plans through some airlines. Depending on your length of stay, your package may include a cocktail party, dancing, daily poolside activities, or nightly social activities. Although there is often some savings through airline package plans, they are primarily used for their convenience rather than for their savings. By arranging one, you can pay all at once in advance for most of the expenses of your trip. Call you local travel agent for information on specific plans available from your area.

GOING BY BUS

Bus lines across the United States offer daily service to all of the major cities in Florida. The two major lines are Greyhound and Trailways; you can check with your local travel agent for information on other bus companies servicing the state from your area.

Both Greyhound and Trailways have special touring tickets—Ameripasses and Eagle Passes. The passes come in 7-day, 15-day, and 30-day varieties. These tickets are good for unlimited travel anywhere for as long as the time specified on the ticket. All passes may be renewed for an additional $10.70 per day. If you purchase an ordinary ticket and stay on the regularly scheduled route toward your destination, you can stop over at any place on the way for as long as you want and your ticket will still be honored when you continue your trip. If you pay the regular fare for a round trip ticket, it is good for up to one year.

At various times both Greyhound and Trailways have had special discount rates for the elderly, although these are not always in effect year-round. Both companies also have trips to certain cities "on sale" from time to time. You will need to check with your local bus company to find out more about these offers.

Many bus companies and tour operators offer charter tours, available from all parts of the country. There are coaches, large enough to accommodate 40 people, complete with air conditioning, bars, snacks, and lavatories. Some bus lines offer escorted tours. On one of these, a guide not only points out sights along the bus ride, but also remains with the group after its arrival at its destination, continuing to help its members make the most of their trip. Evenings are usually left up the individuals—but the escort is still available for advice. Charter tours are also available without escorts, in case your group prefers to guide itself.

Some bus companies will arrange custom-made package tours—guided or unguided. (Sometimes a preformed group of around 35 people is required.) Besides bus fare, a package can also include accommodations, meals, rental cars, sightseeing tours, and cocktails. The bus companies can even arange to have a convention site ready for your group.

Unescorted package tours usually mean a savings—bus rates are lower per person, and discounted accommodations and attraction rates are often available, too. To see about arranging a package tour or charter to Florida from your area, call your local travel agent.

STATE FACTS

Motto: In God we trust
Song: "Old Folks at Home"
Flower: Orange blossom
Bird: Mockingbird
State Animal: Florida Panther
State Mammal: Freshwater: Manatee
　　　　　　　　Saltwater: Dolphin
Fish: Freshwater: Largemouth bass
　　　Saltwater: Atlantic sailfish
Nickname: Sunshine State
Capital: Tallahassee
Statehood: March 3, 1845, the 27th state
Boundaries: Alabama and Georgia to the north, the Atlantic Ocean to the east, the Straits of Florida and the Gulf of Mexico to the south, Alabama and the Gulf of Mexico to the west
Time zones: Eastern and Central
Total area: 58,560 square miles
Water area: 4,470 square miles
Population: 9,739,992
Elevation: 0 (sea level)–345 feet (Walton County)
Largest city in population: Jacksonville
Number of Counties: 67
Principal rivers: Apalachicola; Aucilla, Blackwater, Chipola, Choctawatchee, Escambia, Hillsboro, Kissimmee, Ochlockonee, Perdido, St. Johns, St. Marys, Suwanee
Principal lakes: Apopka, Crescent, George, Harris, Istokpoga, Kissimmee, Okeechobee, Orange, Tohopekaliga
Major springs: Spring Creek Springs, Crystal River Springs, Silver Springs, Rainbow Springs, Alapaha Rise, St. Marks Spring, Wakulla Springs, Wacissa Springs Group, Ichetucknee Springs, Holton Spring
Drinking age: 19
Right turn on red: yes
Origin of state name: Ponce de Leon landed near St. Augustine in 1513 during the Easter season, or *Pascua florida*

INDUSTRIES

Tourism, sports, and thoroughbred horses.
Agriculture: citrus fruits, vegetables, horticulture, livestock
Manufacturing: food products, chemicals and chemical products, paper and paper products, miscellaneous manufacturing (including ordnance), printing and publishing, electrical machinery
Mining: phosphate, kaolin, fuller's earth, limestone, sand, gravel, peat, titanium, zirconium, hafnium
Lumbering
Fishing: shrimp, menhaden, sponges
Defense activities

CLIMATE

Florida's mild climate is made possible by three factors: latitude (Florida has an overall range of 7° 30'); elevation above sea level; and proximity to the Atlantic Ocean and the Gulf of Mexico. The mean temperature in January is between 60° and 70° F, while the hottest months, June through September, have a mean temperature of between 80° and 83° F.
Average annual temperature: 72° F
Summer mean: 81° F
Winter mean: 63° F
Record high: 109° F
Record low: −2° F
Average annual precipitation: 52.76"
Average snowfall: less than 1"
Hurricanes threaten the state from late summer through the fall, especially along the Keys and the lower Peninsula.

TOPOGRAPHY

Coastal Lowlands: Region rising less than 100 feet above sea level. Encircles the peninsula and extends inland from 10 to 125 miles from the coast.

Western Highlands: A section lying within the northwestern section of Florida, between the Perdido River on the west, and the Apalachicola River to the east, and from the Alabama border to the coastal lowlands. Much of the area is covered with pine woods, and it is hilly in the north.

Marianna Lowlands: A region surrounded by the western highlands, including Jackson, Holmes, and Washington counties. Covered with hills and hollows.

Tallahassee Hills: A region occupying the area east of the Marianna Lowlands, between the Apalachicola and Withlacoochee Rivers, and the Georgia state line and the coastal lowlands. The section is composed of rolling hills with gentle slopes. In the western end Mt. Pleasant stands on a level plain 300 feet above sea level.

Central Highlands: A diversified natural area running from the Tallahassee Hills to the St. Marys River, south-southeast from the Georgia border for 250 miles along the crest of the Florida Plateau. Within the area are the southern edge of the Okefenokee Swamp, the hills around Live Oak, hills, hollows, and plain, and thousands of lakes.

CAMPGROUNDS

The camper who heads for Florida will find an infinite variety of facilities available—from the primitive to the most deluxe. But, like many of the state's accommodations, space for camping is at a premium during peak vacation periods, so advance reservations are a must in the "high seasons" and in areas of popular tourist attractions.

Information for this directory of public and private campgrounds has been supplied either through personal inspection by field representatives or from correspondence with the campground managers. Every effort has been made to verify the facts as given, but the publisher cannot be responsible for inaccuracies or information that is no longer valid at the time of publication.

The directory offers two kinds of information: (1) the state and city maps and (2) campground listings. By using both you can plan all of your overnight or destination stops.

HOW TO USE THE MAPS

The state and city maps are not intended for use as driving maps. They show only the major highways and large cities, and since most campgrounds are in remote areas the maps are of little help in plotting complete travel routes. Their purpose is to provide the base for the locator numbers that represent the campgrounds. Each map number corresponds to a number assigned to a campground in the listing pages. The position of the number shows the approximate location of the campground within the state, or, on the city maps, in relation to the city and its surrounding area. As you plan your itinerary you can check the maps and see immediately what facilities are available on your route.

HOW TO USE THE LISTINGS

In some of the listing categories symbols and letters are used to indicate special circumstances. These are explained in the legend shown at the top of page 110. For several of the other categories the following information may prove helpful:

Park number. As explained above, this number matches a number on the state or city map. Where several campgrounds of the same category are clustered in a small area a single number is shown, for easier readability, and this same number is assigned to all of the campgrounds in that area. Therefore you will find numbers duplicated in the listings. Occasionally a number has been omitted. This is done to provide space for future campgrounds.

The sequence of the numbers is: lower numbers indicate public campgrounds—those in state parks; state forests; national parks; national forests; city, county, or civic parks. The higher numbers represent privately owned campgrounds.

Map reference. If you find a campground in the listing pages that has all of the facilities you want but you don't know its location, the map reference letters and numbers will give you that information. The letters match the letters on the vertical borders of the maps; the numbers are on the horizontal borders. The red grid lines extending from the two reference points outline the area in which the campground is located. In some listings an asterisk (*) follows the reference. This means that the campground is keyed to the city, not the state, map.

Park name. In public camping areas the name of the individual campground is indented under the headquarters name.

Access. Driving directions are given in reference to the nearest town or city; turnpike, freeway, or interstate exits; junctions of major highways; distance and direction from state or county roads. These abbreviations are used:

N	north	nr	near
E	east	PO	post office
S	south	Pk	park
W	west	Pkwy	parkway
adj	adjacent	PUA	public use area
CA	camping area	RA	recreation area
CG	campground	Res	reservoir
Co	county road	RS	ranger station
ext	exit	Rsrt	resort
fr	from	SF	state forest
FH	forest highway	SP	state park
FM	farm road	SU	special use area
FR	forest road	tpke	turnpike
Hwy	state highway	US	US highway
I	interstate expressway	Vil	village
jct	junction	WA	wayside area
mi	miles		

Maximum trailer size. By industry definition a travel trailer is 35 feet or less in length. If a campground can accommodate a unit larger than 35 feet, the letter "U" is used to indicate unlimited space is available. If it cannot, a figure is shown indicating the largest travel trailer that can be parked. This does not imply that all sites can handle the maximum size specified.

Fees. Separate fees are indicated for tents and for trailers. These fees are the approximate cost for two adults to occupy a site. They do not include such extras as firewood, electric hookups, etc., unless the site cannot be rented without these facilities. Please note that rates may vary according to location, season, and size of family and that they are subject to change without notice.

Many of the public areas have entrance fees separate and in addition to overnight camping fees. These fees are for all travelers who visit federal and state recreational parks.

Special information on the public areas. Fees for camping in the state parks in Florida are explained on page 87. See this page also for reservation information and details on conditions and restrictions in effect in the state-administered campgrounds.

From the Atlantic to the Gulf, from the Panhandle to the Keys, whether you're tenting, trailering, or driving a motor home, Florida has a campground for you. Happy camping!

FLORIDA

FOR MAP, SEE PAGE 114 MIAMI MAP, SEE PAGE 119

MAP REFERENCE & NAME
m area north of map
* see city map
UC under construction

FEES REFLECT MINIMUM RATE FOR 2 ADULTS AND ARE SUBJECT TO INCREASE

FEES
C contribution
F entrance fee required
Credit cards accepted
A American Express
M MasterCard
V Visa

SITES
A adults only
E tents rented
N no specific number
P primitive
S self-contained vehicles
U unlimited trailer size
V trailers rented

PHYSICAL ENVIRONMENT
1-5 Miles from National Forest site to facilities
B 10,000 acres or more
H over 9,000 feet
access to ocean
access to lake
access to river
desert area
heavily wooded
mountainous terrain
prairie land
rural area
urban area
♿ handicapped facilities

RV & CAMPER SERVICES
• at the campground
○ within one mile
$ on the grounds; extra charge
R reservations required
Z reservations accepted

SEASON
LD Labor Day
MD Memorial Day
U unlimited length of stay
w open some off-season weekends
** limited winter facilities

RECREATION
Within 5 miles
g 18 hole golf course
h marked hiking trails
k marked bike trails
m full service marina
s riding stable
t tennis courts

Public areas
n no drinking water
y boil drinking water
Boating on site
d dock
l launch
r ramp

Park Number	Map Reference	Name	Fee	Electric / Water / Sewer	Credit Cards	Tent Sites	Trailer Sites	Pull-thru / Trailer Size	Bottled Gas / Sanitary Service / Maximum Amps	Nearest Town/Access	Physical Environment	Elevation	Acres	Season	Reservations	Time Limit / Pets Permitted / Motor Bikes Permitted	Flush Toilets / Showers	Tables / Firewood / Recreation Hall	Store / Cafe / Laundry / Ice	Playground / Swimming Pool / Other Swimming / Fishing / Boating	Other	Telephone	Mail Address
		STATE PARKS																					
1	G4	Collier Seminole SP	7.00	$ •		130	130	U	•	**Naples**, 17 mi SE on US 41		1	6423	All year		14	••	•		• • dl		813-394-3397	Gen Del, Marco 33937
2	A4	Fort Clinch SP	7.00	$ •		62	62	U	•	**Fernandina Beach**, 3 mi N on Hwy A1A		1	1085	All year	Z	14	••	•		• •• dl		904-261-4212	2601 AtlanticAve,FernadinaBch
3	C4	Blue Spring SP	6.00	$ •			44	30	•	**DeLand**, 4 mi S on Hwy 17			945	All year	Z	14	••	•	•• •	• •• dlr		904-775-3663	Star Rt 3 Orange City 32763
4	G3	Florida Caverns SP	6.00	$ •			32	30	•	**Marianna**, 3 mi N on Hwy 167		1	1784	All year	Z	14	••	•		• •• l	g	904-482-3632	2701 Caverns Rd,Marianna32446
5	B3	Mike Roess Gold Head SP	6.00	$ •		107	107	• 26	•	**Keystone Heights**, 6 mi NE on Hwy 21		1	1481	All year	Z	14	••	•	•• •	• •• dlr		904-473-4701	Rt 1,Bx 545,Keystone Hghts
6	E4	Highlands Hammock SP	6.00	$ •			136	• U	•	**Sebring**, 6 mi W on US 27 & 98 and Hwy 634		1	3800	All year	Z	14	••	• •	•• •	•		813-385-0011	Rt 1 Bx 310, Sebring 33870
7	D3	Hillsborough River SP	6.00	$ •		118	118	30	•	**Zephyrhills**, 6 mi SW on US 301		1	2964	All year	Z	14	••	•	•• •	•• • lr	g	813-986-1020	Rt 4 Bx 250L, Zephyrhill33599
8	E5	Jonathan Dickinson SP	7.00	$ •		135	135	• U	•	**Stuart**, 13 mi S on US 1		1	B	All year	Z	14	••	• •	•• •	• •• dlr	gh	305-546-2771	14800 SE Fed Hwy, Hobe Sound
9	C2	Manatee Springs SP	6.00	$ •		74	74	30	•	**Chiefland**, US 19/98 ext, 6 mi W on Hwy 320		1	2074	All year	Z	14	••	•	•• •	• •• dlr	g	904-493-4288	Rt 2 Bx 362,Chiefland 32626
10	E3	Myakka River SP	6.00	$ •		76	76	28	○ •	**Sarasota**, 17 mi E on Hwy 72		1	B	All year	Z	14	••	•	• •	• • lr		813-924-1027	Rt 1 Bx 72, Sarasota 33577
11	B3	O'Leno SP	6.00	$ •			64	• 27	•	**Lake City**, 20 mi S on US 41		1	5898	All year•	Z	14	••	• •		• ••		904-454-1853	Rt 2 Bx 307, High Spgs 32643
12	H2	St Andrews SRA	7.00	$ •			179	30	•	**Panama City Beach**, 3 mi E on Hwy 392		1	1062	All year	Z	14	••	• •	• •	• •• dlr		904-234-2522	4415 Thomas Dr,PanamaCty32407
13	A2	Suwannee River SP	6.00	$ •		32	32	30	•	**Live Oak**, 13 mi W on US 90		1	1831	All year		14	••	•		• • l		904-362-2746	Rt 8 Bx 297, Live Oak 32060
14	C4	Tomoka SP	7.00	$ •		100	100	27	•	**Ormond Beach**, 3 mi N on N Beach St		1	914	All year	Z	14	••	•	• •	• • dlr		904-677-3931	Bx 695, Ormand Bch 32074
14	C4	Flagler Beach SRA	7.00	$ •		34	34	U	•	**Flagler Beach**, 2 mi S on US A1A		1	145	All year	Z	14	••	•		• •• l		904-439-2474	Bx 717, Flagler Bch 32036
15	G3	Torreya SP	6.00	$ •		35	35	U	•	**Bristol**, 13 mi NE on Hwy 12		1	1063	All year		14	••	•		•		904-643-2674	Star Rt,Bristol 32321
16	G3	Three Rivers SRA	6.00	$ •		65	65	30	•	**Sneads**, 1 mi N on US 90		1	834	All year		14	••	•		• • dl		904-593-6565	Rt 1 Bx 15-A, Sneads 32460
17	H5	Pennekamp Coral Reef SP	8.00	$ •			47	U	•	**Key Largo**, N on US 1		1	2289	All year	Z	14	••	•	• •	• •• dlr		305-451-1202	PO Bx 487, Key Largo 33037
18	C3	Lake Griffin SRA	6.00	$ •		47	47	• 25	○ •	**Fruitland Park**, 2 mi N on US 27-441		1	415	All year		14	••	•		• • dlr		904-787-7402	Bx 608,Fruitland Pk 32731
19	H4	Bahia Honda SRA	8.00	$ •			69	U	•	**Bahia Honda Key**, on US 1		1	276	All year	Z	14	••	•	• •	• •• dlr		305-872-2681	R 1 Bx 782, Big Pine Key33043
20	B4	Anastasia SRA	7.00	$ •			139	30	•	**St. Augustine Beach**, on Hwy A1A		1	888	All year	Z	14	••	•		• ••		904-829-2668	Bx 167, St Augustine 32084
21	G3	Falling Waters SRA	6.00	$ •		34	34	30	•	**Chipley**, 3 mi S on Hwy 77A		1	154	All year		14	••	•		•		904-638-4030	Rt 5 Bx 660, Chipley 32428
22	F3	Koreshan SRA	7.00	$ •		60	60	30	•	**Fort Myers**, 13 mi S on US 41, at Estero		1	156	All year		14	••	•		• • l		813-992-0311	PO Bx 7, Estero 33928
23	A4	Little Talbot SP	7.00	$ •		40	59	U	•	**Jacksonville**, 17 mi NE on Hwys 105 & A1A		1	2500	5/15-10/1**	Z	14	••	•		• •• l		904-251-3231	PO Bx 246, Ft George 32226
24	G2	Fred Gannon Rocky Bayou	6.00	$ •		50	50	U	•	**Niceville**, 3 mi E on Hwy 20		1	632	All year		14	••	•		• •• dl		904-897-3222	PO Bx 597, Niceville 32578
25	H2	Grayton Beach SRA	7.00	$ •		36	36	U	•	**Grayton Beach**, on Hwy 30A		1	356	All year	Z	14	••	•	•	• •• l		904-231-4210	Bx 25,Santa Rosa Bch 32458
26	F5	Pahokee SRA	6.00	$ •		40	40	30	•	**Pahokee**, on US 441		1	30	All year	Z	14	••	•	•	• •• dl		305-924-7832	Drawer 719, Pahokee 33476
27	B1	Ochlockonee River	6.00	$ •		30	30	30	•	**Sopchoppy**, 4 mi S on US 319		1	392	All year	Z	14	••	•		• •• dl		904-962-2771	PO Bx 5, Sopchoppy 32358
28	H3	T H Stone Memorial	5.00	$ •		115	115	28	•	**Port St Joe**, 10 mi S on Hwys 98 & 30		1	2516	All Year	Z	14	••	•	• •	• •• dlr		904-227-1327	Bx 909, Port St Joe, 32456
29	G2	Basin Bayou SRA	6.00	$ •		20	20	U	•	**Freeport**, 7 mi W on Hwy 20		1	287	All year		14	••	•		• • l		904-835-2633	Rt 1 Bx 68-V,Freeport 32439
30	B4	Faver-Dykes SP	6.00	$ •		30	30	30	•	**St. Augustine**, 15 mi S to US 1-I-95 jct, E to Park Rd		1	752	All year		14	••	•		• • dl		904-794-0997	Rt 4 Bx 213 J-1,St Aug 32084
31	G2	Blackwater River SP	6.00	$ •		18	18	24	•	**Milton**, 15 mi NE on US 90, 3 mi N of Harold		1	360	All year		14	••	•		• •• l		904-623-2363	Rt 1 Bx 47-C,Holt 32564
32	H3	Dead Lakes SRA	6.00	$ •		30	30	28	•	**Wewahitchka**, 4 mi N on Hwy 71, E on park road		1	41	All year		14	••	•		• • l		904-639-2702	PO Bx 989,Wewahitchka 32465
33	H4	Long Key SRA	8.00	$ •		60	60	25	•	**Long Key**, on US 1		1	849	All year		14	••	•		• •• l		305-664-4815	Bx 776, Long Key 33001
34	E3	Oscar Sherer SRA	7.00	$ •		104	104	• U	•	**Osprey**, 2 mi S on US 41		1	462	All year		14	••	•	•• •	• •• r		813-966-3154	Bx 398 S Trail, Osprey 33559
35	D5	Sebastian Inlet SRA	7.00	$ •		90	90	30	•	**Sebastian**, on Hwy A1A		1	578	All year		14	••	•	•• •	• •• dl		305-589-3754	PO Bx 728, Wabasso 32970
36	G5	Chekika SRA	6.00	•		20	20	30	•	**Homestead**, 11 mi NW, SW 237th St & Grossman Dr		1	640	All year		14	••	•		• ••		305-253-0950	Bx 1313, Homestead 33030
37	D4	Lk Kissimmee SP	6.00	$ •		30	30	• U	•	**Lake Wales**, 15 mi E		1	B	All year		14 •	••	•		•		813-696-1112	L4248 Camp Mack,Lk Wales33853
38	C4	*Hontoon Island SP*	6.00	$ •		24				**DeLand**, 6 mi W on Hwy 44, Hontoon Rd to St John's Riv; access by boat only		1	1650	All year		14	••	•		• • dr		904-775-3663	Star Rt 3, Orange City 32763
		STATE AREAS																					
		South FL Water Mgmt Dis																					PO Bx V, W Palm Beach 33402
39	E4	Okee-Tantie Rec Area	7.50	$ $ $		250	215	U	○ •	**Okeechobee**, 3 mi S on US 441 to Hwy 78, 4.5 mi W	♿	1	130	All year	Z	14 •	••	• $	•• •	• • dlr		813-763-2622	Rt 4 Bx 644 Okeechobee 33472
40	D4	Southport Pk	7.50	$ $ $		53	53	U	•	**Kissimmee**, SW on US 17/92, 7 mi S on rd 531, 6 mi E on Southport Rd		1	30	All year	Z	14 •	••	• $	••••	• • dlr		305-348-5822	2001 Southpt, Kissimmee 32741
40	D4	Big Lagoon SRA	7.00	$		50	50	• U		**Pensacola**, 10 mi SW off SR292		1	698	All year		14 •	••	••	○ •	• •• l		904-492-1595	12301 Gulf Bch,Pensacola32507
		STATE FORESTS																					
41	H2	Pine Log	None				20	20	○ •	**Ebro**, 1 mi S on Hwy 79		1	6911	All year		14	••	••	○○ ○	•• l			715 W 15th,Panama City 32401
42	B1	Newport Fire Tower	5.25			13	13	20		**Newport**, on US 98, on St Marks River		1	10	All year		14 •	••	•	○○	• l		904-488-8180	1214 Tower,Tallahassee 32301
44	E5	Donald McDonald Pk	5.25			30	30	20	•	**Vero Beach**, 15 mi N, 1 mi W on Co 505		1	37	All year		14 •	••	•	○○	• dl			Okeechobee
45	G2	Blackwater River	5.25	$ •		58	58	20	•	**Milton**, jct Hwys 191 & 4, 1 mi E, 1 mi N on paved rd	♿	1	B	All year		14	••	••		•• d	h	904-957-4111	Rt 1 Bx 77, Milton 32570
46	D3	Withlacoochee	5.25	$ •		120	120	20	•	**Brooksville**, approx 11 mi E on US 98, 4 mi N on Croom Rd	♿	1	B	All year		14	••	••		•• l		904-796-4958	15023 Broad, Brooksvlle 33512
47	C4	Orange City Fire Tower	5.25			14	14	20		**Orange City**, 1 mi S on US 17/92		1	10	All year		14 •	••	•	○○○○			904-445-2488	Rt 1 Bx 20F, Bunnell 32010

FLORIDA

CAMPGROUNDS

FOR MAP, SEE PAGE 114   MIAMI MAP, SEE PAGE 119

Map Ref	Name	Fee	Electric/Water/Sewer	Credit Cards	Tent Sites	Trailer Sites	Pull-Thru	Trailer Size	Bottled Gas	Sanitary Service	Max Amps	Nearest Town / Access	Physical Environment	Elevation	Acres	Season	Reservations	Time Limit	Pets Permitted	Motor Bikes Permitted	Flush Toilets	Showers	Tables	Firewood	Recreation Hall	Store	Cafe	Laundry	Ice	Playground	Swimming Pool	Other Swimming	Fishing	Boating	Other	Telephone	Mail Address
	NATIONAL PARKS																																					
	Everglades																																					
48 G5	Long Pine Key	5.00			107	107	U					Homestead, 16 mi SW on Hwy 27		1	B	All year		14	•	•	•	•	•								o		dlr			305-247-6211	PO Bx 279, Homestead 33030
49 H4	Flamingo	5.00			308	170	U	•	•			Homestead, 50 mi SW on Hwy 27		1	B	All year		14	•	•	•	•	•								•		dlr				
50 G4	Backcountry CS (26 areas)	F			P36				o			Homestead, 50 mi SW on Hwy 27, in Everglade City, boat access only		1	B	All year		14	•	•	•	•	•								o		d				
	Biscayne NP																																					
51 G5	Elliott Key CG	None			P35							Homestead, 9 mi E on North Canal Dr to Convoy Point Headquarters and launch ramp, by boat		0	B	All year		14	•	•	•	•	•								•		d			305-247-7275	Bx 1369, Homestead 33030
	Fort Jefferson NM																																					
52 H4	Garden Key				9							Key West, 68 mi W over open water		1	B	All year		14	•	•	•	•	•													305-247-6211	PO Bx 279, Homestead 33030
	NATIONAL SEASHORES																																					
	Gulf Islands																																					
53 H1	Fort Pickens CG	6.00	$ •		84	81	U		•			Pensacola, E on US 98, S on Hwy 399		0	B	All year		14	•	•	•	•	•		5	5						•		d			904-932-3192 904-932-5018	PO Box 100 Gulf Breeze 32561 Gulf Breeze 32561
	NATIONAL FORESTS																																					
	Osceola NF																																					
56 B3	Ocean Pond	3.00			12	39	21		•			(See HOW TO USE YOUR GUIDE for Nat Forest Development Scale) Olustee, 1.1 mi E on US 90, 4 mi N on Co 250A, 1.2 mi S on Fr 268		1	25	All year		14	•	•	•	•	•								1	1	dl			904-752-2577	Olustee
	Ocala NF																																					
57 C4	Juniper Springs	5.00			79	79	21		•			Ocala, 28 mi E on Hwy 40		1	47	All year		14	•	•	•	•	•		1	•					1	2	dlr			904-625-2520	Ocala
57 C4	Mill Dam	4.00			10	3	21		•			Ocala, 19 mi E on Hwy 40, 1.3 mi N on FR 58		1	4	All year		14	•	•	•	•	•		1	•					1		dlr			904-625-2520	Ocala
57 C4	Hopkins Prairie	3.00			10	4						Ocala, 24.2 mi E on Hwy 40, 6.3 mi N on FR 88, 4.6 mi E on FR 86, .6 mi N on FR 86F		1	5	All year		14	•	•	•	•			1											904-625-2520	Ocala
58 C3	Lake Eaton	4.00			12	12	21					Ocala, 19 mi E on Hwy 40, 4.2 mi N on Co 314A, .4 mi E on FR 79A, 1 mi N on FR 96		1	2	All year		14	•	•	•	•											d			904-625-2520	Ocala
59 C4	Salt Springs	6.00	•		209	209	31		•			Ocala, 10.9 mi E on Hwy 40, 18.4 mi N on Hwy 314, .8 mi N on Hwy 19		1	85	All year		14	•	•	•	•	•		1	1	1	1					dlr		n	904-625-2520	Ocala
60 C3	Johnson Field	3.00			19	7	15					Palatka, 17.2 mi SW on Hwy 19, .3 W on FR 77		1	5	10/1-4/30		14	•	•	•	•	•								1		dl			904-357-3721	Palatka
60 C3	Grassy Pond	3.00			6	6	31					Ocala, 11 mi E on Hwy 40, 19.8 mi NE on Hwy 314, 5.2 mi NW on Hwy 316, .6 mi N on FR 88E		1	2	All year		14	•	•	•	•	•		2	2										904-625-2520	Ocala
60 C3	Lake Delancy	3.00			15	15	31					Ocala, 11 mi E on Hwy 40, 19.8 mi NE on Hwy 314, 5.7 mi N on Hwy 19, 2 mi W on FR 75		1	88	All year		14	•	•	•	•	•								1		dlr			904-625-2520	Ocala
60 C3	Mason Bay	None			12	12	31					Ocala, 11 mi E on Hwy 40, 10 mi NE on Hwy 314		1	10	10/20-1/15	R	U		•	•					1	4	dl			904-625-2520	Ocala
61 C3	Fore Lake	4.00			29	16	21					Ocala, 11 mi E on Hwy 40, 6 mi NE on Hwy 19		1	10	All year		14	•	•	•	•			1	4	dl			904-625-2520	Ocala
62 C4	Lake Dorr	4.00			34	34	21	4				Umatilla, 5.6 mi N on Hwy 19		1	10	All year		14	•	•	•	•	•		2	1	•						dl			904-357-3721	Umatilla
62 C4	River Forest	None			20	20	31					Paisley, 10.5 mi E on Hwy 42		1	8	All year		14	•	•	•	•			2	4					1		dlr			904-357-3721	Paisley
62 C4	Clearwater Lake	4.00			42	42	21		•			Umatilla, 2.6 mi N on Hwy 19, 6.2 mi E on Hwy 42		1	10	All year		14	•	•	•	•	•		1	4					1		dl			904-357-3721	Umatilla
62 C4	Big Scrub	40.00			33	33	21					Altoona, 6.2 mi N on Hwy 19, 7 mi W on FR 73		1	9	All year		14	•	•	•	•			1	1					3	d	dlr			904-357-3721	Altoona
62 C4	Alexander Springs	5.00			67	67	21		•			Umatilla, 7.8 mi N on Hwy 19, 5.2 mi NE on Hwy 445		1	30	All year		14	•	•	•	•	•		4	•							dlr			904-357-3721	Umatilla
	Apalachicola NF																																					
64 B1	Whitehead Lake	3.00			4	2	21					Bristol, 11.4 mi E on Hwy 20, 3.2 mi S on Hwy 65, 15.1 mi SE on Hwy 67, 3.2 mi E on FR 111		1	2	All year		U		•	•	•														904-643-2477	Bristol
64 B1	Hitchcock Lake	3.00			6	4	15					Bristol, 11.4 mi E on Hwy 20, 3.2 mi S on Hwy 65, 22.8 mi SE on Hwy 67, 1.5 mi E on FR 184		1	3	All year		U		•	•	•											dl			904-643-2477	Bristol
65 H3	Wright Lake	3.00			21	6	21					Bristol, 12.8 mi S on Hwy 12, 22 mi NE on Hwy 379, 2 mi S on Hwy 65, 2 mi W on FR 101		1	8	All year		U		•	•	•										1	dl			904-643-2477	Bristol
65 H3	Hickory Landing	3.00			10	10	21					Bristol, 12.8 mi S on Hwy 12, 22 mi NE on Hwy 379, 2 mi S on Hwy 65, 1.8 mi SW on FR 101		1	2	All year		U		•	•	•											dl			904-643-2477	Bristol
65 H3	Cotton Landing	3.00			6	6	21					Bristol, 12.8 mi S on Hwy 12, 13.2 mi NE on Hwy 379, 2.8 mi SW on FR 123, .7 mi W on FR 123B		1	7	All year		U		•	•												dl			904-643-2477	Bristol
65 H3	Camel Lake	3.00			6	5	21					Bristol, 12.1 mi S on Hwy 12, 2 mi E on FR 105		1	4	All year		U		•	•	•											l			904-643-2477	Bristol

112 CAMPGROUNDS

FLORIDA

FOR MAP, SEE PAGE 114   MIAMI MAP, SEE PAGE 119

PARK NUMBER	MAP REFERENCE	NAME	FEE	ELECTRIC	WATER	SEWER	CREDIT CARDS	TENT SITES	TRAILER SITES	PULL-THRU	TRAILER SIZE	BOTTLED GAS	SANITARY SERVICE	MAXIMUM AMPS	NEAREST TOWN/ACCESS	PHYSICAL ENVIRONMENT	ELEVATION	ACRES	SEASON	RESERVATIONS	TIME LIMIT	PETS PERMITTED	MOTOR BIKES PERMITTED	FLUSH TOILETS	SHOWERS	TABLES	FIREWOOD	RECREATION HALL	CAFE	STORE	LAUNDRY	ICE	PLAYGROUND	SWIMMING POOL	OTHER SWIMMING	FISHING	BOATING	OTHER	TELEPHONE	MAIL ADDRESS
		NATIONAL FORESTS (CONT'D) *Apalachicola NF (Cont'd)*																																						
66	B1	Buckhorn	3.00					10							Crawfordville, 6.4 mi N on US 319, 12 mi NW on Hwy 267, 2 mi S on FR 350		1	8	11/1-1/31	U		•																	904-926-3561	Crawfordville
66	B1	Silver Lake	4.00	•				15	30	21		•			Tallahassee, 4.1 mi W on US 90, 5.2 mi SW on Hwy 20, 3 mi S on Co 260		1	7	All year	14		•	•	•	•	•		5			•								904-926-3561	Tallahassee
		CORP OF ENGINEERS *Lake Seminole*																																						
69	G3	East Bank Area	6.00	•	•			45	45	•	U	•	•		Chattahoochee, 2 mi N on Jim Woodruff Dam Rd	♿	1	158	All year	14		•	•	•	•	•													912-662-2814	Bx 96, Chattahoochee 32324
70	G3	Neal's Landing	None					15	15		U		○		Donalsonville GA, 12 mi W		1	121	All year	14		•	•			•					○			dl						
		Okeechobee Lake																																						
71	E5	St Lucie Lock & Dam	5.00					10	S10	U					Stuart, 6 mi S on Hwy 76		1	15	All year	14		•	•	•	•	•								l						Bx 1327, Clewiston 33440
72	F4	Ortona Lock	None					10	S10	U					La Belle, 8 mi E on Hwy 78		1	5	All year	14		•	•	•	•	•								dl			813-983-8101	
73	F4	WP Franklin Lock & Dam-N	5.00					12	S12	U					Bayshore, jct of Hwys 31 & 78, 5 mi E on Hwy A1A (boat access only)		1	2	All year	14		•	•	•	•	•					○			dl				
73	F4	WP Franklin Lock & Dam-S	5.00					13	13	•	U		○		Fort Myers, 15 mi E on Hwy 80		1	10	All year	14		•	•	•	•	•								l				
		CITY, COUNTY AND CIVIC																																						
80	F4	Moore Haven RA	5.00	•	•		MV	15	S31	U		•		30	Moore Haven, N on Hwy 27 to Moore Haven Locks	▲ 🏕	1	27	All year	N 14		•	•	•	•	•		•						dlr		m	813-983-2662	PO Bx 68, Moore Haven 33471
83	A2	Markham Pk	8.50	• • $				70	80	32,	○	•			Fort Lauderdale, I-95, 14 mi W on Hwy 84	▲ 🏕	1	607	All year	Z 14	•	•	•	•	•	•	•	○			•		•	lr			305-472-5882	16001 W 84, Ft Lrdrl 33326
84	D5	Grange Island South	None					P50	95		U				Melbourne, 12 mi S on Hwy 19 (boat access only)	▲ 🏕		30	All year	N 21		•	•	•	•	•		○						d			305-727-9762	Melbourne 32901
84	D5	Long Point Recreation Pk	7.61	$ $ $				45	P20	U		•			Melbourne Beach, 18 mi S on Hwy A1A	▲ 🏕		100	All year	N 21		•	•	•	•	•								dl			305-723-3839	Melbourne Bch 32951
84	D5	Grange Island North	None					P20			U				Melbourne, 12 mi S (boat access only)	▲ 🏕		5	All year	N 21		•	•	•	•	•								d			305-727-9762	Melbourne 32901
85	E5	The Savannas	5.50	• •				64	64	U		•			Fort Pierce, US 1, 1 mi E on Hwy 712	▲ 🏕	1	25	All year	Z 7	•	•	•	•	•	•		○						lr	g		305-464-7855	1400E Midway Rd,FtPierce33450
87	D4	Wickham Pk	7.62	• •				85	85	30	○	•			Melbourne, US 1 N, 1 mi W on Parkway Dr	▲ 🏕	1	480	All year	N 21	•	•	•	•	•	•	•	○			○				gmt		305-254-1764	Melbourne 32935
88	C4	Eustis Municipal RV Pk	8.00	• •				1400	45	35	○	•		20	Eustis, .75 mi N on Hwy 19, 25 mi W on Hwy 452A	▲ 🏕		100	All year	Z U	•	•	•	•	•	•		○						lr	g		904-357-8882	PO Bx 509, Eustis 32726
89	G5	Milton Thompson Pk	8.00	•				25	45	U					Hialeah, US 27, 2 mi S on State Hwy 27	▲ 🏕		30	11/1-5/1	N 21		•	•	•	•	•		○						d			305-821-5122	Rt 1 Bx 659C, Hialeah 33010
94	D4	Turkey Lake Pk	12.00	• • $				200	32	U		•		30	Orlando, 7 mi W on I-4, ext on SR 535, fol signs to Hiawassee Rd	▲ 🏕	0	175	All year	N 21	•	•	•	•	•	•		○					•	dl	ghkt		305-299-5581	3401 S Hiawassee, Orlndo 32811
96	A3*	John D Easterlin Pk	10.00	•				45	45	22	U		•		Oakland Park, I-95, E on Oakland Pk Ave, N on NW 9th Ave, W on NW 38th	▲ 🏕	1	46	All year	Z 14		•	•	•	•	•		○							g		305-776-4466	1000 NW 38th, Ft Lrdrl 33309
97	D5	Jetty Park	10.00	•	$			15	117	U					Cape Canaveral, in town	▲ 🏕	0	38	All year	N 21		•	•	•	•	•	•	○			•				gt		305-783-7222	400 E Jetty, Cp Canaveral32920
99	E3	Fort DeSoto Pk	9.00	• •				85	150	30	○	•		20	Tierra Verde, US 19, 2-1/4 mi W on Hwy 682, 4-3/4 mi S on Hwy 693	▲ 🏕	1	900	All year	N 14		•	•	•	•	•		○						l	gt		813-866-2662	Tierra Verde 33715
		PRIVATE																																						
100	B4	Lazy J Trlr Ranch	6.00	•					S22	U					St. Augustine, Hwy 16, btw US 1 & I-95, on Woodland Ave	▬ 🌿	1	4	All year	Z U	•	•	•	•	•	•					○			dl	g		904-829-8745	Rt10 Bx121C,St Augustine32084
101	C3	Silver Spgs Cmprs Garden	10.95	• •				184	184	U		•		50	Silver Springs, I-75, 10 mi E on Hwy 40	▬ 🌿	1	15	All year	R U	•	•	•	•	•	•	•	○	○	○	•	•	•		g		904-236-3700	Bx 7, Silver Springs 32688
101	C3	Craft Motel Trlr Pk	10.00	• •	AMV			27	27	•	U	•	•	30	Silver Springs, 1 blk W	▬ 🌿	1	10	All year	Z U	•	•	•	•	•	•		○			•				g		904-236-2782	PO Bx 25, Silver Spgs 32688
102	E4	Goff's Oak Acres CG	7.35	• •				50	V25	•	U	•	○		Lake Placid, 16 mi S on US 27, 4 mi W on Hwy 731	▬ 🌿	1	20	10/1-5/30	Z U	•	•	•	•	•	•		○						d	g		813-465-2795	Rt 2 Bx 383, Lk Placid 33852
103	C4	Lake Crescent Trlr Pk	8.00	• • $$$					V6		U	•			Crescent City, US 17	▬ 🌿	1	5	All year	Z U	•	•	•	•	•	•					○			dlr			904-698-2322	1100 N Summit,Crscnt Cty32012
103	C4	KOA Crescent City	8.50	• • $$$				10	83	•	U	•	•	50	Crescent City, 1 mi N on US 17	▬ 🌿	1	30	All year	R U	•	•	•	•	•	•	•	○			•		•	dlr	g		904-698-2020	Rt 1 Bx 25,Crescent City 32012
104	B2	Suwannee Gables Motel	10.00	• •	MV				4		U	•		30	Old Town, 1.5 mi N on US 19/98/27A	▬ 🌿	1	3	All year	Z 14	•	•	•	•	•	•								dl			904-542-7752	Rt. 3, Bx 567 Old Town 32680
105	C3	Silver Waldena Rsrt	7.50	• •				30	65	•	U	•	•		Silver Springs, 8 mi E on Hwy 40	▲ 🏕	1	55	All year	Z U	•	•	•	•	•	•		○			○			dr	g		904-625-2851	Rt 4 Bx 300, SilverSpgs 32688
106	D4	Torchlite Trvl Trlr Pk	8.00	• •				10	40	•	U	•	•		Clermont, 3.5 mi S on US 27	▲ 🏕	1	13	All year	Z U	•	•	•	•	•	•		○						dr	g		904-394-3716	Rt 1, Bx 8AA, Clermont 32711
107	D3	Riverlawn Trlr Pk	7.00	• •					15	•	U	•			Riverview, US 301, 1 mi E on Stoner Rd	▲ 🏕	1	15	All year	Z U		•	•	•	•	•		○						dr	gt		813-677-6622	Stoner Rd., Riverview 33569
107	D3	Oakside Mbl Pk	10.00	• •					15	•	U				Riverview, 1 mi N on US 301	▲ 🏕	1	5	All year	Z U		•	•	•	•	•		○						dlr	gt		813-677-1086	Bx 70, Riverview 33569
108	A3*	Kozy Kampers	3.99	• •	MV			20	V87	•	U	•		30	Fort Lauderdale, FL tpke, ext 20, 1/2 mi E on Commercial Blvd	▲ 🏕	1	6	All year	Z U		•	•	•	•	•		○						dl	g		305-731-8570	3631 W Cmmrcl,Ft Lrdrl 33309
110	H2	Sandy Beach CG	6.00	• •				E50	V150	•	•	•	•	30	Gulf Breeze, jct Hwy 399/US 98, 10 mi E on US 98	▲ 🏕	1	50	All year	Z U		•	•	•	•	•		○			○			dr	g		904-932-4248	6401 Gulf Breeze,Glf Brz32561
110	H2	Navarre Bch Family CG	8.00	• •				160	160	•	U	•			Pensacola, 27 mi E on US 98, 1.5 mi E Navarre Bridge on US 98	▲ 🏕	1	10	All year	Z U		•	•	•	•	•		○							g		904-939-2188	Rt 1 Bx 24, Mary Esther 32569
110	H2	Squirrel's Tent City	6.00	• •				50	150	U		•			Pensacola, 15 mi E on US 98	▲ 🏕	1	150	All year	Z U		•	•	•	•	•		○						dl	g		904-932-4248	Gulf Breeze 32561
111	F4	Shady Acres Trvl Pk	10.00	• •	MV			10	300	U		•		30	Fort Myers, 12 mi S on US 41	▲ 🏕	1	23	All year	Z U		•	•	•	•	•	•	○							g		813-481-3361	PO Bx 740, Estero 33928

CAMPGROUNDS   113

FLORIDA

Population: 9,746,342 (1980 Census)
Area: 54,153 Sq. Miles
Capital: Tallahassee

Cities and Towns

Alachua	B-3
Apalachicola	H-3
Apopka	C-4
Arcadia	E-3
Atlantic Beach	B-4
Auburndale	D-4
Avon Park	D-4
Bartow	D-3
Belle Glade	H-3
Blountstown	H-3
Boca Raton	F-5
Bonifay	F-5
Boynton Beach	F-5
Bradenton	E-3
Bristol	H-3
Bronson	C-3
Brooksville	D-3
Bushnell	C-3
Cantonment	G-1
Cape Canaveral	D-5
Cape Coral	E-3
Chattahoochee	A-1, G-3
Chipley	G-3
Clearwater	D-3
Clermont	D-4
Cocoa	D-5
Cocoa Beach	G-5
Coral Gables	C-4
Crawfordville	B-1
Crescent City	C-4
Crestview	B-2
Cross City	E-3
Crystal River	E-3
Dade City	D-3
Dania	F-5
Daytona Beach	C-4
Deerfield Beach	F-5
De Funiak Sprs.	G-2
De Land	F-5
Delray Beach	F-5
Dunedin	D-3
E. Naples	F-4
Florida City	G-5
Ft. Lauderdale	F-5
Ft. Meade	E-3
Ft. Myers	E-3
Ft. Ogden	E-3
Ft. Pierce	E-5
Ft. Walton Beach	H-2
Frostproof	E-4
Gainesville	G-5
Goulds	B-4
Green Cove Sprs.	A-2
Greenville	D-4
Haines City	D-4
Hallandale	G-5
Hialeah	B-3
High Springs	B-3
Holly Hill	C-4
Hollywood	G-5
Homestead	C-3
Inverness	C-3
Jacksonville	B-4
Jacksonville Beach	B-4

FLORIDA

One inch equals approximately 50.3 miles

FLORIDA (WESTERN SECTION)

One inch equals approximately 57.8 miles

Jasper	A-2
Kenansville	D-4
Key West	H-4
Kissimmee	D-4
La Belle	F-4
Lake Butler	B-3
Lake City	B-3
Lakeland	D-3
Lake Placid	E-4
Lake Wales	D-4
Lake Worth	F-5
Lawtey	B-3
Leesburg	C-3
Live Oak	B-2
Macclenny	B-3
Madison	A-2
Marathon	H-4
Marianna	A-2
Mayo	B-2
Melbourne	D-5
Mexico Beach	H-3
Miami	G-5
Miami Beach	G-5
Miami Shores	G-5
Milton	G-1
Monticello	A-2
Moore Haven	F-4
Naples	F-4
New Port Richey	D-3
New Smyrna Beach	C-3
Ocala	C-3
Okeechobee	E-4
Opa-Locka	G-5
Orange City	C-4
Orlando	D-4
Ormond Beach	C-4
Palatka	C-3
Palm Beach	F-5
Palmetto	E-3
Panama City	H-3
Pensacola	H-1
Perrine	G-5
Perry	B-2
Plant City	D-3
Pompano Beach	F-5
Punta Gorda	E-3
Quincy	A-1
Riviera Beach	F-5
St. Augustine	B-4
St. Cloud	D-4
St. Petersburg	E-3
Sanford	C-4
Sarasota	E-3
Sebring	E-4
Starke	B-3
Stuart	E-5
Tallahassee	A-1
Tampa	D-3
Tarpon Sprs	D-3
Tavares	C-4
Titusville	C-4
Trenton	B-3
Venice	E-3
Vero Beach	E-5
Warrington	H-1
Watertown	B-3
Wauchula	E-3
W. Palm Beach	F-5
W. Pensacola	H-1
Wewahitchka	H-3
Winter Haven	D-4
Winter Park	D-4

FLORIDA

FOR MAP, SEE PAGE 114   MIAMI MAP, SEE PAGE 119

PARK NUMBER / MAP REFERENCE	NAME	FEE	ELECTRIC / WATER / SEWER	CREDIT CARDS	TENT SITES	TRAILER SITES	PULL-THRU / TRAILER SIZE	BOTTLED GAS / SANITARY SERVICE / MAXIMUM AMPS	NEAREST TOWN/ACCESS	PHYSICAL ENVIRONMENT / ELEVATION	ACRES	SEASON	RESERVATIONS / TIME LIMIT / PETS PERMITTED / MOTOR BIKES PERMITTED / FLUSH TOILETS / SHOWERS / TABLES / FIREWOOD / RECREATION HALL / STORE / CAFE / ICE / LAUNDRY / PLAYGROUND / SWIMMING POOL / OTHER SWIMMING / FISHING / BOATING / OTHER	TELEPHONE	MAIL ADDRESS
	PRIVATE (CONT'D)														
111 F4	Woodsmoke Cmpg Rsrt	14.50	•••	MV	14	292	• U	• 30	Fort Myers, 9 mi S on US 41	▲≋≋ 1	35	All year	N U ••••• ••••••• • •• gt	813-992-1772	19251 US 41 SE,Ft Myers 33908
112 D3	Camp Nebraska Trvl Trl Pk	10.00	•••		3	70	• U	• 30	Fowler, .5 mi S on NE Ave (US 41) in Tampa	▲≋≋ 1	5	All year	N U •• ••••• •• ••••	813-971-3460	10314 N Nebraska, Tampa 33612
112 D3	Busch Trvl Pk	11.21	••S	AMV		134	• U	• 30	Tampa, I-75, Busch Blvd ext, 2.5 mi E, .5 mi N on McKinley (40th) Dr	▲⛺ 1	17	All year	N 7 •• •••••• ••• g	813-971-0008	10001 McKinley Dr,Tampa 33612
112 D3	Marty's Trlr Pk	9.50	•••			32	• U	• 30	Tampa, I-75, Fowler ext, 1 blk E, S on Nebraska Ave (US 41)	▲⛺ 1	5	All year	N U •• ••• ••• •• g	813-977-1102	10510 Nebraska Av, Tampa 33612
113 D3	Camper's Holiday Pk	7.50	•••			65	• U	•	Brooksville, 7.5 mi S on Hwy C581	▲≋≋ 1	45	All year	N U •• r ••••••• •• •••	904-796-3707	2092 Culbreath, Brksvll 33512
114 H2	Gulf Hills CG	6.00	•••	MV	40	V20	• U	• 30	Destin, 15 mi E on US 98, 5 mi on C30A	▲⛺≋ 1	40	3/1-12/1	Z U ••• ••••• $ •• •• a	904-267-2446	Box 142, Santa Rosa Bch 32459
115 D3	KOA Ft Lauderdale	10.00	•••			A45	• U	• 50	Fort Lauderdale, I-95, .5 mi W on Hwy 84, 1/4 mi S	▲⛺ 1	12	All year	Z U ••• •••••••••• l ••• a	305-584-5404	3400 SW 26 Trrc,Ft Ldrdl33312
116 E3	Trailer Villa	10.00	••S	MV		400	• U	• 30	Bradenton, S on Bus US 41, 2 blks E on 53rd Ave W	⛺ 1	20	All year	Z U ••••• •••• •• ••	813-755-5680	1101-53 Ave W,Bradenton 33507
116 E3	Sugarcreek Country Club	15.00	•••				• U	• 30	Bradenton, US 41 N, 2 mi E on 26th Ave	▲⛺ 1	40	All year	N U ••• ••••• •••• ••	813-747-6331	3300 26th E, Bradenton 33508
116 E3	Arbor Terrace Pk	10.00	$••	MV		A62	• U	• 15	Bradenton, Bus US 41, .5 mi E on 57th Ave W	⛺≋ 1	30	All year	N U ••••• ••• •• gt	813-755-6494	405 57 Ave W Bradenton 33507
117 E3	Sarasota Lks Cmpg Rsrt	10.00	•••			298	• U	• 50	Sarasota, US 41 W at DeSota Rd to US 301, N on 301 to University Pkwy to CG	⛺≋ 1		All year	Z U ••••• ••••••••• • •• g	813-355-8585	1674 Univ Pkwy,Sarasota 33580
117 E3	Windward Isle	11.50	•••			A58	• U		Sarasota, I-75, ext 37 Hwy 72, 1/4 mi W	⛺ 1	30	All year	N U ••• ••• ••	813-922-3090	1 Catamaran Dr,Sarasota 33583
118 B3	Travelers Campground	8.00	•••		20	100	• U	•	Alachua, I-75 & US 441, Alachua ext, 200 yds S on US 441, 1 mi N on Access Rd	⛺≋ 1	40	All year	N U ••• ••••• ••• • g	904-462-2505	Rt 2 Bx 307, Alachua 32615
120 C4	Salt Springs CG	8.40	$••		74	135	• U	• 30	Palatka, Ocala NF on Hwy 19, at jct of Hwys 316 & 19	▲⛺ 1	150	All year	Z U ••••••• d ••• gt	904-685-2048	Rt 2 Bx 1560, Ft McCoy 32637
121 D4	Silver Glen Springs	10.50	$••		100	V50	• U	• 30	Fort McCoy, I-95, 35 mi W on Hwy 40, 4 mi on Hwy 19	▲⛺ 1	1015	All year	Z U ••••••• dlr ••• g	904-685-2514	Rt 2 Bx 3000, Ft McCoy 32637
121 D4	The Best Holiday Trvl Pk	11.00	•••	MV	200	200	• U	• 30	Winter Haven, US 27, 1 mi W on Hwy 540	⛺ 1	22	All year	Z U ••• •••••• o ••• gt	813-324-7400	7400 Cprss Gdns,Wntr Hvn33880
121 D4	Hammondell CS	11.00	•••		20	V130	• 49	• 30	Cypress Gardens, 2-1/2 mi E on Cypress Gardens Rd	▲⛺≋ 1	14	All year	Z U ••• ••••••• dlr •••	813-324-5775	5601 Cprss Gdns,Wntr Hvn33880
121 D4	Lakeshore Palms Trvl Pk	10.00	•••				• 49	• 15	Cypress Gardens, 2 mi S on Helena Rd	⛺ 1	2	All year	Z U ••• •••••• o ••	813-324-1339	4800 Eloise Rd,Wntr Hven33880
122 H3	Magnolia Bch Cottage & CG	8.00	$••		75	75	• 32	• 30	Panama City, US 98, 3 mi S on Hwy 3031, 1.5 mi E on Hwy 747	▲⛺ 1	7	All year	N U •• ••••••• dl ••	904-234-2108	7800 Magnolia Rd,Panama 32401
123 H4	Big Pine Key Fishing Ldg	9.00	•••		70	112	U		Bahia Honda, 3 mi S on US 1, at Spanish Harbor Bridge, mi mrkr 33	⛺ 0	9	All year	Z U •• ••••••• dlr •••	305-872-2351	Bx 513, Big Pine Key 33043
123 H4	Sea Horse CG	9.00	•••		71	42	30, U	o •	Big Pine Key, Spanish Harbor Brdg, 2 mi SW on US 1, .25 mi Nat mi mrkr 31	▲⛺ 1	8	All year	Z U ••••••• dlr •••	305-872-2443	Rt 1 Bx 533, Big Pine Key33043
123 H4	Halcyon Beach Trlr Pk	11.00	•••			A18	31		Marathon, US 1, btw mi mrkr 31 & 30, 1.5 mi N at Key Deer Blvd on Watson Blvd, corner Ave 8	▲⛺ 1	9	All year	N U ••• ••••• d •••	305-872-2699	PO Bx 56, Big Pine Key 33043
124 D3	KOA Tampa East		•••	MV	47	112	• U	• 30	Tampa, 12 mi E on I-4, McIntosh ext, .25 mi S to US 92, 350 ft W	▲⛺ 1	18	All year	Z U ••• •••••••••• • ••• g	813-754-3027	Rt. 3, Box 280, Dover 33527
124 D3	Tampa-East Green Acres CG	11.00	•••		40	260	• U	• 30	Dover, I-4, McIntosh Rd ext #9, .25 mi S, .25 mi W on US 92	▲⛺ 1	30	All year	Z U ••• ••••••• o ••• g	813-659-0002	12720 US Hwy 92, Dover 33527
125 C4	Daytona Beach Trlr Pk	8.00	••S			14	o U	•	Daytona Beach, jct US 92 & US 1, 1 mi N, 2 blks E on Madison	▲⛺ 1	3	All year	N U •• ••••• ••• g	904-258-6652	646 N Bch St,Daytona Bch32014
125 C4	Daytona Beach CG	10.00	•••	MV	60	180	• U	• 30	Daytona Beach, I-96, S Dayton (SR400) to Clyde Morris Blvd, 3 mi S	⛺ 1	17	All year	N U ••• ••••• ••• dl ••• g	904-761-2663	Daytona Beach 32019
125 C4	Rose Bay Trvl Pk	9.00	•••			289	U	•	Daytona Beach, 6 mi S on US 1, 1 .5 mi W on Nova Rd	▲⛺ 1	31	All year	N U ••• •••••• ••• g	904-767-4308	5401 S Nova, Pt Orange 32019
125 C4	Orange Isles CG	11.77	•••		100	150	U		Daytona Beach, I-95, ext S Daytona, E on Hwy 400, 1.5 mi S on S-5A/Nova	▲⛺ 1	22	All year	N U •• •••••• ••••• d ••• g	904-767-9170	Bx 1609 RR 6,Daytona Bch32019
125 C4	Nova Family CG	8.50	••S		100	V150	• U	• 30	Daytona Beach, US 1, 1.5 mi W on Herbert St	▲⛺≋ 1	17	All year	Z U ••• ••••••• dl ••• gt	904-767-0095	RR6 Bx 1569,Daytona Bch 32019
125 C4	Seaside Trlr Pk on Ocn	13.00	••S	V		38	U		Daytona Beach, N to Hwy 40, 2 mi N on Hwy A1A	⛺ 1	4	All year	N U •• •••••• •• ••	904-401-0900	1093 Ocean Shr,Ormnd Bch32074
126 G1	West Florida MHP	6.50	•••			7	• U		Pensacola, US 29, 1 mi E on US 90A	⛺ 1		All year	N U ••• •••••• •••	904-477-2059	550 E 9 Mi Rd,Pensacola 32514
128 D3	Holiday Springs Trav-L-Pk	12.00	$••	MV		A248	• 28	• 30	Weeki Wachee Springs, 7 mi S on US 19	▲≋≋ 1	60	10/1-5/1	R U ••• •••••••• lr ••• g	904-683-0034	Bx 500, Weeki Wachee 33512
129 C4	KOA Daytona North/Bulow	12.50	•••		150	350	• 20	• 30	Daytona Beach, 14 mi N on I-95, ext 90 Marco Polo Blvd 1/4 mi E, 3 mi N on 5-A	▲⛺≋ 1	90	All year	N U ••• ••••••••• $ •• g	904-439-2549	Bx 1328, Flagler Bch 32036
129 C4	Beverly Bch Surfside Camp	12.95	•••		100	124	• U	• 30	Flagler Beach, jct Hwy A1A/100, 3 mi N	▲⛺ 1	10	All year	N U •• •••••• ••• g	904-439-3111	PO Bx 1048, Flagler Bch 32036
129 C4	Picnickers' CG, North	10.00	•••		10	40	U	• 30	Flagler Beach, jct Hwy A1A/100, 2 mi N	⛺ 1	3	All year	N U •• •••• ••• g	904-439-2495	Rt 1 Bx 254,Flagler Bch 32036

116   CAMPGROUNDS

FLORIDA

FOR MAP, SEE PAGE 114 — MIAMI MAP, SEE PAGE 119

Park #	Map Ref	Name	Fee	Credit Cards	Electric/Water	Sewer	Tent Sites	Trailer Sites	Pull-Thru	Bottled Gas	Sanitary Service	Max Amps	Nearest Town/Access	Physical Env	Elevation	Acres	Season	Reservations	Pets	Time Limit	Motor Bikes	Flush Toilets	Showers	Tables	Firewood	Recreation Hall	Store	Cafe	Laundry	Ice	Playground	Swimming Pool	Other Swimming	Fishing	Boating	Other	Telephone	Mail Address
		PRIVATE (CONT'D)																																					
129	C4	Picnickers' CG, South	10.00		•		10	50	•	o o		30	Flagler Beach, jct Hwy A1A/100, 2 mi N		1	5	All year	N	U	•	•	•	•	•				•	•		•					904-439-5473	Rt 1 Bx 258, Flagler Bch 32036
130	D3	Spanish Main Travel Rsrt	12.00		•		50	300	• U			30	Tampa, I-4, 6.5 mi N on US 301		1	35	All year	N	U		•	•	•	•	o	o	o	•	•				ghk		813-986-2415	Thonotosassa 33592
130	D3	Happy Traveler RV Pk & CG	14.00		•		20	185	• U			30	Tampa, I-75 bypass, .5 mi E on Fowlers Ave		1	18	All year	N	U	•	•	•	•	•	o	o	o	•	•				g		813-986-3094	Bx 290A, Thonotasassa 33592
131	C3	Camper's World	14.00		•		40	60	• U			30	Lake Panasoffkee, I-75, 8 mi W on Hwy 44		1	35	All year	N	U		•	•	•	•	o		o	•	•	dlr			g		904-748-2237	Rt 2 Bx 456, Lk Pnsfkee 33538
131	C3	Midtown Trlr Pk	9.50		•			28	U				Inverness, US 41		1	1	All Year	N	U		•	•	•	•				•					g		904-726-2961	110 S Pk Ave, Inverness 32651
132	D3	Country-Aire Estates	5.75		•		45	150	• U			30	Dade City, 2 mi W off US 301		1	10	All year	N	U		•	•	•	•			o	•	•	dl			g		305-567-3630	800 McDonald Dade City 32525
133	E3	ARC Rsrt	9.00		•			150	• U			30	Miami, 9 mi S on US 41, 2.5 mi E on Gibsonton Dr		1	22	All year	N	U		•	•	•	•	o			•	•				g		813-677-1997	9812 Gibsonton, Riverview 33569
134	D3	Son-Mar Trvl Pk	12.00		$			303	• U			30	Port Richey, 10 mi N on US 19		1	16	All year	N	U		•	•	•	•				•	•				g		813-868-2285	300 S Duncan, Clrwtr 33515
135	B3	Old Bellamy Rd Cmpg Pk	7.00		•		20	48	• U			30	Gainesville, 20 mi N on I-75, 1/4 mi W on Hwy 236, 1000 ft N on Co		1	6	All year	N	U		•	•	•	•				•					g		904-454-1098	Rt 1 Bx 332, High Spgs 32643
137	G4	Enchanting Acres MHP	12.00		•			A57	• U			30	Naples, 2.5 mi E on US 41		1	28	All year	N	U		•	•	•	•				•		dlr			g		813-774-2822	2 Enchanting Blvd, Naples 33942
138	D4	Lake Wales CG	9.50		•		5	70	o U			30	Lake Wales, jct US 27 & Hwy 60, 3 mi S on US 27		1	14	All year	N	U		•	•	•	•	o			•	•				g		813-638-9011	3430 Hwy 27 S, Lk Wales 33853
138	D4	Camp Inn Resort	12.00		•		15	325	• U			30	Lake Wales, 8.5 mi S on US 27		1	75	All year	N	U		•	•	•	•		o		•	•	•			g		813-635-2500	3455 N Hwy 27, Frstprf 33843
138	D4	Camp 'n Aire	9.50		•		10	80	• U			30	Lake Wales, 3 mi S on US 27		1	13	All year	N	U		•	•	•	•	o			•	•				g		813-638-3853	3532 Hwy 27 S, Lk Wales 33853
138	D4	Sandy Cove Trlr Pk	8.00		$			AS16	U			30	Lake Wales, 5 mi S on US-27A, 1 mi SE on N Crookes Lk Dr		1	4	All year	N	U		•	•	•	•				•		l			g		813-638-1139	159 Crooked Lk, Babson Lk 33827
139	D4	Lazy K Family KG	8.00		•		20	87	• U			30	Haines City, 6 mi S on US 27, 1 blk W on Hwy 542		1	15	All year	N	U		•	•	•	•	o			•	•				g		813-439-1107	Bx 1799, Dundee 33838
139	D4	Paradise Island KG	9.00		•		8	167	• U			30	Haines City, 2-1/2 mi N on US 17		1	10	All year	N	U		•	•	•	•	o	o	o	•	•	dlr			g		813-439-1350	Hwy 27 S, Haines City 33844
140	H4	Jolly Roger Travel Pk	8.00		$ $		60	145	• U			30	Marathon, N on US 1, at mi mrkr 59		1	15	All year	N	U		•	•	•	•	o		o	•					g		305-289-0404	Bx 525 Rt 1, Marathon 33050
140	H4	Lions Lair Travel Pk	10.00		$ $		10	60	o U			30	Marathon, Grassy Key, #59 mi mrkr		1	8	All year	N	U		•	•	•	•	o	o		•	•	dlr			g		305-289-0606	RR 1 Bx 390, Marathon 33050
144	B3	Casey Jones CG	5.00		$		15	34	• U			30	Lake City, I-75, Lake City Hwy 47 ext, 1/8 mi to 242, W 1/ 8 mi		1	3	All year	N	U		•	•	•	•				•	•				ght		904-752-9789	RR 9 Bx 1088, Lake City 32055
146	D2	Wynken Blynken & Nod Pk	14.00		•			10	U	o			Hialeah, US 27 at 2775 W Okeechobee Rd		0	13	1 year	N	U		•	•	•	•	o		o	•		lr			gh		305-887-6570	2775 W Okchbee, Hialeah 33010
147	F5	The Anchorage MHP	9.00		•		810	17	• U	810			Delray Beach, 1-1/2 mi N on E side of US 1		1	10	All year	N	U		•	•	•	•				•		dlr			gt		305-278-2020	1925 Fed Hwy, Delray Bch 33444
149	E4	Crystal Lakes RV Rsrt	12.00		•			810	31				Okeechobee, S on US 441		1	165	All year	N	U		•	•	•	•	o			•	•				gt		305-763-0231	US 441 S, Okeechobee
149	E4	Vantage Oaks Camp	8.00		•		A30	168	• U			30	Okeechobee, 2.5 mi SE on St Rd 710 (Beeline), 1 mi S on Everglades Blvd		1	15	All year	N	U		•	•	•	•	o					lr			ght		813-763-9935	4351 SE 26 St, Okeechobee 33472
150	E2	Tamiami Trlr Pk	10.00		•		23	203					Miami, in town		1	12	All year	N	U		•	•	•	•	o			•					g		305-649-9170	3038 SW 8th St, Miami 33135
151	D3*	KOA Miami North	14.75		•			295	31	•			Miami, 1-1/2 mi N on US 17		1	9	All year	N	U		•	•	•	•	o	o	o	•	•				g		305-940-4141	14075 Biscayne, Miami 33181
152	E3	Shell Creek Pk	11.00		•		12	176	• U				Punta Gorda, 4-1/2 mi E on US 17, 4-1/2 mi E on Hwy 764		1	20	All year	N	U		•	•	•	•				•	•	dlr			g		813-639-4234	Rt 1 C-764, Punta Gorda 33950
152	G4	Peace River Fishing Camp	9.50		•		15	V32	U			50	Punta Gorda, 10 mi N on Hwy 17		1	10	All year	N	U		•	•	•	•				•	•				g		305-892-7010	Rt 1 Bx 411, Punta Gorda 33950
154	G4	Marco Naples Hitching Pst	14.00		•			295	• U				Naples, 6 mi E on US 41		1	23	All year	N	U		•	•	•	•	o		o	•	•	dl			g		813-774-1259	100 Barefoot Wms Rd, Npls 33962
154	G4	KOA Naples	10.75		•	MV	18	155	• U				Naples, 7 mi SE on US 41, 1/4 mi S on Co 951, 1/8 mi E on Henderson Creek Dr		1	15	All year	N	U		•	•	•	•	o	o		•	•	dl			gt		813-774-5455	1700 Barefoot Wms, Naples 33962
154	G4	M & E Trlr Pk	13.00		•			A100	U			50	Naples, jct FL tpke, 4-1/2 mi E on Hwy 826, 1 mi S on US 1		1	6	All year	N	U		•	•	•	•				•					gt		813-774-5414	13 Chrry Tree Ln, Naples 33962
156	D4	Canoe Creek CG	9.50		•		50	171	• U			30	St. Cloud, 6 mi S on Hwy 523		1	30	All year	N	U		•	•	•	•				•	•	dlr			g		305-892-7010	Rt 2 2440, St Cloud 32769
157	E3	Caroline Trlr Ct	8.50		•			28	U			20	St. Petersburg, 6418 Haines Rd		1	3	All year	N	U		•	•	•	•	o			•					g		813-525-3250	6418 Haines, St Prtsbrg 33702
157	E3	KOA St Petersburg	14.00		•		50	392	• U			30	St. Petersburg, 2 mi NW on Alt US 19 to 95th St N		1	40	All year	N	U		•	•	•	•	o		o	•	•	dl			gt		813-392-2233	5400 95 St N, St Prtsbrg 33708
159	E5	Twin Rivers Mbl Pk	10.00		•			20	• U			30	Stuart, 8 mi S on US 1		1	6	All year	N	U		•	•	•	•				•	•				g		813-283-3631	7770 Fed Hwy, Hope Sound 33455
160	E3	Gulf Beach Trlr Pk	11.75		$			37	32				Siesta Key, US 41, 1 mi W on Hwy 72, 2 mi S on Midnight Pass Rd		1	2	All year	N	U		•	•	•	•				•					g		813-349-3839	8862 Midnight Pass, Srsta 33581
162	B4	Bing's Fmly CG	8.00		•		12	52	• U			30	Marineland, 3.5 mi S on Hwy A1A		1	8	All year	N	U		•	•	•	•				•		dlr			g		904-445-3242	Rt 1 Bx 134, St Augustine 32084
163	C3	Tall Timber Trvl Trlr Pk	6.00		•			154	• U			30	Silver Springs, 10 mi E on Hwy 40, 1 mi N at Lynne		1	43	9/1-5/30	N	U		•	•	•	•				•					g		904-625-2783	Rt 4 Bx 950, Silver Sprgs 32688
163	C3	Forest Cove CG	6.00		•		18	16	• U			30	Silver Springs, 6 mi E on Hwy 40, .5 mi S		1	5	All year	N	U		•	•	•	•				•					g		904-625-1295	R 6 Bx 397 FC, Slvr Spgs 32688
164	C4	Trail Boss CG	8.00		•		5	V22	U			30	Welaka, US 17, 5 mi N on Hwy 309, River Rd to CG		1	4	All year	N	U		•	•	•	•				•	•	dlr			gmt		904-467-2319	PO Bx 52, Welaka 32093
165	G5	DeSoto Park	12.00		•			A100	• U			50	Homestead, US 1, opposite Chamber of Commerce		0	30	All year	N	U		•	•	•	•				•					g		305-248-0232	100 NE 6th Ave, Homestead 33030
165	G5	Isla Gold MHP	12.00		•	MV		100	A32				Homestead, 4 mi W on Hwy A1A		0	17	All year	N	U		•	•	•	•				•		dlr			g		305-258-0818	26401 S Fed Hwy, Naranja 33032
165	G5	Coral Roc MHP	7.50		$			200	U				Homestead, FL Tpke, 137th Ave ext, S to Biscayne Dr, 1.5 mi E to 152nd Ave, .5 blk N		1	30	All year	N	R		•	•	•	•				•							305-247-1328	28201 152nd, Homestead 33030
166	E5	Zachary Taylor Cmpg Rsrt	9.75		•	MV	50	49	• U			30	Okeechobee, jct US-441/Hwy 70, 5 mi S on US 441/98		1	20	All year	N	U		•	•	•	•	o			•	•	dlr			gm		813-763-3377	361 US 441S, Okeechobee 33472
168	H2	Sand Dollar CG	8.00		$		49	49	• U			30	Panama City, 20 mi W on US 98, 7 mi W on 30A		1	3	All year	N	N		•	•	•	•				•					ghs		904-231-4358	Rt 2 Bx 627, Seagrv Bch 32459

CAMPGROUNDS 117

FLORIDA

CAMPGROUNDS

PARK NUMBER / MAP REFERENCE	NAME	FEE	ELECTRIC / WATER / SEWER	CREDIT CARDS	TENT SITES	TRAILER SITES	PULL-THRU	TRAILER SIZE	BOTTLED GAS / SANITARY SERVICE / MAX MAPS	NEAREST TOWN/ACCESS	PHYSICAL ENVIRONMENT	ELEVATION	ACRES	SEASON	RESERVATIONS	PET/MOTOR BIKES/FLUSH TOILETS/SHOWERS/TABLES/FIREWOOD/REC HALL/STORE/CAFE/LAUNDRY/ICE/PLAYGROUND/SWIM POOL/OTHER SWIM/FISHING/BOATING	OTHER	TELEPHONE	MAIL ADDRESS
	PRIVATE (CONT'D)																		
169 D3	Lakewood Trlr Pk	7.00	•••			75	•U	30		New Port Richey, Hwy 19, 4.5 mi E on Hwy 52	▲ ≋	1	12	All year	R		g	813-856-1306	4500 St Rd 52, Hudson 33562
169 D3	Shady Acres MH & Trvl Pk	9.00	•••	5		26	•U	30		Hudson, US 19, 2.5 mi N of Hwy 52	♨	1	10	All year	N			813-868-5628	14417 US 19N, Hudson 33567
170 E3	Lone Oak Trlr Pk	8.00	•••			S37	•U	30	o	Palmetto, jct US 301 & US 41	♨	1	4	All year	Z		gst	813-722-2039	115 10th St, Palmetto 33561
170 E3	Palm Bay Trvl Trlr Pk	8.00	•••			A5	•U	30		Palmetto, US 41, 1 blk E on US 301	♨	1	4	5/1-10/31	N		g	813-722-7048	751 US 301 N, Palmetto 33561
171 E4	Bonnie Brae Mbl Estates	9.45	•••			23	•U	30	o	Avon Park, S City Limits, 1 Blk W on Cornell St	⊞ ♨	1	17	All year	N		g	813-453-6395	1201 W Cornell, Avon Park 33825
172 C3	Crystal River MHP	6.00	•••			9	U	50		Crystal River, 1.5 mi N on US 19, 1.5 mi W on NW 19th St	▲	0	8	All year	N		g		2200 NW 15th, Crstl Riv 32629
172 C3	Crystal Isles Rsrt CG	11.00	•••	25		272	•U	30	•	Crystal River, US 19, 4 mi W on Hwy C-44W	▲ ≋	1	33	All year	N	dl	gt	904-795-3774	Rt 4 Bx 400, Crystal Riv 32629
172 C3	Thunderbird MHP	7.50	•$$			S15	•U	30	•	Crystal River, 2 mi N on US 19	≋	1	12	All year	N		g	904-795-3911	Rt 3 Bx 796, Crystal Riv 32629
174 H4	Homer's Trlrs By The Sea	10.00	•$$			19	U			Marathon, 4 mi E on US 1, at mi mrkr 58-1/2	♨	0	2	All year	N	d	g	305-289-0307	RR 1 Bx 354, Marathon 33050
175 D3	Safari Camp St Catherine	7.00	•••	25		100	U	30		Bushnell, I-75, Webster ext, 1 mi E on Hwy 476B, 1 mi N on C	▲ ≋	1	117	All year					Rt 1 Bx 60, Bushnell 33513
175 D3	Ridge Manor CG	8.00	•••	10		70	U			Ridge Manor, I-75, 4 mi E on Hwy 50, btw US 98 & US 301	≋	1	4	All year	N			904-793-5345	R 1 Bx 340, Rdg Manor 33525
177 C4	Chisholm Trail CG	7.00	•••	50		30	•U	30		Altoona, 3 mi N on Hwy 19, in the Ocala NF	▲	1	5	All year		$	h	904-669-5995	Rt 1 Bx 209, Altoona 32702
177 C4	KOA Kelleys Ocala Forest	11.75	•••	50		70	•U	30		Altoona, Star Rt 19, 5 mi N on Star Rt 42	▲	1	25	All year	N	dr	g	904-669-3888	Rt 1 Bx 437, Umatilla 32704
180 D3	Bay Bayou Traveler	9.50	•$$			62	•U	30		Tampa, 275, ext 30 W, 11 mi Rt 580	⊞	6	10	All year	N		g	813-855-1000	12201 W Hlsbrgh, Tampa 33615
181 D2	Medley MHP	14.00	•••			15	U			Miami, Palmetto Expy, South Riv Dr Ext, .5 mi SE on S Riv Dr	♨	1	18	All year	N		gh	305-885-7070	8181 NW S River, Miami 33166
182 F3	Gaylord Mbl Garden	9.00	•••			S30	U	30		North Fort Myers, ext 27 off 75, S to US Bus 41, 1 mi E on Laurel, 1/4 mi N on Garden St	≋	1	5	All year		dl		813-995-7417	2867 Garden, N Ft Myers 33903
183 E3	East Myakka River RV Pk	8.50	•••			71	U	30		Venice, ext 34, 7 mi S on US 41	▲	1	27	All year	N		gt	813-426-5040	10400 S Tamiami, Venice 33595
184 F3	Tamiami Trvl Pk	13.50	•••			245	U	20		North Fort Myers, 2757 US 41 N	⊞	1	15	All year	N	l	g	813-995-5747	2757 US 41N, N Ft Myers 33903
185 E3	Avalon Trvl Trlr Pk	9.00	•••			SA25	U	31	o	Clearwater, US 19S, 2.5 S of Hwy 60	⊞	1	15	All year	N		g	813-531-6124	1960 19S, Clrwtr 33516
185 E3	Trvl Towne Trvl Trlr Rsrt	13.00	•••	20		340	U			Clearwater, 6 mi N on US 19	⊞	1	18	All year	N		gh	813-784-2500	3330 US 19N, Clearwater 33575
185 D3	Dunedin Beach CG	11.50	•••	25		233	•U	30		Dunedin, Hwy 586, .5 mi N on US 19A	▲	1	18	All year	N	dr	gh	813-784-3719	2920 Alt 19N, Dunedin 33528
185 E3	Alcove MHP	12.00	•••			A25	32			Clearwater, US 19, .5 mi W on Hwy 588 (Sunset Point Rd), .5 mi S on Coachman Rd	▲	1	12	All year	N		g	813-797-5438	1600 Coachman, Clrwtr 33575
185 D3	Belle Haven Mbl Pk	8.00	•••			A22	28			Clearwater, jct 19N & Hwy 580, 1/4 mi N on 19	⊞	1	5	All year	N		gt	813-796-1450	2790 US Hwy 19N, Clrwtr 33515
185 D3	Kapok Trvl Pk	12.00	•••			45	U			Clearwater, 1 mi E of US 19 on Hwy 60	⊞	1	5	All year	N	$ l	gh	813-797-6300	3070 Gif to Bay, Clrwtr 33519
186 C4	St John's River CGs	7.50	•••	20		50	•U	30		Barberville, 6 mi W on Hwy 40	▲	1	9	All year	N		g	904-749-2850	PO Bx 64 Hwy 40, Astor 32002
186 C4	Parramore's Fishing Camp	9.00	•••	40		50	50			Astor, Hwy 40	⊞	1	8	All year	N		g	904-749-2721	Rt 2 Bx 156, Astor 32002
187 F3	KOA Miami South	13.75	•••	35		273	U	30		Perrine, US 1, 5.5 mi W on Quail Roost Dr (SW 200th St), .5 mi S on 162nd Ave	⊞	1	50	All year	N	o dlr		305-233-5300	20675 SW 162, Perrine 3157
188 F4	Up River CG	11.75	•••	25		275	U			North Fort Myers, jct Hwy 78/31, 1.5 mi W on Hwy 78 (1 mi E of I-75)	⊞	1	26	All year	N	dl	g	813-995-6807	Rt 2 Bx 142, N Ft Myers 33903
188 F4	Seminole CG & Trlr Rsrt	10.00	•••	5		125	U	30		North Fort Myers, jct I-75 ext 26 & Hwy 78, 500 ft E, 1/4 miN on Wells	⊞	1	20	All year	N	o dlr		813-995-1449	Rt 21 Bx1150, N Ft Myers 33903
189 D3	Mockingbird MHP	7.00	•••			S17	•U	30		Zephyrhills, 2 mi N on US 301	⊞	1	10	All year	N			813-782-3787	33 Robin, Zephyrhills 33599
190 D4	Yogi Bear's Jellystone Pk	16.50	•$	100		433	•U	30		Apopka, 2 mi S on Hwy 435	▲	1	112	All year	N	dlr	g	305-889-3048	R 1 Bx 2000, Apopka 32703
190 D4	Apopka-Clarcona CG	10.00	•••	20		60	•U	30	o	Apopka, 2.5 mi S on Hwy 435	⊞	1	16	All year	N		g	305-886-3745	3400 Clarcona Rd, Apopka 32703
191 D3	Camp-A-Wyle Lake Resort	12.00	•••	25		200	U	30		Weeki Wachee Springs, 3 mi N on US 19	▲	1	198	All year	N	dlr	gt	904-596-2139	9206 Cmmrcl Way, Brksvll 33512
191 D3	Weeki Wachee N Trlr & MHP	9.00	•••			57	U	30		Weeki Wachee Springs, 6 mi N on US 19	⊞	1	47	All year	N		g	904-596-0300	10400 Amity, Brooksville 33512
192 D3	Seven Oaks Travel Pk	12.00	•••	30		140	U	30		Hudson, Hwy 2 mi N	⊞	1	10	All year	N		g	904-862-3016	2948 2nd Ave, Hudson 33567
193 E3	Brook-To-Bay Trlr Ranch	11.00	•••			AS12	U			Englewood, US 41, 4 mi S on Hwy 775	⊞	1	20	All year	N		g	813-474-1941	1891 Englewood, Englwd 33533
193 E3	Gulf to Bay Park	12.00	•••			AS15	30	50	o	Englewood, Manasota Key, Hwy 776, N on N Beach Rd	♨	1	4	All year	R	$ l	g	813-474-4841	2295 N Beach, Englewood 33533
193 E3	Holiday Travel Park	9.00	•••			100	•30			Englewood, jct US 41/Hwy 775, 9 mi S, 2 mi E on Hwy 76, Alt 45	≋	1	33	All year	Z	dl	gt	813-474-5078	1475 Flamingo, Englwd 33533
194 E5	Outdoor Rsrt of America	18.00	•••			350	35			Stuart, 9 mi N on Hwy A1A, on Hutchinson Island	▲ ≋	1	144	All year	N	dl		305-229-1300	Box 1116 Jensen Beach 33457
195 D3	Bide-A-While Trlr Pk CG	6.00	•••			38	U			Lakeland, 5 mi E on US 92E	▲	1	5	All year	N		g	813-665-3303	4535 US 92E, Lakeland 33801
195 D3	Sanlan Ranch CG & TT Pk	14.00	•••	50		250	•U	30		Lakeland, 5 mi S on US 98	▲ ≋	1	1300	All year	N	dlr	g	813-665-1726	3929 US 98 S, Lakeland 33801

FOR MAP, SEE PAGE 114   MIAMI MAP, SEE PAGE 119

MIAMI AND VICINITY

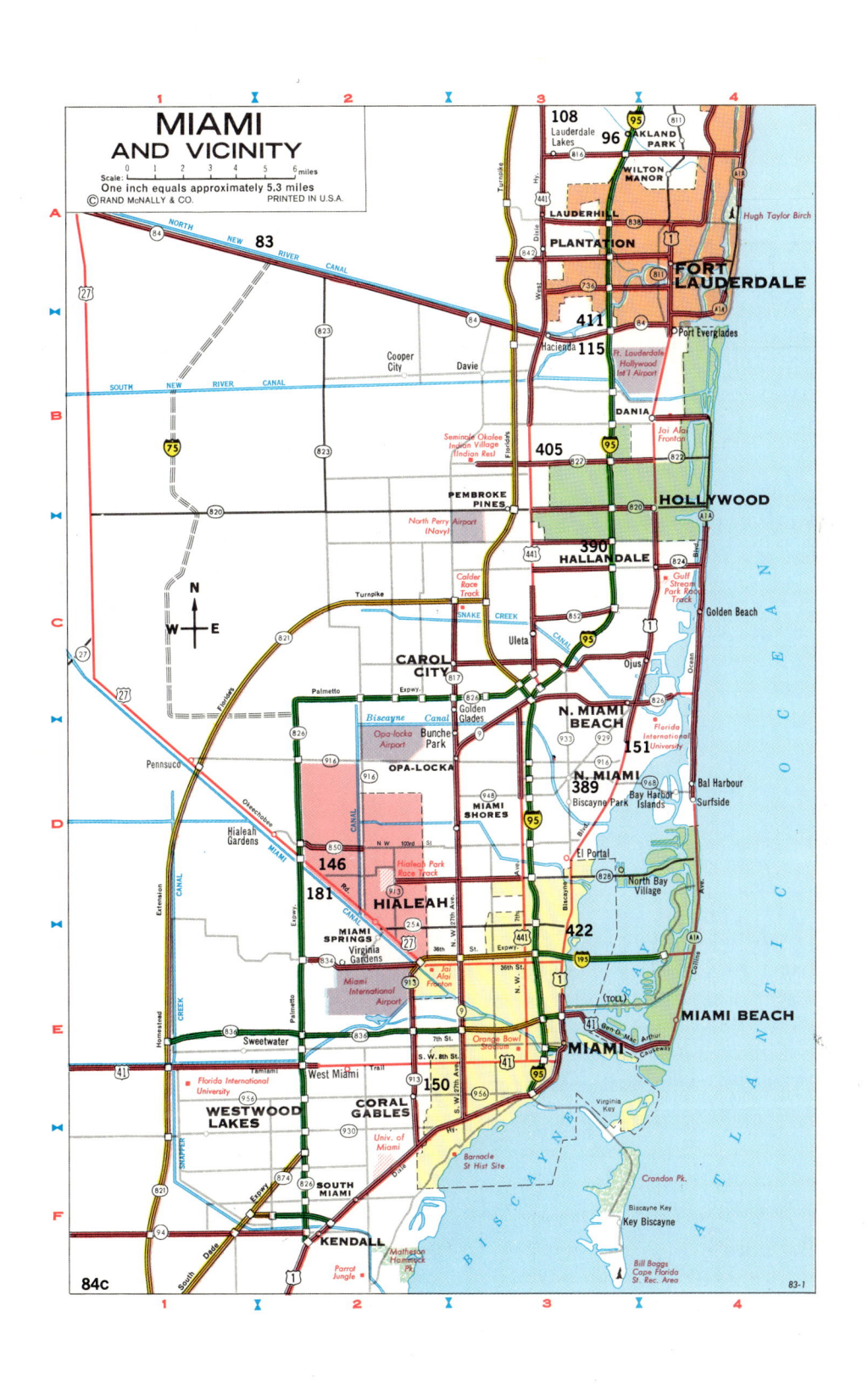

Scale: One inch equals approximately 5.3 miles
0 1 2 3 4 5 6 miles
© RAND McNALLY & CO.   PRINTED IN U.S.A.

CAMPGROUNDS 119

FLORIDA

FOR MAP, SEE PAGE 114 MIAMI MAP, SEE PAGE 119

PARK NUMBER / MAP REFERENCE	NAME	FEE	ELECTRIC / WATER / SEWER	CREDIT CARDS	TENT SITES	TRAILER SITES	PULL-THRU	BOTTLED GAS / SANITARY SERVICE / MAXIMUM AMPS	NEAREST TOWN/ACCESS	PHYSICAL ENVIRONMENT	ELEVATION	ACRES	SEASON	RESERVATIONS	TIME LIMIT / PETS PERMITTED / MOTOR BIKES PERMITTED / FLUSH TOILETS / SHOWERS / TABLES / FIREWOOD / RECREATION HALL / STORE / CAFE / LAUNDRY / ICE	PLAYGROUND / SWIMMING POOL / OTHER SWIMMING / FISHING / BOATING	OTHER	TELEPHONE	MAIL ADDRESS
	PRIVATE (CONT'D)																		
196 D4	Lake Wales Trlr Pk	7.00	•••			A10	•U	30	Lake Wales, Bus Sec, 5 blks N on US 27-A		1	3	All year	N		○	gt	813-676-9118	705 Scenic Hwy, Lk Wales 33853
196 D4	Sunny Acres MHP	7.00	•••		5	30	•U	30	Lake Wales, 5 mi N on US 27A		1	20	All year	N		○○		813-439-3911	5143 Alt 27N, Lk Wales 33853
198 G5	Goldcoaster Pk	14.00	•••	MV	10	400	U		Homestead, 1 mi S on US 1, 1-1/3 mi W on Hwy 27 (Palm Dr)		1	82	All year	N	••••	••○		305-248-5462	34850 SW 187, Homestead 33034
200 F3	Lake Wood Trvl Rsrt	13.75	•••		20	360	•U	30	St. James City		0		All year	N	••••	• l	gt	813-283-2415	St James City 33956
201 B3	Shady Oak Trlr Pk	6.00	•••		20	52	•U		Starke, 8 mi S on US 301		1	20	All year	N	••		g	904-468-1338	Star Rt Bx 26, Hampton 32044
202 E3	Sun-N-Fun Rsrt	15.00	•••			A1061	•U		Fruitville, I-75, ext 39, 1 mi E on Hwy 780		1	188	All year	N	••••	dl	g	904-371-2505	7125 Fruitville, Sarasota 33582
204 F5	Palm Beach Traveler Pk	13.00	•••			A100	35	30	Lantana, FL Pkwy, ext 38, E to Jog Rd, S to Lantana Rd, E to Lawrence Rd		1	7	All year	N	••••	l	gh	305-967-3139	6159 Lawrence, Lantana 33462
204 F5	Palm Bch-Lk Worth CG	10.50	••• $		132	132	U	30	Lake Worth, FL tpke, ext 36, 3 mi E on Hwy 802		0	12	All year	N	••••	dl	g	305-965-1653	5332 Lk Worth Lk Worth 33463
205 B3	KOA Starke CG	9.00	•••		10	64	•U	30	Starke, S on Hwy 301		1	16	All year	N	••••		g	904-964-8484	1463 S Walnut, Starke 32091
207 F3	Punta Gorda Kampground	7.00	•••		8	200	•U	30	Fruitville, I-75, ext 161, W to CG		1	20	All year	N	••••	lr	g	813-639-2010	3701 Baynard, Punta Gorda 33950
208 E3	Charlotte Harbor Cmpg	10.50	••• $			28	U	20	Charlotte Harbor, Punta Gorda Bridge, 1/4 mi N on US 41		1	2	All year	N	••••	dl	g	813-625-5695	Charlotte Harbor 33950
210 F5	Vacation Inn Travel Pk	18.00	•••	AMV		390	•U	30	West Palm Beach, S-bnd FL tpke ext 44, E on PGA Blvd, 3 mi S on Hwy 809		1	40	All year	N	••••	•••		305-848-6166	6566 N Mltry, W Plm Bch 33407
211 E5	Suni Sands Trvl Trlr Pk	10.00	•••			25	U		Jupiter, US 1, 1000' E on Hwy A1A		1	12	All year	N	••••	○	gt	305-746-7000	A1A Ocean Dr, Jupiter, 33458
211 E5	Yogi-By-The-Sea/Jupiter	16.00	•••		50	245	U		Jupiter, 4 mi S on US 1		1	23	All year	N	••••	dlr	g	305-622-7500	1745 US 1, Jupiter 33408
211 E5	KOA Palm Beach Gardens	13.50	•••	MV	30	75	U		Lake Park, I-95, 1/4 mi W on PGA Blvd, 1.5 mi N on Military Trail, 1/4 mi E on Hood Rd		1	10	All year	N	••••	r	ght	305-622-8212	4063 Hood Rd Lake Park 33410
212 C4	Orange City Country Vil	9.50	•••	MV		550	33	30	Orange City, I-4, ext 15A, fol signs		1	30	All year	N	••••	l	g	904-775-2275	2300 E Graves, Ornge Cty 32763
212 C4	Lakeside Mbl Pk	7.00	•••			14	•U		DeLand, 2.5 mi S on US 17-92		1	8	All year	N	•••		g	904-734-1574	Rt 4 Bx 101, Deland 32720
213 D4	Ponderosa Pk of Kissimmee	11.00	•••		20	160	U		Kissimmee, FL tpke ext 65, 4 mi W on US 192/441, 1 mi E on Hwy C530		1	14	All year	N	••••		g	305-847-6002	Rt 1 Bx 137, Kissimmee 32741
214 E4	Jack's Lk Letta CG	7.00	•••			16	•U		Avon Park, Hwy 17		1	7	11/1-5/1	R	•••			813-385-3825	2455 S Lk Letta, Avon Pk 33825
214 E4	Dolan City Trvl Trlr Pk	10.00	•••			AS170	U		Sebring, Southgate Center, 3 mi N on US 27		1	13	9/1-6/1	U	••••		g	305-385-3870	1200 US 27 N, Sebring 33870
214 E4	Ohrt's Mobile Village	8.00	•••			6	U		Avon Park, 10 mi S on US 27		1	10	All year	N	••	lr	g	813-385-3289	1100 US 27N, Sebring 33870
214 E4	Whispering Pines Village	11.00	•••			A175	32		Sebring, 2 mi N on US 27, 1-1/2 mi W on Hwy 634, 1-1/4 mi N on Brunn rd		1	20	All year	N	•••	○ d	gmt	813-385-4806	2323 Brunns Rd, Sebring 33870
214 E4	Lake Bonnet Village CG	11.00	•••	MV	197	197	35	30	Avon Park, 5 mi S on Hwy 17		1	20	All year	N	••••		gt	813-385-7010	2900 Lk Bonnet, Avon Pk 33825
215 D4	Merry D Sanctuary	9.00-	•••		25	25	35		Sebring, US 17/82/531, .5 mi S, 7 mi S on 531		1	54	All year	N	••••	dlr	gt	813-385-5837	4261 Pleasanthill, Sebring 32471
215 D4	Harbor Oaks Marina & CGs	9.00	•••		20	16	28		Kissimmee, US 17/92 & US 192/441, 4 mi SW on US 17/92, .5 miN on Pleasant Hill Rd, US 531, 900 ft on Marsh Rd		1	2	All year	N	••		g	305-846-1321	3605 Marsh, Kissimmee 32741
215 E3	Aloha Trvl Pk	14.00	•••		12	100	U		Kissimmee, 5 mi SW on US 17/92		1	8	All year	N	••••	•	gt	305-348-5730	Rt 2 Bx 399A, Kissimmee 32741
216 E3	Venice CG Trvl Trlr Pk	11.00	•••			100	U		Venice, I-75, ext 34 (River Rd), 3/4 mi S to Venice Ave, 1 mi E		1	23	All year	N	••••	○	gt	813-488-0850	4085 E Venice Ave, Venice 33595
216 E3	Royal Coachmen Rsrt	19.00	•••		68	308	•U	30	Venice, I-75, Venice ext, W to US 41, S to Laurel Rd, 1 mi E		1	104	All year	N	••••	dl	gt	813-488-9674	PO Bx 398, Venice 33595
216 E3	King's Gate Trlr Pk	18.00	•••			AS30			Nokomis, US 41, 1.5 mi E on Laurel Rd		1	50	9/1-6/30	U	••••	dlr	g	813-485-8139	1500 King's Way, Nokomis 33555
216 E3	Ramblers Rest Rsrt	9.00	•••	M	18	450	U	30	Venice, I-75, ext 34 (river Rd) 2.5 mi S		1	75	All year	N	••••	dlr	g	813-493-4354	Rt 1 Bx 800, Venice 33595
217 D4	Lake Whippoorwill Rsrt	7.50	•••		60	144	U	30	St. Cloud, Beelone Expy, 4 mi S on Hwy 15		1	20	All year	N	••••		gt	305-277-5075	Rt 5 Bx 121, Orlando 32812
218 H4	KOA Fiesta Key	12.00	•••	MVA	100	288	•U	30	Long Key, US 1, at mi mrkr 70		1	28	All year	N	••••	dlr	gt	305-664-4922	Long Key 33001
218 H4	Outdoor Rsrts-Long Key	18.00	•••			550	•U		Long Key, US 1 at mi mrkr 66		1	48	All year	N	••••	dlr	t	305-664-8166	PO Bx 438, Long Key 33001
220 D4	Sherwood Forest RV Pk	15.50	•••	M	60	494	•U		Kissimmee, I-4, 3 mi E on US 192		1	60	All year	N	••••	dlr	ght	305-396-7431	5300 Space Coast, Kssmm 32741
220 D4	John Fowlers Port O'Call	17.00	•••		100	500	•U		Kissimmee, jct I-4/US 192, 4 mi E on US 192		1	60	All year	N	••••	dlr	gh	305-396-0110	5195 US 192, Kssmm 32741
220 D4	Kissimmee CG	12.00	•••		5	46	35		Kissimmee, 4 mi W on US 192		1	8	All year	N	••••	dlr		305-396-6851	2643 Alligator Ln, Kssmm 32741
220 D4	Twin Lakes CG	9.00	•••		50	150	35		Kissimmee, I-4, 5 mi E on US 192		1	40	All year	N	••••	dl	g	305-396-8101	5044 Spacecoast, Kssmm 32741
220 D4	Orange Grove CG	13.00	•••		48	191	U		Kissimmee, 3 mi W on US 192		1	15	All year	N	••••		g	305-396-6655	2425 Old Vineland, Kssmm 32741
220 D4	Holiday Village CG	15.00	•••		450	V450	U		Kissimmee, I-4, 1.5 mi E on US 192		1	80	All year	N	••••	r	g	305-396-4595	2650 Holiday Trl, Kssmm 32741
220 D4	KOA Kampground	16.00	•••	MV	64	380	U		Kissimmee, Disney World, 5 mi E on US 192		1	73	All year	N	••••	sgt	800-432-9198	Drawer 939, Kissimmee 32741
222 D4	Peace River Village	7.00	•••			19	U		Bartow, 1/4 mi E on Hwy 60		1	12	All year	N	••••		g	813-533-7823	2405 E Hwy 60, Bartow 33830

120 CAMPGROUNDS

FLORIDA

FOR MAP, SEE PAGE 114   MIAMI MAP, SEE PAGE 119

MAP REFERENCE / PARK NUMBER	NAME	FEE	ELECTRIC / WATER / SEWER	CREDIT CARDS	TENT SITES	TRAILER SITES	PULL-THRU	TRAILER SIZE	BOTTLED GAS / SANITARY SERVICE / MAXIMUM AMPS	NEAREST TOWN ACCESS	PHYSICAL ENVIRONMENT	ELEVATION	ACRES	SEASON	RESERVATIONS	TIME LIMIT / PETS PERMITTED / MOTOR BIKES PERMITTED / FLUSH TOILETS / SHOWERS / TABLES / FIREWOOD / RECREATION HALL	STORE / CAFE / LAUNDRY / ICE	PLAYGROUND / SWIMMING POOL / OTHER SWIMMING / FISHING / BOATING	OTHER	TELEPHONE	MAIL ADDRESS
	PRIVATE (CONT'D)																				
224 F4	KOA Clewiston	13.00	•••	MV	50	119	U		••	Clewiston, 2 mi W on US 27, 700 ft N on Hwy 720		1	12	All year	N	•U••••••	•••	••••	gmt	813-983-7078	Rt 2 Bx 242, Clewiston 33440
225 C4	Paradise Lakes	7.00	•••		25	175	U		••	Deltona, I-4, DeBary Deltona ext, 3.5 mi E on DeBary and Doyle, ext 53		1	48	All year	N	•U••••••	••	••• r	g	305-574-2371	Bx 339, Deltona 32725
226 F3	Gulf Air Trvl Pk	13.00	•••		6	200	U		•• 30	Fort Myers, I-75, ext Daniels Rd, Hwy 41 S, 865 Beaches		1	15	10/1-5-1	N	•U••••••	••	••••	g	813-466-8100	Rt 3 Bx G Ft Myers 33908
226 F3	Ft Myers Beach KG	15.00	•••	MV	100	400	U		•• 30	Fort Myers, 10 mi SW on Hwy 867, 1 mi S on Hwy 865		1	30	All year	N	•U••••••	••	••••	g	813-481-0655	Rt 3 Bx 462, Ft Myers 33908
226 F3	San Carlos Trlr Pk & Isls	11.00	•••		9	V90	U		•• 30	Fort Myers, jct Hwy 867 & 865, 3 mi S on 865		1	15	All year	N	•U••••••	o o •••••	••• dlr	gt	813-463-9237	Ft Myers Beach 33931
226 F3	Ebb Tide Trlr Pk	11.50	•••			5	U		•• 30	Fort Myers, 10 mi SW on Hwy 867, 3 mi S on Hwy 865, .5 mi E on Main St		1	12	5/1-10/30	N	•U••••••	o o •••••	••	g	813-463-5444	1725 Main, Ft Myers Bch 33931
226 F3	Indian Creek Pk	16.00	•••		16	A850 78	U 31		••	Fort Myers, 3 mi W to S-865, 2 mi S on S-867		1	150	All year	R	•U••••••	••	••• dlr	gt	813-446-6060	2121 San Carlos, Ft Myers Bch
229 E5	The Fijian RV Park	8.50	•••							Okeechobee, 9 mi S on US 441 & 98, 1 mi N on Co S 15A		1	4	All year	N	•U••••••	o ••••	••••		813-763-6200	895 Hwy 441S,Okchbee 33472
230 D3	Lazy A CG	10.00	•••		10	50	U		••	Pinellas Park, US 19, 2.5 mi W on Hwy 694		1	4	All year	R	•U••••••	•••	•	g	813-544-5570	6710 Pk Blvd,Pinellas Pk33565
230 D3	Robert's MH & RV Pk	10.00	•••			347	U		•• 50	St. Petersburg, I-75, 1 mi W on Hwy 694 (Gandy Blvd)		1	60	All year	N	•U••••••	••	••• dlr	g	813-577-6820	3390 Gandy,St Ptrsbrg 33702
231 C3	Turtleback Camp	9.00	•••		15	80	U		•• 30	Lake Panasoffkee, I-75, Lk Panasoffkee ext, 1/4 mi W on Hwy 470		1	16	All year	N	•U••••••	••	••	mt	904-793-2051	Rt1 Bx102,Lk Panasoffkee33533
231 C3	Ri La Ca Marina & CG	6.50	•••		15	15				Lake Panasoffkee, I-75, Lk Panasoffkee ext, 3 mi W on Hwy 470, N on Co Rd 439		1	8	All year	N	•U••••••	••	•••		904-793-6339	Bx 1099, Lk Panasoffkee 33538
232 D3	West's Oakdale Trlr Ct	5.00	•••			A5	30			Zephyrhills, 1 mi S on US 301		1	2	All year	N	•U••••••	•		ght	813-782-9097	602 S Gall, Zephyrhills 33599
232 D3	Country-Aire Village	12.00	•••		20	190	U			Zephyrhills, US 301, 1.5 mi E on Hwy 54E		1	30	All year	N	•U••••••	••••	o	sg	813-782-8270	1920 23rd, Zephyrhills 33599
232 D3	Ralph's Travel Park	6.00	•••			400	U		••	Zephyrhills, 4 mi W on Hwy 54		1	27	10/15-5/15	N	•U••••••	o •••			813-782-8223	3455 Hwy 54W,Zephyrhills33599
232 D3	Palm View Gdns Trvl Rsrt	10.00	•••			508	U		••	Zephyrhills, US 301, 1 mi S on US 301		1	40	All year	N	•U••••••	o o •••••	••• dlr		813-782-8665	1706 S US301,Zephyrhills33599
232 D3	Bahr's Travel Park	10.00	•••			50	32			Zephyrhills, US 301, 1 mi N on Co Rd 41		1	5	10/1-6/1	N	•U••••••	o o •••		gt	813-782-3587	708 Ft King,Zephyrhills 33599
233 F5	Lake City Trlr Pk	12.00	•••			S10	35			Boynton Beach, US 1 at 2649 N Federal Hwy		1	3	All year	N	•U••••••	o o •••••	••• dlr	gmst	813-645-1098	2649 Fed Hwy, Byntn Bch 33435
234 E3	Hawaiian Isles Trvl Rsrt	11.00	•••			A803	U		•• 30	Ruskin, 2 mi S on US 41, 1 mi W on Bay Rd		1	130	All year	N	•U••••••	••••	———	—	813-634-2395	Bx 525, Ruskin 33570
234 E3	Little Manatee River MHP	9.00	•••			100	U		•• 30	Riverview, Hwy 674, 4 mi S on US 301		1	77	All year	N	•U••••••	••••	—	—	813-645-2439	4337 Hamlin, Riverview 33569
234 E3	Little Manatee River CG	9.00	•••			100	U		•• 30	Ruskin, 4 mi S on US 41, 3 mi E on Stephen Rd		1	70	All year	N	•U••••••	o o •••	—	—	813-645-2439	201 Stephen Rd., Ruskin 33570
234 E3	Camp Bayou	6.00	•••		10	65	U		•• 20	Ruskin, US 41, 2 mi S on US 41, 3 mi W on Hwy 674, 3 mi S on 24th St SE		1	150	All year	N	•U••••••	o o •••		dr	813-645-3608	3013-24 St SE, Ruskin 33570
234 E3	Paradise Mbl Ct	9.50	•••			15	U		•• 30	Ruskin, 1-1/4 mi S on US 41, on Little Manatee Riv		1	10	All year	N	•U••••••	••	• dl	g	813-645-3635	2201 Stamiami Tr, Ruskin 33570
234 E3	Tampa S Trvl Trlr Rsrt	9.00	••• S			120	U		•• 30	Tampa, 20 mi S on US 41		1	13	All year	N	•U••••••	o o •••••	••• dlr	g	813-645-1202	2900 Tamiami Trl,Ruskin 33570
234 E3	Hide-A-Way CGs	10.50	•••		13	300	U		•• 30	Ruskin, 2.5 mi S on US 41, 3/4 mi E on Studio Blvd		1	100	All year	N	•U••••••	o o •••••	••• dlr	g	813-645-6037	2206 Chaney Dr, Ruskin 33570
235 E3	Linger Lodge	6.75	•••			98	U		•• 30	Bradenton, I-75, ext 41 (SR70), 1 mi W to Braden River Rd		1	10	All year	N	•U••••••	•••	•• lr		813-755-2757	7205 Linger Ldg, Bradntn 34202
236 E3	Lettuce Lake CG	9.00	•••		12	98	U		•• 30	Arcadia, 10 mi S on US 17, 2 mi W on Co 761, in Fort Ogden		1	30	All year	N	•U••••••	•••	••• dlr		813-494-6057	PO Bx 97, Fort Ogden 33842
237 H4	Boyd's Key West CG	10.00	••• S		60	60	U		••	Key West, N on US 1 to Mi 5, 3 blk S on McDonald Ave		1	12	All year	N	•U••••••	o •••••	•	gkmt	305-294-1465	Stock Island, Key West 33040
237 H4	Jabour's Trlr Ct	15.00	••• S		30	V60	U		•• 50	Key West, US 1 to US 1 Downtown (K.W.), Right at City Marina, cross brdg W to Eaton St SW, W on William or Elizabeth St to Gulf		1	2	All year	N	•U••••••	o o •••	•	gm	305-294-5723	223 Elzbth, Key West 33040
237 H4	Key West Seaside Pk	18.00	•••			199	U		•• 50	Key West, 6 mi N on US 1, at mi mkr 11		1	20	All year	N	•U••••••	••••	• dlr		305-294-9515	US 1 & Boca Chica,Key W 33040
237 H4	Leo's CG	8.50	•••			V30	U			Key West, US 1, E at 2nd light on Stock Isl (btw mi mrks 4 & 5)		0	5	All year	N	•U••••••	o	o	gt	305-296-5260	Stock Isl, Key West 33040
239 D4	Ray's Trvl Trlr Pk	8.00	•••	MV	250	S12	U		•• 30	Orlando, city limits, 3.5 mi E on Hwy 50		1	2	All year	N	•U••••••	o o •••••	••• dr	gt	305-277-4593	8424 E Colonial,Orlando 32817
240 C4	Twelve Oaks CG	10.00	•••			250	U		••	Sanford, I-4 Sanford ext 51, 2 mi W on Hwy 46		1	24	All year	N	•U••••••	o o •••••	•• dr	g	305-323-0880	Rt 1 Bx 176, Sanford 32771
240 C4	Wekiva Falls Rsrt	8.50	•••		47	746	U		••	Sanford, I-4, Sanford ext 51, 5 mi W across Wekiva River on Hwy 46, 1 mi W on Wekiva River Rd, fol signs		1	140	All year	N	•U••••••	•••••	••••		904-383-8055	Rt 1 Bx 378, Sorrento 32776
240 C4	Town & Country RV Resort	8.00	•••	MV	50	V150	U		•• 30	Sanford, I-4, Sanford ext 51, 1.5 mi W on Hwy 46, fol signs		1	30	All year	N	•U••••••	•••	o		800-323-5540	Bx 279, Lake Monroe 32747
243 F3	Alligator Pk	11.50	••• S			V180	U		•• 30	Punta Gorda, I-75, .5 mi W on N Jones Loop Rd, 1 mi S on Taylor Rd (765A)		1	50	All year	N	•U••••••	••	•	g	813-639-7916	Punta Gorda 33950
243 F3	Sun-N-Shade Family CG	9.50	••• S		20	70	U		•• 30	Punta Gorda, 8 mi S on US 41		1	15					•		813-639-5388	Rt 2 Bx 950, Punta Gorda 33950

CAMPGROUNDS 121

FLORIDA

FOR MAP, SEE PAGE 114   MIAMI MAP, SEE PAGE 119

Map Ref	Park #	Name	Fee	Electric/Water/Sewer	Credit Cards	Tent Sites	Trailer Sites	Pull-Thru	Trailer Size	Bottled Gas	Sanitary Service	Max Amps	Nearest Town, Access	Physical Env	Elev	Acres	Season	Reservations	Time Limit	Pets	Motor Bikes	Flush Toilets	Showers	Tables	Firewood	Rec Hall	Store	Cafe	Laundry	Ice	Playground	Pool	Other Swim	Fishing	Boating	Other	Telephone	Mail Address
		PRIVATE (CONT'D)																																				
243 F3		KOA Punta Gorda	12.50	•••	MV	7	182	•	U			30	Punta Gorda, 5 mi S on US 41, 1/2 mi W on Burnt Store Rd	≋≋ 1		16	All year	N				•	•	•		•	•		•		•	•				l	813-639-3978	6001 Burnt Store, Pnt Grd 33950
244 E4		Buckhead Ridge Marina	6.50	$•$		7	107	•	U				Okeechobee, 8 mi S on Hwy 78, 1 mi S on Hwy 78B	▲ 1		15	All year	N				•	•	•		•	•					•		•		g	813-763-2826	Hwy 78B, Okeechobee 33476
246 F5		Del-Raton Trvl Trlr Pk	14.00	•••			A85	•	32	•			Delray Beach, 2 mi S on US 1, 1 mi N of Boca Raton	▲ 1		5	All year	N				•	•	dlr		•			•								305-278-4633	3008 Fed Hwy, Delray Bch 33444
247 C4		Sugar Mill Ruins TT Pk	10.50	•••		100	100	•	U			30	New Smyrna Beach, I-95, 3 mi E on Hwy 44, 1 mi S on Old Mission Rd	▲ 1		80	All year	N				•	•	•		•	•		•		•					g	904-427-2284	Rt 2 Old Mssn, New Smyrna 32069
247 C4		KOA New Smyrna Beach	12.75	$$$	MV	36	101	•	U				New Smyrna Beach, I-95, ext 84A, Hwy 44, 3.5 mi E, 1-3/4 mi S on Mission Rd	▲ 0		17	All year	N				•	•	dlr		•	•		•		•					g	904-427-3581	1300 Old Mssn, NwSmrnaBch 32069
249 D4		Days Pk of Orlando	13.00	•••	MV		254	•	U				Orlando, I-4 ext 33rd St, 2 blks E	▲ 1		38	All year	N				•	•	•		•	•		•		•					sg	305-423-7646	1600 W 33rd, Orlando 32805
249 D4		Green Acres of Orlando		•••		450	450	•	U			30	Orlando, jct I-4/Hwy 436, 2 mi W on Hwy 436, 1.5 mi S on Hwy 431	▲ 1			All year	N				•	•	•													305-295-3461	9701 Forest Cty, Orlando 32810
250 G4		Outdoor Rsrt/Chokoloskee	10.00	•••	MV	14	216	•	U			30	Chokoloskee Island, US 41, 8 mi S on Hwy 29, on Chokoloskee Island	▲ 1		25	All year	N				•	•	dlr		•			•								813-695-2881	Bx 1503, Chokoloskee 33925
250 G4		Chokoloskee Island Pk	10.00	•••		A16	100	•	25			15	Chokoloskee Island, US 41, 8 mi S on Hwy 29, fol signs	≋ 1		5	All year	N				•	•	$		•	•		•		•					t	813-695-2414	Bx C, Chokoloskee 33925
255 A1		Bell Trlr Pk	7.00	•••		5	5		U				Tallahassee, 5 mi W on US 90, ext 263 S to 90 W, 1 mi	≋ 1		10	All year	N				•	•			•										m	904-576-2915	Rt 4 Bx 382, Tallahassee 32301
255 A1		Bennets O/N Trlr Pk	6.30	•••		8	53	•	U				Tallahassee, jct I-10/Hwy 263, 1/2 mi S on Hwy 263, 1/4 mi W on US 90	▲ 1		91/2	All year	N				•	•			•										gh	904-576-2306	Rt 14 Bx 355, Tallahassee 32304
255 A1		Southern Bell Trlr Pk	6.00	•••		10	20		U				Tallahassee, 4-1/2 mi W on US 90	▲ 1		20	All year	N				•	•	dlr		•	•		•								g	904-576-2165	5876 W Tenn, Tallahassee 32304
256 B1		Sea Breeze CG	7.00	$$		24	28		U				Carrabelle, 4 mi E on US 98	≋ 1		2	All year	N				•	•			•	•		•		•					g	904-697-2130	Star Rt 11, Carrabelle 32322
257 D3		Florida Campland	5.00	$$		100	150	•	U				Dade City, 8 mi N on US 90	▲ 1		43	All year	N				•	•			•										g	904-583-2091	5300 N Hwy 98, Dade Cty 33525
258 A1		Home Trlr Pk	5.00	•••			8		U				Quincy, 2 mi W on US 90	▲ 1		12	All year	N				•	•	$		•										gt	904-627-6772	Quincy 32351
259 F3		America Outdoors Ft Myers	18.00	•••			271	•	50				Fort Myers, city limits, 5 mi W on US 41	▲ 1		38	All year	N				•	•	dlr		•	•		•		•					g	813-481-4294	Rt 13 Bx 600, Ft Myers 33908
259 F3		Fort Myers CG	12.00	•••	MV	76	269	•	U			30	Fort Myers, 6 mi S on US 41	▲ 1		30	All year	N				•	•	dl		•	•		•		•					g	813-481-1007	Rt 13 Bx 650, Ft Myers 33908
262 F4		Rock Creek CG	12.00	•••		210	210	•	U			50	Naples, US 41, E to CO 31, 1 mi N	▲ 1		11	All year	N				•	•			•					•					g	813-775-3100	3100 North Rd, Naples 33942
262 F4		Lake San Marino RV Park	10.00	•••			100	•	U			30	Naples, US 41 & S888	▲ 1		30	All year	N				•	•			•										g	813-597-4202	1000 Wiggins Pass, Npls 33940
262 F4		Naples Trlr Pk & Motel	12.00	•••			26		32	•			Naples, on Tamiami Trail (US41), N edge of Naples	▲ 1		12	All year	N				•	•			•										gt	813-261-3870	2630 9th N, Naples 33940
263 D2		Bay Aire TT Pk	10.00	•••			172	•	U			30	Palm Harbor, 1/10 mi N on US Alt-19	▲ 1		10	All year	N				•	•			•										g	813-784-4082	2242 US-Alt 19, Plm Hrbr 33563
263 D2		Bayshore MHP & Apts	9.50	•••			15		33				Tarpon Springs, Hwy 19A, 6 blks E via Orange, Spring Blvd & Riverside Dr (over drawbridge)	▲ 1		5	All year	N				•	•	dl		•			•									813-937-1661	403 Rvrside, Tarpon Spgs 33589
263 D2		Caladesi Trvl Trlr Pk	10.50	•••			86		U			30	Palm Harbor, jct US-19A & Hwy 584	▲ 1		6	All year	N				•	•			•	•		•									813-784-3622	205 Dempsy Rd, Plm Harbor 33563
263 D2		Holiday Trvl Trlr Pk	12.50	•••		525	125	•	U			30	Holiday, jct US 19N, 19A	▲ 1		30	All year	N				•	•			•	•		•									813-934-6782	3999 US 19N, Holiday 33589
263 D2		Ross Trlr Pk	5.00	•••			A6		26				Holiday, jct US-19A, 500 ft S on 19A	▲ 1		2	All year	N				•	•														813-934-9108	3727 Alt 19N, Holiday 33590
263 D2		Sherwood Forest	10.00	•••	MV	30	95	•	U			30	Palm Harbor, jct US 19A/584	▲ 1		13	All year	N				•	•	dl		•	•		•		•					g	813-784-4582	251 Alt 19S, Palm Harbor 33563
263 D2		RV Cypress Pointe CG	12.00	•••			394	•	U			30	Palm Harbor, jct US 19 & Hwy 584, 2.5 mi N on 19	▲ 1		44	All year	N				•	•			•	•		•								gt	813-938-1966	4600 US 19N, Palm Harbor 33563
263 D2		Wall Springs Trlr Pk	5.00	•••		6	7		U			20	Tarpon Springs, 3 mi N on US 19A, 1 blk W on Bravard St 1 blk S	▲ 0		7	All year	N				•	•														813-937-8060	604 Hlsbrgh, Palm Harbor 33563
263 Q2		KOA Clearwater/Tarpon Spg	13.00	•••	MV	32	80	•	U			30	Tarpon Springs, 2.5 mi N on US 19	▲ 1		12	All year	N				•	•	dl		•	•		•		•					g	813-937-8412	3906 US 19, Palm Harbor 33563
263 D2		Linger Longer Trvl Rsrt	11.50	•••			145	•	U			30	Tarpon Springs, US 19A, 1/4 mi W on Anclote Rd	▲ 1		20	All year	N				•	•			•	•				•						813-937-1463	Bx 320 Anclt, Tarpon Spgs 33589
268 D3		Lake Padgett Mbl Village	8.00	•••			5		30				Lutz, 3 mi N on US 41	▲ 1		15	All year	N				•	•			•			•		•						813-992-0120	Bx 57, Land O Lakes 33539
269 F4		Palm Lk Trlr & Cmpg Rsrt	8.00	•••			80	•	U			30	Bonita Springs, Old US 41, 1 mi E on Carrel Rd	▲ 1		7	All year	N				•	•	dl		•			•		•						813-992-3030	11253 Carrel, Bonita Spgs 33923
269 F4		Citrus Pk RV & Trvl Trlr	12.00	•••		30	689	•	U				Bonita Springs, Bus Rt 41, fol signs or I-75 Exit Bonita Springs - fol signs	▲ 1		320	All year	N				•	•					s								ght		25501 Trost, Bonita Spgs 33923
269 F4		Bamboo Mbl Village	10.00	•••			AS15		30				Bonita Springs, Old US 41, in town	≋ 1		7	All year	N				•	•			•										g	813-992-2822	Rt 5, Bonita Springs 33923
269 F4		Bonita Lk Resort	13.00	•••			166	•	50	•			Bonita Springs, 1/2 mi N on Old US 41 (Hwy C-887)	▲ 1		10	All year	N				•	•	dl		•	•		•								g	813-992-2481	26070 Old US 41, BntaSpgs 33923
270 D4		KOA Cape Kennedy	12.00	•••			138	•	U				Titusville, I-95, Star Rt 46 ext, .5 mi W	▲ 1		15	All year	N				•	•			•	•		•		•					g	305-269-7361	Rt 2 Bx 250, Titusville 32780
271 H2		Frangista Trlr Pk	15.00	•••			12		U				Destin, 7 mi E on US 98	▲ 1		2	All year	U				•	•			•			•								g	813-837-9878	Destin 32541
271 H2		Holiday Travel Pk	15.00	•••	$	260	260	•	U				Destin, 9 mi E on US 98	▲ 0		25	All year	N				•	•			•			•								g	904-837-6334	5380 Hwy 98E, Destin 32541
272 F4		Crooked Hook CG	13.00	•••	MV	171	171	•	U			30	Clewiston, 3 mi E on US 27	▲ 1		22	All year	N				•	•			•										gt	813-983-7112	Box 366, Lk Harbor 33459
275 C4		Ocean Village CG Trlr Pk	13.50	•••	MV	40	69		U				Ormond Beach, SR 40, 4 mi N on Hwy A1A	▲ 1		9	All year	N				•	•														g	904-441-1808	2162 Ocean Shr, OrmondBch 32074
278 B2		Dandridge Trvl Trlr Pk	5.50	•••		30	20		U				Perry, US 19/98/27A at jct Co 361	▲ 1		7	All year	N				•	•			•										g	904-584-7755	Rt 3 Bx 290, Perry 32347
278 B2		Town & Country Camper Ldg	6.00	•••			22		U				Perry, on US 19/98/27A S	▲ 1		10	All year	N				•	•			•										g	904-584-3095	2785 S US 19, Perry 32347

FLORIDA

FOR MAP, SEE PAGE 114 · MIAMI MAP, SEE PAGE 119

Map Ref	Park #	Name	Fee	Electric	Water	Sewer	Credit Cards	Tent Sites	Trailer Sites	Pull-Thru	Trailer Size	Bottled Gas	Sanitary Service	Max Amps	Nearest Town/Access	Physical Env	Elevation	Acres	Season	Reservations	Time Limit	Pets	Motor Bikes	Fish/Toilets	Showers	Tables	Firewood	Rec Hall	Store	Cafe	Laundry	Ice	Playground	Swimming	Other Swim	Boating	Other	Telephone	Mail Address
		PRIVATE (CONT'D)																																						
278 B2		Carrin's Trailer Pk	6.00	•	•	•		6	6	U	•				Perry, 3 mi E on US 27		1	2	All year	N		•			•	•		•			•	•					g	904-584-5235	Rt 3 Box 68, Perry 32347
278 B2		Westgate Mtl & CG	8.00	•	•	•	AMV	60	60	• U	•		50		Perry, at 1627 S US Hwy 19/98/27A		1	6	All year	U		•			•	•		•			•	•					gt	904-584-5235	1627 S B Bltr, Perry 32347
280 D4		KOA Cocoa Beach	16.00	•	•	•	MV	36	154	• U	•		30	•	Rockledge, I-95, Rockledge/Fiske ext (74), 200 yds E on Barnes Blvd		1	22	All year	U		•			•	•	•	•	•		•	•			•		ght	305-636-3000	820 Barnes, Rockledge 32955
281 D4		Biblia Village	10.25	•	•	•			150	• U	•		30		Cocoa, 5 mi S on I-95, ext Fiske Blvd, 100 yds W		1	230	All year	N		•			•	•		•	•		•	•		l				305-636-9550	4200 S Fiske Blvd, Cocoa 32922
282 E3		Manatee RV Pk	10.00	•	•	•	MV	50	118	• U	•		30		Palmetto, 2 mi N on US 41		1	100	All year	N		•			•	•	•	•	•		•	•					g	904-645-7652	6302 US 41N, Palmetto 33561
283 E3		Holiday Cove Trvl Trlr Pk	12.50	•	•	•			112	• U	• 32		30		Cortez, US 41, 6 mi W on Hwy 684 (Cortez Rd)		1	9	All year	U		•			•	•		•	•		•	•		dl			gt	813-792-1111	11900 Cortez Rd W, Cortez
284 F5		Pied Piper Camp Resort	11.95	•	•	$			194	• 32		30		West Palm Beach, FL Tpke ext 40, 1 mi W on Okeechobee Blvd		1	15	All year	U		•			•	•	•	•	•		•	•					gt	305-686-0714	7000 Okeechobee, W Palm 33411
289 B4		KA Hanna Pk CG	9.00	•	•	•	MV	300	300	• U	•		30		Atlantic Beach, Hwy 10, 4 mi N on A1A (Mayport Rd)		0	50	All year	N		•			•	•		•			•			r		•	g	904-299-2316	301 Campground, AtlnticBch32233
290 B4		Regency Trvl Trlr Park	10.00	•	•	•			40	• U	•		30		Jacksonville, 8 mi SE on Atlantic Blvd (SR 10), 1.5 mi E of Regency Mall, 7 mi W of beaches		1	5	All year	N		•			•	•	•	•	•		•	•					g	904-641-2273	10557 Atlantic, Jcksnvll 32211
290 B4		Golfair Trlr Pk	7.00	•	•	•			14	U					Jacksonville, E on US 90 to Jacksonville Beach, rear of Beach Plaza Shopping Cntr		1	12	All year	N		•			•	•		•						o o	dlr		g	904-249-8451	1300 Shetter, Jcksnvll 32250
290 B4		Fleetwood MHP	10.00	•	•	•			79	• U	•		30		Jacksonville, I-95, 1 mi W on University Blvd, 1/4 mi N on US 1		1	10	All year	N		•			•	•		•			•						g	904-737-4733	5001 Philips Hwy, Jcksnvll32207
291 E3		Winterset Trvl Trlr Pk	12.84	•	•	•			218	U			30		Bradenton, 6-1/2 mi N on US 41		1	22	All year	U		•			•	•	•	•	•		•	•					g	813-722-6154	8515 US 41N, Palmetto 33561
291 E3		Frog Creek CG	11.00	•	•	•		56	125	• U	•		30		Palmetto, 6 mi N on US 41, 1/4 mi W on Bayshore Rd		1	16	All year	U		•			•	•		•			•		s				g	813-722-7661	8515 Bayshore, Palmetto 33561
291 E3		Fiesta Grove Cmpr Rsrt	10.00	•	•	•			205	• U	•		50		Palmetto, jct US 19/US 41, 4 mi N on US 41, 1/4 mi W on Bayshore Rd		1	18	All year	U		•			•	•	•	•	•		•	•					g		8615 Bayshr Rd, Palmetto 33561
291 E3		Tree Lk Trvl Trlr Rsrt	12.00	•	•	•			A254	• U	•		50		Manatee River, 6 mi N on US 41, 500 ft W on Erie Rd		1	40	All year	U		•			•	•	•	•	•		•	•					gt	813-729-1913	PO Bx 1786, Bradenton 33506
292 D5		Outdoor Rsrts of America	17.00	•	•	•	MV		576	U					Melbourne Beach, jct Hwy 192/Hwy A1A, 4 mi S on Hwy A1A		1	50	All year	N		•			•	•	•	•	•		•	•					gt	305-724-2600	3000 S A1A, MelbourneBch32951
293 F3		Pink Citrus Trlr Pk & CG	8.00	•	•	•		30	76	• U	•		30		Bokeelia, jct Hwy 78 & 767, 6-1/2 mi N on 767		1	20	All year	Z		•			•	•		•			•				dlr			813-283-0346	Box 1 Bx 140, Bokeelia 33922
293 F3		Pineland Marina and CG	10.50	•	•	•			S33	U			30		Pineland, US 41, 13 mi W on Hwy 78 to Pine Island, 5 mi N on Hwy 767, 1-1/2 mi W on Pineland Rd		0	20	All year	Z		•			•	•		•							dl			813-283-0080	Box 13, Pineland 33945
294 D4		Woodlands CG	9.00	•	•	•		34	100	• U					Winter Garden, FL Tpke, ext 85, S on US 27, 3.5 mi E on Hwy 50, 1/2 mi N on Hwy 455 to CG		1	150	All year	N		•			•	•		•									h	305-469-2792	Rt 2 Bx 137AA, Wntr Grdn 32787
294 D4		Stage Stop CG	9.00	•	•	•		248	248	• U	•		30		Winter Garden, FL Tpke, ext 80, 3 mi W on Hwy 50		1	22	All year	U		•			•	•	•	•	•		•	•					g	305-656-8000	Box 1366, Winter Garden 32787
294 D4		Killarney Mbl Ct	9.00	•	•	•			S18	• U	•		30		Winter Garden, FL Tpke, 4 mi W on Hwy 50 to Killarney, 1/2 mi N fol sign		1	4	All year	N		•			•	•		•									g	305-656-2525	Box 97, Killarney 32740
294 D4		Orlando/Winter Garden	10.00	•	•	•		25	320	• U	•		30		Winter Garden, FL Tpke, ext 80, 2 mi W on Hwy 50		1	28	All year	Z		•			•	•	•	•	•		•	•					g	305-656-1415	279 W Hwy 50, Wntr Grdn 32787
296 D4		Myakka CG & Stables	9.00	•	•	•		15	25	• U			20		Sarasota, jct US 41, /Hwy 72, 7.5 mi E on Hwy 72		1	160	All year	Z		•			•	•		•	•		•						gh	813-924-8435	RR 1 Bx 74, Sarasota 33583
297 D4		KOA St Augustine/Jcksnvl	11.75	•	•	$		55	108	• U	•		30		Jacksonville, S on I-95, ext Hwy 210		1	34	All year	U		•			•	•		•	•		•	•					g	904-824-8309	Rt 8 Bx 32, Jcksnvll 32224
298 D3		Trvl Trlr Cty	8.00	•	•	•	MV		20	• U			30		Port Richey, 3-1/2 mi N on US 19		1	7	All year	Z		•			•	•		•	•		•	•		r			gh	813-868-1629	11310 US 41 N, Pt Richey 33568
299 D3		Cloverleaf Forest	12.00	•	•	•	MV		AS261	U			30		Brooksville, 1 mi W on US 41		1	12	All year	U		•			•	•	•	•	•		•	•						904-796-8016	910 US 41 N, Brooksville33512
299 D3		Brentwood Lake Cmpg	6.00	•	•	•		60	100	• U	•		20		Brooksville, 2 mi N on US 41		1	20	All year	N		•			•	•		•									g	904-796-5760	11089 Ancient Tr, Brksvll3512
300 B4		Frog Hollow	6.00	•	•	•			15	• U			30		St. Augustine, 4 mi N on US 1		1	7	All year	R		•			•	•		•	•		•						ght	904-829-6665	Rt 3 Bx 48, St Augustine 32084
300 B4		Beachcomber CG	8.38	•	•	•		12	48	• U			30		St. Augustine, 2 mi N on Hwy A1A		1	4	All year	U		•			•	•		•	•								g	904-824-4853	2000 N Hwy A1A, St Augstn32084
301 E5		Tropical Pk	9.00	•	•	•		20	92	• U	•		30		Wabasso, US 1		1	18	All year	U		•			•	•	•	•	•		•	•		dl			g	305-589-5665	Bx 148 8850 US 1, Wabasso32970
302 B2		Cragg's Corner CG	6.00	•	•	•		12	20	• U	•		30		Old Town, E on US 19		1	2	All year	U		•			•	•		•									g	904-542-7315	Rt 3 Bx 431, Old Town 32680
302 B2		Dilger's Suwanee Riv CG	4.50	•	•	•		15	30	• U					Old Town, 3 mi S on US 19/98/27A, 2 blocks N off Suwannee River Bridge		1	30	All year	Z		•			•	•		•						lr		•		904-542-7183	US 19, Old Town 32680
304 E4		Lykes Fisheating CG	8.00	•	•	$		156	156	• U			30		Palmdale, US 27, 1/2 mi N of Hwy 29		1	2000	All year	U		•			•	•		•			•						ht	813-675-1852	PO Box 100, Palmdale 33944
304 E4		Shady Acres CG	8.00	•	•	•		20	25	• U	•		30		Palmdale, US 27, 1/2 mi N		1	4	All year	U		•			•	•		•	•								h	813-675-4369	Box 23, Palmdale 33944
306 C3		Three Flags Trvl CG	9.00	•	•	•			80	• U	•		30		Wildwood, I-75, 1 mi E on Hwy 44		1	10	All year	U		•			•	•	•	•	•		•	•		dl			g	904-748-3870	Rt 2 Bx 48A, Wildwood 32785
306 C3		Rail's End MH & RV Pk	10.00	•	•	•		15	46	• U			30		Wildwood, 3 mi E on Hwy 44		1	15	All year	Z		•			•	•		•	•								g	904-748-1224	Rt 3 Box 358C Wildwood 32785
307 D3		Hidden Valley CG	9.00	•	•	$			50	• U			30		Brooksville, I-75, Brooksville ext, 8 mi W on US 50	8		11	All year	Z		•			•	•		•				•					g	904-796-8710	22329 Cortez, Brksvll 33512
307 D3		Frontier CG	9.50	•	•	•		29	110	• U			30		Weeki Wachee Springs, 6 mi E on Hwy 50		1	21	All year	U		•			•	•	•	•	•		•	•					g	904-796-9988	5102 Hwy 50W, Brksvll 33512
311 B3		Robert's Trlr Pk	5.00	•	•	•			5	U					Crestview, US 19, 10 mi W on Hwy 90		1	4	All year	U		•			•	•		•									g	904-682-3333	1641 E US 90, Crestview 32536
313 B2		Gulf Breeze Trlr Pk	6.00	•	•	•	MV	16	45	• U	•		30		Steinhatchee, US 19, 1 mi E on Hwy 51		1	7	All year	Z		•			•	•		•						dlr			g	904-498-3948	Bx 236, Steinhatchee 32359

CAMPGROUNDS 123

124 CAMPGROUNDS

FLORIDA

FOR MAP, SEE PAGE 114 MIAMI MAP, SEE PAGE 119

Park Number / Map Reference	Name	Fee	Electric / Water / Sewer	Credit Cards	Tent Sites	Trailer Sites	Pull-Thru / Trailer Size (RV Services)	Bottled Gas / Sanitary Service / Maximum Amps (RV Services)	Nearest Town/Access	Physical Environment	Elevation	Acres	Season	Reservations	Time Limit / Pets Permitted / Motor Bikes Permitted	Flush Toilets / Showers	Tables / Firewood / Recreation Hall	Store / Cafe / Laundry / Ice (Camper Services)	Playground / Swimming Pool / Other Swimming / Fishing / Boating	Other (Recreation)	Telephone	Mail Address
	PRIVATE (CONT'D)																					
315 D3	Hollingsworth Trvl Trlr P	7.95	• • •		20	75	• U	• • 30	**Lakeland,** I-4, 2.5 mi N on US 98 N		1	10	All year	Z	U •	• •	• •	○ ○ • ○		g	813-858-2026	6211 US 98 N, Lakeland 33805
315 D3	Tiki Village CG	10.00	• • •		10	100	U	• •	**Lakeland,** I-4, US 98 ext, 1 blk N, 3/8 mi, E to CG		1	15	All year	Z	U •	• •	•	• ○ • •	• • ○ ○ l	g	813-858-5364	Crevasse St, Lakeland 33805
315 D3	Oakridge MHP	10.00	• • •		A8	A8	32		**Lakeland,** 6 mi N on Hwy 33 (2 mi S of I-4)		1	8	All year	Z	U	• •	• •	•	• •	g	813-683-4257	5210 Hwy N 33, Lakeland 33805
318 E5	Pine View Mbl Pk	11.00	• • •			S12	• U	○ •	**Fort Pierce,** 1 mi S of Sears Town on US 1		1	5	All year	Z	U		•	○ ○ • ○			305-461-3741	3265 S Federal, Ft Pierce33450
319 E5	Ocean Resort CO-OP	20.00	• • •	MV		400	U	• 50	**Fort Pierce,** 7 mi N on Hwy A1A		0	26	All year	Z	U •	• •	• •	• • •	• • • •	gt	305-465-1003	5101 N A1A, Ft Pierce 33450
320 H2	Raccoon River Rsrt	12.00	• • •	MV	40	100	• U	• •	**Panama City Beach,** 10 mi W on US 98 Alt, 1 mi N on Hwy 392 (Middle Beach Rd)		1	28	All year	Z	U •	• •	• $ •	• • • •	• • • • r	gh	904-234-0181	12405 Mid Bch, PnmaCtyBch32407
320 H2	Beach CG	10.00	$ • $	MV	116	100	• 30	○ • 30	**Panama City,** 4.5 mi W on Alt 98		1	32	3/1-9/30	Z	U •	• •	• • •	• • • •	• • ○ •	gh	904-234-3833	11826 W Hwy 98, Pnma Cty 32401
320 H2	Sea Gull Trlr Pk & CG	10.00	• • •		45	74	• U	•	**Panama City,** 7 mi W on US 98		0	20	All year**	Z	U •	• •	•	○ ○ ○ •	• • •	g	904-234-2253	14700 W Hwy 98, Pnma Cty 32401
320 H2	Long Beach Camp Inn	8.22	• • •	AM	48	300	• U	• •	**Panama City Beach,** 10511 W Hwy 98 Alt		1	25	All year	Z	U	• •	• • •	• • • •	• • • •	g	904-234-3584	Bx 9110, Panama Cty Bch 32407
322 C3	Covered Wagon CG	8.57	• • •		20	20	• U	○ 30	**Homosassa Springs,** 2 mi S on US 19/98		1	6	All year	Z	U •	• •	• •	○ ○ ○ ○	○ ○	g	904-628-4669	Rt 4 Bx 207, Homosassa 32646
322 C3	Turtle Creek CG	8.50	• • •	MV	75	250	U	• • 30	**Homosassa Springs,** 3/4 mi W of US 19 on Hwy S490A		1	20	All year	Z	U • •	• •	• • •	• • •	• • ○ • dlr	gmt	904-628-2928	Bx 1029, Homosassa Sprngs32647
322 C3	Nature's CG	8.00	• • $		100	150	• U	• • 30	**Homosassa Springs,** 1.5 mi W of US 19 on Hwy S490A		1	100	All year	Z	U •	• •	• $ •	• • •	• • • dlr	g	904-628-2892	Bx 429, Homosassa Spgs 32647
323 D4	Cozy Grove CG	8.50	• • •	MV	25	156	• U	○ •	**Kissimmee,** I-4, 192 W .5 mi, past Disney entrance, Star Rt 545 S 5 mi, E 1/8 mi on Star Rt 532		1	20	All year	Z	U •	• •	• •	• • • •	• • ○	gh	813-424-2791	Rt 1 Bx 205, Davenport 33837
323 D4	Lakewood South CG	9.00	• • •		264	264	• U	•	**Orlando,** I-4 W, ext US 192, 1 mi W to Hwy 545, 5 mi S		1	20	All year	Z	U •	• •	• • •	• • • •	• • ○		813-424-2669	Rt 1 Bx 210, Davenport 33837
323 D4	Three Worlds Camp Rsrt	12.00	• • •	MV	73	200	• U	• •	**Kissimmee,** 16 mi S on US 17/92		1	120	All year	Z	U •	• •	• •	• • •	• • • r		813-424-1286	Rt 1 Box 54B, Davenport 33837
324 D4	Central Pk	8.00	• • •		20	180	• U	• • 30	**Haines City,** jct 27/17/92, 1/4 mi N on 27		1	22	All year	Z	U •	• •	• •	○ ○ • •	• ○	g	813-422-5322	1501 Commerce, Haines Cty33844
324 D4	Haines City Mbl Pk	6.50	$ • •			18	U	○ • 30	**Haines City,** jct 27/17/92, 1/4 mi N on 27		1	40	All year	Z	U •	• •	• •	○ ○ • ○	• •		813-422-2475	1300 Plk Cty, Haines Cty 33844
324 D4	Kennard Mbl Pk	7.00	• • •			12	30	○ • 30	**Haines City,** 1 mi W on US 17/92		1	3	All year	Z	U	• •	•	○ ○ • ○	○ dlr	g	813-422-2947	Kennard Pk, Haines City33844
324 D4	Flamingo RV Park	8.00	• • •		4	31	• U	○ • 30	**Haines City,** 4 mi W on US 17/92		1	4	All year	Z	U •	• •	•	○ ○ • ○	• • dlr	g	813-956-4511	PO Bx 1261, Lake Alfred 33850
324 D4	Horizons End Camp Rsrt	14.00	• • •		100	190	• U	○ • 50	**Davenport,** I-4, 3 mi S on US 27		1	60	All year	Z	U •	• •	• •	○ ○ • •	• •		813-422-1114	PO Bx 848, Barnum City 33837
325 A3	Ridley's O/N Trlr Pk	6.00	• • •		20	20	• U	•	**Hilliard,** 5 mi N on US 1/301		1	6	All year	Z	U •	• •	•	• •	•		904-845-2941	Rt 1, Hilliard 32046
327 B2	Shady Oaks MHP	7.00	• • •		30	30	• U	•	**Cross City,** 3 mi S on US 98/19/27A		1	15	All year	Z	U •	• •	• ○ •	• ○ • •	• • ○		904-498-3725	Rt 3, Old Town 32680
328 D3	Ja-Mar Travel Park	10.00	• • •			A396	U	• 50	**Port Richey,** Hwy 52, 1.5 mi S on US 19			24	All year	Z	U •	• •	•	○ ○ • ○	• •	g	813-863-2040	11203 US 19, Port Richey 33568
328 D3	Suncoast CG	11.00	• • •	MV	15	88	• U	• 30	**Port Richey,** 1.5 mi N on US 19, 3 mi S of Hwy 52		1	10	All year	Z	U • •	• •	• •	• ○ • •	• • ○ ○ dlr	g	813-842-9324	9029 US 19 N, Pt Richey 33568
329 H3	Gulfview CGs	7.00	• • •		55	30	• U	• 30	**Apalachicola,** 10 mi E on US 98		1	3	All year	Z	U •	• •	•	○ •	• • l		904-670-8970	US 98, Eastpoint 32328
329 H3	KOA Apalachicola Bay	9.00	• • $	MV	14	59	• U	•	**Apalachicola,** 6 mi E on US 98		1	6	All year	Z	U • •	• •	• •	• ○ • •	• • ○ dlr		904-670-8307	PO Bx 621, Eastpoint 32328
334 E4	River Ranch Rsrt CG	14.50	• • •	AMV	35	100	U	• •	**Lake Wales,** Yeehaw Jct (FL tpke), 20 mi W on Hwy 60		1	6	All year	Z	U •	• •	• • •	• • • •	• • ○ • dlr	gmst	813-692-1321	24700 Hwy 60 E, Lk Wales 33853
335 B3	Ginnie Springs	10.00	$ •	MV	100	55	• U	•	**High Springs,** I-75, ext Alachua-High Spgs, 6 mi W on US 441, 1/2 mi S on US 41, 6.5 mi W on Hwy 340, 1 mi N on Ginnie Spgs Rd		1	200	All year	Z	U •	• •	• •	• •	• • lr		904-454-2202	Rt 1 Bx 153, High Spgs 32643
337 D3	Oak Harbor CG	9.50	• • •		54	V146	• U	• •	**Haines City,** 4.5 mi W on US 92, N on Experiment Sta Rd, E on Old Dixie Hwy, 2.5 mi N on Lk Lowery Rd		1	75	All year	R	U •	• •	• •	•	• • • dl	g	813-956-1341	Haines City 33844
350 C3	Nautilus Trlr Pk	8.50	• • •			30	• U	• 30	**Ocala,** jct US 27/441/301 & Star Rt 200, 1.5 mi S		1	15	All year	Z	U • •	• •	• •	○ ○ • ○		g	904-629-6242	3441 S Pine St, Ocala 32670
350 C3	Cross Country Trvl Pk	7.00	• • •		5	17	30	○ • 50	**Ocala,** jct 441/301/27 & Hwy 200, 4 mi S		1	3	All year	Z	U • •	• •	•	○ ○ • ○		gt	904-622-7403	5100 S Pine, Ocala 32670
381 D2	Lake Seminole CS	8.00	• • •		18	A50	• 31	○ • 30	**Seminole,** jct 19A/694 (74th Ave), 1 blk E		1	16	All year		U	• •	• •	○ ○ • •	○	g	813-392-4378	10550 74th Ave, Seminole 33542
381 D2	A19A Fmly CS	7.50	• • •		20	40	32	• • 30	**Largo,** Hwy 688, .5 mi S on Hwy A19A		1	3	All year		U •	• •	•	• ○ • •	• •	g	813-531-3231	12474 66th St N, Largo 33543
381 D2	Roycroft Trvl Trlr Pk	12.00	• • •			140	U	• •	**Seminole,** Alt US 19, 1 blk E on 70th Ave		1	7	All year	Z	U •	• •	•	○ ○ • ○	○ ○ l	g	813-391-4581	10562 70th Ave N, Smnl 33542
381 D2	Bay Drive Trlr Pk	6.50	• • •			15	30	• 30	**Largo,** US 19 Alt, 1/4 mi W on Co 686		1	5	All year	Z	U • •	• •	•	○ ○ • ○	○ ○ l	g	813-584-6375	1665 W Bay Dr, Largo 33540
381 D2	Bay Pines Annex	13.00	• • •			AS6	31	○ • 20	**Seminole,** jct 19A/699, 1/4 mi N		1	15	All year	R	U • •	• •	•	○ ○ • ○	○ ○ dlr	gh	813-392-3807	5640 Seminole, Seminole 33542
381 D2	Vacation Village	10.00	$ • •			A293	U	• • 50	**Largo,** US 19, 1/4 mi W on Hwy 688		1	17	All year	Z	U	• •	• •	○ ○ • ○	•	g	813-531-5589	6850 Ulmerton Rd, Largo 33541
381 D2	Rainbow Village	12.00	• • •			AS305	U	• • 50	**Largo,** A19A, 3/4 mi S of Hwy 688		1	20	All year	Z	U •	• $	• •	○ ○ • ○	•	g	813-536-3545	11911 66 St N, Largo 33543
381 D2	Lees Travel Pk	10.00	• • •			140	• U	• •	**Largo,** I-75, Hwy 688 ext, 3 mi W, 1/4 mi N on Belcher Rd		1	10	All year	Z	U	• $	• •	○ ○ • ○	•	g	813-536-2050	1610 S Belcher, Largo 33541
381 D2	Holiday CG	12.00	• • •	MV	50	150	U	• • 30	**Seminole,** jct 19A/694, .5 mi E		1	50	All year	Z	U •	• •	• •	• ○ • •	• • dr	gh	813-391-4960	10000 Pk Blvd, Seminole 33543
381 D2	Travel World	16.00	• • •			A340	• 32	• 30	**Clearwater,** I-75, 3 mi W on Hwy 688, 1/4 mi S on US 19		1	22	All year	Z	U	• $	• •	○ ○ • ○	•	g	813-536-1765	12400 US 19S, Clrwtr 33516
381 D2	Camper's Cove	9.00	• • •			10	U		**Largo,** US 19, 10 mi W on Hwy 688, 10 ft S on Hamlin, 1/2 blk W to CG		1	5	All year	Z	U	• $	• •	○ ○ • ○	○ ○	g	813-595-5722	14750-118th Ave N, Largo 33544
381 D2	Yankee Traveler Trlr Pk	12.00	• • •			S10	U	• •	**Largo,** US 19, 2 mi W on Hwy 688		1	10	All year	Z	U	•		○ ○ • ○	•		813-531-7998	8500 Ulmerton Rd, Largo 33541
382 E4	Brighton Camparina	8.50	• • •			70	• U	○ • 30	**Okeechobee,** 15 mi SW on Hwy 78, 3 mi N on Hwy 721		1	42	All year	Z	U •	• •	• • •	• • • •	• • • • dlr	h	813-763-8531	RR 6 Bx 770, Okeechobee 33472
383 F5	Neasham's Holiday Pk	12.50	• • •			140	U	• • 50	**Deerfield Beach,** I-95, ext 37, 2.5 mi W on Hillsboro Blvd, W to Power Line Rd, 1 blk S		0	11	All year	Z	U • •	• •		• • • •	○ •	gt	305-421-4671	100 S Pwrln, Drfld Bch 33441
384 B4	Pacetti's Marina & CG	8.00	• • •	MV	25	125	• U	• •	**St. Augustine,** 17 mi W on Hwy 16		1	18	All year	Z	U •	• •	• • •	• • • •	• • • dlr	g	904-284-5356	Bx366 Orngdl, Grn Cv Spgs32043

FLORIDA

FOR MAP, SEE PAGE 114 · MIAMI MAP, SEE PAGE 119

PARK NUMBER MAP REFERENCE	NAME	FEE	ELECTRIC	WATER	SEWER	CREDIT CARDS	TENT SITES	TRAILER SITES	PULL-THRU	BOTTLED GAS	SANITARY SERVICE	MAX AMPS	NEAREST TOWN/ACCESS	PHYSICAL ENVIRONMENT	ELEVATION	ACRES	SEASON	RESERVATIONS	TIME LIMIT	PETS PERMITTED	MOTOR BIKES PERMITTED	FLUSH TOILETS	SHOWERS	TABLES	FIREWOOD	RECREATION HALL	STORE	CAFE	LAUNDRY	ICE	PLAYGROUND	SWIMMING POOL	OTHER SWIMMING	FISHING	BOATING	OTHER	TELEPHONE	MAIL ADDRESS
	PRIVATE (CONT'D)																																						
385 H4	Lazy Lakes CG	8.00	S ·	·			60	29	·	30			Key West, US 1, 15 mi NE at 20 mi mkr, 3 blks S on Johnson Rd		0	22	LD-MD	N	U	·	·	·	·	·	·	·	·		·	·	·	·				305-745-1079	Bx 154, Sugarloaf Key 33044
385 H4	Venture Out-Cudjoe Cay	15.00	· ·	·		MV		200	· U	30	·		Key West, 18 mi NE on US 1, at mi mkr 23		1	65	All year	N	U	·	·	·	·	·	·	·	·	·	·	·	dl				305-745-3233	Rt 2 Bx 38, Smmrlnd Key 33042
386 H5	Camper's Cove	14.00	· ·	·			4	26	o	30	o		Key Largo, 6 mi S on gulf side of US 1, bet mi mkrs 101 & 102		1	3	All year	N	U	·	·	·	·	·	·	·	·		·	·	dl	t			305-451-0561	101640 N Overseas, Ky Lrgo33047
386 H5	Calusa Camp Rsrt	15.00	· ·	·		MV	43	200	· U	30	·		Key Largo, 1 mi N on US 1, btw mi mkrs 101 & 102		0	30	All year	N	U	·	·	·	·	·	·	·	·	·	·	·	dl	t			305-451-0232	325 Calusa, Key Largo 33037
386 H5	Key Largo Ocean Rsrts	17.00	· ·	·		MV		40	· U	30	·		Key Largo, 3 mi S on US 1 at mi marker 95			20	All year	N	U	·	·	·	·	·	·	·	·	·	·	·	dl	t			308-852-3011	Overseas Hwy, Key Largo 33037
386 H5	Glen's Trlr Pk	13.00	· ·	·			10	15	· U	30	·		Key Largo, PenneKamp SP, 1 mi S on US 1, btwn mi markers 102 & 101		1	6	All year	N	U	·	·	·	·	·	·	·	·		·	·	dl				305-852-2911	Overseas Hwy, Key Largo 33037
386 H5	Amer Outdoors-Key Largo	14.00	· ·	·		MV	106	151	· 33	30			Key Largo, Bus sect, 2-1/2 mi S on US 1, btwn mi mkrs 97 & 98		1	12	All year	N		·	·	·	·	·	·	·	·	·	·	·	d				305-852-8054	Rt 1 Box 38A, Key Largo 33037
386 H5	King's Kamp & Marina	12.00	· ·	·			13	47	· U	30	o		Key Largo, Jewfish Cr, 4 mi S, btwn mi mrkrs 103 & 104		1	3	All year	N	U	·	·	·	·	·	·	·	o		·	·	dlr				305-451-0010	Rt 3 Bx 294, Key Largo 33037
386 H5	Key Largo KG & Marina	13.00	· ·	·		MV	32	177	· U	30	·		Key Largo, John Pennekamp St Pk, 1 mi S on US 1, 1/4 mi E atmile marker 101.5		1	40	All year	N	U	·	·	·	·	·	·	·	·	·	·	·					305-451-1431	R 4 Bx 118-A,Key Largo 33037
386 H5	Travel Trailer Town	12.00	· ·	·				2	o	30	o		Key Largo, US 1, btw mi markers 101 & 102		0	2	All year	N	U	·	·	·	·	·	·	·	·		·	·	d				305-852-5908	Rt 1 Bx 72, Key Largo 33037
387 C3	Bushnell Trlr Ct	6.00	· ·	·				18	· U	30	o		Bushnell, I-75, 1 mi E on Hwy 48, 1 blk S on US 301		1	5	All year	N	U	·	·		·	·	·	·	·	·	o		dl				904-793-3511	Box 456, Bushnell 33513
387 C3	Red Barn CG	10.00	· ·	·			20	263	· U	30	·		Bushnell, I-75, ext, 1000 ft off N side of Hwy 48		1	40	All year	N	U	·	·	·	·	·	·	·	·		·	·	dl				904-793-6220	Bushnell 33513
388 H3	Presnell's Camp	7.00	· ·	·			12	17	· U	30	o		Port St. Joe, 4.5 mi N on Hwy C30		1	4	All year	N	U	·	·	·	·	·	·	·	·			·	d				904-227-1821	PO Bx 386, Port St Joe 32456
389 D3	Kobe's Trvl Trlr Pk	12.80	· ·	·		MV	A10	A40	o 32	30	·		Miami, I-95, 135th St ext, E to NE 16th Ave, S to 11900 NE 16th Ave		1	2	All year	N	U	·	·	·	·	·	·	·	·	·	·	·	dlr				305-893-5121	11900 NE 16th Ave,Miami 33161
390 C3	DBA Trinity Towers	14.00	· ·	·				175	· 32				Hollywood, I-95, 1/4 mi W on Pembroke Rd		1	6	All year	N	U	·	·	·	·	·	·	·	·	·	·			g			305-962-7400	3300 Pembroke,Hollywood 33021
390 C3	Holiday Pk	13.50	· ·	·			500	130	· U	30	·		Hallandale, I-95, exit 21 1/4 mi W on Hallandale Bch Blvd		1	5	All year	N	U	·	·	·	·	·	·	·	·	·	·		dlr	g			305-981-4414	3140 Hallandale, Hlndle 33009
391 E4	Buttonwood Bay	12.00	· ·	·				500	· U	30	·		Sebring, US 27		1	60	All year	N	U	·	·	·	·	·	·	·	·	o		·		gms			813-655-1122	1000 US 27S, Sebring 33870
392 E4	Sebring Grove CG	9.00	· ·	·				80	· U	50	·		Sebring, 1/4 mi S on US 27		1	10	All year	N	U	·	·	·	·	·	·	·	·		·	·	l	ght			813-382-1660	4105 US 27 S, Sebring 33870
397 B4	KOA St Augustine Bch	11.00	· ·	·		MV	68	126	· U	30	·		St. Augustine, 4 mi S on Hwy A1A, 300 ft SW on Hwy 3		1	12	All year	N	U	·	·	·	·	·	·	·	·	·	·	·	dlr	t			904-471-3113	Rt 5 Bx 9E, St Augustine32084
397 B4	Bryn Mawr Ocean Rsrt	16.00	· ·	·		MV		250	· U	30	·		St. Augustine, I-95, E thru St. Augustine on Hwy 16, 8 mi S on A1A		1	38	All year	N	U	·	·	·	·	·	·	·	·	·	·	·		g			904-471-3353	Rt 5 Bx 18P, St Augustine32084
397 B4	Cooksey's Cmpg Pk	11.00	· ·	·			115	225	· U	30	·		St. Augustine, Hwy A1A, S at St Augustine Beach on Hwy S-3		1	120	All year	N	U	·	·	·	·	·	·	S ·	·	·	·	·	dlr	gt			904-471-3171	Rt 5 Bx 12, St Augustine32084
397 B4	Ocean Grove Camp Rsrt	10.00	S ·	·		MV	50	150	· U	30			St. Augustine, 6.5 mi S on Hwy A1A		1	18	All year	N	U	·	·	·	·	·	·	·	·	·	·	o	dlr				904-471-3414	RFD 5,Bx 16K, StAugustine32084
399 G1	Adventures Unlimited	7.00	· ·				25	14	U	30			Milton, 12 mi N on Hwy 87, 4-1/2 mi E at Coldwater Brdg		1	24	All year	N	U	·	·	·	·		·	·	o		o	·					904-623-6197	209 Broad St, Milton 32570
401 H4	Key Trlr Ct	10.00	· ·	·				125	30	30	·		Marathon, on US 1, mi mrkr 50		1	12	All year	N	U	·	·	·	·	·	·	·	·		·		dlr				305-743-9994	6099 Overseas, Marathon 33050
401 H4	Knights Key Pk	10.00	· ·	·		MV	80	150	· 30	30	·		Knights Key, US 1, by 7 mi brdg, 1/2 mi S of Marathon, at mi mrkr 47		1	25	All year	N	U	·	·	·	·	·	·	·	·	·	·	·	dlr	g			305-743-9994	Box 525, Marathon 33050
403 B3	KOA Lake City N	9.50	· ·	·		MV	18	51	· U	30	·		Lake City, I-75, E on I-10, 1 mi N on US 441		1	80	All year	N	U	·	·	·	·	·	·	·	·	·	·	·	dlr	g			904-752-9131	Rt 1 Bx 103, Lake City 32055
404 B3	Suwannee Riv-Ponderosa CG	20.00	· ·	·			40	119	· U	30	·		White Springs, I-75, ext Star Rt 136, 3 mi E		1	30	All year	N	U	·	·	·	·	·	·	·	·	·	·	·	dlr	g			904-397-2292	Rt 1 Bx 93, White Sprgs 32096
405 B3*	Seminole Pk	15.00	· ·	·				102	· 31	20	·		Hollywood, FL tpke, Hollywood ext, 2 mi N on US 441		1	20	All year	N	U	·	·	·	·	·	·	·	o	o	o	·	dlr	gmst			305-987-6961	3301 N St Rd 7,Hollywood3021
407 C3	Blue Parrot Camping Pk	10.00	· ·	·		MV	325	325	· U	30	·		Ocala, 24 mi S on US 27/441, 1-1/2 mi N at Lady Lk on C25A		1	40	All year	N	U	·	·	·	·	·	·	·	·	·	·	·	dlr	g			904-753-2026	Rt 1 Bx 1240, Lady Lake 32659
407 C3	Pine Is CG & Fish Camp	10.00	· ·	·			30	30	· U	30	·		Fruitland Park, 4 mi N on US 27, E on Lemon St, 6 mi on Lk Griffin Rd		1	9	All year	N	U	·	·	·	·	·	·	·	·		o	·	dlr				904-753-2972	Rt 2 Bx 630, Lady Lake 32659
410 C3	Lake Weir Trlr Pk & CG	5.50	· ·	·			10		· U	30	·		Belleview, E on Co 25 to Okiawaha, 1 mi S		1	4	All year	N	U	·	·	·	·	·		o o	·			·	dlr				904-288-2614	Rt 1 Bx 2282, Okiawaha 32679
411 B3*	Yacht Haven Trlr Resort	10.00	· ·	·			10	200	· 31	30	·		Fort Lauderdale, I-95, 2 blks W on Hwy 84		1	20		N	U	·	·	·	·	·	·	·	·	·	·	·	dl	g			305-583-2322	2323 St Rd 84, Ft Ldrdl 33312
413 C3	Tee Pee Trvl Pk	9.00	· ·	S ·			12	137	· U				Leesburg, 6 mi S on US 27		1	15		N	U	·	·	·	·	·	·	·	·	·	·	·		gt			904-787-1504	6745 S Hwy 27, Leesburg 32748
413 C3	Holiday Trvl Pk	14.00	· ·	·			25	935	· U				Leesburg, 3 mi S on US 27, .5 mi W on Hwy 33		1	103		N	U	·	·	·	·	·	·	·	·	·	·	·	dlr				904-787-5151	4519 S SR 33,Leesburg 32748
420 D4	Lake Maika'i CG	10.50	· ·	·		MV	V125		· U	30			Barnum City, jct US 27/ 192, 1 mi E on 192, 1 mi N on Hwy 545		1	10		N	U	·	·	·	·	·	·	·	·		·	·	r				305-239-8774	SR 545, Bx 142, Wntr Grdns32787

CAMPGROUNDS 125

FLORIDA

FOR MAP, SEE PAGE 114 MIAMI MAP, SEE PAGE 119

PARK NUMBER	MAP REFERENCE	NAME	FEE	ELECTRIC/WATER/SEWER	CREDIT CARDS	TENT SITES	TRAILER SITES	PULL-THRU	TRAILER SIZE	BOTTLED GAS	SANITARY SERVICE	MAXIMUM AMPS	NEAREST TOWN/ACCESS	PHYSICAL ENVIRONMENT	ELEVATION	ACRES	SEASON	RESERVATIONS	TIME LIMIT	PET PERMITTED	MOTOR BIKES PERMITTED	FLUSH TOILETS	SHOWERS	TABLES	FIREWOOD	RECREATION HALL	STORE	CAFE	LAUNDRY	ICE	PLAYGROUND	SWIMMING POOL	OTHER SWIMMING	FISHING	BOATING	OTHER	TELEPHONE	MAIL ADDRESS
		PRIVATE (CONT'D)																																				
420	D4	Captain Kidd's RV Rsrt	16.00	•••$	MV	85	500	•	U	•		50	Kissimmee, jct I-4/US 192, 4 mi on US 192			100	All year	N		U		•	•	•	•		o	o		•	•	•	•		gh	305-396-6101	8550 Spacecst, Kissimmee 32741
420	D4	Yogi Bear-US 192/Orlando	14.00	•••$	MV		615	•	U	•		50	Kissimmee, US 27, 1.5 mi E on US 192, 15 mi fr Kissimmee			70	All year	N		U		•	•	•	•	o	o	o		•	•	dlr			g	305-423-4751	Kissimmee 32741
420	D4	Ft Wilderness Rsrt	20.00	•••$	AM	90	735	•	U	•		50	Orlando, jct I-4 & US 192, W on US 192, inside Walt Disney World			640	All year	R	14	U		•	•	•	•	•	•	•	•	•	•	dr			ght	305-824-2727	Bx 40, Lk Buena Vista 32830
422	E3*	Little Farm Mbl Ct	10.00				AV5		30			30	Miami, 8500 Biscayne Blvd			20	All year	N		U		•	•							•					g	305-754-3303	4485 Meridian, Miami 33140
423	E5	Enchanted Forest Trlr Pk	6.00	••			S28		U				Okeechobee, jct US 441/Hwy 70, 2 mi E on 70, .5 mi N on Padgett Co, 1/4 mi W of Hwy 710			10	All year	N		U		•	•		•											gmt	813-763-1050	Bx 3010 Padgett, Okchbee 33472
424	B4	Pellicer Creek Cmpg Pk	8.00	••		30	54	•	U	•		30	St. Augustine, ext 92 jct I-95/US 1, .5 mi S on US 1			8	All year	N		U		•	•	•	•		o		o					•		g	904-797-5377	Rt 4 Box 209E, St Agstn 32086
425	D4	Yogi Bear-Orlando/I-4	16.75	•••$	MV	29	469	•	U	•		30	Orlando, 8 mi S on I-4 ext 528-A, ext 528-A W, 1 mi S on Turkey Lk Rd			73	All year	N		U		•	•	•	•	•	o	o	o	•	•	dlr				305-351-4394	9200 Turkey Lk, Orlando 32809
426	E3	KOA Peace River	12.00	••		15	183	•	U	•			Arcadia, 2 mi W on Hwy 70			150	All year	N		U		•	•	•	•	o	o		o			lr			gh	813-494-0214	Rt 7 Bx 303, Arcadia 33821
427	C3	Arrowhead CS	9.50	••	MV	20	110		U				Ocala, I-75, ext 70, 1/8 mi W on US 27, 1/8 mi S on NW 38th ve			25	All year	N		U		•	•	$	•	o	o		o					•			904-622-5627	1720 NW 39th Ct, Ocala 32670
428	C3	Oaktree Village CG	8.50	••		70	137	o	U	•		30	Ocala, jct I-75/US 27, 800 ft W			40	All year	N		U		•	•		•	o	o					lr			g	904-629-1569	4039 NW Blitchon, Ocala 32670
428	C4	Holiday Trvl Pk	12.00	••	MV	50	156	•	U	•		30	Daytona Beach, 15 mi N on I-95, ext 90 Marco Polo Blvd, NW corner			35	All year	N		U		•	•	•	•	o	o				•				t	904-672-8122	Star Rt Bx 54A, Bunnell 32010
429	D3	Camp Lemora	11.00	••			302		U	•		30	Zephyrhills, 13 mi N of jct I-4 & US 301			70	All year	N		U		•	•	•	•	o	o		o					•		hk	813-986-4456	50 Dead Rv, Thonotsasa 33592
430	B3	KOA Space Coast Resort	17.00	••	MV	36	154	•	U	•			Cocoa Beach, I-95, ext 74, E to Barnes Blvd (SR 502)			38	All year	N		U		•	•	•	•	o	o		o							gmst	305-636-3000	820 Barnes, Rockledge 32955
432	E5	Road Runner Trvl Pk	10.00	••			330		U	•		50	Fort Pierce, Sunshine Tpke ext 56, 5 mi N on Hwy 713, 1 1/4 mi E on Hwy 8				All year	N		U		•	•		•	o	o									g	305-464-0969	Box 235, Rt 5, Ft Pierce 33450
433	H3	Rustic Sands Rsrt CG	8.00	••		16	42		U	•		30	Panama City, 25 mi E on US 98, 3/4 mi N on C386A			17	All year	N		U		•	•	•	•	o	o		o					•		mt	904-648-5229	Bx 13146, Mexico Bch 32410
433	H3	El Governor	8.00	••		12	26		U	•		30	Mexico Beach, on US 98			5	All year	N		U		•	•			o	o		o									904-648-5432	Bx 13156, Mexico Beach 32410
434	B3	Florida Camp Inn	10.00	••			450		U				Davenport, I-4, 4-1/2 mi N on US 27			35	All year	N		U		•	•		•	o	o		o					•			813-424-2494	Rt 1 Bx 235, Davenport 33837
439	C3	Lykes Chassahowitzka Rive	7.00	•• $		25	52		U				Homosassa Springs, jct US 19/Hwy 480, 1.7 mi W on Hwy 480			50	All year	N		U		•	•	•			o					dlr		•		g	904-382-2200	PO Bx 890, Homosassa Spgs 32647
440	A2	Outdoor Rsrts	8.95				104		U				Jennings, I-75, 1st ext in Fl (Jennings Ext)			50	All year	N		U		•	•		•		o					r					904-938-3321	Rt 1 Bx 221, Jennings 32053
443	H3	Cape San Blas Cmpg Rsrt	9.00	••			V26	•	30			20	Port St. Joe, 1 mi SE on US 98, 7 mi S on Hwy C30, 1.5 mi W on Cape San Blas Rd C30E			7	All year	N		U		•	•	$	•		o		o					•			904-229-6800	Bx 645, Port St Joe 32456
443	H3	Ski Breeze Camp Sites	9.00	••		15	V40		U				Port St. Joe, 8.5 mi SE on Hwy 30C			12	All year	N		U		•	•	•			o							•		g	904-229-6105	Rt 3C Bx 48, Port St Joe 32456
444	B2	KOA Madison	9.00	••		10	62	•	U	•			Madison, Interchange of I-10 & Hwy 53			15	All year	N		U		•	•	•	•	o	o		o			lr				g	904-973-2504	Rt 1 Bx 3095, Madison 32340
445	C3	Safari Camp-E Pensacola	8.50	••		25	68	•	U	•			Milton, N on Hwy 87 to Entrance			20	All year	N		U		•	•	•	•	o	o		o							g	904-623-3936	Rt 4 Bx 185, Milton 32570
445	G1	KOA Pensacola/Milton	9.50	••	MV	39	39	•	U	•			Bagdad, jct I-10/Hwy 191			9	All year	N		U		•	•	•	•	o	o		o							g	904-623-9203	Box 238, Bagdad 32530
446	C3	Holiday Trvl Pk	9.50	••	MV	20	88	•	U	•			Ocala, I-75, 500 ft W on Hwy 40			10	All year	N		U		•	•	•	•	o	o		o							g	904-622-5330	4001 SW Broadway, Ocala 32671
446	C3	Camper Village	9.95	••			70	•	U				Ocala, I-75, ext Hwy 200, 1/4 mi W			10	All year	N		U		•	•		•		o		o							gh	904-237-3236	3931 SW College, Ocala 32674
446	C3	Scottish Inn	8.00	••	Amv	30	160	•	U				Ocala, I-75 & Hwy 40			21	All year	N		U		•	•			o	o		o									904-629-6902	3601 SW Broadway, Ocala 32671
446	C3	KOA Ocala	12.25	••	MV	25	225	•	U	•			Ocala, I-75, ext Hwy 200, 1/4 mi W on 38th Ave			14	All year	N		U		•	•	•	•	•	o	o	o	•	•							904-237-2138	3200 SW 38th Ave, Ocala 32670
447	G5	Southern Comfort CG	12.00	••	MV	194	194	•	U	•			Homestead, 1 mi S at jct US 27/US 1, & at S End of Fl tur 1 blk E of US #1 on Palm Dr, Fl City			25	All year	N		U		•	•		•	o	o		o							g	305-248-6909	345 E Palm Dr, Fl City 33030
447	G5	Aquarius Trlr Pk	12.00	••			250		U			50	Homestead, 1 blk E of US 1			30	All year	N		U		•	•		•		o		o							gmt	305-248-9383	451 SE 8th, Homestead, 33030
448	D4	Clerbrook RV Rsrt	12.00	••		50	V600	•	U	•		50	Clermont, 8 mi N on Hwy 27 or FL tpke ext 85			650	All year	N		U		•	•	•	•	o	o		•			lr		•		gh	904-394-5513	Rt 2 Bx 107, Clermont 32711
450	C3	Village Pines	6.00	••		10	15		U			30	Inglis, 7 mi N on US 19			23	All year	N		U		•	•		•		o		o					•		t	904-447-2777	SR 1 Bx 52A, Dunnellon 32630
451	F5	Boca Trvl Pk	17.00	••		20	V102	•	U	•		50	Boca Raton, FL tpk ext 28, 1/8 mi W on SR 808, 1/4 mi S on Boca Rio Rd			10	All year	N		U		•	•		•		o		o			o				ght	305-482-8222	21000 Boca Rio, Boca Raton
452	C3	Pine Manor MHP	6.50	••	MV		23		U			30	Ocala, 1 mi W on Hwy 27, on US 441/301			10	All year	N		U		•	•		•		o		o							g	904-622-7089	2815 NW Pine, Ocala 32670
452	C3	Ocala Springs RV Pk	9.50	••	MV	100	V100	•	U	•		50	Silver Springs, 4 mi W on Baseline Rd			600	All year	N		U		•	•	•	•	o	o		o			lr				g	904-236-9918	PO Bx 9, Silver Springs 32688
453	C3	Webster MH & Trvl Park	7.00	••		45	75		U	•		30	Webster, 1 mi W on W Central Ave			25	All year	N		U		•	•	•	•	o	o		o							ghst	904-793-6765	RT 2 Bx 515, Webster 33597
454	G2	Holiday Lake Trav-L-Pk	8.00	••	AMV		33		U				Crestview, jct I-10/Hwy 85, ext #85			5	9/1-5/1	N		U		•	•		•		o							•			904-682-6111	Bx 1355, Crestview 32536
455	D3	Orchid Lake Trvl Trlr Pk	7.50	••		15	300		U	•		30	New Port Richey, I-295, ext Wilson, 1/8 mi W on Wilson 587W			55	All year	N		U		•	•	•	•	o	o	o	o					•		ghst	813-847-1925	4802 Orchid Lk, Pt Richey 33552
457	B4	The Pine Villa MHP	7.00	••			S16		U				Jacksonville, I-295, ext Wilson, 1/8 mi W on Wilson			18	All year	N		U		•	•				o											904-771-5034	7621 Wilson, Jcksnvll 32210
458	G3	Pt Laura Marina CG	13.60	••		30	30		U				Cross Key, US 1, mi marker 112.5			3	All year	N		U		•	•				o							•	•	mst	305-248-6233	999 Morris Ln, Cross Key 33035
459	G1	Breezy Ridge RV Pk	7.35	••			S10		U				Milton, 3 mi W on US 90			3	All year	R		U		•	•				o											904-994-9799	1750 Hwy 90 W, Milton 32570
460	G2	Ponce de Leon CG	7.80	••		10	40		U				Ponce de Leon, I-10 ext 15, 300 yds S of interchange on Hwy 81			10	All year	N		U		•	•				o							•		ht	904-836-4555	Rt 1 Bx 5A, Pnc de Leon 32455

ACCOMMODATIONS & RESTAURANTS

On these pages is a selection of motels, hotels, inns, resorts, and restaurants located throughout Florida. Due to space limitations it has not been possible to list every fine establishment. The omission of any motel, hotel, or restaurant does not mean, therefore, that it is inferior in quality to those included. In the metropolitan areas and areas of popular tourist attractions, particularly, there is a multiplicity of accommodations available, so representative facilities in various size and price ranges have been chosen.

The emphasis is on accommodations for the vacationing family interested in overnight or brief stays rather than on those that cater to the visitor who spends the complete "season" in one location.

All information has been supplied by the establishments, and the publisher is not responsible for inaccuracies in the facts as given or for the possibility that they may not be valid at the time of publication. However, if you find serious discrepancies between the information listed and the quality or availability of services or facilities, please notify Guide Editors, Publishing Group, Rand McNally & Company, PO Box 7600, Chicago, IL 60680.

RATE INFORMATION

- A State sales tax of 4% is added to all charges for accommodations and meals.
- Unless otherwise indicated, all rates are based on the European plan: lodging only, no meals. Some establishments offer the American plan: lodging plus three meals a day; or the modified American plan: lodging plus two meals per day.
- In most instances rates vary throughout the year, based on the "high season" of each area. Rates given are for the high season, with months and dates indicated. Lower rates would be in effect during other times.

CREDIT CARDS

Major credit agencies are indicated by these abbreviations:
  A—American Express
  C—Carte Blanche
  D—Diners Club
  MC—MasterCard
  V—Visa

If you wish to use a card from an agency not listed check with the management at the time your reservation is made to be sure your card will be honored.

LOCATION INFORMATION

Highway and mileage directions are given in reference to the downtown area of the city or town under which the establishments are listed. Services or facilities "adj" (adjacent) are within 100 feet, and "opp" (opposite) facilities are across the closest thoroughfare.

ARCADIA

BEST WESTERN M & M MOTEL. 504 S Brevard (33821), on US 17. 813/494-4884. 37 A/C rms. Early Jan-Mar: S, $32-$38; D, $35-$45; each addl, $5; under 12 free; rest of yr: lower rates avail. Crib, $4; cot, $7. Color TV. Pool. Cafe adj, 8 am-2 pm. Cr cds: A, C, D, MC, V.

BARTOW

EL JON. 1460 E Main St (33830), ¾ mi E on FL 60 Business, ½ blk E of 17, 98. 813/533-8191. 38 A/C rms. Dec-Apr: S, D, $35-$38; each addl, $4; rest of yr: lower rates. Color TV. Pool. Cafe adj, 6 am-11 pm. Cr cds: A, C, D, MC, V.

BELLE GLADE

HOLIDAY INN. 1075 S Main St (33430), on FL 80 bet 27, 441. 305/996-7222. 104 A/C units, 2 story. Dec-Mar: S, $44-$52; D, $48-$54; each addl, $6; under 18 free; rest of yr: varied lower rates. TV. Pool. Cafe, 6 am-10 pm. Bar. Cr cds: A, D, MC, V.

TRAVELERS MOTOR LODGE. 1300 S Main St (33430), ½ mi S on FL 80. 305/996-6761. 26 A/C rms. Dec-Apr: S, $30; D, $36-$42; each addl, $5; under 10 free; rest of yr: varied lower rates. TV. Cr cds: A, MC, V.

BOCA RATON

BEST WESTERN UNIVERSITY INN. 2700 N US1 (33431), 1 mi N on 1. 305/395-5225. 90 A/C rms, 2 story. Dec-Apr: S, $59; D, $69; each addl, $6; under 12 free; family rates avail; rest of year: varied lower rates. TV. Pool. Cafe, 7 am-10 pm. Bar. Coin lndry.

BOCA RATON HOTEL & CLUB. Camino Real (33432), ¾ mi. S, 2 blks E of 1. 305/395-3000; res: 800/327-0101. 921 A/C units, 6-27 story, (60 with kit.) in 3-story villas. Dec-May: Mod Amer plan: S, $180-$225; D, $205-$280; each addl, $45; parlor, $80; kit units, $215-$340; suites avail; Eur, golf plans avail; rest of yr: varied lower rates. Reservation required. Color TV. 3 pools, 2 Olympic-size. Cafe (public by reservation), 7 am-9:30 pm. Bar, 11-2 am; closed Sun. Golf. Tennis. Dancing, movies, entertainment. Many rms with balcony overlook Lake Boca Raton. Cr cds: A, MC, V.

BRIDGE. 999 E Camino Real (33432), 10 blks E off FL A1A. 305/368-9500. 198 A/C units. Dec-Apr: S, D, $97; each addl, $10; suites, $160-$240; rest of yr: varied lower rates. Color TV. Pool. Cafe, 7 am-6 pm; dining rm, 6-10:30 pm. Bar; entertainment, dancing exc Mon. Cr cds: A, MC, V.

HOLIDAY INN LAKESIDE. 8144 Hwy 808 (33433), just W of FL Tpke exit 28. 305/482-7070. 100 A/C rms, 2 story. Dec-Apr: S, $54-$56; D, $66-$72; each addl, $5; under 18 free; rest of yr: varied lower rates. Color TV. Pool. Cafe, 7 am-2 pm, 5-10 pm. Bar; entertainment, dancing exc Sun. Coin lndry. Golf. Tennis. Cr cds: A, C, D, MC, V.

Restaurants

LA VIEILLE MAISON. 770 E Palmetto Park Rd, 2½ mi E of I-95, Boca Raton exit. 305/391-6701. Hrs: May-Oct, 6:30-10:30; Nov-Apr, 6-10. Closed Memorial Day, July 4, Labor Day. Reservation required. A/C. French, Italian menu. Liquor, wine, beer. Wine list. Dinner, prix fixe, $28, excluding beverage. Specialties: rack of lamb, la crêpe soufflé au citron, Terrine de truite de truffes, crevettes au pernod. Jackets required. Cr cds: A, MC, V.

NEW ORLEANS BAYOU. 501 E Palmetto Park Rd, 5 blks E on 1. 305/395-1682. Hrs: 5:30-11 pm; Reservation required. French menu. Bar. Semi-a la carte. Dinner, $11.95-$18.95. Specialties: shrimp creole, veal, scampi. Entertainment, dancing. Jacket at dinner. Cr cds: A, MC, V.

BONITA SPRINGS

BEACH & TENNIS CLUB. 1070 Hickory Blvd (33923), 2 mi W of 41. 813/992-1121. 150 A/C kit. units,

10 story. Mid-Dec-mid-Apr: S, D, $60; rest of yr: lower rates avail. Color TV. Pool. Cafe, 7 am-3 pm, Bar 5-11:30 pm. Coin lndry. Tennis. Gulf opp. Cr cds: A, C, D, MC, V.

Restaurant

ROOFTOP RESTAURANT. (Box 210.) Casa Bonita Plaza, 4 mi W of 41. 813/992-0033 or 597-4445. Hrs: 11:30 am-2:30 pm; 5-10 pm; Fri, Sat, 5-11 pm; Sun, 10 am-2:30 pm, 5-10 pm. Closed Mon (mid-May-Nov); also Dec 25. A/C. Bar. Dinner, semi-a la carte, $3.25-$13.00. Specialties: seafood, prime rib, Sun brunch. Entertainment exc Sun, Mon. Cr cds: MC, V.

BRADENTON

BEST WESTERN BRADENTON RESORT INN. 2303 1 St (33505), 2 mi SE on 41. 813/747-6465. 237 A/C rms, 2 story. Mid-Dec-late-Apr: S, D, $54-59; each addl, $6; under 12 free; rest of yr: some lower. Color TV. Pool. Cafe, 7 am-11 pm. Bar, 11 am-midnight. Cr cds: A, C, D, MC, V.

CATALINA APTS & BEACH RESORT. (1325 Gulf Dr N, Bradenton Beach 33510), ½ mi N on Anna Maria Island. On SR 789. 813/778-1013. 27 kit units, 2 story. Mid-Dec-early Jan, Feb-Apr: S, D, $55; each addl, $5; 1-bdrm apt $79; 2-bdrm apt $89; 3-bdrm apt $100; under 3 yrs free; family, wkly rates avail; rest of yr: lower rates. Color TV. Pool. Coin lndry. Beach; dock. Cr cds: A, D, MC, V.

SHORELINE. (Box 1344; 33506.) 303 9 St W, 1 blk E of 41 Business. 813/746-1076. 19 rms, 17 A/C. Mid-Dec-mid-Apr: S, D, $34-$38; each addl, $4; rest of yr: varied lower rates. Color TV. Pool. Cr cds: MC, V.

Restaurant

PETE REYNARD'S. (5325 Marina Dr at 54 St, Holmes Beach.) 3 mi N of Bradenton Beach on Anna Maria Island, ¾ mi N of FL 64. 813/778-2233. Hrs: 11:30 am-10 pm; Sun, hols, from noon. A/C. Bars. Semi-a la carte. Lunch, $3.50-$7.00 up; dinner, $6.00-$7.00. Specialties: steak, prime rib, seafood. Salad bar. Entertainment Wed-Sat. Dockage for guests. Cr cds: A, C, D, MC, V.

BROOKSVILLE

HOLIDAY INN. (Box 97; 33512.) At Weeki Wachee Spring, W on 19 at jct FL 50. 904/596-2007. 122 A/C rms, 2 story. Mid-Dec-late Apr: S, $36; D, $42; each addl, $6; family rates avail; rest of yr: varied lower rates. Color TV. Pool; wading pool. Cafe, 7 am-10 pm. Coin lndry. Cr cds: A, D, MC, V.

HOLIDAY INN. (Box 998, Rte 3; 33512.) 12 mi E at jct FL 50, 98, I-75. 904/796-9481. 122 A/C rms, 2 story. Mid-Dec-Apr: S, $34; D, $38; suite avail; family rates avail; rest of yr: lower rates. Color TV. Pool; wading pool. Cafe, 6:30 am-2 pm, 5-10 pm. Bar. Coin lndry. Lighted tennis. Cr cds: A, C, D, MC, V.

BUSHNELL

BEST WESTERN GUEST HOUSE. (33513.) 1 mi W at jct FL 48, I-75. 904/793-5010. 47 A/C rms, 2 story. Mid-Dec-mid-Apr: S, $28-$30; D, $30-$34; each addl, $4; rest of yr: lower rates. Color TV. Pool.

CAPE CORAL

CAPE CORAL COUNTRY CLUB INN. 4003 Palm Tree Blvd (33904), 3 mi W of Cape Coral Bridge. 813/542-3191. 100 A/C rms, 2 story. Mid-Dec-mid-Apr: S, $50-$60; D, $55-$65; each addl, $5; under 17 free; rest of yr: lower rates. Color TV. Pool. Cafe, 7 am-2:30 pm. Dining rm 5-10 pm. Bar; entertainment, dancing exc Mon, Tu. Lighted tennis; pro. Golf; pro. Cr cds: A, C, D, MC, V.

DEL PRADO INN. 1502 Miramar St & Del Prado Blvd (33904), 1 mi W of Cape Coral Bridge. 813/542-3151. 100 A/C rms, 2 story. Mid-Dec-mid-Apr: S, $50-$60; D, $55-$65; each addl, $5; under 12 free; studio rms avail; rest of yr: lower rates. Color TV. Pool. Cafe (see TWISTY'S). Bar; entertainment, dancing exc Sun, Mon. Cr cds: A, MC, V.

MALAGA. 1721 SE 46 Lane (33904), ½ mi N of Cape Coral Bridge. 813/542-3464. 24 A/C kit. units, 2 story. Dec-Apr: 1-2 bdrm $350-$400/wk; kit units $225/wk; rest of yr: lower rates. Color TV. Pool. Coin lndry. Boat docks.

Restaurant

TWISTY'S. (See Del Prado Inn above.) 813/542-3151. Hrs: 7-11 am, 11:30 am-2:30 pm, 5-10 pm; Sun, 7 am-1 pm, 5-8 pm. A/C. Bar. Semi-a la carte. Bkfst, $2.50-$5.25; lunch, $3.25-$5.25; dinner, $4.95-$11.95. Child's plates $1 less. Specialties: steak, shrimp. Entertainment, dancing exc Sun, Mon. Cr cds: A, MC, V.

CEDAR KEY

BEACH FRONT. (Box 400; 32625.) 3 blks W on 1 St. 904/543-5113. 24 A/C rms, 2 story, 7 kits. S, D, $30-$34; each addl, $4; kit. units, $42-$44; under 4 yrs free; family rates avail. Color TV. Pool. Cafe adj, 6:30 am-10 pm. On Gulf. Cr cds: MC, V.

Restaurant

THE CAPTAIN'S TABLE. (Box 279.) On the West Pier. 904/543-5441. Hrs: 4-10:30 pm; Sat, Sun, 11:30 am-10:30 pm. Closed lunch Mon-Fri. Bar. Semi-a la carte. Lunch, $2.50-$6; dinner, $6.50-$16.00. Specialties: seafood, island lime pie, pineapple pie.

CLEARWATER

BAY QUEEN. 1925 Edgewater Dr (33515), 2 mi N on 19A. 813/441-3295. 18 A/C units, 1-2 story, 16 kits. Mid-Dec-mid-Apr: S, D, $40-$46; each addl, $3; wkly rates avail; rest of yr: lower rates. Color TV. Pool. Bkfst adj, 7-11 am. Bay opp. Cr cds: A, MC, V.

BELLEVIEW BILTMORE. Belleview Blvd (33517), ¼ mi W of 19A in Belleair. 813/442-6171. 320 A/C rms. Jan-Apr: S, $56-$81; D, $86-$126; each addl, $24; suites, $136-$182; under 5, $13; serv charge $3/day. Closed rest of yr. Color TV. Olympic-size pool. Cafe, 7:30 am-9:30 am, noon-1:30 pm, 7-8:30 pm (public by reservation, dress requirements). Bars, 11-1 am; Sun, 1 pm-midnight; entertainment, dancing exc Sun. Tennis; pro. Golf; pro. Entertainment, dancing. 1,500-ft beach. On Intracoastal Waterway. Cr cds: A, C, D, MC, V.

BEST WESTERN CLEARWATER CENTRAL. 100 Hwy 19N (33515), 1 blk N of FL 60. 813/799-1565. 117 A/C rms, 2 story. Feb-late Apr: S, D, $28-$42; each addl, $5; under 12 free; family rates avail; rest of yr: lower rates. Color TV. Cafe adj, 7 am-10 pm. Bar, 4 pm-midnight; closed Sat, Sun. Coin lndry. Tennis. Cr cds: A, C, D, MC, V.

CLEARWATER DOWNTOWN TRAVELODGE. 711 Cleveland St (33515), 7 blks E on FL 60, 2 blks E of 19A. 813/446-9183. 48 A/C rms, 3 story. Feb-Apr: S, $44-$50; D, $61-$67; each addl, $10; rest of yr: lower rates. Color TV. Pool. Cafe adj, 5 am-9 pm. Cr cds: A, C, D, MC, V.

CLEARWATER PALMS. 1735 Gulf-to-Bay Blvd (33515), 2 mi E on FL 60. 813/461-0669. 24 A/C rms, 1-2 story, 12 kits. Mid-Dec-Apr: S, $34; D, $38; each addl, $3; kit. units, $2 addl; rest of yr: lower rates. Color TV. Cafe opp, open 24 hrs. Cr cds: MC, V.

HOLIDAY INN. 400 Hwy 19S (33515), at jct FL 60. 813/797-8173. 196 A/C rms, 2 story, 7 kits. Jan-Apr: S, D, $55; each addl, $4; family rates avail; rest of yr: lower rates. Color TV. Pool. Cafe, 6 am-2 pm, 5-10 pm. Bar, 11-2 am; entertainment, dancing exc Sun. Coin lndry. Cr cds: A, C, D, MC, V.

HOWARD JOHNSON'S. 410 Hwy 19S (33515), at jct FL 60. 813/797-5021. 88 A/C rms, 2 story. Mid-Dec-Apr: S, $30-$50; D, $40-$70; each addl, $6; under 18 free; family rates avail; rest of yr: lower rates. Color TV. Pool; wading pool. Cafe open 6:30 am-11 pm. Coin lndry. Cr cds: A, C, D, MC, V.

QUALITY INN ROYAL. 120 Hwy 19N (33515), 1 blk N of FL 60. 813/796-1116. 145 A/C rms, 2 story. Feb-Apr: S, D, $44-$50; each addl, $4.50; under 16 free; family, wkend rates avail; rest of yr: lower rates. Color TV. Pool. Cafe, 6 am-midnight. Bar, noon-2 am; entertainment, dancing. Coin lndry opp. Cr cds: A, C, D, MC, V.

RAMADA INN-COUNTRYSIDE. 2560 Hwy 19N (33515), opp Countryside Mall, 1 blk S of FL 580. 813/796-1234. 130 A/C rms, 5 story, 9 kits. Mid-Dec-late Apr: S, $51-$58; D, $61-$68; each addl, $6; under 18 free; kit. units, $72-$82; family rates avail; rest of yr: lower rates. Color TV. Pool. Cafe. Bar. Coin lndry. Lighted tennis. Cr cds: A, C, D, MC, V.

Restaurants

KAPOK TREE INN. 923 McMullen Booth Rd, 1 mi N of FL 60. 813/726-4734. Hrs: noon-9:00 pm; Sun to 9 pm. A/C. Bar. Semi-a la carte. Lunch, $4.95-$6.25; dinner, $6.75-$11.75, min, $1.50. Specialties: chicken, fried shrimp. Cr cds: A, C, D, MC, V.

SAVOY. 924 McMullen Booth Rd, 1 mi N of FL 60 on FL 593. 813/726-3312. Hrs: 11:30 am-2 pm, 5-10 pm; Sun 11:30 am-2:30 pm, 5-9 pm. A/C. Continental menu. Bar. Table d'hôte: brunch, $6.95-$9.99; lunch, $4.95-$10.95; dinner, $11.95-$19.95. Specialties: prime rib, snapper. Background music. Cr cds: A, C, D, MC, V.

SIPLE'S GARDEN SEAT. 1234 Druid Rd S, 3 blks W of 19A, 1 mi S of FL 60. 813/442-9681. Hrs: 11:30 am-3 pm, 5:30-9:30 pm; Sun, hols, 11:30 am-8:30 pm. A/C. Bar. Semi-a la carte. Lunch, $4.75-$10.50; dinner, $9.25-$15.00 up. Child's plates, $3.50-$6. Specialties: prime rib, veal, seafood, roast duckling. Overlooks bay. Jackets. Cr cds: A, C, D, MC, V.

MORRISON'S. (Cafeteria). 1315 E Cleveland St. On FL 60, 1 blk E of US 19A. 813/446-2673. Hrs: 11 am-2 pm; 4 pm-8 pm; Sun, 11 am-7:30 pm. Avg ck: lunch, $3.10; dinner $4. Specializes in

CLEARWATER BEACH

ADAM'S MARK/CARIBBEAN GULF HOTEL. 430 S Gulf View Blvd (33515), ¼ mi S of FL 60. 813/443-5714. 206 A/C units, 14 story. Jan-Apr: S, D, $55-$110; each addl, $8; studio rms, $125; suites, $125-$325; under 18 free; rest of yr: varied lower rates. Color TV. Pool. Cafe, 7 am-2 pm,

128 ACCOMMODATIONS & RESTAURANTS

5-10 pm. Bar noon-2 am; entertainment, dancing exc Mon. Coin lndry. On Gulf. Cr cds: A, C, D, MC, V.

BEST WESTERN SEA WAKE INN. 691 S Gulf View Blvd (33515), ½ mi S of FL 60. 813/443-7652. 110 A/C units, 6 story, 50 kits. Mid-Dec-Apr: S, D, $62-$80; each addl, $6; kit $68-$86; 2 under 12 free; family rates avail; rest of yr: varied lower rates. Color TV. Pool. Cafe, 7 am-9 pm. Bar, 11:30 am-1:30 pm; entertainment exc Sun. Coin lndry opp. On Gulf. Cr cds: A, C, D, MC, V.

CLEARWATER BEACH HILTON. 715 S Gulf View Blvd (33515). 813/447-9566. 210 A/C rms, 2-10 story. Mid-Dec-mid-May: S, D, $79-$104; each addl, $12; suites, $195-$295; Amer plan avail; family rates avail; golf, tennis package plans avail; rest of yr: varied lower rates. Color TV; free in-rm movies. Pool; wading pool. Cafe, 7 am-10 pm. Sat to 11 pm. Bars; entertainment exc Sun. Coin lndry. 1,000-ft beach; sailboats, boats, motors avail. Cr cds: A, C, D, MC, V.

GULF SANDS BEACH RESORT. 655 S Gulf View Blvd (33515). 813/442-7171. 154 A/C units, 5 story, 113 kits. Mid-Jan-Apr: S, D, $40-$72; each addl, $6; suites, $67-$92; kit. units, $6 more; under 13 free; rest of yr: varied lower rates. Color TV. Pool. Cafe, 7 am-2 pm, 4-9:30 pm. Bar. Coin lndry opp. On beach. Cr cds: A, C, D, MC, V.

ISLANDER. 692 Bayway Blvd (33515), ½ mi S of 60. 813/442-4005. 24 A/C units, 2 story, 21 kits. Mid-Dec-Apr: S, D, $28-$58; each addl, $4; kit. units, $44; wkly rates avail; under 12 free; rest of yr: varied lower rates. Color TV. Pool. Cafe opp, 24 hours, Dec-June; 6 am-2 am rest of year. Coin lndry. Boat dock; pier. Cr cds: MC, V.

ISLAND QUEEN. 158 Brightwater Dr (33515), ½ mi S of 60. 813/442-8068. 14 A/C kit. units, 2 story. Mid-Dec-mid-Apr: D, $58-$68; each addl, $6-$10; rest of yr: varied lower rates. Color TV. Pool. Dock. Cr cds: MC, V.

NEW YORKER. 332 Hamden Dr (33515), 1 mi N on Brightwater Dr. 813/446-2437. 16 A/C units, 2 story, 14 kits. Mid-Dec-Apr: S, $38; D, $40-$45; each addl, $8; kit. units, $45-$48; rest of yr: varied lower rates. Color TV. Pool. Cr cds: MC, V.

RED CARPET RESORT. 530 S Gulf View Blvd (33515), ½ mi S of FL 60. 813/447-6407. 26 A/C units, 2 story, 20 kits. Feb-Apr: S, D, $50-$53; each addl, $4; kit. units, $55-$60; under 5 yrs free; wkly rates avail off-season; rest of yr: varied lower rates. Color TV. Pool. Cafe opp, open 24 hrs. Boat dock, pier. On bay. Cr cds: A, MC, V.

RITZ. 355 S Gulf View Blvd (33515). ¼ mi S of FL 60. 813/441-9905. 34 A/C units, 3-5 story, 31 kits. Mid-Feb-Apr: S, D, $53; each addl, $5; kit units, $52-$55; rest of yr, varied lower rates. Pool. Cafe ½ blk, 6 am-11 pm. Cr cds: A, C, D, MC, V.

SEA CAPTAIN. 40 Devon Dr (33515). 1 blk S of FL 60. 813/446-7550. 21 A/C rms, 2-story, 23 kits. Jan-May: S, $35; D, $35-$40; each addl, $5; kit units, $40-$45; wkly rates, rest of yr: varied lower rates. Pool.

SEA STAR. 326 Hamden Dr (33515). ¼ mi S of FL 60. 813/445-6174. 19 A/C rms, 2-story, 16 kits. Feb-Mar: S, D, $46; each addl, $4; kit units, $45-$52; wkly rates, rest of yr: varied lower rates. Pool. Cr cds: MC, V.

SPY-GLASS. 215 S Gulf View Blvd (33515). ¼ mi S of FL 60. 813/446-8317. 64 A/C units, 9 story, 56 kits. Mid-Dec-late Apr: S, $35; D, $45-$60; kit. units, $45; each addl, $5; rest of yr: varied lower rates. Color TV. Pool. Cafe opp, 7 am-3 pm. Gulf opp. Cr cds: A, MC, V.

WELLS MANOR. 333 Hamden Dr at Brightwater (33515), ¼ mi S of 60. 813/442-6865. 20 A/C units, 2 story, 16 kits. Mid-Jan-Apr: S, D, $28-$55; each addl, $4; kit. units, $47-$48; family rates avail; under 5 yrs free; rest of yr: varied lower rates. Color TV. Pool. Dock. Some rms face bay. Cr cds: MC, V.

Restaurants

THE BANK 1890'S RESTAURANT. 601 S Gulfview Blvd, ½ mi S of FL 60, 5 blks S of Causeway. 813/446-4787. Hrs: 8-11 am, 11:30 am-3:30 pm, 4:30-10 pm; Sun, noon-9 pm. A/C. Bar, 8 am-11 pm. Buffet. Bkfst, $3.25; lunch, $3.50; dinner, $5.50; Sun, $4.75. Child's plates. Specialties: roast beef, seafood, roast chicken. Salad buffet. Entertainment exc Mon.

CURRENTS. 521 S Gulfview Blvd. 813/447-6461. Hrs: 6 am-2 pm, 5:30-10 pm. Bkfst, $3.50; lunch, $5-$6; dinner, $7.50-$12; serv plate $1.50; child's plates half price. Bar. Entertainment. Cr cds: A, MC, V.

HEILMAN'S BEACHCOMBER. 447 Mandalay Ave, 1 blk N of FL 60. 813/442-4144. Hrs: 11:30 am-midnight; Sun, noon-10:30 pm. A/C. Bar. Semi-a la carte. Lunch, $1.95-$9.50 up; dinner, $6.95-$17.95. Child's plates. Specialties: charcoal-broiled steak, skillet-fried chicken, prime rib, fresh seafood. Organist exc Sun. Cr cds: A, D, MC, V.

PELICAN. 470 Mandalay Ave, 4 blks N of FL 60. 813/442-3151. Hrs: 11:30 am-10:30 pm; Sun, noon-10 pm. A/C. Bar. Semi-a la carte. Lunch, $3.95-$7.95; dinner, $7.95-$11.95; serv plate $1.50. Child's plates, $2.95-$3.95. Specialties: stuffed-fried shrimp, sweetbreads, steak. Cr cds: A, D, MC, V.

CLERMONT

DAYS INN. (Box 105K, Rte 2; 32711.) 8 mi N at jct 27, FL 19, Florida Tpke. exit 85. 904/429-2151. 183 A/C rms, 2 story. S, $26.88-$30.88; D, $30.88-$40.88; each addl, $4; under 18, $1; under 5 free. Color TV. Pool. Cafe 6:30 am-10 pm. Coin lndry. Cr cds: A, MC, V.

ORLANDO VACATION RESORT. (Box 25-E3, Rte 1; 32711.) On US 27, 1 mi N of 192. 904/394-6171. 230 A/C rms, 2 story. S, $38-$44; D, $42-$48; each addl, $8; under 18 free. Mod Amer plan avail; rest of yr: lower rates. Color TV. Pool. Cafe, 7:30 am-10 pm. Bar, noon-1 am; entertainment, dancing exc Sun. Coin lndry. Tennis; pro. Cr cds: A, C, D, MC, V.

RODWAY INN WESTGATE. (32711.) On 192 just E of jct 27. 904/424-2621. 195 A/C rms, 2 story. Mid-Dec-early Jan, mid-Feb-Apr, June-early Sep: S, D, $52-$57; under 18 free; rest of yr: lower rates. Color TV. Pool. Cafe, 6:30 am-10 pm. Bar. Coin lndry. Cr cds: A, C, D, MC, V.

CLEWISTON

CLEWISTON INN. (PO Drawer 1297; 33440.) 108 Royal Palm Ave, at 27. 813/983-8151. 56 A/C rms, 2 story. Jan-Mar: S, $35; D, $42-$50; each addl, $4; family rates avail; rest of yr: lower rates. Color TV. Cafe, 6:30 am-9:30 pm. Bar. Lighted tennis adj. On river. Cr cds: A, C, D, MC, V.

Restaurant

GLADES. 316 Sugarland Hwy, on FL 27. 813/983-7118. Hrs: 6 am-9 pm; Fri, Sat, to 10 pm. Closed Dec 25. A/C. Bar. Semi-a la carte: bkfst, $2.95-$5.95; lunch, $3.25-$13.95; dinner, $5.95-$13.95. Specializes in alligator steak. Cr cds: C, D, MC, V.

COCOA

BEST WESTERN-COCOA INN. 4225 W King St (32922), at jct I-95, SR 520. 305/632-1065. 120 A/C rms, 2 story. Sep-Mar: S, D, $26-$45; each addl, $4; under 12 free; special events higher; rest of yr: lower rates. Color TV. Pool. Cafe, 7 am-2 pm, 5:30-9:30 pm. Bar, 4 pm-2 am. Cr cds: A, C, D, MC, V.

HOLIDAY INN I-95. (Box 3884; 32922.) 900 Friday Rd, at jct FL 524, I-95. 305/631-1210. 142 A/C rms, 2 story. Mid-Dec-mid-Apr: S, D, $32-$40; each addl, $5; under 18 free; family rates avail; rest of yr: lower rates. Color TV. Pool. Cafe, 7 am-2 pm, 5-10 pm. Bar, 4:30-11 pm. Coin lndry. Cr cds: A, C, D, MC, V.

HOWARD JOHNSON'S. 860 N Cocoa Blvd (32922), 1 mi N on 1. 305/632-4210. 53 A/C rms, 2 story. Dec-Apr: S, $32-$43; D, $38-$48; each addl, $8; under 18 free; rest of yr: lower rates. Color TV. Pool. Cafe, 6:30-1 am; Coin lndry. Cr cds: A, C, D, MC, V.

Restaurant

NEPTUNE. (1022 Old Dixie Hwy, Rockledge.) 1 blk E of US 1. 305/636-0655. Hrs: 7 am-11 pm. Closed Sun, hols. A/C. Bar. Semi-a la carte. Lunch, $2.75-$4.25; dinner, $4.95-$11.95. Child's plates to $3.75. Specialties: seafood, baked stuffed shrimp, steak Neptune. Cr cds: A, MC, V.

COCOA BEACH

CROSSWAY INN. 3901 N Atlantic Ave (32931), 2 blks S of jct A1A & Fl 520. 305/783-2221. 94 A/C rms, 40 kits. Apr-Dec: S, D, $40-46; kit units, $6 addl; each addl, $5; family, wkly, group rates avail; under 12 free; special events (3-5-day min) higher; rest of yr: lower rates. Color TV. Pool. Cafe, 11 am-2 pm, 5-11 pm. Bar. Coin lndry. Lighted tennis; pro. Cr cds: A, C, D, MC, V.

HOLIDAY INN. 1300 N Atlantic Ave (32931), on FL A1A, 1½ mi S of FL 520. 305/783-2271. 313 A/C rms, 2 story. S, $40-$55; D, $47-$62; each addl, $7; under 18 free; Amer plan, family, group rates avail; oceanside suites, $110. Color TV. Olympic-size pool. Cafe, 6:30 am-10 pm. Bar; entertainment, dancing. Coin lndry. Tennis. Cr cds: A, C, D, MC, V.

SURF STUDIO. 1801 S Atlantic Ave (32931), on FL A1A, 1½ mi N of Patrick AFB. 305/783-7100. 11 A/C kit. units. S, D, $30-$80; each addl, $8; family, wkly rates avail. Color TV. Cafe adj, 7 am-9 pm. Coin lndry. Tennis. On beach. Cr cds: A, MC, V.

Restaurants

BERNARD'S SURF. 2 S Atlantic Ave, 3 mi S on FL A1A, S of Causeway. 305/783-2401. Hrs: 11 am-11 pm; Sun, 5-10:45 pm. Closed Dec 24-25. Reservation required. A/C. Bar. Semi-a la carte. Lunch, $1.95-$6.95; dinner, $5.95-$25.95; serv plate, $3. Specialties: avocado stuffed with shrimp salad, Maine lobster, steak. Cr cds: A, D, MC, V.

MOUSETRAP. 5600 N Atlantic Blvd, on FL A1A, 1½ mi N of FL 520. 305/784-0050. Hrs: 11-2 am; Sat, Sun from 5 pm. A/C. Continental menu. Bar. Semi-a la carte. Lunch, $2.25-$5.00; dinner, $4.00-$13.00. Specialties: steak, seafood, veal. Salad bar. Entertainment, dancing. Cr cds: A, MC, V.

RAMON'S. (Box 1368.) 204 Cocoa Beach Causeway, on FL 520 at FL A1A. 305/783-7444. Hrs: 11 am-midnight; Sun, 4-11 pm. Closed Dec 25. A/C. Bars. Semi-a la carte. Lunch, $2.95-$7.95; dinner,

$4.95-$24.95; serv plate, $4.00. Child's plates, $4.75. Specialties: prime rib, seafood. Cr cds: A, C, D, MC, V.

CORAL GABLES

CHATEAUBLEAU INN. 1111 Ponce de Leon Blvd (33134). ½ mi N, 4 blks S of 8th, 41. 305/448-2634. 117 A/C rms, 3-4 story, 3 kits. Dec-Mar: S, $50; D, $60; each addl, $10; under 12 free; rest of yr, varied lower rates. Pool. Cafe, 6 am-midnight. Cr cds: A, C, D, MC, V.

DAVID WILLIAM. 700 Biltmore Way (33134), ¼ mi W. 305/445-7821. 200 A/C units (85 transient), 63 with kit. Mid-Nov-Apr: S, D, $75-$85; each addl, $5; kit. units, $85-$90; under 12 free; suites, $85-$225; rest of yr: lower rates. Color TV. Rooftop pool; poolside serv. Cafes (see CHEZ VENDOME, 700 CLUB). Bar; entertainment exc Sun. Coin lndry. Health club; sauna. Some balconies. Cr cds: A, C, MC, V.

HOLIDAY INN DOWNTOWN. 2051 Le Jeune Rd (33134) 7 blks S of US 41. 305/443-2301. 168 A/C rms, 6 story. Dec-mid-Apr: S, $59-$63; D, $67-$73; each addl, $5; family rates avail; rest of yr: lower rates. Color TV. Pool; wading pool. Cafe, 6:30 am-11 pm. Bar; entertainment exc Sun. Cr cds: A, D, MC, V.

HOLIDAY INN-SOUTH. 1350 S Dixie Hwy (33146), 3 mi S on 1. 305/667-5611. 155 A/C rms, 3 story, 12 kits. Mid-Dec-Apr: S, $52-$57; D, $59-$64; each addl, $5; kit. units, $63-$70; family rates avail; rest of yr: lower rates. Color TV. Pool. Cafe, 6:30 am-2:30 pm. Bar, 11-1 am; entertainment, dancing. Coin lndry. Cr cds: A, C, D, MC, V.

RIVIERA COURT. 5100 Riviera Dr (33146), 2½ mi S on 1. 305/665-3528. 30 A/C rms, 2 story, 14 kits. Mid-Dec-mid-Apr: S, D, $50-$55; each addl, $4; kit. units, $60-$65/ rest of yr: lower rates. Color TV. Pool. On waterway, dock. Cr cds: A, C, D, MC, V.

Restaurants

CHEZ VENDOME. (See David William Hotel above.) 305/445-7821. Hrs: 11:30 am-3 pm, 5:30-11:30 pm; Sun from 5:30 pm. A/C. French, Amer menu. Bar. Small wine list. Semi-a la carte. Lunch, $4.95-$6.25; dinner, $9.95-$16.00. Specialties: steak au poivre Vendôme, frogs' legs, strawberries Vendôme. Strolling guitarists exc Sun. Jacket required after 7 pm. Cr cds: A, C, D, MC, V.

700 CLUB. (See David William Hotel above.) 305/445-7821. Hrs: 7:15-11 am, 11:30 am-2:30 pm, 7-11 pm; Sun, noon-3 pm. Closed Sat lunch; some hols. A/C. French, Amer menu. Bar. Semi-a la carte. Bkfst, $4.50-$7.50; lunch, $4.95-$5.25; dinner, $10.25-$14.25. Specialties: steak, prime rib, veal. Pianist. Jacket required. Cr cds: A, C, D, MC, V.

CROSS CITY

CARRIAGE INN. (Box 5C; 32628.) 3 blks S on 19, 27A, 98. 904/498-3910. 25 A/C rms, 2 story. S, $22; D, $27; each addl, $3; Pool. Cafe, 6 am-10 pm. Cr cds: A, D, MC, V.

CRYSTAL RIVER

CRYSTAL LODGE. (Box 456; 32629.) ½ mi N on 19, 98. 904/795-3171. 50 A/C rms, 1-2 story, 5 kits. S, $22-$39; D, $24-$40; each addl, $3.50; under 12 free; wkly rates avail. Color TV. Pool. Cafe, 6 am-2 pm, 5-9:30 pm. Bar. Dock; launching ramp; boats, guides avail. On Crystal River. Cr cds: A, D, MC, V.

PLANTATION INN & GOLF RESORT. (Box 1116; 32629.) Kings Bay Rd, 12 mi S on FL 44W, then take Plantation Rd. 904/795-4211. 124 A/C rms, 1-2 story, 12 golf villas. Jan-Apr: S, D, $58-$68; each addl, $6; golf villas, $125; under 12, free; wkly rates in villas; Amer, Mod Amer plans; golf, tennis packages; rest of yr, lower rates. Cafe, 7 am-9 pm. Bar; entertainment, dancing. Coin lndry. Cr cds: A, C, D, MC, V.

DADE CITY

RIDGE MANOR. 7555 US 301-N Ridge Manor (33525). 8 mi N on US 301. 904/583-2109. 13 A/C rms. Dec-Apr: S, $21-$33; D, $24-$33; each addl, $2; under 12 free. Cr cds: A, MC, V.

Restaurant

PEEKS. 406 S 7th St, 4 blks S on Business US 301. 904/567-2484. Hrs: 7 am-8 pm; in summer, Sat to 11:30 pm, Sun to 2 pm. Bar, 3 pm-11:30 pm. Semi-a la carte, bkfst, $2.35-$3.25; lunch, $3.25-$6.25; dinner, $3.25-$6.25. Child's plates. Specializes in fried chicken and steak. Entertainment. Cr cds: A, MC, V.

DAYTONA BEACH

ACAPULCO INN. 2505 S Atlantic Ave (32018), 3 mi S on FL A1A. 904/761-2210. 133 A/C units, 8 story, 84 kits. Late May-early Sep: S, D, $42-$48; each addl, $6-$8; kit. units, $48-$52; under 12 free; Easter, race wks, special events higher (5-day min); rest of yr: lower rates. Color TV. Pool; wading pool. Cafe, 7 am-9:30 pm. Bar, 11-2 am; entertainment, dancing exc Sun. Ck-out, 11 am. Coin lndry. On ocean. Cr cds: A, C, D, MC, V.

ALADDIN INN. 2323 S Atlantic Ave (32018), 3 mi S on FL A1A in Daytona Beach Shores. 904/255-0476. 120 A/C rms, 6 story, 46 kits. Sept-Dec: S, D, $33-$47; each addl, $6-$7; kit. units, $48-$53; under 17 free; higher rates during Easter, race wks (5-day min); Amer, Mod Amer plans avail; wkly rates avail; rest of yr: lower rates. Color TV. Pool. Bar, 9 pm-1:30 am. Coin lndry. On beach. Cr cds: A, C, D, MC, V.

BEACHCOMER INN. 2000 N. Atlantic Ave (32018), 2½ mi N on FL A1A. 904/252-8513. 174 A/C units, 7 story, 98 kits. Late Feb-Labor Day: S, D, $48-$58; each addl, $6; kit. units, $50-$58; wkly rates avail; spring break, Easter, July 4, Thanksgiving, Christmas, race wks higher (5-day min); rest of yr: varied lower rates. Color TV. Pool; wading pool. Cafe, 7 am-1 pm, 5 pm-10 pm. Bar; entertainment exc Sun. Ck-out, 11 am. Coin lndry. Tennis. On ocean. Cr cds: A, D, MC, V.

BEST WESTERN AMERICANO BEACH LODGE. 1260 N Atlantic Ave (32018), 12 blks N on FL A1A. 904/255-7431. 199 A/C units, 9 story, 86 kits. June-Labor Day: S, D, $36-$65; each addl, $7; kit. units, $38-$65; kit. apt, $65-$120; under 12 free; hols, race wks (5-day min), special events, higher; rest of yr: varied lower rates. Color TV. Olympic-size pool; wading pool. Cafe, 7 am-2 pm. (also see KING'S CELLAR). Bars, entertainment, dancing. Coin lndry. Ocean front. Cr cds: A, C, D, MC, V.

BEST WESTERN LA PLAYA MOTOR INN. 2500 N Atlantic Ave (32018), on FL A1A. 904/672-0990. 239 A/C units, 9 story, 102 kits. Mid-Dec-mid-Aug: S, D, $42-$54; each addl, $6; kit. units, $65-$85; under 12 free; Amer plan, family, group, wkly rates avail; hols, race wks, special events higher (5-day min); rest of yr: varied lower rates. Color TV. Pool; wading pool. Cafe, 7 am-2 pm. Bar; entertainment, dancing exc Sun. Coin lndry. Lighted tennis. Cr cds: A, C, D, MC, V.

CARRIAGE HOUSE. 800 N Atlantic Ave (32018), on FL A1A. 904/252-6491. 117 A/C rms, 6-7 story, 55 kits. June-Sep: S, D, $36-$42; kit. units, $43-$48; under 12 free; family, group, wkly rates avail; special events, race wks (5-day min), hols higher; rest of yr: varied lower rates. Color TV. Pool; wading pool. Cafe, 7 am-2 pm. On beach. Cr cds: A, C, D, MC, V.

DAYS INN-BEACHSIDE. 1909 S Atlantic Ave (32018). 2½ mi S on FL A1A. 904/255-4492. 196 A/C units, 9 story, 49 kits. Feb-late Apr: S, $45-$47; D, $51.53; each addl, $4; kit units, $52-$55; under 18, $1; under 2, free; special events higher rates; family rates; rest of yr, lower rates. Pool, wading pool. Cafe, 7 am-1 pm, 5-9 pm. Coin lndry. Cr cds: A, MC, V.

DAYTONA BEACH TRAVELODGE. (749 Ridgewood Ave, Holly Hill 32017.) 8 blks N on 1. 904/255-6511. 38 A/C rms, 2 story. Jan-Labor Day: S, $30-$40; D, $38-$45; each addl, $5; family rates avail; Easter, July 4, race wks higher; rest of yr: lower rates. Color TV. Pool. Cafe adj, noon-9 pm. Coin lndry opp. Cr cds: A, C, D, MC, V.

DAYTONA BEACH TRAVELODGE OCEANFRONT. 3135 S Atlantic Ave (32018), 5 mi S on FL A1A. 904/767-8533. 115 A/C units, 8 story, 71 kits. S, D, $32-$65; each addl, $5-8; kit. units, $53-$55; under 17 free; July 4, race wks, special events higher (5-day min); Amer, Mod Amer plans avail; family rates avail; rest of yr: varied lower rates. Color TV. Pool; wading pool. Cafe, 7 am-2 pm. Coin lndry. Cr cds: A, C, D, MC, V.

DAYTONA HILTON. 2637 S Atlantic Ave (32018), 3¼ mi S on FL A1A. 904/767-7350. 220 A/C rms, 11 story, 5 kits. Mar-Apr, mid-June-Aug: S, $48-$104; D, $72-$130; each addl, $24; kit. units, $106; suites, $140-$400; studio rms, $93; Easter, July 4, race wks higher. Amer, Mod Amer plans avail; family, wkly rates avail; rest of yr: varied lower rates. Color TV; free in-rm movies. Pool; wading pool. Cafe, 7 am-3 pm; dining rm, 5-11 pm. Bars, 7-1:30 am; entertainment, dancing wkends. Coin lndry. Lighted tennis. Dock. On ocean. Cr cds: A, C, D, MC, V.

DAYTONA INN-BROADWAY. 219 S Atlantic Ave (32018). 2 mi S at jct 92, A1A. 904/252-3626. 150 A/C rms, 4 story, 62 suites, 66 kits. Mid-Feb-late Apr; late June-mid-Aug: S, D, $44-$52; each addl, $6; suites, $50-$60; under 16, free; hols, special events, higher rates; family, wkly rates; sr cit rates; rest of yr, varied lower rates. Pool, wading pool. Cafe, 7 am-2 pm, 5-10 pm. Bar, 4 pm-2 am; entertainment. Coin lndry. Cr cds: A, C, D, MC, V.

HAWAIIAN INN. 2301 S Atlantic Ave (32018), 3 mi S on FL A1A. 904/255-5411. 211 A/C units, 5 story, 110 kits. Feb-Labor Day: S, D, $52-$68; each addl, $6; kit. units, $58-$68; under 12 free; family, wkly rates avail; higher rates during race wks (5-day min), hols, special events; rest of yr: varied lower rates. Color TV. 3 pools, 1 indoor; wading pool. Cafe, 7:30 am-2:30 pm; dining rm, 6 pm-2 am. Bar, 5:30 pm-2 am. Polynesian entertainment, dancing exc Mon. Coin lndry. On beach. Cr cds: A, C, D, MC, V.

HOLIDAY INN-OCEANSIDE. 905 S Atlantic Ave (32018). 9 blks S on FL A1A. 904/255-5432. 108 A/C rms, 5 story, 24 kits. Mar-late Apr: S, D, $55-$80; each addl, $6; kit units, $63-$80; under 18 free; sr cit rates; Easter, July 4, race wks higher (3-day min); family rates; varied lower rates rest of yr. Pool. Bar, 4 pm-2 am; dancing. Coin lndry. Cr cds: A, C, D, MC, V.

HOWARD JOHNSON'S-AIRPORT. (Box 25, Rte 1, 32014.) At jct 92, I-4, I-95. 904/255-7412. 144 A/C rms, 2 story. S, $36-$42; D, $43-$50; each addl, $8; under 18 free; Amer, family, group, golf,

130 ACCOMMODATIONS & RESTAURANTS

plans avail; race wks, Easter higher. Color TV. Large pool; wading pool. Cafe open 24 hrs. Bar. Coin lndry. Cr cds: A, C, D, MC, V.

HOWARD JOHNSON'S-AIRPORT. (Box 25, Rte 8, 32014.) At jct 92, I-4, I-95. 904/255-7412. 144 A/C rms, 2 story. S, $35-$42; D, $43-$50; each addl, $8; under 18 free; sr cit rates; race wks, Easter higher. Pool, wading pool. Cafe open 24 hrs. Bar, 4 pm-2 am. Cr cds: A, C, D, MC, V.

HOWARD JOHNSON'S OCEANSIDE. 2560 N Atlantic Ave (32018), 3 mi N on FL A1A. 904/672-1440. 140 A/C rms, 4-8 story, 26 kits. Early June-Labor Day: S, D, $45-$55; each addl, $5; kit. (3-day min), $54; under 18 free; hols, special events, race wks (5-day min) higher; Amer plan, family, wkly, group rates avail; rest of yr: varied lower rates. Color TV. Pool; wading pool. Cafe open 24 hrs. Coin lndry adj. Tennis. On beach. Cr cds: A, C, D, MC, V.

INN ON THE BEACH. 1615 S Atlantic Ave (32018), 2 mi S on FL A1A. 904/255-0921. 196 A/C units, 7 story, 8 kits. Mid-Apr-late June, early July-early Sep: S, D, $55-$64; each addl, $5; kit. units, $70; suites, $68 up; under 14 free; hols, special events higher (4-day min); Mod Amer plan avail; wkly rates avail; rest of yr: varied lower rates. Color TV. Pool; wading pool. Cafe, 7 am-2 pm. Bar, 11-2 am; entertainment Tu-Sat. Coin lndry. On ocean. Cr cds: A, C, D, MC, V.

INTERNATIONAL INN. 313 S Atlantic Ave (32018), 3 blks S on FL A1A. 904/255-7491. 153 A/C units, 6 story, 70 kits. Feb-late May, late May-Labor Day: S, D, $25-$70; each addl, $8-$10; under 17 free; hols, race wks, special events higher (5-day min); family, wkly rates avail; rest of yr: lower rates. Color TV. Pool; wading pool. Cafe, 7:30 am-3 pm; Bar, 7:30 pm-2 am; entertainment, dancing in season. Coin lndry. On ocean. Cr cds: A, C, D, MC, V.

QUALITY INN PERRY'S OCEAN-EDGE. 2209 S Atlantic Ave (32018), 2¾ mi S on FL A1A. 904/255-0581. 145 A/C units, 2-6 story, 80 kits. Feb-Apr, mid-June-Aug: D, $46-$63; each addl, $6-$8; kit. units, $54-$71; Easter, race wks higher (6-day min); rest of yr: varied lower rates. Color TV. 2 pools, 1 indoor; wading pool. Cafe, 7 am-2 pm. Coin lndry. Oceanfront. Cr cds: A, C, D, MC, V.

QUALITY INN REEF. 935 S Atlantic Ave (32018), 9 blks S on FL A1A. 904/252-2581. 241 A/C units, 2-6 story, 125 kits. Early Feb-mid-Apr, early June-early Sep: S, D, $38-$60; kit units, $60; each addl, $6; Easter, race wks, special events higher (5-day min); family plans avail; rest of yr: varied lower rates. Color TV. 2 pools; wading pool. Cafe, 7 am-2 pm. Bars, 6 pm-3 am, entertainment, dancing Fri-Sat. Coin lndry. Cr cds: A, C, D, MC, V.

SURFSIDE INN. 3125 S Atlantic Ave (32018), 5 mi S on FL A1A. 904/788-1000. 115 A/C rms, 7 story, 80 kits. Late May-late June, early July-late Aug: S, D, $57-$99; each addl, $5-$8; studio rms, $46-$54; kit. units, $62-$64; under 17 free; Amer, Mod Amer plans avail; wkly rates avail; rest of yr: lower rates. Color TV. Pool; wading pool. Cafe, 7 am-8 pm. Bar, 11-2 am; entertainment, dancing. Coin lndry. On beach. Cr cds: A, C, D, MC, V.

TRAVELODGE DAYTONA BEACH. (749 Ridgewood Ave, Holly Hill 32017.) 2 mi N on US 1. 904/255-6511. 38 A/C rms, 2 story. Jan-Labor Day: S, $30-$40; D, $38-$45; each addl, $5; under 17 free; sr cit rates; race wks higher; rest of yr, lower rates. Pool. Cafe, noon-9 pm. Cr cds: A, C, D, MC, V.

TREASURE ISLAND INN. 2025 S Atlantic Ave (32018), 2½ mi S on FL A1A. 904/255-8371. 232 A/C units, 11 story, 116 kits. S, D, $33-$37; each addl, $5-$8; kit. units, $60-$64; under 12 free;

hols, special events higher (5-day min); family, wkly rates avail; rest of yr: varied lower rates. Color TV. Pool; wading pool. Cafes, 7 am-10 pm. Bar, 11-2 am; entertainment, dancing exc Sun. Coin lndry. Cr cds: A, C, D, MC, V.

VOYAGER BEACH. 2424 N Atlantic Ave (32018), 3 mi N on FL A1A. 904/677-7880. 251 A/C rms, 6 story, 84 kits. Mid-Feb-late Apr, late June-early July: S, D, $40-$55; each addl, $4-$8; under 12 free; Easter, July 4, race wks, special events higher (4-day min); family, wkly, mthly rates avail; rest of yr: varied lower rates. Color TV. 2 pools; 2 wading pools. Cafe, 7 am-2 pm, 5 pm-2 am. Bar; entertainment, dancing exc Mon. Coin lndry adj. Tennis. Cr cds: A, C, D, MC, V.

WHITEHALL INN. 640 N Atlantic Ave (32018). 6 blks N on FL A1A. 904/258-5435. 210 A/C units. S, D, $44-$59; kit units, $54-$59; under 18 free; wkly rates, sr cit rates; race wks, Easter, higher rates. Pool; wading pool. Cafe, 7 am-9 pm. Bar, 5 pm-2 am; dancing in season. Coin lndry. Cr cds: A, C, D, MC, V.

Restaurants

ANCHOR INN. (608 W Dunlawton St, Port Orange 32019.) 1 mi W of Port Orange Bridge. 904/767-0845. Hrs: 4:30-9:30 pm. Closed Mon; also mid-Dec-late Dec. A/C. Liquor, beer. Wine list. Dinner, semi-a la carte, $4.50-$13.95. Child's plates. Specialties: seafood, steak. Cr cds: MC, V.

CHEZ BRUCHEZ. 304 Seabreeze Blvd (32018), 3 blks W of FL A1A. 904/252-6656. Hrs: 11:30 am-2 pm, 5-9 pm. Closed Dec 25; also Sep-Oct. A/C. French, Amer menu. Imported wine, beer. Semi-a la carte. Lunch, $4.75-$8; dinner, $8.50.$15; Child's plates half price. Specialties: roast filet Nivernaise, frogs' legs provençale, mousse au chocolat. Cr cds: A, C, D, MC, V.

JUAN 92. 200 Volusia Ave. 4 mi W on 92, opp Speedway, dog track. 904/253-9812. Hrs: 11:30 am-2 pm, 4-10 pm; Fri, Sat to 11 pm. A/C. Mexican, Amer menu. Bar. Semi-a la carte: lunch, $2.95; dinner, $3.95-$11.95. Serv plate, $1. Child's plates. Background music. Cr cds: A, MC, V.

KING'S CELLAR. (See Best Western Americano Beach Lodge above.) 904/255-3014. Hrs: 5-11 pm. Closed Tues. A/C. Bars. Dinner, table d'hôte, $4.95-$30; Child's plates, $3.50 up; Specialties: seafood, prime rib, Italian dishes. Entertainment, dancing. Cr cds: A, C, D, MC, V.

KLAUS. 144 Ridgewood Ave. 1 mi N on US 1. 904/255-7711. Hrs: 5-10 pm. Closed Mon, Thanksgiving, 2 wks late Dec. A/C. Bar, wine list. Semi-a la carte: dinner, $8.95-$18.50; min $7.95. Background music. Cr cds: A, D, MC, V.

MARKO'S HERITAGE INN. (Box 397, Port Orange.) 900 S Ridgewood Ave, 2 mi S of Port Orange Bridge on US 1. 904/767-3809. Hrs: 4:30-10 pm. A/C. Semi-a la carte: dinner, $6.89-$15.99; sr cit rates. Child's plates. Specializes in steak, seafood. Background music. Cr cds: A, D, MC, V.

DE FUNIAK SPRINGS

BEST WESTERN CROSSROADS INN (Box 852; 32720.) Jct I-10, 331. 904/892-5111. 98 A/C rms, 2 story. Late May-Labor Day: S, $35-$37; D, $40-$42; each addl, $6; under 18 free; rest of yr: lower rates. Color TV. Pool. Cafe, 6:30 am-9 pm. Bar; entertainment, dancing Fri, Sat. Cr cds: A, C, D, MC, V.

DE LAND

TROPICAL APARTMENTS & MARINA. (1485 Lakeview Dr., 32720.) 4 mi W of FL 44, 2 mi S on Old New York. 904/734-3080. 14 A/C kit units, 1 bdrm, $31; 2 bdrm, $36; each addl, $4; under 12 $1; wkly, family, mthly rates avail. TV. Coin lndry. On river.

DESTIN

RIVIERA ON THE GULF. (Box 455; 32541.) 1¼ mi E on 98. 904/837-6144. 42 A/C units, 1-2 story, 8 kits., 24 A/C kit. cottages. Late May-Labor Day: S, D, $57; kit. cottages $89-$110; each addl, $3; rest of yr: varied lower rates. Color TV. Indoor pool. Cafe adj, 6 am-10 pm. Ck-out, 11 am. On Gulf.

SANDESTIN. (32541.) 8 mi E on 98. 904/874-3950. 170 A/C in 6-story inn, 1-3 bedrm kit villas: 1 bdrm $140; 2 bdrm $155; 3 bdrm $175; each addl, $8; villa rates, package plans avail; rest of yr: varied lower rates. Maid serv avail. Color TV. Pool; wading pool. Cafe, 7 am-10 pm. Bar; dancing. Golf. Lighted tennis. Entertainment, dancing. Along Gulf, bay shores. Cr cds: A, C, D, MC, V.

DUNEDIN

JAMAICA INN. 150 Marina Plaza (33528), at end of FL 580 on 19A. 904/733-4121. 50 A/C units, 2 story, 32 kits. Mid-Jan-Apr: S, D, $62-$67; each addl, $5; kit. units, $62-$67; rest of yr: lower rates. Color TV. Pool. Cafe (see BON APPETIT). Bar. On St Joseph's Sound; marina opp. Cr cds: MC, V.

Restaurant

BON APPETIT. 150 Marina Plaza, at end of FL 580 on 19A. 904/733-2151. Hrs: 8-1 am; Sun, 9 am-4 pm. Reservation recommended. A/C. Bar. A la carte. Entrees. Lunch, $5.95-$10.95; dinner, $10.50-$18.95; Sun brunch, $11.95. Specialties: rack of lamb, veal Oscar, spinach salad, onion soup. Overlooks St Dunedin Marina. Cr cds: MC, V.

EUSTIS

LAKE SHORE ACRES. 926 N Bay St (32726), 6 blks N on FL 19, 44, 2¾ mi N of 441. 904/357-3433. 22 A/C rms, 6 kits. Dec-mid-Apr: S, $20-$33; D, $22-$26; each addl, $3; kit. units, $95 wkly; under 6 yrs free; wkly, group rates avail; rest of yr: lower rates. Color TV. Pool. Cafe, 5:30 am-8:30 pm. Dock. On Lake Eustis. Cr cds: A, MC, V.

FORT LAUDERDALE

BEST WESTERN FORT LAUDERDALE INN. 5727 N Federal Hwy (33308), 8 mi N on 1. 305/491-2500. 172 A/C rms, 2 story. Late Dec-Apr: S, $42-$56; D, $48-$62; each addl, $10; rest of yr: varied lower rates. Color TV. Olympic-size pool; wading pool. Cafe, 7:30 am-2:30 pm, 5:30-9:30 pm. Bar; entertainment, dancing exc Mon. Coin lndry. Cr cds: A, C, D, MC, V.

BEST WESTERN MARINA & YACHT HARBOR (formerly Marina Inn & Yacht Harbor). 2150 SE 17 St Causeway (33316), on FL A1A, 3 mi E of I-95. 305/525-3484. 174 A/C rms, 3 story. Mid-Dec-mid-Apr: S, $65-$75; D, $75-$85; each addl, $6; under 18 free; rest of yr: varied lower rates. Color TV. Pool; poolside serv. Cafe, 7 am-2 pm, 5-10 pm. Bars; entertainment. Tennis. Golf. Dock; boating. Marina, on Intracoastal Waterway. Cr cds: A, C, D, MC, V.

CARRIAGE HOUSE MOTOR LODGE. 1180 N US 1 (33304). ½ mi N on US 1 & Sunrise Blvds, 3 mi E of I-95. 305/564-6411. 53 A/C units, 2 story, 17 kits. Mid-Dec-Apr: S, D, $45-$55; each addl, $5;

ACCOMMODATIONS & RESTAURANTS 131

kit units, $44-$46; under 12 free in summer; wkly rates; lower rates rest of yr. Color TV. Pool. Cafe opp; open 24 hrs. Coin lndry. Cr cds: A, C, D, MC, V.

DAYS INN. 2460 Hwy 84 (33312), 7 mi SW on FL 84 at jct I-95. 305/792-4700. 288 A/C rms, 3 story. Mid-Dec-Apr: S, $49; D, $53; each addl, $4; family rates avail; rest of yr: varied lower rates. Color TV. Pool. Cafe, 6 am-9 pm. Coin lndry. Cr cds: A, D, MC, V.

DAYS INN OF AMERICA. 1700 Broward Blvd, adj to I-95. 305/463-2500. 144 A/C units, 5 story. Elvtr. S, D, $49-$54; each addl, $5; under 14 $1; wkly rates. Crib, cot free. TV. Pool. Playground. Cafe open 24 hrs. Ck-out noon. Meeting rms. Sundries. Picnic tables, grills. Nonsmoking area. Cr cds: A, MC, V.

FORT LAUDERDALE BEACH HILTON INN. 4060 Galt Ocean Dr (33308). 5 mi NE on FL A1A. 305/565-6611. 226 A/C rms, 12 kits. Mid-Dec-May: S, D, $88-$130; each addl, $5; suites, $195-$250; under 18 free; rest of yr: varied lower rates. Color TV. Pool. Cafe, 7 am-10 pm, dining rm, 5-10 pm. Bars, 11-2 am; entertainment, dancing. On beach. Cr cds: A, C, D, MC, V.

HAPPY HOLIDAY. 3055 Harbor Dr (33316), 2½ mi SE off FL A1A, 3 mi E I-95. 305/525-3158. 28 A/C units, 2 story, 18 kits. Mid-Dec-mid-Apr: S, D, $55-$65; each addl, $10; kit. units, $65-$90; rest of yr: varied lower rates. Color TV. Pool. Cafe, 8 am-10 pm. Coin lndry. Private patios, balconies. Picnic tables, grills. Cr cds: MC, V.

HOLIDAY INN-LAUDERDALE-BY-THE-SEA. (4118 Ocean Dr, Lauderdale-by-the-Sea 33308.) 6 mi NE on FL A1A. 305/776-1212. 187 A/C rms, 5 story, 18 kits. Dec-Mar: S, $70-$82; D, $75-$87; each addl, $10; kit. units, $100; rest of yr: varied lower rates. Color TV. Pool. Cafe, 6 am-10 pm. Bars, 11-2 am. Entertainment exc Mon; dancing. Coin lndry. Lighted tennis. Ocean opp. Cr cds: A, C, D, MC, V.

HOLIDAY INN-OCEANSIDE. 3000 E Las Olas Blvd (33316), 2½ mi E on FL A1A, 3 mi E of I-95 Sunrise Blvd exit. 305/463-8421. 224 A/C rms, 2-6 story. Mid-Dec-Apr: S, $44-$82; D, $50-$90; each addl, $5; under 18 free; rest of yr: varied lower rates. Color TV. Rooftop pool. Cafe, 7 am-3 pm, 4-11 pm. Bar; entertainment, dancing exc Sun. On ocean. Cr cds: A, MC, V.

HORIZON. 607 N Atlantic (33304), 6 blks N on A1A. 305/564-5211. 57 A/C rms, 4 story, 36 kit. apts. Dec-Apr: S, D, $52-$57; each addl, $8; kit apts, $100-$105; studio rms, $76-$90; under 16 free; family rates avail. Color TV. Pool. Cafe 1 blk, 24 hrs. Coin lndry. Tennis, golf privileges. On beach. Cr cds: A, C, D, MC, V.

HOWARD JOHNSON'S. 700 N Atlantic Blvd (33304), 30 blks NE on FL A1A; 3½ mi E of I-95. 305/563-2451. 144 A/C rms, 9 story. Mid-Dec-Apr: S, D, $75-$93; each addl, $7; under 18 free; rest of yr: varied lower rates. Color TV. Pool. Cafe open 24 hrs. Bar, 6 pm-2 am; dancing exc Mon. Beach opp. Cr cds: A, C, D, MC, V.

IRELAND'S INN. 2220 N Atlantic Blvd (33305), 1 blk E of FL A1A. 305/565-6661. 83 A/C units, 51 kits. Mid-Dec-Apr: S, D, $50-$100; kit. units, $70-$130; penthouse, $175; each addl, $10; rest of yr: varied lower rates. Children over 12 only in winter. Color TV. 2 pools. Cafes, 7:30 am-3 pm, 5:30-10:30 pm. Bar; patio bar; entertainment, dancing Fri, Sat. On beach. Cr cds: A, MC, V.

JOLLY ROGER. 619 N Atlantic Blvd (33304), 3½ mi N on FL A1A, 3½ mi E of I-95. 305/564-3211. 100 A/C units, 3-5 story. Elvtr. Mid-Dec-mid-Apr:
S, D, $50-$68; each addl, $7; kit. units $64-$76; apts $60-$82; under 16 free (limit 2); varied lower rates rest of yr. Crib free, cot $10. TV. Pool; poolside serv. Cafe 8 am-3 pm, 6-9:30 pm. Bar 11-2 am; from noon Sun, Mon. Ck-out 11 am. Coin lndry. Gift shop. Beauty shop. Game rm. Private patios, balconies. Opp ocean. Cr cds: A, MC, V.

MARK 2100. 2100 N Atlantic Blvd (33305). 4 mi E of I-95, 1 blk E of FL A1A. 305/566-8383. 130 A/C rms, 3-4 story, 64 kits. Mid-Dec-Apr: S, D, $62-$72; each addl, $10; kit units $76-$118; sr cit rates in summer; lower rates rest of yr. Color TV. 3 pools. Cafe, 7 am-3 pm, 5:30-9:30 pm. Bar, 11-1:30 am; entertainment, dancing exc Mon. Cr cds: A, C, D, MC, V.

OAKLAND PARK INN. 3870 N Andrews Ave (33309). 3 mi N 305/563-1351. 69 A/C units, 3 story. Mid-Dec-mid-Apr: S, $55; D, $59; each addl, $10; kit units, $80; under 12 free; wkly rates; varied lower rates rest of yr. Color TV. 2 pools. Whirlpool. Coin lndry. Cr cds: A, MC, V.

RAMADA-OCEAN FRONT. 4240 Galt Ocean (33308), 7 blks E on FL A1A. 305/566-8631. 94 A/C rms, 3 story, 20 kits. Mid-Dec-Apr: S, D, $75-$85; each addl, $8; kit. units, $80-$85; under 18 free; rest of yr: varied lower rates avail. Color TV. 2 pools. Cafe, 7 am-11 pm. Bars; entertainment, dancing exc Sun, Mon. Coin lndry. On ocean. Cr cds: A, C, D, MC, V.

SEA CHATEAU. 555 N Birch Rd (33304), 2 blks W on FL A1A, 3 mi E of I-95, Sunrise Blvd exit. 305/566-8331. 19 A/C units, 2 story, 5 kits. Mid-Dec-Apr: S, D, $40-$45; each addl, $10; kit. units, $45-$50; rest of yr: varied lower rates. Over 6 yrs only. Color TV. Pool.

THREE CROWNS. 3030 Harbor Dr (33316), 2½ mi SE & 1 blk W of FL A1A, 3 mi E of I-95, State Rd 84 exit. 305/525-6633. 35 A/C units, 6 story, 20 kits. Mid-Dec-early-May: S, D, $55-$65; studio rms, $68-$75; apts, $95; penthouse apt to 6, $135; each addl, $8-$9; rest of yr: varied lower rates. Color TV. Pool. Coin lndry. Cr cds: MC, V.

PIER 66 HOTEL & MARINA. (Drawer 9177; 33310.) 2301 SE 17 St Causeway, 2½ mi SE on FL A1A. 305/524-0566; res: 800/327-3796. 258 A/C rms. Mid-Dec-late Apr: S, D, $110-$160; each addl, $15, exec suites, $400-$650; rest of yr: varied lower rates. Color TV. 2 pools; wading pool. Cafe, 7 am-11 pm. Bars; entertainment. Coin lndry. Lighted tennis. Marina. Golf. On Intracoastal Waterway. Cr cds: A, C, D, MC, V.

SHERATON YANKEE TRADER. 303 N Atlantic Blvd (33304), 1 mi E on FL A1A. 305/467-1111. 443 A/C rms. Mid-Dec-mid-Apr: S, D, $59-$85; each addl, $10; suites, $175; under 18 free; rest of yr: lower rates. Color TV. Pool. Cafe, 7 am-11 pm; dining rm, 6-11 pm; musical show exc Mon. Bar; supper club, entertainment, dancing. Tennis. Beach opp. Cr cds: A, C, D, MC, V.

Restaurants

BRAUHAUS. 1701 E Sunrise Blvd, 10 blks N on 1. 305/764-4104. Hrs: 5-10 pm; Fri, Sat to 11 pm. Off-season closed Mon. A/C. German menu. Bar from 4 pm. Semi-a la carte: lunch, $4.95-$6.95; dinner, $8.95-$14.95. Child's plates. Entertainment, dancing exc Mon & Tues. Cr cds: A, MC, V.

CASA VECCHIA. 209 N Birch Rd (33304), 2 blks W of FL A1A. 305/463-7575. Hrs: 6-10:30 pm. A/C. Northern Italian menu. Bar. Dinner, semi-a la carte, $13-$20. Specialties: Cornish hen primavera, ossobuco. Cr cds: A, MC, V.

DANTE'S. 2871 N Federal Hwy, 3½ mi N on 1. 305/564-6666. Hrs: 5:30 pm-midnight. Closed Dec
25. Reservation required. A/C. French, Amer menu. Bar. Dinner, semi-a la carte, $11-$11.95. Child's plates avail. Specialties: prime rib, seafood, veal Cordon Bleu. Cr cds: A, MC, V.

THE DOWN UNDER. 3000 E Oakland Park Blvd, 4 mi N bet FL A1A, 1. 305/563-4123. Hrs: 11:30 am-2 pm; 6-11 pm, Sun, 6-11 pm. Reservation required. A/C. French menu. Bar. Semi-a la carte. Lunch, $7.50-$15; dinner, $13.95-$21.50. Specialties: canard au poivre vert, beef Wellington, trout Imperial. Cr cds: A, V.

GIBBY'S STEAKS & SEAFOOD. 2900 NE 12th Terrace, 3½ mi off 1. 305/565-2929. Hrs: 11:30 am-2:30 pm, 5-11 pm. Reservation required. A/C. Bar. Semi-a la carte. Lunch $5.95-$6.95; dinner, $12.95-$22.95. Specialties: prime ribsteak, rack of lamb, lobster Newburg. Cr cds: A, C, D, MC, V.

MAI-KAI. 3599 N Federal Hwy, 4½ mi N on 1. 305/563-3272. Hrs: 5 pm-midnight. A/C. Cantonese, Amer menu. Bar. Dinner, semi-a la carte, $10.95-$22.95 up; early dinner to 6:30 pm, $10.95-$18.95. Specialties: Mai-Kai beef, Peking duck, shrimp Lee Lin Ark. Background music. Polynesian entertainment; cover, $1.50-$2.95. Cr cds: A, MC, V.

94TH AERO SQUADRON. 2500 NW 62 St, 2 mi W of I-95 on Cypress Creek Rd. 305/491-4570. Hrs: 11 am-3 pm, 4-10 pm. Closed Dec 25. A/C. French, Amer menu. Bar. Semi-a la carte. Lunch, $3.95-$6.50; dinner, $4.50-$17.50. Child's plates, $3.95. Specialties: lemon veal, steak, snapper. Cr cds: A, MC, V.

SEA GRILL. 1619 NE 4 Ave, 2 mi NE on 4th Ave. 305/763-7211. Hrs: 11:30 am-11 pm; 11:30 am-10 pm Sun. Closed Thanksgiving, Dec 25. A/C. Bar. Semi-a la carte. Lunch, $4.50-$7.50; dinner, $6-$15; serv plate, $1.95. Child's plate, $3.50-$5. Specialties: lobster Imperial, red snapper. Cr cds: MC, V.

STOUFFER'S ANACAPRI. 1901 N Federal Hwy. 305/563-1111. Hrs: 7 am-9:15 pm. Reservation required. A/C. Bar. Semi-a la carte. Bkfst, $2.25-$5.95; lunch, $3.95-$4.95; dinner, $6.95-$14.95. Child's plates avail. Specialties: prime rib, red snapper, chicken. Cr cds: A, D, MC, V.

FORT MYERS

BEST WESTERN ROBERT E LEE MOTOR INN. 6611 N Hwy 41 (33903), ½ mi N on 41. 813/997-5511. 108 A/C rms, 6 story. Dec-late Apr: S, $35-$45; D, $42-$52; each addl, $3; under 12 free; rest of yr: lower rates. Color TV. Pool. Cafe adj, open 24 hrs. Bar, noon-2 am; entertainment, dancing. Coin lndry. Dock. Private patios, balconies. Cr cds: A, C, D, MC, V.

DAYS INN-NORTH. 1099 N US 41 (33903). Just N of Caloosahatchee River, 1 mi S of FL 78, on US 41. 813/995-0535. 127 A/C rms, 2 story. Mid-Dec-Mar: S, $37.88; D, $44.88; each addl, $4; under 18 $1; lower rates rest of yr. Color TV. Pool. Cafe, 6:30 am-9:30 pm. Cr cds: A, MC, V.

FORT MYERS TRAVELODGE. 2038 W 1 St (33901), 2 blks W of 41. 813/334-2284. 49 A/C rms, 2 story. Mid-Dec-mid-Apr: S, D, $44-$54; each addl, $3; family rates avail; rest of yr: lower rates. Color TV. Pool. Cr cds: A, C, D, MC, V.

ROCK LAKE. 2930 Palm Beach Blvd (33901), 1 mi E of 41 Business. 813/334-3242. 18 A/C rms in 9 cottages. Jan-Apr: S, D, $25-$26; each addl, $3; rest of yr: varied lower rates. TV.

SAN CARLOS INN & SPA. (Box 800, Rte 22; 33908), 10 mi S on US 41 at Constitution Blvd. 813/481-

3818. 47 A/C rms, 2 story. Mid-Dec-Apr: S, $46; D, $52; each addl, $10; under 12 free; lower rates rest of yr. Color TV. Pool; mineral spring; sauna closed Thurs (am). Cafe, 7 am-10 pm. Bar, 3 pm-midnight. Cr cds: MC, V.

TA KI-KI. 2631 1 St (33902), 6 blks E on FL 80. 813/334-2135. 23 A/C rms, 5 kits. Mid-Dec-Apr: S, D, $45; each addl, $3; kit. units, $290-$315 wk; rest of yr: varied lower rates. Color TV. Pool. On river; boat dock. Cr cds: A, C, D, MC, V.

Restaurants

SMITTY'S. 2240 W 1st St (33901). 813/344-4415. Hrs: 11 am-10:30 pm; Sun, noon-9:30 pm. A/C. Bar. Semi-a la carte. Lunch, $4-$8.25; dinner, $8.50-$20. Child's plates, $4.25-$6.25. Specialties: prime rib, New York strip steak. Entertainment, dancing exc Sun. Cr cds: A, D, MC, V.

THE SHALLOWS. 5833 Winkler Rd (33907), ¾ mi S of airport at College Pkwy. 813/481-4644. Hrs: 5-10:30 pm; Sat, 5-10:30 pm; Sun, to 9:30 pm. Closed Dec 25. Reservation required. A/C. Bar, 4-11:30 pm. Dinner, semi-a la carte, $9.50-$15; serv plate, $1.50. Child's plate avail. Specialties: red snapper with crab, veal Oscar, ice cream pie. Salad bar. Cr cds: A, D, MC, V.

THE VERANDA. 2d St & Broadway (33901), 3 blks E of 41 on FL 82. Hrs: 11:30 am-2:30 pm, 5:30-11 pm. Closed Sun. A/C. Bar, 11-1 am. Continental menu. Semi-a la carte. Lunch, $4.25-$9; dinner, $8.95-$14.95. Specialties: veal marsala, table side desserts, authentic New Orleans "poor boy" sandwiches (lunch only). Entertainment. Cr cds: A, D, MC, V.

FORT PIERCE

DOCKSIDE INN. 1152 Seaway Dr (33450), 2 mi E on FL A1A. 305/461-4824. 17 A/C units, 2 story, 16 kits. Mid-Dec-mid-Apr: S, $30-$40; D, $35-$40; each addl, $5; kit. apts, $33-$44; wkly rates avail; rest of yr: varied lower rates. Color TV. Pool. Dockage. Cr cds: A, MC, V.

HOLIDAY INN PARKWAY. (Box 1628; 33450.) 5 mi W on FL 70, jct. FL Tpke exit 56, FL 70. 305/464-5000. 163 A/C rms, 2 story. Mid-Dec-Apr: S, $34-$42; D, $40-$48; each addl, $6; under 18 free; rest of yr: lower rates. Color TV. Pool. Cafe, 7-10 pm. Bar, 11-10 pm; entertainment, dancing. Coin lndry. Cr cds: A, D, MC, V.

HOWARD JOHNSON'S. (Box 610 A, Rte 4, 33450.) 5 mi W on FL 70, Okeechobee Rd at jct FL 70, FL Tpke, exit 56 FL, FL 70. 305/646-4500. 64 A/C rms, 2 story. Mid-Dec-Apr: S, $34-$42; D, $35-$59; each addl, $8; under 18 free; family rates avail; rest of yr: varied lower rates. Color TV. Pool; wading pool. Cafe open 24 hrs. Cr cds: A, C, D, MC, V.

FORT WALTON BEACH

CAROUSEL. 571 San Rosa Blvd, ¾ mi SW on US 98 (32548). 904/243-7658. 105 A/C rms, 2-4 story, 93 kits. May-Labor Day: S, D, $55-$70; each addl, $3; kit units $70-$88; family rates; lower rates rest of yr. Color TV. 2 Pools. Cafe adj, 7-4 am. Bar, 4 pm-4 am; entertainment, dancing. Coin lndry. Cr cds: A, MC, V.

DAYS INN. 135 Miracle Strip Pkwy SW (32548), 1 mi W on 98. 904/244-6184. 62 A/C rms, 2 story. May-Labor Day: S, D, $44-$48; each addl, $4; under 18, $1; rest of yr: lower rates. Color TV. Pool. Cafe, 6 am-9 pm. Gulf opp. Cr cds: A, D, MC, V.

HOWARD JOHNSON'S. 314 Miracle Strip Pkwy SW (32548), 1¾ mi W on 98. 904/243-6162. 140 A/C rms, 2 story. Mid-May-Labor Day: S, $25-$35; D, $35-$50; each addl, $5; suites, $38-$53; under 18 free; rest of yr: lower rates. Color TV. Pool; wading pool. Cafe open 24 hrs; dining rm, 5-11 pm. Bar; entertainment exc Sun. Coin lndry. Launch ramp; dockage. Cr cds: A, C, D, MC, V.

ISLANDER BEACH RESORT. 790 Santa Rosa Blvd (32548). 1½ mi SW of US 98. 904/244-4137. 111 A/C units, 88 kit suites, 7 story. May-Labor Day: S, D, $38-$74; kit units, $60-$140; each addl, $3; varied lower rates rest of yr; family rates. Color TV. Pool. Cafe, 7-4 am. Bar, 11-4 am; entertainment, dancing. Coin lndry. On beach. Cr cds: A, MC, V.

RAMADA INN. (32548.) 2 mi SE on 98. 904/243-9161. 454 A/C rms, 2-6 story. May-Labor Day: S, D, $50-$85; each addl, $10; suites, $130-$150; under 18 free; rest of yr: varied lower rates. Color TV. 3 pools; wading pool. Cafes, 6 am-10 pm. Bars; entertainment, dancing. Lighted tennis. Cr cds: A, MC, V.

Restaurants

THE LANDING. 225 Miracle Strip Pkwy SW. 904/244-7134. Hrs: 11 am-3:30 pm, 5-10 pm. Closed Jan 1, Thanksgiving, Dec 24 & 25. A/C. Bar, 11 am-midnight. Wine list. Semi-a la carte: lunch, $3.85-$5; dinner, $6.95-$13.95. Specializes in prime rib & seafood. Salad bar. Background music. Entertainment. Cr cds: A, MC, V.

PERRI'S. 300 Eglin Pkwy NE, 3¼ mi N on FL 85, 3 mi N of 98. 904/862-4421. Hrs: 5-10 pm; Fri, Sat to 10:45 pm. Closed Sun, Mon; also Mid-Dec-early Jan. A/C. Italian, Amer menu. Bar. Semi-à la carte. Dinner, $4.95-$10.75. Child's plates. Specialties: veal dishes, lasagne & manicotti dinner.

GAINESVILLE

GATOR COURT. 4170 SW 13 St (32608), 2 mi E of FL 121. 904/376-4667. 14 A/C rms. S, $19-$23; D, $21-$25; each addl, $3; under 8 free; special events higher. Color TV. Cr cds: MC, V.

HILTON. 2900 SW 13 St (32608), 1¼ mi S on 441. 904/377-4000. 197 A/C rms, 2-4 story. S, $38-$48; D, $44-$58; each addl, $10; under 18 free; family rates avail; football wkends higher. Color TV. Pool. Cafe, 7 am-6 pm. Bars, 11-2 am; entertainment, dancing exc Sun. On lake. Cr cds: A, C, D, MC, V.

HOLIDAY INN-UNIVERSITY CENTER. (Box 1406; 32601.) 1250 W University Ave, 6 blks W on 441 at FL 26. 904/376-1661. 167 A/C rms, 6 story. S, $45-$49; D, $50-$55; each addl, $6; under 12 free; special events (2-day min) higher. Color TV. Cafe, 6:30 am-2 pm, 5-10 pm. Bar; entertainment, dancing. Coin lndry ½ mi. Cr cds: A, C, D, MC, V.

HOLIDAY INN-WEST. (32601.) 3 mi W on FL 26 at jct I-75. 904/376-3221. 279 A/C rms, 2 story. S, $37-$44; D, $43-$50; each addl, $4; wkly rates avail. Color TV. Pool; wading pool. Cafe, 6 am-10 pm. Bar; entertainment, dancing exc Sun, Mon. Coin lndry. Cr cds: A, C, D, MC, V.

HOWARD JOHNSON'S IN-TOWN. 2820 NW 13 St (32601), 1½ mi N on 441. 904/376-1211. 82 A/C rms, 2 story. S, $37-$43; D, $48-$64; each addl, $8; under 18 free; special events (2-day min) higher. Color TV; free in-rm movies. Pool. Cafe open 7-1:30 am. Coin lndry. Cr cds: A, C, D, MC, V.

QUALITY INN. 1901 SW 13th St (32601), ½ mi S on 441, ½ mi S of FL 26. 904/376-2222. 100 A/C rms. S, $28; D, $35; each addl, $4; under 16 free; special events (2-day min) higher; family, group rates avail. Color TV. Pool. Cafe, 7-11 am, 5-9 pm. Bar; entertainment, dancing. Tennis. Cr cds: A, C, D, MC, V.

TABOR. 4041 SW 13 St (32608), 2¾ mi S on 441 at jct FL 121, 331. 904/376-4423. 10 A/C rms. S, $17-$20; D, $21-$24; each addl, $3; under 5 yrs free; special events higher. Color TV.

Restaurants

MORRISON'S (Cafeteria). 2620 NW 13 St, 1½ mi N on 441 in Gainesville Mall. 904/378-7422. Hrs: 11 am-8 pm. A/C. Avg ck: lunch, dinner, $4.

PRIMROSE INN. 214 W University Ave, 1 blk W on FL 26, 10 blks E of 441. 904/376-9348. Hrs: 11:30 am-2:20 pm, 5-8:45 pm. Closed Sat, Memorial Day, July 4, Labor Day wknd, Christmas and New Year's weeks. A/C. Bar. Table d'hôte. Lunch, $3-$4; dinner, $4-$8. Child's dinner, $2.95.

HALLANDALE

RIVIERA. 2080 S Ocean Dr (33009), ¾ mi SE on FL A1A. 305/454-6666. 170 A/C rms, 2 story, 40 kits. Dec-Apr: S, D, $60-$65; each addl, $5; under 12 free; villas avail; rest of yr: varied lower rates. Color TV. Pool. Cafe, 7 am-10 pm. Bar, 11-6 am. Coin lndry. Tennis. Cr cds: A, D, MC, V.

SUNAQUA. 1945 S Ocean Dr (33009), ¾ mi SE on FL A1A. 305/457-7600. 78 A/C rms, 1-2 story, 25 kits. Dec-May: S, D, $55-$60; each addl, $4; kit. units, $65; under 12 free; family rates in summer; rest of yr: varied lower rates. TV; color in most. Pool. Cafe, 6:30 am-4 pm. Coin lndry. Docking facilities. Beach opp. Cr cds: A, MC, V.

Restaurant

VALLE'S STEAK HOUSE. 1000 E Hallandale Beach Blvd, 2 mi E. 305/454-9556. Hrs: 11 am-11 pm; Sun from noon. A/C. Bar. Semi-a la carte. Lunch, $3-$6.95; dinner, $6.95-$15.95. Child's plate, $2.95. Specialties: steak, seafood, prime rib. Cr cds: A, C, D, MC, V.

HIALEAH

HOLIDAY INN. 1950 49 St (33012), just E of Palmetto Expwy exit NW. 103 St. 305/823-2000. 255 A/C rms, 4 story. Mid-Dec-Apr: S, $50-$60; D, $60-$70; rates higher during Orange Bowl; each addl, $5; family rates avail; rest of yr: varied lower rates. Color TV. Pool; wading pool. Cafe, 6 am-2 pm, 5-10 pm (limited menu to 3 am). Bar; entertainment, dancing exc Mon. Coin lndry. One of chain. Cr cds: A, D, MC, V.

SHERATON AMERICUS. (103d St NW at Palmetto, Hialeah Gardens 33016) 305/825-1000. 263 A/C rms. S, $75-$105; D, $82-$90; each addl, $8; under 18 free; sr cit rates. Color TV; in-rm movies, free cable. Pool; whirlpool, sauna. Cafe, 7 am-11 pm. Bar, 11-5 am; entertainment. Cr cds: A, C, D, MC, V.

HOLLYWOOD

HOLIDAY INN-DOWNTOWN. 1925 Harrison St (33020), 2 blks W off 1. 305/927-3341. 95 A/C rms, 6 story. Dec-mid-Apr: S, D, $58; each addl, $5; family rates avail; rest of yr: varied lower rates. Color TV. Pool. Cafe, 6 am-10 pm. Bar, 11:30-2 am. Coin lndry. Cr cds: A, D, MC, V.

HOLIDAY INN-HOLLYWOOD BEACH. 4000 S Ocean Dr (33019), 3 mi SE on FL A1A, 4 mi E of I-95. 305/458-1900. 320 A/C rms, 10 story. Mid-Dec-late Apr: S, $80-$122; D, $82-$122; each addl $12; under 9 free. Rest of yr: varied lower rates. Color TV. Pool. Cafe, 7 am-10 pm. Bars, 11-2 am; entertainment, dancing Fri, Sat in season. Tennis. Beach Opp. Cr cds: A, C, D, MC, V.

HOLLYWOOD LAKES COUNTRY CLUB & INN. 14800 Hollywood Blvd (33026), 14 mi W on FL 820 at Hollywood Lakes, 3 mi E of FL 27. 305/431-8800. 101 A/C rms, 2 story. Mid-Jan-Apr: S, $54-$59; D, $64-$78; each addl, $8; under 12 free; golf package plan; lower rates rest of yr. Color TV. Pool. Cafe, 6:30 am-9 pm. Bar, 11 am-10 pm; entertainment, dancing Wed. Coin lndry. Cr cds: A, D, MC, V.

HOWARD JOHNSON'S. 2900 Polk St (33020), 2 mi W on FL 820, just E of I-95 Hollywood Blvd exit. 305/923-1516. 72 A/C rms, 2 story. Dec-May: S, $48; D, $64; each addl, $6; under 18 free; rest of yr: varied lower rates. Color TV. Pool. Cafe open 24 hrs. Cr cds: A, C, D, MC, V.

HOWARD JOHNSON'S. 2501 N Ocean Dr (33019), 5 mi E on FL A1A. 305/925-1411. 242 A/C rms, 11 story, 6 kits. Dec-Apr: S, $64-$84; D, $75-$82; each addl, $10; kit. units, $85; under 18 free; rest of yr: varied lower rates. Color TV. Pool. Cafe 10 am-4 pm. Bars, 11-3 am; entertainment, dancing exc Sun. Coin lndry. On beach. Cr cds: A, C, D, MC, V.

Restaurants

GEPETTO'S TALE OF THE WHALE. 1828 Harrison, at Federal Hwy off Young Circle. 305/920-9009. Hrs: 5-10 pm. Reservation required. A/C. Continental menu. Bar. Dinner, semi-a la carte, $7.95-$20; Child's plate, $5.95. Specialties: fettuccine Gepetto, sole Portofino. Appetizer, salad bar. Cr cds: MC, V.

NEPTUNE SEAFOOD. 1824 Harrison St. On Young Circle. 305/929-3581. Hrs: noon-2 pm, 4:30-10 pm. Res required. A/C French menu. Serv bar. Table d'hote: dinner $9.95-$11.95. Specialties: snapper New Orleans, escargots en croute. Background music. French decor. Cr cds: MC, V.

HOMESTEAD

CORAL ROC. (1100 N Krome Ave, Florida City 33034.) On FL 27, 1 blk W of US 1. 305/247-4010. 16 A/C rms, 4 kits. Mid-Dec-Apr: S, D, $38-$44; each addl, $3; kit units $322-$350/wk, 5-day min; under 12 free; varied lower rates rest of yr. Color TV. Pool. Cafe opp 11 am-11 pm; closed Sun. Coin lndry. Cr cds: MC, V.

RAMADA INN. 51 Homestead Blvd, ½ mi E on US 1 (33030). 305/245-1260. 109 A/C rms, 2 story. Mid-Dec-Mar; S, D, $47-$52; each addl, $10; under 18 free; sr cit rates; family rates; varied lower rates rest of yr. Color TV. Pool. Cafe, 6:30 am-2 pm. Bar, 11-2:30 am; entertainment, dancing exc Sun. Cr cds: A, C, D, MC, V.

Restaurants

CAPRI. (935 N Krome Ave, Florida City.) On FL 27. 305/247-1544. Hrs: 11 am-11 pm; Fri, Sat to midnight. Closed Sun, Dec 25. A/C. Bar. Italian, Amer menu. Semi-a la carte. Lunch, $2-$3.95; dinner, $5.50-$8.50. Specialties: veal, prime rib. Entertainment Tu-Sat. Food to go. Cr cds: A, MC, V.

HOMOSASSA SPRINGS

RIVERSIDE VILLAS RESORT. (Box 258, Homosassa 32646.) 3 mi W on FL 490, 3 mi W of 19, 98. 904/628-2474. 72 A/C rms, 2 story, 24 kits. S, D, $41-$44; each addl, $4; kit. units, $51-$62; under 17 free. Color TV. Pool. Cafe (see YARDARM). Bar; entertainment, dancing exc Mon. Coin lndry. Tennis. Marina; boats, paddleboats, guides avail. Cr cds: A, C, D, MC, V.

SHERATON INN. (Box 8; 32647.) 3 blks S on 19, 98, just S of jct FL 490. 904/628-4311. 104 A/C rms, 2 story. Mid-Dec-Apr: S, $36-$38; D, $40-$43; each addl, $4; under 17 free; family rates avail; rest of yr: lower rates. Color TV. Pool. Cafe (see LOUIS PAPPAS' HOMOSASSA SPRINGS). Bar. Tennis. Cr cds: A, C, D, MC, V.

Restaurants

LOUIS PAPPAS' HOMOSASSA SPRINGS. (See Sheraton Inn above.) 904/628-2311. Hrs: 6:30 am-10 pm. A/C. Bar. Semi-a la carte: bkfst, $1.50-$3; lunch, $3-$6.25; dinner, $3.75-$6.25. Child's plates, $1.50-$3. Entertainment, dancing Wed, Fri, Sat. Cr cds: A, C, D, MC, V.

YARDARM. (See Riverside Villas Resort above.) 904/628-2474. Hrs: 6:30 am-10 pm. A/C. Bar. Semi-a la carte. Bkfst, $3-$5; lunch, $5-$8; dinner, $8-$16. Specialties: seafood, prime rib, steak. Salad Bar. Entertainment, dancing Tu-Sat. Cr cds: A, C, D, MC, V.

ISLAMORADA

CHEECA LODGE. (Box 527; 33036), mi marker 82½. 305/327-2888. 86 A/C rms, 10 kits., 10 cottages. Mid-Dec-Apr: S, D, $125-$155; kit. cottages, $135-$165; under 18 free; family rates avail; rest of yr: lower rates avail. Color TV. Pool. Bar, 11-2 am; entertainment, dancing exc Mon. Lighted tennis, pro. Golf. On beach. Cr cds: A, C, D, MC, V.

CHESAPEAKE. (Box 909; 33036.) 2 mi N on US 1. 305/644-4662. 38 A/C rms, 2 story, 18 A/C kit villas. S, D, $53-$55; each addl, $6; 1-2 bdrm villas, $50-$110; 2-day min hols. Color TV. Pool. Cafe, 11:30 am-10 pm. Bar. Cr cds: A, MC, V.

DROP ANCHOR. (Box 222; 33036.) 3 mi N on 1. 305/664-4863. 12 A/C rms, 2 story, 8 kits. Mid-Dec-late Apr: S, D, $45-$48; each addl, $10; kit. units, $55-$60; rest of yr: varied lower rates. Color TV. Pool. On Beach. Cr cds: A, C, D, MC, V.

HOWARD JOHNSON'S. (Box 224; 33036.) 2½ mi N on 1. 305/664-2711. 56 A/C rms, 2 story. Mid-Dec-Apr: S, $36-$70; D, $41-$74; each addl, $10; under 18 free; rest of yr: varied lower rates. Color TV. Pool. Cafe open 24 hrs. Coin lndry. On beach. Cr cds: A, C, D, MC, V.

THE ISLANDER. (Box 766; 33036.) ½ mi S on 1. 305/664-2031. 114 A/C units in motel, villas, 92 kits. Mid-Dec-Apr: S, D, $45-$65; with kit., $51-$65; each addl, $6; villas, $55-$58; rest of yr: lower rates. Color TV. 2 pools (1 saltwater). Cafe, 6:30 am-2 pm, 6-10 pm. On ocean. Cr cds: A, D, MC, V.

SUNSET INN. (Box 269; 33036.) On 1. 305/664-4427. 60 A/C rms, 1-2 story, 28 kits. Mid-Dec-Apr: S, D, $50-$60; kit. units, $45-$62; apts, $55-$65; suites, $90-$140; each addl, $7; rest of yr: lower rates. TV. 2 pools, 1 on private island. Cafe, 7 am-2 pm. Bars; entertainment, dancing Fri-Sat. Coin lndry opp. Boat ramp, dockage. On Gulf. Cr cds: MC, V.

Restaurants

THE CONCH. (Box 943.) ¼ mi E on 1. 305/664-4590. Hrs: 5-10 pm. Reservation required in season. Closed Thurs; also Labor Day-early Oct. A/C. Bar. Semi-a la carte. dinner, $8-$16.50; serv plates, $1.50. Child's plates, $3.75-$6.25. Specialties: seafood, veal, turtle. Player piano; guests "sing-a-long." Cr cds: MC, V.

CORAL GRILL. (Box 373.) On 1, ½ blk S of Whale Harbor Bridge. 305/664-4803. Hrs: 4:30-9:30 pm; Sun, noon-3 pm, 3:30-9 pm. Closed Mon, Dec 25, Labor Day-Oct. A/C. Bar. Buffet dinner, $11.95. Specialties: prime rib, steamed shrimp. Cr cds: MC, V.

JACKSONVILLE

BEST WESTERN INN I-95 SOUTH. 5221 University Blvd W (32216). 5 mi S on I-95, University Blvd exit. 904/737-1690. 187 A/C rms, 2 story. S, $34-$40; D, $40-$50; each addl, $5; under 12 free; sr cit rates. Color TV. Pool. Cafe, 6 am-10 pm. Bar; entertainment; dancing Cr cds: A, C, D, MC, V.

BEST WESTERN INTERNATIONAL AIRPORT. 1351 Airport Rd (32229), 12 mi N on Airport Rd at I-95. 904/757-9150. 116 A/C rms, 2 story. S, $27-$30; D, $30-$34; each addl, $4; under 12 free. Color TV. Pool. Cafe, 6:30 am-10 pm. Bar, 4 pm-2 am; entertainment. Cr cds: A, MC, V.

DAYS INN-SOUTH. 5649 Cagle Rd (32216), 5 mi S at jct I-95 University Ave exit. 904/733-3890. 214 A/C rms, 2-3 story, 52 kits. S, $33; D, $37; each addl, $4; kit. units, $25.88-$27.88; suites, $31.88; under 2 yrs free. Color TV. 2 pools. Cafe, 6 am-9 pm. Coin lndry. Cr cds: A, MC, V.

HILTON. 565 S Main St (32207), ½ mi S on 1, adj I-95 in Gulf Life Center. 904/398-8800. 292 A/C rms. S, $63-$95; D, $67-$97; each addl, $13; suites, $275-$400; studio rms, $150. Color TV. Pool. Cafe, open 7 am; dining rm (see WHETBY'S WHARF). Bar, entertainment, dancing exc Sun. Some wet, dry bars. Cr cds: A, C, D, MC, V.

HOLIDAY INN-AIRPORT. (Drawer 18409; 32229.) 12 mi Airport Rd at I-95. 904/757-3110. 188 A/C rms, 2 story. S, $42-$50; D, $48-$56; under 18 free. Color TV. Pool; wading pool. Cafe, 6:30-10 pm. Bar, 11:30-2 am; entertainment, dancing, exc Sun. Coin lndry. Lighted tennis. One of chain. Cr cds: A, C, D, MC, V.

HOLIDAY INN-ORANGE PARK. (100 Park Ave, Orange Park 32073.) On 17 at jct I-295 Bypass. 904/264-9513. 308 A/C rms, 2 story. S, $32-$36; D, $36-$42; each addl, $3; under 18 free; family rates avail; football wkends (2-day min) higher. Color TV. Pool. Cafe, 6 am-10 pm; Fri, Sat to 11 pm (also see SEVENTEEN SOUTH). Bar; entertainment, dancing exc Sun. Coin lndry. Cr cds: A, C, D, MC, V.

HOWARD JOHNSON'S-WEST. 6545 Ramona Blvd (32205) 5 mi W at I-10 exit 3. 904/781-1940. 63 A/C rms, 2 story. S, $32-$49; D, $35-$55; each addl, $8; under 18 free; sr cit rates. Color TV. Pool; wading pool. Cafe, 6 am-11 pm. Coin lndry. Cr cds: A, C, D, MC, V.

LA Quinta. 8555 Blanding Blvd (32244). 15 mi S on I-295, Blanding Blvd exit. 904/778-9539. 122 A/C rms, 2 story. S, $30-$36; D, $34-$38; each addl, $5; under 18 free; sr cit rates. Color TV. Pool. Cafe, open 24 hrs. Cr cds: A, C, D, MC, V.

RAMADA INN-WEST. 510 Lane Ave S (32205), 5 mi W at I-10 Lane Ave exit. 904/786-0500. 220 A/C rms, 2 story. S, $32-$35; D, $36-$42; each addl, $4; under 18 free; football wkends, special events (3-day min) higher. Color TV. Pool. Cafe, 6 am-10 pm. Bar, 11-2 am; entertainment, dancing. Coin lndry. Cr cds: A, C, D, MC, V.

THUNDERBIRD. 5865 Arlington Expwy (32211), 3½ mi SE on 1A, 90A. 904/724-3410. 276 A/C rms, 2 story. S, $35-$45; D, $39-$49; each addl, $4; under 18 free; special events higher. Color TV. Pool.

Cafe, 6:30 am-10 pm. 2 bars; entertainment, dancing, Dec 25. A/C. Italian, Amer menu. Wine, beer. Cr cds: A, C, D, MC, V.

Restaurants

PATTI'S. 7300 Beach Blvd, 6 mi E on 90, ½ mi W of 1A. 904/725-1662. Hrs: 5-10 pm; Fri, Sat to 11:30 pm; Sun, 4:30-10 pm. Closed Mon; Thanksgiving, Dec 25. A/C. Italian, Amer menu. Wine, beer. Dinner, semi-a la carte, $4.15-$12.75. Child's plates, $1.50-$2.50. Specialties: boneless chicken à la parmigiana, lasagne. Cr cds: A, C, D, MC, V.

SEVENTEEN SOUTH. (See Holiday Inn-Orange Park Motel above.) 904/264-9513. Hrs: 6-10 pm, Fri, Sat, to 11 pm. A/C. Bar. Semi-a la carte. Dinner, $7.50-$12.75. Child's plates, $3.50. Salad bar. Entertainment, dancing exc Sun. Cr cds: A, C, D, MC, V.

STRICKLAND'S TOWN HOUSE. 3510 Phillips Hwy, 3 mi S on US 1. 904/396-1682. Hrs: 11:30 am-2:30 pm, 5:30-10:30 pm. Closed Sun (exc Easter, Mother's Day); also Jan 1, Memorial Day, July 4, Labor Day, Dec 25. A/C. Bar. Semi-a la carte. Lunch, $3.50-$6 up; dinner, $6.95-$15 up. Specialties: "Town House" salad, prime rib, seafood. Entertainment. Cr cds: A, C, D, MC, V.

WHETBY'S WHARF. (See Hilton Hotel above.) 904/398-5235. Hrs: 11:30 am-10:30 pm. A/C. Continental menu. Bar. A la carte. Entrees: lunch, $4-$7; dinner, $10-$17; Sun brunch. Child's plates, $2-$4; Specialties: stuffed shrimp Wellington, seafood, prime rib. Salad bar. Entertainment, dancing exc Sun. Cr cds: A, C, D, MC, V.

JACKSONVILLE BEACH

FRIENDSHIP INN GOLD COAST. 731 1 St N (32250), 2 blks E of FL A1A. 904/249-9071. 32 A/C rms, 1-2 story, 6 kits. Memorial Day-Labor Day, special events: S, $30-$54; D, $38-$58; each addl, $3; kit. units, $42-$60; under 12 free; rest of yr: lower rates. Color TV. Pool. Cafe opp, 6 am-9 pm. On beach. Cr cds: A, C, D, MC, V.

HOLIDAY INN. 1617 N First St (32250), 2 blks E of FL A1A bet 15 & 16 Aves N. 904/249-9071. 150 A/C rms, 7 story, 13 kits. June-mid-Sep: S, $58-$69; D, $68-$80; each addl, $6; kit. units, suites, $69-$90; football wkends (2-day min) higher; rest of yr: lower rates. Color TV. Pool; wading pool. Cafe, 7 am-2 pm, 5:30-10 pm; Sun from 7 am. 2 bars, entertainment, dancing. Coin lndry. On beach. Cr cds: A, C, D, MC, V.

JASPER

BEST WESTERN. (Box 136E, Rte 3; 32052.) 7 mi W on FL 6 at I-75. 904/792-1234. 57 A/C rms, 2 story. S, $22-$26; D, $24-$34; each addl, $6; under 12 free. Color TV. Pool. Cafe, 6 am-9 pm. Cr cds: A, C, D, MC, V.

JUPITER

JUPITER HILTON INN. (33458.) 20 mi N of West Palm Beach on 1. 305/746-2511. 194 A/C units, 35 kits. Dec-Apr: S, $70-$135; D, $80-$150; each addl, $10; kit. units, $125-$200; under 18 free; rest of yr: varied lower rates. Cafe, 7 am-10 pm. Bar, 11-2 am; entertainment, dancing. Golf. Lighted tennis, pro. On ocean. Cr cds: A, C, D, MC, V.

KEY BISCAYNE

BISCAYNE MOTOR LODGE AND BEACH CLUB. 798 Crandon Blvd (33149), 7 mi SE of US 1. 305/361-5426. 54 A/C rms, 40 kit. units. Mid-Dec-Apr: S, D, $59; each addl to 4 free; kits., $89; under 18 free; rest of yr: lower rates. Color TV. Pool. Coin lndry. Cr cds: A, C, D, MC, V.

KEY BISCAYNE HOTEL & VILLAS. 701 Ocean Dr (33149), 7½ mi SE of 1. 305/361-5431. 101 A/C rms in hotel, 75 1-3 bedrm A/C villas with kits. Mid-Dec-Apr: S, D, $110-$125; each addl, $15; villas to 6, $150-$500; rest of yr: varied lower rates; Mod Amer plan avail in summer. Color TV. Pool. Cafe, 7-11 am, noon-2:30 pm, 6-9 pm. Bars; entertainment, dancing Sat in season. Coin lndry. Golf. Tennis. On ocean. Cr cds: A, MC, V.

KEY LARGO

GILBERT'S. (Box 272, RR 1; 33037.) On 1 at Jewfish Creek Bridge. 305/451-1133. 36 A/C rms, 2 story, 6 kits. Mid-Dec-Apr: S, D, $46; each addl, $5; kit. units, $76; 1 under 17 free; rest of yr: varied lower rates. Color TV. Pool. Cafe, 7 am-11 pm. Bar, 11-1 am; entertainment, dancing Fri, Sat. Coin lndry. Marina; boats; boat storage (24 ft); dockage. On Intracoastal Waterway. Cr cds: A, MC, V.

HOLIDAY INN. (Box 708; 33037.) M M 100. 305/451-2121. 100 A/C rms, 2 story. Mid-Dec-mid-Apr: S, $42-$58; D, $48-$66; each addl, $5; rest of yr: varied lower rates. Color TV. Pool; wading pool. Cafe, 6 am-10 pm. Bar, 11-1 am; entertainment, dancing. Coin lndry. Lighted tennis. Boats, scuba diving avail. On Deepwater Channel; marina. One of chain. Cr cds: A, C, D, MC, V.

HOWARD JOHNSON'S. (Box 1169; 33037.) On 1 at mi marker 102. 305/451-1400. 100 A/C rms, 2 story. Mid-Dec-Apr: S, $60-$70; D, $64-$74; each addl, $10; under 18 free; hol wkends higher; rest of yr: lower rates. Color TV. Cafe open 24 hrs. Bar, 6 pm-3 am; entertainment. Coin lndry. On Gulf. Cr cds: A, C, D, MC, V.

KEY WEST

BEST WESTERN KEY AMBASSADOR. 1000 S Roosevelt Blvd (33040), 2 mi SE on FL A1A. 305/296-3500. 100 A/C rms, 2 story, 29 kits. Late-Dec-mid-Apr: S, $78-$108; D, $98-$108; each addl, $10; rest of yr: varied lower rates. Color TV. Pool. Coin lndry. Cr cds: A, C, D, MC, V.

MARRIOTT'S CASA MARINA RESORT. 1500 Reynolds St (33040), on the ocean. 305/296-3535. 251 A/C rms. Mid-Dec-Apr: S, D, $120; each addl, $25; under 18 free, suites, $360; family rates avail; rest of yr: lower rates. Color TV. Pool. Bar, 11-2 am; entertainment. Lighted tennis. On ocean. Cr cds: A, C, D, MC, V.

PIER HOUSE. 5 Duval St at Front St (33040), 9 blks NW of 1. 305/294-9541. 120 A/C rms, 2-3 story. S, D, $95-$220; under 5, free; rest of yr: some lower rates avail. Color TV. Pool. Cafe, 7:30 am-10 pm. Bar; dancing Fri-Sun. Cr cds: A, MC, V.

SANTA MARIA. 1401 Simonton St at South (33040), 6 blks S on FL A1A. 305/296-5678. 51 A/C rms, 2 story, 16 kits. Mid-Dec-Apr: S, D, $52-$85; each addl, $10; 2 under 10 free; hols, special events higher; 2-wk min in suites, efficiencies during Christmas hols, Feb-Mar; rest of yr: lower rates. Color TV. Pool. Cafe, 7-11:30 am, noon-2:15 pm, 5:30-11 pm. Bar; entertainment in season. Cr cds: A, C, D, MC, V.

SOUTHEAST OCEAN INN. 1300 Simonton St (33040), 4 blks SE. 305/294-6663. 45 A/C rms, 2 story, 6 kits. Mid-Dec-Apr: S, D, $58-$68; each addl, $8; kit. units, $54; rest of yr: varied lower rates. Color TV. Pool. Cafe, noon-3 pm. Bar. Cr cds: A, MC, V.

SOUTHERNMOST. 1319 Duval St (33040), end of FL A1A. 305/296-6577. 50 A/C rms, 2 story, 15 kits. (no ovens). Late Dec-early Apr: S, $42; D, $65; each addl, $7; kit. (5-day min), $5 more; rest of yr: lower rates. Color TV. Pool. Cafe, 8 am-4 pm. Cr cds: A, MC, V.

SUGAR LOAF LODGE. (Box 148, Sugar Loaf Key 33044.) 13 mi NE on 1. 305/745-3211. 55 A/C rms, 10 kits. Mid-Dec-late Apr, holidays, last wk July: S, D, $60; each addl, $5; kit. units, $70; 2 under 12 free; rest of yr: varied lower rates Color TV. Cafe, 7:30 am-10 pm. Bar; entertainment, dancing. Coin lndry. Tennis. Marina; motor boats, canoes. Cr cds: A, C, D, MC, V.

Restaurants

CHEZ EMILE. 423 Front St in Old Key West just off Duval St. 305/294-6252. Hrs: 6-11 pm. May-Sept: 7-10:30 pm; Fri, Sat, to 11 pm. Closed Sun, Jan 1, Dec 25. Reservation recommended. A/C. French Menu. Wine, beer. Dinner, semi-a la carte, $9.95-$16.50. Child's plates half price. Specialties: red snapper-sauce nantua, tournedos Rossini, shrimp bordelaise. Locally popular. Cr cds: A, MC, V.

HENRY'S. (See Marriott's Casa Marina Resort) 305/296-3535. Hrs: 7-11 am, 11 am-2:30 pm, 5-11 pm. A/C. Bar. Semi-a la carte: bkfst $2-$5.95; lunch $3.95-$7.95; dinner $10.95-$17.95. Outdoor dining. Own baking. Background music; piano 7 days. Valet parking. Jacket, tie at dinner. Cr cds: A, C, D, MC, V.

PIER HOUSE. 5 Duval St, 9 blks NW of US 1, on Key West Harbour. 305/294-9541. Hrs: 11:30 am-2:30 pm, 6-10:30 pm; Fri, Sat to 11:30 pm; Sun brunch 10 am-2 pm. A/C. Bar 11-3 am. Wine list. Continental menu. Semi-a la carte: soup & salad buffet lunch $5.50; dinner $14.50-$22.50; sunset special (6 pm-sunset) $9.50-$12.50; Sun brunch $8.25-$9.50. Specialties: lamb provencale, zazuella. Own pastries, ice cream. Background music. Entertainment, dancing. Built over water facing the sunset. Cr cds: A, MC, V.

KISSIMMEE

HOLIDAY INN. (Box 1707; 32741.) 2145 E Vine St, on 192, 441. 305/846-4646. 150 A/C rms, 2 story. S, $36; D, $54; each addl, $5; under 18 free. Color TV. Pool. Cafe, 7 am-2 pm, 5:30-10 pm. Bar; entertainment, dancing exc Sun. Coin lndry. One of chain. Cr cds: A, C, D, MC, V.

HYATT ORLANDO. 6375 Spacecoast Pkwy (32741), on 192 at I-4. 305/846-1234. 960 A/C rms, 2 story. S, D, $67-$87; under 18 free; suites, $170-$240. Color TV. 4 pools; wading pools. Cafe, 6 am-midnight. Bar; entertainment, dancing exc Sun. Coin lndry. Lighted tennis; pro. Cr cds: A, C, D, MC, V.

KNIGHTS INN ORLANDO SOUTH. 2800 Poincia Blvd (32741), off 192, 2 mi E of I-4. 305/846-8186. 103 A/C rms, 23 kits. S, $44; D, $50; each addl, $3; kit. units, $2 addl. Color TV. Pool. Cafe adj open 24 hrs. Cr cds: A, MC, V.

LARSON'S LODGE-KISSIMMEE RED CARPET INN (formerly Kissimmee Red Carpet Inn). 2009 W Vine St (32741), 3 mi W on 192, 7 mi E of I-4. 305/846-2713. 120 A/C rms, 3 story, 12 kits. Jan-Apr, June-Aug, hols: S, $42-$62; D, $45-$65; each addl, $5; kit., $6 more; under 18 free; rest of yr: varied lower rates. Color TV. Pool. Cafe, 7 am-11 pm. Bar, 11 am-1 am; entertainment exc Mon. Coin lndry. Cr cds: A, C, D, MC, V.

QUALITY INN-KISSIMMEE EAST. 2661 E Spacecoast Hwy (32741). 3 mi E on US 192, 441, FL Tpke exit 65. 305/846-2221. 374 A/C units, 2-3 story, 22

ACCOMMODATIONS & RESTAURANTS 135

kits. Elvtr. Feb-Apr, June-Aug: S, $42; D, $48; each addl, $6; kit. units $10 addl; under 18 free; sr citizen rates; lower rates rest of yr. Crib $4, cot $5. TV, 2 pools. Cafe 7 am-noon, 5:30-10 pm. Bar, entertainment, dancing exc Sun. Coin lndry. Meeting rms. Some refrigerators. Picnic tables, grills. Cr cds: A, C, D, MC, V.

REGENCY INN. 8660 Hwy 192 (32741), 14 mi W. 305/396-4500; res: 800/327-9129; FL 800/432-9194. 226 A/C rms, 2 story. S, D, $70; under 18 free. Color TV. 2 pools. Cafe, 7 am-11:30 am, 5-10 pm. Bar, 5 pm-2 am; entertainment, exc Sun. Coin lndry. Lighted tennis; pro. Cr cds: A, C, D, MC, V.

Restaurant

SPINELLI'S. 1200 Pennsylvania Ave, ½ blk N of US 441 & 192, 5 mi SE of FL tpke exit 65. 305/892-2435. Hrs: 11 am-2 pm; 6-10; Sun 5-9. Closed lunch, Sat, Sun; Thanksgiving, Dec. 25. A/C. Continental, Italian menu. Bar. Wine list. Dinner, semi-a la carte $9.75-$18; serv plate, $2.50. Specialties: saltimbocca alla Romana, pitto di polla alla Spinelli, fruitti di mare. Cr cds: A, C, D, MC, V.

LAKE BUENA VISTA

HOWARD JOHNSON'S RESORT. (Box 22204; 32830.) Preview Blvd, just off I-4. 305/828-8888. 323 A/C rms. Early Feb-mid-Apr, mid-June-early Sep: S, D, $80-$115; each addl, $8; suites, $220-$360; under 18 free; rest of yr: lower rates. Color TV. Pool. Cafe open 24 hrs. Bar, 11:30-2 am. Coin lndry. Cr cds: A, C, D, MC, V.

ROYAL PLAZA. (Box 22038; 32830.) 1905 Preview Blvd, just off FL 535, I-4. 305/828-2828; res:800/327-2990. 396 A/C rms, 2 kits. S, D, $88-$118; each addl, $5; under 18 free. Color TV. Pool. Cafe, 7 am-midnight; (also see EL CID). Bar, 11-3 am; entertainment, dancing. Coin lndry. Lighted tennis; pro. Cr cds: A, C, D, MC, V.

VISTANA RESORT. 13800 Vistana Dr (32830), 1 mi S of I-4. 305/239-3100; res: 800/327-9152. 98 A/C kit. units, 1-2 story. Mid-Dec-mid-Apr, June-Aug: 2 bdrm villas, $140-$225; 2-3 bdrm $120-$250; under 17 free; rest of yr: lower rates. Color TV. Pool. Coin lndry. Lighted tennis; pro. Cr cds: A, MC, V.

Restaurants

EL CID. (See Royal Plaza above.) 305/828-2828. Hrs: 6-11 pm. Reservation requested. A/C. Continental, French menu. Bar, 11-2:30 am. Dinner, semi-a la carte, $8-$25. Child's plates, $4-$7. Specialties: steak Diane, scampi, fresh Maine lobster.

LAKE BUENA VISTA CLUB. 2200 Club Lake Dr, 3 mi SW of I-4, W of Disneyworld. 305/828-3735. Hrs: 7-11 am, 11:30 am-3 pm, 6-9:30 pm; Fri, Sat, 6-11 pm; Sun, 7 am-1:45 pm. Reservations required. A/C. Continental, French menu. Bar. A la carte. Entrees: Bkfst, $2.25-$6.65; lunch, $4.50-$7.50; dinner, $11.25-$16.25; Sun brunch. Specialties: French onion soup, Chateaubriand, steak Diane. Entertainment. Jacket at dinner. Cr cds: A, MC.

LAKE CITY

AMERICAN INN. (Box 2337; 32055.) 3½ mi W on 90, ¼ mi W of jct I-75. 904/752-5400. 20 A/C rms. S, $18-$20; D, $20-$23; each addl, $3. Color TV. Cafe adj, 6:30 am-10 pm. Bar, noon-11 pm. Tennis. Cr cds: MC, V.

BEST WESTERN INN-LAKE (formerly Best Western Inn- Lake City). (Box 258; 32055.) Rte 8, 3½ mi W on 90. 904/752-3801. 57 A/C rms, 2 story. S, $25-$34; D, $28-$36; each addl, $3; under 12 free; suite, $25; lower rates Sep-Nov, May. Color TV. Pool. Cafe 6 am-11 pm. Cr cds: A, C, D, MC, V.

DAYS INN. (Box 265, Rte 8; 32055.) 3½ mi W on 90 at I-75. 904/752-9350. 190 A/C rms, 2 story, 70 kits. (equip avail). S, $26.88; D, $31.88; each addl, $5; kit. units, $31.88. Color TV. 2 pools. Cafe, 6 am-9 pm. Coin lndry. Cr cds: A, MC, V.

HOLIDAY INN. (Drawer 1239; 32055.) 3½ mi W on 90 at I-75. 904/752-3901. 332 A/C rms, 2 story. S, $30-$33; D, $39-$42; Color TV. 2 pools. Cafe, 6:30 am-2 pm; 5:30-10 pm. Bar, 11 am-midnight. Disco exc Sun. Coin lndry. Lighted tennis. Cr cds: A, C, D, MC, V.

HOWARD JOHNSON'S. (Box 260, Rte 8; 32055.) 3½ mi W on 90 at I-75. 904/752-6262. 96 A/C rms, 2 story. S, $29-$36; D, $37-$45; each addl, $8; under 18 free; family rates avail. Color TV. Pool. Cafe open 24 hrs. Coin lndry. Cr cds: A, C, D, MC, V.

RODEWAY INN. (Box 201, Rte 13 32055.) 3½ mi W on US 90 at I-75. 904/752-7720. 100 A/C rms, 2-story, S, $25-$30; D, $30-$32; each addl, $5; under 16 free; sr citizen rates. Crib $2, cot $5. TV Pool. Cafe, open 24 hrs. Coin lndry. Cr cds: A, C, D, MC, V.

Restaurant

WAYSIDE. Hwy 90 at I-75, 4 mi W on 90. 904/752-1581. Hrs: 6 am-11 pm, Sun to 10. Closed Dec 25. A/C. Bar. Table d'hôte. Bkfst, 75¢-$4.95; lunch, dinner, $2.95-$16.95, also sandwiches. Child's menu. Specialties: steak, seafood. Cr cds: MC, V.

LAKELAND

BEST WESTERN MEMORIAL MOTOR LODGE. 508 E Memorial Blvd (33801), 1 mi N on 92, 98. 813/683-7471. 145 A/C rms, 2 story, 58 kits. Jan-mid-Apr: S, $34-$40; D, $40-$46; each addl, $6; kit. units $40-$48; rest of yr: lower rates avail. Color TV. Pool. Cafe open 24 hrs. Coin lndry. Tennis. Cr cds: A, C, D, MC, V.

HOLIDAY INN. (Drawer E, Plant City 33566.) 2011 N Wheeler St, 11 mi W at jct FL 39, I-4. 813/752-3141. 268 A/C rms, 2 story, 8 kits. Feb-mid-Apr: S, $34-$44; D, $42-$50; each addl, $5; under 18 free; family, Disney World package plans avail; rest of yr: lower rates. Color TV. Pool. Cafe (see FAMOUS 1776). Bar; entertainment, dancing exc Sun. Coin lndry. Cr cds: A, C, D, MC, V.

LAKELAND. 1224 E Memorial Blvd (33801), 1½ mi E on 92, 1 blk E of 98. 813/682-2106. 20 A/C rms. Mid-Dec-Apr: S, $30-$35; D, $35-$40; each addl, $3; under 6 yrs free; rest of yr: lower rates. Color TV. Pool. Cr cds: A, C, D, MC, V.

RED CARPET INN. 3410 Hwy 98 (33805), 2 mi N at jct I-4. 813/858-3851. 100 A/C rms, 2 story. Mid-Dec-Mar: S, $22.50-$28.50; D, $26.50-$48.50; each addl, $4-$5; under 18 free; rest of yr: lower rates. Color TV. Pool. Cafe, 6 am-midnight. Bar. Coin lndry. Cr cds: A, C, D, MC, V.

Restaurants

BRANCH RANCH DINING ROOM. (Box 3896, Rte 2, Plant City.) Thonotosassa Rd, 1 mi N of I-4 Branch Forbes Rd exit. 813/752-1957. Hrs: 11:30 am-9:30 pm. Closed Mon; also Dec 24-25. A/C. Semi-a la carte. Dinner, $7-$12.50; serv plate, $3. Child's plates, $3-$3.75. Specialties: country ham, chicken pot pie, Florida lobster. Cr cds: D, MC, V.

FAMOUS 1776. (See Holiday Inn above.) 813/752-3141. Hrs: 6 am-11 pm. A/C. Bar; closed Sun. Semi-a la carte. Bkfst, $1.50-$5.50; lunch, $1.75-$5.95; dinner, $5.95-$16.95 up. Child's plates, senior citizens menu avail. Specialties: prime rib, Maine lobster, steak, fisherman's platter. Salad bar. Entertainment, dancing exc Sun. Cr cds: A, C, D, MC, V.

FOXFIRE. (Drawer AV.) On 98 at jct. I-4. 813/858-1481. Hrs: 5:30-2 am. Closed Sun, Easter, Dec 25. Reservation required. A/C. Bar. Dinner, $5.95-$15.95 up. Child's plates, $1 less. Specialties: steak, seafood, prime rib. Salad bar. Entertainment, dancing exc Sun. Cr cds: A, C, D, MC, V.

LAKE PLACID

HOLIDAY INN. (Box 180, Rte 3; 33852.) 4 mi S on 27, 2 mi N of FL 70. 813/465-3133. 100 A/C rms, 2 story. Mid-Jan-mid-Apr: S, $45-$60; D, $50-$65; each addl, $6; under 12 free; higher during Sebring races, (3-day min); rest of yr: varied lower rates. Color TV; free in-rm movies. Pool. Cafe, 7 am-2 pm. Bar, 11 am-2 am; entertainment, dancing exc Mon. Coin lndry. Cr cds: A, D, MC, V.

PLACID LAKES INN AND COUNTRY CLUB. 111 Club Rd Circle NW (33852). 4½ mi SW, 5 mi W of US 27. 813/465-4333. 68 A/C rms, 26 kits. Jan-Apr: S, D, $32-$37; each addl, $6; kit units $37; under 12 free; monthly rates, golf package plan; special events higher; lower rates rest of yr. Pool; lifeguard. Cafe, 7-9:30 am, 11:30 am-2:30 pm, 6-9 pm. Bar 11:30 am-midnight; entertainment, dancing wkends. Cr cds: A, C, D, MC, V.

LAKE WALES

LANTERN. (Box 45, Rte 6; 33853.) 3949 Hwy 27N, 3½ mi N on 27. 813/676-1387. 18 A/C rms, 2 kits. Feb-Apr: S, D, $35; each addl, $3; kit. units, wkly, $165-$195; rest of yr: lower rates. Color TV. Pool. Cafe, 8 am-9 pm; Sun to 7 pm. Bar, 11 am-midnight; entertainment Fri, Sat. Cr cds: A, D, MC, V.

LAUREL. 801 Hwy 27 S (33853), on 27, ¼ mi S of FL 60. 813/676-3317. 13 A/C rms, 3 mobile homes. Jan-Apr: S, $32.95; D, $35.95; mobile homes, $35; each addl, $2.50; rest of yr less. Color TV. Pool. Cafe opp, 7 am-9 pm. Coin lndry. Paddleboats. Private beach. Cr cds: C, D, MC, V.

SANDS. 830 Hwy 27S (33853), ½ mi S of FL 60. 813/676-3917. 20 A/C rms. S, $32-$40; D, $36-$50; each addl, $4; family rates avail off-season; rest of yr: varied lower rates. Color TV. Pool. Cafe, 7 am-8 pm. Beer. Cr cds: A, C, D, MC, V.

Restaurant

CHALET SUZANNE. (Drawer AC.) 4 mi N on 27. 813/676-6011. Hrs: 8 am-9:30 pm. Closed Mon, June-Nov. A/C. Continental menu. Bar. Table d'hôte. Bkfst, $4.25-$8.25; lunch, $16.50-$20.50; dinner, $32.95-$36.95; serv plate, 16%. Child's plates. Specialties: chicken Suzanne, lobster Newburg, homemade soups, baked grapefruit. Entertainment in season. Cr cds: A, C, D, MC, V.

LAKE WORTH

COUNTRY SQUIRE INN. 7859 Lake Worth Rd (33463), 7 mi W on FL 802 at FL tpke exit 36. 305/968-5000. 114 A/C rms, 2 story. Dec-mid-Apr: S, $46-$48; D, $48-$52; each addl, $6; under 18 free; family rates avail, rest of yr: varied lower rates. Color TV. Pool. Cafe, 6:30 am-10 pm. Bar; entertainment, dancing exc Sun. Coin lndry. Lighted tennis; pro. Cr cds: A, C, D, MC, V.

MARTINIQUE. 801 S Dixie Hwy (33460), 8 blks S on 1. 305/585-2502. 24 A/C rms, 1-2 story, 3 kits. Mid-Dec-Apr: S, D, $30-$50; each addl, $5; kit. units, $270-$280 wk; family rates avail; rest of yr: lower rates. Color TV. Pool. Cr cds: MC, V.

Restaurants

ALIVE & WELL. 612 Lake Ave, 2 blks off 1. 305/586-8344. Hrs: 11:30 am-2:30 pm, 5:30-9;30 pm; Sat, Sun 5:30-10 pm. Closed Mon, July 30-Nov. A/C. Bar. Semi-a la carte. Lunch, $3.25-$4.25; dinner, $5.75-$14.50. Child's plate half price. Specialties: spinach pie, stuffed shells.

KRISTINE'S. 1132 N Dixie Hwy, 12 blks N on 1. 305/582-1307. Hrs: 4:30-9 pm; Sun, 3:30-8:30 pm. Closed Mon; also Aug-Sep. A/C. French, Amer menu. Liquor, wine, beer. Dinner, semi-a la carte, $6.50-$10.50. Specialties: coq au vin, roast duckling. Salad bar.

LEESBURG

HOLIDAY INN. 1308 N 14 St (32748), 2 mi N on 27, 441. 904/787-1210. 130 A/C rms, 2 story. S, $36-$50; D, $44-$60; each addl, $6; under 18 free; Mod Amer plan, group, family rates avail. Color TV. Pool. Cafe, 6 am-2 pm, 5-10 pm. Bar; entertainment, dancing exc Sun. Coin lndry. Cr cds: A, C, D, MC, V.

MARATHON

HOLIDAY INN. (Box 186 33050.) On US 1 at mi marker 54. 904/289-0222. 134 A/C rms. 2 story. Dec-mid Apr: S, $63-$76; D, $69-$82; each addl, $5; family rates; sr citizen rates; varied lower rates rest of yr. Pool; wading pool, poolside serv. Cafe, 7 am-10 pm. Rm serv from 9 am. Bar; entertainment exc Sun. Coin lndry. Marina; dockage, boats, motors, charter boats. Cr cds: A, C, D, MC, V.

HOWARD JOHNSON'S. (Box T; 33050.) 2½ mi N on 1. 305/289-1400. 78 A/C rms, 2 story. Mid-Dec-Mar: S, D, $60-$80; each addl, $10; under 18 free; hols, more; rest of yr: varied lower rates. Color TV. Pool. Cafe open 24 hrs. Bar. Coin lndry. Dock. Cr cds: A, C, D, MC, V.

RUTTGER'S KEYS. (Box 3407, Marathon Shores 33052.) 3½ mi E, ½ mi S of 1 at Key Colony Beach. 305/289-0525. 53 A/C rms, 3 story. Late Dec-late Apr: S, D, $52-$58; each addl, $3; rest of yr: varied lower rates. Color TV. Pool. Cafe, 7-2 pm, 6-10 pm. Sand beach. Cr cds: MC, V.

Restaurants

PERRY'S. 6900 Overseas Hwy, at mi marker 51. 904/743-3108. Hrs: 11 am-11 pm. A/C. Service bar. Semi-a la carte: lunch, $2.50-$6.95, dinner, $6.95-$16.95. Child's plates. Specializes in seafood & steak. Salad bar. Background music. Large fish tank on premises. Cr cds: A, D, MC, V.

SOUTH SEAS SEAFOOD HOUSE. 1477 Overseas Hwy, ¾ mi N of 7 mi bridge on US 1. 305/743-5600. Hrs: 5-10 pm. Closed Sun off season, Dec 25; also Sep. A/C. Bar, 5 pm-midnight. Dinner, semi-a la carte, $9.95-$13.95. Specialties: flounder, seafood en casserole, seafood platter. Salad bar. Cr cds: A, MC, V.

MARCO ISLAND

MARCO VILLA GARDEN APTS. 475 Tallwood St (33937), 2 blks S of 953, 2 mi N of FL 92. 813/394-2611. 30 A/C kits. Early Jan-Mar: 2-4 person, $46-$60; each addl, $5; wkly rates avail; rest of yr: lower rates. Color TV. Pool. Cr cds: D, MC, V.

MARRIOTT'S MARCO BEACH HOTEL & VILLAS. (Box 178; 33937.) 400 Collier Blvd, ¼ mi S of FL 92. 813/394-2511. 740 A/C rms in hotel, 1-2 bedrm villas, 55 kits. Mid-Dec-mid-June: S, $125-$140; D, $140-$150; kit. units: 1-2 bedrm apt, $275-$400; 1-2 bedrm penthouses, $400-$600; villas to 4, $350-$375; each addl, $10; under 5 yrs free; Amer, Mod Amer plans avail; rest of yr: varied lower rates. Color TV. 3 pools. Cafe, 7 am-midnight. (also see MARCO DINING ROOM & QUINN'S). Bar; entertainment, dancing. Lighted tennis, instruction avail. Launching ramp; dockage; boats, sailboats, guides avail. Cr cds: A, C, D, MC, V.

Restaurants

MARCO DINING ROOM. (See Marriott's Marco Beach Hotel & Villas above.) 813/394-2511. Hrs: 6:30-10 pm. Reservation required. A/C. Continental, Amer menu. Bar. Wine list. Dinner, semi-a la carte, $15-$23. Child's plates. Specialties: rack of lamb, steak au poivre, Dover sole. Entertainment, dancing exc Sun. Jacket required. VOYAGER ROOM. Cr cds: A, C, D, MC, V.

O'SHEAS'. 1069 Jackson Ave, 2½ mi N of FL 92, adj to Marco Bay Yacht Club. 813/394-7531. Hrs: 11 am-3 pm, 5:30-10:30 pm. A/C. Bar. Semi-a la carte. Lunch, $6.95-$12.95, dinner, $9.95-$14.95; light dinner, $5.95-$7.50. Specialties: oysters, seafood, New England clam chowder. Entertainment, dancing exc Sun. Cr cds: MC, V.

QUINN'S. (See Marriott's Marco Beach Hotel & Villas above.) 813/394-2511. Hrs: 9 am-4 pm, 6-10 pm. A/C. Bar. Lunch, a la carte. $3.75-$6.50; dinner, semi-a la carte, $10-$15. Specialties: bouillabaisse, sirloin steak. Entertainment. Cr cds: A, C, D, MC, V.

MARIANNA

HOLIDAY INN. (Box 979; 32446.) 2 mi E on 90. 904/526-3251. 80 A/C rms, 2 story. S, $21-$24; D, $37-$45; under 18 free. Color TV. Pool. Cafe, 6 am-2 pm; 5-9 pm. Coin lndry. Cr cds: A, D, MC, V.

MARINELAND

QUALITY INN MARINELAND. (Box 122, Rte 1, St. Augustine 32084.) On FL A1A. 904/471-1222. 125 A/C rms, 2-5 story, Elvtrs. S, $36-$41; D, $38-$43; each addl, $5, under 16 free; sr citizen rates; wkly rates. Crib, cot $5. 2 pools; wading pool. Playground. Cafe, 7:30 am-9:30 pm. Bar. Ck-out 11 am. Coin lndry. On beach. Cr cds: A, C, D, MC, V.

MELBOURNE

BEST WESTERN HOST OF AMERICA. 420 S Harbor City Blvd (32901), 4 mi N on 1. 305/723-5320. 100 A/C rms, 2 story. Jan-Apr: S, $40-$50; D, $50-$55; each addl, $5; under 12 free. Easter, races higher; Amer plan, family, wkly group rates avail; rest of yr: lower rates. Color TV. Pool. Cafe, 6:30 am-11 pm. Bar; entertainment, dancing. Cr cds: A, C, D, MC, V.

HOLIDAY INN-MIDTOWN (formerly Holiday Inn-East). (Box 817; 32901.) 440 S Harbor City Blvd, 4 mi N on 1. 305/723-3661. 154 A/C rms, 2 story. Dec-May: S, $37-$44; D, $44-$51; each addl, $5; family rates avail; rest of yr: lower rates. Color TV. Pool. Cafe, 6 am-midnight; Sat, Sun to 1 am. Bar; entertainment, dancing. Coin lndry. One of chain. Cr cds: A, C, D, MC, V.

RAMADA INN. (Box 1268.) 964 S Harbor City Blvd (32901), ½ mi N on 1. 305/724-4422. 122 A/C rms, 6 story. S, $36-$42; D, $44-$51; each addl, $8; under 18 free; suites, $50-$70. Color TV. Pool. Cafe, 6:30 am-9;30 pm; wkends from 7:30 am-9:30 pm. Bar; entertainment, exc Sun; dancing. Cr cds: A, C, D, MC, V.

Restaurants

POOR RICHARD'S INN. 522 Ocean Ave, Melbourne Beach. 2 mi S of FL 192, 3 blks E of FL A1A. 305/723-6659. Hrs: 6-10:30 pm. Reservation required. A/C. Bar; piano bar. Dinner, semi-a la carte, $10.95-$15.95. Specialties: prime rib, filet mignon, fresh grouper. Entertainment Tu-Sat. Restored 1889 home. Cr cds: A, MC, V.

STEAK HOUSE OF MELBOURNE BEACH. 903 Oak St. 2 mi S of US 192 on Oak St (FL A1A). 305/723-6659. Hrs: 11 am-11 pm; Sat from 4 pm; Sun noon-10 pm. Closed lunch Sat, hols. A/C. Bar. Wine list. Semi-a la carte: lunch, $3.50-$9.95; dinner, $7.95-$18.95; discount on dinner 4-6 pm. Child's plates $3.95-$5.95. Specializes in Pompano en papilotte, Delmonico prime rib. Background music. Cr cds: A, MC, V.

MIAMI

COCONUT GROVE. 2649 S Bayshore Dr (33133), 5 mi S. 305/858-2500; res: 800/327-8771. 144 A/C rms, 56 suites; S, $85-$105; D, $90-$115; each addl, $5; under 12 free; rest of yr: lower rates. Color TV. Pool. Cafe. Bars, 11-3 am; entertainment, dancing exc Sun. Coin lndry. Lighted tennis; pro. Cr cds: A, C, D, MC, V.

DUPONT PLAZA. 300 Biscayne Blvd Way (33131), ½ blk E of 1. 305/358-2541; res: 800/327-3480. 295 A/C rms, 8 kits. Dec-Apr: S, $68; D, $79; each addl, $10; under 12 free; rest of yr: lower rates. Color TV. Pool. Cafe, 7 am-10 pm. Bar; entertainment exc Sun. Dock; on Biscayne Bay. Cr cds: A, C, D, MC, V.

EVERGLADES. (Box 013621, 33101.) 244 Biscayne Blvd, at 3d St; ¼ mi NE on US 1, 305/379-5461; res: 800/527-5700. 371 A/C rms. Dec-Apr: S, $73; D, $81; each addl, $10; under 17 free; lower rates rest of yr. Crib free, cot $10. Rooftop pool. Cafe 7 am-10:30 pm. Bar; pianist, dancing Fri-Sun in season. Cr cds: A, C, D, MC, V.

HOLIDAY INN. 2500 Brickell Ave (33129), 2 mi S on 1. 305/854-2070. 54 A/C rms, 3 story. Mid-Dec-Apr: D, $52.60-$54.60; each addl, $10.50; under 12 free; wkly rates avail; rest of yr: varied lower rates. Color TV. Pool. Cafe, 7 am-3 pm, 5:30-10 pm. Bar, 11-3 am; entertainment, dancing exc Sun, Mon. Cr cds: A, D, MC, V.

HOLIDAY INN-BISCAYNE. 11190 Biscayne Blvd (33161) at 112 St, 9 mi N on 1, I-95 exit 125 St. 305/893-4110. 276 A/C rms, 5 story. Mid-Dec-mid-Apr: S, $47; D, $55; each addl, $10; family rates avail; rest of yr: varied lower rates. Color TV. Pool. Cafe, 7 am-11 pm. Bar, 11 am-2 am; entertainment, dancing exc Mon. Coin lndry. Cr cds: A, C, D, MC, V.

HOLIDAY INN-CALDER RACE COURSE. 21485 NW 27th Ave (33055), jct 27, FL Tpke exit 4. 305/621-5801. 210 A/C rms, 8 story, 16 kits. Dec-late Apr: S, $48-$63; D, $54-$69; each addl, $4; kit. units, $50-$60; under 18 free; rest of yr: varied lower rates. Color TV. Pool; sauna. Cafe, 7-11 pm, Bar; entertainment, dancing exc Sun. Coin lndry. Cr cds: A, D, MC, V.

HOLIDAY INN-CIVIC CENTER. 1170 NW 11 St (33136) at NW 11 Pl, 2 blks S of FL 836 Civic Center exit. 305/324-0800. 182 A/C rms, 8 story. Late Dec-Apr: S, $49-$53; D, $53-$57; each addl, $4; family plan avail; rest of yr: lower rates. Color TV. Pool. Cafe, 7 am-11 pm. Bar; entertainment, dancing. Coin lndry. Cr cds: A, C, D, MC, V.

ACCOMMODATIONS & RESTAURANTS 137

HOLIDAY INN-CUTLER RIDGE. 10779 SW 200th St (33157), 1½ blks W of 1 at Caribbean Blvd. 305/253-9960. 100 A/C rms, 6 story. Dec-Apr: S, $34.50-$45.50; D, $42.50-$65.50; under 18 free; boat show, special events higher; rest of yr: lower rates. Color TV. Pool. Cafe, 7 am-2 pm, 5:30-10:30 pm. Bar; entertainment, dancing exc Sun. One of chain. Cr cds: A, D, MC, V.

HOWARD JOHNSON'S-BROAD CAUSEWAY. 12210 Biscayne Blvd (33181). At 123 St, 10 mi N on 1. 305/891-7350. 100 A/C rms, 4 story. Mid-Dec-late Apr: S, $45; D, $50-$55; each addl, $8; under 18 free; rest of yr: lower rates. Color TV. Pool. Cafe open 7 am-midnight. Bar. Coin lndry opp. Cr cds: A, C, D, MC, V.

HOWARD JOHNSON'S-GOLDEN GLADES. (16500 NW 2 Ave, N Miami 33169.) 8 mi N on FL 826, 1 blk E of jct I-95. 305/945-2621. 256 A/C rms, 2-4 story. Mid-Dec-Apr: S, $50-$60; D, $65-$75; each addl, $8; under 18 free; rest of yr: lower rates. Color TV. 2 pools. Cafe open 24 hrs. Bar; entertainment, dancing. Cr cds: A, C, D, MC, V.

HOWARD JOHNSON'S-MIDTOWN. 1100 Biscayne Blvd (33132), ½ mi N at jct 1, FL 836. 305/358-3080. 115 A/C rms, 7 story. Mid-Dec-Apr: S, $68; D, $69-$75; each addl, $8; under 18 free; rest of yr: varied lower rates. Color TV. Rooftop pool. Cafe, 6 am-midnight. Bar, noon-1 am. Cr cds: A, C, D, MC, V.

HOWARD JOHNSON'S-PLAZA. 200 SE 2 Ave (33131), just off I-95. 305/374-3000. 256 A/C rms, 1 kit. Mid-Dec-Mar: S, $80; D, $90; each addl, $8; under 18 free; special events higher; rest of yr: lower rates. Color TV. Pool. Cafe 6 am-midnight, Fri, Sat to 1 am. Bar; entertainment, dancing exc Mon. Cr cds: A, C, D, MC, V.

MARRIOTT AIRPORT. 1201 NW Le Jeune Rd (33126). 4 mi NW. 305/649-5000. 799 A/C rms. Dec-May: S, $80-$100; D, $90-$110; each addl $8; studio rms, suites, family rates avail; rest of yr: varied lower rates. Color TV. Pool. Cafe open 24 hrs; dining rm (see KING'S WHARF). Bars, 5 pm-2 am; entertainment, dancing exc Sun. Lighted tennis; pro. Cr cds: A, C, D, MC, V.

MIAMI LAKES INN & COUNTRY CLUB. NW 154 St (33014), 15 mi NW, 1 blk E of FL 826. 305/821-1150. 102 A/C rms, 5 kits. Mid-Jan-mid-Apr: S, $65; D, $75; one addl, $12; under 12 free; golf package plans avail; rest of yr: varied lower rates. Color TV. Pool. Cafes, 7 am-2:30 pm, 6-11pm. Bar, 11-1 am; entertainment, dancing exc Mon. Golf. Lighted tennis; handball; racquetball. Cr cds: A, C, MC, V.

OMNI INTERNATIONAL. Biscayne Blvd at 16th St (33132), 4 blks N on Biscayne Blvd, 4 blks N of I-95. 305/374-0000. 556 A/C rms. Mid-Dec-mid-Apr: S, $70-$130; D, $130-$145; each addl, $20; under 12 free; rest of yr: lower rates. Color TV. Rooftop pool. Cafe, 7 am-11 pm (also see MAISON). Bar; entertainment, dancing. Lighted tennis; pro. Cr cds: A, C, D, MC, V.

SHERATON RIVER HOUSE. 3900 NW 21 St (33142) 5 mi N at Int'l Airport. 305/871-3800. 408 A/C rms, 10 story. Sept-Apr: S, $85-$105; D, $90-$125; each addl, $8; rest of yr: lower rates. Color TV. Pool. Cafe, 7 am-11 pm (also see DAPHNE'S). Bar, 11-2 am; entertainment, dancing exc Sun. Lighted tennis; pro. Golf. Cr cds: A, C, D, MC, V.

Restaurants

CAFE CHAUVERON. (9561 E Bay Harbor Dr, Bay Harbor Island.) 7½ mi N. 305/866-8779. Hrs: 5:30-10:30 pm. Reservation required. Closed June-Nov 1. French menu. Bar. Wine cellar. Dinner, a la carte entrees, $15.50-$42.50. Specialties: bouillabaisse a la marseillaise, chicken in champagne cream, veal escalopine, sweetbreads with chestnuts. View of bay. Jacket required. Cr cds: A, C, D, MC, V.

CENTRO VASCO. 2235 SW 8 St, 2 mi N on 41. 305/643-9606. Hrs: noon-midnight. A/C. Spanish, Amer menu. Bar. Semi-a la carte. Lunch, $6-$16; dinner, $4.50-$15.50; serv plate, $1. Child's plates half price. Specialties: seafood à la Basque, filet madrilène, angulas. Cr cds: A, D, MC, V.

DAPHNE'S. (See Sheraton River House above.) 305/871-3800. Hrs: 7-2 am. Reservation required. A/C. Bar. Semi-a la carte. Bkfst, $3.50-$5.75; lunch, $4.25-$7.95; dinner, $9.25-$20. Specialties: baby back ribs, chocolate mousse pie. Entertainment, dancing. Cr cds: A, C, D, MC, V.

KALEIDOSCOPE. (3112 Commodore Plaza, Coconut Grove.) 305/446-5010. Hrs: 11:30-3 pm, 6-11 pm; Fri, Sat, to midnight; Sun brunch, noon-3 pm. A/C Serv bar. Continental menu. Semi-a la carte: lunch, $4.50-$7.95; dinner, $7.95-$14.95. Specialties: chicken breast Kaleidoscope, Veal paprika, toast Hawaii. Own pastries. Background music, strolling guitarist. Outdoor dining. European cafe interior. Cr cds: A, C, D, MC, V.

KING'S WHARF. (See Marriott Hotel above.) 305/649-5000. Hrs: 11:30 am-2:30 pm, 6-10:30 pm; Fri, Sat to 12:30 am. A/C. Bar. Lunch, $4.25-$10.95; dinner, semi-a la carte, $7.95-$19. Specialties: rib roast veal Oscar, Salad bar. Entertainment, dancing. Cr cds: A, C, D, MC, V.

LA BELLE EPOQUE. (1045 95th St, Bay Harbor Island.) 7 mi N. 305/865-6011. Hrs: 5:30-11 pm. Closed Sun in summer. Reservation recommended. A/C. French menu. Bar. Dinner, semi-a la carte, $20-$28. Specialties: scampis Provençales, escargots bourguignons, poulet Josephine en croute. Jacket required. Cr cds: A, D, MC, V.

LA PALOMA. 10999 Biscayne Blvd. 7 mi N on US 1. 305/891-0505. Hrs: 5 pm-midnight. Closed Sep. Res required. A/C. Continental menu. Bar; piano bar. Wine cellar (dining by res). Semi-a la carte: dinner, $8.75-$13.95. Specializes in scampi, veal. Background music; pianist. Jacket requested. Cr cds: A, C, D, MC, V.

MAISON. (See Omni International Hotel above.) 305/374-0000. Hrs: 6:30-11:30 pm. Closed Sun. Reservation recommended. A/C. Continental menu. Bar. Dinner, $14.50-$20. Specialties: rack of lamb, duckling roti au poivre, roast sirloin. Jacket required. Cr cds: A, C, D, MC, V.

PRINCE HAMLET INN. 8301 Biscayne Blvd. 305/754-4400. Hrs: 11 am-2 pm, 5-10 pm; Sat to 10:30 pm; Sun brunch, 11 am-2 pm; off season, 11:45 am-2:30 pm, 6-10 pm. Closed Rosh Hashanah, Yom Kippur, Dec 24. A/C. Danish, Amer menu. Bar. Table d'hôte. Lunch, dinner, $9.95-$23.95; Sun brunch, $10.55. Specialties: duck Danoise, veal Oscar, bouillabaise Copenhagen. Complimentary cold table. Cr cd: A.

RAIMONDO. 201 NW 79 St, 5½ mi N, 5 blks E of I-95. 305/636-9355. Hrs: 6-11 pm. Reservation required. Closed Jan 1, Easter, Thanksgiving, Dec 25. A/C. Italian menu. Wine, beer. A la carte entrees, $10-$40. Specialties: zuppa di pesce alla Peppino, spaghetti carbonara, steak Diane. Advance notice required for special dishes.

TIBERIO. (9700 Collins Ave, Bal Harbour.) In Bal Harbour shopping mall. 305/861-6161. Hrs: noon-3 pm, 6-11 pm; Fri, Sat, to 11:30 pm; Sun, 6-11:30 pm. Res recommended. A/C Northern Italian menu. Bar. A la carte: lunch, $3.95-$11.95; dinner, $16.95-$24.50. Specializes in homemade pasta. Cr cds: A, C, D, MC, V.

MIAMI BEACH

ATLANTIC TOWERS. 4201 Collins Ave (33140). 2 mi N on FL A1A. 305/534-4751; res: 800/327-4735. 166 air-cooled rms, 28 kits. Mid-Dec-mid-Apr; S, $20-$22; D, $26-$28; each addl, $6; Mod Amer plan; kit units, $31; under 10 free; lower rates rest of yr. Saltwater pool. Cafe, 7 am-noon, 5:30-9 pm. Bar. Coin lndry. Cr cds: A, C, D, MC, V.

BEST WESTERN BEAU RIVAGE. (9955 Collins Ave, Bal Harbour 33154.) 7½ mi N on FL A1A. 305/865-8611. 295 A/C units, 4 story, 140 kits. Late Jan-mid-Mar: S, D, $69-$90; each addl, $8; studio rms $69-$90; kit units, $8 addl; Mod Amer plan, $17.50/person; family rates; lower rates rest of yr. TV; free in-rm movies. Pool; wading pool. Cafe, 7:30 am-11 pm; dining rm, 5:30-9 pm. Bars; entertainment, dancing exc Mon. Cr cds: A, C, D, MC, V.

CHATEAU. 19115 Collins Ave (33160). 14 mi N on FL A1A. 305/931-8800. 164 A/C rms, 2-4 story; 77 kits. Mid-Dec-early Jan, Feb-mid-Apr: S, $38-$68; under 12 free; each addl, kit units, $6 more; rest of yr: lower rates. Color TV. Pool; wading pool. Cafe, 8 am-5 pm. Bar; entertainment, dancing. Coin lndry. On ocean. Cr cds: A, D, MC, V.

COLONIAL INN. 18101 Collins Ave (33154). 13 mi N on FL A1A. 305/932-1212. 300 air-cooled rms, 2-3 story, 77 kits. Mid-Dec-mid-Apr: S, D, $50-$67; each addl, $5; studio rms with kit, $5 addl; lower rates rest of yr. Pool; wading pool. Cafe, 7:30 am-8:30 pm; also dining rm, noon-2 am; entertainment, dancing exc Mon. Coin lndry. Cr cds: A, C, D, MC, V.

DEAUVILLE. 6701 Collins Ave (33141), 2½ mi N of I-195 on FL A1A. 305/865-8511. 500 air-cooled rms. Mid-Dec-Mar: S, D, $86-$106; each addl, $14; modified Amer plan, each addl, $19; rest of yr: lower rates. Color TV. Saltwater pool; wading pool. Cafe, 7 am-10 pm; dining rm, 5:30-10 pm. Bars; entertainment, dancing. Tennis; pro. On ocean. Cr cds: A, C, D, MC, V.

DI LIDO. 155 Lincoln Rd (33139), 1 blk E on FL A1A. 305/538-0811. 350 air-cooled rms, 53 kits. Mid-Dec-Apr: S, $48-$66; D, $50-$68; 1st addl, $6, 2nd addl free; family rates avail; rest of yr: lower rates. Color TV. Olympic-size pool. Cafe, 7:30 am-11 pm. Bars; entertainment; dancing Wed, Fri, Sat. Coin lndry. On ocean. Cr cds: A, D, MC, V.

DORAL-ON-THE-OCEAN. 4833 Collins Ave (33140), 2¾ mi N on FL A1A. 305/532-3600; res: 800/327-6334. 420 A/C rms. Mid-Dec-Apr: S, D, $120-$134; one addl, $20; suites, $145-$400; golf package plan avail; rest of yr: lower rates. Color TV. Pool; wading pool. Cafe, 7-1:30 am; rooftop dinning rm, 7 pm-midnight. Bar. On ocean. Cr cds: A, C, D, MC, V.

EDEN ROC. 4525 Collins Ave (33140), ¼ mi N of I-95 on FL A1A. 305/532-2561; res: 800/327-8337. 350 A/C rms, 10 kits. Mid-Dec-Apr: S, D, $95-$135; each addl, $12; suites, $160-$450; under 6 free; rest of yr: lower rates. Color TV. Pool. Cafe, 7 am-11 pm. Bar. Coin lndry. Health club; solarium; sauna. Soc dir. On ocean. Cr cds: A, C, D, MC, V.

HAWAIIAN ISLE. 17601 Collins Ave (33160), 12 mi N of FL 826 on FL A1A. 305/932-2121; res: 800/327-5275. 210 A/C rms, 2 story, 72 kits. Mid-Dec-mid-Apr: S, D, $41-$64; each addl, $7; kit units, $49-$72; rest of yr: lower rates. Color TV. 2 pools; 2 wading pools. Cafe, 7:30 am-11 pm. Bar; entertainment, dancing. Coin lndry. Tennis. On ocean. Cr cds: A, C, D, MC, V.

HILTON-FONTAINBLEAU. 4441 Collins Ave. (33140). 2½ mi N on FL A1A. 305/538-2000. 1,224

138 ACCOMMODATIONS & RESTAURANTS

A/C units. Dec-Apr: S, D, $115-$175; each addl $15; suites $255-$525; children free; package plans; lower rates rest of yr. Color TV; in-rm movies. ½ acre lagoon pool; whirlpools. Cafe, 7-2 am; dining rms, 6 pm-2 am. Bars; entertainment, dancing. Dockage. Catamarans, windsurfing. Cr cds: A, C, D, MC, V.

HOLIDAY INN. 8701 Collins Ave (33154), 7½ mi N on FL A1A. 305/866-5731. 216 A/C rms. Mid-Dec-Apr: S, $56-$92; D, $61-$99; each addl, $8; family rates avail; rest of yr: lower rates. Parking free. Color TV. Pool. Cafes, 7 am-10 pm. Bar. On ocean. Cr cds: A, C, D, MC, V.

HOLIDAY INN-CONVENTION CENTER. 2201 Collins Ave (33139), ½ mi N on FL A1A. 305/534-1511. 351 A/C rms, 3-12 story. Mid-Dec-Apr: S, $63; D, $72; each addl, $8; family rates, suites avail; rest of yr: lower rates. Color TV. Pool. Cafe, 7 am-10:30 pm. Bar; entertainment (in season), dancing exc Mon. Coin lndry. On ocean. Cr cds: A, C, D, MC, V.

HOLIDAY INN-SUNNY ISLES. 18001 Collins Ave (33160). 12¾ mi N on FL A1A. 305/932-1800. 115 A/C units, 3 story. Mid-Dec-Apr: S, $50-$60; D, $55-$65; each addl, $6; under 18 free; lower rates rest of yr. Color TV. Pool. Cafe, 7 am-2 pm, 6-10 pm. Bar 6 pm-2 am. Coin lndry. Cr cds: A, C, D, MC, V.

HOTEL PULITZER. 4000 Alton Rd (33140), at E end of I-195. 305/532-4411. 137 air-cooled rms, 8 story. Elvtrs. Mid-Dec-Apr: S, $66; D, $74; each addl, $8; studios, $90; suites, $170; under 5 free; lower rates rest of yr. Color TV. Pool; wading pool. Cafe, 7 am-midnight. Rm serv, 7 am-10 pm. Rooftop bar, 11:30-2 am; entertainment in season exc Mon. Cr cds: A, C, D, MC, V.

MARCO POLO RESORT. 19201 Collins Ave (33160), 14 mi N on FL A1A. 305/932-2233; res: 800/327-6363. 509 A/C rms, 269 kits. Mid-Dec-mid-Apr: S, D, $60-$90; each addl, $8; kit units, $76-$85; family rates avail; rest of yr: lower rates. Color TV. Pool; wading pool. Cafe, 7 am-midnight. dining rm, 5-10 pm. Bar; entertainment, dancing. Coin lndry. On ocean. Cr cds: A, C, D, MC, V.

MONACO. 17501 Collins Ave (33160), 12 mi N on FL A1A. 305/932-2100. 113 A/C rms, 2 story, 39 kits. Mid-Dec-mid-Apr: S, D, $43-$66; each addl, $7; kit units, $7 more; modified Amer plan avail; rest of yr: varied lower rates. Color TV. Pool; wading pool. Cafe, 7:30 am-9 pm. Bar; entertainment, dancing exc Mon. Coin lndry. On ocean. Cr cds: A, C, D, MC, V.

NEWPORT. (Box 6646, Bal Harbour 33154.) 16701 Collins Ave at jct FL A1A, 826. 305/949-1300; res: 800/327-5476. 355 A/C rms, 10 story. Elvtr. Mid-Dec-mid-Apr: S, D, $73-$98; each addl, $12; lower rates rest of yr. Color TV. 2 pools; wading pool. Cafe, 7 am-4:30 pm; dining rm, 5-11 pm. Bars; entertainment nightly, some dancing. Coin lndry. Cr cds: A, MC, V.

OCEAN ROC. 19505 Collins Ave (33160), 14 mi N on FL A1A. 305/931-7600; res: 800/327-0553. 95 air-cooled rms, 3 story, 25 kits. Mid-Dec-late-Apr: S, D, $44-$52; each addl, $6; kit., $6 more; under 10 free; rest of yr: lower rates. Color TV. Pool; wading pool. Cafe, 8 am-7:30 pm. Coin lndry. On ocean. Cr cds: A, C, D, MC, V.

PAN AMERICAN. 17875 Collins Ave (33160), 12½ mi N on FL A1A. 305/932-1100. 146 air-cooled rms, 2-3 story, 45 kits. Mid-Nov-Apr: S, D, $108-$198; each addl, $5; kit., $5 more; rest of yr: lower rates. Color TV. Large pool. Cafe, dining rm, 7 am-midnight. Bar, 11-2 am; entertainment, dancing exc Mon. Coin lndry. On ocean. Cr cds: A, MC, V.

SEA VIEW. (9909 Collins Ave, Bal Harbour 33154.) 5 mi N on FL A1A. 305/866-441. 128 A/C rms. 13 kits. Mid-Dec-late Apr: S, D, $78-$145; each addl, $12; kit units, $6 addl; lower rates rest of yr. Color TV. Pool. Cafe 7:30 am-4 pm; dining rm, 6-10 pm (closed Mon & Tu in summer). Bar; entertainment, dancing. Cr cds: A, C, MC, V

SEVILLE. 2901 Collins Ave (33140), 1 mi N on FL A1A. 305/532-2511; res: 800/327-1641. 279 air-cooled rms. Mid-Dec-mid-May: S, $58-$60; D, $60-$68; 3d person $6; modified Amer plan avail; rest of yr: lower rates. Color TV. Pool; wading pool. Cafe, 24 hours. Bar. Some balconies. On ocean. Cr cds: A, D, MC, V.

SINGAPORE. (9601 Collins Ave, Bal Harbour 33154) 7 mi N on FL A1A. 305/865-9931; res: 800/327-4911. 238 A/C units, 7 story, 109 kits. Mid-Dec-late-Apr: S, D, $46-$80; each addl, $5; kit. units $4 more; modified Amer plan avail: $12 more each, under 10, $6.50; rest of yr: varied lower rates. Color TV. Cafe, 8 am-3 pm; dining rm, 5-8:30 pm. Bar; entertainment, dancing exc Mon. Coin lndry. On ocean. Cr cds: A, C, D, MC, V.

THUNDERBIRD. 18401 Collins Ave (33160), 13 mi N on FL A1A. 305/931-7700; res: 800/327-2044 or 2045. 176 air-cooled units, 5 story, 90 kits. Mid-Dec-late-Apr: S, D, $68-$89; each addl, $8; kit., $6 more; rest of yr: lower rates. Color TV. Large saltwater pool; wading pool. Cafe, 7:30 am-10 pm (also see CHRISTINE LEE'S GASLIGHT). Bar. Coin lndry. Tennis; pro. On ocean.

Restaurants

CHRISTINE LEE'S GASLIGHT. (See Thunderbird Motel above) 305/931-7700. Hrs: 5 pm-3 am. A/C. Chinese, Amer menu. Bar. Dinner, semi-a la carte, $9.95-$17.50 up. Specialties: Chinese steak, Mandarin lemon chicken. Cr cds: A, D, MC, V.

THE DINING GALLERIES. (On grounds of Hilton-Fountainbleau.) 305/538-2000. Hrs: 6 pm-1 am; Oct-May, Mon-Fri, 11 am-2 pm; Sun, 10 am-3 pm, 6 pm-midnight. Res recommended. A/C. Bar. Wine list. A la carte: dinner, $14-$18.50. Table d'hote: Sun brunch, $18.50. Child's plates. Specialties: veal Romanoff, pompano with crab. Entertainment, dancing. Jacket requested. Cr cds: A, C, D, MC, V.

THE FORGE. 432 Arthur Godfrey Rd, 2½ mi N, 3 blks W of FL A1A. 305/538-8533. Hrs: 6 pm-2:30 am. A/C. Bar. Wine cellar. Continental menu. Dinner, semi-a la carte, $12.95-$19.95 up; Specialties: steak Java, veal O.J., Forge Blacksmith pie. Cr cds: A, C, D, MC, V.

MASA-SAN. 19355 NW 2d St. 25 mi N, I-95N to exit 441N (18). 305/651-7782. Hrs: 11:30 am-2:30 pm, 5-11 pm; Sun, 5-10 pm. Closed Sat, Sun lunch, Dec 25. A/C. Japanese menu. Wine, beer. A la carte: lunch, $3.25-$6.95; dinner, $7.95-$17.95. Specializes in sushi bar, tempura, teriyaki. Background music. Cr cds: A, MC, V.

RONEY PUB. 2301 Collins Ave. ½ mi N of FL A1A. 305/532-3353. Hrs: 5-11 pm. Fri, Sat, to 10:45 pm. A/C. Bar. Semi-a la carte: dinner, $6.25-$19.95. Serv plate, $1.55. Specializes in steak, barbequed ribs, cheesecake. Background music. Cr cds: A, C, D, MC, V.

MOUNT DORA

MT DORA MOTOR LODGE. (Box 406; 32757.) ½ mi N on 441, 1 mi E of FL 19. 904/383-2181. 50 A/C rms, 1-2 story. Dec-Apr: S, $30-$35; D, $35-$45; each addl, $5; under 12 free with family; rest of yr: lower rates. Color TV. Pool. Cafe. Bar; entertainment Thurs, Sat, Sun. Cr cds: MC, V.

Restaurant

CAPT APPLEBY'S. (Box 1245). 1 mi N on FL 441. 904/383-6662. Hrs: 11:30 am-9:30 pm; Sat, from 4:30 pm; Sun, to 8:30 pm. Closed Thanksgiving, Dec. 25. A/C. Bar. Semi-a la carte: lunch, $2.29-$8; dinner, $5.30-$13. Child's plates. Specializes in seafood, prime rib. Salad bar. Background music. Bake shop. Cr cds: A, MC, V.

NAPLES

BEST WESTERN BUCCANEER. (Box 1616, 33940.) 2329 Tamiami Trail, 2 mi N on US 41. 813-261-1148. 110 A/C kit. units, 2-3 story. Feb-mid-Apr; S, D, $75-$90; each addl, $6; children free; lower rates rest of yr. Color TV; in-rm movies. Pool. Cafe, 7 am-2 pm, 4:30 pm-8 pm. Cr cds: A, C, D, MC, V.

DUTCHESS MOTOR LODGE. 9853 Tamiami Trail N (33940), 8 mi N on 41. 813/597-3533. 19 A/C rms, 10 kits. Mid-Dec-mid-Apr: S, D, $26.50-$34.50; each addl, $5; kit. units, $36-$42; rest of yr: lower rates. Color TV. Pool. Coin lndry. Cr cds: A, D, MC, V.

RAMADA INN. 11000 Gulf Shore Dr. N, (33940). 1 mi W of US 41 at Vanderbilt Beach. 813/597-3151. 148 A/C units, 2 story, 16 kits. Mid-Dec-Apr: S, D, $80; kit. units, $98; under 18 free; sr citizen rates; lower rates rest of yr. Color TV. Pool; wading pool; poolside bar. Cafe, 7:30 am-4 pm, 5-9 pm. Bar; entertainment, dancing exc Mon. Coin lndry. Cr cds: A, C, D, MC, V.

THE TIDES. 1801 Gulf Shore Blvd N (33940). 1 mi W of US 41. 813/262-6196. 36 A/C units, 24 kits, 2 story. Mid-Nov-Apr: S, D, $50-$69; 1 bedrm suites, $101-$140; 2 bedrm suites, $152-$205; kit units, $68-$94; under 3 free; lower rates rest of yr. Color TV. Pool. Free coffee, continental bkfst in season. Cr cds: MC, V.

Restaurants

THE PEWTER MUG. 14120 N Tamiami Trail, 9 mi N on 41. 813/597-3017. Hrs: 5-10 pm; Fri, Sat, 5-11 pm. Closed major hols. Reservation recommended. A/C. Bar. Semi-a la carte. Dinner, $6.95-$14.95. Child's plates. Specialties: beef, prime rib. Salad bar. Cr cds: A, D, MC, V.

PICCADILLY PUB. 625 5 Ave S, 3 blks W of 41. 813/262-7521. Hrs: 11:30 am-3:30 pm, 5:30-9:30 pm. Closed Sun, Jan 1, Thanksgiving, Dec 25. A/C. Bar. A la carte, lunch, $2.75-$7.50 up; semi-a la carte, dinner, $9.50-$14.75 up. Specialties: conch chowder, steaks, almond fried shrimp. Jacket required in main dining rm only. Cr cds: A, MC, V.

NEW PORT RICHEY

DAYS INN. (Box 1898, Port Richey 33568) 4 mi N on 19. 813/863-1502. 157 A/C rms, 2 story, 35 kits. Jan-late Apr: S, $30; D, $37-$39.88; each addl, $3; kit units, $49-$51.88; under 18, $1; rest of yr: lower rates. Color TV. Pool. Cafe, 6 am-10 pm. Coin lndry. Cr cds: A, D, MC, V.

HOLIDAY INN. 5015 US 19 N (33552). 813/849-8551. 135 A/C rms, 2 story. Late Dec-late Apr: S, D, $43-$50; each addl, $4; under 12 free; rest of yr: lower rates. Color TV. Pool; wading pool. Cafe, 7 am-2:30 pm, 5-10 pm. Bar, 11-midnight; entertainment Tu-Sat. Coin lndry adj. Cr cds: A, C, D, MC, V.

Restaurants

SEAPORT INN. 11217 Hwy 19 N at Port Ritchey ½

mi S of FL 52. 813/863-5402. Hrs: 5-10 pm; Fri, Sat to 11 pm; Sun, 4-10 pm. Closed Mon. A/C. Bar. Continental menu. Dinner, semi-a la carte, $9.75-$15.95 up; serv plate, $1. Specialties: bouillabaisse, four course gourmet dinner. Cr cds.: A, C, D, MC, V.

NEW SMYRNA BEACH

BEST WESTERN ISLANDER BEACH LODGE. 1601 S Atlantic Ave (32069). 904/427-3452. 150 A/C units, 7 story, 75 kits. Feb-Easter, Memorial Day-Labor Day: S, D, $34-$70; each addl, $6, kit units, $44-$76; suites, $46-$78; under 18 free; special events higher (5 day min); group, monthly, wkly rates avail; rest of yr: lower rates. Color TV. Olympic-size pool; wading pool. Cafe, 7 am-2:30 pm, 5-11 pm. Bar; entertainment, dancing. Coin lndry. On beach. Cr cds: A, C, D, MC, V.

SMYRNA. 1050 N Dixie Frwy (32069), 1½ mi N on 1. 904/428-2495. 10 A/C rms. Mid-Dec-mid-Apr: S, $18; D, $22-$24; each addl, $3; racing events higher; rest of yr: lower rates. Color TV. Cafe opp, 5 am-midnight. Cr cds: MC, V.

OCALA

BEST WESTERN SOUTHERN HOST. 3520 SW Broadway (32670), 3 mi W on FL 40, 4 blks E of I-75. 904/629-7961. 38 A/C rms. S, $21; D, $25; each addl, $2. Color TV. Pool. Cafe adj, 6:30 am-10 pm. Cr cds: A, C, D, MC, V.

DAVIS BROS. 3924 SW Broadway (32670), 3 mi W on FL 40 at I-75. 904/629-8794. 96 A/C rms, 2 story. Jan-Apr, June-Labor Day: S, $24; D, $32-$38; each addl, $3; under 12 free; rest of yr: lower rates. Color TV. Pool; wading pool. Cafe, 7 am-8 pm; Coin lndry. Cr cds: A, C, D, MC, V.

DAYS INN. 4040 SW Broadway (32670), ¼ mi W on FL 40 at jct I-75. 904/629-8850. 140 A/C rms, 2 story. Summer, S, $26; D, $33; each addl, $4; under 18, $1; lower rates rest of yr. Color TV. Pool. Cafe open 24 hrs. Cr cds: A, D, MC, V.

FAIRWAYS. 2829 NE Silver Springs Blvd (32670), 2½ mi NE on FL 40. 904/622-7503. 26 A/C rms. S, $20; D, $20-$24; each addl, $3. Color TV. Pool. Cr cds: A, C, D, MC, V.

FRENCH COURT. 2425 E Silver Springs Blvd (32670), 2 mi E on FL 40. 904/732-3146. 23 A/C rms, 1-2 story. S, D, $20-$26; each addl, $3. Color TV. Pool. Coin lndry. Cr cds: A, C, D, MC, V.

OCALA TRAVELODGE. 1626 SW Pine St, (32670). 1 mi S on US 27, 301, 441. 904/622-4121. 68 A/C rms, 2 story. S, $24-$26; D, $31-$34; each addl, $4; under 16 free; sr cit rates. Color TV. Pool. Free coffee in rms. Cafe open 24 hrs. Cr cds: A, C, D, MC, V.

Restaurants

1890 BEEF HOUSE. 917 E Silver Springs Blvd, 9 blks E on FL 40. 904/629-2000. Hrs: 5-10 pm. Closed Sun, Jan 1, Thanksgiving, Dec 24 and 25. A/C. Bar. Dinner, semi-a la carte, $5.95-$13.95, also sandwiches; serv plate, $1. Specialties: prime rib, fried grouper, steak. Cr cds: A, D, MC, V.

MORRISON'S. 1602 E Silver Springs Blvd, 16 blks W on FL 40, 3 mi W of I-75. 904/622-7447. Hrs: 11 am-8 pm. A/C. Avg ck: lunch, $5; dinner, $6.50. Specialties: beef, custard pie.

PETER DINKEL'S. 725 E Silver Springs Blvd, 7 blks W. 904/732-8003. Hrs: 11 am-11 pm; Sat, from 4:30; Sun, 4:30-9:30; Closed Mon. A/C. Bar. Semi-a la carte. Lunch, $3-$18.50; dinner, $5-$19.50.

Child's plate, $1 less. Specialties: prime rib, steak, seafood. Piano, Tu-Sat. Cr cds: A, D, MC, V.

OKEECHOBEE

OHIO. 507 N Parrott Ave (33472), 5 blks N on 441. 813/763-1148. 24 A/C rms. Nov-Apr: S, $29; D, $29-$35; each addl, $3; wkly rates avail; rest of yr: lower rates. Color TV. Cr cds: MC, V.

Restaurant

FAT JOHNNIE'S ROYAL BUFFET. 119 Parrott Ave. 813/763-3300. Open 24 hrs. A/C. Semi-a la carte. Bkfst, $1.25-$3.50; lunch, $3.50-$7; dinner, $3.95-$8.95; Child's plates, $2.50. Specialties: prime rib, fresh catfish, "all-u-can-eat buffet" (7 hot meats with all the trimmings). Salad bar.

ORLANDO

CARAVAN RESORT INN. 5827 Caravan Ct (32819). 5 mi SW at jct FL 435, I-4. 305/351-3800. 261 A/C units, 2 story. S, D, $60; each addl, $5; suites, $70-$195; under 17 free. Color TV. Pool; wading pool. Cafe, 7 am-noon, 5-10 pm. Bar 5 pm-midnight. Coin lndry. Cr cds: A, C, D, MC, V.

COLONIAL PLAZA MOTOR INN. 2801 E Colonial Dr (32803), 3 mi W on FL 50, 2 mi E of I-4. 305/894-2741. 226 A/C units, 2 story, 7 kits. S, $39.50-$43.50; D, $46.50-$49.50; each addl, $7; under 17 free; Color TV. 2 pools. Cafe adj, 7 am-11 pm. Bar, noon-midnight exc Sun, Mon. Cr cds: A, C, D, MC, V.

GOLD KEY INN. 7100 S Orange Blossom Trail (32809), 6 mi S on 17, 92, 441, 3 mi S of I-4; 2 mi N FL Tpke exit 70. 305/855-0050. 210 A/C rms, 2 story. S, $54-$60; D, $60-$66; each addl, $6; suites, $156-$212; under 18 free. Color TV. Pool. Cafe (see PICCADILLY). Bar; entertainment, dancing exc Sun. Tennis; pro. Cr cds: A, C, D, MC, V.

HILTON INN ORLANDO. 3200 W Colonial Dr (32808). 2½ mi W on FL 50, 2 mi W of I-4. 305/395-5270. 320 A/C rms, 2 story, 4 kits. Jan-Dec: S, $42-$66; D, $57-$81; each addl, $12; kit units, $80; children free with parents; rest of yr: lower rates. Color TV; free in-rm movies. 2 pools. Cafe, 7 am-2 pm, 6-10 pm. Bar, entertainment exc Sun. Coin lndry. Cr cds: A, C, D, MC, V.

HOLIDAY INN-AIRPORT. 7900 S Orange Blossom Trail (32809), on 441 at jct Sand Lake Rd. 305/859-7900. 259 A/C rms, 2 story. Dec-Feb, June-Aug: S, $37-$47; D, $45-$55; each addl, $6; under 18 free; rest of yr: varied lower rates. Color TV. Pool; wading pool. Cafe, 7 am-2 pm, 4:30-10 pm. Bar; entertainment, dancing. Coin lndry. Cr cds: A, C, D, MC, V.

HOLIDAY INN-MIDTOWN. 929 W Colonial Dr (32804), ¾ mi W of I-4. 305/843-1360. 154 A/C rms, 2 story. S, $52-$58; D, $44-$58; each addl, $6; suites, $61; under 18 free. Color TV. Pool. Cafe, 6 am-10 pm. Bar, 11-2 am; entertainment, dancing, piano exc Sun. Coin lndry opp. Cr cds: A, D, MC, V.

HOLIDAY INN-ORLANDO WEST. (Rte 50W, Ocoee 32761.) 8 mi W on FL 50 at Maguire Rd; Fl Tpke exit 80. 305/656-5050. 172 A/C rms, 1-2 story. June-early Sep: S, $45; D, $47; each addl, $5; under 12 free; rest of yr: lower rates. Color TV. Pool. Cafe, 6:30 am-2 pm, 5-10 pm. Bar entertainment, dancing exc Sun. Coin lndry. Cr cds: A, MC, V.

HOLIDAY INN-SOUTH. 4049 S Orange Blossom Trail (32805), 3 mi S on 17, 92, 441, ¼ mi S of I-4. 305/843-1350. 178 A/C rms, 2 story. S, $41-$43; D, $48-$53; each addl, $6; Color TV;

free in-rm movies. Pool. Cafe, 6:30 am-2:30 pm, 5:30-10:30 pm. Bar; entertainment exc Sun.

HOWARD JOHNSON'S-AIRPORT (formerly Howard Johnson's Orange Blossom). 8820 S Orange Blossom Trail (32809), 7 mi S on 17, 92, 441, just N of FL Tpke exit 70. 305/851-8200. 195 A/C rms, 2 story. S, $65; D, $68; each addl, $5; under 18 free. Color TV. Pool; wading pool. Cafe, 6-1 am. Bar. Coin lndry. Cr cds: A, C, D, MC, V.

HOWARD JOHNSON'S EXECUTIVE CENTER. (Box 1072; 32802.) 304 W Colonial Dr at jct FL 50, I-4. 305/843-8700. 262 A/C rms, 14 story. Mid-Jan-mid-Apr, mid-June-Aug: S, $52-$60; D, $58-$62; each addl, $8; under 18 free; rest of yr: lower rates. Color TV. Pool. Cafe 6 am-midnight; Fri, Sat to 2 am; Bar, 11-2 am; entertainment, dancing. Coin lndry. Cr cds: A, C, D, MC, V.

HOWARD JOHNSON'S MIDTOWN. 2014 W Colonial Dr (32804), at Tampa Ave, 2 mi W on FL 50, 1½ mi W of I-4. 305/841-8600. 111 A/C rms, 2 story. Mid-Feb-Aug: S, $34-$48; D, $34-$58; each addl, $5; group rates avail; under 18 free with parents. Color TV. Pool. Cafe, 6:30 am-11 pm. Bar, 10:30-midnight. Coin lndry. Cr cds: A, C, D, MC, V.

INTERNATIONAL INN. 6327 International Dr (32809). 9 mi SW at jct FL 528A, I-4. 305/351-4444. 315 A/C rms. S, $32-$38; D, $35-$45; each addl, $3-$5; suites, $100-$150; under 18 free. Color TV. Pool. Cafe, 7-11 am, 6-9 pm. Bar, 6 pm-11 am. Cr cds: A, C, D, MC, V.

JAMAICA INN. 3300 W Colonial Dr (32808), 3 mi W on FL 50, 2 mi W of I-4. 305/293-7221. 101 A/C rms, 1-2 story, 7 kits. S, $32-$36; D, $36-$39; each addl, $4; kit. units, $39-$42; suites, $50-$60; under 17 free; family rates avail; higher rates during Daytona Races, Tangerine Bowl game, Christmas, Easter wks. Color TV. Pool. Cafe, 7 am-2:30 pm. Bar, 11-1 am. Cr cds: A, C, D, MC, V.

QUALITY INN INTERNATIONAL. 7600 International Dr (32809), 9 mi SW at jct FL 528A, I-4. 305/351-1600. 320 A/C rms, 2 story. Mid-Dec-May, June-early Sep: S, $33; D, $39; each addl, $5; under 18 free. Color TV. Pool; wading pool. Cafe, 6:30-10:30 am, 5:30-9:30 pm. Bar. Coin lndry. Cr cds: A, C, D, MC, V.

QUALITY INN UNIVERSITY (formerly Best Western University Inn). 11731 E Colonial Dr (32817), 8 mi E on FL 50. 305/273-1500. 122 A/C rms, 2 story. Dec-Aug: S, D, $36-$40; each addl, $5; under 16 free; wkly rates avail; rest of yr, lower rates. Pool. Cafe, 7 am-2 pm, 6-10 pm. Bar; entertainment, dancing exc Sun, Mon. Cr cds: A, C, D, MC, V.

RAMADA INN CENTRAL. 4919 W Colonial Dr (32808), 5 mi W on FL 50. 305/299-8180. 210 A/C rms, 2 story. S, D, $41-$52; each addl, $5; suites, $60; under 18 free. Crib free. Color TV. Pool; wading pool. Cafe, 7 am-10 pm. Bar; entertainment, dancing exc Sun. Coin lndry. Cr cds: A, C, D, MC, V.

RAMADA INN WEST. (PO, Ocoee 32761.) 10 mi W on FL 50, ¼ mi E of FL Tpke exit 80. 305/656-3333. 300 A/C rms, 7 story. S, D, $28; each addl, $4. Color TV. Pool; wading pool. Cafe, 7-11 am, 7-11 pm. Bar; entertainment. Coin lndry. Lighted tennis; pro. Cr cds: A, C, D, MC, V.

1776 INN. 5858 International Dr (32809), 9 mi SW at jct FL 528A, I-4. 305/351-4410. 232 A/C rms, 2 story. S, $34-$54; D, $34-$56; children free. Color TV. Pool. Bar; entertainment, dancing Wed-Sat. Coin lndry. Cr cds: A, C, D, MC, V.

SHERATON WORLD. 10100 International Dr

(32809). 305/352-1100. 807 A/C units, 2-3 story. Feb-Apr: S, D, $74; each addl, $10; under 18 free; lower rates rest of yr. 3 pools; 2 wading pools. Cafe, 7 am-2 pm, 5-10 pm. Dining rm. Coin lndry. Cr cds: A, C, D, MC, V.

SUNSHINE PARKWAY INN. 9301 S Orange Blossom Trail (32809), jct 17, 92, 441, FL Tpke exit 70. 305/851-8730. 144 A/C rms, 2 story. Feb-Apr, June-Aug: S, $44; D, $56; each addl, $6; under 18 free. Color TV. Pool. Cafe, 7 am-10 pm. Bar. Cr cds: A, C, D, MC, V.

Restaurants

ANGELO'S. 6223 S Orange Blossom Trail. On US 441, 17, 92. 305/855-6623. Hrs: Mon-Thurs, 11:30 am-2:30 pm, 5-10 pm; Fri, Sat to 11 pm; Sun, 4-10 pm. Closed Thanksgiving, Dec. 25. A/C. Italian menu. Bar. Semi-a la carte: lunch, $2.95-$4.95; dinner; $4.75-$12.95. Serv. plate. Child's plates, $2.50-$3.95. Specializes in veal, steak, seafood. Antipasto salad bar. Background music. Cr cds: A, C, D, MC, V.

DUFF'S FAMOUS SMORGASBORD. 4442 Curry Ford Rd in Conway Shopping Center. 305/277-5090. Hrs: 11 am-3 pm, 4-8 pm; Sun, hols. 11 am-8 pm. Closed Dec 25. A/C. Table d'hôte. Lunch, $3.25; dinner, $4.25; Sat, Sun, brunch $3.25-$4.25. Child's plates, $2.25. Specialties: fried chicken, hot & cold desserts. Salad bar.

HOUSE OF BEEF. 801 John Young Pkwy, 3 mi W on FL 50. 305/295-1931. Hrs: 11:30 am-11 pm, Sun champagne brunch 11:30 am-2 pm. Res advisable. A/C. Bar. Semi-a la carte. Lunch, dinner, $5.30-$17.75. Specialties: prime rib, steak. Salad bar. Cr cds: A, D, MC, V.

LA CANTINA. 4721 E Colonial Dr, on FL 50. 305/894-4491. Hrs: 5-11 pm; Fri, Sat to midnight. Closed Sun, Mon; Jan 1, July 4, Thanksgiving, Dec 25; also late July-mid-Aug. A/C. Italian, Amer menu. Bar. Dinner, semi-a la carte, $4.25-$15.95; serv plate, $2.50. Child's plates, $2-$2.50. Specialty: steak. Cr cds: A, C, D, MC, V.

MORRISON'S (Cafeteria). (Box 6123C.) 1840 E Colonial Dr, 1½ mi E of FL 50, 2 mi E of I-4. 305/896-2091. Hrs: 11 am-8 pm. A/C. Avg ck: lunch, $3; dinner, $4. Specialties: roast beef, string beans, apple pie. Also at 7440 International Dr. 351-0051.

94TH AERO SQUADRON. 4200 E Colonial Dr 6 mi E on FL 50. 305/898-4251. Hrs: 11 am-3 pm, 5-11 pm; Sun 4-10 pm. Closed Dec 25. A/C French, Amer menu. Bar. A la carte: lunch, $3.45-$6.50, dinner, $4.50-$18. Child's plates. Specializes in prime rib, steak. Big band, top 40 Thurs-Sat. WWI decor. Cr cds: A, D, MC, V.

PICCADILLY. (See Gold Key Inn above.) 305/855-0050. Hrs: 7-10:30 am, 11:30 am-1:30 pm, 6-10 pm; Fri, Sat, to 11 pm; Sun, 8-10 am, brunch, 11:30 am-2 pm, dinner 6-10 pm. A/C Continental menu. Bar, 11-2 am. Table d'hote. Bkfst, $3.25-$6.50; lunch, $5.50-$12.50; dinner, a la carte, $10-$17; Sun brunch, $5.50-$12. Specialties: prime rib, veal Oscar, rack of lamb. Entertainment, dancing exc Sun. Cr cds: A, C, D, MC, V.

ORMOND BEACH

CASA DEL MAR. 621 S Atlantic Ave (32074), 1¼ mi S on FL A1A. 904/672-4550. 151 A/C rms, 7 story, 57 kits. Early Feb-Apr: D, $40-$60; each addl, $5; kit. units, $60-$66; special events higher; wkly rates avail, rest of yr: varied lower rates. Color TV. Pool; wading pool. Cafe, 11 am-2 pm, 5-8 pm. Bar. Coin lndry. On ocean. Cr cds: A, C, D, MC, V.

IVANHOE BEACH LODGE. 205 S Atlantic Ave (32074), 2 blks S on FL A1A. 904/672-6711. 147 A/C units, 7 story, 70 kits. S, D, $32-$43; kit. units, $35-$49; each addl, $3; under 16 free; Easter, July 4, Christmas, race wks higher. Color TV. Pool; wading pool. Cafe (see IVANHOE). Bar. Coin lndry. Tennis. On beach. Cr cds: A, D, MC, V.

MAINSAIL. 281 S Atlantic Ave (32074), 3¼ blks S on FL A1A. 904/677-2131. 50 A/C units, 2-4 story, 33 kits. S, D, $38-$42; each addl, $3-$5; kit. units, $50; Easter, July 4, special events, race wks (4-day min) higher; wkly rates avail. Color TV. Pool; wading pool. Cafe adj, open 24 hrs. Coin lndry. Tennis. On beach. Cr cds: A, MC, V.

MAVERICK. 485 S Atlantic Ave (32074), 1¼ mi S on FL A1A. 904/672-3550. 138 A/C units, 7 story, no ground floor rms, 50 kits. Feb-late Apr: S, D, $24-$60; each addl, $6; kit. units, $29-$70; under 16 free; wkly rates avail; Easter, July 4, race wks, special events (3-day min) higher; rest of yr: varied lower rates. Color TV. Pool; wading pool. Cafe, 7 am-2 pm. Bar. Coin lndry. Tennis. On beach. Cr cds: A, C, D, MC, V.

TREASURE COVE. 145 S Atlantic Ave (32074). ½ mi S on FL A1A. 904/677-1446. 84 A/C units, 7 story, 48 kits. Mar-Apr, late June-mid-July: S, D, $32-$53; each addl, $5; kit units, $38-$55; hols, special events (5-day min) higher; varied lower rates rest of yr. Color TV. Pool. Cr cds: A, D, MC, V.

Restaurants

IVANHOE. (See Ivanhoe Beach Lodge above.) 904/672-6711. Hrs: 7 am-10 pm. A/C. Bar. Semi-a la carte. Bkfst, $1-$4.75; lunch, $1.60-$5.75; dinner, $3.95-$17. Child's plates half price. Specialties: seafood, prime rib. Cr cds: A, C, D, MC, V.

JULIAN'S. 88 S Atlantic Ave, 1 blk S on FL A1A. 904/677-6767. Hrs: 4-11 pm. A/C. Bar. Semi-a la carte. Dinner, $5-$10.95. Child's plates, $1 less. Specialty: prime beef. Entertainment; organist exc Tu. Cr cds: A, C, D, MC, V.

MORRISON'S (Cafeteria). 135 E Granada Ave, 1 blk W on FL A1A. 904/677-0724. Hrs: 11 am-8 pm. Semi-a la carte. Lunch, $3.25; dinner, $4.10. Specialties: seafood, chicken. Salad bar.

PALATKA

HOLIDAY INN PALATKA. 201 N 1st St (32077), 2 blks S on US 17. 904/328-3481. 125 A/C rms. S, $32-$41; D, $36-$45. Color TV. Pool. Cafe, 6 am-3 pm, 5-10 pm. Bar. Coin lndry. Boat dock. Cr cds: A, D, MC, V.

Restaurant

HOLIDAY HOUSE. (Box 16.) Rte 17 S, 1 blk S of Bridge. 904/325-2125. Hrs: 11 am-9 pm. Closed Dec 24. A/C. Semi-a la carte. Lunch, $4.35; dinner, $5.25. Specialties: lamb, roast beef, ham. Salad bar. Cr cds: MC, V.

PALM BEACH

THE BREAKERS. S County Rd (33480), 6 blks NE on FL A1A, 5 mi E of I-95 exit Okeechobee Blvd. 305/655-6611. 567 A/C rms. Dec-Apr: modified Amer plan (serv charge in lieu of tipping): S, $175-$270; D, $185-$275; parlor, $110-$125 more, one addl, $60; under 12 free. June-Sep: Eur, golf, tennis package plans avail. Color TV. 2 pools, 1 indoor-outdoor. Dining rm (public by reservation), 7-10:30 am, 6-10 pm; beach club lunch from 11:30 am. Bar, 11-2 am. Golf; pro. Tennis; pro. Boats avail. Dancing, entertainment. On ocean; cabana, beach clubs. Cr cds: MC, V.

THE COLONY. 155 Hammon Ave (33480), ¼ mi S on FL A1A. 305/655-5430. 100 A/C rms. Mid-Dec-mid-May: S, D, $80-$125; 1-2 bedrm suites, $185-$275; penthouse suites avail; rest of yr: lower rates avail. Closed (Maisonette only) mid-May-Nov. Color TV; in-rm movies avail. Pool. Cafe, 7 am-3 pm, 5 pm-midnight. Bar; entertainment, dancing. Cr cds: A, MC, V.

HEART OF PALM BEACH. 160 Royal Palm Way (33480), 1 blk W on FL A1A, 3 mi E of I-95. 305/655-5600. 88 A/C rms, 3 story. Dec-Apr: S, D, $78-$110; each addl, $8; under 12 free; rest of yr: varied lower rates. Color TV. Pool. Café, 7 am-9 pm. Bar, 11 am-9 pm. Cr cds: A, C, D, MC, V.

HILTON PALM BEACH. 2842 S Ocean Blvd (33480). 30 blks S on FL A1A. 305/586-6542. 134 A/C units, 6 story. Dec-Apr: S, $93-$154; D, $104-$165; each addl, $15; children free; lower rates rest of yr. Color TV. Pool. Cafe, 7 am-10 pm. Bar, 11-1 am; entertainment, dancing. Cr cds: A, C, D, MC, V.

HOWARD JOHNSON'S. 2870 S County Rd at Lake Worth Rd (33480), 6 mi S on FL A1A, E of FL Tpke exit 36. 305/582-2581. 99 A/C rms, 3 story. Dec-Apr: S, D, $64-$80; each addl, $5; under 18 free; rest of yr: varied rates. (Rates subject to change.) Color TV. Pool. Cafe, 6:30 am-11 pm. Bar. Coin lndry. Cr cds: A, C, D, MC, V.

Restaurants

CAPRICCIO. 336 Royal Poinciana Plaza, 4 blks NW on FL A1A, 4 mi N on I-95, exit Okeechobee Blvd. 305/659-5955. Hrs: 11:30 am-3 pm, 6-11 pm. Closed Sun, months of May & Sep early Oct, Jan 1, Dec 25. A/C. Continental menu. Bar. Semi-a la carte. Lunch, $8-$9.50; dinner, $11-$15.75. Specialties: scampi Capriccio, lamb, Pompano snapper. Jacket required for dinner. Cr cds: A, C, D, MC, V.

PETITE MARMITE. 315 Worth Ave, 2 blks W on FL A1A. 305/655-0115. Hrs: 11:30 am-11 pm; summer: 11:30 am-3 pm, 6-10 pm; closed Sun. A/C. Continental, Amer menu. Bar. Semi-a la carte. Lunch, $9-$15; dinner, $13.75-$20. Specialties: broiled scampi, Marmite special veal chop, breast of chicken. Jacket required at dinner. Cr cds: A, C, D, MC, V.

PANAMA CITY

CASA LOMA. 13615 W US 98A (32407). 12½ mi W. 904/234-1100. 100 A/C units, 4 story, 37 kits. May-Labor Day; S, $42-$50; D, $44-$64; each addl, $10; suites, $75-$95; kit units, $50-$64; under 18 free; higher rates during hols, special events; lower rates rest of yr. Color TV. Pool. Cr cds: A, MC, V.

HOLIDAY LODGE. 6400 W Hwy 98 (32407), 7½ mi W on 98, on Bay off Hathaway Bridge. 904/234-2114. 113 A/C rms, 2 story, 16 kits. Mid-Apr-mid-Sep: S, $30-$36; D, $40-$48; each addl, $3; kit. units, $48; under 12 free; rest of yr: some lower. Color TV. Pool. Playground. Cafe, 6 am-10 pm. Bar; entertainment, dancing. Coin lndry adj. Marina; sailboats, charter boats. On bay. Cr cds: A, C, D, MC, V.

HOWARD JOHNSON'S. 4601 W US 98 (32401). 4 mi W on US 98. 904/785-0222. 126 A/C rms. 1-3 story. Mid-May-Labor Day: S, $35-$39; D, $45-$55; each addl, $5-$7; under 18 free; sr cit rates; higher rates during hols; lower rates rest of yr. Color TV; cable. Pool. Cafe, open 24 hrs. Bar. Cr cds: A, C, D, MC, V.

PALMETTO COURT. 17255 W Hwy 98A (32407), 16¼ mi W in Panama City Beach. 904/234-2121. 51 A/C units, 2 story, 45 kits. Mid-May-Labor Day: S, D, $60; kit. units to 6, $65-$100; rest of yr: lower rates. Color TV. Pool; wading pool. Playground. Tennis. On Gulf. Cr cds: A, MC, V.

ACCOMMODATIONS & RESTAURANTS 141

RAMADA INN. 3001 W 10 St (32401), 2½ mi W on 98 Business. 904/785-0561. 150 A/C rms, 2 story. May-Labor Day: S, $42-$52; D, $48-$58; each addl, $7; under 18 free; rest of yr: lower rates. Color TV. Pool. Cafe (see HARBOUR HOUSE). Bar; entertainment, dancing Tu-Sat. Marina adj; charter boats avail. On bay. Cr cds: A, C, D, MC, V.

SEA AQUA. 17643 W Hwy 98A (32407), 17½ mi W in Panama City Beach. 904/234-2163. 52 A/C units, 2 story, 26 kits. May-Sep: S, D, $46-$51; each addl, $2; kit. units, $51-$52; rest of yr: lower rates. Color TV. Pool. Coin lndry opp. On Gulf. Cr cds: A, MC, V.

SHALIMAR PLAZA. 17545 W Hwy 98A (32407), 17¼ mi W in Panama City Beach. 904/234-2133. 50 A/C units, 3 story, 47 kits. Memorial Day wkend-Labor Day (3-day min wkends): D, $49-$59; each addl, $5; kit. units to 6, $49-$59; rest of yr: lower rates. Color TV. Pool. Playground. Tennis. On Gulf. Cr cds: MC, V.

Restaurants

CAPT. ANDERSON'S. 5551 N Lagoon Dr, at Thomas Dr on Grand Lagoon, 10 mi SW, 3 mi S of 98. 904/234-2225. Hrs: 4-10:30 pm. Closed Sun; Dec-mid-Jan. A/C. Bars. Dinner, semi-a la carte, $8.95-$18.95. Specialties: charcoal-broiled steak, red snapper, Gulf seafood, grouper. Cr cds: A, D, MC. V.

HARBOUR HOUSE. (see Ramada Inn above). 904/785-9053. Hrs: 6 am-10 pm. Closed Dec 25. A/C. Bar. Semi-a la carte. Bkfst, $1.75-$6.50; dinner, $5.75-$15; Specialties: prime rib, steak, seafood. Salad bar. Cr cds: A, D, MC, V.

PENSACOLA

BEST WESTERN SEVILLE INN. 223 E Garden St (32501), 3 blks E on Palafox on 98 Business. 904/433-8331. 172 A/C rms, 2 story. S, $30-$33; D, $40-$44; each addl, $4; suites, $55-$60; special events, hols higher; under 18 free. Color TV. 2 pools, 1 indoor. Cafe, 6:30 am-2 pm, 4:30-9 pm. Bar, 11-2 am; entertainment, dancing; closed Sun. Coin lndry. Cr cds: A, C, D, MC, V.

DAYS INN. 6911 Pensacola Blvd (32505), 6 mi N on 29, ½ mi S of jct I-10. 904/477-9000. 180 A/C rms, 2 story. S, $32; D, $38; each addl, $4; under 18, $1. Color TV. Pool. Cafe, 6 am-10 pm. Cr cds: A, C, D, MC, V.

HOLIDAY INN-NORTH. (Box 12685; 32754.) 6501 Pensacola Blvd, 5 mi N on 29, ¾ mi S of I-10. 904/476-7200. 219 A/C rms, 2 story. Mid-May-Labor Day: S, $38-$47; D, $44-$53; each addl, $6; under 18 free; rest of yr: lower rates. Color TV. Pool; wading pool. Cafe, 6 am-10 pm. Coin lndry. Cr cds: A, D, MC, V.

LENOX INN. 710 N Palafox (32501). ¾ mi N on US 29 at jct US 90, 98. 904/438-4922. 157 A/C rms, 3 story. Elvtr. S, $35-$38; D, $40-$50; each addl, $4; suites, $50; studio rms, $35-$45; under, 18 free; lower rates rest of yr. Color TV. Pool. Cafe, 8:30 am-9:30 pm; Sun, to 2 pm. Bar; closed Sun. Cr cds: A, C, D, MC, V.

RAMADA INN-NORTH. 6550 Pensacola Blvd (32505), 5 mi N on 29, 4 mi S of 90A, 1½ mi S of I-10 exit 29 (S). 904/477-0711. 104 A/C rms, 2 story. S, $42 D, $52; each addl, $8; suites, $60; under 18 free. Color TV. Pool; wading pool. Playground. Cafe, 6:30 am-10 pm. Bar; dancing exc Sun. Cr cds: A, C, D, MC, V.

SHERATON INN. 224 E Garden St (32501), at Alcaniz St, 3 blks E on 98 Business. 904/434-3201.
202 A/C rms, 4 story. S, D, $44-$52; each addl, $4; studio rms, $30-$38; suites, $100-$150. Color TV. Pool. Cafe, 6 am-10 pm. Bar; entertainment, dancing. Cr cds: A, C, D, MC, V.

Restaurants

DRIFTWOOD. 27 W Garden St, ½ blk SE on 98 Business. 904/433-4559. Hrs: 11 am-3 pm, 5-10 pm. Closed Sun, major hols. A/C. Revervation recommended. Bar. French, Amer menu. Semi-a la carte. Lunch, $4.75-$5.95; dinner, $8.25-$12.75. Specialties: crabmeat, eggplant, horseradish salad. Cr cds: A, D, MC, V.

MORRISON'S (Cafeteria). Town & Country Mall, 3 mi NW on FL 29. 904/438-5691. Hrs: 11 am-9 pm. A/C. Specialties: prime round of beef, shrimp, fried fish almondine.

SKOPELOS SEAFOOD & STEAK. 1842 W Cervantes St. 1½ mi NW on US 90, 98. Hrs: 4-11 pm; Sun, from 3 pm. Closed Mon, Dec 25. A/C Bar. Semi-a la carte: dinner, $4.95-$16.95. Child's plates. Specializes in seafood, char broiled steaks, homemade Greek baklava. Background music. Cr cds: A, MC, V.

PERRY

HOWARD JOHNSON'S. 2277 S US 19 (32347). 1¾ mi S at jct US 19, 27A, 98. 904/584-5311. 60 A/C rms, 2 story. S, $23-$35; D, $26-$37; each addl, $5; under 18, free; sr cit rates. Color TV. Pool. Cafe, open 24 hrs; Sun, Mon, to 9:30 pm. Cr cds: A, C, D, MC, V.

POMPANO BEACH

BEACHCOMBER HOTEL & VILLAS. 1200 S Ocean Blvd (33062), 12 blks S on FL A1A. 305/941-7830. 137 A/C hotel rms, 68 kit. studio rms, 7 kit. apts, 8 kit. villas; A/C; 2-8 story. Dec-Apr: S, D, $55-$104; studio rms, $75-$133; villas, $110-$1,421; each addl, $10-$12; summer: lower rates. Color TV. Olympic-size pool; wading pool; poolside serv. Cafe, 5-10 pm. Bar; entertainment, dancing exc Sun. Coin lndry. Tennis. Golf. 300-ft beach. Cr cds: A, MC, V.

BEST WESTERN SEA GARDEN. 615 N Ocean Blvd (33062), 6 blks N on FL A1A. 305/943-6200. 126 A/C units, 2-4 story, 79 kits. Dec-Apr: S, D, $58-$110; studio apts, $72-$105; suites, $150-$175; each addl, $10; rest of yr: lower rates. Color TV. 2 Olympic-size pools; poolside serv. Cafe, 7 am-3 pm, 5-9 pm. Bar; entertainment, dancing exc Mon, Sep. Tennis. Golf. On beach; some rms across hwy. Also 40 apts for 4 avail in season. Cr cds: A, C, D, MC, V.

OCEAN RANCH. 1110 S Ocean Blvd (33062), on FL A1A. 305/941-7100. 84 A/C units, 1-6 story, 54 kits. S, D, $59-$79; kit. studio rms, $68-$88; kit. apts, $71-$102; each addl, $8; rest of yr: lower rates. Color TV. 2 Olympic-size pools. Cafe, 8 am-10 pm. Bar; entertainment, dancing. Coin lndry. On beach. Cr cds: A, MC, V.

POMPANO BEACH MOTOR LODGE. 1112 N Ocean Blvd (33062), 11 blks N on FL A1A. 305/943-0630. 55 A/C units, 6 story, 34 kits. Dec-Apr: S, D, $52-$65; each addl, $6; studio rms, $60-$70; kit. units, $62-$75; rest of yr: lower rates. Color TV. Pool; poolside serv. Cafe, 8 am-3 pm, 6-9 pm. Bar, 11 am-11 pm. Tennis. On ocean. Cr cds: A, C, D, MC, V.

SANDS HARBOR HOTEL & MARINA. 125 N Riverside Dr (33062), 2 blks W of FL A1A. 305/942-9100. 56 A/C rms, 9 story, 31 kits. Dec-Apr: S, D, $50-$60; kit. units, studio rms, $45-$50; apts avail;
each addl, $5; under 10 $2.50; family rates avail; rest of yr: lower rates. Color TV. Pool; poolside serv. Cafe, 8 am-11 pm. Bars; entertainment, dancing Fri-Sat. Marina; yacht slip adj. On Intracoastal Waterway. Cr cds: A, D, MC, V.

SUN CASTLE CLUB. 1380 S Ocean Blvd (33062), 13 blks N on FL A1A. 305/941-7700. 105 A/C units, 4 story, 31 kits. Dec-mid-Apr: S, D, $66-$94; kit. units, $67.90-$102; each addl, $6.50; rest of yr: varied lower rates. Color TV. Olympic-size pool. Cafe, 7:30 am-2 pm, 6-9:30 pm. Bar; entertainment, dancing exc Mon. Tennis. Dockage opp. On beach. Cr cds: A, C, D, MC, V.

SURFSIDE. 710 S Ocean Blvd (33062), 7 blks S on FL A1A. 305/942-2400. 30 A/C rms, 2 story, 27 kits. Dec-Apr: S, D, $33-$39; studio rm $41-$50; apts for 2-4, $60-$86; each addl, $5; under 10 free; rest of yr: lower rates. Color TV. Pool. Coin lndry. On ocean. Cr cds: MC, V.

TRADERS RESORT. 1600 S. Ocean Blvd (33062). 16 blks N on FL A1A. 305/941-8400. 93 A/C units, 3 story, 47 kits. Feb-mid-Apr: S, D, $47-$56; each addl, $5; kit. units, $92-$152; kit studios, $60-$80. Color TV. Pool Cafe, 7-11 am, 11:30 am-2 pm, 5:30-10 pm. Bar; entertainment, dancing exc Sun. Cr cds: A, C, D, MC, V.

Restaurants

CAPTAIN'S COVE. 700 S Federal Hwy, 15 blks S on Fed 1, 4 mi E of I-95 (Atlantic Ave). 305/943-4100. Hrs: 4-11 pm, Sun to 10 pm. Closed Dec 25. A/C. Bar. Seafood & steak menu. Semi-a la carte. Dinner, $7.95-$17. Child's plates. Specialties: broiled Maine lobster, shellfish lovers' delight, NY steaks. Salad bar. Entertainment, dancing. Nautical decor. Cr cds: A, MC, V.

HARRIS IMPERIAL HOUSE. 50 N Ocean Blvd, on FL A1A at jct Atlantic Blvd. 305/941-2201. Hrs: 11:30 am-2:30 pm; Mon-Sat, 5-10:30, Sun 4-10. Reservation required. A/C. Cantonese, Amer menu. Bar. Semi-a la carte. Lunch, $3.75-$7.50; dinner, $6.95-$13.95. Child's plates. Specialties: sesame chicken, Cantonese steak, South Seas supreme. Salad bar. Cr cds: A, C, D, MC, V.

HEINI'S PLACE. 3332 Atlantic Blvd ½ blk W of FL A1A. 305/941-7859. Hrs: Oct-May: 4-10 pm. Closed Sun; mid-June-mid July. A/C. Dinner, semi-a la carte, $8.95-$16. Specialties: veal Normande, cheese fondue, filet of sole. Background music. Cr cds: MC, V.

PORT CHARLOTTE

PORT CHARLOTTE. 137 S Tamiami Dr NE (33952), just E of 41. 813/625-4177. 31 A/C rms, 4 kits. Dec-Apr: S, $24-$33; D, $27-$36; each addl, $3; kit. units, $30-$35; rest of yr: lower rates. Color TV. Pool. Whirlpool. Cafe opp, 6 am-midnight. On canal; dockage. Cr cds: MC, V.

PUNTA GORDA

HOLIDAY INN. 300 Retta Esplande (33950), at Cross St, 1 blk W of 41. 813/639-1165. 102 A/C rms, 1-2 story. Mid-Dec-late Apr: S, $50-$55; D, $60-$65; each addl, $3; family rates avail; rest of yr: lower rates. Color TV. Pool. Cafe 6 am-10 pm. Bar; entertainment, dancing exc Sun. Coin lndry. Cr cds: A, D, MC, V.

HOWARD JOHNSON'S. 33 Tamiami Trail (33950), on 41. 813/639-2167. 102 A/C rms, 2 story. Feb-Mar: S, $50-$62; D, $56-$68; each addl, $10; suites, $100-$150; under 18 free; lower rates rest of yr. Color TV. Pool. Cafe 6:30 am-11 pm. On Charlotte Harbor. Cr cds: A, C, D, MC, V.

142 ACCOMMODATIONS & RESTAURANTS

ST. AUGUSTINE

BY THE SEA COURT. 57 Comares Ave (32084), 6½ blks E of FL A1A. 904/829-8646. 22 A/C rms, 8 kits. S, D, $40-$55; each addl, $10. Color TV. Pool. Cafe, noon-midnight. Bar. Tennis. Private beach. Boats, sailboats avail. Cr cds: MC, V.

DAYS INN. 2800 Ponce de Leon Blvd, (32084), 1¾ mi N on 1 Business. 904/829-6581. 124 A/C rms, 2 story. S, $28.88-$38.88; D, $29.88-$32.88; each addl, $4; under 2 free; races, hols higher rates. Color TV. Pool. Cafe, 6 am-9 pm. Cr cds: A, MC, V.

HOLIDAY INN DOWNTOWN. 1300 Ponce de Leon Blvd (32084), 1¼ mi NW on US 1. 904/824-3383. 122 A/C rms, 2 story. Mid-June-Aug: S, $40; D, $45-$50; each addl, $3; suites, $35-$39; under 19 free; special events higher; rest of yr: lower rates. Color TV. Pool. Cafe, 6 am-10 pm. Bar; entertainment. Cr cds: A, C, D, MC, V.

HOWARD JOHNSON'S WEST. (Box 365; 32084.) 9 mi W on FL 16. 904/829-5686. 64 A/C rms, 2 story. June-Aug: S, $34-$50; D, $38-$60; each addl, $6; under 18 free; races, hols higher rates; rest of yr: lower rates. Color TV. Pool; wading pool. Playground. Cafe, 6 am-midnight. Coin lndry. Cr cds: A, C, D, MC, V.

LION. 420 Anastasia Blvd (32084), 6 blks S on FL A1A. 904/824-8931. 36 A/C rms, 6 kits. June-Labor Day, Feb-Apr: S, D, $26-$40; each addl, $3; kit. units, $5 more; special events & hols higher. Color TV. Pool. Cafe, 8 am-9 pm. Cr cds: A, D, MC, V.

MONTEREY. 16 Bayfront (32084), across from Ft Castillo de San Marcos, FL A1A. 904/824-4482. 53 A/C rms, 2 story, kits., 1 efficiency apt. S, D, $24-$38; each addl, $3; kit. units, suites, $25-$35; family, wkly rates avail; special events, hols higher rates. Color TV. Pool. Cafe adj, 7 am-10 pm. Matanzas Bay opp. Cr cds: A, C, D, MC, V.

PONCE DE LEON. (Box 98; 32084.) Ponce de Leon Blvd, 3 mi N on US 1. 904/824-2821. 200 A/C rms, 1-4 story. S, $41-$50; D, $48-$57; each addl, $5; under 18 free; Mod Amer plan avail; golf & tennis package plans avail. Color TV. Pool. Playground. Cafe, 7 am-2:30 pm, 6-9 pm. Bar, entertainment, dancing exc Sun. Tennis. Golf. Cr cds: A, D, MC, V.

QUALITY INN CARAVAN. 2500 Ponce de Leon Blvd (32084), 1 mi N on US 1, 4 mi E of I-95. 904/824-2883. 91 A/C rms, 2 story. Late Dec-Oct: S, $34-$42; D, $38-$46; each addl, $4; under 16 free; special events, Daytona races, Easter hols higher; rest of yr: lower rates. Color TV. Pool. Cafe, 11 am-9 pm. Bar, 11:30 am-9:15 pm; entertainment exc Sun. Cr cds: A, D, MC, V.

SCOTTISH INN OF ST AUGUSTINE. (Box D-1; 32084.) One Corporate Square, 5 mi W at jct FL 16, I-95. 904/829-5643. 144 A/C rms, 2 story. Mid-Feb-mid-Apr, mid-June-Labor Day; S, $22.95-$24.95; D, $24.95-$26.95; each addl, $3; under 12, free; sr cit rates; races, hols higher rates. Color TV. Pool; wading pool. Cafe, 6:30-10:30 am, 5-10 pm. Bar 5-10 pm Cr cds: A, C, D, MC, V.

Restaurants

CHIMES. 12 Avenida Menendez, ½ mi N on FL A1A. 904/829-8141. Hrs: 7 am-10 pm. Closed Dec 25. A/C. Italian-Spanish menu. Bar. Semi-a la carte. Bkfst, $1.85-$3.75; lunch, $2.75-$12.50; dinner, $5.25-$15. Specialties: fresh seafood, steak. Cr cds: A, D, MC, V.

COLUMBIA. 98 St George St. In center of historical area. 904/824-3341. Hrs: 11 am-midnight. A/C. Bar, to 1 am. Spanish menu. Semi-a la carte: lunch, dinner, $2.95-$12.95. Specializes in snapper all-cante, paella, black bean soup. Background music. Entertainment. Cr cds: A, C, D, MC, V.

RAINTREE. 102 San Marco Ave. 904/824-7211. Hrs: 5-10 pm. A/C. Bar. Wine list. Continental menu. Semi-a la carte: dinner, $9.95-$25.50. Child's plates. Specialties: brandy pepper steak, raintree cream shrimp. Own baking. Background music. Entertainment. Cr cds: A, MC, V.

ST. AUGUSTINE BEACH

HOLIDAY INN-BY THE SEA. Ocean Trace Rd (32084), 1 blk E of FL A1A. 904/471-2626. 103 A/C rms, 4 story. Elvtrs. Early Feb-Sep: S, $35-$60; D, $40-$65; each addl, $5; under 18 free; special events higher rates; rest of yr: lower rates. Color TV. Pool; poolside snack bar. Free Continental bkfst. Bar, 5 pm-1 am; entertainment, dancing exc Mon. Coin lndry. On ocean. Cr cds: A, C, D, MC, V.

LA FIESTA MOTOR LODGE. 1001 FL A1A (32084), ¾ mi S. 904/824-2827. 37 A/C rms, 2 story, 2 kits. Early Feb-early Sep: S, D, $35-$55; each addl, $5; kit units, $5 more; family rates avail. Daytona races, Easter, hols higher rates; rest of yr: lower rates. Color TV. Pool. Cafe, 11 am-10 pm. Coin lndry. Cr cds: A, C, D, MC, V.

SHERATON ANASTASIA INN. Pope Rd, 10 mi S on FL A1A (32084), 2 blks E on Pope Rd. 904/824-8321. 143 A/C rms, 2 story, 20 kits. Mid-May-Aug: S, D, $30-$67; each addl, $5-$6; kit units, $42-$64; suites, $80; under 18 free; special events higher rates; rest of yr: some lower. Color TV. Pool; poolside serv. Cafe, 7 am-2 pm, 5-10 pm. Bar; entertainment, dancing exc Mon. Coin lndry. On ocean. Cr cds: A, C, D, MC, V.

ST. PETERSBURG

THE BAYFRONT CONCOURSE. 333 1 St S (33701). 813/896-1111. 305 A/C rms, 12 story. Nov-Apr: S, D, $65-$70; each addl, $5; suites, $80-$150; rest of yr: lower rates. Color TV. Pool; wading pool; poolside serv. Cafe, 7-11 am; dining rm. Bar 11 am-2 am; entertainment, dancing exc Mon. Cr cds: A, C, D, MC, V.

BEACH PARK. 300 Beach DR NE (33701), ¼ mi E of 275. 813/898-6325. 26 A/C units, 2 story, 11 kits. Jan-Apr: S, D, $35-$45; each addl, $5; kit. units, $45-$83; rest of yr: varied lower rates. Color TV. Cr cds: A, D, MC, V.

BEST WESTERN NORTH. 2595 54th Ave N (33714), at I-275. 813/522-3191. 160 A/C rms, 2 story. Mid-Dec-Apr: S, $31-$33; D, $38-$48; each addl, $5; rest of yr: lower rates. Color TV. Pool; wading pool. Cafe, 6 am-11 pm; wkends to midnight. Bar. Coin lndry. Cr cds: A, C, D, MC, V.

DAYS INN NORTH ST. PETE. (9359 US 19N, Pinellas Park 33565) 1½ mi N. 813/577-3838. 154 A/C rms, 2 story. Mid-Dec-late May; S, $36.88; D, $40.88; each addl, $4; under 18, $1; lower rates rest of yr. Color TV. Pool. Cafe, 6:00 am-9 pm; winter, to 10 pm. Coin lndry. Cr cds: A, C, D, MC, V.

HOLIDAY INN-NORTH. 5005 34 St N (33714), 8 mi N on 19. 813/525-1181. 180 A/C rms, 2 story. S, $30-$45; D, $54-$66; each addl, $6; under 18 free. Color TV. Pool; wading pool. Cafe, 7 am-2 pm, 5-10 pm. Bar; entertainment exc Sun. Coin lndry. Cr cds: A, C, D, MC, V.

HOLIDAY INN-SOUTH. 4601 34 St S (33711), 3 mi S on 19. 813/867-3131. 134 A/C rms, 2 story. Late Dec-mid-Apr; S, $52; D, $54-$66; each addl, $6; family rates avail; suites avail; rest of yr: varied lower rates. Color TV. Pool; poolside serv. Cafe, 7 am-2 pm, 5-10 pm. Bar; entertainment, dancing exc Sun. Coin lndry. Marina adj. Cr cds: A, D, MC, V.

QUALITY INN. 2260 54th Ave N (33714). 4 mi N at I-275. 813/521-3511. 120 A/C rms, 5 story. Mid-Jan-mid-Apr: S, $37-$39; D, $41-$44; each addl, $5; under 16, free with family; sr cit rates; lower rates rest of yr. Color TV. Pool. Cafe, 7 am-2 pm, 6-9 pm. Bar; entertainment, dancing Tu-Sat in season. Cr cds: A, C, D, MC, V.

SHERATON-ST PETE MARINA AND TENNIS CLUB. 6800 34 St S (33711), 6 mi S on 19. 813/867-1151. 138 A/C rms, 2 story, 46 kits. Mid-Feb-Apr: S, D, $36-$109; each addl, $10; kit units, $75-$125; under 18 free; rest of yr: varied lower rates. Color TV. 2 pools; wading pool; poolside serv. Playground. Cafe, 7 am-2 pm, 5-10 pm. Bar; entertainment, dancing Mon-Sat. Coin lndry. Lighted tennis; pro. Marina sailing school. On bay. Cr cds: A, C, D, MC, V.

Restaurants

AUNT HATTIE'S. 625 1 St S, 6 blks SE, opp Albert Whitted Airport, adj Bayfront Center. 813/822-4812. Hrs: 11:30 am-9 pm. Closed Labor Day, Dec 25. A/C. Serv bar. Semi-a la carte. Lunch, $3.75-$4.65; dinner, $6.50-$10.25. Child's plates avail. Specialties: chicken & dumplings, grilled roast beef hash, langostinos. Cr cds: A, D, MC, V.

BRADFORD'S COACH HOUSE. 1900 4 St N. 813/822-7982. Hrs: 11:30 am-10 pm; Sat to 11 pm; Sun to 9 pm. Closed Memorial Day, July 4, Labor Day. A/C. Bar. Semi-a la carte. Lunch, $3.50 up; dinner, $5-$16; 15% serv charge. Specialty: prime rib. Salad bar. Entertainment exc Sun. Cr cds: A, MC, V.

FISHERMAN'S INN. 9595 4 St N, ¼ mi S of Gandy Blvd. 813/576-4252. Hrs: 11 am-10 pm, Fri to 11. A/C. Bar. Semi-a la carte. Dinner, $5-$10. Specialties: hot seafood platter, NY cheesecake, key lime pie. Cr cds: A, MC, V.

MAAS' SUNCOAST ROOM. (Maas Bros Dept Store). 3 St & 1 Ave N. 813/895-7525. Hrs: 11 am-3 pm; Mon, Fri, also 4-6:30 pm; Sun, noon-4 pm. Closed Jan 1, Dec 25. A/C. Liquor, wine, beer. Semi-a la carte. Lunch, $3.50-$3.95; dinner, $5.50-$9. Child's plates. Specialties: baked chicken, lamb, seafood. Cr cd: A.

ROLLANDE & PIERRE. 2221 4 St N, 2½ mi N on 92. 813/822-4602. Hrs: 5-10:30 pm. Closed Sun, Dec 25. A/C. French, Amer menu. Bar. Semi-a la carte. Dinner, $9-$15. Specialties: chicken Véronique, frogs' legs, veal Oscar. Pianist Fri, Sat. Cr cds: A, C, D, MC, V.

SAND DOLLAR. 2401 34 St S, 2 mi S on 19. 813/327-5264. Hrs: 4-11 pm. Closed Labor Day. A/C. Rotating bar. Semi-a la carte. Lunch, $2.45-$4.95; dinner, $5.95-$13.95. Child's plates ½ price. Specialties: prime rib, almond-fried shrimp. Salad bar. Entertainment, dancing Tu-Sat. Tropical decor. Cr cds: A, C, D, MC, V.

ST. PETERSBURG BEACH AREA

ALPAUGH'S GULF BEACH NORTH. (1912 Gulf Blvd, Indian Rocks Beach 33535.) 813/595-9421. 16 A/C kit. units, 2 story. Mid-Dec-Apr: 1 bedrm, $50-$53; each addl, $5; under 12, $3; rest of yr: varied lower rates. Color TV. Coin lndry. On Gulf.

ALPAUGH'S GULF BEACH SOUTH. (68 Gulf Blvd, Indian Rocks Beach 33535.) 813/595-2589. 16 A/C kit. units, 2 story. Mid-Dec-Apr: S, D, $46-$53;

ACCOMMODATIONS & RESTAURANTS 143

under 12 free; rest of yr: varied lower rates. Color TV. Coin lndry. On Gulf.

BILMAR BEACH RESORT. (Box 9188, 10650 Gulf Blvd, Treasure Island 33706) at Causeway on FL 699. 813/360-5531. 174 A/C rms, 3-8 story, 61 kits. Jan-Apr: kit. units, S, D, $67-$125; each addl, $4; suites, $98; studio rms, $60-$108; under 12 free; rest of yr: varied lower rates. Color TV. 2 pools; poolside serv. Cafe, 7 am-10 pm. Bar, 11-2 am; entertainment, dancing. Tennis. On beach. Cr cds: A, C, D, MC.

BEACHCOMBERS. (6200 Gulf Blvd, St. Petersburg Beach 33706.) ¾ mi S of Causeway on FL A19A/699. 813/367-1902; res: 800/237-0707. 100 A/C rms, 2 story, 50 kits. Feb-mid-Apr: S, D, $86-$104; each addl, $4; kit units, $87-$115; under 12, free; family rates; advance res discount rates; lower rates rest of yr. Color TV. Pool. Cafe, open 24 hrs. Cr cds: A, C, D, MC, V

CORAL REEF. (5800 Gulf Blvd, St Petersburg Beach 33706) 1 mi S of St Petersburg Causeway. 813/360-0821. 130 A/C units, 2-6 story, 123 kits. Feb-late Apr: S, D, $54-$100; each addl, $4; kit. units, $58-$110; rest of yr: varied lower rates. Color TV. Pools. Cafe, 8 am-9 pm. Rm serv. Bar. On Gulf. Cr cds: A, C, D, MC, V.

DOLPHIN BEACH RESORT. (4900 Gulf Blvd, St Petersburg Beach 33706) ¼ mi N of Pinellas Bayway, 1½ mi S of Causeway on FL A19A/699. 813/360-7011. 258 A/C units, 3 story, 148 kits. Feb-Apr: S, D, $70-$90; each addl, $5; kit units, $80-$100; penthouse suite,$175; under 12 free; rest of yr: most lower. Color TV. Pool; poolside serv; lifeguard. Cafe, 7 am-10 pm. Bar, 11-2 am; entertainment, dancing exc Sun. Tennis. Marina adj; boats, charter boats avail. On Gulf. Cr cds: A, C, D, MC, V.

HOLIDAY INN. (Box 6245, St Petersburg Beach 33706) 5300 Gulf Blvd, 1½ mi S of St Petersburg Causeway. 813/360-6911. 120 A/C units, 8 story, 34 kits. Late Dec-mid-Jan, early Feb-Apr: S, D, $58-$66; each addl, $6; kit. units, $67-$78; rest of yr: varied lower rates. Color TV. Pool; poolside serv. Cafe, 7 am-11:30 pm; dining rm, 10:30 am-10 pm. Bar 11-2 am; entertainment, dancing exc Sun. Coin lndry. Sailboat, paddleboat rental. On Gulf; private beach. Cr cds: A, C, D, MC, V.

HOLIDAY INN. (15208 Gulf Blvd, Madeira Beach 33708) just N of Madeira Bridge. 813/392-2275. 157 A/C rms, 4 story. Late Dec-Apr: S, D, $85-$95; each addl, $5; under 19 free; rest of yr: varied lower rates. Color TV. Pool. wading pool; poolside serv. Cafe, 7 am-11 pm, Sun to 10 pm. Bar; entertainment, dancing exc Mon. Coin lndry. Tennis. On Gulf. Cr cds: A, C, D, MC, V.

HOLIDAY ISLES. (2200 N Gulf Blvd, Indian Rocks Beach 33535) 1 mi N of FL 688 on FL 699. 813/596-3488. 20 A/C kit. units, 1-2 story. Mid-Dec-early Apr: kit units, $35-$46.25; each addl, $7; wkly rates avail; rest of yr: varied lower rates. Color TV. Private Beach. On Gulf.

HOWARD JOHNSON'S. (11125 Gulf Blvd, Treasure Island 33706) 5 blks N of TI Causeway on 699. 813/360-6971. 84 A/C rms, 3 story. Mid-Dec-Apr: S, D, $50-$66; each addl, $10; family rates avail; rest of yr: varied lower rates. Color TV. Pool. Playground. Snack bar, open 24 hrs. Coin lndry. Cr cds: A, C, D, MC, V.

ISLAND INN. (9980 Gulf Blvd, Treasure Island 33706) 1 mi S of TI Causeway. 813/367-3731; 800/237-6425. 101 A/C rms, 6 story, 50 kits. Late Feb-Apr, D, $25-$75; each addl, $5; suites, $40-$110; rest of yr: varied lower rates. Color TV. Pool; poolside serv. Coin lndry. On Gulf. Cr cds: A, C, D, MC, V.

NORMANDY. (Box 6307, St Petersburg Beach 33736.) 5606 Gulf Blvd, 1¼ mi S of Causeway on FL A19A/699. 813/360-7002. 67 A/C units. 1-3 story, 53 kits. Feb-mid-Apr: S, D, $59-$76; 1-2 bedrm apts, $68-$125; each addl, $4; under 12, free; golf, tennis, other package plans; advance res rates; varied lower rates rest of yr. Color TV. Pool. Cafe, 8 am-3:30 pm. Coin lndry. Cr cds: A, C, D, MC, V.

QUALITY INN TRAILS END. (11500 Gulf Blvd, Treasure Island 33706) 8 blks N of TI Causeway. 813/360-5541. 54 A/C units, 1-2 story, 32 kits. Feb-Apr: S, D, $45-$50; each addl, $4; kit units, $53-$70; rest of yr: varied lower rates. Color TV. Pool. Cafe adj, 7 am-3:30 pm. On beach. Cr cds: A, C, D, MC, V.

RAMADA INN. (12000 Gulf Blvd, Treasure Island 33706.) 813/360-7051. 121 A/C rms, 4 story, 23 kits. Mid-Dec-Apr: S, $70; D, $75; each addl, $4; kit units, $78-$82; under 18 free; wkly rates avail; rest of yr: lower rates. Color TV. Pool. Playground. Cafe, 7 am-10 pm. Bar; entertainment exc Sun, Mon; dancing exc Sun-Tu. Coin lndry. Boat rental, waterskiing. On Gulf. Cr cds: A, C, D, MC, V.

SEA CHEST. (11780 Gulf Blvd, Treasure Island 33706) 10 blks N of TI Causeway. 813/360-5501. 20 A/C units, 2 story, 14 kits. Mid-Jan-Apr: S, D, $33-$46; each addl, $3; kit. units, $40-$49; each addl, $3; apts, $50-$58; rest of yr: varied lower rates. Color TV. Pool. On beach. Cr cds: A, MC, V.

TROPIC TERRACE. (11730 Gulf Blvd, St. Petersburg Beach 33706.) 813/367-2727. 42 A/C units, 2-3 story. Mid-Jan-Apr; S, D, $34; each addl, $7; 1 bedrm apts, $43; wkly rates; lower rates rest of yr. Color TV. Coin lndry. Cr cds: A, MC, V.

TRADE WINDS. (10300 Gulf Blvd, Treasure Island 33706) on FL 699. 813/360-0490. 21 A/C units, 2 story, 16 kits. Jan-Apr: S, D, $37-$39; each addl, $5; kit units, $43; 1 bedrm, $48-$55; rest of yr: varied lower rates. In season: adults only. Color TV. Pool. On Gulf. Cr cds: D, MC, V.

Restaurants

CARELESS NAVIGATOR. (11595 Gulf Blvd, Treasure Island) ½ mi N of FL 699. 813/367-2797. Hrs: 4-10 pm, Fri, Sat to 11, Sun 1-10. Reservation recommended. A/C. Bar, 4-1 am. Dinner, semi-a la carte, $9-$15.90; Specialties: native Florida snapper, captain's steak, seafood combo. Entertainment, dancing. Cr cds: A, D, MC, V.

KING CHARLES. (See Don Cesar Beach Resort Hotel above.) 813/360-1881. Hrs: 10:30 am-2 pm; hol, noon-8; off-season, 6:30-10 pm. A/C. Continental menu. Bar. Dinner, semi-a la carte, $18.95-$25.95. Specialties: rack of lamb, steak Diane, chateaubriand. Jacket required. Cr cds: A, C, D, MC, V.

LE POMPANO. (19325 Gulf Blvd, Indian Shores.) 813/596-0333. Hrs: 4-10 pm. A/C. French menu. Bar. Semi-a la carte. Dinner, $8-$16. Entertainment, dancing exc Sun, Mon. Waterfront dining. Cr cds: A, D, MC.

RED CAVALIER. (17855 Gulf Blvd, Redington Shores.) 813/393-8741, 393-8742. Hrs: 4 pm-midnight; Sun from 1 pm. A/C. Bar to 2 am. Semi-a la carte: dinner, $4.95-$14.95. Serv charge 15%. Child's plates. Specializes in Danish lobster tails, prime rib. Background music. Entertainment, dancing Tu-Sat. Cr cds: A, C, D, MC, V.

RICHARD'S. (5001 Duhme Rd, Madeira Beach.) ½ mi N of FL 699. 813/393-3497. Hrs: 11:30 am-9 pm; Sun, to 8:30 pm. Closed Mon. A/C. Bar. Semi-a la carte: lunch, dinner, $5.95-$16.95; 15% serv charge. Child's plates. Specializes in ethnic foods, prime rib, fried & broiled seafood platters. Own pies. Background music. Entertainment, Tu-Sat. Overlooks gardens. Cr cds: A, C, D, MC, V.

TRADER FRANK'S. (19601 Gulf Blvd, Indian Shores) 2½ mi S of FL 688 on FL 699. 813/595-2567. Hrs: 11:30 am-4 pm, 4:30-10 pm. A/C. Chinese, Japanese, Polynesian, Amer menu. Dinner, $4.50-$7.50. Specialties: hula tailed shrimp, Fung Wung Kai, teriyaki steak. Salad bar. Entertainment, dancing exc Mon. Cr cds: A, C, D, MC, V.

SANFORD

HOLIDAY INN-SANFORD/LAKE MONROE. (Box 2838; 32771) 530 N Palmetto Ave 14, Sanford Exit & Sanford Mt Dora exit. 305/323-1910. 100 A/C rms, 2 story. S, $30; D, $45; each addl, $5; under 12 free; family rates avail. Color TV. Pool; poolside serv. Cafe, 6:30 am-10 pm. Bar; entertainment. Coin lndry. Complex on Lake Monroe; marina. Cr cds: A, D, MC, V.

Restaurant

MOLLY MAGEE'S. 2544 S Park Ave., 1 blk E of US 17, 92. 813/322-9450. Hrs: 11:30-2 am. Closed Sun. A/C. Bar. Semi-a la carte: lunch, dinner $3.95-$13. Specializes in king crab legs, prime rib. Salad bar. Own baking. Background music. Entertainment, dancing. Cr cds: A, MC, V.

SANIBEL & CAPTIVA ISLANDS

CASA YBEL. 2255 W Gulf Dr. (33924), 3 mi W of Causeway on Sanibel Island. 813/472-3145. 72 A/C kit. units, 2 story. Mid-Dec-Apr: 1 bedrm for 2, $150; 2 bedrm for 4, $180; (3 day min for 2 bedrm units); each addl, $10; wkly rates avail; rest of yr: lower rates. Color TV. Pool; poolside serv. Cafe, 10 am-10 pm (also see THISTLE LODGE). Cr cds: A, D, MC, V.

ISLAND INN. (Box M, Sanibel; 33924.) 3111 W Gulf Dr, 4½ mi W of Causeway on Sanibel Island. 813/472-1561. 57 A/C units in motel, lodges, 2-3 story, 29 kits. Mod Amer plan: mid-Nov-late Apr (4-day min hols): S, D, $86-$115; each addl, $25; under 10, $10-$15; rest of yr: varied lower rates, Eur plan only. Serv charge, 10% in season. Color TV. Pool. Cafe, 7:30-9 am, 6:30-7:45 pm. Coin lndry. Tennis. On beach. Cr cds: MC, V.

JOLLY ROGER. 3201 W Gulf Dr (33924), 6 mi W of Causeway on Sanibel Island. 813/472-1700. 45 A/C units, 2 story, 34 kits. Mid-Dec-Apr (3-day min hols; 1-wk min Christmas, Easter): S, D, $55-$75; each addl, $5; kit. units, $80-$90; suites, $125-$160; rest of yr: lower rates. Color TV. Pool. Cafe, 5:30-9:30 pm. Coin lndry. Tennis. On Beach. Cr cds: A, MC, V.

RAMADA. 1131 Middle Gulf Dr on Sanibel Island (33924). 813/472-4123. 98 A/C rms, 2 story. Mid-Dec-Apr: S, D, $51.50-$56.50; each addl, $6; suites, $76; under 18 free. Color TV. Pool; poolside serv. Cafe, 7:30-2 am, 5-10 pm. Bar; entertainment, dancing. Tennis. On beach. Cr cds: A, C, D, MC, V.

SANIBEL MOORINGS. (PO, Sanibel 33924.) 800 Gulf Dr, ½ mi S of Causeway on Sanibel Island. 813/472-4119. 112 A/C kit. units, 2 story. Mid-Dec-late Apr: wkly: 1-3 bedrm apts, $524-$840 week; each addl, $70 week; in season wkly only; off season 3-day min; rest of yr: lower rates. Color TV. 2 pools; wading pool. Coin lndry. Tennis. On beach.

SANIBEL SIESTA. 1246 Fulger St (33924), 3½ mi W of Causeway on Sanibel Island, 1½ mi S of FL 867. 813/472-1767. 52 2 bedrm A/C kit. units, 3 story. Mid-Dec-Apr: $581/wk to $847 wk. (rentals wkly in season, 4 night min in summer); each addl, $70/wk; rest of yr: lower rates. Color TV. 2 pools. Coin lndry. On beach.

SOUTH SEAS PLANTATION. (Box 194, Captiva 33924.) 12 mi W of Causeway at end of Captiva Island. 813/472-5111; res: 800/282-3402 (FL), 800/237-3102 (exc FL). 20 A/C rms, 2 story; 500 A/C 1-3 bedrm kit apts; beach & tennis, bayside & marina villas. Mid-Dec-Apr: S, D, $100; each addl, $15 kit units, $120-$200; kit cottages, $245-$350; lower rates rest of yr. Color TV. 16 pools; 2 whirlpools. Child's program. Cafe, 7-11 am; 11:30 am-5 pm, 5:30-10 pm (also see CHADWICK'S). Box lunches. Bar. Coin lndry. Sundries. Marina. Sailing charters; sailing school. Fish/hunt guides, fish/game clean/store. Bicycles. Cr cds: A, C, D, MC, V.

SUNDIAL BEACH & TENNIS RESORT. 1246 Middle Gulf Dr (33924). 3 mi W of Causeway on Tulipa Way on Sanibel Island. 813/472-4151. 215 kit. units, 4 story. Mid-Dec-mid-Apr: 1 bedrm, $130-$175; 2 bedrm, $175-$230; each addl, $10; under 10 free, family, tennis, vacation, honeymoon package plans avail; rest of yr: lower rates. Color TV, 3 pools; poolside serv. Cafe, 8-10 am, 11:30 am-2:30 pm, 5:30-9:30 pm (jacket required). Bar; entertainment, dancing. Coin lndry. Tennis. Boat, bicycle rentals. On Gulf. Cr cds: A, C, D, MC.

WEST WIND INN. (Box F, Sanibel; 33924.) W Gulf Dr, 6½ mi W of Causeway on Sanibel Island. 813/472-1541. 104 A/C units, 2 story, 64 kits. Mid-Dec-mid-Apr (3-day min hols): S, D, $70-$78; each addl, $7; kit units, $79-$85; suites, $136-$219; lower rates rest of yr. Color TV. Pool. Cafe, 5:30-9:30 pm. Coin lndry. Cr cds: A, C, D, MC, V.

Restaurants

CHADWICK'S. (See South Seas Plantation above.) 813/472-5111. Hrs: 7 am-2 pm, 6-midnight; Sun, 9 am-2 pm, 5-11 pm. A/C. Continental menu. Bar, 11-2 am. Bkfst buffet, table d'hôte, $4.50-$6.50. Semi-a la carte. Lunch, $4.25-$7.95; dinner, $9.95-$18. Specialties: beer batter shrimp, chicken Tahiti, sole Vèronique. Seafood buffet Fri eve. Entertainment, dancing Tu-Sat (winter only). Cr cds: A, D, MC, V.

COCONUT GROVE. (PO, Sanibel.) Periwinkle Way at Tarpon Bay Rd, 2½ mi W of Causeway on Sanibel Island. 813/472-1366. Hrs: 11 am-10 pm. Closed 1 wk after Labor Day for 7 days. A/C. Bar. Semi-a la carte. Lunch, $1.95-$5.95; dinner, $8.95-$12.95. Child's plates, $3.95-$6.50. Specialties: baklava, stuffed shrimp, roast sirloin of beef. Salad bar. Will cook your cleaned fish. Cr cds: MC, V.

NUTMEG HOUSE. (PO, Sanibel.) 2761 Gulf Dr, 3½ mi W of Causeway on Sanibel Island. 813/472-1141. Hrs: 5:30-9:30 pm; Sun, champagne brunch, noon-2 pm. Reservation suggested in winter. Closed Mon. A/C. Dinner, semi-a la carte, $12-$18. Specialties: veal marsala, roast duck l'orange.

THISTLE LODGE. (See Casa Ybel Motel above.) Hrs: 10 am-10 pm; Sun from 9 am. Closed Mon. A/C. Continental menu. Bar. Semi-a la carte. Brunch, $5-$9; dinner $12-$17; Specialties: Sun brunch, paella, bouillabaisse, stuffed pork chops. 19th century mansion furnished in Victorian elegance. Cr cds: A, D, MC, V.

SARASOTA

BEST WESTERN GOLDEN HOST. 4675 N Tamiami Trail (33580), 2 mi N on 41. 813/355-5141. 80 A/C rms, 2 story, 7 kits. Mid-Dec-mid-Apr: S, $28-$56; D, $32-$56; kit units, $42-$56; each addl, $4; rest of yr: lower rates. Color TV. Pool. Cafe adj, 7 am-9 pm. Bar. Cr cds: A, C, D, MC, V.

BEST WESTERN ROYAL PALMS. 1701 N Tamiami Trail (33580), 1 mi N on 41. 813/365-1342. 37 A/C rms, 10 kits. Late Dec-mid-Apr: S, D, $30-$48; each addl, $4; kit. units, $45; under 12 free; wkly, monthly rates avail; rest of yr: lower rates. Color TV. Pool. Cafe, 24 hrs. Cr cds: A, C, D, MC, V.

BEST WESTERN SARASOATA MOTOR INN. 8150 N Tamiami Trail (33580), 6 mi N on 41. 813/355-7747. 158 A/C rms, 3 story. Jan-Apr: S, $25-$60; D, $40-$70; each addl, $4; under 18 free; rest of yr: lower rates. Color TV; free in-rm movies avail. Pool. Cafe, 7-10 am, 11:30 am-3 pm, 5-10 pm. Bar; entertainment, dancing exc Mon. Cr cds: A, C, D, MC, V.

CADILLAC. 4021 N Tamiami Trail (33580), 2 mi N on 41. 813/355-7108. 25 A/C rms, 3 kits. Mid-Dec-Apr: S, $32; D, $34; each addl, $2; kit. units, $34; rest of yr: lower rates. Color TV. Pool. Cr cds: A, D, MC, V.

FLAMINGO COLONY. 4703 N Tamiami Trail (33580), 2¼ mi N on 41. 813/351-2088. 26 A/C rms, 11 kits. Mid-Dec-Easter: S, D, $42; each addl, $4; rest of yr: lower rates. TV, color in many. Pool. Cafe adj, 7 am-9 pm. Coin lndry. Cr cds: MC, V.

RAINBOW MOTOR LODGE. 4200 N Tamiami Trail (33580), 2 mi N on 41. 813/355-7616. 36 A/C rms, 1-2 story, 29 kits. Jan-mid-Apr: S, $32; D, $34; kit. units, $275/wk; rest of yr: lower rates. Color TV. Cr cds: D, MC, V.

RAMADA INN. 6545 N Tamiami Trail (33580), 4 mi N on 41. 813/355-7771. 110 A/C rms, 2 story. Feb-late Apr: S, D, $62-$79; each addl, $7; under 18 free; rest of yr: lower rates. Color TV. Pool. Cafe, 6:30 am-10 pm. Bar; entertainment, dancing exc Sun. Coin lndry. Cr cds: A, C, D, MC, V.

RODEWAY INN. 1 N Tamiami Trail (33577). ¼ mi N on US 41 at Gulf Stream Ave. 813/365-1900. 105 A/C rms, 6 story, 5 kits. Elvtrs. Feb-Mar: S, D, $53-$63; each addl, $6; suites, $70-$75; under 17 free; lower rates rest of yr. Color TV. Pool. Cafe, open 24 hrs. Bar. Coin lndry. Cr cds: A, C, D, MC, V.

SARASOTA HYATT HOUSE. 1000 Blvd of the Arts (33577) at Watergate Center, ¼ mi N, 3 blks W of 41. 813/366-9000. 285 A/C rms. Mid-Dec-May: S, $82-$92; D, $97-$107; each addl, $15; suites, 1 bedrm, $250; 2 bedrm, $300; rest of year: lower rates. Color TV. Pool; poolside serv. Cafe, 11-12:30 am. Bar; entertainment. Tennis. Dockage. Cr cds: A, C, D, MC, V.

SUNSET TERRACE. 4644 Tamiami Trail (33580), 2 mi N on 41. 813/355-8489. 24 A/C rms, 22 kits. Mid-Jan-mid-Apr: S, D, $38-$50; kit. units, $38-$50; $250/wk; under 10 free; rest of yr: lower rates. Color TV. Pool. Cafe opp, 7 am-9 pm. Coin lndry. Cr cds: MC, V.

Restaurants

MEL-O-DEE. 4685 N Tamiami Trail, 2 mi N on 41. 813/355-5768. Hrs: 7 am-9 pm. A/C. Semi-a la carte. Bkfst, $2.25-$4.25; lunch, $2.35-$4.50; dinner, $4.25-$8.25. Child's plates. Specialties: steak, roast turkey, homemade pies. Salad bar. Cr cds: MC, V.

WINDJAMMER. 'Jammer Family Room. 6700 S Tamiami Trail, 7 mi S on 41, opp Gulf Gate Shopping Center. 813/924-1121. Hrs: 4-9 pm; Sun, 11:30 am-8:30 pm. Closed Dec 25. A/C. Bar. Dinner, semi-a la carte, $2.85-$9.95. Specialties: prime rib, barbecued shortribs, seafood. Salad bar. Cr cds: MC, V.

ZINN'S. 6101 N Tamiami Trail on 41. 813/355-5417. Hrs: 5-10 pm. Closed Dec 25, also after Labor Day-mth of Sep. A/C. Bar, 11 am-2 pm; 3:30-10 pm. Dinner, semi-a la carte, $6.95-$16.95; serv plate, $2; Sun brunch buffet, 11 am-2 pm, $6.50. Specialties: boned chicken under glass, plank-broiled red snapper, prime rib. Pianist. Cr cds: A, MC, V.

SEBRING

SAFARI INN. 1406 US 27 North (33870), 2 mi N on 27. 813/382-1148. 37 A/C rms. Jan-mid-Apr: S, $33.60-$35.70; D, $35.70-$44.10; each addl, $5; kit. units, $5 addl; special events higher rates; rest of yr: lower rates. Color TV. Pool; whirlpool. Playground. Coin lndry. Cr cds: A, C, MC, V.

SUNSET BEACH. 2221 SE Lakeview Dr (33870), on Hwy 27. 813/385-6129. 42 A/C rms, 1-2 story, 23 kits. Dec-Apr: S, $24-$36; D, $26-$38; each addl, $5; kit. units, $26-$38; higher rates during races; rest of yr: lower rates. Color TV. Cafe adj, open 24 hrs. On beach. Cr cds: MC, V.

SILVER SPRINGS

BEST WESTERN MUSTANG MOTOR INN. (Box 395; 32688.) 5001 Silver Springs Blvd, 4 blks W on FL 40. 904/236-2891. 56 A/C rms, 2 story. Mid-Jan-mid-Apr, mid-June-mid-Sep: S, D, $36; each addl, $4; under 12 free; rest of yr: lower rates. Color TV. Pool. Playground. Cafe adj, 6 am-10 pm. Tennis. Cr cds: A, C, D, MC, V.

HOWARD JOHNSON'S. (Box 475; 32091.) 1 blk E on FL 40. 904/236-2616. 44 A/C rms, 2 story, 4 kits. Jan-mid-Apr, mid-June-early Sep: S, $34-$42; D, $42-$50; each addl, $5; kit units, $275/wk; under 18 free; sr cit rates; races, hols, football wkends, special events higher; lower rates rest of yr. Color TV. Cafe open 24 hrs. Cr cds: C, D, MC, V.

SUN PLAZA. (Box 216; 32688.) Silver Springs Blvd, on FL 40. 813/236-2343. 48 A/C rms, 9 kits. June-Labor Day: S, $26; D, $34; each addl, $3; rest of yr: lower rates. Color TV. Pool. Playground. Cafe adj, open 24 hrs. Cr cds: A, D, MC, V.

STARKE

STARKE MOTOR INN. (Drawer 1090; 32091.) 7 blks N on US 301. 904/964-7600. 100 A/C rms, 2 story. S, $29-$33; D, $29-$33; each addl, $5; under 18 free. Color TV. Pool; poolside serv. Playground. Cafe, 6 am-2 pm, 5-10 pm. Bar; entertainment Wed-Sat. Coin lndry. Cr cds: A, C, D, MC, V.

STUART

HOLIDAY INN. (Box 566; 33494.) 1209 S Federal Hwy, 1 mi S on 1. 305/287-6200. 120 A/C rms, 2 story. Mid-Dec-late Apr: S, $48; D, $60; each addl, $5; rest of yr: varied lower rates. Color TV. Pool. Playground. Cafe, 6 am-2 pm, 5-10 pm. Bar; entertainment, dancing exc Sun. Coin lndry. Cr cds: A, D, MC, V.

HOWARD JOHNSON'S. 950 S Federal Hwy (33494), jct 1 & FL 76. 305/287-3171. 82 A/C rms, 2 story. Mid-Dec-late Apr: S, D, $50-$70; each addl, $8; under 18 free; rest of yr: lower rates. Color TV. Pool. Cafe open 24 hrs. Rm serv. Bar. Coin lndry. Tennis. Cr cds: A, C, D, MC, V.

INDIAN RIVER PLANTATION. (Box 569; 33494.) 385 NE Plantation Rd, 3 mi E on FL A1A. 305/225-3700. 110 A/C kit. apts. Mid-Dec-mid-Apr: 1-bedrm for 1-4, $85-$150; 2-bedrm for 4-6, $95-$190; family package plan avail; special events higher rates (3-day min); rest of yr: lower rates.

Color TV. 3 pools; poolside serv. Dining rm. Coin lndry. Golf. Tennis. Private beach.

TALLAHASSEE

DAYS INN. 2800 N Monroe St (32303). 2½ mi N on US 27 at I-10. 904/385-0136. 115 A/C rms, 1-3 story. S, $32-$33; D, $36-$38; each addl, $4; under 18, $1; under 2 free. Color TV. Pool. Cafe, 6 am-9 pm. Cr cds: A, C, D, MC, V.

HOLIDAY INN APALACHEE. 1302 Apalachee Pkwy (32301), 1 mi E on 27, 1 mi S of 90. 904/877-3141. 167 A/C rms, 2 story. S, $37-$43; D, $41-$48, each addl, $4; under 18 free. Color TV. Pool; wading pool. Cafe, 6:30 am-2 pm, 5:30-10 pm. Bar; entertainment, dancing exc Sun.

HOLIDAY INN DOWNTOWN. 316 W Tennessee St (32301), 3 blks W on 90. 904/222-8000. 160 A/C rms, 12 story. S, $39-$45; D, $44-$49; studio rms avail; under 18 free. Color TV. Pool; poolside serv. Cafe, 6:30 am-2 pm, 5:30-10 pm. Bars; entertainment, dancing. Cr cds: A, C, D, MC.

PONCE DE LEON. 1801 W Tennessee St (32304), 1½ mi W on 90. 904/222-4950. 25 A/C rms. S, $18-$22; D, $24-$28; each addl, $3; special events higher rates. Color TV. Pool. Cafe, 24 hrs. Cr cds: A, C, D, MC, V.

QUALITY INN SOUTHERNAIRE. Hwy 90 W at Brevard St (32304), 1½ mi W on 90. 904/224-7116. 103 A/C rms, 1-2 story. S, $31-$35; D, $35-$39; each addl, $4; suites, $35-$50; under 16 free. Color TV. Pool. Playground. Cafe adj, open 24 hrs. Bar; entertainment, dancing exc Sun. Cr cds: A, D, MC, V.

RAMADA INN-WEST. 2121 W Tennessee St (32304), 2½ mi W on 90; I-10 Capital Circle exit. 904/576-6121. 150 A/C rms, 2 story. S, $36-$40; D, $44-$48; each addl, $6; suite, $70-$80; under 18 free. Color TV. Pool; sauna. Playground. Cafe, 6 am-10 pm. Bar; entertainment, dancing exc Sun. Cr cds: A, C, D, MC, V.

TALLAHASSEE MOTOR HOTEL. 1630 N Monroe St (32302), on 27 southwest I-10, downtown. 904/224-6183. 92 A/C units, 1-2 story. S, $23-$29; D, $27-$35; each addl, $3. Color TV. Pool. Cafe, 6:30 am-9:30 pm. Cr cds: A, C, D, MC, V.

Restaurants

ADAMS ROOM. 101 S Adams St, 2 blks N of Capitol. 904/224-5000. Hrs: 11 am-11 pm. Closed Sun. A/C. Bar. Semi-a la carte. Lunch, $4.95-$9.95; dinner, $8.95-$15.95. Specialties: steak, seafood. Early Amer decor.

BROWN DERBY. 2415 N Monroe St in Tallahassee Mall, on US 27 N, 1 mi S of Interchange I-10 exit US 27. 904/386-1109. Hrs: 11:30-12:30 am; Sat, from 4 pm; Sun 11:30 am-10 pm. Closed Dec 25. A/C. Bar. Semi-a la carte. Lunch, $1.85-$5; dinner, $3-$10. Specialty: beef. Salad bar. Entertainment, dancing exc Sun. Cr cds: A, C, D, MC, V.

MORRISON'S (Cafeteria). 2415 N Monroe Ave, 3 mi N on 27N, in Tallahassee Mall. 904/385-3471. Hrs: 11 am-8 pm. A/C. Avg ck: lunch, dinner, $3.25-$3.75. Specialty: Southern cooking.

TAMPA

ADMIRAL BENBOW INN. 1200 N Westshore Blvd (33607). ½ blk N of I-275. 813/879-1750. 240 A/C rms, 5 story. S, $45-$47; D, $52-$57; each addl, $4; suites, $80-$100; under 12 free; wkend rates. Color TV; in-rm movies. Pool; wading pool. Cafe, 6:30 am-3 pm, 5-10 pm. Bar, 11 am-2 am; entertainment, dancing exc Sun. Cr cds: A, C, D, MC, V.

BAY HARBOR INN. 7700 Courtney Campbell Causeway (33607), 8 mi W on FL 60, 3 mi W of airport. 813/885-2541; res: 800/237-7773. 260 A/C rms, 6 story. S, $60-$75; D, $70-$85; each addl, $9; suites, $110-$115; under 16 free. Color TV; in-rm movies avail. Pool; poolside serv. Playground. Cafe, 7 am-11 pm. Bar; entertainment, dancing exc Sun. Coin lndry. Tennis. On Tampa Bay. Cr cds: A, C, D, MC, V.

CAUSEWAY INN BEACH. 7627 W Columbus Dr (33607) on Courtney Campbell Causeway, 7 mi W on FL 60. 813/884-7561. 152 A/C rms, 2 story. Dec-late Apr: S, $37-$59; D, $42-$69; each addl, $12; suites, $115; sr cit rates; package plans, lower rates rest of yr. Color TV; in-rm movies. Pool. Cafe, 7 am-11 pm. Bar 11 am-2 am; entertainment, dancing. Coin lndry. Cr cds: A, C, D, MC, V.

DAYS INN-BUSCH GARDENS. 2901 E Busch Blvd (33612), 1¾ mi E of I-75 on FL 580. 813/933-6471. 179 A/C rms, 2 story. Mid-Dec-mid-Apr: S, $38; D, $44; each addl, $4; rest of yr: lower rates. Color TV. Pool. Cafe, 6:30 am-9:30 pm. Coin lndry. Cr cds: A, D, MC, V.

EXPRESSWAY INN-NORTH. 3693 Gandy Blvd (33611), ½ blk E of 92, 4½ mi S of I-75. 813/837-1921. 60 A/C rms, 2 story, 2 kits. Mid-Dec-mid-Apr: S, $34; D, $38; each addl, $4; rest of yr: lower rates. Color TV. Pool. Cafe, 6 am-1 pm Coin lndry adj. Cr cds: A, C, D, MC, V.

HOLIDAY INN-NORTH. 400 E Bearss Ave (33612), 10 mi N at I-75. 813/961-1000. 171 A/C rms, 2 story. Mid-Dec-mid-Apr: S, $44-$48; D, $52-$58; each addl, $6; suites, $75; under 12 free; rest of yr: varied lower rates. Color TV; free in-rm movies. Pool; wading pool; poolside serv. Cafe, 6:30 am-10 pm. Bar; entertainment, dancing exc Sun. Coin lndry. Orange grove; guests may pick own oranges. Cr cds: A, C, D, MC, V.

HOLIDAY INN-STATE FAIR I-4 EAST. 2708 N 50 St (33619), 4 mi SE on 41, 1 mi N of FL 60; I-4 exit 50 St. 813/621-2081. 183 A/C rms, 2 story. Mid-Dec-mid-Apr: S, $42-$46; D, $48-$60; each addl, $6; studio rms, $30; under 18 free; rest of yr: lower rates. Color TV; in-rm movies. Pool; wading pool; poolside serv. Cafe, 6 am-11 pm. Bar; entertainment, dancing exc Sun. Coin lndry. Cr cds: A, C, D, MC, V.

HOLIDAY INN WEST-STADIUM. 4732 N Dale Mabry (33614), 2½ mi NE on I-75. 813/877-6061. 252 A/C rms, 5 kits, 2 story. Mid-Dec-mid-Apr: S, $29-$33; D, $36-$42; each addl, $5; under 19 free; $3 addl/person during stadium special events; rest of yr: lower rates. Color TV. Pool; wading pool. Cafe, 5:30-10:30 pm. Bar; entertainment, dancing exc Mon. Coin lndry. Cr cds: A, C, D, MC, V.

LA QUINTA. 4730 Spruce St (33607). On I-75 at Westshore Blvd exit. 813/879-3970. 122 A/C rms, 2 story. S, $37; D, $43; each addl, $5; suites, $35-$75; under 18 free; sr cit rates. Color TV; in-rm movies. Pool. Cafe, open 24 hrs. Bar. Nonsmoking area. Cr cds: A, C, D, MC, V.

MARRIOTT-TAMPA AIRPORT. (Box 241107; 33622.) At Int'l Airport, 1½ mi N of jct FL 60, I-75. 813/879-5151. 300 A/C rms, 6 story. Mid-Dec-mid-Apr: S, $75-$85; D, $85-$95; each addl, $8; studio rms, $100-$110; suites, $160-$325; under 18 free; sr cit rates. Color TV; in-rm movies. Pool. Cafe, 6 am-midnight; (also see C.K.'S). Bar, 11 am-2 am; entertainment, dancing. Cr cds: A, MC, V.

QUALITY INN-NORTH. 210 E Fowler Ave (33612), 6 mi N at I-75 Fowler Ave exit. 813/933-6487. 147 A/C rms, 2 story, 35 kits. Jan-Apr: S, $40-$51; D, $46-$56; each addl, $7; kit. units, $56-$64; under 16 free; tour package avail; rest of yr: varied lower rates. Color TV. Pool; wading pool; poolside serv; lifeguard. Playground. Cafe open 6 am-2 am. Bar. Coin lndry. Cr cds: A, C, D, MC, V.

RODEWAY INN. 2520 N 50 St (33619), 4 mi SE at jct 41, I-4. 813/247-3941. 294 A/C rms, 2 story. Mid-Dec-mid-Apr: S, $46-$52; D, $54-$60; each addl, $8; rest of yr: varied lower rates. Color TV. Pool; poolside serv. Cafe, 7 am-2:30 pm, 5-10 pm. Bar; entertainment, dancing. Cr cds: A, C, D, MC, V.

Restaurants

BERN'S STEAK HOUSE. 1208 S Howard Ave, 3 blks SW, 4 blks N of Bayshore Blvd. 813/251-2421, also 800/282-1547. Hrs: 5-11 pm. Closed Dec 25. A/C. Bar. Wine cellars. Dinner, semi-a la carte, steak $14.10-$90. Other entrees, $10-$14.90. Child's plates. Specialties: organically grown vegetables, aged prime beef, blended imported coffee. Accordionist Tu-Sat. Antiques, paintings, statuary. Cr cds: A, C, D, MC, V.

CAFE de PARIS. 4430 W Kennedy Blvd. On FL 60, 4 blks W of US 92. 813/876-5422. Hrs: 11:30-2:30 pm, 5:30-11 pm. Closed lunch Sat, Sun; Jan 1, Dec 25. A/C. French menu. Wine, beer. Wine list. Semi-a la carte: lunch, $5-$8; dinner, $8.95-$26. Specialties: Chateaubriand Bouquetiere, shrimp Monte Carlo. Background music. Wine displays. Cr cds: A, C, D, MC, V.

C.K.'S. (See Marriott-Tampa Airport above.) 813/879-5151. Hrs: 11:30 am-2:30 pm, 5:30-11 pm; Sun to 10 pm. A/C. Continental, Amer menu. Bar. Semi-a la carte. Lunch, $4.75-$9.25; dinner, $11.50-$16.50. Specialties: prime rib, chicken Florentine, red snapper. Cr cds: A, MC, V.

COLUMBIA. 22 St & 7 Ave, 4 blks S of I-4 exit 21 St in Ybor City. 813/248-4961. Hrs: 11 am-2 am. Reservation recommended. A/C. Spanish, Amer cuisine. Bars. Wine cellar. Semi-a la carte. Lunch, $3.95-$10.95; dinner, $7.95-$22. Child's plates, $4.75-$7.95. Specialties: red snapper Alicante, chicken & yellow rice, filet steak Columbia. Entertainment, dancing exc Sun. Violinist; flamenco dancers. 10% entertainment charge in some rms. Also THE CAFE AT THE COLUMBIA. Hrs: 11-2 am. Reservation recommended. Spanish, Amer menu. Bar. Specialties: Australian lobster tail, 2002 T-bone porterhouse, red snapper El Greco. Modern decor. Live entertainment. Cr cds: A, C, D, MC, V.

OLD SPAGHETTI WAREHOUSE. 1911 N 13th St (33605). 1 mi S I-4, Ybor City exit. In Ybor Square. 813/248-1720. Hrs: 11 am-2:30 pm, 5-10 pm; Fri to 11 pm, Sat noon-11 pm, Sun noon-10 pm. Closed Thanksgiving, Dec 25. A/C. Italian menu. Bar. Semi-a la carte: lunch, $1.75-$5.95; dinner, $3.40-$7.25. Serv. plate. Child's plates. Specializes in baked lasagne, San Francisco sourdough bread. Background music. Cr cds: A, C, D, MC, V.

SPANISH PARK. 3517 E 7 Ave, 3 mi E, 4 blks W of I-40 exit 40 St in Ybor City. 813/248-6138. Hrs: 11 am-11 pm. Closed Sun; major hols. A/C. Spanish, Amer menu. Bar. Semi-a la carte. Lunch, $4.50-$6; dinner, $6.50-$13.50. Child's plates. Specialties: trout almendra, shrimp Valdes, paella valenciana. Cr cds: A, C, D, MC, V.

TARPON SPRINGS

BEST WESTERN TAHITIAN. 2337 Hwy 19N (33589), N in Tahitian Gardens. 813/937-4121. 140 A/C rms, 2 story, 18 kits. Mid-Dec-Apr: S, D, $45-$55; each addl, $5; under 12 free; rest of yr: varied lower rates. Color TV. Pool. Cafe. Bar. Cr cds: A, C, D, MC, V.

GULF MANOR. 548 Whitcomb Blvd (33589), ½ mi W of 19A. 813/937-4207. 29 A/C rms, 18 kits. Dec-Apr: S, D, $25-$32; each addl, $3; kit. units, $23-$29; rest of yr: lower rates. Color TV. Pool. Playground. Cafe, 7 am-9 pm. Cr. cds.: MC, V.

INNISBROOK. (Drawer 1088; 33589.) 1 mi SE on 19. 813/937-3124; res: 800/237-0157. 1,211 A/C units in 25 lodges, 2 story, 840 kits. Mid-Jan-Apr: S, D, $115; kit. units, $135-$160; 1-2 bedrm kit. units for 1-6, $250-$275; each addl, $10; Amer plan, Mod Amer plan, family rates, package plans avail; rest of yr: varied lower rates. Color TV. 5 pools; poolside serv; sauna. Cafe, 7-10 am, 11:30 am-2 pm, 6:30-10 pm. Bar, 3-midnight. Free lndry facilities. Tennis. Golf. Wildlife preserve. On 1,000 acres. Cr cds: A, C, D, MC, V.

Restaurant

LOUIS PAPPAS' RIVERSIDE. 10 W Dodecanese Blvd, on 19A at Sponge Dock. 813/937-5101. Hrs: 11:30 am-11 pm. A/C. Greek, Amer menu. Bar. Semi-a la carte. Lunch, $3.95-$8.95; dinner, $4.95-$12.95. Specialties: Greek salad, mousaka, seafood. Cr cds: A, MC, V.

TAVARES

SUNDOWN. ¼ mi N on 441, FL 19. 813/343-4666. 34 A/C rms, 2 story, 3 kits., 2 apts. Rm phones. S, $22-$32; D, $25-$38; each addl, $4; kit units, $32-$40; family, wkly rates avail. Color TV. Pool. Playground. Cafe adj, open 24 hrs. Coin lndry. Cr cds: A, D, MC, V.

MISSION INN GOLF & TENNIS RESORT. (Box 441, Howey-in-the-Hills 32737.) FL 19 & Hwy 48, 6½ mi S on FL 19, 6½ mi S of Hwy 48, 5 mi N of FL Tpke exit 85. 813/324-3101; res: 800/874-9053. 147 A/C rms, 4 kits. Dec-Apr: S, $95-$155; D, $95-$245; each addl, $7-$10; kit units, $155-$245; villas $170-$220; under 12 free; golf, tennis package plans avail; rest of yr: varied lower rates. Color TV. Pool; poolside serv. Playground. Cafe, 7 -10:30 am, 11:30 am-2 pm, 6:30-10 pm. Bar, 6 am-1 pm; entertainment, dancing. Coin lndry. Tennis. Golf. Cr cds: A, C, D, MC, V.

TITUSVILLE

L-K MOTOR INN. 3755 Cheney Hwy (32780). 4 mi W on FL 50, 2 blks W of I-95. 305/269-4480. 152 rms, 5 kits. Feb-Apr: S, $24-$27; D $27-$50; each addl $3; sr citizen rates; wkly rates. Crib free, cot $4. TV. Pool. Cafe 6 am-10 pm. Bar. Ck-out 11 am. Coin lndry. Meeting rms. Sundries. Airport, bus depot transportation. Oversize beds. Lawn games. Cr cds: A, MC, V.

QUALITY INN APOLLO. 3810 S Hwy 1 (32780), 2 mi S on 1. 305/267-9111. 112 A/C rms, 2 story. S, $20-$27; D, $30; each addl, $2. Color TV. Pool. Playground. Cafe adj. View of space shots. Cr cds: A, C, D, MC, V.

RAMADA INN. 3500 Cheney Hwy (32780), on FL 50 at I-95. 305/269-5510. 126 A/C rms, 2 story, 26 kits. S, $23-$43; D, $39-$48; each addl, $6. Kit. suites, $76/daily; under 18 free; higher rates during Daytona Speedway. Color TV. Pool. Cafe, 6:30 am-2 pm, 4:30-9 pm. Bar. Coin lndry. Tennis. Cr cds: A, C, D, MC, V.

Restaurants

JACK BAKER'S SAND POINT INN. 801 Marina Rd, 1 mi N. 305/269-1012. Hrs: 11:30 am-10 pm; Sun noon-9 pm. Closed Dec 25. A/C. Bar. Semi-a la carte. Lunch. 2.99-$4.99; dinner, $4.50-$12.99. Specialty: Maine lobster. Nautical atmosphere. Cr cds: A, D, MC, V.

ROYAL OAKS. (On grounds of Royal Oaks Country Club Resort). 305/269-4500. Hrs: 7 am-3 pm, 5-10 pm. Res recommended. A/C. Bar, 11-2 am, Sun, 1 pm-midnight. Wine list. Semi-a la carte. Bkfst, $1.25-$4.75; lunch, $1.65-$4.95; dinner, $7.95-$15.20; super saver package; lower rates rest of yr. Table d'hote: dinner, $7.95-$16.95. Specializes in steak, veal, seafood. Salad bar. Own baking. Background music. Entertainment Wed-Sat (bar). Cr cds: A, MC, V.

VENICE

BEST WESTERN VENICE MOTOR INN. 455 Venice Bypass (33595). 1 mi on US 41. 813/485-5411. 160 A/C rms, 2 story. Jan-mid-Apr: S, $44-$68; D, $50-$70; each addl, $6; under 12, free; suites, $65-$120; super saver package; lower rates rest of yr. Color TV. Pool. Cafe, 6:30-10:30 am, 11 am-3 pm, 4-8 pm. Bar; entertainment, dancing. Coin lndry. Cr cds: A, C, D, MC, V.

HOLIDAY INN. (1660 S Tamiami Trail, Osprey 33559.) 5 mi N on US 41. 813/966-2121. 100 A/C rms, 2 story. Mid-Dec-mid-Apr: S, $60; D, $64; each addl, $4; under 17, free; family rates; lower rates rest of yr. Color TV. Pool. Cafe, 7 am-2 pm; dining rm, 5-10 pm. Bar 11 am-2:30 am; entertainment, dancing; dinner theatre Sept-May. Coin lndry. Cr cds: A, C, D, MC, V.

Restaurant

ITALIAN VILLA. 200 St Augustine Ave, 1 blk W of 41 Business. 813/488-4674. Hrs: 5-10 pm; Fri, Sat to midnight. Closed Tu; Easter, Thanksgiving, Dec 25. A/C. Italian, Amer menu. Wine, beer. Dinner, semi-a la carte, $4-$6.95. Specialties: chicken cacciatora, veal scallopini, lasagne. Cr cds: MC, V.

VERO BEACH

AQUARIUS. 1526 S Ocean Dr, 4 mi SE (32960). 2 blks SE of FL A1A. 305/231-5218. 22 A/C units, 2 story, 19 kits. Dec-Apr: S, D, $30-$40; each addl, $5; suites, $60-$100; kit units, $40-$60; under 12, free; wkly rates; lower rates rest of yr. No maid serv Sun. Color TV. Pool. Cafe opp.

HOLIDAY INN-OCEANSIDE. 3384 Ocean Dr (32960) on FL 60, 1 blk E of FL A1A. 305/231-2300. 104 A/C rms, 2-3 story, 16 kits. Mid-Dec-Apr: S, $55-$61; D, $65-$125; each addl, $6; under 19 free; rest of yr: varied lower rates. Color TV. Pool; wading pool; poolside serv. Cafe, 7 am-10 pm. Bar; entertainment. Coin lndry. Tennis. Cr cds: A, D, MC, V.

SHERATON REGENCY. 4700 N US 1 (32960). 3 mi N of FL 60. 813/231-1600. 108 A/C rms, 4 story. Elvtr. Dec-Apr: S, $64-$70; D, $68-$74; each addl, $8; suites, $90; under 18, free; lower rates rest of yr. Color TV. Solardome. Pool. Cafe, 7 am-10 pm. Bar; entertainment, dancing. Cr cds: A, C, D, MC, V.

SURF 'N SAND. 1516 S Ocean Dr (32960), 2 mi S of FL 60, 2 blks E of FL A1A. 305/231-9623. 15 A/C units, 2 story, 9 kits. S, $37; D, $54; each addl, $5; kit. units, $45-$54; wkly rates avail. Color TV. Pool. Cafe 2 mi, 7 am-2 pm. On ocean. Cr cds: D, MC, V.

Restaurant

THE PATIO. 1103 Miracle Mile, 1 blk N on 1 & 60. 305/562-2880. Hrs: 11 am-3:30 pm, 5-10 pm. Closed Thanksgiving, Dec 25. A/C. Italian, Amer menu. Bar. Semi-a la carte. Lunch, $3-$8.95; dinner, $6.95-$15. Child's plate. Specialties: shrimp scampi, chicken Kiev, filet mignon. Salad bar. Entertainment Thurs-Sat, dancing Sat. Cr cds: A, C, D, MC, V.

WALT DISNEY WORLD

CONTEMPORARY RESORT. (Box 40, Lake Buena Vista 32830.) Off 192, I-4 on Disney World grounds. 305/824-1000. 1,046 A/C rms. S, D, $105-$125; each addl, $4; under 18 free; suites, $115-$270. Color TV. 3 pools, 1 Olympic size; wading pool; poolside serv; lifeguard. Playground. Cafes (see GULF COAST ROOM & TOP OF THE WORLD). Snack bar open 24 hrs. Bars; entertainment, dancing. Coin lndry. Tennis. Health club. Exercise rm. Spacious lobby with monorail stop. On lake. Cr cds: A, MC.

GOLF RESORT. (Box 40, Lake Buena Vista 32830.) On Disney World grounds. 305/824-2200. 151 A/C units. S, D, $100-$120; each addl, $4; under 18 free. Color TV. Pool; poolside serv; lifeguard. Cafe, 7 am-10 pm. Bar. Coin lndry. Tennis. Golf. Cr cds: A, MC.

POLYNESIAN RESORT. (Box 78, Lake Buena Vista 32830.) Off 192, I-4 on Disney World grounds. 305/824-2000. 636 A/C rms, 2 kits. S, D, $100-$125; each addl, $4; under 18 free; suites, $250-$310. Color TV. Pool; wading pool; poolside serv; lifeguard. Playground. Cafe, 8 am-10 pm. Bar (also see PAPEETE BAY VERANDAH). Bar; entertainment. Tennis. Golf. On lake. Cr cds: A, MC.

Restaurants

GULF COAST ROOM. (See Contemporary Resort Hotel above.) 305/842-1000. Hrs: 6:30-10 pm. A/C. Continental menu. Bar. Dinner, a la carte, $10.75-$14.75. Child's plates. Specialties: grilled duck, fresh seafood. Entertainment. Jacket required. Cr cds: MC.

PAPEETE BAY VERANDAH. (See Polynesian Resort Hotel above.) 305/824-2000. Hrs: 8-11:30 am, 5:30-10 pm, Sun champagne brunch, 11 am-2:30 pm. Res required for dinner. A/C. Polynesian menu. Bar. Dinner, a la carte, $9.50-$15. Child's plates. Specialties: chicken Pago-Pago, prime rib, "Papeete Lovo." Salad bar. Entertainment. Cr cds: A, MC.

TOP OF THE WORLD. (See Contemporary Resort Hotel above.) 305/824-1000. Hrs: 8-10:30 am, 11:30 am-2:30 pm, 6:30 & 9:45 pm sittings; Sun, champagne brunch, 11 am-2:30 pm. A/C. Dinner, a la carte, $9.95-$14.50. Child's plates. Specialties: roast duckling Curacao, veal Romanoff. Lunch salad bar. Entertainment, dancing. Jacket required at dinner. Cr cds: A, MC.

WEST PALM BEACH

PARKVIEW. 4710 S Dixie Hwy (33405), 3 mi S on 1. 305/833-4644. 28 A/C rms, 1-2 story. Dec-Apr: S, D, $46-$60; each addl, $5; rest of yr: lower rates. Color TV. Cafe adj, 7 am-10 pm; closed Sat. Cr cds: MC, V.

RAMADA INN. 1800 Palm Beach Lakes Blvd (33401), at I-95 5 mi E of FL Tpke exit 40. 305/683-8810. 203 A/C rms, 2 story. Dec-Apr: S, $59-$65; D, $71-$77; each addl, $5; under 18 free; rest of yr: lower rates. Color TV. Pool; poolside serv. Cafe, 6:30 am-10 pm; dining rm, 5-10 pm. Bar; entertainment, dancing exc Sun. Tennis. Golf. Cr cds: A, C, D, MC, V.

HOLIDAY INN. 100 Datura St (33401), 3 blks S at Flagler Dr. 305/655-8800. 163 A/C rms. Dec-Apr: S, $66-$100; D, $68-$100; each addl, $4; under 20 free; rest of yr: varied lower rates. Color TV. Pool; poolside serv. Cafe, 7 am-10 pm. Bar; entertainment, dancing exc Sun, Mon. Cr cds: A, D, MC, V.

Restaurants

HOWLEY'S. 4700 S Dixie Hwy, 3 mi S on 1. 305/833-5691. Hrs: 7 am-10 pm. Closed Sat; Dec 25. A/C. Beer, wine. Semi-a la carte. Bkfst, $1.75-$3.25; lunch, $3-$3.50; dinner, $9.95-$18.95. Specialties: prime rib, seafood, baked ham.

S & S (Cafeteria). 7925 S Dixie Hwy, 7 mi S on 1. 305/585-8549. Hrs: 11 am-2 pm. 4-8 pm. Closed Dec 25. A/C. Avg ck: lunch $3.10; dinner, $3.55. Specialties: roast beef, chicken, seafood. Salad bar.

WINTER HAVEN

BANYAN BEACH. 1630 6th St NW (33880), 1 mi N on 17. 813/293-3658. 18 A/C rms, 6 kit. Mid-Dec-mid-Apr: S, $30-$40; D, $40-$50; each addl, $4; kit units, $50-$60; rest of yr: lower rates. Color TV. Pool. Private dock. Lake opp. Cr cds: MC, V.

BEST WESTERN DRIFTWOOD MOTOR LODGE. 970 Cypress Gardens Rd (33880), 2 mi SE on FL 540. 813/294-4229. 22 A/C rms, 3 kits. Mid-Dec-Easter wk: S, D, $34-$58; each addl, $6; rest of yr: lower rates. Color TV. Pool. Cafe, 11:30 am-11 pm. Cr cds: A, C, D, MC, V.

GARDEN COURT. 2345 8th St NW (33880), 1 mi N on 17. 813/294-3537. 27 A/C rms, 3 kits. Mid-Dec-mid-Apr: S, $36-$40; D, $42-$46; each addl, $3; kit. units (3-day min), $5 more; rest of yr: lower rates. Color TV. Pool. Cafe 1 blk, 7 am-11 pm. Cr cds: MC, V.

GARDEN LODGE. 2000 Cypress Gardens Blvd (33880), 3½ mi SE on FL 540, ¾ mi W of Cypress Gardens. 813/324-6334. 26 A/C rms, 1-2 story, 4 kits. Late Dec-mid-Apr: S, $40-$50; D, $45-$60; each addl, $5; kit. units, $5 more; rest of yr: lower rates. Color TV. Pool. Cafe opp, 6 am-10 pm. Lake Ina opp.

HOLIDAY INN. ½ mi S on 17 (33880). 813/294-4451. 225 A/C rms, 2 story, Dec-Apr: S, $40-$50; D, $56-$64; each addl, $8; kit. units, suites, $42-$50; under 18 free; rest of yr: lower rates. Color TV. 2 pools; wading pool. Cafe, 6:30 am-10 pm. Bar; entertainment, dancing exc Mon. Coin lndry. Cr cds: A, C, D, MC, V.

QUALITY INN CYPRESS GARDENS. (Box 7, Cypress Gardens 33880). On 540, 3 mi E of US 17, W of US 27, at Cypress Gardens entrance. 813/324-5950. 158 A/C rms, 3-5 story. Dec-Apr: S, $45-$50; D, $50-$55; each addl, $5; under 17 free; suites, $150; rest of yr: lower rates. Color TV. Olympic-size pool. Cafe, 7 am-9 pm, (also see GAZEBO). Bar, 11-2 am; entertainment, dancing exc Mon. Cr cds: A, C, D, MC, V.

RANCH HOUSE. 1911 Cypress Gardens Blvd (33880), 3 mi SE on FL 540, 2 mi W of Cypress Gardens. 813/324-5994. 53 A/C units, 2 story, 37 kits. Mid-Dec-Easter: S, $50; D, $50-$54; each addl, $3; kit. units, $54-$58; family, wkly rates avail; rest of yr: lower rates. Color TV. Pool. Cafe, 6:30 am-10 pm. Ck-out, 11 am. Cr cds: A, D, MC, V.

Restaurants

CHRISTY'S SUNDOWN. Ave K & 3 St SW, 3 blks S on 17. 813/293-0069. Hrs: 11:30 am-11 pm. Closed Sun; Jan 1, Easter, Thanksgiving, Dec 25. A/C. Bar to 1:30 am. Semi-a la carte. Lunch, $3.25-$5.25; dinner, $6.95-$12.95. Child's plates. Specialties: shish kebab, fresh snapper, prime rib. Entertainment, dancing exc Sun. Cr cds: A, MC, V.

GAZEBO. (See Quality Inn Cypress Gardens Motel.) 813/324-5950. Hrs: 7 am-2 pm, 5-10 pm; Sun, noon-8 pm. A/C. Bar. Dinner, semi-a la carte, $5.75-$9.95. Child's plates. Specialties: veal, Chateaubriand for 2, prime rib. Cr cds: A, C, D, MC, V.

MORRISON'S (Cafeteria). 140 Winter Haven Mall, 2 mi S on 17. 813/293-1003. Hrs: 11 am-8 pm. A/C. A la carte. Lunch, dinner, $1.50-$4.50. Specialties: shimp, roast beef, homemade custard pie.

WINTER PARK

ALTAMONTE SPRINGS INN & RACQUET CLUB. (151 N Douglas Ave, Altamonte Springs 32701.) Just NW of jct FL 436, I-4. 305/869-9000. 216 A/C rms, 2 story. Mid-Dec-mid-Apr: S, $50-$52; D, $56-$58; each addl, $6; under 12 free; suites, $150-$200; rest of yr: lower rates. Color TV. Pool. Playground. Cafe open 24 hrs. Bar. Coin lndry. Tennis. Cr cds: A, C, D, MC, V.

BEST WESTERN MT VERNON MOTOR LODGE. 110 S Orlando Ave (32789), 1 mi W on 17, 92, 1¼ mi E of I-4 Fairbanks Ave exit. 305/647-1166. 134 A/C rms, 2 story. S, $53-$66; D, $59-$72; each addl, $6; under 12 free; family, group rates avail. Color TV. Pool. Cafe, 7 am-2:30 pm. Bar, 11-2 am; entertainment exc Sun. Cr cds: A, C, D, MC, V.

SUNDANCE INN. (225 W Semoran Blvd, Altamonte Springs 32701.) Just W of jct FL 436, I-4. 305/862-8200. 150 A/C rms, 3 story. Mid-Feb-mid-Apr: S, $36; D, $44; each addl, $6; under 12 free; rest of yr, lower rates. Color TV. Pool. Cafe, 6:30 am-10 pm. Bar, 11-2 am; entertainment, dancing. Coin lndry. Cr cds: A, C, D, MC, V.

HOLIDAY INN-ALTAMONTE SPRINGS. (Box 636, Altamonte Springs 32701.) 231 Wymore, on Hwy 436, just SW of I-4. 305/862-4455. 202 A/C rms, 2 story. S, $45-$65; D, $52-$65; each addl, $8; suites, $125-$175; under 18 free. Color TV. Pool; wading pool. Cafe, 6:30 am-10 pm. Bar, noon-2 am; entertainment, dancing exc Sun. Coin lndry. Tennis. Cr cds: A, C, D, MC, V.

LANGFORD. (Box 970; 32789.) 300 E New England Ave at Interlachen, 1 mi E of 17, 92, 1¾ mi E of I-4 Fairbanks exit. 305/644-3400. 220 A/C rms, 2-7 story, 56 kits. Mid-Dec-mid-May: S, $45-$50; D, $55-$65; suites, $130-$200; each addl, $5; kit., $5 more; under 17 free; monthly rates avail; rest of yr: lower rates. Color TV. Pool; poolside serv; lifeguard. Cafe, 7 am-10:30 pm; dining rm, 7-11:30 pm. Bar, 10-2 am; entertainment, dancing exc Sun. Cr cds: A, D, MC, V.

QUALITY INN OF WINTER PARK. 901 N Orlando Ave (32789), 1½ mi NE on 17, 92, 1 mi E of I-4 Lee Rd exit. 305/644-8000. 103 A/C rms, 2 story. June-Aug, Oct-May: S, $35-$50; D, $40-$50; each addl, $5; under 16 free; rest of yr: lower rates. Color TV. Pool. Cafe, 6 am-11:30 pm. Cr cds: A, C, D, MC, V.

Restaurants

FREDDIE'S STEAK HOUSE. (Box 781, Fern Park.) 3 mi N on 17, 92, 3 mi E of I-4 Altamonte Springs exit. 305/339-3265. Hrs: 4:30 pm-1:30 am. Closed Sun; Jan 1, Dec 25. Reservation suggested. A/C. Continental, Amer menu. Bar; piano bar. Dinner, table d'hôte, $9.95-$17.95. Child's plates, half price. Specialties: roast prime rib, veal, seafood. Entertainment exc Sun. Jacket suggested. Cr cds: A, C, D, MC, V.

MAISON & JARDIN. (430 S Wymore Rd, Altamonte Springs.) ½ mi S of jct FL 436, I-4. 305/862-4410. Hrs: 6:30-10:30 pm; Sun, 11 am-2 pm, 5:30-9 pm. Closed Mon; Jan 1, July 4, Thanksgiving, Dec 25. Reservation requested. A/C. Continental, Amer menu. Bar. Wine list. Dinner, semi-a la carte. $11.75-$19.50 up; Sun brunch, 7.95-$8.95. Child's plates half price. Specialties: beef Wellington, veal Oscar, rack of lamb Diable. Strolling guitarist. Jacket required. Cr cds: A, C, D, MC, V.

MAISON DES CREPES. 348 N Park Ave. 1½ mi E of 17, 92, E of I-4 Fairbanks exit. 305/647-4469. Hrs: 11:30 am-3 pm, 6:30-10 pm. Closed Sun, major hols; also first 2 wks in July. A/C. French menu. Semi-a la carte: lunch, $3.50-$6.95 (min $3, serv plate $1); dinner, $7.95-$18 (min $7) serv plate $3. Child's plate, half price. Specialties: crepes, filet Royal. Background music. Country French decor. Cr cds: A, C, D, MC, V.

VILLA NOVA. 839 N Orlando Ave. 1½ mi NW on US 17, 92, 1 mi E of Lee Rd exit. 305/644-2060. Hrs: 11:30 am-2:30 pm, 6 pm-midnight. Closed Sun; major hols. Res recommended. A/C. Continental menu. Bar to 1 am. A la carte: lunch, $3.95-$8.25; dinner, $8.95-$18.50. Child's plates half price. Specializes in seafood, veal, steak. Background music, entertainment, dancing Mon-Sat. Cr cds: A, C, D, MC, V.

ZEPHYRHILLS

BEST WESTERN. (Box 876; 33599.) 1034 Gall Blvd, ½ mi S on 301. 813/782-5527. 36 A/C rms, 2 story. Dec-Mar: S, $28; D, $34; each addl, $4. Cot, $3. Color TV. Pool. Cr cds: A, C, D, MC, V.

DAYS INN. At jct FL 54, I-75 (33599). 813/973-0155. 122 A/C rms, 2 story. Jan-May: S, D, $25.88-$38.88; each addl, $4; under 18 free; rest of yr: lower rates. Color TV. Pool. Cafe open 24 hrs. Coin lndry. Golf. Cr cds: A, D, MC, V.

INDEX

A

accommodations (motels and hotels), 127–49
Air Force Museum, Duyton, Ohio, 99
Air Force Space Museum, Cape Canaveral, 33
airboat rides, Everglades National Park, 65
A. L. Anderson Park, Tarpon Springs, 61
Alamo, The, San Antonio, Tex., 100
Alfred B. Maclay State Ornamental Garden, Tallahassee, 22, 88
Amelia Island, 27, 30
American Amateur Golf Classic, Pensacola, 12
American Invitational Horse Show, Tampa, 61
American Museum of Science and Energy, Oak Ridge, Tenn., 99
American Police Hall of Fame and Museum, Punta Gorda, 56
Anastasia State Rec. Area, St. Augustine, 35, 90
Andersonville National Historic Site, Ga., 100
Anhinga Trail, Flamingo, 66
Annapolis, Md., 96
Annie Russell Theatre, Winter Park, 49
Antique Car Meet, Ormond Beach, 34
Antique Auto Show, Mount Dora, 44
Antique Car Collection, Silver Springs, 21
Apalachicola National Forest, Apalachicola, 16, 17, 21
Apopka, 40
Arcadia, 40, 126
Arrivas House, St. Augustine, 36
Art Deco District, Miami Beach, 84
Art Show, Mount Dora, 44
Artists Unlimited, Key West, 70
Arts and Crafts Festival, St. Augustine, 34
Arts and Crafts Show, Tarpon Springs, 61
Arts Festival, Jacksonville, 30
Art Show and Foliage Festival, Apopka, 40
Asolo Theater, Sarasota, 58
Astrodome, Houston, Tex., 100
Astroworld, USA, Houston, Tex., 100
Atlanta, Ga., 99–100
Atlantic Beach, 30, 126
Aucilla Game Management Area, Tallahassee, 23–24
Audubon Center, Lake Wales, 43
Audubon House, Key West, 70
Avon Park, 40
Azalea Festival, Palatka, 34

B

Bach Festival, Winter Park, 49
Bahamas, 101–2
Bahia Honda State Rec. Area, Marathon, 64, 68, 92
Barbados, 105
Barnacle State Historic Site, The, Miami, 82, 93
Barry College, Miami Shores, 84
Bartow, 40, 126
Basin Bayou State Rec. Area, Niceville, 10, 88
Bass Museum of Art, Miami Beach, 84
Bayfront Center, St. Petersburg, 56, 57
Bayfront Park, Homestead, 72
Bayfront Park, Miami, 81
Bayhill Classic, Orlando, 46
Bayview Park, Key West, 71
Bayview Park, Pensacola, 12
Beach Festival, Jacksonville, 30
Beach Marathon, Jacksonville, 30
Beal Maltbie Shell Museum, Winter Park, 49
Beaux Arts Exhibit, Fort Walton Beach, 9
Belle Glade, 63, 64, 126
Belle Glade Marina, 64
Belle Glade Regatta, 64
Belle of Louisville, 99
Belleview Biltmore, Clearwater, 52
Bellingrath Gardens, Ala., 100
Bellm's Cars and Music of Yesterday, Sarasota, 59
Bethune-Cookman College, Daytona Beach, 29
Bicentennial Flag Pavilion, Jacksonville Beach, 31
Big Cypress Bend, Everglades City, 65
Big Cypress National Preserve, 65
Big Cypress Seminole Indian Reservation, Immokalee, 73
Big Cypress Swamp, 51, 55, 65
Big Lagoon State Rec. Area, Pensacola, 12, 88
Big Pine Key, 68–69
Big Tree Park, Sanford, 47
Bill Baggs Cape Florida State Rec. Area, Key Biscayne, 81, 93
Billy Bowlegs Festival, Fort Walton Beach, 9
Biscayne National Park, 5, 72
Black Gold Jubilee Celebration, Belle Glade, 64
Black Hills Passion Play, Lake Wales, 43
Blacksmith Shop, St. Augustine, 36
Blackwater River State Forest and Game Management Area, Milton, 7, 10
Blackwater River State Park, Milton, 10, 88
Blessing of the Fleet, Destin, 8
Blessing of the Fleet, St. Augustine, 34
Blue Angels, Pensacola, 12
Blue Angels Air Show, Pensacola, 12
Blue Spring State Park, De Land, 30, 90
Boat-a-Cade, Belle Glade, Kissimmee, 41, 64
Boca Grande, 52, 126
Boca Raton, 76, 77, 126–27
Bok Tower Gardens, Lake Wales, 39, 43
Bonita Springs, 52, 127
Bradenton, 52–53, 127
Breakers, The, Palm Beach, 84
Bristol, 16
British Leewards, 104
British Windwards, 105
Brokaw-McDougall House, Tallahassee, 22
Brookgreen Garden, S.C., 98
Brooksville, 16, 127
Broward County Fair, Fort Lauderdale, 79
Buccaneer Bay, Weeki Wachee, 25
Bulow Plantation State Historic Site, Bunnell, 28, 90
Busch Gardens, Tampa. See Dark Continent/Busch Gardens
Bushnell, 40, 127

C

Cable Car, St. Petersburg, 56
Ca'd'Zan, Sarasota, 51, 58
Caladesi Island State Park, Dunedin, 53, 92
Calloway Gardens, Ga., 100
Camden, N.J., 95
Camel Lake, Apalachicola, 16
Camellia Gardens, Marshallville, Ga., 100
Camellia Show, Pensacola, 13
campgrounds, 110–126
Canadian Festival, Daytona Beach Shores (Daytona Beach), 29
Canaveral National Seashore, Kennedy Space Center, 33, 34, 37
Cape Canaveral, 28
Cape Canaveral Air Force Station, 28, 33, 44
Cape Coral, 52
Captiva Island, 58, 145
Caribbean Gardens, Naples, 5
Caribbean islands, 101–6
Cartoon Museum, Orlando, 45
Casa del Hidalgo, St. Augustine, 36
Castillo de San Marcos National Monument, St. Augustine, 27, 35, 36
Castle Dracula, Panama City, 11
Cathedral of St. Augustine, 37
Cayman Islands, 103
Cecil M. Webb Wildlife Management Area, Punta Gorda, 55
Cedar Key, 16, 127
Cedar Key Art Festival, 16
Cedar Key Seafood Festival, 16
Cedar Key State Museum, 16, 88
Cedar Keys National Wildlife Refuge, 16
Central Florida, 39–49; map, 46; parks, 91–92
Central Florida Civic Theatre, Orlando, 45
Central Florida Dragway, Orlando, 46
Central Florida Fair, Orlando, 46
Central Florida Zoological Park, Sanford, 46
Century Tower, Gainesville, 18
Chalet Suzanne, Lake Wales, 39, 44
Chalo Nitka Festival, Moore Haven, 73
Chasco Fiesta, New Port Richey, 19
Chassahowitzka National Wildlife Refuge, Brooksville, 16
Chattahoochee, 17
Chattahoochee National Forest, Ga., 98
Chautauqua Festival, De Funiak Springs, 8
Chekika State Recreation Area, Homestead, 73, 92
Chiefland, 17
Chipley, 8, 127
Christmas Boat Parade, Pompano Beach, 85
Christmas Concerts, White Springs, 25
Churchill Downs, Louisville, Ky., 99
Cincinnati, Ohio, 99
Cincinnati Zoo, 99
Circus Clown College, Venice, 61
Circus World, Orlando, 39, 44, 46
Citrus Bowl Football Classic, Orlando, 46
Citrus Invitational Basketball Tournament, Orlando, 46
Citrus World, Lake Wales, 43
City of Miami Marine Stadium, 82
City Recreation Center, Naples, 55
Civic Center, Lakeland, 43
Classic Car Meet, Winter Haven, 48
Clearwater, 51, 52, 127–28
Clearwater Beach, 128
Clermont, 39, 128
Clewiston, 63, 64, 128
Cloisters of the Monastery of St. Bernard de Clairvaux, Miami, 81
Cocoa, 27, 28, 33, 128–29
Cocoa Beach, 28, 129
Coconut Grove Bayfront Park, Miami, 81
Collier-Seminole State Park, Marco, 55, 65, 93
Columbia, The, Tampa, 60
Community Concert Association, Sarasota, 58
Conch Tour Train, Key West, 69
Conservation Center, Sanibel, 58
Constitution Convention State Museum, Port St. Joe, 13, 88
Contemporary Arts Center, Cincinnati, 99
Coral Castle, Homestead, 72
Coral Gables, 76, 77, 129
Corkscrew Swamp Sanctuary, Immokalee, 51, 52, 63, 65, 73
Crandon Park, Key Biscayne, 81
Crandon Park Zoo, Key Biscayne, 81
Crawfordville, 17
Crestview, 8
"Cross and Sword," St. Augustine, 34–35
Cross City, 129
Cross Creek, 15
Crystal River, 17
Crystal River State Archaeological Site, Crystal River, 17, 88
Cumberland Gap National Historic Park, 99
Cummer Gallery of Art, Jacksonville, 32
Cyclorama, Atlanta, Ga., 99
Cypress Gardens, Winter Haven, 39, 41, 44, 47–48
Cypress Gardens Festival Month, Winter Haven, 48
Cypress Knee Museum, Palmdale, 73
Cypress Point Reptile Institute, Silver Springs, 5, 21

D

Dade Battlefield State Historic Site, Bushnell, 39, 40, 91
Dade City, 18, 129
Dade City Arts and Crafts Festival, 18
Dade County Art Museum, Miami, 82
Dania, 78

INDEX 149

Dania Jai-Alai Palace, 78
Dark Continent/Busch Gardens, The, Tampa, 5, 39, 51, 60
Days in Spain Festival, St. Augustine, 34
Daytona Beach, 27, 28–29, 129–30
Daytona 500, 29
Daytona 200 Motorcycle Classic AHA Camel Pro Race, Daytona, 29
Daytona International Speedway, 29
Daytona Playhouse, 29
Dead Lakes State Rec. Area, Wewahitchka, 13, 88
De Bary, 29
De Bary Hall, 29
Deer Park, Silver Springs, 21
Deer Point Dam, Panama City, 10
De Funiak Springs, 8, 130
De Land, 29–30, 130–31
De Land Museum, 30
De Leon Springs, 30
De Leon Springs State Rec. Area, De Leon Springs, 30
Delius Cottage, Jacksonville, 30
Delius Festival, Jacksonville, 30
Delray Affair, Delray Beach, 78
Delray Beach, 78
De Mesa-Sanchez House, St. Augustine, 36
Dent Smith Trail, Melbourne, 34
Derby Lane, St. Petersburg, 57
De Soto Celebration, Bradenton, 52
De Soto National Memorial, Bradenton, 5, 52
Destin, 7, 8–9, 131
Devil's Millhopper State Geological Site, Gainesville, 89
Dinner Key, Miami, 81
Dirksen Garden. See Senator Everett McKinley Dirksen Garden
Discount Fashion Row, Hallandale, 80
Disney World, Lake Buena Vista. See Walt Disney World
Dr. Julian Bruce St. George Island State Park, Apalachicola, 16, 89
Dogwood Trail, Brooksville, 16
Dominican Republic, 103–4
Don CeSar, St. Petersburg, 51, 57
Donald Duck Citrus World, Lake Wales, 39
Donnelly Mansion, Mount Dora, 44
Driftwood Inn, Vero Beach, 85
Dry Tortugas, 64, 72, 73
DuBois Home, Jupiter, 81
Dunedin, 53, 131
Duval Street, Key West, 71

E

East Bay Racetrack, Tampa, 61
Easter Sunrise Service, St. Augustine, 34
Eden State Ornamental Garden, Point Washington (Grayton Beach), 9, 88
Edison National Historic Site, West Orange, N.J., 96
Edison Pageant of Light, Fort Myers, 54
Edison's Winter Home, Fort Myers, 54
Eglin Air Force Base, Fort Walton Beach, 7, 9
Eglin Wildlife Management Area, Fort Walton Beach, 7
Ellenton, 53
Elliot Museum, Stuart, 85
Eola Park, Orlando, 45
EPCOT—Experimental Prototype Community of Tomorrow, Walt Disney World, Lake Buena Vista, 42
Ernest Hemingway House, Key West, 68, 70
Etowah Mounds, Ga., 99
Eustis, 41, 47
Everglades, 4, 5, 51–52, 53
Everglades Area Chamber of Commerce Welcome Station, Everglades City, 64
Everglades City, 64–65
Everglades Experiment Station, 63
Everglades Jungle Cruise, Fort Myers, 54
Everglades National Park, 5, 55, 63–64, 65; Visitor Center, Flamingo, 66
Everglades National Park Boat Tours, 64

Everglades Reclamation State Historic Site, Belle Glade, 61, 93
Everglades Wonder Gardens, Bonita Springs, 52

F

Fakahatchee Strand (Everglades City), 65
Fairchild Tropical Garden, Coral Gables, 5, 78
Fall Festival of the Islands, Sanibel, 58
Falling Waters State Rec. Area, Chipley, 8, 88
Fantasy Festival, Key West, 71
Faver-Dykes State Park, St. Augustine, 35, 90–91
Fernandina Beach, 27, 30
Festival of States, St. Petersburg, 58
Fiesta in the Park, Lake Eola (Orlando), 46
Fiesta Day, Tampa, 61
Fiesta of Five Flags, Pensacola, 7, 13
Firecracker 400, Daytona Beach, 29
First Presbyterian Church, Tallahassee, 22
fishing and fishing tournaments, 8, 9, 17, 30, 34, 44, 57, 58, 66, 73, 85
Flagler Beach State Rec. Area, 30, 91
Flagler College, St. Augustine, 36
Flagler Memorial Presbyterian Church, St. Augustine, 37
Flamingo, 63, 65–66
Flamingo Gardens, Fort Lauderdale, 79
Flipper's Key West, Marathon, 64, 68
Florida A & M University, Tallahassee, 22
Florida Air Show, Kissimmee, 41
Florida Atlantic University, Boca Raton, 77
Florida Attractions Association, 109
Florida Caverns State Park, Marianna, 9, 88
Florida Citrus Festival, Winter Haven, 47
Florida Citrus Invitational Golf Tournament, Orlando, 46
Florida Citrus Showcase, Winter Haven, 39, 47
Florida Citrus Tower, Clermont, 39, 41
Florida Community College Activities State Basketball Tournament, De Land, 29
Florida Derby Festival, Hallandale, 80
Florida Folk Festival, White Springs, 25
Florida Forest Festival, Perry, 19
Florida Grapefruit League, 28, 43, 46, 47, 52, 53, 54, 57, 59, 61, 79, 83, 85
Florida Gulf Coast Art Festival, Clearwater, 53
Florida High School Championship Track Meet, Winter Park, 49
Florida Hiking Trail, Umatilla, 47
Florida Institute of Technology, Melbourne, 34
Florida Keys, 63–64, 66–72
Florida Marine Welcome Station, Fernandina Beach, 30
Florida Pioneer Museum, Homestead, 73
Florida Seafood Festival, Apalachicola, 16
Florida's Historic Highlights, 1
Florida Southern College, Lakeland, 43
Florida's Silver Springs. See Silver Springs
Florida's Sunken Gardens, St. Petersburg, 5, 52, 56
Florida State Fair, Tampa, 61
Florida State Museum, Gainesville, 18
Florida State University, Tallahassee, 22
Florida's Weeki Wachee. See Weeki Wachee
Florida Symphony Orchestra, Orlando, 45
Florida 12-Hour International Grand Prix of Endurance, Sebring, 47
Florida West Coast Symphony, Sarasota, 58
Flying High Circus, Tallahassee, 22
Fontainebleau State Park, La., 100
Forest Amusement Park, Daytona Beach, 29
Forest Capital Center, Perry, 19
Forest Capital Park, Perry, 19
Forest Capital State Museum, Perry, 15, 19, 89
Fort Barrancas, 12
Fort Caroline National Memorial, Jacksonville, 5, 32
Fort Clinch State Park, Fernandina Beach, 30, 91
Fort Cooper State Park, Inverness, 39, 91
Fort De Soto Park, St. Petersburg, 57
Fort Foster State Historic Site, Zephyrhills, 25, 89
Fort Frederica National Monument, Ga., 98
Fort Gadsden State Historic Site, Apalachicola and Sumatra, 16, 21, 89

Fort Jefferson National Monument, 5, 64, 71, 73
Fort Lauderdale, 76, 79, 131–32
Fort Matanzas, St. Augustine, 5, 35
Fort Mellon Park, Sanford, 46
Fort Myers, 51, 53–54, 132
Fort Pickens, Pensacola, 13
Fort Pierce, 75, 79, 132
Fort Pierce Inlet State Rec. Area, Fort Pierce, 79, 93
Fort Sumter National Monument, S.C., 98
Fort Walton Beach, 7, 9, 132
Fountain of Youth Park, St. Augustine, 36
Foxbower Wildlife Exhibit, Weeki Wachee, 25
Fredericksburg, Va., 97
Fred Gannon Rocky Bayou State Rec. Area, Niceville, 10, 88
French Leewards, 104–5
Fruit and Spice Park, Homestead, 73
Fun 'n' Sun Festival, Clearwater, 52

G

Gainesville, 15, 18, 132–33
Gainesville Dragway, 18
Gallegos House, St. Augustine, 36
Gamble Plantation State Historic Site, Ellenton, 53, 92
Garden of Our Lord, Coral Gables, 78
Gasparilla Pirate Invasion, Tampa, 61
Gator Bowl Festival, Jacksonville, 30
Gator Bowl Football Game, Jacksonville, 30
Gatorland and Zoo, Orlando, 39, 45
Gatorland Zoo, Kissimmee, 41
Georgia Veterans Memorial State Park, 100
Gilbert Plant, Mount Dora, 44
Gold Coast Railroad, Fort Lauderdale, 79
Golden Apple Dinner Theatre, Sarasota, 58
Gomez House, St. Augustine, 36
Gonzales-de Hita Houses, St. Augustine, 36
Goodyear Blimp, Pompano Beach, 85
Grace S. Turner House, St. Petersburg, 57
"Grand Strand," S.C., 96
Grant Seafood Festival, Melbourne, 33
Gray Line, St. Petersburg, 56
Grayton Beach, 9
Grayton Beach State Rec. Area, 9, 88
Great Gulf Coast Arts Festival, Pensacola, 13
Great Healing Spring, De Leon Springs, 30
Great Smoky Mountains National Park, 98
Great White Heron National Wildlife Refuge, Florida Keys, 64, 68
Greek Easter Week, Tarpon Springs, 61
Greek Festival Bazaar, Pensacola, 13
Green Cove Springs, 3, 30
Greenfield Village, Mich., 98
Gregory House, Bristol, 16
Greynolds Park, Miami, 81
Gulfarium, Fort Walton Beach, 9
Gulf Coast Junior College, Panama City, 10
Gulf Islands National Seashore, 5, 8–9, 12
Gulf World, Panama City, 10
Gulfstream Park, Hallandale, 80
Gulfstream Polo Field, West Palm Beach, 85
Gumbo-Limbo Trail, Flamingo, 66
Gusman Concert Hall, Coral Gables, 77

H

Haas Museum, St. Petersburg, 57
Haiti, 103
Halifax Area Art Festival, Ormond Beach, 34
Hallandale, 80, 133
Hampton Roads, Port of Va., 97
Harvest Festival, Homestead, 73
Haulover Beach Park, Miami Beach, 83
"Heart of Florida" Fair, Dade City, 18
Hemingway Days, Key West, 71
Henry Ford Museum and Greenfield Village, Mich., 98
Henry Morrison Flagler Museum, Palm Beach, 84
Henry Plant Museum, Tampa, 60
Hermitage, Nashville, Tenn., 99
Hernando County Fair, Brooksville, 16

150   INDEX

Hertzberg Circus Collection, San Antonio, Tex., 100
Hialeah, 80, 133
Hialeah Park, 80
Hialeah Speedway, 80
Highland Games & Festival, Dunedin, 53
Highlands Hammock State Park, Sebring, 39, 47, 91–92
Hillsborough River State Park, Sebring, 39, 47, 89
Historical Museum of South Florida, Miami, 82
Hobe Sound National Wildlife Refuge, Jupiter, 81
Hollywood, 76, 80, 133
Homestead, 63, 72–73, 133
Homosassa, 18
Homosassa Springs, 18, 133
Hontoon Island State Park, De Land, 30, 90
House of Presidents, Clermont, 41
House of Refuge, Stuart, 85
Hugh Taylor Birch State Rec. Area, Fort Lauderdale, 79, 93
Huntington Beach State Park, S.C., 98
Hurricane Monument, Florida Keys, 66

I

Ichetucknee Springs State Park, Lake City, 19, 89
Immokalee, 73
IMSA National Championship, Daytona Beach, 29
Indian Key Festival, Florida Keys, 66
Indian Temple Mound Museum, Fort Walton Beach, 9
Indian World Museum, Kissimmee, 41
Indiatlantic Art Show, Melbourne, 34
International Powerboat Races, Key West, 71
Intracoastal Waterway, 7, 27, 75
Islamorada, 66, 133–34
Islamorada Public Beach, 66
Island Bay National Wildlife Refuge, Boca Grande, 52
Island Shrimp Festival, Fort Myers, 54
Isle of Eight Flags Shrimp Festival, Fernandina Beach, 30

J

Jack Island, Fort Pierce, 79, 93
Jacksonville, 27, 30–33, 134
Jacksonville and All That Jazz Festival, Jacksonville, 31
Jacksonville Art Museum, 32
Jacksonville Beach, 31, 134
Jacksonville University, 33
Jacksonville Zoological Park, 32
jai-alai, 29, 49, 61, 80, 83
Jamaica, 102–3
Jamestown, Va., 97
Janes Scenic Drive, Copeland (Everglades City), 65
Japanese Garden, Miami, 82
Jasper, 134
Jazz Holiday, Clearwater, 52
Jeannie With The Light Brown Hair auditions, White Springs, 25
Jefferson County Watermelon Festival, Monticello, 19
Jekyll Island, Ga., 98
J. N. "Ding" Darling National Wildlife Refuge, Sanibel, 58
John Gorrie State Museum, Apalachicola, 16, 89
John Pennekamp Coral Reef State Park, Key Largo, 64, 66, 93
John Young Science Center and Planetarium, Orlando, 45
Jonathan Dickinson State Park, Jupiter, 81, 93
Joseph Verner Reed Wilderness Sanctuary, Jupiter, 81
Judah P. Benjamin State Historic Memorial, Ellenton, 53
Judge P. White Methodist Parsonage, Quincy, 20
Jungle Larry's African Safari and Caribbean Gardens, Naples, 55
Jungle Queen, Fort Lauderdale, 79
Junior Museum of Bay County, Panama City, 10
Junior Museum Market Day, Tallahassee, 22
Junior Orange Bowl Parade, Coral Gables, 78
Juniper Springs, Umatilla, 47
Jupiter, 75, 81, 134
Jupiter Lighthouse and Museum, 81

K

Kapok Tree Inn, Clearwater, 53
Katherine Abbey Hanna Park, Jacksonville, 32
Kelly Park, Apopka, 40
Kennedy Space Center, Cape Canaveral, 27, 28, 33, 37, 45
Key Biscayne, 74, 81, 91, 134–35
Key Colony Beach, 68
Key Deer National Wildlife Refuge, Florida Keys, 64, 69
Key Largo, 66, 135
Keystone Heights, 33
Key West, 63, 64, 69–72, 76, 135
Key West Art Center, 70
Key West Cemetery, 71
Key West Fragrance and Cosmetic Factory, 70
Key West Hand Print Fabrics, 70
Key West Hospitality House, 70
King Neptune Frolics, Sarasota, 60
Kings Island, Ohio, 99
Kingsley Plantation State Historic Site, Jacksonville, 30, 91
Kissimmee, 39, 41, 135
Kissimmee Valley Livestock Show, 41
Koreshan State Historic Site, Estero, 54, 92

L

Lake Alice Wildlife Preserve, Gainesville, 18
Lake Apopka, 40
Lake Buena Vista, 42–43, 135–36
Lake Buena Vista Resort Community, 42
Lake Butler, 18
Lake City, 19, 136
Lake County Historical Society, Tavares, 47
Lake Griffin State Rec. Area, Leesburg, 39, 44, 92
Lake Ida County Park, Delray Beach, 78
Lake Jackson Mounds State Archaeological Site, Tallahassee, 22, 89
Lake Kissimmee State Park, Lake Wales, 39, 44, 92
Lakeland, 43, 136
Lake Louisa State Park, Clermont, 39, 41, 92
Lake Maggiore Park, St. Petersburg, 57
Lake Manatee State Rec. Area, Bradenton, 52, 92
Lake Okeechobee, 44, 63, 73
Lake Placid, 43–44, 136
Lake Placid Day, 43
Lake Talquin State Rec. Area, Tallahassee, 22, 89
Lake Verona, 40
Lake Wales, 43–44, 136
Lake Worth, 136
Lake Worth Playhouse, 81
Latin American Fiesta, Tampa, 61
Layton, 67–68
Lazy Bones, Fort Myers, 54
Leesburg, 39, 44, 136–37
LeMoyne Art Foundation, Tallahassee, 22
Leu Gardens, Orlando, 45
Lexington, Ky., 99
Lighthouse Museum, Key West, 71
Lightner Museum, St. Augustine, 36
Lignumvitae Key State Botanical Site, Islamorada, 66–67, 93
Lincoln Road Mall, Miami Beach, 84
Lion Country Safari, West Palm Beach, 85
Little Gallery, Tallahassee, 22
Little Talbot Island State Park, Jacksonville, 31, 91
Little White House, Warm Springs, Ga., 100
Live Oak, 19
Lloyd Beach State Rec. Area, Dania, 78, 93
Loch Haven Art Center, Orlando, 45
Loch Haven Park, Orlando, 45
London Wax Museum, St. Petersburg, 57
Long Key State Recreation Area, Florida Keys, 67, 93
Long Pine Key, Flamingo, 66
Louisiana State University, Baton Rouge, La., 100
Louisville, Ky., 99
Lowe Art Museum, Coral Gables, 78
Lowe House, St. Petersburg, 57
Loxahatchee National Wildlife Refuge, Delray Beach, 78

M

Maclay State Ornamental Garden, Tallahassee, 22, 28
Madira Bickel Mound State Archaeological Site, Terra Ceia, 61, 92
Magic Kingdom, Walt Disney World, 42–43
Mahan Nurseries, Monticello, 15
Mahogany Hammock, Flamingo, 66
Mammoth Cave National Park, Ky., 98
Manatee Springs State Park, Chiefland, 17, 89
Marathon, 68, 73, 137
Marco Island, 51, 54–55, 137
Mardi Gras, Pensacola, 13
Mardi Gras Fun Center, Daytona Beach, 29
Marianna, 9, 137
Marie Selby Botanical Gardens, Sarasota, 5, 59
Marineland, 5, 33, 137
Marine Stadium, Miami, 82
Marjorie K. Rawlings State Historic Site, Cross Creek (Gainesville), 18, 89
Marquesas Keys, 64
Marriott's Marco Beach Hotel and Villas, Marco Island, 55
Marsh Museum, Ormond Beach, 34
Martello Gallery and Museum, Key West, 71
Martinique, 105
Matheson Hammock Beach and Park, Coral Gables, 77
Matheson Mansion, Florida Keys, 66
McLarty Museum, Sebastian, 85
Mead Botanical Gardens, Winter Park, 48
Medieval Fair, Sarasota, 60
Melbourne, 27, 33–34, 137
Merchant's Home Show, New Port Richey, 19
Merritt Island National Wildlife Refuge, Kennedy Space Center, 27, 33
Metro-Dade Department of Tourism, 81, 83
Metrozoo, Miami, 83
MGM's *Bounty,* St. Petersburg, 56
Miamarina, Miami, 81
Miami, 76, 77, 79, 81–83, 137–38
Miami Beach, 76, 83–84, 138–39
Miami Beach Garden and Conservatory, 84
Miami Beach Theater of the Performing Arts, 84
Miami-Dade Cultural Center, Miami, 82
Miami International Boat Show, Miami Beach, 84
Miami Marine Stadium, City of, 82
Miami Seaquarium, 5, 82–83
Miami Serpentarium, 5, 83
Miami Wax Museum, 82
Midway Fun Fair, Daytona Beach, 29
Mike Roess Gold Head Branch State Park, 33, 91
Milton, 10
Mineral Springs, Green Cove Springs, 30
Miracle Strip, 6, 7, 11
Miracle Strip Amusement Park, Panama City Beach, 11
Miracle Strip Parkway, Daytona Beach, 29
Miss Cheerleader U.S.A., Winter Haven, 48
Miss Florida-USA Pageant, Fort Lauderdale, 79
Mission of Nombre de Dios, St. Augustine, 36
Mission Trail, San Antonio, Tex., 100
Monkey Jungle, Goulds (Miami), 83
Monroe County Beach and Garden Center, Key West, 71
Monticello, 15, 19
Moore Haven, 73
Morikami Park, Delray Beach, 78–79
Morristown National Historical Park, Morristown, N.J., 96

INDEX 151

Morse Gallery of Art, 49
Morven, Princeton, N.J., 96
Mount Dora, 44, 139
Mount Vernon, Va., 95
Mug Race (sailboats), Palatka, 34
Municipal Aquarium, Key West, 70
Municipal Marina, St. Petersburg, 57
Museum of Art, Fort Lauderdale, 79
Museum of Arts and Sciences, Daytona Beach, 29
Museum of Fine Arts, St. Petersburg, 57
Museum of Food Containers, Kissimmee, 41
Museum of Japanese Culture, Delray Beach, 78
Museum of Old Dolls and Toys, Winter Haven, 47
Museum San Augustin Antiguo, St. Augustine, 36
Museum of Science and Industry for Tampa/Hillsborough, 61
Museum of Science and Space Transit Planetarium, Miami, 82
Museum of Southern Florida and the Caribbean, Miami, 82
Museum of Sunken Treasure, Cape Canaveral, 28–29
Museum of the Arts, Fort Lauderdale, 79
Museum of the Circus, Sarasota, 59
Museum of the Sea and the Indian, Destin, 9
Myakka River State Park, Sarasota, 59, 92
Myrtle Beach State Park, S.C., 97–98
Mystery Fun House, Orlando, 45

N

Naples, 51, 55, 139–40
Naples Pier, Naples, 55
NASA Lyndon B. Johnson Space Center, Houston, Tex., 100
National Audubon Society. See Audubon Society
National Police Hall of Fame and Museum, Port Charlotte, 56
Natural Bridge Battlefield State Historic Site, Woodville (Tallahassee), 24, 89
Naval Aviation Museum, Pensacola, 7, 12
Neil Armstrong Air and Space Museum, Wapakoneta, Ohio, 97
Netherlands Antilles, 105–6
New College, Sarasota, 58
New Echota, Ga., 98
New Orleans, La., 94
Newport Recreation Area, Newport (St. Marks), 20
New Port Richey, 19, 140
New Smyrna Beach, 34, 140
New Smyrna Sugar Mill Ruins State Historic Site, 34, 91
Niceville, 10
Nine Mile Pond, Flamingo, 66
Noell's Ark Chimpanzee Farm, Tarpon Springs, 61
Norris Dam, Tenn., 98
Norris, Tenn., 98
North Central Florida, 14–25; map, 23; parks, 88–89
Northeast Florida, 26–37; map, 31; parks, 90–91
North Florida Fair, Tallahassee, 22
North Shore Olympic Pool, St. Petersburg, 57
Northwest Florida, 6–13; map, 11; parks, 88
Norton Gallery and School of Art, West Palm Beach, 85

O

Oak Ridge, Tenn., 98
Ocala, 19, 140
Ocala National Forest, Ocala and Umatilla, 19, 41, 47
Ocean Front Amusements, Daytona Beach, 29
Ocean World, Fort Lauderdale, 79
Ochlockonee River State Park, Sopchoppy, 21, 89
Ochopee, 65
Ocmulgee National Monument, Ga., 99
Okalee Seminole Indian Village, Hollywood, 80

Okeechobee, 44, 140
Okeechobee Waterway, Belle Glade, 64
Okefenokee Swamp, Ga., 98
Old Capitol, Tallahassee, 22
Oldest House, St. Augustine, 27, 36
Oldest House Museum, Key West, 71
Oldest School, St. Augustine, 27, 36
Old Fort, New Smyrna Beach, 34
Old Island Days, Key West, 71
Old Mallory Square, Key West, 69
Old Pensacola Lighthouse, Pensacola, 12
Old Protestant Cemetery, St. Augustine, 37
Old Seville Square, Pensacola, 7, 12, 13
Old Spanish Treasury, St. Augustine, 36
Old Sugar Mill, St. Augustine, 36
Old Town Trolley, Marathon, 69
O'Leno State Park, Lake Butler, 18, 89
Olustee, 19
Olustee Battlefield State Historic Site, 19, 89–90
Orange Bowl, Miami, 83
Orange County Historical Museum, Orlando, 45
Orange Cup Regatta, Lakeland, 43
Orchid Jungle, Homestead, 5, 63, 72
Orlando, 39, 44–47, 140–41
Orlando Sports Stadium, 46
Ormond Beach, 27, 34, 141
Oscar Scherer State Rec. Area, Osprey, 56, 92
Osceola Arts Festival, Kissimmee, 41
Osceola National Forest, Lake City, Olustee, 19

P

Paddlewheel Queen, Fort Lauderdale, 79
Pahokee State Rec. Area, Belle Glade, 64, 93
Pahokee Observation Tower, Belle Glade, 64
Palatka, 27, 34, 141
Palatka Horseman's Rodeo, Palatka, 34
Palm Beach, 27, 75, 84, 141–42
Palm Beach Fairgrounds Speedway, West Palm Beach, 85
Palmdale, 73
Panama City, 7, 10, 142
Panhandle Watermelon Festival, 8
Parrot Jungle, Miami, 83
Pasco County Fair, Dade City, 18
Pasco County Fair Raceway, Dade City, 18
Patrick Air Force Base, Cocoa Beach, 28
Paurotis Pond, Flamingo, 66
Payne's Prairie State Preserve, Micanopy (Gainesville), 18, 89
Peabody Auditorium, Daytona Beach, 29
Pelican Island National Wildlife Refuge, Sebastian, 85
Pensacola, 5, 7, 8, 11, 142
Pensacola Art Center, 12
Pensacola Beach, 7
Pensacola Historical District, 12
Pensacola Historical Museum, 12
Pensacola Museum of Art, 12
Pensacola Naval Air Station, 7, 12
Pensacola PGA Open, 13
Pensacola Seafood Festival, 7, 13
Performing Arts Center, Clearwater, 52
Perry, 15, 19, 142
Peso de Burgo-Pellicer Houses, St. Augustine, 36
Petticoat Junction, Long Beach Resort (Panama City), 11
Philippe Park, Safety Harbor, 56
Pier Place, St. Petersburg, 56
Pineland Trail, Flamingo, 66
Pioneer Florida Museum, Dade City, 18
Pirate's Alley, Key West, 70
Pirate's Island, 9
Planetarium, St. Petersburg, 57
Planet Ocean, Miami, 5, 83
Plantation Key, 66
Plantation Paradise, Lake Placid, 43
Playalinda Beach, Kennedy Space Center, 33
Players, The, Sarasota, 59
Plaza de la Constitucion, St. Augustine, 36
Plaza Ferdinand VII, Pensacola, 12
Polk County Historical and Genealogical Library, Avon Park, 40
Pompano Beach, 84–85, 142–43

Pompano Park Harness Raceway, Pompano Beach, 84
Ponce de Leon Park, Punta Gorda, 56
Ponce de Leon Springs State Rec. Area, De Funiak Springs, 8, 88
Port Canaveral, 28
Port Charlotte, 56, 143
Port St. Joe, 13
Potter's Wax Museum, St. Augustine, 36
Princeton, N.J., 96
Puerto Rico, 104
Punta Gorda, 56, 143
Put-in-Bay, Ohio, 98

R

R. A. Grey Archives, Library, and Museum Building, Tallahassee, 22
Raft Races, Key West, 71
Rattlesnake Festival and International Championship Gopher Race, Dade City, 18
Ravine State Ornamental Garden, Palatka, 27, 34, 91
recipes, Florida food, 110–11
Redland Fruit and Spice Park, Homestead, 5, 63, 72
Reptile World Serpentarium, Kissimmee, 41
restaurants, 126–49
Ribera House, St. Augustine, 36
Ringling Bros.-Barnum & Bailey. See Circus World
Ringling Museums, Sarasota, 51, 58
Ripley's Believe It Or Not Museum, St. Augustine, 36
Rocky Mount, N.C., 97
Rodman Dam and Reservoir, Palatka, 34
Rodeo Frontier Days, Homestead, 73
Rodriguez-Avero-Sanchez House, St. Augustine, 36
Rogers' Christmas House and Village, Brooksville, 16
Rollins College, Winter Park, 49

S

Safety Harbor, 56
Safety Harbor Spa, 56
Sailor Circus, Sarasota, 60
St. Andrews State Rec. Area, Panama City Beach, 7, 10, 88
St. Armands Key, Sarasota, 59
St. Augustine, 3, 27, 34–37, 143
St. Augustine Alligator Farm, 3, 36
St. Augustine Beach, 143
St. Augustine National Cemetery, 37
St. George Island, State Park, 16
Saint Leo Abbey, Dade City, 18
St. Leo College, Dade City, 18
St. Lucie County Fair, Fort Pierce, 80
St. Lucie County Historical Museum, Fort Pierce, 79
St. Lucie State Museum, Fort Pierce, 79, 93
St. Marks, 19–20
St. Marks National Wildlife Refuge, Apalachicola and St. Marks, 20
St. Nicholas Greek Orthodox Cathedral, Tarpon Springs, 61
St. Petersburg, 39, 51, 54, 56–57, 143–44
St. Petersburg Beach Area, 144
St. Petersburg Historical Museum, 57
Sandy Shoes Festival, Fort Pierce, 80
Sanford, 46–47, 144–45
Sanibel Island, 51, 58, 145
Sanibel Shell Fair, 58
San Marcos de Apalache State Historic Site, St. Marks, 21, 90
Santa Rosa Island, 7, 12
Sarasota, 51, 58–60, 145–46
Sarasota Jungle Gardens, 5, 52, 59
Sarasota Opera Company, Sarasota, 58
Savannah, Ga., 98
Science Museum and Planetarium, West Palm

152 INDEX

Beach, 85
Science Center of Pinellas County, Inc., St. Petersburg, 57
Seabreeze Yacht II, Daytona Beach, 29
Sea Islands, Ga., 98
Sea World of Florida, Orlando, 5, 39, 44, 45
Sebastian, 75, 85
Sebastian Inlet, 27
Sebastian Inlet State Rec. Area, 85, 93
Sebring, 39, 47, 146
Seminole Harness Raceway, Casselberry (Winter Park), 49
Seminole Indian Reservation, Moore Haven, 73
Seminole Indian Reservation, Okeechobee, 44, 45
Senator Everett McKinley Dirksen Garden, Tallahassee, 21
Seven Lively Arts Festival, Hollywood, 80–81
Shark Rodeo, Pensacola, 13
Shark Valley Loop Road, Everglades City, 65
Shell Factory, Fort Myers, 54
Shell Island, Panama City, 10
Sherman Field, Pensacola, 12
Shipwreck Island, 11
Sidewalk Art Fair, Coral Gables, 78
Sidewalk Art Festival, Kissimmee, 41
Sidewalk Art Festival, Winter Park, 49
Silver Lake, Apalachicola, 16
Silver Springs, 3, 15, 19, 20, 146
Silver Spurs Rodeo, Kissimmee, 39, 41
Singing Tower, Bok Tower Gardens, Lake Wales, 39
Six Flags Over Georgia, 100
Six Flags' Stars Hall of Fame, Orlando, 46
Six-Gun Territory, Silver Springs, 21
Smather's Beach, Key West, 71
Snake-A-Torium, Panama City Beach (Panama City), 10
Snowball Derby, Pensacola, 13
Sopchoppy, 21
South Central Florida, 62–73; map, 67; parks, 92–93
South Eastern Bible College, Lakeland, 43
South Florida State Fair and Exposition, West Palm Beach, 85
Southeast Florida, 74–85; map, 78; parks, 93
South Florida Junior College, Avon Park, 40
South Florida Museum and Bishop Planetarium, Bradenton, 52
Southland Sweepstakes Regatta, St. Petersburg, 57
Southwest Florida, 50–61; map, 55; parks, 91–92
Southwest Florida Championship Rodeo, Fort Myers, 54
Space Coast Art Festival, Cocoa Beach, 28
Spanish Military Hospital, St. Augustine, 36
Spanish National Tourist Office, St. Augustine, 36
Sponge Exchange, Tarpon Springs, 61
Spongeorama Exhibit Center, Tarpon Springs, 61
Spook Hill, Lake Wales, 44
Spring Creek Springs, St. Marks, 20
Springtime Tallahassee, 22
state facts, 107
State Parks, 86–93
State Theatre of Florida, Sarasota, 59
Stephen Foster State Folk Culture Center, White Springs, 25, 90
Stetson University, De Land, 29

Stuart, 75, 85, 145
Sugar Mill Gardens, Daytona Beach, 29
Sumatra, 21
Summerland Orchid Gardens, Florida Keys, 64, 68
Sunshine Skyway, St. Petersburg, 57
Sunshine Speedway, St. Petersburg, 58
Suwanee County Fair and Livestock Show, Live Oak, 19
Suwanee River State Park, Live Oak, 19, 90
Swamp Buggy Races, Naples, 55
Sweet Corn Festival, Zellwood (Apopka), 40

T

Tallahassee, 15, 21, 146
Tallahassee Junior Museum, 23
Tamiami Trail, Everglades City, 64, 65
Tampa, 39, 51, 54, 60–61, 146–47
Tampa Bay Downs, Tampa, 61
Tampa Municipal Beach, 60
Tampa Museum, 61
Tampa Stadium, 61
Tampa Tarpon Tournament, Tampa, 61
Tampa Theatre, 61
Tarpon Springs, 51, 61, 147
Tavares, 47, 147
Tavernier, 66
Temple Mound, Fort Walton Beach, 9
Ten Thousand Islands, Everglades City, 51, 64, 65
Terra Ceia, 61
Theater of the Sea, Florida Keys, 66
Three Rivers State Rec. Area, Marianna, 9, 88
T. H. Stone Memorial St. Joseph Peninsula State Park, Port St. Joe, 13, 88
Tour of Homes, Monticello, 19
Tourist Center, Fort Myers, 54
Tournament Players Championship, Jacksonville, 30
Tovar House, St. Augustine, 36
Trimble Park, Mount Dora, 44
Trinidad, 105
Trinity Church, Apalachicola, 16
Trinity Episcopal Church, St. Augustine, 37
T. T. Wentworth Jr. Museum, Pensacola, 12
Turtle Kraals, Florida Keys, 66
Twenty-Mile Bend, Delray Beach, 78
Tyndall Air Force Base, Panama City, 10

U

Umatilla, 47
Underwater Coral Gardens, Islamorada, 66
Universalist Church, Tarpon Springs, 61
University Art Gallery, Gainesville, 18
University of Central Florida, Orlando, 45
University of Florida, Gainesville, 18
University of Miami, Coral Gables, 76, 78
University of North Florida, Jacksonville, 33
University of South Florida, Tampa, 61
University of Tampa, 3, 60–61
U.S. Naval Air Station, Pensacola, 7, 12
U.S. Naval Ship Research and Development Laboratory, Panama City, 10

V

Vacation Kingdom, Lake Buena Vista, 42
Van Wezel Performing Arts Hall, Sarasota, 58

Venetian Municipal Pool, Coral Gables, 77–78
Venetian Sun Festival, Venice, 61
Venice, 51, 61, 147
Vero Beach, 85, 147–48
Veteran's Day Parade, Homestead, 73
Villa Vizcaya Museum and Gardens, Miami, 82
Virginia Beach Park, Miami, 81
Virgin Islands, 104
Visitors' Information Center, St. Augustine, 35–36
Voyager Sightseeing Train, Fort Lauderdale, 79

W

Wacissa Springs Group, Tallahassee, 23–24
Wacissa River Canoe Trail, Tallahassee, 24
Wadeview Park, Orlando, 45
Walk of Fame, Winter Park, 49
Walt Disney World Team Championships, Orlando, 46
Walt Disney World, Lake Buena Vista, 39, 42–43, 44, 148
Walt Disney World Village, Lake Buena Vista, 42
Walton County Fair, De Funiak Springs, 8
Walton House, Pensacola, 12
Warm Mineral Springs and Cyclorama, Venice, 61
Washington, D.C., 96
Washington Oaks State Ornamental Garden, Marineland, 33, 91
Washington's Birthday Celebration, Eustis, 41
Waterfront Playhouse, Key West, 70
Watermelon Festival, Chiefland, 17
Wauchula, 47
Wax and Historical Museum, Panama City, 11
Weeki Wachee, 16, 24–25
Wekiwa Springs State Park, Apopka, 39, 40, 91
Wells Studio Gallery, Islamorada, 66
West Florida Museum of History, Pensacola, 12
West Lake Trail, Flamingo, 66
West Palm Beach, 85, 148
West Palm Beach Speedway, 85
Wet 'n' Wild, Orlando, 39, 46
Wewahitchka, 13
Wheelmen's Rendezvous, Homestead, 73
White Springs, 25
Wiggins Pass State Rec. Area, Bonita Springs, 52, 92
Wild Waters, Silver Springs, 22
Winter Haven, 39, 47, 148
Winter Park, 39, 48–49, 148–49
Wirick-Simmons House, Monticello, 19
Withlacoochee State Forest, Inverness, 18
Women's South Atlantic Open, Ormond Beach, 34

Y

Ybor City, Tampa, 60
Ybor City State Museum, Tampa, 60, 92
Ybor Square, Tampa, 60
Yulee Sugar Mill Ruins State Historic Site, Homosassa Springs, 18, 90

Z

Zephyrhills, 25, 149
Zorayda Castle, St. Augustine, 36